District Gazetteers of India Series 133

MADRAS DISTRICT GAZETTEERS

MALABAR

District Gazetteers of India Series 133

MADRAS DISTRICT GAZETTEERS

MALABAR

C. A INNES

EDITED BY

F. B EVANS

23 VOLUMES (IN 25 BINDINGS)

(VOL. 2nd)

GYAN

Published by

Gyan Publishing House
5, Ansari Road
Daryaganj, New Delhi-110002
Phone: 011-47034999, 9811692060
E-mail: books@gyanbooks.com

Distribution Network
gyanbooks.com
India, USA, Canada, UK, Australia, France

ISBN: 978-93-6208-562-7 (Set) 23 Volumes (In 25 Bindings)
978-81-212-5855-5 (PB)

First Published, 1933

2nd Impression 2024

Printed at: Gyan Press, Delhi.

MADRAS DISTRICT GAZETTEERS (Vol. 2nd)
Author: C. A INNES
Editor: F. B EVANS

LIST OF VOLUMES

S. NO.	ISBN NO.	VOLUME	TITLE	AUTHOR	PRICE	PAGES
			ASSAM DISTRICT GAZETTEERS			
1	9788121285926	1st	Cachar	B. C. Allen	600	300
2	9788121285919	2nd	Sylhet	B. C. Allen	750	378
3	9788121285902	3rd	Goalpara	B. C. Allen	400	203
4	9788121285896	4th	Kamrup	B. C. Allen	675	344
5	9788121285889	5th	Darrang	B. C. Allen	725	364
6	9788121285872	6th	Nowgong	B. C. Allen	560	280
7	9788121285865	7th	Sibsagar	B. C. Allen	675	343
8	9788121285858	8th	Lakhimpur	B. C. Allen	690	347
9	9788121285841	9th	Naga Hills and Manipur	B. C. Allen	580	294
10	9788121285834	10th	The Khasi And Jaintia Hills, The Garo Hills And The Lushai Hills	B. C. Allen	675	363
11	9788121285827	11th	The Sadiya and Balipara Frontier Tract	B. C. Allen	375	190
			BENGAL DISTRICT GAZETTEERS			
12	9788121218672	1st	Angul	L. S. S. O'Malley	340	168
13	9788121259637	2nd	Bakarganj	J. C. JACK	970	194
14	9788121218696	3rd	Balasore	L. S. S. O'Malley	450	228
15	9788121259590	4th	Bankura	L. S. S. O'Malley	1000	199
16	9788121218375	5th	Bhagalpur	J. Byrne	390	194
17	9788121218290	6th	Birbhum	L. S. S. O'Malley	300	150
18	9788121259651	7th	Eastern Bengal and Assam - Bogra	J. N. Gupta	940	188
19	9788121218351	8th	Burdwan	J. C. K. Peterson	450	227
20	9788121259538	9th	Calcutta District Gazetteer - Statistics, 1901 - 02		340	68
21	9788121218313	10th	Champaran	L. S. S. O'Malley	410	205
22	9788121259613	11th	Eastern Bengal District Gazetters - Chittagong	L. S. S. O'Malley	1080	216
23	9788121259552	12th	Chota Nagpur Tributary		130	26
24	9788121259415	13th	The Cooch Behar Gazette: Statistics		1460	292
25	9788121218412	14th	Cuttack	L. S. S. O'Malley	490	248
26	9788121261357	15th	Eastern Bengal District Gazetteers Dacca	B. C. Allen	400	207
27	9788121218436	16th	Darbhanga	L. S. S. O'Malley	360	180
28	9789362089335	17th	Darjeeling	L. S. S. O'Malley	500	248
29	9788121259453	18th	Eastern Bengal District Gazetteers - Dinajpur	F. W. Strong	890	178
30	9788121259392	19th	Faridpur	L. S. S. O'Malley	700	140
31	9788121218474	20th	Gaya	L. S. S. O'Malley	540	270
32	9788121214032	21st	Bihar and Orissa District Gazetteer: Hazaribagh	E. Lister	715	234
33	9788121218337	22nd	Hooghly	L. S. S. O'Malley	680	340
34	9788121218191	23rd	Bengal District Gazetteer Howrah	L. S. S. O'Malley	390	199
35	9788121259293	24th	Eastern Bengal and Assam - Jalpaiguri	John F. Gruning	890	178
36	9788121259279	25th	Jessore	L. S. S. O'Malley	960	192
37	9788121259231	26th	Khulna	L. S. S. O'Malley	1100	220
38	9788121259217	27th	Malda	G. E. Lambourn	670	134
39	9788121267854	28th	Manbhum	H. Coupland	600	313
40	9788121218498	29th	Midnapore	L. S. S. O'Malley	500	252
41	9788121218597	30th	Monghyr	L. S. S. O'Malley	560	280
42	9788121259156	31st	Murshidabad	L. S. S. O'Malley	1250	250
43	9788121259576	32nd	Bengal District Gazetteers - Muzaffarpur	L. S. S. O'Malley	940	188
44	9788121259132	33rd	Mymensingh	F. A. Sachse	960	192
45	9788121259118	34th	Nadia	J. H. E. Garrett	1070	214
46	9788121259095	35th	Eastern Bengal and Assam - Noakhali	J. E. Webster	580	115
47	9788121218450	36th	Feudatory States of Orissa	L. E. B. Cobdenramsay	790	395
48	9788121259071	37th	Pabna	L. S. S. O'Malley	710	142
49	9788121218511	38th	Palamau	L. S. S. O'Malley	380	190
50	9788121218634	39th	Patna	L. S. S. O'Malley	500	250
51	9788121218535	40th	Puri	L. S. S. O'Malley	650	328
52	9788121218757	41st	Purnea	L. S. S. O'Malley	440	220
53	9788121258937	42nd	Rajshahi	L. S. S. O'Malley	1080	216
54	9788121256681	43rd	Bihar and Orissa District Gazetteers: Ranchi	M. G. Hallett	1350	278
55	9788121258913	44th	Eastern Bengal and assam - Rangpur	J. A. Vas	890	178
56	9788121218559	45th	Sambalpur	L. S. S. O'Malley	480	242
57	9788121214056	46th	Santal Parganas	L. S. S. O'Malley	940	308
58	9788121218610	47th	Saran	L. S. S. O'Malley	380	190
59	9788121218658	48th	Shahabad	L. S. S. O'Malley	380	190
60	9788121256704	49th	The Gazetteer of Sikhim	H. H. Risley	960	481
61	9788121218573	50th	Singhbhum, Saraikela And Kharsawan	L. S. S. O'Malley	560	280
62	9788121259439	51st	Eastern Bengal District Gazetteers - Tippera	J. E. Webster	730	146
63	9788121259033	52nd	24 Parganas	L. S. S. O'Malley	1420	284

CENTRAL PROVINCES DISTRICT GAZETTEERS

S. NO.	ISBN NO.	VOLUME	TITLE	AUTHOR	PRICE	PAGES
64	9789362081728	1st, Vol. A	Akola (Descriptive)	A. E. Nelson, C. Brown	870	436
65	9789362085481	2nd, Vol. A	Amraoti (Descriptive)	S. V. Fitzgerald, A. E. Nelson	1050	524
66	9789362089267	3rd,Vol. A	Balaghat (Descriptive)	R. V. RUSSELL	430	216
67	9789362083494	4th, Vol. A	Betul (Descriptive)	R. V. RUSSELL	610	306
68	9789362085146	5th, Vol. A	Bhandara (Descriptive)	R. V. RUSSELL	580	292
69	9789362088390	6th, Vol. A	Bilaspur (Descriptive)	R. V. RUSSELL	870	434
70	9789362086044	7th, Vol. A	Buldana (Descriptive)	A. E. Nelson	1090	543
71	9789362089014	8th, Vol. B	Chanda (Descriptive)	R. V. RUSSELL	470	234
72	9789362086938	9th	Chhattisgarch Feudatory State	E. A. De Brett	880	440
73	9789362082961	10th	Chhindwara (Descriptive)	R. V. RUSSELL	550	274
74	9789362089342	11th, Vol. A & B	Damoh (Descriptive and Statistical Tables 1891-1901)	R. V. RUSSELL	830	414
75	9789362081230	12th, Vol. A	Durg (Descriptive)	A. E. Nelson	460	232
76	9789362086037	13th, Vol. A	Hoshangabad (Descriptive)	R. V. RUSSELL	860	430
77	9789362086792	14th, Vol. A	Jubbulpore (Descriptive)	A. E. Nelson	950	474
78	9789362089663	15th, Vol. A & B	Mandla (Descriptive and Statistical Tables 1891-1901)	R. V. RUSSELL	370	186
79	9789362086419	16th, Vol. A	Nagpur (Descriptive)	R. V. RUSSELL	790	394
80	9789362080646	17th, Vol. A	Narsinghpur (Descriptive)	R. V. RUSSELL	510	257
81	9789362084835	18th, Vol. A	Nimar (Descriptive)	R. V. RUSSELL	600	299
82	9789362087737	19th, Vol. A	Raipur (Descriptive)	A. E. Nelson	790	396
83	9789362080264	20th, Vol. A	Saugor (Descriptive)	R. V. RUSSELL	570	285
84	9789362081117	21st, Vol. A	Seoni (Descriptive)	R. V. RUSSELL	460	232
85	9789362084965	22nd, Vol. A	Wardha (Descriptive)	R. V. RUSSELL	600	302
86	9789362083401	23rd, Vol. A	Yeotmal (Descriptive)	R. V. RUSSELL	550	277
87	9789362080325	24th, Vol. I, Pt. I	Gwalior (Text and Tables)	R. V. RUSSELL	980	489
88	9789362087133	24th, Vol. I, Pt. II	Gwalior (Maps)	R. V. RUSSELL	400	198
89	9789362086341	24th, Vol. I, Pt. III	Gwalior (Village List)	R. V. RUSSELL	810	406
90	9789362085467	24th, Vol. I, Pt. IV	Gwalior (Photos)	R. V. RUSSELL	1400	698
91	9789362087393	25th, Vol. II	Indore (Text and Tables)	C. E. Luard	1050	524
92	9789362084422	26th, Vol. III	Bhopal (Text and Tables)	C. E. Luard	540	272
93	9789362086815	27th, Vol. IV	Rewah (Text and Tables)	C. E. Luard	500	250
94	9789362087584	28th, Vol. V, Pt. A	Western States - Malwa (Text)	C. E. Luard	1520	762
95	9789362087300	29th, Vol. VI, Pt. A	Eastern States - Bundelkhand (Text)	C. E. Luard	930	463
96	9789362082169	30th, Vol. VI, Pt. B	Eastern States - Bundelkhand (Tables)	C. E. Luard	830	417

GAZETTEER OF THE BOMBAY PRESIDENCY:

S. NO.	ISBN NO.	VOLUME	TITLE	AUTHOR	PRICE	PAGES
97	9788121283441	1st, Part I	History of Gujarat	Ed.: James M. Campbell	3220	644
98	9788121285582	1st, Part II	History of the Konkan Dakhan and Southern Maratha Country	Ed.: James M. Campbell	4200	840
99	9788121285568	2nd	Gujarat, Surat and Broach	Ed.: James M. Campbell	2990	598
100	9788121285544	3rd	Kaira and Panch Mahals	Ed.: James M. Campbell	1690	339
101	9788121285520	4th	Ahmedabad	Ed.: James M. Campbell	1860	372
102	9788121285506	5th	Cutch, Palanpur, and Mahi Kantha	Ed.: James M. Campbell	2390	478
103	9788121285483	6th	Rewa Kantha, Narukot, Cambay, and Surat States	Ed.: James M. Campbell	1450	290
104	9788121285469	7th	Baroda	Ed.: James M. Campbell	3260	652
105	9788121285445	8th	Kathiawar	Ed.: James M. Campbell	3790	758
106	9788121285421	9th, Part I	Gujarat Population - Hindus	Ed.: James M. Campbell	3170	636
107	9788121285407	9th, Part II	Gujarat Population - Musalmans and Parsis	Ed.: James M. Campbell	1520	304
108	9788121285384	10th	Ratnagiri and Savantvadi	Ed.: James M. Campbell	2500	501
109	9788121285360	11th	Kolaba and Janjira	Ed.: James M. Campbell	2550	513
110	9788121285346	12th	Khandesh	Ed.: James M. Campbell	3190	638
111	9788121285322	13th Part I	Thana	Ed.: James M. Campbell	2050	413
112	9788121285308	13th Part II	Thana	Ed.: James M. Campbell	1770	357
113	9788121285285	14th	Thana - Places of Interest	Ed.: James M. Campbell	3290	659
114	9788121285261	15th Part I	Kanara	Ed.: James M. Campbell	2340	348
115	9788121285247	15th Part II	Kanara	Ed.: James M. Campbell	1740	348
116	9788121285223	16th	Nasik	Ed.: James M. Campbell	3490	698
117	9788121285209	17th	Ahmadnagar	Ed.: James M. Campbell	3860	772
118	9788121285186	18th Part I	Poona	Ed.: James M. Campbell	2930	586
119	9788121285162	18th Part II	Poona	Ed.: James M. Campbell	2680	537
120	9788121285148	18th Part III	Poona	Ed.: James M. Campbell	2500	503
121	9788121285124	19th	Satara	Ed.: James M. Campbell	3450	692
122	9788121285100	20th	Sholapur	Ed.: James M. Campbell	2730	547
123	9788121285087	21st	Gazetteer of the Bomaby Presidency: Belgaum	Ed.: James M. Campbell	2570	514
124	9788121285063	22nd	Dharwar	Ed.: James M. Campbell	4200	841
125	9788121285049	23rd	Gazetteer of the Bombay Presidency:Bijapur	Ed.: James M. Campbell	3550	712
126	9788121285025	24th	Kolhapur	Ed.: James M. Campbell	2250	450

S. NO.	ISBN NO.	VOLUME	TITLE	AUTHOR	PRICE	PAGES
127	9788121285001	25th	Botany	Ed.: James M. Campbell	2040	408
128	9788121284981	26th, Part I	Materials Towards a Statistical Account of the Town and Island of Bombay - History	Ed.: James M. Campbell	2500	504
129	9788121284967	26th, Part II	Materials Towards a Statistical Account of the Town and Island of Bombay - Trade and Fortifications	Ed.: James M. Campbell	2690	538
130	9788121284943	26th, Part III	Materials Towards a Statistical Account of the Town And Island of Bombay - Administration	Ed.: James M. Campbell	2450	702
131	9788121284929	27th	General Index	Ed.:R. E. Enthoven	2190	428
			MADRAS DISTRICT GAZETTEERS			
132	9788121258814	1st	Anantapur	W. Francis	1140	227
133	9788121258555	2nd	Malabar	C. A Innes & F. B Evans	3010	602
134	9788121258791	3rd	Bellary	W. Francis	1890	377
135	9788121258777	4th	Statistical Appendix For Chingleput		280	56
136	9788121258753	5th	Coimbatore	K. N. Krishnaswami Ayyar	3420	628
137	9788121232814	6th	Madras District Gazetteers District Gazetteer Cuddapah	C. F. Brackenbury	1120	285
138	9788121258715	7th	Statistical Appendix For Ganjam		370	73
139	9788121256766	8th, Vol. 1st	Godavari District Gazetteer	F. R. Hemingway	650	320
140	9788121256803	8th, Vol. 2nd	Godavari District Gazetteer	F. R. Hemingway	160	83
141	9788121258678	9th	Statistical Appendix For Kistna		640	127
142	9788121258654	10th	Statistical Appendix For Kurnool		270	54
143	9788121258616	11th	Madura	W. Francis	1900	379
144	9788121258579	12th	Statistical Appendix For Madura		740	148
145	9788121258630	13th	The Nilgiris	W. Francis	2190	437
146	9788121234276	14th	Madras District Gazetteers Gazetteer Of The Nellore District Brought Upto 1938		1150	386
147	9788121258517	15th	North Arcot		590	118
148	9788121258494	16th, Vol. 1, Part I	Salem	F. J. Richards	1710	343
149	9788121258593	16th, Vol. 1, Part II	Salem	F. J. Richards	1800	360
150	9788121258456	17th	South Arcot	W. Francis	2400	480
151	9788121258470	18th	Statistical Appendix For South Canara		400	80
152	9788121258432	19th, Vol. 1st & 2nd	Tanjore: Main Volume and Statistical Appendix		2070	401
153	9788121258395	20th	Tinnevelly	H. R. Pate	2740	547
154	9788121258418	21st	Statistical Appendix For Tinnevelly		320	64
155	9788121258371	22nd, 1st & 2nd	Trichinopoly: Main Volume and Statistical Appendix	F. R. Hemingway	2440	487
156	9788121241953	23rd	Vizagapatam District Gazetteer	W. Francis	760	385
			PUNJAB DISTRICT GAZETTEERS			
157	9788121255943	1st	Ambala District 1883-84		620	124
158	9788121255967	2nd	Amritsar		1180	236
159	9788121255981	3rd	Delhi		1300	260
160	9788121256001	4th	Ferozepore		950	188
161	9788121256025	5th	Faridkot		350	70
162	9788121256049	6th	Gujranwala 1893-94		1270	254
163	9788121256063	7th	Gujrat	C. E. Luard	1140	228
164	9788121256087	8th	Gurdaspur 1891-92		1260	252
165	9788121256100	9th	Gurgaon 1883-4		1020	203
166	9788121256124	10th	Hazara	H. D. Watson	2290	458
167	9788121256148	11th	Hissar district and Lohar State		1840	367
168	9788121256162	12th	Hoshiarpur		1420	283
169	9788121256186	13th	Jhang		1070	213
170	9788121256209	14th	Jhelam		1010	202
171	9788121256223	15th	Jalandhar District 1883-84		540	108
172	9788121256247	16th, Vol. XIV-A	Jullundur District, with maps and Kapurthala		1990	398
173	9788121256261	17th, Pt. I	Kangra (Proper)		1450	290
174	9788121256285	17th, Pt. II	Kangra (Kulu, Lahual, Spiti)		1800	357
175	9788121256308	18th	Karnal		1930	386
176	9788121256322	19th	Kohat		1540	307
177	9788121256346	20th	The Lahore District 1883-84		1220	244
178	9788121256384	21st	Ludhiana and Maler Kotla		1680	335
179	9788121256407	22nd	Lyallpur		735	147
180	9788121256421	23rd	Mianwali		1170	234
181	9788121256445	24th	Montgomery	P. J. Fagan	1590	318
182	9788121258364	25th	Multan (1901-02)	E. D. Maclagan	2400	480
183	9788121258708	26th	The Rohtak District 1883-84		980	196
184	9788121258746	27th, Vol. III A	Dujana State 1904		500	16
185	9788121256483	28th	Shahpur District		1780	356
186	9788121256506	29th	Simla District		800	159

S. NO.	ISBN NO.	VOLUME	TITLE	AUTHOR	PRICE	PAGES
187	9788121256520	30th	The Chamba State		2040	408
188	9788121256544	31st	The Chenab Colony 1904		1550	310
189	9788121256568	32nd	Kalsia State		270	53
190	9788121256582	33rd	Suket and Mandi		770	154
191	9788121256605	34th	Phulkian States, Patiala Jind And Nabha 1904		2070	414
192	9788121256643	35th	Simla Hill States		2220	443
193	9788121256667	36th	Sirmur		920	183
			RAJPUTANA DISTRICT GAZETTEERS			
194	9789362088994	1st, Vol. I-A & B	Ajmer-merwara (Text and Statistics Tables)	C. C. Watson	1230	246
195	9789362080882	2nd. Vol. II-A & B	Mewar Residency (Text and Statistics Tables)	K.D. Erskine	1700	339
196	9789362088444	3rd, Vol. III-A & B	The Western Rajputana States Residency And The Bikaner Agency	K.D. Erskine	3590	718
			UNITED PROVINCES OF AGRA AND OUDH DISTRICT GAZETTEERS			
197	9789362087560	Vol. I	Agra	H. R. Nevill	2260	452
198	9789362082466	Vol. II	Aligarh	H. R. Nevill	1300	260
199	9789362089779	Vol. III	Allahabad	H. R. Nevill	2050	409
200	9789362081346	Vol. IV	Almora	H. G. Walton	1670	333
201	9789362085658	Vol. V	Azamgarh	D. L. Drake Brockman	1750	349
202	9789362080547	Vol. VI	Bahraich	H. R. Nevill	1410	281
203	9789362085214	Vol. VII	Ballia	H. R. Nevill	1750	350
204	9789362084668	Vol. VIII	Banda	D. L. Drake Brockman	1750	349
205	9789362086518	Vol. IX	Bara Banki	H. R. Nevill	1720	344
206	9789362084101	Vol. X	Bareilly	H. R. Nevill	1640	327
207	9789362086631	Vol. XI	Basti	H. R. Nevill	1610	321
208	9789362083814	Vol. XII	Benares	H. R. Nevill	2290	458
209	9789362086105	Vol. XIII	Bijnor	H. R. Nevill	1820	363
210	9789362081674	Vol. XIV	Budaun	H. R. Nevill	1890	378
211	9789362086891	Vol. XV	Bulandshahr	H. R. Nevill	2100	419
212	9789362081520	Vol. XVI	Cawnpore	H. R. Nevill	2210	442
213	9789362088031	Vol. XVII	Dehra Dun	H. G. Walton	1710	342
214	9789362088710	Vol. XVIII	Etah	E. R. Neave	1600	320
215	9789362082992	Vol. XIX	Etawah	D. L. Drake Brockman	1390	277
216	9789362082220	Vol. XX	Farrukhabad	E. R. Neave	1620	324
217	9789362083869	Vol. XXI	Fatehpur	H. R. Nevill	1890	377
218	9789362085962	Vol. XXII	Fyzabad	H. R. Nevill	1700	339
219	9789362087997	Vol. XXIII	Garhwal	H. G. Walton	1270	254
220	9789362089892	Vol. XXIV	Ghazipur	H. R. Nevill	1600	320
221	9789362085436	Vol. XXV	Gonda	H. R. Nevill	1650	330
222	9789362080271	Vol. XXVI	Gorakhpur	H. R. Nevill	1890	378
223	9789362086129	Vol. XXVII	Hamirpur	D. L. Drake Brockman	1390	277
224	9789362087638	Vol. XXVIII	Hardoi	H. R. Nevill	1680	336
225	9789362081636	Vol. XXIX	Jalaun	D. L. Drake Brockman	1180	236
226	9789362084309	Vol. XXX	Jaunpur	H. R. Nevill	1750	350
227	9789362084187	Vol. XXXI	Jhansi	D. L. Drake Brockman	1960	391
228	9789362089168	Vol. XXXII	Kheri	H. R. Nevill	1650	330
229	9789362086778	Vol. XXXIII	Lucknow	H. R. Nevill	1760	352
230	9789362088635	Vol. XXXIV	Mainpuri	H. R. Nevill	1740	348
231	9789362080424	Vol. XXXV	Meerut	H. R. Nevill	2170	434
232	9789362081087	Vol. XXXVI	Mirzapur	D. L. Drake Brockman	2430	486
233	9789362085443	Vol. XXXVII	Moradabad	H. R. Nevill	1900	380
234	9789362082763	Vol. XXXVIII	Muttra	D. L. Drake Brockman	2140	428
235	9789362089915	Vol. XXXIX	Muzaffarnagar	H. R. Nevill	2260	451
236	9789362086143	Vol. XL	Naini Tal	H. R. Nevill	1890	377
237	9789362086761	Vol. XLI	Partabgarh	H. R. Nevill	1560	312
238	9789362081124	Vol. XLII	Pilibhit	H. R. Nevill	1570	314
239	9789362084453	Vol. XLIII	Rai Bareli	H. R. Nevill	1610	322
240	9789362088284	Vol. XLIV	Rampur	H. R. Nevill	1170	234
241	9789362083654	Vol. XLV	Saharanpur	H. R. Nevill	2190	438
242	9789362083142	Vol. XLVI	Shahjahanpur	H. R. Nevill	1510	302
243	9789362083623	Vol. XLVII	Sitapur	H. R. Nevill	1590	317
244	9789362089939	Vol. XLVIII	Sultanpur	H. R. Nevill	1330	266
245	9789362080851	Vol. XLIX	Unnao	H. R. Nevill	1530	305

MADRAS DISTRICT GAZETTEERS

MALABAR

VOLUME I

MADRAS DISTRICT GAZETTEERS

MALABAR

BY

C. A. INNES, I.C.S.

EDITED BY

F. B. EVANS, I.C.S.

REPRINTED BY THE SUPERINTENDENT
GOVERNMENT PRESS
MADRAS

PREFATORY NOTE

The Malabar District Gazetteer was published in 1908. Volume II containing the statistical portion was republished in 1915 and again in 1933. On the latter occasion, a supplement containing additions and corrections to Volume I was incorporated in Volume II. The demand for Volume I of the Gazetteer was so great that all the copies were soon sold out, and the volume has been out of print for a number of years. the Government, demand to therefore, ordered that the Gazetteer should be reprinted. The work of reprinting was, however, delayed, to some extent, owing to the pressure of work in the Government Press.

The Supplement to Volume I contained in the 1933 edition of Volume II has been incorporated in the present edition. Chapter XVII of the Gazetteer relating to Anjengo district has been deleted from this Reprint, as the enclaves of Anjengo and Tangasseri were transferred,

No fresh edition of Volume II of the Gazetteer is being now reprinted. In view of the fact that it contains only statistical information which is now out of date, and consequently not of much general interest, and in view of the fact that a large number of copies of this volume is available in stock in the Government Press, the Government ordered that it was not necessary to reprint that volume.

EGMORE,
18*th October* 1933.

B. S. BALIGA,
Curator, Madras Record Office.

PREFATORY NOTE TO THE FIRST EDITION

This Gazetteer follows the plan prescribed by the Government for the series of district gazetteers. Statistics have for the most part been given in a separate volume of Appendices, which is to be revised decennially after each census.

The greater part of the book was written in 1904–1905 by Mr. C. A. Innes, I.C.S., then Settlement Officer in Malabar ; but owing to his appointment to the Secretariat of the Government of India, he was unable to finish it or to revise the proofs of what he had written.

Most of the details of the account of the higher castes in Chapter III have been contributed by Mr. A. R. Loftus-Tottenham, I.C.S., who compiled a valuable series of notes on caste customs when he was Special Assistant Collector at Malappuram ; and wrote a rough draft of a large part of the chapter. Chapter XVI on the Laccadive Islands was contributed by Mr. C. W. E. Cotton, I.C.S. The whole work has subsequently been revised by Mr. F. B. Evans, I.C.S., whose responsibility extends particularly to the sections on the Early History and the Portuguese period in Chapter II, Chapter III, most of the section on the Economic Position of the Ryots in Chapter IV, and the whole of the account of the Land Tenures in Chapter XI.

Free use has been made of the old Malabar Manual published in 1887 by Mr. W. Logan, Collector of Malabar, whose intimate knowledge of the district and the people renders his work a permanent authority of the utmost value. Other authorities to which reference has been made, have been quoted as far as possible in the footnotes. A list of the principal books consulted is appended. The literature dealing with Malabar is extensive, and it has often been impossible, within the circumscribed limits of an official compilation such as this, to do more than indicate where fuller and more interesting information may be found.

BOOKS AND PUBLICATIONS REFERRED TO

ALBUQUERQUE, ALPHONSO D': *Commentaries.* (Translated by Birch for the Hakluyt Society. 1875–83.)

BADEN-POWELL, B. H.: *The Indian Village Community.* (Longmans. 1896.)

———: *The Land Systems of British India.* (Clarendon Press. 1892.)

BARBOSA, DUARTE: *The Coasts of East Africa and Malabar.* (Translated by the Hon'ble H. E. J. Stanley for the Hakluyt Society. 1866.)

BARROS E DE COUTO: *Da Asia.* (Decadas I–III, 1497–1530, by Joao de Barros. Decadas IV–XII, 1530–1600, by Diego de Couto.)

BARTOLOMEO: *Voyage to the East Indies.* (Translated by W. Johnston. London. 1800.)

BIDDULPH, Col. J.: *The Pirates of Malabar.* (Smith Elder & Co. 1907.)

BUCHANAN, Dr. FRANCIS: *A Journey through Mysore, Canara and Malabar.* (3 vols. London. 1807.)

BURNELL, A. C.: *South Indian Palæography.* (Trubner. 1878.)

CASTANHEDA, FERNAO LOPES DE: *Historia do Discobrimenta e Conquista da India pelos Portugueses.* (Translated in Kerr's Collection of Voyages and Travels, Vol. II. London. 1811.)

Cochin Ethnographical Survey. Monographs, Nos. 1–12.

CORREA, CASPAR: *Das Lendas.* (Translated by Lord Stanley of Adderley for the Hakluyt Society. 1869. *The Three Voyages of Vasco da Gama.*)

DANVERS, F. C.: *The Portuguese in India.* (Allen & Co. 1894.)

DAY, FRANCIS: *The Land of the Perumals.* (Madras. 1863.)

East India Company's Records: *Letters received by the East India Company.* (Vol. I. 1602–1613. Edited by F. C. Danvers. Vols. II–VI, 1613–1617. Edited by W. Foster. Allen & Co. 1896–1902.)

Epigraphia Indica. I, III, IV, VI, VII, VIII.

FERGUSSON, JAMES: *History of Indian and Eastern Architecture.* (Murray. 1876.)

Fifth Report of the Select Committee on the East India Company. (London. 1812.)

FORBES, JAMES: *Oriental Memoirs.* (London. 1813.)

FRANCIS, W.: *Madras Census Report,* 1901. (Census of India. Vol. XV.)

FRYER, J.: *A New Account of the East Indies and Persia.* (London. 1698.)

GOPAL PANIKKAR, T. K.: *Malabar and its Folk.* (Natesan, Madras. 1901.)

GRÆME's Report on the District of Malabar. 1822.

HAMILTON, Capt. ALEXANDER: *A New Account of the East Indies.* (London. 1744.)

IBN BATUTA: *Travels.* (Translated from an abridged MSS. by S. Lee. Murray. 1829.)

India in the Fifteenth Century. (Travels edited by R. H. Major for the Hakluyt Society. 1857.)

Indian Antiquary, Volumes II, VI, XVIII, XIX, XX, XXI, XXVI, XXX, XXXI.

Joint Commissioners, Report of the — deputed to Malabar. 1793.

JORDANUS, FRIAR: *Wonders of the East.* (Translated by Col. Yule for the Hakluyt Society. 1863.)

KANAKASABHAI, V.: *The Tamils Eighteen Hundred Years Ago.* (Higginbotham, Madras. 1904.)

LINSCHOTEN, JOHN HUYGHEN VAN: *Voyage.* (Edited by Burnell and Tiele for the Hakluyt Society. 1884.)

LOGAN, W.: *Malabar.* (2 vols. Madras. 1887.)

———: *A Collection of Treaties, Engagements, etc., relating to British Affairs in Malabar.* (Madras. 1891.)

LOGAN, W.: *The Malabar Land Tenures.* (Malabar Special Commission, 1883. Madras Government Press.)

MACKENZIE, G. T.: *Christianity in Travancore.* (Trivandrum. 1901.)

Madras Government Museum Bulletins. Vol. I, No. 2. Vol. II, Nos. 1 and 3. Vol. III, Nos. 1, 2 and 3. Vol. IV, Nos. 1 and 3.

Madras Journal of Literature and Science, Volumes XI, XIII and XXII.

Malabar Land Tenures. (A collection of official papers on the subject, 1880–85. Madras Government Press.)

Malabar Land Tenures Committee, 1885. Report. (Madras Government Press, 1887.)

Malabar Marriage Commission. Report. (Madras. 1894.)

Malabar Quarterly Review. Volumes I–V.

MALLESON: *History of the French in India.*

MARCO POLO: *Travels.* (Translated by Col. Yule.)

MATEER, S.: *Native Life in Travancore.* (Allen & Co. 1883.)

MAYNE, J. D.: *Hindu Law and Usage.* (Higginbotham, Madras. 1906.)

MCCRINDLE, G. W.: *Ancient India as described by Megasthenes and Arrian.* (Trubner. 1877.)

MOORE, LEWIS: *Malabar Law and Custom.* (Higginbotham, Madras. 1905.)

NAGAM AIYAR, V.: *The Travancore State Manual.* (Trivandrum. 1906.)

ORME, ROBERT: *History of Indostan.* (London. 1803.)

PIETRO DELLA VALLE: *Travels to India.* (Edited by Grey for the Hakluyt Society. 1891.)

PYRARD DE LAVAL: *Voyage to the East Indies.* (Translated by Gray and Bell for the Hakluyt Society. 1887.)

RAE, G. MILNE: *The Syrian Church in India.* (Blackwood. 1892.)

RAMUSIO, GIO BATTISTA: *Navigatione e Viaggi.* (3 vols. Venice. 1556–74.)

RISLEY, Sir H.: *Census Report,* 1901. (Census of India, Vol. I.)

Roteiro Il.; *A Journal of the First Voyage of Vasco da Gama.* (Translated by Ravenstein for the Hakluyt Society.)

SANKARA MENON, M.: *Cochin Census Report,* 1901. (Census of India, Vol. XX.)

SUBRAMANIA AIYAR, N.: *Travancore Census Report,* 1901. (Census of India, Vol. XXVI.)

Selections from the Records of the Madras Government, Revenue. Vols. I–III.

SEWELL, R.: *A Forgotten Empire* (Vijayanagar). (Swan, Sonnenschein & Co. 1900.)

South Indian Inscriptions, II and III.

TAVERNIER: *Travels in India.* (Translated by V. Ball. Macmillan. 1889.)

THEVENOT: *Travels into the Levant.* (London. 1687.)

THURSTON, EDGAR: *Ethnographic Notes in Southern India.* (Madras Government Press, 1906.)

TURNER, Sir CHARLES: *Minute on the Draft Bill relating to Malabar Land Tenures.* (Madras. 1885.)

VARTHEMA, LUDOVICO DI: *Travels.* (Edited by Badger for the Hakluyt Society. 1864.)

WALKER, Major: *The Malabar Land Tenures.* 1801.

WELSH, Col.: J.: *Military Reminiscences in the East Indies.* (Smith Elder & Co. 1830.)

WHITEHOUSE, T.: *Lingerings of Light in a dark Land.* (Brown & Co. London. 1873.)

WILKS, Col.: *History of Mysore.* (3 vols. London. 1810.)

YULE: *The Book of Ser Marco Polo.* (2 vols. Murray. 1903.)

ZEIN-UD-DIN: *Tahafut-ul-Mujahidin.* (Translated by Rowlandson for the Oriental Translation Fund. London. 1833.)

PLAN OF CONTENTS

TABLE OF CONTENTS

CHAPTER I.

PHYSICAL DESCRIPTION.

CHAPTER II.

POLITICAL HISTORY.

CHAPTER III.

THE PEOPLE.

CHAPTER IV.

AGRICULTURE AND IRRIGATION.

CHAPTER V.

FORESTS.

CHAPTER VI.

OCCUPATIONS AND TRADE.

CHAPTER VII.

MEANS OF COMMUNICATION.

CHAPTER VIII.

RAINFALL AND SEASONS.

PAGE

CHAPTER IX.

PUBLIC HEALTH.

CHAPTER X.

EDUCATION.

CHAPTER XI.

LAND REVENUE ADMINISTRATION.

CHAPTER XII.

SALT, ABKARI AND MISCELLANEOUS REVENUE.

CHAPTER XIII.

ADMINISTRATION OF JUSTICE.

CHAPTER XIV.

LOCAL SELF-GOVERNMENT.

CHAPTER XV.

GAZETTEER.

CHAPTER XVI.

THE LACCADIVE ISLANDS AND MINICOY.

GAZETTEER

OF THE

MALABAR DISTRICT.

CHAPTER I.

PHYSICAL DESCRIPTION.

GENERAL DESCRIPTION—Boundaries—Taluks and chief towns—Etymology of name—Scenery. HILLS—The Western Ghats—Outlying hills—Passes and the Palghat gap. THE RIVER SYSTEM—Valarpattanam river—Kotta river—Beypore river—Kadalundi river—Ponnani river—Cochin river—Tributaries of the Cauvery. THE COAST LINE—Islands—Mud banks—Their origin—*Ketta vellam*. SOILS—Soils of the Wynaad. RAINFALL. CLIMATE—Temperature—Climate of Wynaad—Humidity—Winds. GEOLOGY—Geological formation of the plains—Laterite—Geology of Wynaad—Gold fields of the Wynaad—Gold washing—Gold in the plains—Iron—Other minerals—Building stones. FLORA, FAUNA—Domestic animals—Sheep, goats and pigs—Big game—The lesser animals—Crocodiles—Birds, butterflies and snakes—Fish.

CHAP. I.
GENERAL DESCRIPTION.

Boundaries.

MALABAR, one of the two districts of the Madras Presidency situated on the west coast of India, lies between N. Lat. 10° 15′ and 12° 18′ and E. Long. 75° 14′ and 76° 15′, and stretches along the shores of the Arabian Sea for a distance of 150 miles. Bounded on the north by South Canara and on the south by Cochin State, the district is divided on the east from Coorg, the Nilgiris and Coimbatore by the Western Ghats, an almost continuous mountain wall broken only by the Palghat Gap. Only in two places does Malabar rise above the crest of the ghats, in the Wynaad taluk, a part of the great Mysore plateau, and in the Attapadi and Silent Valleys behind the irregular ridge stretching from the Kundahs to the lofty hills north of Palghat. The breadth of the district varies from less than five miles in the extreme south of the Ponnani taluk to upwards of seventy miles in the middle, where Palghat taluk penetrates the line of the ghats.

Malabar proper is made up of the nine taluks of Chirakkal, Kottayam, Kurumbranad, Calicut, Wynaad, Ernad, Walavanad, Ponnani, and Palghat. Cochin taluk, which is also a part of the district, includes the town of British Cochin and seventeen *pattams* or small isolated estates situated within

CHAP. I. GENERAL DESCRIPTION. Taluks and chief towns.

the boundaries of Cochin State. The Laccadive islands off the coast are also administered by the Collector. Excluding the extent of the islands, the area of the district is 5,787·45 square miles. Its capital is the Cantonment and Municipality of Calicut, and other towns of importance are Palghat, Tellicherry, Cannanore, Cochin, Badagara and Ponnani.

Etymology of name.

The etymology of the name Malabar has given rise to much controversy. Al Biruni (970–1039 A.D.) appears to have been the first to call the country Malabar; but long before his time the Egyptian merchant, Cosmas Indicopleustes, mentions a town Male on the west coast of India, as a great emporium of the pepper trade. Malabar has therefore been derived from Male, but more probably it is a compound of the Dravidian *mala*, a hill, and either the Arabic *barr* a continent, or the Persian *bar* a country. Malibar, Manibar and the Melibar of Marco Polo are perhaps the most common among the many variants of the name found in the ancient Muhammadan and European writers.[1] The vernacular name for the district is Malayalam 'the land of hills'; the ancient name Kerala, which properly includes Cochin and Travancore, is also used.

Scenery.

The scenery of the district is varied in the extreme, and ranges from the radiant beauty of the coral reefs of the Laccadives, with their blue sea, white foam, and green lagoons, fringed with feathery palms and sparkling sand, to the stern majesty of the mighty Western Ghats. In the warm wet air vegetation runs riot, and many of the exotics, which grow hardly under glass in the hot houses of Kew, here flourish in the open air in the wildest profusion. Along the narrow strip of sand near the coast, the green of palm and jack tree contrasts vividly with the red of the roads that run beneath them. Beneath the shade of the trees nestle the houses of the natives, not huddled together as in an East Coast village, but each in its own compound surrounded by a stout thorn fence, and full of giant plantains with their broad leaves and of the many coloured flowers of the *hibiscus*. A mile or two inland the scene changes, and the country begins to swell towards the barrier of the ghats, at first in range after range of low red laterite hills with paddy flats fringed with cocoanut gardens winding in and out of their recesses, and later in the long spurs, deep ravines and thick jungles that mark the rise of the hills. Towering over all, their slopes clad in dense forests, the majestic mountains of the Western Ghats keep watch over the favoured land at their feet.

HILLS. The Western Ghats.

The chief glory of Malabar is the long array of these ghats, which maintain an average elevation of 5,000 feet, but occasionally soar up into peaks upwards of 8,000 feet high. From the extreme north of the district they run parallel with

[1] *Indian Antiquary*, XXXI, p. 347.

CHAP. I.
HILLS.

the coast, at a distance of some twenty miles, as far as Vavul Mala or Camel's Hump abreast of Calicut. At Vavul Mala they turn sharply eastward, and, after bending northwards round the Nilambur Valley, recede inland as far as the Vada Malas north of the Palghat Gap. South of the gap they rise again in the Tenmalas or southern hills, some four or five thousand feet high, and gradually swell once more into the giant Anamalas. Mukurti (8,380 feet), Nilgiri Peak (8,118 feet), Gulikal hill (8,096 feet) and Anginda Peak (7,828 feet), the highest peaks of the Malabar section of the Western Ghats, are all on the Nilgiri boundary overlooking the Nilambur Valley. In Malabar proper, Vavul Mala (7,677 feet), a landmark conspicuous far out to sea, and Vellari Mala (7,364 feet) take pride of place; and hills between 4,000 and 7,000 feet high are too numerous to mention.

Outlying hills.

Detached from the main range, several outlying hills break the monotony of the undulating laterite downs of the low country. Pranakkod (1,792 feet) and Ananga Mala (1,298 feet) in the Walavanad taluk, Pandalur hill and Urot Mala (1,533 feet) in Ernad taluk, and Alattur hill in Palghat are the highest of these hills; but the most famous is the bold, bluff eminence of Mount Deli (720 feet) on the coast of Chirakkal taluk a few miles north of Cannanore. Marco Polo touched here, and describes the surrounding country under the name of the kingdom of Eli. The hill has always been a well-known land mark, and Vasco da Gama's pilots foretold that the first land to be sighted would be "a great mountain which is on the coast of India in the kingdom of Cannanore, which the people of the country in their language call the mountain Delielly, and they call it of the rat, and they call it Mount Dely because in this mountain there were so many rats that they never could make a village there."[1] The etymology of the name is, however, very uncertain.

Passes and the Palghat Gap.

Many passes pierce the wall of the Western Ghats. The Perambadi Ghat gives access to Coorg, the Periya and Tamarasseri Ghats to the Malabar Wynaad and Mysore and the Karkkur Ghat to the Nilgiri district. Excellent roads ascend all these passes, and they are to-day the most important arteries of road-borne traffic in Malabar. But as channels of trade the passes are dwarfed into insignificance by the Palghat Gap. For some miles on either side of Palghat town the hills have been rolled aside by some world convulsion, and the unique physical character of this the sole break in a mountain chain 600 miles long is equalled only by its economic importance. Through the Gap twenty-five miles broad the south-west winds bring moist air and fruitful showers to the thirsty plains of Coimbatore, and road and railway link the east and western coasts of the presidency.

---

[1] *The Three Voyages of Vasco da Gama* (Hakluyt series), p. 145.

CHAP. I. HILLS.

THE RIVER SYSTEM.

The river system of Malabar, in itself as simple as it is extensive, is complicated by the ramifications of a network of backwaters near the sea. Apart from the three great tributaries of the Cauvery, which drain the Attapadi Valley and nearly the whole of the Wynaad taluk, all the rivers of the district flow down from their watersheds in the Western Ghats to the Arabian Sea. With the single exception of the Ponnani river, none of them exceeds a hundred miles in length; and only when the south-west monsoon is blowing, and the rainfall on the ghâts is measured in scores of inches, do they roll down in heavy flood. For nine months in the year the majority are shallow streams, and, unable to force their way through the sand banks formed along the coast by the persistent action of the littoral current, lose themselves in back waters and creeks and arms of the sea. Many of these backwaters have been linked up by artificial canals, forming important means of communication ; and, in the south of the district, there is an uninterrupted waterway from Tirur to Travancore.

Valarpattanam river.

The Valarpattanam river in Chirakkal taluk, though not the longest river in Malabar, probably discharges into the sea the greatest volume of water. The river rises in the slopes of Periya Mala in the extreme north-west corner of the Wynaad, and is joined before Iritti by two great feeder streams. It is 70 miles long, and enters the sea at the thriving Mappilla towns of Valarpattanam, from which it takes its name. Timber is floated down the stream from the ghat forests, and small boats laden with salt and salt-fish ascend at all times of the year as far as the once important Mappilla village of Irukkur to return with rich cargoes of pepper. The wide and deep estuary of the river, which forms the port of Valarpattanam or Baliapatam, opens out on the north into a backwater, into which falls the Taliparamba river with the drainage water of the north-east of the taluk. The Sultan's canal connects this backwater with the creeks and arms of the Mount Deli river, which again joins the Nileswaram river. The major portion of the last-named stream lies in South Canara, but for some miles it is the northern boundary of Malabar.

Kotta river.

The Anjarakkandi and Mahe rivers, which drain the rich pepper country of Kottayam and northern Kurumbranad, are navigable for a few miles only from their mouths, and are unconnected with one another and with other streams. But the Kotta river in the centre of the latter taluk, which takes its name from a fort (Mal. *Kotta*), which commanded its entrance in the days when the Kottakkal pirates harried the shipping along the coast, opens up a long chain of inland waterways. From its catchment area among the dense masses of virgin forest on the Western Ghats, it gathers in its course of only 46 miles an immense volume of water, and is navigable as far as Kuttiyadi, whence a pack bullock track leads into North Wynaad. A short canal connects the river on the north with Badagara, the chief port of Kurumbranad; and the Payyoli and Conolly canals link it on the south with the Agalapuzha, Elattur, Kallayi and Beypore rivers and with Calicut, the capital of the district.

Beypore river.

The Beypore river or Chaliar, 96 miles long, famed of old for its auriferous sands, is the only river of Malabar which draws a great part of its waters from above the crest of the ghat ranges. It has three main branches, which unite a few miles above Nilambur. The eastern branch, or Karimpuzha, rises below Mukurti peak, and drains the densely wooded valley between Gulikal hill and the Nilagiri and Mukurti peaks. The middle branch, the Ponpuzha or gold river, drains the Ouchterlony valley and the south-east of the Marappanmadi or Needlerock range in the Nambalakod amsam of the Nilgiri-Wynaad (where it is called the Pandi), and passes over the ridge of the ghats in a succession of rocky cataracts a few miles south of the Karkkur pass. The westernmost branch, or Chaliyar, leaps down from the crest of the Wynaad hills in a magnificent water-fall near the Choladi pass, and drains the valley east of the Vavul Mala or Camel's Hump. The three streams, reinforced by many large feeders, unite in the heart of the famous teak plantations in the middle of the Nilambur valley, and thence flow into the sea at Beypore, six miles south of Calicut, once the terminus of the Madras Railway.

The monsoon floods scour out the bar sufficiently to admit country craft into the mouth of the river, and even in the driest seasons boats of light draught can ascend the stream as far as the Mappilla village of Mambad under the very shadow of Chekkunnu, one of the spurs of Camel's Hump range. Vast quantities of timber are floated down from the forests to Beypore, and thence through the Conolly canal to Kallayi, close to the Calicut bazaar, one of the greatest timber marts in India.

Kadalundi river.

The Kadalundi river, which is connected with the Beypore river by a creek, flows down through the Ernad and Walavanad taluks from the wilds of the Silent Valley, and empties itself into the sea at Kadalundi after a course of some 75 miles. An attempt, continued down to 1857, was made by several Collectors to complete an uninterrupted system of water communication from Badagara in Kurumbranad to Trivandrum in Travancore, by constructing a navigable canal from this river to one of the arms of the Ponnani river; but the cutting, though still in existence, is impassable except for the smallest boats at the height of the monsoon. The oily mud, which oozes up from below into the water of the

CHAP. I. THE RIVER SYSTEM.

canal, is the great obstacle to navigation. In rainy weather the Kadalundi river is navigable for small boats as far as Karuvarakkundu at the foot of the ghats, but in the dry season they cannot ascend higher than Puttur amsam in Ernad taluk.

Ponnani river.

The Ponnani river, the longest of all the rivers that penetrate to the Arabian Sea through Malabar, is of less commercial importance than is either the Valarpattanam or the Beypore river. The main stream 156 miles long comes from the Anamalai hills through the Pollachi taluk in Coimbatore, and its drainage area among the mountains exposed to the full force of the south-west monsoon is comparatively small. In the hot weather the wide sandy bed of the river is almost dry except for a few miles from its mouth, but in the monsoon laden boats ascend for considerable distances. The river traverses the taluks of Palghat and Ponnani, skirts the southern boundary of Walavanad, and, after receiving between the railway stations of Pallippuram and Kuttipuram the drainage-water of the last taluk from its great tributary, the Tutha river, discharges itself into the sea at the port of Ponnani. North of the town a wide reach of backwater stretches away to the railway system at Tirur, and to the south the river is linked by a canal with the Veliyangod and Chettuvayi backwaters, and ultimately with the long line of waterways that ends only at Trivandrum.

Cochin river.

The so-called Cochin river is hardly a river at all. It is rather the tidal opening of these inland waters and of the many rivers that rise in the high ranges of Cochin State and Travancore. The swift rush of water across the bar maintains a minimum depth of eleven feet of water at low tide; and, though steamers generally lie out in the open roadstead, native ships of considerable size enter the harbour of Cochin, and take in cargo in smooth water off the quays of the town.

Tributaries of the Cauvery.

The three tributaries of the Cauvery which have their water-sheds in Malabar are the Kabbani, the Rampur and the Bhavani rivers. The first two drain nearly the whole of the Wynaad taluk, but their streams are too swift and their beds too rocky for any but timber traffic. The Bhavani river, rising in the Kundahs near Kudikadubetta, falls rapidly in a series of cataracts from the highest range of the Kundahs into the Attapadi valley to the east of Anginda peak, gathers volume from one large and innumerable small feeder streams in the valley, and at its north-east corner flows northwards into the Coimbatore district.

The seaboard of Malabar trends north-north-west by south-south-east throughout its length of 150 miles. Cochin boasts the only harbour worthy of the name; and, though ships of shallow draught can cross the bars of one or two rivers, the

CHAP. I. THE COAST LINE.

coast affords scanty shelter to shipping against the gales of the south-west monsoon. There is no deep water close in shore; the muddy bottom shelves gradually for thirty to forty miles from the coast to a depth of 100 fathoms, whence it drops suddenly to 1,000 fathoms; but except for Sacrifice rock about eight miles out to sea off the mouth of the Kotta river, and the dangerous reefs at Calicut, Tellicherry and Tangasseri, navigation is not complicated by hidden rocks. The littoral current flows from south to north in the south-west monsoon, and southwards at other times. It is strong from May to October, and traces of a long battle for supremacy between land and sea are everywhere visible. North of Calicut, the coast line as far as the solitary eminence of Mount Deli is fringed with low cliffs alternating with reaches of sand, and denuded headlands and bays hollowed out by the waves on their southward side betray the action of the ocean current. South of Calicut the shore is one unbroken stretch of sand, partly thrown up by the waves, partly formed by alluvial deposits brought down by the rivers and backwaters. There is reason to believe that two thousand years ago the eastern shore of the backwater from Cranganore nearly to Quilon was the coast line of the country; but, if this be so, the sea has since been claiming its own again. Tradition tells of a church buried out to sea some hundred yards west of Vypeen on the north bank of the Cochin river, and on the south bank the process of erosion is going on steadily year by year. Hamilton's story of a 'sunken town built by the Portuguese' on Coote's reef off Calicut lacks confirmation, but there is no doubt that the sea now covers what was once the site of the tomb of the Arab Priest, Shaikh Mammu Koya.

Islands.

The Laccadives, 'the hundred thousand islands' attached to Malabar, lie at a distance varying between 139 and 218 miles off the coast, and consist of a group of four inhabited and ten uninhabited islands. They lie generally north and south in a crescent shape, with usually a shallow lagoon enclosed by a reef on the western and north-western sides. They are coral formations and their highest points are not more than thirty feet above sea level. They are covered with dense masses of vegetation, consisting in the cultivated parts of cocoanuts, with a few jacks and lime trees, and elsewhere of screw pine and scrubby undergrowth. Minicoy, with its dependant quarantine islet of Viringilli, lies further south at a distance of 243 miles from Calicut. In general appearance it is similar to the Laccadives; but the inhabitants speak Mahl, and the island is really an offshoot of the Maldive group.

Mud Banks.

The mud banks, that occur at rare intervals along the seaboard from the Kotta river to Cape Comorin, are peculiar to this part of the west coast of India, and from time

CHAP. I. THE COAST LINE. immemorial have been known to mariners as safe and smooth anchorages, even in the gales of the south-west monsoon. The most famous are the banks at Alleppy in Travancore and at Narakkal just north of Cochin; but there are smaller banks at Calicut and Pantalayini Kollam in Malabar proper. Ordinarily, when the sea is smooth, the banks are discoverable only by soundings for mud; but, with the onset of the monsoon, the bed of mud at the bottom of the sea is stirred up, and the anchorages calm down as if oil had been poured on their waters. The mud itself, which is peculiar and is not found elsewhere along the coast, is dark-green in colour, fine in texture and oily to the touch. Another curious feature of the banks is that they are not stationary, but are carried slowly along by the littoral currents. The Alleppy bank is peculiar in that at times its smooth surface is disturbed by 'mud volcanoes' rivers or huge cones of mud and water, which come bubbling up from below, often bringing with them dead fish and roots and trunks of trees.

Their origin. The bank of Alleppy is the only one which has been scientifically investigated, but *mutatis mutandis* the same explanation holds good for all. The nature of the coast line from Cranganore to Quilon has already been alluded to. The narrow mouth of the Cochin river is the sole outlet of a long line of backwaters, which fed by countless streams run paralled with the sea for a hundred miles and more, and are only separated from it by a strip of sand. At Alleppy, beneath the sand and an underlying stratum of chocolate-coloured sandsstone, boring has revealed a layer of mud of precisely the same nature as that found in the sea outside the town, and the connection between the two is obvious. In the monsoon, when the rivers come down in flood and the pressure increases, the swollen backwaters are driven to find another egress to the sea. A subterranean river forces its way through the yielding mud below Alleppy, and, carrying part of it along in its impetuous course, forms the mud bank off the town. Similar subterranean rivers and substrata of mud must lie below Narakkal, Calicut and Pantalayini Kollam, and the absence of 'mud volcanoes' is due to the fact that they lie nearer to the mouths of rivers, and the pressure of water in the neighbouring lagoons is less. The transquillising effect of the mud is due to the oil therein. Samples sent for assay to the laboratory of the Geological Survey at Calcutta, 'when subjected to distillation, gave a brownish-yellow oily matter lighter than water and looking not unlike petroleum.' The oil is derived partly no doubt from the decomposition of organic matter in the mud, and is also possibly generatedund er the influence of moderate heat in the subjacent lignitiferous deposits belonging presumably to Warkilli Strata.[1]

[1] See *Madras Journal of Literature and Science*, XXII, N.S. 132–136. Records of Geological Survey of India, XVII and XXIII.

CHAP. I. THE COAST LINE.

Ketta vellam.

The suffocation of the fish in heavy monsoons, when the Alleppy bank is violently stirred up, possibly connects the banks with another curious and unexplained phenomenon often observed in Malabar, which is locally known as the *ketta vellam* or stinking water. At various periods of the year, but chiefly towards the close of the rains, the sea and some of the backwaters exhale very offensive effluvia. The water is at times of a dark porter colour, at other times it leaves a deposit of black mud on the sand. It is invariably fatal to fishes of all sorts, which float dead and dying on the surface, and are thrown up in thousands by the waves upon the beach. Local fishermen believe that in seasons when the monsoon is weak, the stagnant backwaters are poisoned by the emptying of the pits in which the husks of cocoanuts are left to rot in mud and water for months together.

SOILS.

Geologically, the plains of Malabar consist for the most part of a low laterite tableland, fringed on the seaward side by a narrow belt of recent alluvial formations. Except for a thin line of arenaceous soil on the very shore of the sea in some of the coast taluks, the soils of this part of the district belong without exception to the red ferruginous series, and are composed of a mixture of clay and river sand in varying proportions. The percentages borne by each class of soil to the total area of each taluk are exhibited in the following table :—

—	Red ferruginous series.			Arenaceous series.
	Clay.	Loam.	Sand.	
Chirakkal ..	1·85	89·75	8·40	..
Kottayam ..	·47	96·80	2·73	..
Kurumbranad ..	1·20	85·91	11·33	1·56
Calicut	·15	92·25	6·87	·73
Ernad	·52	94·03	5·40	·05
Walavanad ..	·01	83·04	16·95	..
Palghat	..	90·40	9·60	..
Ponnani	4·15	39·89	51·06	4·90
Cochin	8·8	2·7	88·5	..

Clayey and sandy soils.

Except in the Ponnani and Cochin taluks, red loam is the prevailing soil. Clay preponderates only in a few lands inundated yearly during the monsoon, and in the beds of the shallow lakes and lagoons of Ponnani, which dry up or are baled out by Persian wheels sufficiently to admit of a single crop of paddy being snatched in the hot weather months. The alluvial deposits, a mixture of river sand and silt, are a

[1] See Day's *Land of the Permauls*, pp. 416 and 417 ; and *Madras Government Museum Bulletin*, Vol. iii, No. 2, pp. 127–129.

CHAP. I. Soils.

light sandy soil slightly impregnated with salt and peculiarly suited to the growth of the cocoanut palm. They are found chiefly along the shores of the backwaters and near the mouths of the rivers on the coast, and it is in places such as these that the cocoanut grows with the greatest luxuriance. The soil has the advantage of being easily worked, and paddy grows well upon it provided that rain be plentiful and the crop generously manured. Its power of retaining surface moisture is small, and the ryots rarely attempt to grow more than one crop of paddy upon this soil.

Red loam.

The loamy soils of the tableland are lateritic in their origin. Laterite, a form of decomposed gneiss, and in itself a soil rather than a rock, is peculiarly sensitive to the action of the weather, and, when exposed thereto, rapidly disintegrates into its component parts. The most valuable of these in its fertilizing power is the white or yellow clay, which fills the tubes which penetrate laterite in every direction. This clay contains both iron and potash. To the former the soil owes both its name and its reddish colour. The latter in small quantities is a valuable ingredient, and its excess is rapidly got rid of by water. The process of disintegration is continually going on, and the most valuable parts of the laterite are washed down yearly by heavy rains from the surrounding hills into the paddy flats below. The resultant soil is a well-balanced mixture of clay and sand, poor perhaps in organic matter, but on the whole, well suited to paddy. Cocoanuts, arecanuts and jack trees flourish well with careful cultivation in the gardens on the borders of the flats, and pepper, the Malabar money of old, grows vigorously in the interior of the northern taluks near the foot of the ghats, where the soil is richer in organic matter. The slopes of the laterite hills are too stony and gravelly to be really fertile; but, even on them, successive crops of hill rice and oil seeds repay the most casual cultivation once in every three or four years, and not infrequently patches of loamy soil occur, where ginger, another of Malabar's most distinctive crops, grows at intervals to the great profit of the enterprising ryot.

Soils of the Wynaad.

The Wynaad has been excluded from the above table for the reason that its paddy flats alone have been classified. The soils of these flats belong to the red ferruginous series with a sprinkling (4 per cent) of regar soils in the north of the taluk. The red ferruginous soils are of various shades of red and brown, due to the presence of iron in the original rocks which they now represent. They are of different degrees of fertility, mostly good, varying with the quantity of carbonaceous matter (derived from the decomposition of organic substances) which they contain. The soils are coloured by sesquioxide of iron resulting from the disintegration of pyrites, which is largely disseminated through the gneiss. Laterite is comparatively

CHAP. I. Soils.

scarce, but crystals of magnetic and grains of titaniferous iron ore are by no means uncommon, and occasional bands of haematite occur. Hence the large impregnation of the soils with iron. The regar soils are dark in colour, mostly black and blackish brown, and are of remarkable natural fertility, containing in addition to finely comminuted minerals much organic matter derived from the decay of the luxuriant vegetation of the tract.

RAINFALL.

Detailed statistics of the rainfall are given in the separate Appendix to this volume and in Chapter VIII below. The district average, which is more than 116 inches, is exceeded in the presidency only in South Canara.

CLIMATE. Temperature.

Systematic meteorological observations are made daily at Cochin and Calicut, and it is only just to the much abused climate of Malabar to say that nowhere is it more unpleasant than at these two places. The following statement gives the average maxima, minima, and mean temperatures in degrees Fahrenheit at 8 a.m. :—

—	Cochin.			Calicut.		
	Average maximum.	Average minimum.	Mean.	Average maximum.	Average minimum.	Mean.
January	89·1	71·5	80·3	87.6	69·6	78·6
February ..	89·9	73·7	81·8	88.7	72·6	80·7
March	91·2	77·0	84·1	90·3	76·1	83·2
April	91·5	78·4	85·0	91·3	77·9	84·6
May	89·6	77·6	83·6	90·4	77·9	84·1
June	85·0	74·7	79·8	84·6	74·7	79·7
July	83·5	74·1	78·8	82·5	73·9	78·2
August	83·7	74·3	79·0	82·8	74·1	78·4
September ..	84·6	74·5	79·6	84·3	74·4	79·3
October	86·2	74·6	80·4	86·2	74·5	80 4
November ..	87·5	74·4	80·9	87·4	73·1	80·2
December ..	88·5	72·9	80·7	87·6	70·5	79·1
The year ..	87·55	74·8	81·2	86·9	74·1	80·5

The most striking feature of these statistics is the extraordinary uniformity of the temperature. Great extremes of heat and cold are unknown, and the fierce hot weather of the Ceded districts and their pleasant cool season are both absent. In the hottest months, the average maximum is only 91° ; but, though at first sight this compares favourably with the 103° of Bellary, it is oppressive enough in the moisture-laden atmosphere of Malabar to make life a burden. In the monsoon, when the sun is obscured by clouds and the landscape blotted out in rain, the diurnal range of the thermometer is very limited ; but the air is damp and chilly rather than cold, and, even in the nights of the so-called cold weather, the thermometer rarely sinks below 70°. The net result is a

CHAP. I. CLIMATE.

climate which though not unhealthy cannot be called exhilarating. Europeans find it trying to the nerves and conducive to all forms of rheumatism, and in the damp months of the monsoon the thinly clad native suffers from dysentery and pneumonia. In the rains too, clothes, saddlery, books, guns and the like must be looked after with peculiar care, and have to be kept in hermetically sealed cases or in cupboards in which a lamp is kept constantly burning.

Climate of Wynaad.

The climate of the Wynaad plateau, 3,000 or 4,000 feet above the sea, is much cooler. During the cold weather, the thermometer falls as low as 60°, but in March, April and May a temperature of 84° and more is often recorded. These are the unhealthy months when malarial fever of a severe type is prevalent. From October to the end of February, when the climate is dry, cool and salubrious, the Wynaad is the sanitarium of Malabar.

Humidity.

As is natural in a district exposed to the full force of the south-west monsoon, the average percentage of humidity in the atmosphere (82·5) is exceptionally high. It rises to 90 per cent in the months of June, July and August when the monsoon prevails, and sinks to 72 in January, when the average rainfall is less than one-fourth of an inch.

Winds.

Statistics of the average daily velocity and the normal direction of the wind at Cochin, the only station where these observations are recorded, are given in the margin. The curious persistence with which the wind blows from the north-west, even in the months of the so-called south-west monsoon, is noticeable. The explanation is that the monsoon current, which approaches the Peninsula of India from an almost due westerly direction, there encounters an elevated land surface, the trend of which is towards the south-south-east, and, though a considerable portion surmounts the ghats and enters India, yet a large part of the surface air is deflected southwards and becomes a north-westerly wind.[1]

Month.	Direction.	Velocity.
January ..	N. 63 W.	6
February ..	N. 72 W.	37
March ..	N. 77 W.	54
April ..	N. 78 W.	59
May ..	N. 78 W.	55
June ..	W.	44
July ..	N. 78 W.	54
August ..	N. 75 W.	64
September ..	N. 75 W.	70
October ..	W.	45
November ..	N. 88 W.	25
December ..	N. 66 W.	20

The south-west monsoon breaks early in June with fierce squalls and floods of rain. After the first violent burst, persistent rain sets in, and on the coast the air current is steady

[1] *The Winds and Monsoons of the Arabian Sea and Indian Ocean* by W. L. Dallas, p. 37.

CHAP. I. CLIMATE.

rather than strong. But inland, as it advances nearer to the funnel of the Palghat Gap, its velocity increases, and furious gusts sweep the rain along almost parallel with the ground. In September the current grows weak, and from October onwards, growing stronger as the weather gets hotter, land winds blow at night and in the mornings. In the forenoon there is a lull, and about 2 P.M., with the punctuality almost of clockwork, cool breezes from the sea spring up to supply the place of the atmosphere rarified by the heat. The land winds are most unpleasant and dangerous both to man and beast. In the Palghat taluk especially during February, March and April a hot wind rushes in from the burning plains of Coimbatore, and dries up every green thing for miles around. The value of the south-west monsoon to Western navigation was discovered as early as the beginning of the Christian Era by Hippalus the pilot;[1] but scientific opinion is still divided whether it is merely drawn from a reservoir of air over the equatorial zone fed by the south-east trades, or whether it is the trade wind itself deflected by the specific gravity of the air and by the physiographic features of the region over which it blows.[2]

GEOLOGY.

The only parts of Malabar that have been examined by the Geological Survey of India are the gold fields of the Wynaad and the region between the Beypore and Ponnani rivers. Geologically however these two tracts taken together are typical of the whole district above and below the ghats.

Geological formation of the Plains.

Between the Beypore and Ponnani rivers the country consists for the most part of a laterite plateau rising to its greatest height between the village of Kolattur in the Walavanad taluk and the three outlying hills of Urot Mala, Pranakkod and Ananga Mala. The plateau is seamed with deep valleys and gorges, the result of sub-aerial erosion, and contains some isolated hills of gneiss rising above the laterite; on the west it ends abruptly and is divided from the sea by a belt of sand of recent formation resting upon a stratum of sandstone; to the east low hills of gneiss rise gradually to the range of the Western Ghats. There are many indications that originally Malabar lay some 500 feet below its present level and that the sea washed the foot of the ghats, and the terraced character of the laterite plateaus is probably the result of marine denudation before the general elevation of the country, the sea eroding the face of the ghats and the isolated hills, and laying sedimentary deposits around them.

Rocks.

The rocks found in the plateau in order of ascension are gneiss, intrusive dykes and sheets, laterite and recent deposits. The last are found only near the coast, and the intrusive dykes and sheets are not of much importance. The gneiss is almost

---

[1] See the Periplus Maris Erythræi *M'Crindle's* Translation.

[2] See Dallas' *Winds and Monsoons of the Arabian Sea and Indian Ocean.*

CHAP. I. GEOLOGY.

everywhere very fine-grained, and is usually well laminated. Quartz, horneblende, felspar, mica, garnets, magnetite and hæmatite are the chief minerals found in the gneiss, the first two being the most abundant.

Laterite.

The laterite is of two varieties, vesicular and pellety. The former is a ferruginous hardened clay permeated by numerous vesicular branching and anastomosing tubes half an inch or less in diameter. Where the laterite has not been exposed to the air, the tubes are filled with a whitish yellow clay containing a smaller percentage of iron and a greater percentage of potash than the walls of the tubes. The deeper one digs, and the less affected the laterite is by the weather, the fainter becomes the distinction between the walls and their contents. Finally it disappears altogether, and what is laterite above is clay below. The pellety variety is more solid, and consists of small irregular nodules of red oxide of iron cemented together by similar material. It is a more advanced stage of laterite induced by exposure to the elements, and the process of its formation may be seen going on in many places. The contents of the tubes are washed out by the rains, and the exposed parts of the vesicular laterite break up. The tube walls disintegrate into little sub-angular, irregular pieces, and washed down by rain and rivers are deposited in lower levels. The origin of laterite has been much discussed since the name was first invented by Dr. Buchanan in the year 1800. The latest explanation is that it has been formed in Malabar by 'the decomposition of gneiss and the partial rearrangement by the mechanical action of water of the resulting materials.' In other words it is properly a soil rather than a rock, and the low laterite hills, which bulk so largely in the landscape of the district, are in reality gneissic hills covered with layers or caps of laterite of varying thickness.[1] This theory is however not free from objection.

Geology of Wynaad.

The present physical aspect of the Wynaad is due to sub-aerial denudation, and the principal agent in bringing about its wonderfully varied scenery has undoubtedly been water. With the possible exception of Edakkal Mala, there are no indications of any of the hills having been extruded. Ample geological grounds exist for regarding them merely as the remnants of ancient crystalline rocks which, thanks to the superior hardness of their component minerals, have withstood the enormous waste of centuries. The principal rocks are gneiss, members of the Charnockite series, intrusive rocks, and, most interesting of all from an economic point of view, auriferous quartz reefs. The gneissic rocks are typically biotite gneisses, their chief constituents being quartz, felspar, biotite and garnet. Charnockite is a name invented in 1893 for a rock common in the

---

[1] Conf. *Memoirs of the Geological Survey of India*, Vol. XXIV, Part 3; and Oldham's *Geology of India*, pp. 383–87.

Wynaad taluk, which is not only younger than biotite gneisses, but is intrusive in them. The whole range of Vellari Mala and most of the hills north of Vayittiri are composed of this rock, which is highly garnetiferous and horneblendic. The most important of the other intrusive rocks are the great masses of biotite gneiss, which occur at Sultan's Battery and between Kalpatta and Meppadi. Pegmatite veins composed chiefly of quartz, not of the auriferous variety, and felspar are common both in the gneiss and charnockite.

Gold fields of the Wynaad.

The hard crystalline quartz reefs, usually white and barren looking at the outcrop, which are common in the rectangular tract of country enclosed between Minangadi and Sultan's Battery on the north and Meppadi and the head of the Choladi Pass on the south, are known to be auriferous. Pyrites is the chief source of gold, but its proportion to quartz is usually small and its distribution irregular. The reefs seem to have been worked by the natives at least two centuries ago, but the official history of the industry begins only in 1793, when the Governor of Bombay applied to the local officials for information on the subject of gold mining and washing. The matter was taken up again in 1828, and in 1831 the Collector reported that the privilege of collecting gold in the Wynaad and the Nilambur Valley below it had been farmed out for the preceding forty or fifty years, and that the metal was chiefly obtained by washing the soil in streambeds, paddy flats and hillsides. Lieut. Woodly Nicholson of the 49th Native Infantry and a Swiss watchmaker of Cannanore, named H. L. Huguessin, then explored the neighbourhood of Devala and the Nilambur Valley, where they found a regular set of mines with shafts from 10 to 50 feet deep worked by 500 or 600 Mappillas belonging to the Nilambur Tirumulpad. They reported to Government in enthusiastic terms on the capabilities of the mines; but a committee subsequently appointed threw cold water on their proposals, and the matter was dropped.

The next important attempt to work the mines on a large scale began in the sixties of the last century, when the Wynaad had begun to be opened up for coffee and the traces of the old gold workings attracted the attention of the planters, some of whom had seen the Australian Gold Fields; and in 1874 was started the Alpha Gold Mining Company (nominal capital six lakhs), which began operations in a valley about a mile and a half south of Devala. Next year Government deputed Dr. W. King of the Geological Survey to examine the country, and he reported that in the Nambalakod amsam at any rate quartz crushing should be a success. Other companies were started, and in 1879 the Government of India employed Mr. Brough Smyth (for many years Secretary for Mines in Victoria and held

CHAP. I. GEOLOGY.

to be the greatest authority on the subject in Australia) to examine the Wynaad reefs. He reported in detail and concluded :—

"The reefs are very numerous and are more than of the average thickness of those found in other countries, . . . they are strong and persistent and highly auriferous at an elevation of less than 500 feet above the sea and they can be traced thence upwards to a height of nearly 8,000 feet . . . . . and the country possessing facilities for prosecuting mining operation at the smallest cost, sooner or later gold mining will be established as an important industry in South India."

In another place he wrote :—

"It is not however unlikely that the first attempts will fail. Speculative undertakings, having for their objects the making of money by buying and selling shares, are commenced invariably by appointing Secretaries and Managers of high salaries and the printing of a prospectus. This is followed by the erection of costly and not seldom wholly unsuitable machinery ; no attempts are made to open the mine and then, after futile endeavour to obtain gold, etc., worth of capital, it is pronounced and believed that gold mining on a large scale will never prove remunerative."

The latter prophecy was fulfilled to the letter ; the former was altogether falsified. The result of his report was the great boom of 1880. The London stock markets were just then ripe for any speculation ; 33 English Companies were floated with an aggregate nominal capital of over four million pounds sterling ; expensive machinery was sent out and sensational reports came home ; and shares were quoted at 50, 75 and even 100 per cent. premium. But of the four millions of capital more than half was allotted for payment for the lands in which the supposed mines were located ; and actual crushing was slow to begin. The experts sent out were often impostors, few of the reefs were opened out and little of the machinery erected. The results of the first crushings fell far below the exaggerated prophecies, and the inevitable slump quickly followed. In two years fifteen of the 33 companies had passed into the hands of the liquidators, and the yields obtained by the others were so poor (up to the first quarter of 1883, 3,597 tons had yielded only 9,641 dwts. of gold on an average of 2·7 per ton), that operations were gradually suspended ; and nothing now remains but melancholy relics of past activity in the shape of rusty machinery, derelict bungalows and abandoned roads.

In 1901 a local syndicate attempted unsuccessfully to reopen some of the reefs in the Nilgiri-Wynaad, and about the same time the Government of India deputed Mr. Haydon of the Geological Survey and Dr. Hatch, the Survey's mining specialist, to examine the mines and test the "belief undoubtedly still current in many quarters that the previous failures were in large part due to unsuitable appliances as well as to insufficient

CHAP. I. GEOLOGY.

supervision." Samples were taken systematically from numerous reefs not only in the Nilgiri-Wynaad, but also in the neighbourhood of Meppadi and Vayittiri ; and the conclusion arrived at was that "it is clear that with the methods at present available for the treatment of low grade ores, there is no hope of goldmining in the Wynaad becoming remunerative.[1]"

Gold washing.

The gold that decked Solomon's temple in the halcyon days of Jewish sovereignty is said to have come from the Malabar Coast whence came ivory, peacocks, apes and sandalwood that formed the cargo of Hiram's shipmen "that had knowledge of the sea".[2] In such names as Ponnani, Ponmudi, Ponmana and Ponnoorkode, the prefix *Pon* denotes gold, and the words supply philological evidence of the existence of gold in or about them. The sands of many of the rivers of South Malabar are highly auriferous but the sources of the gold must be looked for higher up in the Wynaad and the Attapadi valleys ; and Ponnarippu or tax on washing for gold was one of the sources of revenue of the early Malabar Rajahs.[3]

Gold in the Plains.

On the plains gold is found in the Nilambur valley, the soil of which originated in the detritus of the decomposed strata of superincumbent gneiss, which once connected the Nilgiri and Vellari Mala ranges, and receives additions yearly from the wash of the surrounding hills of the auriferous tract. To this day the Tirumulpad of Nilambur pays a small royalty for the privilege of washing for gold in the upper streams of the Beypore river and traces of ancient surface workings are visible here and there in the valley.

There has been no mining for gold, iron or other minerals in the district since 1915. A licence for prospecting for gold was granted to a European Engineer of Trichinopoly in 1926, but it was cancelled in 1929.

Iron.

The whole of the district, hill and plain alike, as is apparent from the above description of its geological formation, contains iron ore in inexhaustible quantities ; and, if only there were coal near at hand, Malabar might become one of the greatest industrial centres in India. One hundred years ago, when Dr. Buchanan travelled through the district, as many as thirty-four forges were at work in the vicinity of Angadippuram in Walavanad ; and in 1848 iron works were started at Beypore. But the works failed, and the native industry, killed by the influx of cheaper English material, is moribund ; and only at

[1] See Messrs. Haydon and Hatch's paper in Memoirs of the Geological Survey of India, Vol. XXXIII, Part 2 (1891) ; also Dr. King's preliminary note on the Gold Field's Records, Geol. Survey of India, VIII, 29 (1875) ; his note on progress there, *ibid.*, XI, 235 (1878) ; Mr. R. Brough Smyth's report of 1879 (Madras Government Press, 1880) and Mr. D. E. W. Leighton's *Indian Gold Mining Industry* (Higginbotham, 1883).

[2] *Indian Antiquary*, Vol. 1, page 230.

[3] *Padmanabha Menon's History of Kerala*, Vol. 1, pages 111–112.

CHAP. I. GEOLOGY.

one or two forges near Karuvarakkundu in the Ernad taluk are small quantities of iron still smelted by the primitive processes described by Buchanan.[1]

Other minerals.

Apart from gold and iron, the mineral wealth of Malabar is insignificant. Mica is fairly common, and seams of coal or rather carboniferous strata occur at Beypore, Cannanore and near Tritala in the Ponnani taluk.[2] Some excitement was also caused a few years ago by the discovery of a small pocket of quicksilver in the free state near Tellicherry. But none of these minerals exist in sufficient quantities to justify mining operations.

Building stones.

Of building stones of the common sort the district has great store. Grey granite of excellent quality crops out at frequent intervals. Laterite is universal, and on account of its cheapness is in great demand for buildings, culverts and bridges. In the mass, before exposure to the atmosphere, it is soft and yielding, and therefore easily quarried. Under the action of the weather it hardens and answers most of the purposes for which bricks are used ; but it varies in quality, and as a building material has its limitations. None but the best varieties can withstand a heavy, crushing weight, and many big laterite bridges, which once spanned the wide rivers of the district, have fallen into ruins.

FLORA.

The flora of a district, which ascends through every variation of soil and climate from the purely tropical zone on the coast to the cold mountain tops of the higher ranges of the Western Ghats, with a rainfall nowhere less than fifty inches and often more than three hundred, demands systematic and expert investigation. The famous *Hortus Malabaricus,* compiled at Cochin more than two hundred years ago by the Dutch Commander Baron Van Rheede and his collaborator the Carmelite monk Matthæus, and published in twelve volumes at Amsterdam between 1686 and 1703 with 794 copper plate engravings, describes under their trivial names most of the trees and plants of the West Coast ; but the list still awaits classification in the light of modern botanical science. In the magnificent evergreen shola forests of the upper ghat slopes, where the trees attain an immense size, and their flowers are not easy to obtain, many varieties still remain to be identified, and even on the plains numerous seemingly common hedgerow plants elude the diagnosis of local experts. The principal garden and timber trees of economic value are mentioned in Chapters IV and V below. Most of the Indian botanical orders are strongly represented, and in the monsoon months the glorious beauty of the vegetation beggars description. Wonderful is the contrast between Malabar in the hot weather and Malabar in the

[1] *A Journey through Mysore, Canara and Malabar* by Dr. Francis Buchanan, Vol. II, p. 494.

[2] *Madras Journal of Literature and Science,* Vol. XI, 1840.

CHAP. I. FLORA.

monsoon. In March, when skies are brass and earth is iron, and hot land winds are blowing, the sun-baked paddy flats are bare and brown, and beneath the shade of the dusty trees the gardens are mere wastes of laterite rock and uncultivated ground. The thunder showers of April and May bring some relief to the parched soil, but Malabar is not its real self till the rains break. In the space of a single night the new grass springs up, and the calladiums push their heads above ground; and soon even the rough laterite sides of the deep ditches between the gardens are clothed with a mass of delicate ferns, and between the bare red hills the winding valleys are one unbroken stretch of the emerald green of growing paddy set off by the darker green of the trees in the overhanging gardens. Along the coast the graceful cocoanut palm (*Cocos nucifera*) is of course the characteristic tree; but jack (*Artocarpus integrifolia*), mango (*Mangifera Indica*), cashew nut (*Anacardium Occidentale*), the talipot palm (*Corypha umbraculifera*), the areca (*Areca catechu*), the casuarina (*Casuarina equisitifolia*) and others too numerous to mention are common. Many familiar trees in the littoral zone are exotics in Malabar. The cocoanut itself is supposed to have come from Ceylon; and the seeds of the custard apple, guava, pineapple, papaya and cashew nut, which last is still known to natives as the foreign mango, were introduced into Cochin from Brazil by the Portuguese admiral Pedro Alvarez Cabral in 1500 A.D. Along the shores of the backwaters the screw pine (*Pandanus odoratissimus*) and the *Dilivaria ilicifolia*, an acanthaceous shrub with the leaf of a holly and a blue flower, are conspicuous. In gardens the plantain (*Musa paradisiaca*) thrives with a luxuriance worthy of the Hindu emblem of fertility and plenty, and wild arrow-root (*Curcuma angustifolia*), calladiums, yams, and other vegetables grow almost like weeds. Further eastward, as the district contracts towards the Palghat gap, the palmyra supplants the cocoanut, and the tamarind flourishes in the drier climate; and typical of the interior of the northern taluks is the pepper vine (*Piper nigrum*) trained on the stem of the scarlet flowered *Erythrina Indica*. Five miles from the foot of the ghat slopes begin the primeval forests, and from this point almost to their topmost peaks magnificent timber trees, bamboos and rattans, giant creepers, orchids, ferns and mosses abound in endless profusion. Flowering trees are a conspicuous feature of the Malabar flora. Among the commoner varieties, which adorn the landscape in the hot weather, the scarlet mantle of the gold mohur tree (*Poinciana regia*), the lilac flowers of the *Lagerstrœmia flos reginæ*, the beautiful wax-like flowers of the frangipani (*Plumeria acuminata*) and the deep red blossoms of the silk cotton tree (*Bombax Malabaricum*) are deserving of mention. The alamander and the hibiscus, one variety of which, *Hibiscus mutabilis*, changes colour as the day lengthens and from pure white gradually assumes a delicate

CHAP. I. FLORA.

pink tint, are the commonest garden flowers; but zinneas, balsams, cannas and Eucharis lilies also grow luxuriantly.

FAUNA. Domestic animals.

Malabar affords another example of the well-known rule that a wet climate is unsuited to cattle. Buffaloes, indeed, for which no climate seems too damp, and no rainfall too heavy, thrive, and bear the burden of most of the arduous work in the field; but the indigenous breed of cattle is miserably weak and under-sized. The climate no doubt is mainly responsible; but lack of selection in breeding, the reluctance of the Hindu to thin down his overgrown herds and his negligence in the matter of proper feeding all make for deterioration. Fodder crops are never grown. Bullocks and buffaloes in hard work are fed on paddy straw; the rest are driven out to graze on the laterite hills near the coast and in the jungles at the foot of the ghats. In the monsoon, when grass is fairly plentiful, they grow sleek and fat, but with the close of the rains in November they revert gradually to their normal, half-starved condition. Draught cattle of good quality are imported from Coimbatore and Mysore, and command good prices at the great annual fair at Kizhur in Kurumbranad taluk and in the important weekly market at Vaniamkulam. But they are invariably gelded animals, and do not help to improve the local stock. There are, however, signs of an awakening interest in the matter. The agricultural associations lately formed in the Palghat, Tellicherry and Malappuram divisions have taken it up, and arrangements have been made to import bulls from Mysore for service in Malabar. The success of the experiment will depend largely on the question of fodder. Thousands of tons of poonac (cocoanut oil-cake), which the district can illspare, are exported annually to Hamburg to feed German cattle, and no attempt is made to utilize the various oil seeds, etc., in the form of cakes as a food for cattle. Lucerne and guinea grass might well be tried in gardens, and cholam (*Sorghum vulgare*) sown thickly on dry lands in the monsoon and cut before it comes to ear would probably do excellently as a fodder crop.

Sheep, goat, and pigs.

There are no sheep in Malabar except in the drier parts of Palghat, but the goat is universal. In some of the coast towns, notably Ponnani, where the Mappillas take great care of them, they are of good quality and fine milkers; but for the most part they differ in no way from their East Coast kindred, and are remarkable only for their voracious appetites and catholic diet. Pigs are reared in large quantities by the Syrian Christians of South Ponnani.

Big game.

The ghat ranges and the belt of forest at their base still abound with the larger wild animals, though the advance of cultivation is gradually driving them from the low country. The elephant still roams the Begur and Chedleth reserves of North Wynaad in large herds, and numbers caught yearly in pitfalls spend the rest of their lives in dragging timber and helping to exploit their native forests. They are also common all along the chain of ghats and in the Nilambur valley. Rogues are fortunately rare, but not many years ago a single tusker held up for weeks the traffic on the Karkkur ghat and killed several people. Bison have suffered too much in the past from murrain and over-shooting to be very abundant, but they are still fairly common, especially in the forests of Brahmagiri in North Wynaad. In the hot weather they seek the cooler air of the higher ghat slopes, but as soon as the rains break they descend into the Nilambur valley and the swampy leech-infested jungles at the back of the Kurumbranad and Kottayam taluks to feed on the tender grass. The haunts and habits of the sambhur are very similar; but the graceful spotted deer or chutah is now almost confined to the Nilambur valley, where it is extraordinarily common all the year round. Tigers are to be found in most places, where there are deer; but they are rarely bagged. They confine themselves to the jungle and do not prey much upon cattle. Worse foes to the cultivator are the panthers which abound on the ghat slopes and in the Wynaad and are occasionally found lurking in lantana thickets far out in the low country, and above all the wild pigs, which haunt every patch of cover within ten miles from the foot of the hills and do untold mischief in the paddy fields. Bears are common above the ghats, and are occasionally met with in the foot-hills. The ibex, or Nilgiri goat (*hemitragus hylocrius*) is now found only on the slopes of the Kundahs and in the hills surrounding the Attapadi valley and the Palghat gap.

The lesser animals. Among lesser denizens of the jungles, monkeys and lemurs are well represented in the ghat forests and in the less populous parts of the plains. The destructive wild dog is unfortunately far too common, and three fine species of squirrels deserve notice. The Malabar squirrel (*Sciurus Malabaricus*) is of two varieties distinguished by their tails, which are wholly black and tipped with yellow respectively. They have a magnificent rich red fur and may often be seen racing from tree to tree in the forests. The large flying squirrel (*Pteromys petaurista*) is equally plentiful, but is rarely seen owing to its nocturnal habits. It also has a beautiful fur. Hares are fairly common in the scrub on the low hills, and otters and crocodiles abound in the rivers and backwaters.

Birds, butterflies, and snake. In birds, butterflies and all manner of creeping things the district is extraordinarily rich. Gorgeous butterflies of rare species flit through the fever haunted swamps and steamy forests at the bottom of the ghats, and in the monsoon every paddy flat is alive with snakes, mostly of harmless varieties. The cobra and Russell's viper and krait take their toll of human life every year, and in the mountains lives the dreaded king-cobra (*Ophiophagus elaps*). Of birds alone 420 different species are well known and have been described by Dr. Jerdon,

CHAP. I. FAUNA.

for many years a resident of Tellicherry. Snipe revel in the swamps of the Wynaad and the paddy flats of the plains, and a few seasons ago 800 couple fell to a single gun in the vicinity of Calicut. Teal, duck and curlew are fairly common in the backwaters in the south of the district; and quail, jungle fowl and peafowl abound, the latter especially in the Nilambur valley. Pigeons are very numerous. Every temple and mosque has its own flock of half tame blue rocks; the lovely green pigeon is often shot among the avenue trees of the interior; and the imperial pigeon (*Carpophaga aenea*) is a common feature of the forests. The melancholy pelican ibis (*Tantalus leucocephalus*) which is so frequently seen feeding in the paddy fields, is rare outside of Malabar. Other noticeable birds are the spoon bill, the pied horn-bill (*Hydrocissa coronata*), the egret (*Babulcus coromandus*) and the fish eagle on the coast; and the big horn bill (*Dichoceros cavatus*), the Malabar blue thrush (*Myiophonus horsfieldii*) and the sun bird (*Cinnyris lotenia*) on the ghats.

Fish.

The sea, rivers and backwaters teem with fishes innumerable. Varieties of economic value are mentioned in Chapter XII below, and are discussed exhaustively in Mr. Thurston's *Sea Fisheries of Malabar and South Canara.*[1] The *karimin* or black fish (*Sacco-branchus fossilis*), is noteworthy for its poisonous pectoral spine, a wound from which often induces gangrene and necessitates amputation of the injured limb. Of fresh water fishes murrel and carp are the most important. The mahseer is commonly said to be plentiful in the head waters of most of the large rivers; but the Malabar carp, *barbus rosapinnis*, is probably often confused with the true mahseer, or *barbus mosal*. In the Wynaad rivers, however, the latter grow to considerable size and in the Kabbani have been known to scale over 150 lb.

---

[1] *Bulletin of the Madras Museum*, Vol. III, No. 2.

CHAPTER II.

POLITICAL HISTORY.

EARLY HISTORY—Dearth of materials—Immigration into Malabar—Parasuramakshetram—Kerala or Chera—Early references to the Cheras—Early trade—Trade with Rome—Identifications of Roman place-names on the West Coast—Karoura, the capital of Chera—Limits of Kerala—Later trade with Rome—The dearth of authorities—Ancient Tamil literature—Chera civilisation—Epigraphic research—Sri Vishnu Varman—King Bhaskara Ravivarman—Other kings known from inscriptions—Sthana Ravi—Ravivarman—Vira Raghava Chakravarti—Foreign invasions—Chinese trade with Kerala—The Keralolpatti and Kerala Mahatmyam—The Brahman colonisation of Kerala—The Perumal period—Cheraman Perumal—The question of his identity and chronology—The story possibly a confusion between two distinct traditions—1320 A.D. to 1498 A.D. THE PORTUGUESE PERIOD, A.D. 1498–1663—Discovery of India, 1498—Arrival of Cabral, 1500—Discovery of Cochin—Joao da Nova, 1501—Vasco da Gama, 1502—D. Francis D'Albuquerque, 1503—Pacheco's defence of Cochin—Almeida the first Viceroy, 1505–1509—D. Alfonso D'Albuquerque, 1509–1515—Vasco da Gama, Viceroy, 1524–1571—Decline of the Portuguese—Loss of the monopoly of trade with Europe—The fall of Cochin, 1663. THE STRUGGLE FOR THE PEPPER TRADE, 1663–1766—The Dutch in Malabar—Rise of the English—Travancore and the decline of the Dutch—The French and the English in North Malabar—North Malabar politics—Peace with Mahe—Darmapattanam Island—The Bednur war—Struggles with the French—Siege of Tellicherry—Fall of Mahe—Events in South Malabar—Zamorin's invasion of Palghat. THE MYSOREAN CONQUEST, 1766–1792—The invasion of 1766—The invations of 1766—Rebellion in Malabar—Negotiations with the Malabar chieftains—Attack on Cochin and Travancore—Capitulation of Mahe—Siege of Tellicherry, 1779–1782—Death of Haidar, 1782—The peace of 1784—Founding of Ferok—Proselytism to Islam—Downfall of Tippu's power in Malabar. BRITISH SUPREMACY—Changes in the district—Administration—Mistaken revenue policy of 1792—The first Pychy rebellion, 1793–1797—Second Pychy rebellion, 1800–1805—Other risings. MAPPILLA OUTBREAKS—Their beginning—General features, 1836–1853—Mambram Tangals—The Mappilla Acts—Murder of Mr. Conolly—Mr. Logan's commission—Its result—Disarming of the Mappilla taluks—The outbreak of 1896—Outbreak of 1898—Conclusion—Condition of the Mappillas before and at the time of the Great War—Outbreaks of 1915 and 1919—The Mappilla Rebellion, 1921–22—Propaganda against Government—First signs of revolt—Outbreak of rebellion—Engagements at Pukkottur—Arrival of reinforcements—Rebel activaties and measures taken against them—Raid on Melmuri and defeat of rebels at Pandikkad—Capture of leaders—General features of the rebellion and after—Mappilla women—Special Courts and offences—Distress and relief measures—Malabar Special Police made a permanent garrison.

CHAP. II. EARLY HISTORY.

Dearth of materials.

LITTLE is known of the early history of Malabar, and with such scraps of reliable information, as have come down to us, it is impossible to weave together a continuous and connected story. The Malayalis, like the Hindus generally, are totally devoid of the historical spirit. The Keralopatti and Kerala Mahatmyam, which embody their traditions, are late compilations of unknown origin, and are so full of inconsistencies, anachronisms and absurdities that it is difficult to separate from the chaff what few grains of truth they contain. The inscriptions of the district have never been systematically

CHAP. II. EARLY HISTORY.

surveyed, and though some of them give us tantalising glimpses into what appears to have been a high state of civilization and a well ordered political system, they are for the most part obscure and their value is much discounted by the difficulty of fixing their dates. Epigraphic research has made great progress in Southern India in the last twenty years, but unfortunately, so far as the ancient history of Malabar is concerned, its results have been mainly negative. It has disproved much that was formerly accepted, but offers little in place of the theories it has destroyed.

Immigration into Malabar.

The aborigines of Malabar are possibly represented by the Cherumans and Pulayans, the agrestic slaves of the soil, and by the jungle tribes of the Kurumbans, Kuricchiyans, Paniyans, etc. The higher castes are all foreigners, and there are many theories of their origin and the order of their coming. In the serpent worship of the Nayars and their matriarchal customs some have found traces of a Scythian origin.[1] Ferguson was led by the striking similarity of Malayalam and Canarese architecture to that of the Newars of Nepal, combined with the prevalence of polyandry amongst the latter, to suggest a connection between the Nayars and the Newars[2]; and Mr. Kanakasabhai relying mainly on literary evidence has attributed a Mongolian origin to the whole Dravidian race of Tamils, amongst whom he includes the Nayars.[3] But anthropometric results are against these theories. The name Nayar seems to be properly a title equivalent to Knight, and it is now generally held that they are a Dravidian race with, no doubt, considerable admixture of Aryan blood; and it is recognised that the date of their arrival in Malabar cannot be even approximately determined.

The word Tiyan is commonly derived from dvipam, an island, as Iluvan is from Simhala (Ceylon); and the accepted tradition is that they came from Ceylon bringing with them the cocoanut (*tenga*, the southern tree ?). From the fact that cocoanuts do not figure in the long list of reports given in the *Periplus Maris Erythrœi* written probably in the first century A.D., but are fully described by *Cosmas Indicopleustes*, who wrote at the beginning of the 6th century, the date of Tiyan immigration has been assigned to one of the early centuries of the Christian era. But cocoanuts were well known to the Tamil poets whose date Mr. Kanakasabhai Pillai would ascribe to the first and second centuries A.D.

The Nambudiri Brahmans seem to have entered Malabar from the North; and probably they found the Nayars and Tiyans already in possession. But later researches point to an earlier date for their settlement than was at one time

---

[1] *Malabar Quarterly Review*, March 1902.

[2] See Ferguson, *Indian amd Eastern Architecture*, pp. 271-2, and Sir Walter Elliot, *Coins of Southern India*, p. 61, note 1, and p. 46, note 2.

[3] *The Tamils Eighteen Hundred Years ago*, V. Kanakasabhai (Higginbotham, Madras, 1904).

CHAP. II. EARLY HISTORY.

supposed. The Hiradgalli and other Pallava grants prove that the Brahmans were settled in Southern India in the fourth or fifth century A.D.,[1] and the Kadamba king, Mayura Varman, whom Canarese and Mahratta accounts credit with having introduced Brahmans into the district, is now known to have lived about the end of the fifth century.[2] It has also been argued from the absence of any allusion in the Mitakshara to the *Sarvasvadhanam* marriage of the Nambudiris as a form of adoption then in general use, that the Nambudiris must have detached themselves in upper India from the main body of Aryans or Aryo-Dravidians before this form of adoption became obsolete, that is, long before the fourth or fifth century A.D.;[3] but the argument is obviously inconclusive.[4]

The Mappillas of course belong to a later period. The community now consists of pure Arab settlers, of the descendants of Arab traders and women of the country, and of converts to Muhammadanism mainly from the lower Hindu castes. The first Muhammadan settlers were probably Arab traders, who came to the west on the revival of the trade which had been interrupted by the period of Islamic conquest; but their numbers were apparently inconsiderable till some centuries later, and it is doubtful whether they made any converts before the eleventh century. The Arab merchant Sulaiman writing in 851 A.D. says that he was not aware of any Indian or Chinese converts to Muhammadanism at that date; but an inscription still existing at Madayi gives 1124 A.D. as the date of the establishment of the Madayi mosque, according to tradition the third of the original mosques founded in Malabar; and some time before the date of Ibn Batuta's visit to Malabar (1342-7 A.D.) the Mappillas were a power in the land.

Parasurama kshetram.

The name Parasurama-kshetram—one of the many names given to Malabar in the past—has its origin in the well-known legend that Malabar was reclaimed from the sea by its patron saint, the Brahman warrior sage, Parasu Raman. This legend is related in several of the Puranas, and is the starting point of all the traditional accounts of the early history of the district. Nor is it so puerile as would at first sight appear. Geologists consider it probable that at some remote period the sea washed the foot of the Western Ghats, and that the narrow strip of land which now divides them has been raised up by some great earthquake or volcanic convulsion; and such a natural phenomenon would of course be ascribed to a personal and superhuman agency. It is futile to conjecture when the great upheaval took place, though its date has been boldly fixed

---

[1] See *Bombay Gazetteer*, Vol. I, Part II, 319, and Epigraphia Indica, I, 8.

[2] *Epigraphia Indica*, viii, 31.

[3] *Malabar Quarterly Review*, March 1902, and I.L.R., Mad., XI, 180.

[4] If a man has a daughter but no son, he may adopt a husband for the daughter, and their son can inherit.

CHAP. II. EARLY HISTORY.

at 1,000 years after the flood,[1] but the part ascribed therein to Parasu Raman has been rationalised in various ways. Some have seen in him a Naga chieftain,[2] others the leader of the earliest Âryan colony into Southern India.[3]

Keral or Cheras.

The name Keralam of Kerala is now generally assumed to mean the land of the Cheras, Keram being according to Dr. Gundert a Canarese dialectical form of Cheram; and thus Malabar is connected with one of the great triarchy of Hindu dynasties, Chera, Chola and Pandya, which loom so large in the annals of ancient Southern India. The identification is not beyond dispute, since in a copper plate recently discovered in the Tanjore district "Pandya, Cherala, Chela (*i.e.*, Chera), and Lanka" are named as the several countries conquered by the Chola king Raja Kesari Varma in the eleventh century; and possibly there is some truth in the tradition that Kerala, the West Coast proper, was only a portion of the older Chera kingdom, which included parts of Mysore, Coimbatore and Salem, and that it subsequently became independent. The name Chera, however, survives in Cheranad, an old taluk of Malabar, now part of Ernad, and in the Cheraman Perumals of Malabar tradition; and in the copper plate deed of Vira Raghava Chakravarti referred to below, a king tracing his descent from "Vira Kerala Chakravarti, King of Kings" confers certain privileges on a merchant of Cranganore who is styled "Merchant prince of the Cheraman world." The *Keralolpatti* derives the name Kerala from an early Perumal named Kerala; but the same authority gives 216 A.D. as the date of the beginning of the Perumal era, while Keralaputra is mentioned as the name of a kingdom in an edict of the Buddhist King Asoka in the third century B.C.[4] Another theory connects the name with the word *keram* meaning cocoanut, found in the commoner *nalikeram*.[5]

Early references to the Cheras or Kerala.

The earliest supposed reference to the Cheras in history occurs in the fourth century B.C., when Alexander the Great made his expedition into Northern India, and Megasthenes, Seleucus Nicator's ambassador to the court of Sandragupta, gathered some scanty information about Southern India. He mentions that the Southern peoples were ruled by queens, and names among them the Pandae and Charmae, who are usually presumed to be the Pandyas and Cheras. It is noteworthy that even now all Malayali chieftains' houses are in theory subject to the eldest female member. To the next century belong the stone inscriptions of Sandragupta's successor Asoka

---

[1] Rev. William Taylor, *Translation of Ancient Manuscripts, II*, 65.

[2] *Malabar Quarterly Review*, III, 287.

[3] *Indian Antiquary*, XXXI, 340.

[4] *Indian Antiquary*, XXXI, 342.

[5] See *Malabar Quarterly Review*, III, p. 57, where Mr. A. Krishna Poduval discusses the origin of the word.

already mentioned; and that at Girnar recites that the system of caring for the sick, as well of cattle as of men, followed by king Devanampriya Priyadesin, had been introduced into the border kingdoms of Chola, Pandya and Keralaputra.

Early trade.

Long before this, however, a flourishing trade had sprung up between East and West, and up to the second century A.D. we are mainly dependent upon foreign sources of information for the little we know of Southern India. Solomon (1000 B.C.), in whose day 'silver was nothing accounted of,' obtained his gold from Ophir, and 'once in three years came the navy of Tharshish, bringing gold and silver, ivory, apes and peacocks.' All these, silver excepted, are products of Malabar; and the Hebrew names for the last two objects, *kapim* and *tukim*, are so obviously the Tamil *kavi* and *thokai*, that perhaps it is not altogether an idle fancy which identifies Ophir with Beypore at the mouth of the river of the same name which is famed for its auriferous sands. The similarity again between the Greek names for rice (*oryza*), ginger (*zinziber*) and cinnamon (*karpion*) and the Malayalam *arisi*, *inchiver* and *karuppu*, indicates a trade in these articles between Greece and Malabar, the only part of India where all these products grow side by side. Eastern merchandise in these early days must have been carried as far as Aden in Arab dhows, which crept along the coast and did not venture to face the open sea, and from that port was distributed along the Red Sea and Mediterranean littorals, so Herodotus (B.C. 484–413) states, by Egyptian and Phoenician merchants. The disruption of Alexander the Great's empire and the rise of the Ptolemies to power in Egypt diverted the trade from Tyre to Alexandria, but otherwise made little change. Aden still bounded the horizon of western navigators on the east, and this absence of direct communication accounts for the profound ignorance of the Greeks as to the true position of India. Eratosthanes (B.C. 267) thought it lay east and west, and notwithstanding the fact that in B.C. 120 Eudoxus of Cyzicus is said to have sailed from Egypt to India and to have returned with an enormously valuable cargo, Strabo (B.C. 67–A.D. 24) was almost equally ignorant.

Trade with Rome.

The Romans changed all this. Their conquest of Egypt made them masters of the trade route to the East, and they were not long in tracking the trade to its sources. Hippalus' discovery of the possibility of sailing straight across the Arabian Ocean by the aid of the south-west monsoon gave an immense impetus to commerce in the first century A.D.; and a few years later we find Petronius reproaching Roman ladies for exposing their charms in diaphanous Indian muslins, Pliny the Elder discussing learnedly the various routes to the

CHAP. II. EARLY HISTORY.

West Coast of India and commenting upon the value of the roman trade with India, and Ptolemy describing more or less correctly the geography of South India.

"Afterwards" wrote Pliny in 77 A.D.[1] "it was ascertained that it was possible to proceed direct from the promontory of Syagrus[2] in Arabia to Patale[3] with the west wind (Favonius), which they call there the Hippalus, a distance reckoned at 1,435 miles. The voyage is now made every year with cohorts of archers on board the ships on account of the pirates who infest these seas. It will be worth while to set forth their whole course from Egypt, accurate information concerning it being now available for the first time. The subject deserves attention, for there is no year in which India does not drain our empire of at least 55,000,000 sersterces, sending us in return wares which are sold for a hundred times their original value. But for those whose course is directed to India it is most advantageous to start from Ocelis. Thence they sail with the wind to the greatest mart of India which is called Muziris[4] but is not much to be recommended on account of the pirates who occupy a place in the vicinity named Nitrias. Nor does it furnish any abundance of merchandise. Moreover the anchorage is far from the land, and cargoes have to be loaded and unloaded in barges. The ruler of the country at the time of which I speak was Caelobothras.[5] There is another more advantageous port which is named Barace[6] and lies in the territory of the Neacyndi. The king of this country was called Pandion[7] who lived far from the port in a city of the interior, Madura by name. But the region from which pepper is brought to Barace in barges hewn out of a single tree goes by the name of Cotonara."[8]

In the Periplus Maris Erythræi, the work of an unkown author probably contemporary with Pliny the Elder, is an interesting description of Southern India. Limurike in the following extract is probably a clerical error for Dimurike, and is generally considered to be the Greek equivalent of Tamilakam, the Tamil country. The Peutingerian tables have Damurike.

---

[1] *Natural History*, VI, 26.

[2] Cape Fartak in Arabia.

[3] Probably Pantalayini Kollam near Quilandi.

[4] Cranganore or Kodungallur.

[5] The Latinised form of the Keralaputra mentioned in Asoka's edict at Girnar. "The ruler of Chera or Kerala."

[6] The Bakare of the Periplus. Possibly Vaikkarai near Kottayam in Travancore.

[7] A clear reference to the Pandya kingdom.

[8] This place has been identified both with Kaddattanad and Kolattanad in North Malabar, but the country lying about 16 miles east of Quilon is still called Kottaram or Royal residence, and it is there probably that the pepper grew. Mr. Kanakasabhai in his *Tamils Eighteen Hundred Years Ago* suggests that it is identical with Kuddanadu, one of the 13 ancient divisions of Tamilakam.

CHAP. II. EARLY HISTORY.

"And after this the island that is called white.[1] Then follow Naoura [2] and Tyndis, [3] the first marts of Limurike, and to these succeed Mouziris [4] and Nelkunda, the seats of Government. Tyndis, a village of great note by the sea, lies in the kingdom of Keprobotros,[5] as does Mouziris, a prosperous city thronged by ships from Ariake and by the vessels of Greek merchants. Mouziris stands on a river twenty stadia from its mouth, and 500 stadia distant from Tyndis, whether you measure from river to river or by the length of the sea voyage. Nearly 500 stadia from Mouziris, but in the kingdom of Pandion, is Nelkunda which also is situated near a river and is 120 stadia from the sea. At the mouth of this river is Bakare whither ships come down empty from Nelkunda [6] and ride at anchor off the shore to take in freight, for the river, it may be noted, is not easy to navigate by reason of sunken reefs and shallows. The ships that frequent these ports are of great size, and take in large and bulky cargoes of pepper and betel. The imports here are treasure in great quantities, topazes, a small assortment of plain cloths, flowered robes, stibium, coral, glass, brass, lead, wine about as much as at Barugaza,[7] cinnabar, arsenic and wheat not for sale but for the use of the crew. Pepper, which is brought only to this port, is the chief export and is called Cottanarikon from the district where it is grown. Other exports are pearls in great quantity and of the best quality, ivory, fine silks, spikenard from the Ganges, betel from the countries further East, precious stones of all kinds, diamonds, jacynths, tortoise-shell from the golden Chersonese and from the islands off the coast of Limurike."

Identifications of Roman places named on West Coast.

The identifications suggested in the footnotes for the various places mentioned in the above passages are by no means beyond dispute. Mouziris and the White Island are usually identified with Cranganore and Sacrifice rock respectively, but the others are merely conjectures about which there is little agreement. Ptolemy (second. century A.D.), whose *yewypaoikn vonynois* summed up the geographical knowledge of the ancient world, and remained a text-book of geographical science till the maritime discoveries of the 15th century, volunteers the important information that Karoura was the royal city of Kerobothros, (*i.e.*, Keralaputra), and gives a longer list of the inland and sea-board towns of Limurike. The river Pseudostomos is clearly the mouth of the Periyar below Cranganore, and is a correct Greek translation of *Alimukam*, as this mouth is still called. Similarly Bramagara

---

[1] Sacrifice rock of Badagara, which is still called in Malayalam Velliyankallu or white rock.

[2] Not identified; but possibly Puthupattanam on the north bank of the Kotta river.

[3] Kadalundi (Burnell), or Thondi about 5 miles north of Quilandi (Kanakasabhai Pillai).

[4] Cranganore.

[5] Ruler of Chera or Kerala—*vide* p. 28.

[6] The Neacyndi of Pliny and Nelkunda of Ptolemy. Possibly Nirkunram near Kottayam in Travancore.

[7] Cambay.

CHAP. II. EARLY HISTORY.

and Palura are probably Brahmakulam and Palayur in the Ponnani taluk, the latter an ancient village with old Jewish and Christian traditions. But the identification of Karoura, and the sea-port towns of Podoperoura, Semne and Koreora between Mouziris and Bakare is not so simple. The last three towns Mr. Kanakasabhai in his *Tamils Eighteen Hundred Years ago* guided by the similarity of their names, has identified with Udiamperur, Sembai and Kothora, and Bakare he takes to be the modern Vaikkarai; and he concludes that in Ptolemy's time the sea washed the eastern shores of the Travancore and Cochin backwaters and that neither the backwaters nor the long strip of land which forms their western bank, and on which now stand the flourishing sea-ports of Cochin and Alleppy, were then in existence.[1]

Karoura was formerly identified with Karur in the Trichinopoly district; and according to the Tamil metrical dictionary Tivakaram and ancient name of Karur is Vanji. But this identification of the modern Karur about a hundred miles to the east of the Palghat gap with Vanji the old Chera capital is still an unsettled question. Tamil scholars are opposed to the view that Vanji and Karur were towns in the West Coast. The authors of *Vanjimanagar*, and *Seran Senguttuvan*, both erudite Tamil Pandits, still identify Vanji with the modern Karur. There is however no epigraphical evidence specifically referring to Karur as the ancient Chera capital, though a Brahmi inscription of the 3rd century B.C. copied from Pugalur ten miles from Karur vouches for the great antiquity of the place, and an inscription of the 12th century A.D. at Nerur, six miles from Karur, refers to it as Vanjimanagar. That Vanji was the name of old Chera capital is clear enough, but a writer in the *Indian Antiquary* (Vol. XXXI, page 43) in discussing the subject says that "early records, known traditions, and old inscriptions all point to Tiruvanji or Tiruvanjikulam, lying adjacent to Cranganore, as the capital of the early rulers of Chera or Kerala." Ptolemy, however, places Karoura further inland and an almost equally probable theory identifies the town with "Tirukarur, three miles from Kothamangalam and 28 miles east by north of Cochin, where the remains of an old temple and other massive buildings are still visible."[2]

Limits of Kerala.

The exact extent of the Kerala kingdom when these authors wrote cannot be easily determined. Nelkunda, the southern extent of the kingdom, must have been somewhere near Kottayam in North Travancore, and the reference in the Periplus to the 'white island' or Sacrifice rock points to the Kotta river as its northern boundary. Similarly in one part of the Keralolpatti the limits of the Kerala division of

---

[1] *The Tamils Eighteen Hundred Years ago*, p. 19.

[2] *The Tamils Eighteen Hundred Years ago*, p. 15.

the Malanad, or hill country, are said to have been Puthupattanam on the Kotta river in the north and Kanetti in Travancore on the south, and working on entirely different lines, Mr. Kanakasabhai Pillai has arrived at almost the same conclusion. Of the thirteen *nads*, into which Tamilakam was of old divided, he places four on the shores of the Arabian Sea. Poolinad, the most northern, he identifies with the more modern Polanad and Payyanad, extending roughly from the Kotta river to Beypore, and Kudinad with that part of the Ponnani taluk which in pre-Mysorean days was called Kutnad. Kuddam, 'the land of lakes,' comprised the country round about Kottayam and Quilon; and Vennad, 'the bamboo land," correspond to South Travancore. The last named in the first and second centuries of the Christian era appears to have belonged to the Pandyas, and the Chera or Kerala king was confined to the narrow strip of territory between the sea and the Western Ghats which extends from the Kotta river to Kottayam in North Travancore.

Later trade with Rome.

For some centuries after the time of Ptolemy trade was carried on steadily with the Roman empire and the Peutingerian Tables, compiled in the third century A.D., mention that a considerable Roman settlement existed at Cranganore which still remained the great metropolis of trade on the coast, that there was a temple dedicated to Augustus there, and that the trade was of sufficient importance to justify the presence of two cohorts in the town for its protection. Roman coins have been dug up at various places on the West Coast, and doubtless found their way into Malabar at this period. They belong to the reigns of Augustus, Tiberius Caligula, Claudius and Nero.

The dearth of authorities.

But later Greek and Roman writers are singularly reticent about the Eastern world, and for some hundreds of years little is known of Kerala, the very name dropping out of authentic records for some centuries after Ptolemy. Early Tamil poets shed some rays of light upon the darkness, and the names of a few kings have been handed down in the Jews' and other ancient deeds, to which reference is made below. But the dates of these kings are very vexed questions, and for the internal history of the kingdom we are still mainly dependent upon late and untrustworthy local chronicles.

Ancient Tamil literature.

The names of several Chera kings are mentioned in ancient Tamil literature. One king is said to have fed both the Pandya and Kaurava troops during the Mahabharata war, and another was humbled by the Chola king Sengannan at Kalumalum.[1] One work, the Paddirrupathi, recently edited by Pandit Swaminatha Iyer of the Presidency College, furnishes

[1] *Indian Antiquary*, XVIII, 259.

CHAP. II. EARLY HISTORY.

the names of no less than nine Chera sovereigns, and the durations of their reigns. But the most interesting account of the kingdom from A.D. 40 to A.D. 150 is contained in *The Tamils Eighteen Hundred Years ago,* in which allusions to Chera in the old epic poems and anthologies of the Tamils have been collated for the first time. Five kings reigned in this period. Athan I (A.D. 40–55) was defeated at the battle of Vennil by the Chola king, Karikala, and unable to bear the disgrace of a wound in the back starved himself to death. Athan II (A.D. 55–90) married a daughter of his father's conqueror. His younger son, Ilanko Adikal, was the author of the still extant epic poem Silapadikaram, and the elder Chenk-ku-davan *alias* Imaya Varman (A.D. 90–125) was the greatest of the line. He sent an expedition by sea against the princes of Northern India who had sneered at the Tamil kings, and is credited with having exhibited two captive Aryan chieftains at the courts of Pandya and Chola. Yanaik-kadchey (A.D. 125–136), who succeeded him, was taken prisoner by a Pandya king, but his son Perunj-Cheral-Irum-porai (A.D. 135–150) slew Adikaman Elini and captured his capital Tagadur, identical with Dharmapuri in the Salem district.

Chera civilization.

These dates are by no means beyond dispute,[1] but it is at least clear that Chera civilization had reached a very high level at a very early period. Vanji, the capital, 'was strongly fortified, and on the battlements were mounted various engines to throw missiles upon those who attacked the fort. The king's palace, a temple of Vishnu called Adakamadam or 'the golden shrine,' a Buddhist Chaitya, and a Nigrantha monastery appear to have been the most conspicuous buildings in the town.' At the mouth of the Periyar was the emporium of trade, 'the thriving town of Muchiri where the beautiful large ships of the Yavanas bringing gold come splashing the white foam on the waters of the Periyar, which belongs to the Cherala, and return laden with pepper.' The monarch's power was limited by the 'five great assemblies,' consisting of priests, astrologers, physicians, ministers and the representatives of the people. One-sixth of all the produce of the land was his rightful share, and customs levied at all seaports and tolls on the trunk roads were his other sources of revenue. The king was the final arbiter in all civil and criminal cases, but special officers were appointed to perform the duties of

---

[1] They are based upon the date furnished by the Mahawamso for the Ceylon king, Gajabahu, mentioned in the Silappadikaram as the contemporary of Chenkku-duvan. Dr. Hultzsch is not prepared to accept these dates "unless the identity of the two Gajabahus is not only supported by the mere identity of his name, but proved by internal reasons, and until the chronology of the earlier history of Ceylon has been subjected to a critical examination.' See *South Indian Inscriptions*, II, 378.

judges and magistrates. Punishments were severe, and crime was rare. A man taken in adultery was put to death, and a thief beheaded.[1]

Epigraphic research. Sri Vishnu Varman.

Epigraphic research has revealed to history the names of eight kings of Kerala ; but unfortunately little is known of them but their names, and it is generally impossible either to fix the period when they lived and reigned, or to correlate them with one another or with better known kings of other dynasties. The earliest of those kings is the Sri Vishnu Várman of the 'Kudumbiya family', mentioned in one of the rock inscriptions in the Edakkal cave near Sultan's battery.[2] A Kadamba king of this name is known,[3] and another king of the same was vanquished by Ravivarman, son of Mrigesa Varman of the same dynasty.[4] But no good grounds exist for identifying the Kerala sovereign either with the Kadamba king or with the conquered foe of Ravivarman. The inscription is in Sanskrit, and therefore probably not earlier than the fifth century A.D. ; and it may perhaps be inferred that in the interval of at least 300 years that had elapsed since Ptolemy wrote, the limits of Kerala had been extended over the Western Ghats so as to include that part of Mysore plateau which is now known as the Wynaad.

King Bhaskara Ravivarman.

Two sets of copper plates—the famous Jews' deed [5] in the possession of the White Jews of Cochin and the Tirunelli plates [6]—and a single stone inscription[7] have come known to us from the reign of the 'king of kings, the glorious Bhaskara Ravivarman'. The plates are written in the ancient Tamil or Vatezhuttu characters, and their dates are well known problems of which every antiquarian has his own solution. That of the Tirunelli deed is 'the 46th year opposed to or after the current year' and the Jews grant was made at Muyirikodu or Cranganore 'in the 36th year opposed to or after the second year.' If the cycle then used in Kerala was the Grahappari-virthi cycle of 90 years, as supposed by Mr. Kanakasabhai Pillai, the dates would be respectively 112 A.D. and 192 A.D., and the grants cannot belong to the same reign, as generally assumed. But these dates seem impossibly early, for the deeds are full of Sanskrit words and epigraphic research has revealed no definite reference to Brahmans in South India earlier than the fourth or fifth century A.D.[8]

---

[1] *The Tamils Eighteen Hundred Years ago*, pp. 109–115, and passim.
[2] Indian Antiquary, XXX, 409–421.
[3] Indian Antiquary, VI, 19.
[4] Bombay Gazetteer, Vol. I, pt. II, 389.
[5] Epigraphia Indica, III, 66–69.
[6] Indian Antiquary, XX, 285–292.
[7] No. 16 of 1901.
[8] See Bombay Gazetteer, Vol. I, pt. II, 319, and Epigraphia Indica, I, 8.

CHAP. II. EARLY HISTORY.

Dr. Burnell assigns the Jews' deed to about the eighth century A.D., and this is probably nearer the truth. Anjuvannam was probably a trading corporation,[1] and the rights and privileges connected therewith granted by Bhaskara Ravivarman to Joseph Rabban are very interesting not only for the light they throw on Malabar civilization, but also because they are still preserved to some extent by the Jews of Cochin. They include among others the light by day, the spreading cloth, the palanquin, the umbrella, the drum and the trumpet ; and by the grant the Jews were also excused, so long as the world and the moon shall exist, from the payment of the usual dues to the royal palace. But the real importance of the deed is in the names of the great feudatory princes who attested it. 'Thus do I know, Govardhana Martandan of Venad. Thus do I know, Kodai Srikantan of Venapalinadu. Thus do I know, Manavipala-Manavyan of Eralanadu. Thus do I know, Irayiram Sattan of Valluvanadu. Thus do I know, Kodai Ravi of Nodumpuraiyurnadu. Thus do I know, Murkham Sattan who hold the office of sub-commander of the forces.' The secretary who wrote the deed came from Tellicherry, and Kerala at this time seem to have extended from Tellicherry on the north to Cape Comorin on the south, and to have included Ernad, Walavanad and part of Palghat. Tirunelli lies in North Wynaad under the shadow of Brahmagiri, and the Tirunelli plates, which regulate the temple dues, show that Wynaad was still under the sway of the kings of Kerala.

Other kings known from inscriptions.

Other kings known from inscriptions are Kodai Ravi,[2] Sthana Ravi, Rama,[3] Jayasimha [4] *alias* Vira Kerala Varman, Ravivarman *alias* Kulasekhara, son of Jayasimha, and Vira Raghava Chakravarti.

Sthana Ravi.

Sthana Ravi or Sthana Ravi Gupta, as Dr. Gundert transliterates his name, bequeathed to posterity one of the two sets of copper plates, preserved by the Syrian Christian community at Kottayam in Travancore.[5] In those plates, 'with the concurrence of Ayyan Adigal, ruler of Vennad, of Anjuvannam and Punnathala's lord,' a free-hold site is granted to the Tarisa church by Maruvan Sapir Iso, and the community is invested with rights and privileges very similar to those bestowed upon Joseph Rabban by Bhaskara Ravi. Its date is assumed to be a little later than that of the Jews' deed.

---

[1] Epigraphia Indica, IV, 294.

[2] Nos. 219 of 1895, 13 of 1901 and 1 of 1903 in Government Epigraphist's collection.

[3] No. 220 of 1895.

[4] See Epigraphia Indica, IV, 293.

[5] Translated by Dr. Gundert in the Madras Journal of Literature and Science XIII, 1.

CHAP. II. EARLY HISTORY.

Ravivarman.

Ravivarman, son of Jayasimha, who was perhaps the founder of a dynasty "in the Kerala country", ascended the throne in 1309 A.D.,[1] and ruled at Kolamba *alias* Kollam *alias* Quilon. Probably taking advantage of the confusion which prevailed in Southern India after the memorable invasion of Malik Kafur, he seems to have extended his conquests as far as Conjeeveram in Chingleput.

Vira Raghava Chakravarti.

Vira Raghava Chakravarti, "descendant of the glorious king of kings Vira Kerala Chakravarti", is known by a single copper plate which is also in the possession of the Syrian Christians of Kottayam. The date of the deed is 'the day of Rohini, a Saturday after the expiration of twenty-first of the Solar month of Mina (of the year during which) Jupiter was in Makara. Assuming the deed to belong to the eighth century, Dr. Burnell arrived at 774 A.D. as the only possible year. But on palæographic grounds Mr. V. Venkayya, the present acting Epigraphist to Government, assigns the document to the 13th or 14th century,[2] and Professor Kielhorn would fix its date as Saturday, 15th March 1320.[3] The question however cannot be said to have been yet settled, and in the Travancore Manual the date 230 A.D. is confidently accepted. The grant has generally been supposed to have created the Syrian Christian principality of Manigramam; but it merely confers the lordship of Manigramam, which was probably a trading corporation like Anjuvannam, and certain honours and privileges connected therewith upon one Iravi Korttan of Mahodevarpattanam, "merchant prince of the Cheraman world", and "there is nothing Christian in the document except its possession by its present owners". Among the witnesses to the deed are the Brahman villages of Panniyur and Sukapuram, and the chieftains of Ernad, Walavanad and Vennad or Travancore. This is the first definite reference to the Brahmans as a power in the land.

Foreign invasions.

References to Kerala or Chera are frequent in the inscriptions of other South Indian dynasties in the long period from the second to the fourteenth century, and the country figures among the vaunted conquests of the Western Chalukyas, the Pallavas and the Rashtrakutas. But in the present state of our knowledge we cannot be sure that there is any truth in these boasts of conquests. Contemporary Chola history, however, after the revival of the dynasty in the ninth century by Vijayalaya, throws occasional side lights upon that of Kerala. It must have been either in Vijayalaya's time or that of his son Aditya I that 'the rival kings Udiya (*i.e.*, Chera) and the king of

---

[1] Indian Antiquary, II, 360, and Epigraphia Indica, IV, 145–152, and VIII, 81.

[2] Epigraphia Indica, IV, 290 to 297.

[3] *Ib.*, VI, 84.

CHAP. II. EARLY HISTORY.

Madura who had never gone behind another, were clothed in rags and made to hold lighted lamps on their heads.'[1] Rajaraja I who ascended the Chola throne in 985 A.D., began his military career by destroying the ships at Kandalur Salai, a port somewhere on the Malabar coast,[2] and appears to have defeated a confederacy of the Pandyas and Cheras in a pitched battle in the Malanadu.[3] If, as is alleged, he established the Sadaya festival in Chera,[4] Chera must have become a province of the Chola kingdom, but in that case the necessity for the repeated military operations of his successors is not apparent. His son Rajendra Chola II (A.D. 1011–12 to 1037–8)[5] conquered Magodai [6] or Tiruvanjikulam, the Chera capital, and seized 'the crown praised by many and the garland of the sun, family treasures which the arrow shooting (king of) Kerala rightfully wore; many ancient islands, whose old and great guard was the sea, which resounds with conches; the crown of pure gold worthy of Lakshmi which Parasurama, having considered the fortifications of Sandimatteva impregnable, had deposited there when in anger (he) bound the kings twenty-one times in battle.'[7] Chola invasions of Kerala seem to have been frequent in the 11th century, and in the reign of Kulottinga I (A.D. 1070–1118) the warriors of Kudamalanadu or the western hill country, the war-like ancestors of the degenerate Nayar, died to the last man in the defence of their independence. At the beginning of the 12th century the Chola power suffered a temporary eclipse, but for Chera it was merely a change of masters, and the country seems to have submitted to the Hoysala king Vishnuvardhana.[8] Kulottinga III of Chola, however, regained some of his former domains and 'cut off a finger of Vira Kerala and saw his back (put him to flight); but when the latter came and bowed to him, he bestowed riches upon him in public, and gave him to eat from the royal plates.'[9] The Hoysalas again asserted their superiority, and for the next two centuries Malabar seems to have been subject in turn to them, to the Yadava king Singhana (A.D. 1210–1247)[10] and finally to the Pandyas. Jatavarman Sundara Pandya I, king of the last named nation from 1251 to 1261 A.D., claims to have uprooted the Kerala race.[11] But Malabar seems to have been left undisturbed by the invasion of South India by Malik Kafur

[1] Indian Antiquary, XIX, 331, verse 22.
[2] South Indian Inscriptions, II, 241.
[3] Madras Christian College Magazine, XII, 356.
[4] South Indian Inscriptions, II, 124.
[5] Epigraphia Indica, VII, 7.
[6] Government Epigraphist's Annual Report for 1895, para. 9.
[7] South Indian Inscriptions, III, 28.
[8] Mysore Gazetteer, I, 335.
[9] South Indian Inscriptions, III, 218.
[10] Bombay Gazetteer, I, pt. II, 525.
[11] Indian Antiquary, XXI, 121.

in A.D. 1310, and possibly the Kerala king Ravivarman, as related above was thereby enabled to subdue the Chola and Pandya countries as far east as Chingleput.

CHAP. II. EARLY HISTORY.

Chinese trade with Kerala.

The gap in our information from external sources during a great part of this long period is doubtless due to the check that trade with the west had received not only from the dissolution of the Roman empire, but from the career of conquest upon which Islam started in the seventh century. Relations with China seem to have been opened a century before, and, when in 638 A.D. the Muhammadan conquest of Egypt closed for a time the Red Sea trade route, Malabar found the chief market for its produce in that country. Arab merchants found their way back to the coast in the ninth century, but as late as 1292–3 A.D., when Marco Polo passed up the West Coast, the Chinese had the chief trade with Malabar :—

"There is in this kingdom a great quantity of pepper and ginger and cinnamon and turbit and nuts of India. They also manufacture very delicate and beautiful buckrams. The ships that come from the east bring copper in ballast. They also bring hither cloths of silk and gold, and sandals ; also gold and silver, cloves and spikenard, and other fine spices for which there is a demand here, and exchange them for the products of these countries. Ships come here from many quarters but especially from the great province of Manzi.[1] Coarse spices are exported hence both to Manzi and to the west, and that which is carried by the merchants to Aden goes on to Alexandria, but the ships that go in the latter direction are not one to ten of those that go to the eastward : a very notable fact that I have mentioned before." [2]

The Keralolpatti and Kerala Mahatmyam

The foregoing summary, though not exhaustive, reviews briefly the more important sources of authentic information about Kerala, and the net result, it must be admitted, is somewhat fragmentary. The many gaps can be filled in only from the Kerala Mahatmyam and Keralolpatti, and we pass at once from sober and ascertained facts to what Mr. Logan has styled 'a farrago of legendary nonsense'. The former work, written in indifferent Sanskrit, purports to be an excerpt from the Agni Purana, and exhibits throughout the tendency of the Brahman to manufacture the sanctions of history for the inflated pretensions of his caste. The Keralolpatti, a Malayalam work, though full of inconsistencies and vain repetitions, suggests a more popular origin, and on that account is worthier of serious analysis. It is probably a collection of folk-lore tales and traditions, jotted down just as the author heard them from the lips of common men. Both are comparatively modern productions, and the names of their authors are unknown.

The Brahman colonization of Kerala.

Both accounts start with the legend that the Malanad was miraculously reclaimed from the sea by Parasu Raman and

[1] China.
[2] Yule's *Marco Polo*, Book III, Ch. XXV.

CHAP. II. EARLY HISTORY.

peopled by him with Brahmans, and the Keralolpatti adds that the first settlers fled the country for fear of the myriad Naganmar or serpent folk. Other Brahmans were then brought in from the north and propitiated the serpents by installing them as their household gods. The new colonists were organized into sixty-four gramams or villages, and were directed by Parasu Raman to adopt the *marumakkatayam* law of succession through the mother—an injunction, which, with the single exception of the Payyanur *gramam* in the Chirakkal taluk, they disobeyed. Sudras were next imported from the country east of the ghats for the protection of the Brahmans, and the Nayars were similarly organized into taras, and entrusted with 'the hand, the eye and the order,' or more prosaically with executive functions. 'Thus was created by Parasu Raman the land of Malabar, the Karmabhumi, where good deeds are the sole way to salvation, and it was bestowed upon the Brahmans as a poured out gift.'

The Perumal period.

Four of the gramams were selected to rule the land, but internal dissensions arose, and a protector was appointed in each of the chosen villages by the Brahmans assembled in conclave, a share of the land being set apart for his maintenance. The protectors held office for three years only, and soon succumbed to the tempation of utilising their short period of power to oppress the people. The Brahmans then bethought them of the institution of a monarchy, and their choice falling upon Keya Perumal of Keyapuram in the country east of the ghats, they brought him to Kerala, and installed him as the first of the Perumals at Allur (Cranganore) in the year of the Kaliyug 'Bhumanbhupoyam Prapya,' corresponding to A.D. 216. A long list of subsequent Perumals follows, but is of little value, and their names, which are given in Sewell's list of antiquities,[1] need not be repeated here. At first they were appointed for a term of twelve years ; but from Kulasekhara, by one account in the Keralolpatti, the fourth Perumal, and by another the fourteenth, they seem to have held their thrones till their death. The constant recurrence of Chola and Pandyan Perumals is noteworthy ; and, all dates in the Keralolpatti being quite untrustworthy, may preserve the memory of the Chola and Pandya subjugation of Kerala in the 10th, 11th and 13th centuries, especially as the Mahatmyam relates that, when Bhutarayar Pandi Perumal invaded Malabar, Parasu Raman said to him angrily 'your arrival in my country is vain. I have given it over to the Southern king Adityavarman,' probably the Chola king Aditya I alluded to above. It is to be noticed that according to the tradition all the Perumals were foreigners.

Cheraman Perumal.

The last of the Perumals, whose memory is still green in the minds of the common people, both Hindu and Muhammdan, was Cheraman Perumal. He reigned over Kerala, which was

[1] Pages 195–197.

then confined within narrower limits and was bounded by the five countries Pandi, Tulu, Kongu, Vayanad and Punnad, for thirty-six years to the great content of the people, and was a wise and liberal king. He encouraged trade, and welcomed to the coast Jonakka Mappillas or Muhammadans, installing one of their number at Kannanur (Cannanore) as the lord of the deep or Ali Raja. Finally he became a convert to Islam, and 'left the sandy isle of Tirunavayi with the people of the Veda, and descended from a ship at Kodungallūr harbour, and entered the palace with a view to proceed to Mecca.' But, before taking his departure, he set his house in order, and divided up his kingdom among the great nobles of the realm. The Travancore, Cochin, Kolattiri, Kuruumbranad, Walavanad and many other Rajas were provided for ; but the Zamorin was left out in the cold, and all that the Perumal bestowed upon him was a single village so small that the crowing of a cock[1] could be heard throughout its length and breadth, and his sword with the advice 'to die, kill and annex.'[2]

The question of his identity and chronology.

This tradition is so strong in Malabar, that there must be some foundation of fact for the story. But who the Perumal was, and when he left for Mecca, is one of the most interesting of the many problems of Malabar history. The earliest authorities for the tradition are the Lusiad of Cameons, the itinerary of Duarte Barbosa, who travelled in Malabar early in the sixteenth century and the Tahafut-ul-Mujahidin written by Sheik Zeinuddin in the latter half of the sixteenth century. Zeinuddin gives a circumstantial account of the Perumal's conversion and the foundation of the earliest mosques in Malabar by Malik Ibn Dinar and three other apostles, who were sent to Malabar from Arabia by the Perumal to propagate the fourth Veda ; and records his opinion that though the inhabitants of Malabar believed that the Perumal's conversion took place in the time of Muhammad, it must really have happened some two hundred years after the death of the prophet. Mappilla manuscripts support this date ; and relying on the report that there exists at Zaphar on the Arabian coast, the tomb of a Hindu king, who became one of the Faithful, with the inscription 'Abdul Rahiman Samiri, arrived A.H. 212 : died A.H. 216,' (corresponding to 827–831 A.D.), Mr. Logan identified Cheraman Perumal with the Sthana Ravi mentioned above, and suggested that the Kollam era, which began in September 824 A.D., and is still in general use in Malabar, dates from his

[1] Calicut is *Kozhi-kotta*, Cock-fort.

[2] Still preserved in the Zamorin's palace. It is also said that it is strictly necessary for each new Zamorin, on succeeding to the title, to make a formal entry into Calicut, in which he has to cross the Kallayi river by boat, receive some betel leaf from a Mapilla woman, and declare that he will only rule "until his uncle returns." But the custom is not now observed. A similar declaration has been said to be required of the Maharajah of Travancore on his coronation ; but that is now denied (*vide* Madras Government Museum Bulletin III, 3, page 295 ; and Travancore State Manual I, p. 225).

CHAP. II. EARLY HISTORY.

disappearance. But the report of the existence of the tombstone has never been confirmed, and quite different theories have been advanced of the origin of the Kollam era. It is also remarakable that the travellers, Christians and Muhammadans, who visited Mālabar between the ninth and fifteenth centuries, do not mention the tradition. The Arab merchant Suleiman, who writes with authority as one who had seen the countries which he describes, states explicitly of Malabar in 851–52 A.D., 'I know not there is any one of either nation (Indian or Chinese), that has embraced Islam or speaks Arabic.' Ibn Batuta, the traveller (1342–1347 A.D.), narrates with awe the wonderful story of the tree of testimony at Baliapatam,[1] but makes no mention of the greater miracle of the dividing moons which 'warmed the Perumal's heart with a holy affection toward Mahomed';[2] and Abdur-razak, who came to Calicut a hundred years later, charged with a mission from the Shah of Persia to convert the Zamorin, is equally reticent. It must be added that there are also stories of the conversion of a Cheraman Perumal to Buddhism and to Christianity; and that a Cheraman Perumal figures as the eponymous hero of nearly every Malabar tradition.

The story a confusion between two distinct traditions.

The story in its present form may possibly be a confusion of two distinct traditions, one relating to the extinction of the rule of the Perumals and the other to the conversion of some Malabar king to Islam. The inscription of Ravivarma of Kerala already referred to, goes to show that in 1300 A.D. the whole of Kerala was brought under the rule of the king of Kollam; and if Professor Kielhorn's date for the Kottayam plate of Viraraghava Chakravarti is accepted, it must be inferred that a Perumal was ruling in 1320 A.D. But 25 years later Ibn Batuta, a careful observer, writes "in the country of Malabar there are twelve kings, the greatest of whom has fifty thousand troops at his command, and the least five thousand or thereabouts". The last of the Perumals may therefore have ceased to rule some time between 1320 and 1342; but had he become a convert to Muhammadanism and gone on a pilgrimage to Mecca, Ibn Batuta could scarcely have failed to mention the fact. On the other hand, according to the Keralolpatti the converted Perumal was not Cheraman Perumal the last of the line, but Bana Perumal from Banapuram; after him came Kulasekhara Perumal, a Pandyan, and many others, the last of whom Cheraman Perumal retained the throne for thirty-six years, and defeated the Pandyan king with the help of two Samantans, Manikan and Vikraman, Eradis of Punthura, whom as a reward he made his heirs. We may perhaps infer from this account that one dynasty reigning at Cranganore came to an end with the abdication of a Perumal who was

[1] Lee's *Travels of Ibn Batuta*, ch. xiii.

[2] Rowlandson's *Tahafut-ul-Mujahidin*, p. 49.

converted to Muhammadanism, possibly in the ninth century; and that subsequently by the 14th century, the last Perumal who attempted to claim sovereignty over Kerala as a whole, was weakened by invasion and had to give place to the rising power of the Zamorin backed by Muhammadan support. Stripped of details at least, the bare outline of the Keralolpatti[1] narrative is true to the type of Dravidian political development, as explained by Mr. Baden Powell. At first there is a tribal organisation in which several joint families, each constituting a separate landholding unit and having certain bonds of local union, are kept together under the rule of a hereditary chief of a *nad*. "In the days of powerful tribal government, such chiefs act in concert and the *nad kuttam* or territorial assembly maintains its influence; but soon the chiefs are forced into more or less unwilling submission to some superior or to the suzerainty of some (possibly foreign) dynasty; in that condition they are scarcely heard of, but when the dynasty is overthrown, they throw off all restraint and resume their freedom . . . . All over the south we find these chiefs with the title of *nayak*, *palayagar* and the like."[2]

CHAP. II. EARLY HISTORY.

1320 A.D.-1498 A.D.

In the fourteenth and fifteenth centuries, Malabar apparently had rest from foreign invasion, and was left to work out its destiny without let or hindrance from without, except possibly from the direction of Vijayanagar[3]. None of the Rajas was able to make himself immediately supreme, and Malabar became a collection of independent states, so small that 'though two steps might be made in one territory, a third must inevitably cross the boundary.' The various Rajas seem to have been constantly at war with one another; the Zamorin was particularly aggressive, and, with the exit of the Perumals, he becomes the protagonist on the Malabar stage. Hailing originally from Nediyiruppu in Ernad, the Zamorins at a very early period overran Polanad, the neighbouring territory of the Porlattiri Raja, and secured the land thus won at the point of the sword by a fort at Velapuram in Calicut. The city which grew up round this fort offered few natural advantages for trade, but the early Zamorins were singularly honest in their dealings, and so encouraged trade that Arab merchants settled in large numbers in their dominions, and the trade of Calicut waxed great. In 1442 A.D., Abdur-razak, though he had been treated with scant courtesy by the Zamorin, was constrained to admit that 'such security and justice reign in that city that rich merchants bring

[1] The Keralolpatti relates two legends turning upon the honesty of the Zamorin whereby two traders, a Muhammadan and a Chetty, were induced to settle at Calicut.

[2] Baden Powell. *The Indian Village Community*, p. 167.

[3] See *A Forgotten Empire* (Sewell), pp. 123, 251 and 374; Barros, *Dec.* I, IX.

CHAP. II. EARLY HISTORY.

to it from maritime countries large cargoes of merchandise which they disembark and deposit in the streets and market places, and for a length of time leave it without consigning it to any one's charge or placing it under a guard.' By the Zamorin's favour these Arab traders were able to drive the Chinese out of the market; and in return not only did they increase his power and wealth by the trade which they attracted to Calicut, but they directly supported him in his campaigns of aggrandisement. It was with their aid, so the Keralolpatti tells us, that the Zamorins succeeded in wresting from the Valluva Kon or Walavanad Raja, the management of the Mahamakham festival at Tirunavayi,[1] the outward and visible sign of the predominant prince in South Malabar, and in robbing him of a great part of his territory. Payyanad at an early date had shared the fate of Polanad, ; and by the end of the fifteenth century, the Kurumbranad, Vettatnad and Parappanad Rajas, the Payyormala Nayars and other chieftains in the vicinity of Calicut bad been forced to acknowledge his suzerainty.[2] Travancore was beyond his reach, and the Kolattiris in North Malabar, who even in Marco Polo's time seem to have been independent princes,[3] were strong enough to resist aggression. But the Zamorin waged constant war with the Raja of Cochin, and at the beginning of the sixteenth century this hostility was one of the cardinal factors in Malabar politics. It seems probable that but for the advent of the Portuguese the Muhammadans would have made the Zamorin supreme in South Malabar, and the check that it gave to the growing power of Islam, was not the least important result to the history of the world of the discovery by Bartholomew Dias of the Cape of Good Hope in A.D. 1487.

THE PORTUGUESE PERIOD, A.D. 1498–1663.

The Portuguese period covers 165 years from A.D. 1498 to 1663, and the limits assigned to this book forbid any attempt to throw into narrative form all the events crowded into this long term of years. Nor is it necessary so to do. Vasco da Gama's discovery of India turned a page in the world's history, but, like the Dutch who succeeded them, the Portuguese have left singularly little impression on Malabar. With the fall of Cochin in 1663 the last relics of Portuguese power were swept away, and their memory lingers on the coast only in the numerous Eurasian and Roman Catholic communities.

Discovery of India, 1498.

Eleven years after Bartholomew Dias had discovered the Cape, on May 18th, 1498,[4] four weather-beaten vessels of

---

1 See p. 484–485.

2 See the map opposite page.

3 Yule's *Marco Polo*, Book III, Ch. XXIV, "The Kingdom of Eli."

4 The account given in the "Roteiro" (Ramusio, Vol. I; translated by Ravenstein in the Hakluyt series, *A Journal of the First Voyage of Vasco da Gama*), which appears to have been followed in the main by Barros, and Castanheda, has been adopted in preference to that of Correa. (*The Three Voyages of Vasco da Gama*, Hakluyt series, p. 270.)

CHAP. II. THE PORTUGUESE PERIOD.

strange design sighted Mount Deli, and, running down the inhospitable coast, anchored two days later at "Capua" which their pilot mistook for Calicut,[1] 'because there commenced the city of Calicut.' The south-west monsoon was threatening, and a few days later they moved to the shelter of the mud bank off Pantalayini Kollam. The strangers were the San Raphael, the San Gabriel the Berrio and a store ship under the command of the Portuguese adventurer, Vasco da Gama. Nearly ten months before, on July 8th, 1498, he had sailed from Belem near Lisbon with the avowed object of capturing for Portugal the trade with the East, and thereby striking a blow at the power of the hated Moors. Negotitations were at once opened with the Zamorin, but the jealousy of the Moorish traders, whose influence was paramount in Calicut, threw many obstacles in the way of the Portuguese. Da Gama nevertheless obtained an audience of the king, and permission to open a factory in the town; and the Zamorin sent a letter to the King of Portugal expressing his pleasure at the prospect of trade with him. Da Gama sailed for home on August 30th, 1498. He had secured samples of the various products of Malabar, and had ascertained what articles were most useful for barter on the coast, and had thus effected his object as a pioneer of Portuguese trade; but the immediate profits of the first voyage do not seem to have been considerable.

Arrival of Cabral, 1500.

On March 9th,[2] a second expedition of 13 ships, of which 10 were to go as far as Calicut, and two to Mozambique and one was a provision boat, sailed under the command of Pedro Alvarez Cabral. One ship was lost on the 23rd March, just after the fleet had passed the Cape Verde islands. The rest of the fleet was driven far to the west, and reached the coast of a new land (Brazil) on the 24th April. The provision ship was sent home with despatches announcing the discovery. The remaining eleven ships set sail for the Cape of Good Hope on the 2nd May; but four foundered in a gale before the Cape was reached and one was temporarily lost after it had been rounded, and only six vessels reached Calicut with Cabral on September, the 13th.

After some preliminary negotiations, a factory was set up on shore, and seventy Europeans were landed to carry on trade; and soon the Portuguese began to feel so safe that they went backwards and forwards on their private business "as if they were in their own country." But pepper came in so slowly that in two months' time only two vessels were laden. The Moors declined to do business with their rivals, or to recognize the right which the Portuguese asserted that the Zamorin had conceded them of a monopoly of the spice. Cabral

[1] Kappat in Kurumbranad taluk, 8 miles north of Calicut.

[2] The account followed that of a pilot who accompanied the expedition—Ramusio, Vol. I.

CHAP. II. THE PORTUGUESE PERIOD.

complained to the Zamorin and getting an evasive reply seized a Moorish vessel which was taking in cargo in the roadstead. An open rupture followed. The Moors suddenly fell on the Portuguese on shore, about seventy of whom took refuge in the factory. After resisting for two hours the Portuguese made a rush for their ships; but only twenty got through, and the rest were killed. Cabral then seized two Moorish ships which were in the port, and slaughtered five or six hundred men whom he found on them. Next day he bombarded the town, and pursued some other ships that were passing down the coast; but they ran ashore and Cabral could not take them. So he sailed on to Cochin.

Discovery of Cochin.

The fleet entered the mouth of the Cochin river, and anchored in the glorious expanse of backwater to which the river gives access on the 24th December 1500. Pledges of friendship were exchanged, and the Portuguese made such good use of their time and the Raja's favour that within a fortnight all their ships were full. On January 10th, 1501, Cabral sailed out to meet a large fleet belonging to the Zamorin, which had been discried the day before in the offing. The Calicut fleet in its turn moved to the attack, but on reconsideration Cabral thought it better to decline the combat and sail for Portugal. Seven Portuguese who were on shore at Cochin were left behind, and two Cochin hostages who were on board accompanied Cabral to Portugal. On his way he put into Cannanore. Thence he sailed direct for home. His voyage had been most important and the Portuguese henceforward ceased to court the Zamorin's favour. Cochin with its magnificent harbour and wonderful inland water communications was in every way superior as a port to Calicut, and there, moreover, the Portuguese had not to contend with the vested trade interests of the Moors. Their common hatred of the Zamorin was a tie between them and the Raja, and the Portuguese could rely upon his consistent support.

The next adventurer to weather the Cape was Joao da Nova, who left Portugal with four vessels in the spring of 1501 before Cabral's return. His expedition is noteworthy for a defeat which he inflicted on a fleet of the Zamorin's, and for the small factory which he established at Cannanore.

Cabral's report in the meantime had fired the King of Portugal with a fierce determinaton to wreak vengeance on the Zamorin and to obtain sovereignty of the seas in the east. A great fleet of twenty vessels was fitted out, and was despatched for India at the beginning of 1502, with Vasco da Gama again in command. On arriving at Cannanore da Gama, acting on the instructions which he had received from the King of Portugal, got the Raja to agree to the adoption

CHAP. II. THE PORTUGUESE PERIOD.

of a fixed scale of prices to prevail in the Portuguese factory.[1] He also arranged for the issue of passes by the factor at Cannanore to ensure a safe passage to all Cannanore merchants. He then proceeded to Calicut, where the Zamorin offered satisfaction for the outrage on Cabral's factory; but Da Gama declined to listen to any proposals for peace, unless the Moors were expelled the country, and, on receiving a refusal from the Zamorin, he hung 34 Moors whom he had captured, and sent their head, hands and feet ashore in an open boat. At Cochin Da Gama concluded agreements with the Raja of Cochin and the Rani of Quilon on the same terms as he had secured at Cannanore; and after regulating the affairs of the factories at Cochin and Cannanore he sailed for home on the 29th December 1502.

Vasco da Gama, 1502.

D. Francisco D'Albuquerque, 1503.

His departure was the signal for hostilities to break out between the Zamorin and the Raja of Cochin. The former demanded the surrender of the Portuguese factors, and followed up his demand by invading Cochin with fifty thousand Nayars. The town of Cochin was taken and burnt; but the Raja refused to give up the Portuguese and retired with them to Vypeen. Here they were beseiged for many months; but the timely arrival on September 2nd, 1503, of D. Francisco D'Albuquerque, with two ships from Portugal and four that had been left behind by Da Gama, raised the seige and forced the Zamorin to retire. A few days later the great Alfonso D'Albuquerque arrived from Portugal with three more ships, and the two Albuquerques, in accordance with the instructions of the King of Portugal, built at Cochin the first European fort constructed in India. Alfonso then proceeded to Quilon to bargain for pepper and was there permitted to open a factory. Francisco had in the meantime gone to Calicut and patched up a truce with the Zamorin, and thither Alfonso followed him leaving Duarte Pacheco with one ship and two caravels to hold the Cochin fort. The two Albuquerques then proceeded to Cannanore where they took in cargo and thence sailed separately to Portugal.

Pacheco's defence of Cochin.

As soon as Alfonso D'Albuquerque had sailed for Portugal the Zamorin collected a large fleet and a strong land force to attack Cochin. Pacheco's defence of Cochin stands out as one of the most brilliant feats of arms in the annals of the

[1] The account followed is that of Thomas Lopez, a clerk who accompanied the expedition (Ramusio I., p. 135). Correa, (*Three Voyages of Vasco da Gama*, p. 324) says that in this expedition formal treaties were concluded with Cannanore and Cochin in which the Portuguese formally claimed the sovereignty of the seas and the monopoly of the pepper trade; but this is probably an anachronism. No doubt the King of Portugal assumed the title of 'Lord of the Navigation, Conquests and Trade of Ethiopia, Arabia, Persia and India', a title which was confirmed by the bull of Alexander VI in 1502; but the Portuguese do not seem to have yet been in a position to enforce their lordship by compelling the Moors to take out passes. (See Barros, dec. I.).

CHAP. II. THE PORTUGUESE PERIOD.

Portuguese occupation of India. For nearly four months from March 10th to July 3rd, 1504, in spite of the disaffection of the Cochin Nayars, he held at bay the flower of the Zamorin's army consisting of 57,000 men with 5 big guns and 160 boats. Again and again the Zamorin's fierce attempts to force a passage across the backwater at the Edappalli ferry were foiled, and Pacheco's resources were strained to the utmost to repel simultaneous onslaughts on the Edappalli and Valanjaca ferries. But his indomitable spirit and heavy guns were proof against all attacks, and when the Zamorin retreated in despair on July 3rd he astonished every one by setting sail in the teeth of the monsoon and putting down a partial outbreak at Quilon. Lopo Soarez De Albergaria had in the meantime arrived with the fleet of the year, and with Pacheco's assistance attacked and burnt Cranganore. The Moors, at this time, disheartened by their trade losses, were leaving the country in large numbers and had assembled a fleet at Pantalayini Kollam to take them back to Arabia. Another of Soarez' exploits was to fall on this fleet and to capture seventeen vessels and slay two thousand of the Moslems.

Almeida, the first Viceroy, 1505–1509.

With a fort at Cochin and a factory at Cannanore, Portuguese interests in the East could no longer be managed by an annual fleet spending a few months only in Indian waters; and in 1505 Francisco D'Almeida was sent out for a term of three years as the first Viceroy of India. His instructions were to secure the Portuguese possessions on the coast by fortresses at Cannanore, Cochin and Quilon, and to cut the Moorish trade communications with East and West by seizing Malacca, Ormuz and Aden. These three places commanded respectively the three great trade routes with China and Europe by way of the Malay Straits, the Persian Gulf and the Red Sea. At Cannanore with the Kolattiri's permissian he laid the foundations of a fort, probably on the site of the existing Fort S. Angelo. At Cochin the fort was strengthened. These preparations and the news that Almeida was to stay for three years on the coast alarmed the Zamorin, and he collected a fleet of some two hundred vessels. Lourenco, Almeida's son, intercepted the armada off Cannanore with eleven vessels, and once more demonstrated Portuguese superiority by defeating it with great slaughter on March 10th, 1506. In 1507 one of their Captains, Gonsalvo Vaz, overhauled a native vessel of Cannanore, and declaring her pass signed by Lourenco DeBrito, Commandant at Cannanore, to be fraudulent, seized her cargo and murdered her crew. The body of a rich merchant was washed ashore, and a new King of Cannanore who had just succeeded and was less friendly to the Portuguese than his predecessor, attributed the blame to DeBrito and attacked the fort. It appears however from the narrative of the Italian Varthema that Calicut merchants had been fraudulently obtaining passes at

CHAP. II. THE PORTUGUESE PERIOD.

Cannanore. The Raja of Cannanore was joined by the Zamorin; and their Nayars, 60,000 in number, laid siege to the fort at Cannanore. The last rat in the place had been devoured, it is said, when a miraculous shoal of crabs came forth from the sea. Tristao da Cunha arrived on the 27th August 1507 when the siege had lasted just four months, with a squadron from Socotra, and the Kolattiri sued for peace. But trouble was already brewing in a different quarter. The Mamaluke Sultan of Egypt, whose revenues had been seriously affected by the Portuguese policy, had decreed that the foreigners must be driven from the East; and in 1508 he sent a fleet of twelve ships and 1,500 men to do his will. The fearless Lourenco met them off Chaul with a few Portuguese ships; but he himself was slain, and the Portuguese drew off with the loss of one ship and 140 men. Almeida swore revenge and a year later he got it. He brought the Egyptian fleet, now reinforced by one hundred small vessels* from Calicut, into action off the coast of Gujarat on February 3rd, 1509, and once more asserted the naval supremacy of the Portuguese. The victory was important, for the sovereignty of the sea was never again seriously challenged from Egypt or from India.

D. Alfonso D'Albuquerque, 1509–1515.

Almeida's policy had been to secure Portuguese trade by the command of the sea, and he had set his face against any thought of territorial conquest. Albuquerque, who succeeded him in November 1509, made a definite attempt to consolidate the Portuguese power in the East. His aim was to fortify the various places at which factories had been established, and to secure a territorial headquarters for the Portuguese dominion of the seas and suzerainty over the native kingdoms. To this end he encouraged the crews of the annual fleets to settle on the coast, and to marry native women, scrupulously baptized for the purpose. His idea was to relieve the heavy drain of men on his own small country by raising up in India half caste subjects of Portugal. His command opened badly. An attack upon the Zamorin's palace at Calicut, carried out against his better judgment, cost him three hundred men; and his occupation of Goa in March 1510 nearly brought him to a premature and disastrous end. A second expedition in November of the same year was more successful, and Goa with its deep water harbour, which afforded shelter to their largest vessels against the monsoon gales, henceforward supplanted Cochin as the Portuguese headquarters in India, though it was not officially recognized as such till 1530. Albuquerque next turned his attention to the trade routes. Malacca was captured in 1511, but an expedition against Aden in the year 1513 ended in failure. In the meantime, much to the discontent of the Kolattiri and the Raja of Cochin, he had been negotiating with the Zamorin for peace. He saw that Portugal's true interest lay in peace

* See Albuquerque's *Commentaries*, Vol. III; and Danvers' *Portuguese in India*, I, p. 259.

CHAP. II. THE PORTUGUESE PERIOD.

and a better understanding with the Zamorin, and he wanted time to re-organise the settlements on the coast. His efforts were crowned with success in 1513, and terms very advantageous to the Portuguese were arranged. The Zamorin agreed to supply the Portuguese with all the spices and drugs which his land produced ; they were to have favourable terms of duty and facilities for their shipping ; and the revenue of the land was to be divided equally between the Zamorin and the King of Portugal. The Portuguese were to help the Zamorin in any war, unless it was against a friendly power, and the Zamorin was to help the Portguese with men on the same condition should occasion arise. The Zamorin also gave the Portuguese permission to construct a fort in Calicut, and to barter European goods for pepper, while all other traders were to pay for it in cash. The fort was built at once on the north bank of the Kallayi river. Albuquerque dealt his last blow at Moorish trade by capturing Ormuz in 1515 ; but, while he was absent on this expedition, the news came that he had been superseded. The slanderous tales of those whose exactions he had repressed had done their work ; and Soarez, the man who had come out to succeed him, had been sent home by Albuquerque himself in disgrace. Albuquerque reached Goa just in time to die on December 17th, 1515.

Vasco da Gama, The Viceroy, 1524.

Apart from the establishment of a factory and a fort at Tangasseri in 1517 and 1519 respectively, and the conclusion of commercial treaties with Quilon in 1516 and 1520, the history of the Portuguese in Malabar during the next few years is of little interest. Their settlements enjoyed a large trade, in which private traders had their share ; and increased opportunities of amassing wealth introduced corruption into the administration. During the Governorship of Soarez a financial adviser was sent out from Portugal to exercise control over expenditure ; but he found himself powerless and soon returned home in disgust. Soarez' successor was recalled as the result of petitions complaining that the Portuguese refused to recognise passes issued by themselves to native vessels ; and the next Governor was accused of caring for nothing but the filling of his own pockets and prostituting justice. The Home Government thought it necessary to send out a strong man to restore order, and in September 1524 'there arrived at the bar of Goa Dom Vasco da Gama who discovered India, as Viceroy of India.' He was now an aged man, and he survived only three months ; but in this short period he did much to stem the rising tide of corruption and to rehabilitate the good name of the Portuguese. The Moorish fleets were chased and dispersed, the Portuguese Settlements were purged, and their administration entrusted to the ablest officers. Vasco da Gama died at Cochin on December 24th, 1524, and his body was interred temporarily in the chancel of the existing Government church.

CHAP. II. THE PORTUGUESE PERIOD. 1524–1571.

The rest of the story of the Portuguese in Malabar need not take long in the telling. A desultory war with the Zamorin broke out on the death of Vasco da Gama, and lasted intermittently till 1559. The fort at Calicut withstood a long siege in 1525; and was finally abandoned at the end of the year, the threat of a Turkish armada from Egypt necessitating the concentration of the Portuguese forces. But the loss was more than counterbalanced. Six years later a successful intrigue with the Raja of Tanur, one of the Zamorin's unwilling feudatories, enabled the Portuguese to erect a fort at Chaliyam at the mouth of the Beypore river. The position was one of great strategic importance. Only six miles from Calicut, Chaliyam commanded the long reaches of the Beypore river and cut in twain the Zamorin's dominions. In 1536, or earlier, a fort was also built at Cranganore. The Portuguese hold on Moorish trade grew stronger, and they pursued their advantage relentlessly. All traffic in pepper, ginger, 'in the bark of spice trees and in the clove jilli-flower, and the herb fennel, and the produce of this kind' was contraband; and Malacca and the Arabian ports being closed to them, the Moors were restricted to petty coasting trade in cocoanuts and cloth. With the aid of the Zamorin they made desperate efforts to throw off the yoke, and waged almost constant war with the Portuguese; but they were invariably worsted, and submission to the hated pass system was always the price of peace. In 1559 they desisted from open warfare, and took to piracy, and Kutti Pokker of Ponnani and the famous Kottakkal Kunhali Marakkars[1] in particular harassed Portuguese trade. The Portuguese retaliated not only by reprisals against property, but by converting many of the Faithful forcibly to Christianity; and the bitter hatred which these acts aroused in the Moslem world still lives in the burning pages of the Tahafut-ul-Mujahidin. They eventually suceeded in building a fort at Ponnani 1585 and Kottakal was reduced in 1600 with the aid of the Zamorin.

Decline of the Portuguese.

The Portuguese retained the monopoly of the trade of the East with Europe till the end of the 16th century. But with the small resources at their command, their power in the East could never be consolidated. They had a string of fortresses round the vast coast line from the Cape of Good Hope to China, and for a century held the command of the eastern seas. But they never became a land power in the East. Fortunately for them, during the first half of the century the Indian kingdoms from which they had most to fear, Bijapur and Vijayanagar, were too much occupied, especially in fighting one another, to be formidable to them. In 1565 the Empire of Vijayanagar fell, and with it the prosperity of Goa, which lost the chief market

[1] See p. 460.

CHAP. II. THE PORTUGUESE PERIOD.

for its European goods and Arab ponies.[1] The political result was soon seen in a combination against the Portuguese of the Muhammadan rulers of India with the Zamorin of Calicut and the King of Achin. Goa was attacked in 1570, by an army estimated at 100,000 with 2,000 elephants; but 700 Portuguese under Luis de Athaide held out, until after ten months the Indian army melted away. Malacca and Chaul also successfully stood sieges; but Chaliyam was taken by the Zamorin before the Portuguese reinforcements, which reached Goa towards the end of the year 1571, could relieve it. After this the Portuguese could scarcely hold their own against their native enemies. Their administration was corrupt; and although large fortunes were made by individuals, the State derived little advantages from the profits of trade, while it had to support a great drain of men and money for the wars in the East. In 1580 Portugal was incorporated with Spain, and from that time travellers who visited the Portuguese settlements in the East comment no longer as earlier travellers had done on the strength of the Portuguese in the East, but on their decadence. Linschoten revealed their weakness to his fellow Dutch, who were not slow to make use of the valuable information he supplied, and Pyrard de Laval to the French; and when the Italian traveller Pietro della Valle visited Goa in 1624, it had ceased to be one of the great cities of the world.

Loss of the monopoly of trade with Europe.

On July 20th, 1581, Holland declared its independence of Spain; and the interest of the next eighty years lies in the attempts of the Dutch, the English and the French to obtain a footing in India. The English were the first of these nations to establish a settlement in Malabar. In 1615 Captain Keeling with three ships touched at Cranganore, and entered into a treaty[2] with the Zamorin. The Zamorin hoped for assistance against the Portuguese, and, when the English ships sailed away after landing ten men to found a factory, he showed scant courtesy to the factors. In 1623 Goa was blocked by a combined English and Dutch fleet. In 1630 a treaty of peace was concluded between England and Spain. It was still a matter of dispute, however, whether England could trade in the East Indies without infringing the vested rights of Spain and Portugal. Finally, in 1635, an agreement, purporting to be merely an agreement to carry out the treaty of 1630, was concluded between the Governor of Goa and the President of the East India Company in India. The English East India Company obtained free access to all Portuguese ports, and a few Englishmen settled in Cochin, whence pepper was exported for the first time direct to England in 1635.

[1] De Couto, Decadas VIII. 15, quoted in *A Forgotten Empire* (Sewell), p. 210.

[2] Printed in Foster's *Letters received by the East India Company*, Vol. IV, p. 64.

CHAP. II. THE PORTUGUESE PERIOD.

The fall of Cochin, 1663.

But it was the Dutch who were destined to step first into the shoes of the Portuguese. Already in 1639 they had blockaded Goa, and in 1661 they attempted to gain possession of Cochin. Their first attack was a failure. Vypeen was occupied with 800 men, and the Roman Catholic church strongly entrenched. With the rest of his forces Van Goens, the Dutch Commander, advanced on the town from the south. The Rani's palace at Muttancheri and the outlying parts of the settlement were captured with ease, but a storming party which attacked the fort on the following day was repulsed. Regular siege works were then begun, but the garrison held out bravely until the arrival of the Raja of Purakkad with six thousand Nayars compelled the Dutch to retreat. They embarked on their ships at dead of night, and the Portuguese woke up next morning to find them gone. Their sentinels had been outwitted by the camp fires which the Dutch had left alight, and by a Jew whom they had engaged to sound the hours as usual; and the opportunity of harrassing the Dutch during the difficult operation of embarkation was lost. They had left seven hundred men in Vypeen, and their absence was only temporary. Tangasseri fell to them the same year and Cranganore the next, and in October 1662 they returned to the attack. The Raja of Purakkad once more came to the assistance of his allies, and threw supplies into the fort, but after a brave resistance his troops were routed by the Dutch. The Portuguese garrison still held out, and the Dutch reinforced by the Nayars of the Cochin Raja determined to storm the fort. For eight days and nights the assault was kept up, the assailants being relieved every three hours. Finally their stock of provisions being almost exhausted, and worn out with continuous fighting, the little garrison capitulated on January 8th, 1663. Cannanore was next taken on the 13th February.

THE STRUGGLE FOR THE PEPPER TRADE. 1663–1766. The Dutch in Malabar.

Except for small English factories at Ponnani and Calicut, the Dutch monopoly of the foreign trade of the coast from the Kavvayi river to Cape Camorin was now complete, and many of the most eligible sites for commerce—Tangasseri, Cochin, Cranganore, Chettuvayi and Cannanore—were in their hands. But, with the trade of the Portuguese the Dutch took over their difficulties. The circumstances compelled them as they had compelled the Portuguese and afterwards compelled the English, to seek trade at the sword's point. They could not support the expenses of war indefinitely, and in 1680 were obliged to adopt a policy of retrenchment which only landed them in further difficulties. In 1691 they abandoned Chettuvayi to the Zamorin, and in 1697 they withdrew from their smaller outposts, dismantled parts of their forts at Tangasseri, Cranganore and Cannanore, and contracted that at Cochin to half its former size. The possession of Chettuvayi gave the Zamorin a commanding position on the flank of Cochin, and he was not slow to follow up the advantage. War

CHAP. II. THE STRUGGLE FOR THE PEPPER TRADE.

broke out in 1701, and for nine years the defence of their ally involved the Dutch in ruinous military operations against the Zamorin. They reoccupied Chettuvayi in 1717; but once more their profits had disappeared, and in 1721 the Dutch East India Company formally withdrew from all interference in native wars. This momentous resolution was the turning point of their fortunes on the West Coast of India.

Rise of the English.

No sooner had Cochin fallen in 1663 than the English factors, who had settled there twenty-eight years before, received notice to quit and retired to Ponnani. A year later a small factory was opened at Calicut, and in these two places, living like ordinary merchants with no other protection than that of the Zamorin, the English laid the foundations of their future influence. The Zamorin however was not prepossessed in favour of foreign settlements, and towards the close of the seventeenth century the English Company sought other sites whence they could trade in greater security. Finally they fixed on Anjengo in Tranvancore and Tellicherry in North Malabar. At the former place, a mere sand-spit with nothing to recommend it save its inland waterways, they obtained a site for a factory from the Rani of Attingal in 1684, and in 1690 permission to build a fort. Tellicherry, where a factory was founded some time before 1699, apart from its proximity to the finest pepper and cardamom lands in Malabar, had even fewer advantages to boast of; and the adjacent Darmapattanam Island, naturally a strong position, would have been a far better site for trade. But the island was at that time in dispute among the country powers, and its occupation would doubtless have led to complications, which the Company was determined at all hazards to avoid. From the first the Company set its face against martial enterprise.[1] In order to attract trade, they paid for their pepper full market prices and exempted for a time all manufactured goods from duty and afforded facilities for shipping. They attracted spinners, weavers and men of wealth to settle within their limits; and scrupulously abstained from interfering with their religious and caste ceremonies. They established Courts of Justice, and made life and property secure. This wise and liberal policy had its due reward, especially after the disputes of the rival companies trading to the East were settled in 1708; and in the early years of the eighteenth century the influence of the English waxed as rapidly as that of the Dutch waned.

[1] The advice of Sir Thomas Roe, ambassador to the Great Moghul, to the English East India Company is worth quoting in full. "The Portuguese, notwithstanding their many rich residences are beggared by keeping of soldiers, and yet their garrisons are but mean. They never made advantage of the Indies, since they defended them. Observe this well. It has also been the error of the Dutch who seek plantations here by the sword. They turn a wonderful stock: they prowle in all places; they possess some of the best, yet their dead pays consume all the gain."

CHAP. II. THE STRUGGLE FOR THE PEPPER TRADE.

Travancore and the decline of the Dutch.

The English were fortunately able at this time occasionally to interfere in native politics to their advantage. Such an occasion occurred in 1721, about the same time as the Dutch resolved to withdraw from their support of the Raja of Cochin. Travancore at this time was in a state of anarchy very unfavourable to trade. The authority of the Rajas was merely nominal, and all real power in the country was vested in the Brahmans of the Trivandrum temple and the heads of the great Nayar houses, the Ettuvittil Pillamar, as they were called. The chiefs of the Anjengo factory had also roused the popular feeling against them by unscrupulous methods of trading. The result was that when in 1721, Mr. Gyfford went in person to Attingal with a large retinue to pay the annual present due to the Rani, the whole party was barbarously murdered. The Honourable Company promptly 'resolved in spite of all money expenses to put down the enemies and to subject the country to the King.'[1] Treaties of friendship and commerce were concluded,[2] but the supremacy of the Tranvancore Raja was not established till the great Martanda Varma ascended the throne in 1729. Backed up by the English Company, this prince soon crushed the power of his refractory chieftains, and in 1731 he atoned for the treacherous murder of the Anjengo chief by ceding the gardens of 'Palatady and Cottudali' which are still part of the Anjengo settlement.[3] In 1733 Martanda Varma attacked Calli-Quilon, the Raja of which was an ally of the Dutch. The Dutch were applied to for assistance, but, in pursuance of their policy of non-intervention, refused to interfere. Other petty princes allied to the Dutch were in turn subdued; and in 1739 the Dutch realized that, if they were to retain their hold on the trade of the country and to prevent it from passing into English hands, they must crush the growing power of the Travancore Raja. Unfortunately for themselves they were at the time engaged in other parts of their possessions in the East and had not sufficient force on the spot to command respect for their wishes, and a formal protest made by the Governor Van Imhoff in person to the Raja ended in failure. War ensued, but was carried on half-heartedly by the Dutch; and they had the mortification of seeing the Travancore army, recently organised by the famous Fleming, Eustachius DeLanoy, formerly a soldier in their service, overrun the territory of their ally the Raja of Cochin. Peace was finally declared in 1753, and the terms, which the Dutch were constrained to accept, extinguished for ever their influence in Malabar. They agreed to abandon all their allies to the mercy of the Tranvancore king, and in return the Raja on his part undertook to supply them with a fixed

[1] Logan's *Treaties*, i. XII.

[2] *Ibid.* i. XI, XII, XXIV and XVIII.

[3] *Ibid.* i. XX.

CHAP. II. THE STRUGGLE FOR THE PEPPER TRADE.

quantity of pepper at a price reduced by As. 4 on every 25 lb. The Raja, however, soon repudiated the obligation, telling the Dutch factors that they were no longer a sovereign power, but merely a number of petty merchants; and that, if they required spices, they must buy them in the open market. The Dutch retained Cochin forty-two years longer; but from the date of this treaty they ceased to be the predominant factor in Malabar history.

The French and the English in North Malabar.

In the meantime the French had appeared on the scene, and had obtained a stable footing in North Malabar. In 1725 a small squadron under the command of M. de Pardaillan, acting under the orders of the Governor of Pondicherry, appeared off Mayyazhi, four miles south of Tellicherry, and summoned the town to surrender. The Governor refused, and the position was one of such natural strength that the French Commodore hesitated to attack. 'On high ground rising up from the sea, and washed on the northern side by a little river, the entrance to which was closed by rocks even for the smallest boats, Mahe seemed to be able to bid defiance to any enemy who should attack it on the side of the sea.'[1] But the strength of the position had no terrors for one of M. de Pardaillan's captains, and he obtained permission to execute a plan which his own genius had devised. Under cover of the guns of the squadron, the troops were landed by a raft dryshod and almost in order of battle. The heights were quickly scaled, and the town stormed without serious difficulty. The captain was Bertrand Francois Mahe de Labourdonnais; and, in honour of the great part he had played in its capture, the settlement was rechristened Mahe. The French and the English were once more face to face, and for the rest of the century they fought out in a new field the ancient question of their supremacy. Both intrigued for the support of the native princes and for the trade of their territories; and thus it was that, as in Travancore so in North Malabar, the English Company for all its good resolutions was drawn into the vortex of native politics as had been the Dutch Company before it.

North Malabar politics.

North Malabar had at one time been united under the sway of the Kolattiri, whose dominions had stretched as far south as the Kotta river, and in the north had included part of the Kasaragode taluk of the South Canara district. But various causes had long been at work, making for the dissolution of the kingdom, amongst the chief of which was the working of the *marumakkatayam* law of inheritance through the sister's son, and the natural impulse of successive Kolattiris to make provision for their own children out of the family estates at the expense of their legal heirs. By the end of the seventeenth century the process of disintegration had gone so far that, like

[1] Malleson, *History of the French in India*, p. 62.

Travancore, North Malabar was in a state bordering on anarchy. Only the modern taluk of Chirakkal remained directly under the Kolatiri's authority; and even within these narrow limits the Muhammadan Ali Raja, had made himself master of Cannanore and the Randattara Achanmar were the semi-independent chieftains of the southern amsams of the taluk. The Kadattanad chief, an offshoot of the Kolattanad family, ruled between the Mahe and Kotta rivers, and another such offshoot in the Malayalam country north of the Kavyayi river. Kottayam taluk was in the possession partly of the Iruvalinad Nambiyars, partly of the Puranad or Kottayam Rajas. These princes were all feudatories of the Kolattiri; but they set his authority at nought whenever they could do so with impunity, and the influence of the family was further weakened by internal dissensions. An arrangement, evidently dating from the time when their dominions were wider, divided the executive power in theory between the five eldest males the Kolattiri, the Tekkelamkur or Southern Regent, the Vadakkelamkur or Northern Regent, the Nalamkur and the Anjamkur. But at this time what really happened was that the ablest member, whether by force or with the consent of the others, seized the reins of government. Thus the grant of the site of the Tellicherry factory was secured, not from the Kolattiri, but from the Northern Regent, who at the time was *de facto* ruler of Kolattanad. On this sea of intrigue, conflicting interests and mutual jealousies, the factors now embarked, and with one exception they steered their way with conspicuous skill.

Peace with Mahe.

The French made the first move. The Kurangot Nayar, one of the chieftains of Iruvalinad, had always resented the intrusion of the English into his domains at Tellicherry, and eagerly welcomed an alliance with the French. An attempt was made with his assistance to seize two of the outlying hills of Tellicherry. The English repelled force with force, and supplied the Kadattanad chief with money to carry on war for the recovery of Mahe; and used their influence with the Northern Regent to gain over to their side four of the Iruvalinad Nambiyars. Mutual protests followed, and, under orders from their respective Governments, the two factories agreed in 1728 to live amicably side by side and to combine to keep down the price of pepper. [1]

Darmapattanam Island.

About the same time the Tellicherry chief was able to turn to the advantage of the settlement a danger which threatened its trade from another quarter. The Dutch still held Fort S.Angelo at Cannanore, and in 1728 in order to obtain command of the rich pepper trade of Randattara they instigated the Ali Raja to defy his suzerain and to seize a place named Codally. Darmapattanam Island was at this time in the Ali Raja's possession; and, as it was the key to Tellicherry, the factors

[1] Logan's *Treaties*, i. XVII.

CHAP. II. THE STRUGGLE FOR THE PEPPER TRADE.

could not afford to see it in unfriendly hands. With the aid of the Kottayam Raja the Ali Raja was promptly dislodged; and two years later, to prevent the Prince Regent from surrendering the island to the Dutch, the factors assisted him with money and stores to carry on war with the Mappillas. In return for their assistance the Prince Regent granted to the Company a monopoly of trade in Iruvalinad, Darmapattanam island and Randattara, and permission to hoist their flag, if the French or Dutch threatened to take possession of any of these places.[1]

The Bednur war.

The effect of this diplomatic success was at once neutralised by a totally unexpected danger, this time from the direction of Canara. The malcontents of the Kolattiri family had carried their feud with the Prince Regent so far as to invite the assistance of the Bednur Raja. Early in 1732 his general, 'Ragonatt,' who had crossed the frontier at the head of a Canarese army, had 'gott as far as Mount Dilly'; and the factors were in desperate straits for food, as Mangalore, the granary of Malabar, was now closed to them. The invasion, though directed against the Prince Regent, jeopardised not only the trade of the European factories, but the safety of Malabar; and for a time, their mutual jealousies forgotten, the English and the Dutch joined in a common effort with the native princes to repel the invader. But, their anxiety as to their food supply being allayed by a welcome consignment of rice from Bombay, the factors' first thought was as usual for the safety of Darmapattanam Island. The Prince Regent had bowed to the storm, and had bought the assistance of the Canarese general against the Ali Raja by ceding all the country north of the Valarpattanam river; and he might at any time surrender the island to the Canarese. English troops, nominally in the Prince Regent's pay, were at once introduced into all the forts in the island. The Bibi of Cannanore was next persuaded to relinquish her claims to its possession, as she could neither keep it herself nor afford to see either the French or the Canarese its masters. The Kottayam Raja withheld his consent for a time, but in 1735 gave in when a Canarese army crossed the Anjarakkandi river and prepared for the invasion of Kottayam;[2] and by virtue of these agreements and their previous treaty with the Prince Regent, the Company acquired an indefeasible title to the Island. The Chief's next care was to organise a confederacy of the native princes against the Canarese. This was no easy task. The French agreed to join, but in the end backed out of their promise, and the jealousies of the native princes were a great obstacle to alliances. No great progress was made till 1736, and then the league included only the English, the Prince Regent and the

[1] Logan's *Treaties*, i. XIX.

[2] Logan's *Treaties*, i. XXVII, XXVIII and XXX.

CHAP. II. THE STRUGGLE FOR THE PEPPER TRADE.

Kottayam Raja. The allied forces at once took the field, and gained their first great success on March 7th, 1736, when they captured the Canarese fort at Madakkara on the Valarpattanam river. The strong position of Cadalay was next invested, and Mr. Stephen Law, the Tellicherry Chief, tried hard to persuade the Dutch to join in the attack. Hitherto the Dutch had contented themselves with lending their moral support to the campaign and with refusing to supply the Canarese with food. They held aloof from active operations for fear lest the English should retain Cadalay, as they had retained Madakkara,[1] and utilize it to interfere with their trade in the pepper country on the north bank of the Valarpattanam river. A written promise that Cadalay would be razed to the ground removed their suspicions, and on March 30th they sent 300 men to assist in the attack. The fort was stormed with great slaughter on April 1st ; and the smaller outposts of the Canarese at Madayi, Taliparamba, Mattalayi and Ayconny were captured soon afterwards in rapid succession. The Dutch took no further part in the campaign. They demanded as the price of their assistance that the Prince Regent should supply them with pepper at less than market rates. Eventually the Prince agreed to deliver annually 1,000 candies of pepper at Rs. 56 per candy, about half its market price. But the English fort at Madakkara gave the Company the command of the Valarpattanam river, and Dutch trade at Cannanore rapidly dwindled away to nothing. An English force in the meantime had been prosecuting the campaign against the Canarese in Nileswaram beyond the Kavvayi river, and in February 1737 the Company was strong enough to make its own terms with Bednur. Certain privileges and concessions were secured in Canara, and the monopoly of trade in Kolattanad ; and the Bednur Raja was debarred from advancing further south than the Valarpattanam river.[2] The war continued between the Prince Regent and the Canarese, but the line of the Valarpattanam river was obstinately maintained, and the Company interfered only occasionally ; and after 1740, when the peace of 1737 was ratined,[3] the Canarese caused them little further trouble.

Struggles with the French.

The French about this time had profited by the English preoccupation with the Canarese, and had been busy in many directions. In 1740 they hoisted their flag at Tanur and attempted unsuccessfully to settle at Chettuvayi ; and in the same year the good relations between Mahe and Tellicherry were disturbed by rumours of war between England and Spain assisted by France. The factors remained perpetually on the

---

[1] Under pressure from the Prince Regent who was afraid lest the Mappillas should occupy the fort. Logan's *Treaties*, i. XXXI.

[2] Logan's *Treaties*, i. XXXIII and XXXIV.

[3] Logan's *Treaties*, i. XLII and XLIII.

CHAP. II. THE STRUGGLE FOR THE PEPPER TRADE.

alert, and on June 17th nipped in the bud an ingenious French design on Andolla Mala, one of the outlying hills attached to Tellicherry. Desultory fighting continued for some months, and in November 1741 the factors were alarmed at the news that Labourdonnais had arrived at Mahe with a squadron of five ships. Fortunately his intentions were pacific, and his labours in the cause of peace culminated in two treaties.[1] Both factories withdrew from the advanced posts which they had seized and fortified in the Iruvalinad Nambiyars' domains. They agreed to combine to keep down the price of pepper 'which rises daily,' and on no pretext to give succour to native princes. The English were to arbitrate in disputes between the French and the Kadattanad Raja, and the French were to return the compliment in those between the English and the Prince Regent of Kolattanad. War broke out again in 1744, but the two factories took little part in the hostilities, and alternated between hope and despair as the fleets of their respective nations gained the upper hand in Indian waters. The fall of Fort St. George in 1746 sent the Tellicherry factors down into the depths; but they prepared for a siege with a stout heart, and were cheered by offers of assistance from the Prince Regent, the Bednur and Nileswaram Rajas, the Randattara Achanmar and other chieftains. The French fleet came and went, and the danger passed away. In 1748 Mahe had its turn of adversity, and two English men-of-war made a daring attempt to cut out a French vessel lying in the roads. The peace of Aix la Chapelle was welcomed by both parties in 1749; and the two factories signalised the occasion by combining and reducing the price of pepper to Rs. 56 per candy, a lower price than it had ever touched before.

Siege of Tellicherry.

Less than two years later Tellicherry was in the throes of a desperate siege. An army of the allied princes of Kolattanad, Kottayam and Kadattanad was at its very gates; several of the outposts had been captured, and many houses within the town had been burnt. The French flag was flying over Nileswaram fort, and over the two small fortresses of Ettikulam and Ramdilly at the foot of Mount Deli. They had occupied the mouth of the Kavvayi river, and had thrown men into the Prince Regent's fort at Valarpattanam. A new chief had brought these misfortunes upon the settlement. In 1750 Mr. Thomas Dorril had taken over charge of the factory, and by a series of blunders had undone all the good work of his predecessors among the native princes. The Company had hitherto consistently made a friend of the ruling prince of Kolattanad, regardless of other claims to the throne. Mr. Dorril had thought fit to interfere in the dissensions of the family and to support another claimant against the *de facto* prince. The latter had naturally turned to the French for aid, and

[1] Logan's *Treaties*, i. CVII and CVIII.

CHAP. II. THE STRUGGLE FOR THE PEPPER TRADE.

had enlisted the sympathies of Kottayam and Kadattanad. Bereft of friends nearer home, Mr. Dorril had tried to create a diversion by suggesting to the Bednur Raja that now was the time to attack the Prince Regent's fort at Nileswaram ; and the French had not been slow to seize the opportunity thus offered them of waging war against the Canarese and establishing themselves along the coast north of the Valarpattanam river. At the end of 1751 the Tellicherry fort was in desperate straits, but the arrival of ships from Bombay relieved the pressure. The chief, moreover, had learnt wisdom in adversity, and had succeeded in detaching the Kottayam Raja from his allies. With his help a dishonourable peace was arranged in 1752. Madakkara fort was surrendered and a sum of Rs. 50,000 paid to the Prince Regent, who on his part undertook to destroy his redoubts on the outskirts of Tellicherry. In the following year the Zamorin was induced to visit the town, and was received with great pomp. The growing power of the Prince Regent and of Kadattanad backed by the French had alarmed him, and he entered into a defensive alliance with Kottayam, the Iruvalinad Nambiyars and the Company, to preserve the balance of power in North Malabar.

Fall of Mahe.

Mr. Dorril was superseded in 1754, and Mr. Hodges reigned in his stead at Tellicherry. The new chief was as skilful an administrator as his predecessor had been the reverse ; and, aided by the mistakes of the French, he soon restored British prestige on the coast. He avoided open rupture, but steadfastly set his face to drive the French out of Nileswaram ; and to that end supplied the third Raja of Nileswaram with the sinews of war against their ally, the head of the family. In 1756 this policy bore fruit. The third Raja defeated the French three times in quick succession, and in June of that year captured their fortress at Mattalayi. This fort was a link in the chain of French communications between Mount Deli and their furthest outpost at Nileswaram ; and the last place must have fallen, had not the Prince Regent intervened on their behalf. He pledged his word that the French would evacuate Nileswaram if Mattalayi were restored to them ; and, in return for his mediation, the French promised to surrender a bond for Rs. 60,000, which they had advanced to him during the war with the Company. Mattalayi was restored ; but the French broke all their promises. War was formally declared between England and France on October 17th, 1756, but Mr. Hodges was ready for the struggle which he had long foreseen. Tellicherry had been provisioned, and matters were well in train for a good understanding with Kottayam, Kadattanad and Iruvalinad Nambiyars. In December the first named threw in his lot with the English ;[1] and in April 1757

[1] Logan's *Treaties*, i. CXXI.

CHAP. II. THE STRUGGLE FOR THE PEPPER TRADE.

the Prince Regent returned to his old allegiance,[1] and definitely abandoned his faithless allies, the French. Neither factory took the offensive for the next three years. The French were exhausted by their long struggle in Nileswaram, and the English, true to their business instincts, took the opportunity of increasing their trade. Every ship sent to Canton at this period was freighted up to £40,000 sterling. On December 27th, 1760, four ships put into Tellicherry, and landed Major Hector Munro and six hundred and thirty-five men; three days later other ships arrived, and the end soon came. On January 31st 'glorious news' of the surrender of Pondicherry on the 16th idem was received; and on February 3rd M. Louet, Commandant of Mahe, was summoned to surrender. Ten days later the British flag waved over Mahe, and the French garrison marched into Tellicherry 'with the honours of war, drums beating, colours flying, each man with a ball in his mouth, four field pieces with one mortar and twelve rounds'[2]. Their forts to the north had been surrendered a day or two previously to a prince of the Kolattiri family; and one of them, Ettikulam near Mount Deli had been surprised by the Ali Raja of Cannanore and its garrison barbarously massacred. This fort Major Munro soon recovered, and razed to the ground. The factors, now supreme on the coast and the monopolists of its trade, cut down their establishments, and withdrew from all their outposts save Mount Deli and Darmapattanam Island. Madakkara fort was blown up.

Events in South Malabar.

In the meantime, while the French and the English were engaged in the struggle in North Malabar, great changes had come over the south and east of the country. The hapless Raja of Cochin, deserted by his allies the Dutch in 1753, soon found himself between the hammer of the Zamorin and the anvil of Travancore. In 1755–6 the former attacked Chettuvayi; and, driving in the Dutch outposts, rapidly possessed himself of Cranganore, Parur and Verapoly. At the same time the Travancore Raja, easily overpowering the forces sent to oppose him, overran the south of the kingdom. In his extremity the Cochin Raja turned to Travancore, and in 1761 by a further cession of territory secured assistance against the Zamorin.[3] The first act of the Travancore Raja was to construct the famous Travancore lines thirty miles long, from the shores of the backwater opposite Cranganore to the foot of the ghats, and protected by a fort at their western extremity and by towers at frequent intervals. With his right flank guarded by these lines, the Travancore General, Eustacius De Lanoy, launched his troops in three divisions on the Zamorin's garrisons, extending in a long weak line into

---

[1] Logan's *Treaties*, i. LXX.

[2] *Ibid.* i. LXXVII.

[3] *Ibid.* i. XXIV and CXXV.

Cochin territory, at Cranganore, Parur and Verapoly; and the Zamorin's troops were soon driven in disorder from Cochin. The Travancore Raja was now master of the whole country from Cranganore to Cape Comorin; and small isolated portions of territory round the palace at Trippunattara on the east of the backwater, and north and south of Cochin on its western bank, were all that remained to the Cochin Raja south of the Travancore lines.

THE MYSOREAN CONQUEST, 1766-1793.

Zamorin's invasion of Palghat.

Unfortunately for Malabar, the Zamorin did not confine his restless aggressions to Cochin. Some years before he had made himself master of the south of Walavanad from his own country of Ernad to the borders of the Palghat Raja's dominions, and in 1756-7 he drove a wedge into the last by capturing the district named Naduvattam, now a part of the Palghat taluk. The conquest of the whole of Palghat would have been a mere matter of time, had not the Raja paved the way for the Mysorean invasion by applying in 1757 to Haidar Ali, then Fouzdar of Dindigul, for assistance. Haidar's reply was a force of two thousand horse, five thousand infantry and five guns under the command of his brother-in-law Makhdum Ali. The Zamorin fell back, and Makhdum Ali carried his arms right up to the sea coast. The Zamorin bought off his opponents by undertaking to restore his conquests in Palghat, and to pay an indemnity of twelve lakhs of rupees. The indemnity was not paid; but Haidar never relinquished his claim, and, when his plans were ripe, he enforced it by invading Malabar.

The invasions of 1766.

The first mutterings of the storm were heard at Tellicherry in January 1763. Urgent messages from Honore and Mangalore that 'Heddor Naigu' was threatening Bednur were followed up before the end of the month by the news that Bednur and Mangalore had fallen, and that the Ali Raja of Cannanore, as usual at logger-heads with the Kolattiri, had invited an invasion of Malabar. In May, the Nileswaram Raja took up arms for the defence of his frontier, and the Company deemed it wise to obtain from the Nabob a 'phurmaund',[1] which secured their food supply from Mangalore and bound each party not to assist the other's enemies. But the time for the conquest of Malabar had not come. Haidar disappeared up the ghats, and nearly three years elapsed before he actually crossed the frontier in February 1766, with the avowed object of settling up with the Zamorin and of collecting an old Bednur claim of two lakhs of pagodas against the Kolattiri. In the interval 'Mahe and its dependencies and the places where fortifications stood' had been restored on October 20th, 1765, to the French, and the Ali Raja had prepared the way for the invasion by espousing the cause of 'Capu Tamban', one of the

[1] Logan's *Treaties*, i. LXXX.

CHAP. II. THE MYSOREAN CONQUEST. 1766–1793.

irreconcileables of the Kolattiri family. Haidar's forces consisted of twelve thousand picked troops, including four thousand horse, and four guns, and a powerful fleet accompanied him along the coast. The Ali Raja was at first the 'High Admiral' of this fleet, but was deprived of his command for a piece of wanton cruelty towards the King of the Maldive Islands. After this, he served on land, and his Mappilla irregulars, eight thousand in number, made very efficient scouts. Haidar swept through the country as far as Calicut without meeting any serious resistance. His army had received general instructions to grant no quarter—an injunction which the Ali Raja's Mappillas especially carried out to the letter, sparing neither man, woman nor child—and the inhabitants fled before them. The Nayars were no match for disciplined troops in open fight, and were defeated, on the sole occasion on which they attempted in force to oppose Haidar, at the Perinkulam ferry on the Kotta river. But they were magnificient light troops in an ideal country for guerilla warfare, and they hung on the flank of the army, and harassed its advance till Haidar was compelled to secure his communications by a cordon of block-houses. Calicut was occupied without a blow being struck in its defence. The Zamorin, unable to meet Haidar's modest demand for an indemnity of a crore of gold mohurs, was confined in his palace and debarred from performing the ceremonies of his religion. Fearing other worse indignities, he set fire to the pile with his own hand, and perished in the flames.

Haidar's attitude towards the Company had been capricious rather than actively hostile. He had confirmed all their privileges of trade in Malabar and had refrained from attacking Tellicherry. But he had ravaged Randattara, which had been mortgaged to the factors in 1741, and had made it a grievance that protection had been afforded to refugees who had fled before his army, and that the factors had refused to supply him with gunpowder and arms. At Cannanore, where he had met the Dutch Commandant, he had hinted at his intention to drive the English out of Malabar, and at Calicut he openly suggested an offensive and defensive alliance with the Dutch. Cochin purchased immunity from invasion by promising to pay a subsidy of two lakhs of rupees and eight elephants; but the Raja of Travancore, though he promised a contribution if the Zamorin and Kolattiri were reinstated, declined to become tributary to the Nabob, and replied to his threats of conquest by strengthening his lines. The monsoon was now approaching and Haidar retired to Coimbatore. A force of 3,000 men was left to overawe Malabar, and Madanna, an experienced revenue officer, was appointed Civil Governor of the new province.

Rebellion in Malabar.

Haidar's departure was the signal for a general revolt. Kottayam and Kadattanad rose in the north; and the

CHAP. II. THE MYSOREAN CONQUEST. 1766-1793.

block-houses, their communications cut by swollen streams, were fiercely attacked by bodies of Nayars. Messengers to the East were intercepted and it was not until the Mysorean forts at Ponnani and Calicut had been invested, that news of the rising was brought to Raza Khan, who had been left at Madakkarai on the frontiers of Coimbatore with 3,000 men. He started at once to quell the outbreak; but his small force, handicapped by lack of cavalry, and harassed at every river-crossing by the Nayars, was finally drawn into a position at the junction of the Tuta and Ponnani rivers whence advance and retreat were alike impossible. Haidar heard at Coimbatore of his lieutenant's peril, and made a characteristically impetuous march to his relief. With his men stripped almost naked [1], and his cavalry riding bare-backed, he pushed rapidly on, laying the country waste as he went, and overtook the Nayars in a strongly entrenched position at Pudiyangadi in Ponnani taluk. The first attack failed, but the valour of a body of European troops turned impending defeat into victory, and the Nayars were driven back in utter rout. Organised resistance was now at an end, and Haidar proceeded to pacify Malabar by making a desert of what once had been a populous and prosperous land. With Manjeri for their headquarters the troops carried fire and sword throughout the country side; and their houses in flames, their fruit trees cut down, and their cattle destroyed, the unhappy inhabitants took refuge in the hills and jungles. The Nayars were the object of his special resentment. They were hunted remorselessly down, and hanged without mercy as soon as captured. Their wives and children were sold into slavery, and Haidar even published an edict degrading the caste below the rank of Pariahs. As more were brought in, he conceived the plan of carrying them into captivity into other parts of his dominions; but very few of the thousands deported from Malabar survived the experiment. These violent measures soon produced outward calm in the province, and Haidar retired once more to Coimbatore with his cavalry. Many of his infantry were distributed over Malabar in block-houses, the rest being quartered at Madakkarai, and a strong fort was erected at Palghat to guard his communications with the West Coast.

Negotiations with the Malabar chieftains.

The calm did not last long. The defeat of a force, sent by Haidar to bring the Travancore Raja to reason, led to another general outbreak early in 1767. A Mysorean force of 4,000 men in Kottayam was attacked and routed by half as many Nayars, and once more Haidar's troops were shut up in their stockades. Haidar himself was fighting for his life on the east of the ghats, and his army might have been driven headlong from Malabar, had not the Malabar chieftains in 1768 been deluded by the 'insidious but skilful' negotiations of

[1] As a precaution against dysentery.

CHAP. II. THE MYSOREAN CONQUEST. 1766–1793.

Madanna. He hinted that '*his master had found his conquest* of Malabar an acquisition hitherto more chargeable than advantageous: that, if the chiefs should consent to reimburse the heavy charges which he had incurred, he would be ready to restore their possessions.' The chieftains, dreaming of independence, assented gladly; and Haidar's troops, laden with treasure retreated safely from a position from which otherwise they could hardly have been extricated. The Ali Raja was left undisturbed in possession of Kolattanad, of which Haidar had made him Civil Governor in 1766, and Palghat was studiously omitted from the negotiations. Thus Haidar retained two points in the south-east and north-west of the Province, from which he could resume at pleasure his designs on Malabar.

Attack on Cochin and Travancore.

The next few years were uneventful, except for the sale in 1771 of Cannanore by the Dutch to the Ali Raja; but at the end of 1773 a Mysorean force descended once more on Malabar by a new and direct route through the Wynaad down the Tamarasseri ghat. The Malayali princes yielded without a struggle; and Srinivasa Row remained in Malabar as Fouzdar or Military Governor, assisted by Sirdar Khan. A year later, in 1775, Haidar resolved upon a rupture with the English; but as a preliminary to the invasion of the Carnatic, he decided first to replenish his coffers by carrying out the long threatened invasion of Travancore. To this end Sirdar Khan was set in motion at the head of 10,000 men in August 1776. North Cochin was overrun and Trichur fort captured; but the Travancore lines stopped further advance, and the next few years were wasted partly in skirmishes with the Dutch round Chettuvayi and Cranganore, partly in fruitless negotiations for an alliance, and for a free passage through the Dutch territory along the coast.

Capitulation of Mahe.

In North Malabar, in the meantime, neither the French nor Haidar had prospered. The Prince Regent had been restored to his dominions owing to the failure of the Ali Raja to pay the stipulated tribute, and had been active in Haidar's behalf. He continued, however, to send the pepper of his country exclusively to Tellicherry; and M. John Law of Lauriston, Commander-in-General of the French Settlements in the East Indies, complained to Warren Hastings of the ruin of French trade on the West Coast. The Tellicherry factory, nevertheless, had not paid its way for many years past, and in 1776 despite the protests of the principal inhabitants who came forward with a voluntary offer to raise a tax upon their 'oarts'[1] and houses, it was reduced to a residency. Two years later the French recognition of American independence brought on war with England, and Haidar became alarmed for the safety of Mahe. Two hundred of his own sepoys were

[1] Gardens.

thrown into the town, and at his bidding the Prince Regent joined the French with 1,500 Nayars. All their efforts were unavailing. Ships and men poured into Tellicherry; and, Kottayam and Kadattanad siding with the English, Mahe was blockaded by land and sea. The position was hopeless, and on March 20th, 1779, the garrison marched out with all the honours of war, and Mahe capitulated for the second time.

Mahe was at this time even more important to Haidar than Pondicherry, as the channel whereby he imported arms, ammunition and French reinforcements; and, though he remained nominally at peace for another year, he troubled no longer to disguise his real feelings towards the Honourable Company. The Kadattanad Raja, who had sided with the English, was deposed in favour of a junior prince more amenable to Haidar's wishes; and by November 1779 Mahe had been evacuated, and all the British troops in Malabar had been concentrated in Tellicherry for the defence of the town against the forces of the Kolattanad and Kadattanad Rajas. Tellicherry was not an easy town to defend, and the garrison, a mere handful of English troops, was too small properly to man the long weak chain of outposts round the fort. But the factors had not built up a reputation for honesty and justice for nothing. Every one in North Malabar with property to lose flocked into the town; and these refugees, aided by the Kottayam Raja's Nayars, fought and watched with the courage and vigilance of despair, and foiled every effort of the enemy to break through the slender line of outworks. On July 8th, 1780, a few days before Haidar finally threw off the mask and descended upon the plains of the Carnatic with ninety thousand men, Sirdar Khan, his lieutenant in Malabar, appeared before Tellicherry with a large army from Seringapatam, and infused fresh energy into the attack. Fortunately the English fleet commanded the sea, and confined Sirdar Khan's operations to the land; but for eighteen months the siege was maintained with unabated vigour. Huge towers were raised to rake the opposing batteries with artillery fire, and mines were sunk under and even within 'the defenders' lines. To add to the troubles of the besieged, their gunpowder ran alarmingly short. But at the end of 1781 reinforcements arrived from Bombay, and on January 8th, 1782, Major Abington in a brilliant sortie stormed the enemies' batteries and captured Sirdar Khan himself. The Mysorean army was destroyed, and Mahe was retaken the following day. The Nayars rose all over the country; Major Abington pushing southwards took Calicut on February 13th, and by the 20th of that month Palghat was reported to be the only place of importance remaining in Haidar Ali's hands in South Malabar.

CHAP. II. THE MYSOREAN CONQUEST, 1766–1793.

Death of Haidar, 1782.

Coorg and Balam[1] rose in rebellion at the same time; and Haidar, abandoning for the present his scheme of conquest in the Carnatic, where he had been defeated in every battle by Sir Eyre Coote, determined to devote all his energies to expelling the English from the West Coast. Makhdum Ali was accordingly despatched to Malabar through the Palghat Gap at the head of 7,000 men. In the meantime, however, General Meadows had arrived at Bombay with an expeditionary force, designed to co-operate with Sir Edward Hughes' squadron in an attack on the Dutch Settlements in Ceylon, war having been declared against that nation in the previous year. Every available man was wanted at that time on the East Coast; but Mr. Sullivan, British Resident in Tanjore, without consulting Sir Eyre Coote, took it upon himself to suggest that part of the force should be landed in Malabar to create a diversion against Haidar. A detachment of one thousand men, far too small for the purpose for which it was designed, accordingly disembarked at Calicut soon after the capture of the town by Major Abington, and under the command of Colonel Humberstone moved to meet Makhdum Ali as he advanced from Palghat. The latter, confident in his superior numbers, gave battle on April 8th in a strong but dangerous position at Tirurangadi, with a deep river in the rear of his right. He paid the penalty for his temerity with his own life and the loss of a great part of his army. A skilful movement of the English troops, who had been joined by a body of Nayars, cut off his retreat on the left, and his army thrust back into the river on his right was defeated with heavy loss. The Mysoreans rallied at Ramagiri[2] fort only to be routed once more; but the onset of the rains prevented Colonel Humberstone from carrying out his intention of reducing Palghat, and he retired to Calicut for the monsoon. The rains were barely over when, without awaiting instructions either from Bombay or Sir Eyre Coote, he was again on the march for Palghat with a force greatly reduced by disease. The fort was fortunately too strong for any thought of attack, and Colonel Humberstone fell back upon Mankara and Ramagiri with Haidar's son, Tipu, in hot pursuit at the head of a formidable army. Baffling his pursuers by crossing at dead of night, the Ponnani river, which Tipu believed to be impassable, at a ford 'so deep as to take ordinary men to the chin,' he was just able to entrench himself at Ponnani before he was overtaken. Fierce fighting followed, directed on the Mysorean side by M. Lally; but Colonel Macleod's[3] skilful tactics were proof against all attacks, and the Mysoreans were

[1] The province of Balam is now the Manjarabad taluk of Mysore.

[2] On the road from Cherpalcheri to Pattambi in Walavanad taluk.

[3] Colonel Macleod had been sent by Sir Eyre Coote to supersede Col. Humberstone. He landed at Ponnani on November 19th, 1782, the day before Col. Humberstone arrived there.

CHAP. II. THE MYSOREAN CONQUEST, 1766–1793.

repulsed leaving 200 dead on the field. Next day Sir Edward Hughes' squadron hove in sight, and reinforced Colonel Macleod with 450 European soldiers; and Tipu fell back to await the arrival of his heavy guns before resuming the attack. A few days later, however, 'the swarm of light troops which had continued to watch the English position was invisible, and successive reports confirmed the intelligence that the whole Mysorean force was proceeding by forced marches to the eastward.' Haidar Ali had died on December 12, 1782, and Tipu had gone in hot haste to secure his father's throne.

The peace of 1784.

Colonel Macleod's force was immediately withdrawn from Malabar to take part in the rash and ill-advised campaign against Bednur which ended in the fall of Mangalore; and the only important military operations in Malabar in 1783 were the capture of Palghat on November 15th by Colonel Fullerton, and the storming of Cannanore, 'that nest of enemies,' a month later by Col. Macleod. Overtures for peace were then being made to Tipu, and the possession of Palghat, the key to Malabar, would have strengthened the hands of the English. But the vacillating Government of Lord Macartney ordered Col. Fullerton to evacuate the fort, and the orders were countermanded only when it was too late. The Zamorin, whose troops had immediately taken possession, despairing of succour, fell back before the advance of a Mysorean army; and Tipu's authority was soon re-established from Palghat to the Kotta river. Malabar had little cause to welcome the peace of 1784. With delicate irony Tipu had included the Malabar chieftains among his 'friends and allies'. Even Kottayam, who had never bowed the neck to the Mysorean yoke, was resigned to his tender mercies, and the restoration of Cannanore was another of the stipulations. Needless to say, the Tellicherry factors had not been consulted in arranging the terms of the peace.

Founding of Ferok.

Tipu's affairs were not well managed in Malabar, and the exactions of his revenue collectors drove even the Mappillas of Ernad and Walavanad into rebellion. Arshad Beg Khan, 'a Musalman of rare talents, humanity, and integrity,' who had been Governor of the province since Haidar's death, was deprived of his military commands in 1784–5, and, powerless to quell the disturbances which broke out on every side, tendered his resignation in 1786, and besought his master to come in person to Malabar to restore his shaken prestige. Two years later Tipu followed this advice, and on April 5th, 1788, the factors at Tellicherry received the 'alarming intelligence,' that he was on 'this side of the Tamalcherry (Tamarasseri) ghat.' They set to work at once to repair their defences, which had been neglected since the close of the siege; but Tipu had come with only 5,000 men, and had

CHAP. II. THE MYSOREAN CONQUEST, 1766–1793.

other projects in hand. He had conceived the idea of transferring the capital of Malabar from Calicut to a new site of his own choosing on the south bank of the Beypore river, and busied himself with building a strong fort at the modern village of Ferok. Many of the inhabitants of Calicut were transferred thither; and the new town was made the centre of a network of roads. But the approach of the monsoon compelled Tipu to retire to Coimbatore, and the people of Calicut took the earliest opportunity to return to their homes. The Kolattanad or Chirakkal Raja, as he is henceforward called in the factor's diary, began to give trouble about the same time. Early in June he seized the island of Darmapattanam, which had been in the undisturbed possession of the Honourable Company since 1733, and later on in the month news was received that he had met with a flattering reception from Tipu at Coimbatore. The factors saw plainly who was the real aggressor, and by the end of June 1788 they had nearly completed the task of putting their lines in a thorough state of repair.

Proselytism to Islam.

But the beginning of the end was at hand. On July 17th a Brahman refused to take a message from Tellicherry to Anjengo, pleading that the sanctity, which had hitherto allowed Brahmans to pass in safety from one end of Malabar to the other, was no longer a protection; and a week later news arrived from Calicut that 'two hundred had been seized and confined, made Musalmen, and forced to eat beef.' Tipu had entered on the campaign of proselytism and social reform, which he himself sketched in a proclamation to the people of Malabar :—

"From the period of the conquest until this day, during twenty-four years, you have been a turbulent and refractory people, and in the wars waged during your rainy season, you have caused numbers of our warriors to taste the draught of martyrdom. Be it so. What is past is past. Hereafter you must proceed in an opposite manner, dwell quietly and pay your dues like good subjects: and since it is the practice with you for one woman to associate with ten men, and you leave your mothers and sisters unconstrained in their obscene practices, and are thence all born in adultery, and are more shameless in your connections than the beasts of the field : I hereby require you to forsake those sinful practices and to be like the rest of mankind ; and if you are disobedient to these commands, I have made repeated vows to honour the whole of you with Islam and to march all the chief persons to the seat of Government."

A Raja of the Parappanad family and 'Trichera Terupa, a principal Nayar of Nelamboor' were among the first of the many thus honoured at Coimbatore. The country rose in horror. Thirty thousand Brahmans fled to Travancore. The Kottayam and Kadattanad Rajas besought the factors at Tellicherry 'to take the Brahmans, the poor and the whole country' under their protection. The Nayars of South

CHAP. II. THE MYSOREAN CONQUEST, 1766–1793.

Malabar, headed by Ravi Varma of the Zamorin's house, turned in desperation on their oppressors. Calicut was invested, and, though a force sent to its relief in December under M. Lally raised the siege, Ravi Varma was never quite driven from the field. Early in 1789 Tipu himself descended the Tamarasseri ghat to enforce his proclamation at the point of the sword. General orders were issued to his army of more than twenty thousand men that 'every being in the district without distinction should be honoured with Islam, that the houses of such as fled to avoid that honour should be burned, that they should be traced to their lurking places, and that all means of truth and falsehood, force or fraud should be employed to effect their universal conversion.' The Kadattanad Raja's fortified palace at Kuttippuram was surrounded, and two thousand Nayars forced to surrender after a resistance of several days were circumcised and regaled with beef. The Chirakkal Raja was killed, and the other Rajas and the richer landowners fled to Travancore. The poorer Nayars retreated into the jungles, and were pitilessly pursued by bodies of Mysorean troops. Tipu himself went to Cannanore and solemnised the preliminary ceremonies of a marriage between the Bibi's daughter and one of his sons; and by bestowing upon her part of the Chirakkal Raja's territory, he attached the Bibi and with her the Mappillas of Malabar firmly to his side. He made no attack upon Tellicherry; but he upbraided the factors bitterly for the protection they had afforded to refugees, and kept them by a cordon of troops in a state of virtual siege.

Downfall of Tipu's power in Malabar.

The final act of the drama was now about to begin. The conquest of Travancore had always been the goal of Mysorean ambition on the West Coast; and Tipu, the more inflamed against the country since it had afforded a safe asylum to the fugitive chieftains of Malabar with their 'tens of lakhs of rupees', spent the rest of the year in negotiations with the Dutch and in spying out ways of entry into Travancore. In 1789 a coalition was formed between the English, the Nizam and the Mahrattas; and the significant omission of his name from the list of rulers in the south against whom the English force was not to be used by the Nizam, warned Tipu that the war which had long been threatening could no longer be delayed, and he set himself to prepare for the struggle by winning Travancore. Cranganore and Ayacotta had been sold on July 31st, 1789, by the 'illustrious and mighty Netherlands East India Company', and the Travancore lines from the ghats to the sea blocked the way when Tipu at length set out from Coimbatore in October 1789. His first attack was repulsed, and Tipu sat down to wait for a siege train from Seringapatam and Bangalore and for reinforcements from Malabar. The lines were stormed on April 15th and immediately demolished; but Tipu had got no further south than

CHAP. II. THE MYSOREAN CONQUEST, 1766–1793.

Verapoly when on May 24th, 1790, the approach of the monsoon and the gathering storm in his rear compelled him to turn his face northwards again and to leave Malabar never to return. The factors had not been idle. The strategic importance of Tellicherry, now strengthened by a double line of defences, had at length impressed itself upon the British authorities; and, as soon as the news arrived of Tipu's first assault on the Travancore lines, the factors were directed to raise Malabar behind him. Major Dow raised the siege of the town by issuing on April 25th with a mixed force of Europeans, sepoys and Nayars; and on the same day Mr. Taylor, the Chief, issued a proclamation guaranteeing to all who joined the Honourable Company's forces protection against Tipu, and warning those who held back that they would be 'considered as enemies and acted against accordingly.' The Chirakkal, Kottayam, Kadattanad and other chieftains readily accepted the terms, and were promised that Tipu would be forced 'to relinquish all future claims upon their allegiance and to agree to their becoming the subjects and dependents of the Honourable Company.' To this promise Lord Cornwallis the Governor-General added the undertaking that 'in order to secure a willing obedience from the Malabar Chiefs, we should be contented with their paying a very moderate tribute, provided that they will give the Company advantageous privileges for carrying on a commerce in the valuable possessions of their country.' The Bibi's attitude, however, was still hostile, and the presence of eight thousand of Tipu's troops in and about Cannanore prevented Major Dow from moving far from Tellicherry. But in South Malabar Tipu's authority was rapidly destroyed. The Cochin Raja and the Zamorin declared for the British, and on September 22nd Palghat fort surrendered to Colonel Stuart. Colonel Hartley, who had been sent to assist the Raja of Travancore in the previous April, marched up the coast clearing Chettuvayi island of the enemy, and capturing Chavakkad fort as he advanced towards Palghat. The isolated bodies of Mysorean troops in the meantime had been collected by Martab Khan, one of Tipu's generals, and on December 10th, by a curious coincidence the last decisive battle of the war took place almost on the exact spot at Tirurangadi where Colonel Humberstone had defeated Makhdum Ali nine years before. Colonel Hartley had only the 75th Highlanders and two battalions of sepoys to oppose Martab Khan's army of 9,000 Mysoreans and 4,000 Mappillas, but the issue was never in doubt. Martab Khan was driven back in confusion with the loss of nearly 2,000 killed, wounded and captured, and fled first to Ferok and then up the Tamarasseri ghat with the remnants of his force.

Cannanore was now the only important town in Malabar still hostile to the Company, and General Abercromby himself came from Bombay with the 77th Regiment to conduct the operations for its capture. The siege began by land and sea on December 14th, and on the 17th Bibi surrendered unconditionally, five thousand of Tipu's troops laying down their arms without a murmur. After this, little remained to be done. The Mappilla settlement at Valarpattanam was reduced, and with the capture soon afterwards of Badagara and Kuttippuram forts Malabar was cleared of the enemy, and the British supremacy in Malabar was complete.

CHAP. II. THE MYSOREAN CONQUEST, 17 6–1793.

BRITISH SUPREMACY.

Changes in the district.

Included in the province of Malabar, formally ceded by the treaties signed at Seringapatam on February 22nd and March 18th, 1792,[1] were Coorg, Cochin State and the whole of the district as at present constituted, except the Wynaad taluk. Since then there have been many changes in the limits of Malabar. The Wynaad, which in 1798 Lord Mornington, Governor-General of India, definitely pronounced to be a part of the dominions of Tipu, was ceded by the partition treaty of Mysore after the fall of Seringapatam in 1799.[2] In the same year a separate political officer was stationed in Coorg; and in 1809 Cochin State was placed under the control of the British Resident in Travancore. Mahe opened its gates for the third time in its history after the declaration of war between France and England and Holland in 1793.[3] Two years later, after the alliance between the republics of France and Holland had been proclaimed, the Stadholder of Holland, who had taken refuge in England, issued orders to all the Governors and Commandants, though he was not competent to do so, to admit British troops into all Dutch 'settlements, plantations, Colonies and Factories in East India.' Major Petrie was sent to take possession of Cochin in July 1795, but the Governor Mr. VanSpall had made preparations for a siege and declined to surrender, considering the orders of the Stadholder to be null and void. A siege train and reinforcements were brought up, and on October 19th 'a shell was cast with excellent skill into the centre of the Government House.' The white flag was hoisted forthwith, and on the following day Mr. VanSpall surrendered on terms.[4] With Cochin the outlying *pattams* and Tangasseri passed into British hands, and the Dutch disappeared finally from Malabar. Mahe was restored to the French after the conclusion of peace in 1817,[5] and the French *loge* at Calicut two years later.[6] Finally in 1853 after long discussions the *aldees* or scattered portions of French territory round Mahe were delivered up by

[1] Logan's *Treaties*, ii VII and XI.
[2] *Ibid.* ii CXIII.
[3] *Ibid.* ii LVII.
[4] Logan's *Treaties*, ii XCVI.
[5] *Ibid.* ii. CCLXVIII.
[6] *Ibid.* ii. CCLXXXIX.

CHAP. II. BRITISH SUPREMACY.

the British Government.[1] From 1830 to 1843, the Nilgiri plateau was a part of the Malabar district. In 1843 the Nilgiris were transferred to Coimbatore leaving the range of the Kundahs to Malabar. The Kundahs were transferred to Coimbatore in 1860, and in 1873 and 1877 respectively the Ouchterlony valley and the three amsams of south-east Wynaad, Nambalakod, Cherankod and Munnanad were placed under the jurisdiction of the Commissioner of the Nilgiris. In 1870, a few small tracts of land in the Walavanad and Ponnani taluks were exchanged for a part of Cochin State.[2] Finally, in 1906, the small settlements at Angongo and Tangasseri were separated from Malabar, and constituted the new revenue District of Anjengo.

Administration.

As soon as the treaties of Seringapatam were signed in 1792, the Company set itself seriously to the task of establishing a stable government in the country and reducing to law and order the chaos left by a generation of alien misrule. Mr. Farmer, a senior merchant of Tellicherry, and Major Dow, commandant of the fort, were appointed commissioners on behalf of the Bombay Government to enquire into the state of the country and to make arrangements with the Malabar chiefs for the revenue of the ensuing year. Mr. Page joined them in September, and Messrs. Duncan and Boddam, who arrived from Bengal in December 1792, completed the famous Joint Commission. Three months later their scheme for the administration of the district received the sanction of Sir Robert Abercromby, Governor of Bombay, and on March 18th Mr. Farmer was installed at Calicut as Supravisor and Chief Magistrate of the Province of Malabar. Subject to his general control, two Superintendents had revenue and magisterial charge of the Northern and Southern Divisions of the Province, with headquarters at Tellicherry and Cherpalcheri, respectively, and a senior assistant was Judge and Magistrate of Calicut. At the beginning of 1796, the office of Supravisor was merged in a commission sent to Malabar to enquire into the charges of bribery brought by the Zamorin against the late Supravisor, Mr. James Stevens; and the commission was abolished in its turn on the score of expense soon after Malabar was transferred on 21st May 1800 from the Bombay to the Madras Presidency. Major Macleod, the first Principal Collector, took over charge of the district on October 1st, 1801, and was assisted by nine Subordinate Collectors in the administration of the revenues and of the Civil Government.

The outlook in 1792 when the Bombay Commissioners entered on their labours was anything but promising. The whole district seethed with discontent, and South Malabar in particular was in a state bordering on anarchy. Trade was at a

---

[1] *Logan's Treaties* ii. CCXC.

[2] *Ibid,* ii. CCXCI

CHAP. II. BRITISH SUPREMACY.

standstill, and of the pepper vines in the south of the district Tipu had left not one in fifty standing. His religious persecutions had engendered a fierce and abiding hatred between Hindu and Muhammadan, and the claims asserted by the Brahman and Nayar landlords, now flocking back in their thousands from Travancore, to lands which for years past had been in the undisturbed possession of Mappilla cultivators widened the breach still further. The Zamorin's Nayars had already come into collision three times with the Mappillas of Ernad; and the intractable Mappillas of Walavanad, who had never been amenable even to Mysorean rule, terrorised the countryside by frequent raids from their fortified posts in the jungles at the foot of the Western Ghats. The Joint Commissioners worked with untiring industry, and introduced many excellent measures. Their first acts were to proclaim the freedom of trade in all articles of merchandise, save pepper, to establish Courts of Enquiry and Justice, presided over by themselves in rotation, and to declare a general amnesty for all the 'manifold enormities' of the past twenty years. But their mistaken revenue policy, adopted under the orders of the Governments of India and Bombay, retarded for years the pacification of the district, and culminated ultimately in the fierce blaze of the Pazhassi (Pychy) rebellion. The Mysoreans had collected their revenue direct from the cultivators through the medium of their own officials. The Company, failing to realise how deeply the old regime and the power of the Malabar chieftains had been undermined by the Mysorean conquest and the introduction of a general land revenue, farmed for a lump sum to the Rajas the collection of the revenues in their former dominions. The leases, at first yearly, were renewed in 1794 for a period of five years. But on October 1st, 1795, of a total revenue of some fourteen lakhs due for the year ending September 30th, a balance of nearly six lakhs remained uncollected. A year later, Palghat and Kavalappara were taken over by the Company; and long before the leases expired in 1799 the system had broken down, and the Company had assumed charges of the revenues of most of the districts. The Rajas had not the power to enforce their demands for the revenue. 'When my people ask for revenue' the Zamorin wrote in 1792 to the Joint Commissioners, 'the Mappillas shake their swords at them'; and the Nayars who formerly had 'paid no revenue to any one' but were bound 'to attend their Rajas when called on to war' and who lived 'in woods and hills with every house separate and that house defensive' barred their doors against the tax gatherer. The assessments of the Rajas again were unequal, and Mappillas were rated more highly than Hindus. The general discontent deepened, and in South Malabar the military had to be employed against the Mappilla banditti headed by the notorious robber Unni Mutta Muppan.

Mistaken revenue policy of 1792.

CHAP. II. BRITISH SUPREMACY

The first Pychy rebellion.

But the system had another undesirable result. Not only did it involve the Commissioners in the family feuds of the old Royal houses, but also it entailed upon them the delicate task of deciding between the conflicting claims of the various Rajas to be entrusted with the collection of the revenue in the different *nads* or divisions of the district. Mistakes were inevitable, and one unfortunate error of judgment had disastrous consequences in North Malabar. The influence of Kerala Varma Raja of the Padinnara Kovilagam of the Kottayam family, or the Pazhassi (Pychy) Raja, as he was usually called, was at this time supreme in the rich pepper district of Kottayam. His uncle, the Raja of Kurumbranad, claimed ascendancy in the district, and the Joint Commissioners, ignoring the claims of the nephew, leased Kottayam to him in 1793 for one year. The Pychy Raja, who objected strongly to the arrangement, promptly showed his contempt for both the alleged authority of his uncle and the regulations of the Company, by stopping all collection of revenue in the district and by taking the law into his own hands against erring Mappillas. In the following year the Kurumbranad Raja's lease was renewed for five years, and till 1797 the Pychy Raja remained in more or less open rebellion. Troops were sent to Kottayam and Manattana in 1795 to protect the Kurumbranad tax gatherers; but the revenue fell more and more into arrears, and in 1796 a determined effort was made to surprise the Raja in his palace at Pazhassi. But regular troops were at a disadvantage in the dense trackless jungles at the back of Kottayam, and the rebel Raja had a secure retreat above the ghats in the wilds of the Wynaad. All efforts at conciliation failed, partly owing to the 'intolerable insolence of the Pychy' partly to the duplicity of his uncle of Kurumbranad, and the situation became very grave. The Pychy Raja made overtures to Tipu, the pepper revenue of Kottayam was endangered, and the disaffection spread to Kurumbranad. Troops were despatched to various places in the Wynaad to hold the passes down into the plains, while the low country was being cleared of the rebels; but they were hampered by difficulties of transport and lack of supplies, and a series of minor reverses culminated on March 18, 1797, in a detachment of 1,100 men being surprised and cut to pieces in the Periya Pass. Men in the dress of Tipu's sepoys were distinguished among the rebels; and the situation was so full of peril that the Governor of Bombay, Mr. Jonathan Duncan, and the Commander-in-Chief came in person to Malabar to investigate the state of the district. One of their acts was to cancel the agreement made with the Kurumbranad Raja for Kottayam, and a few months later by the good offices of the Chirakkal Raja the rebellion was brought to a peaceful end. The Pychy Raja was pardoned for all his misdeeds, and granted

CHAP. II.
BRITISH SUPREMACY.

a pension of Rs. 8,000 per annum; and he acquiesced in a settlement made for Kottayam with the senior Raja of the Kottayam family who had recently returned from Travancore.

Second Pychy rebellion, 1800–1805.

Two years later another cause of dispute cropped up, and the Pychy, 'the most untractable and unreasonable of all the Rajas,' as the Joint Commissioners had called him, once more raised the standard of revolt. After the fall of Seringapatam the Wynaad had been ceded to the British; but the Pychy, who claimed the district, resisted all the attempts of the Amildars of the Mysore Commission to take possession. In support of his pretensions he raised a large body of Nayars, Mappillas and Mussalmans, the last for the most part disbanded soldiers of Tipu, and the Supreme Government decreed that his insolence must not go unpunished. The military control of the Province was transferred to the Madras Government, and in 1800 Colonel Arthur Wellesley, afterwards Duke of Wellington, was appointed Commander of the forces in Malabar, South Canara and Mysore. The state of the season prevented him from doing more than strengthen the military posts in Kottayam and prepare for the campaign by constructing military roads; and before the onset of the rains he returned to Seringapatam. The monsoon was the Pychy's opportunity, and he utilized it by descending into the plains, where he was joined by all the leaders of disaffection in the district, notably the bandit chiefs Unni Mutta Muppan and Manjeri Attan Gurukkal and four of the Iruvalinad Nambiyars. Colonel Wellesley himself had no leisure to take the field in the district, but he drew up the plan of campaign. Two cavalry regiments were despatched to Malabar by way of the Palghat Gap to overawe the south of the district; and early in 1802 Colonel Stevenson entered the Wynaad from Mysore with a regiment of horse, two infantry regiments, four battalions of sepoys and six hundred pioneers. His instructions were to construct a line of posts from Edattara near Sultan's Battery on the Mysore frontier to the head of the Tamarasseri ghat, thus opening up communication with Calicut and cutting off the Pychy from his adherents in South Malabar, and then to push forward upon the Raja's palace in as many divisions as he might deem proper. By May 1802 every place of importance in the Wynaad was in Colonel Stevenson's hands, and the Raja, a homeless wanderer, had taken refuge in the wilds of Chirakkal. His adherents were gradually hunted down, and in the course of 1802 many of the rebel leaders were captured and hanged. The rebellion would probably have soon died out, had not Major Macleod taken charge of Malabar a few months previously. In 1802 he aroused great discontent by attempting to disarm the district; and later on in the year he fanned into flame the dying embers of revolt not only by a grievous enhancement of the land assessments, but by revising the

CHAP. II. BRITISH SUPREMACY.

table of exchange. The first sign of recrudescence was the capture of Panamaram fort in the Wynaad in October 1802 and the massacre of its garrison by the proscribed rebel Edachenna Kunjan at the head of a body of Kuricchiyans; and the supineness of Major Drummond, who, though he had 350 men under his command in a neighbouring outpost, made no effort to avenge the disaster, roused the whole of North Wynaad. Three thousand men collected at the Fish pagoda near Manantoddy, and the rebels soon held the Kottiyur and Periya passes. Troops were poured into the Wynaad from the low country; but the whole district was now ablaze, and before the year was out the rebels had ventured nearly as far as the coast and had laid waste the spice plantations at Anjarakkandi. This, however, was their last important success. Major Macleod resigned his office on March 11th, 1803, and Mr. Rickards, his successor, did much by timely concessions to allay the storm in South Malabar. But it was to Mr. T. H. Baber, Sub-Collector of Tellicherry, and to the Kolkars or police organized by Captain Watson a few years before, that the chief credit of stamping out the rebellion was due. Regular troops tied to their transport waggons were of little use against small mobile bands of rebels in a country peculiarly suited to a guerilla warfare. But the kolkarans, equally mobile and with an equal knowledge of the people, the language and the country, hunted down the small parties of the Pychy's adherents with untiring zeal. Mr. Baber also enlisted the country people in the cause of law and order; and his policy of holding them responsible for refusing to help the rebels and for giving prompt information as to their movements, combined with the vigilance of the kolkarans, soon cleared the low country of rebels, and drove them back into the Wynaad. Here the Madras troops who had recently taken the place of Colonel Stevenson's fever-stricken regiments, pursued them with such energy that by April 1805 all appearance of opposition had died away. On June 16th a proclamation was issued offering rewards for the apprehension of the Pychy Raja, two other members of his family, and nine of his principal adherents, and declaring their estates and property confiscated from that date. Several important arrests were made, but the honour of destroying the arch rebel himself was reserved for Mr. Baber. On November 30th, a little more than a month after he had taken over charge of the Wynaad, he had the 'infinite satisfaction' of reporting to Government that he had 'the good fortune to come up with the Cotiote Kerala Varma Raja *alias* the Pychy Raja and with the assistance of Captain Clapham and 50 sepoys and 100 Kolkars to chastise this rebel chieftain by destroying him and five of his followers.' The rebellion died a natural death soon afterwards, and Mr. Baber received a donation of 2,500 pagodas and the thanks of Government for his services.

Other risings.

The Nayar rising of 1808 and 1809 in Travancore and Cochin State did not seriously disturb the general peace of the district; but on January 19th, 1809, the town of British Cochin was fiercely attacked by the rebels. Under cover of the fire of two guns planted on Vypeen point the Nayars, three thousand strong, advanced boldly to the assault, but the British troops drove them back with 300 casualties. Two days later they burnt the Dutch Governor's house on the outskirts of the town; but a second attack on the fort made on January 26 was not pushed home with any spirit, and the assailants were dispersed without difficulty. Three years later the Kuricchiyans and Kurumbans of the Wynaad resented the exaction of the land revenue in money instead of in kind by placing in a state of siege the detachments at Manantoddy and Sultan's Battery. Troops were hurried into the disaffected tract from Mysore and from the coast, and peace was soon restored.

MAPPILLA OUTBREAKS. Their beginning.

The *pax Britannica* was now firmly established in the land, and for four and twenty years, untroubled by disaffection within or dangers from without, the authorities devoted themselves to internal reforms and the people settled down quietly to their agricultural pursuits. But in November 1836, just when prices had risen and the tide of prosperity seemed fairly to have set in, a Mappila of Pandalur desam in Ernad taluk, after murdering one Hindu and wounding three others, was himself shot by a taluk peon. Similar outrages had been known in Tipu Sultan's time and in 1822 Mr. Baber spoke of them as 'a disgrace to the Mappilla community'; but this crime was the first of the long sequence of outbreaks which at varying intervals of time have since marred the tranquillity of Malabar.

General features.

With rare exceptions these outbreaks have always blazed out within a radius of some fifteen miles from Pandalur hill in the Ernad taluk, the so-called 'fanatical zone.' The Arab strain, strong on the coast, is here very faint, and the followers of 'the way' are for the most part proselytes drawn from the dregs of the Hindu population. They are miserably poor and hopelessly ignorant, and their untutored minds are peculiarly susceptible to the inflammatory preaching of the church militant and to alluring contrasts drawn between their miserable state here on earth and the wondrous joys of Paradise. The Mappilla, brooding, it may be, over some fancied slight to his 'pearl-like' faith or over the tyranny of some Hindu landlord till it assumes in his mind the proportion of a gigantic wrong that can be washed out only in blood, determines to win eternal bliss by a martyr's death. Others join him, and the murder of a landlord or his agent or of an apostate sets the seal on their resolve. The *Sahids*, or saints predestinate, prepare for death. They set their houses in order, divorce their wives, and clad in the white robes of martyrs go out to die

CHAP. II. MAPPILLA OUTBREAKS.

fighting against the unbeliever. Their contempt for death and frenzied bravery almost pass belief. In the dreadful outbreak of 1849 one man whose thigh had been broken in the first collision with the troops at Manjeri remained for seven days in all the agony of his neglected wound. He was further tortured by being jolted in a litter twelve long miles from Manjeri to Angadippuram. Yet when the fanatics were cut to pieces at the latter place 'there he was at the time of the fight, hopping on his sound leg in the encounter, only anxious to get a fair blow at the infidels ere he died.' In 1843 and 1849 well armed sepoys in overwhelming numbers refused to face a handful of *Sahids* armed only with war knives, and in 1851 even British troops recoiled in temporary confusion before their onslaught. In 1894 volleys from Lee-Metford and Snider rifles failed to stop them, and some of the fanatics reached the bayonets 'ere meeting with what they sought, death and entrance into paradise.' Few have ever been captured alive, and nothing can exceed the scorn of their wives and relatives and the whole Mappilla community for '*Minjina Sahids*' or 'all-but martyrs.' Only two of the 34 fanatics who went out in 1894 survived, and both were wounded. 'No words can depict' says Sir Henry Winterbotham [1] 'the abject terror of the Hindus of all ranks and classes when a gang of Mappilla fanatics is on the war path. An invasion by a hostile army could not cause more consternation or a greater panic.' All attempts at conciliation or parleys are as dangerous as they are futile, and 'it is and ever must be the prime duty of the Malabar Magistrate to suppress a Mappilla outbreak without delay at all costs, and the special endeavour should be to prevent the fanatics having the opportunity they covet of personal conflict hand to hand with the troops.'

1836–1853.

Mappilla unrest reached its high watermark between the years 1836 and 1853. In this period of eighteen years no fewer than twenty-two outbreaks took place besides numerous abortive risings and conspiracies. One of the bloodiest tragedies of the whole long series was enacted in Manjeri and Angadippuram in 1849. In August of that year, after the usual preliminary murders, five fanatics under Attan Gurukkal, a descendant of the notorious bandit chief mentioned above, seized the Manjeri Karanamulpad's temple overlooking the taluk office hill. Here their numbers swelled to thirty-two in the few hours that it took to bring up a detachment of the 43rd N.I. from Malappuram. The sepoys behaved disgracefully. Ensign Wyse led a storming party against the temple, but a few of the fanatics came rushing down the hill at them, and all but four of the sepoys refused to stand. The ensign and his little band were slain, and even the troops posted in reserve on the taluk office hill fled in panic. Detachments

[1] See G.O. No. 1567, Judicial, dated 30th September 1896.

CHAP. II. MAPPILLA OUTBREAKS.

of H.M.'s 94th regiment and of the 39th N.I. were brought up by forced marches from Cannanore and Palghat. They arrived at Manjeri on September 3rd, and the same night the fanatics, whose numbers had by this time doubled, retreated to the Bagavathi temple at Angadippuram. The troops followed in pursuit next day and at 5 p.m. on September 4th the encounter took place. The Commanding Officer's report is vivid, if ungrammatical :—

"The enemy came on with the most desperate courage throwing themselves on our bayonets ; after firing off their matchlocks, they took to their war-knives, swords and spears, and when struck to the ground, renewed the fight even on their knees by hurling their weapons at the faces of our men and which continued until literally they were cut to pieces ; others planted on the trees kept up a most destructive fire with their matchlocks loaded with iron slugs."

The losses of the troops were trifling, but of the sixty-four fanatics not one lived to tell the tale. The disastrous outrage at Kolattur in the Walavanad taluk followed two years afterwards. The Kolattur Variyar, an old man of 79 and an influential landlord, was dragged out of his house, and hacked to pieces in the paddyfields close by. The sepoys once more broke and fled, and even a detachment of British troops footsore and weary after marching forty miles in two days over hilly country fell back momentarily before the rush of the Mappillas. Hitherto the fanatics had spared women and children, but in 1852 in the outbreak at Mattanur in the Kottayam taluk, one of the very few that have taken place in North Malabar, 'men, women, children, the very infant at the breast' were put to the sword.

Mambram Tangals.

After this Mr. Strange, a Judge of the Sadr Adalat, was placed on special duty to enquire into the disturbances, their causes and remedies. Tirurangadi had for many years past been the centre of Mappilla fanaticism and the Mambram[1] or Taramal Tangal had been its high-priest. The adhigari of the amsam had been murdered in 1843, and the Tangal had been suspected of inspiring the notorious Hal Ilakkam or 'frenzy raising' sect of Mappillas, to whose door at least two of the outrages of that year had been laid. He had died shortly afterwards, and his tomb had become the chosen shrine where the *Sahid* invoked the blessing of Heaven on his enterprise. His son and successor, Saiyyid Fazl, had acquired an even greater ascendancy over the ignorant Mappilla mind. 'They regard him' says a report of the period 'as imbued with a portion of Divinity. They swear by his foot as their most solemn oath. Earth on which he had spat or walked is treasured up.' It may be that, as he protested to the last,

[1] Opposite Tirurangadi on the other side of the Kadalundi river.

CHAP. II. MAPPILLA OUTBREAKS.

his teaching had been misunderstood; but even the Tangal admitted that his presence in the district had led to deeds of horror, and Mr. Strange was directed to report what measures should be taken against him. On the very day (February 17th, 1852) that the order was passed, ten or twelve thousand Mappillas, many of them armed, assembled at Tirurangadi in secret conclave with the Tangal. Any attempt to arrest him would have led to terrible bloodshed, but fortunately Mr. Conolly, the District Magistrate, prevailed upon him to leave Malabar peaceably. He sailed for Arabia on March 19th, 1852.

The Mappilla Acts.

Rejecting the explanations that the disturbances had their origin in agrarian depression or Mappilla destitution, Mr. Strange found their cause to be religious fanaticism fanned by the preaching of ambitious priests, like the Mambram Tangals. The condition of the Hindus had become 'most lamentable,' and the prestige of Government had been severely shaken. He advocated a stern repressive policy; and at his suggestion a special force of police was raised, and Acts XXIII and XXIV of 1854 passed into law. The latter rendered illegal the possession of the war-knife after February 1st, 1855, and by that date 7,561 had been surrendered. The former empowered the authorities to fine the Mappilla population of amsams implicated in outrages, and to take stringent measures against all persons suspected of complicity in them.

Murder of Mr. Conolly.

A few months later Mr. Conolly, District Magistrate of Malabar and provisional member of Council, was barbarously murdered by four Mappilla convicts. They had escaped from jail on August 4th, 1855, and for nearly six weeks they had roamed over the district. They had prayed at the Taramal Tangal's shrine, and it was generally known that they contemplated some desperate deed. At nightfall on September 12th they made their way into Mr. Conolly's bungalow at Calicut on the hill where the barracks now stand. Mr. Conolly and his wife were seated on low sofas in the verandah on either side of a table bearing lamps. 'He was approached from behind, and even Mrs. Conolly did not catch sight of the first blow which alone would have proved fatal; and the next moment the lights were all swept off the table and the ruffians bounded on their victim slashing him in every direction.' Mr. Conolly lingered for about an hour in intense agony. His assailants made good their escape, but were overtaken five days later in the Ernad taluk and shot down. Nine amsams implicated in the outrage were fined, and the net proceeds of the fines, aggregating nearly Rs. 31,000 were granted to Mrs. Conolly.

Mr. Logan's commission.

Notwithstanding the heavy penalites of the Mappilla acts outbreaks still continued, though at longer intervals, and in

CHAP. II. MAPPILLA OUTBREAKS.

1873, Kolattur was the scene of another tragedy. In 1880, after the Melattur outrage of that year, an anonymous petition was received by Government setting forth the manifold grievances of the agriculturists of Malabar and naming eviction in particular as the root of the Mappilla evil. In reporting on this petition Mr. Logan and Mr. Wigram, District Judge of South Malabar, both agreed that Mr. Strange had given far too little weight to agrarian discontent as a cause of disturbances; and on February 5th, 1881, the former was appointed Special Commissioner to enquire into land tenures and tenant right in Malabar, and to consider the best means of removing another Mappilla grievance of long standing, the difficulty of getting from their Hindu landlords sites for mosques and burial-grounds.

Its result.

Mr. Logan's views on Malabar land tenures are dealt with in greater detail in Chapters IV and XI. Briefly he was of opinion that the true position of the janmi or landlord had been completely misapprehended by the early British administrators and after them by the Courts of Justice. In Mappilla outrages he saw an instrument designed to 'counteract the overwhelming influence, when backed by the British Courts, of the Janmis in the exercise of the novel powers of ouster and of eviction for rent conferred upon them. A Janmi who by the courts evicted, whether fraudulently or otherwise, a substantial tenant was decreed to have merited death; and it was considered a religious virtue, not a fault, to have killed such a man, and to have afterwards died in arms fighting against an infidel Government, which sanctioned such injustice.' He suggested various remedies, which were elaborately discussed by two commissions; and the ultimate results of his proposals were the 'Malabar Compensation for Tenants Improvements Act' (Act I of 1887 amended and improved by Act I of 1900), and the decision of Government after the outbreak of 1894 that in special cases it would consider the advisability of acquiring land for Mappilla cemeteries under the Land Acquisition Act.

Disarming of the Mappilla taluks.

A time of excitement succeeded Mr. Logan's commission, and between 1883 and 1885 no less than five outrages gave point to his plea of urgency. One of these disturbances was suppressed with more than usual difficulty. Its origin was purely fanatical. The preceding outbreak had been a fiasco. The hearts of the *Sahids* had failed them at the last moment, and, instead of dying a glorious death, they had been arrested like common malefactors, and sentenced to transportation for life for attempted murder. The apostate, moreover, whom they had gone forth to kill, had survived his wounds and had even been compensated with a portion of the Mappilla fines. A few months later on December 27th, 1884, a gang of twelve men, mostly illiterate cultivators from the remote Chembrasseri amsam at the foot of the Sispara ghat, set out

CHAP. II. MAPPILLA OUTBREAKS.

to wipe away the stain on the honour of Islam. Their first act was to visit the house of the apostate, not half a mile from and within sight of the barracks at Malappuram and to fire a volley at his brother. After this exploit they formed up and marched boldly through Malappuram past the police station, and finally took up their position in the Trikkalayur temple near Ariyakkod on the north bank of the Beypore river. Mr. Logan with the reserve police from Calicut and the troops from Malappuram arrived next day, but the fanatics, departing from precedent, elected to stay behind the stone walls of the temple. The doorway was blown up by dynamite; but the position was too strong to storm, and the fanatics were killed one by one by volleys as they fired at the troops through their loopholes. Only one private was killed, and one officer and one private were wounded, but the risks run by the party of law and order were so great that the disarming of the Calicut, Ernad and Walavanad taluks was resolved upon. Troops were imported by rail and posted at various centres in the disturbed tracts, and under the superintendence of Mr. Logan this dangerous operation was carried out in February 1885 without resistance. A small outbreak followed in Ponnani, and that taluk was also disarmed in June. More than 20,000 arms were collected including nearly 9,000 guns.

The outbreak of 1896.

In the last twenty years there have been only three outbreaks, but two of them were exceptionally serious. In the Pandikkad outbreak of 1894, the names of thirty-two Mappillas were added to the long roll of martyrs, and the appalling tragedy of 1896 was unprecedented as well for the number of the fanatics that took part in it, as for the swift and terrible retribution that overtook them. The saddest part of the whole affair was its want of reason. The few survivors could point to no single grievance that would bear examination; but it is plain that a plot had already been hatched, when on February 25th, 1896, the arrest of four of the ringleaders precipitated the outbreak before the plans of the fanatics had been fully matured. The same evening a gang of twenty Mappillas went out on the war path from Chembrasseri amsam, and for five days in ever increasing numbers they terrorised the country side. Hindus were murdered, or their *kudumis* were cut off, and they were summarily converted to Islam. Temples were desecrated and burnt. Houses were looted in the search for food, money and arms. Finally on March 1st, hard pressed by the pursuit of the troops, the fanatics entered the Manjeri Karanamulpad's temple, determined to make their last stand in a spot hallowed in their eyes as the scene of the first triumphant act of the tragedy of 1849. Twenty solders were guarding the treasury on the hill opposite the temple, and with them shots were exchanged. At 9 a.m. the District Magistrate with the main body of the troops came up in great anxiety for the safety of the

CHAP. II. MAPPILLA OUTBREAKS.

treasury guard, and occupied a hill overlooking the temple from a distance of some 750 yards across a deep valley covered with trees and bushes. The troops opened fire at once, and the fanatics, instead of taking shelter, deliberately courted death offering themselves as a target to the bullets on the open platform of the temple, ' howling, shouting, waving their arms and firing off their guns. Advancing steadily with frequent volleys over the broken ground, the troops came near enough to the Mappilla stronghold to call upon the fanatics to surrender. Hoarse cries of defiance were their only answer, and pushing on the soldiers entered the temple almost without opposition. A horrible sight met their eyes. Within the narrow precincts were piled up the bodies of ninety-two Mappillas. Some were still breathing, but the great majority were dead, and at least twenty had their throats cut from ear to ear. They had been murdered by their comrades to prevent their being captured alive. A small gang of seven *Sahids* was still at large, but by March 13th they had all been arrested or shot by the police, and the outbreak was at an end. Ninety-nine Mappillas had gone out to die, and all but six had accomplished their purpose. Mr. (now Sir Henry) Winterbotham, a Member of the Board of Revenue, was deputed at once to Malabar to enquire into the circumstances of the disturbance and the means taken to suppress it. His report [1] completely justified the action of the District Magistrate. The history of scores of similar outbreaks showed that the only reply to a formal summons to surrender would have been an immediate charge by the fanatics. To make such summons he would have had to give up his position of advantage, and would probably have sacrificed many valuable lives by exposing the troops to a hand to hand conflict with the Mappillas on ground which was all in favour of the latter.

Outbreak of 1898.

No fines were imposed after this outbreak, partly because it was feared that they would accentuate the already extreme poverty of the fanatical zone, partly because the Mappilla community in general had shown far less sympathy with the outbreak than on former occasions. This was perhaps one of the most hopeful signs and it was even more marked in the small abortive rising of 1898. In this case after assassinating an unpopular Hindu landlord, against whom they had a grudge, the murderers donned the orthodox white robes, and on April 3rd set out on the usual career of *Sahids*. On the following day they retreated to a temple in Payyanad to await their death. The Special Police Force came up, but their services were not required. The feeling of the Mappillas of the desam, which formerly had been a hotbed of fanaticism, was strongly against the *Sahids*, and they gathered in force round the

[1] Printed in G.O. No. 1567, Judicial, dated 30th September 1896.

CHAP. II. MAPPILLA OUTBREAKS.

temple. The Pukkoya Tangal came from Malappuram, and at his exhortation the fanatics surrendered without a struggle.

Conclusion.

The Mappilla outbreaks may be attributed to three main causes, poverty, agrarian discontent and fanaticism, of which the last is probably the chief. Poverty is still extreme in the fanatical zone, and is no doubt to some extent accentuated by the Mappilla practice in the south of dividing up the property of the father among his wives, sons and daughters. The Tenants Improvements Act has done much to protect the tenant from ruinous eviction. Fanaticism however is still strong in the land ; and education, for all the expenditure on Mappilla schools, has made but little progress among the community. The repressive policy initiated in 1854, has had a salutary effect. The fining of whole villages has brought home to the community a sense of its responsibility for its unruly members, as was proved in 1896 and again in 1898 ; the most enlightened Mappillas have been enlisted on the side of law and order ; and the Pukkoya Tangal, who as a descendant of the Prophet is almost worshipped by the Mappillas of Ernad and Walavanad, has issued a pamphlet sternly denouncing outbreaks as opposed to true religion. The fanatical zone has been opened up by good roads ; and during the Ramzan fast, when religious enthusiasm is easily roused, the Special Police Force is distributed over the zone, and signallers keep the various detachments in touch with one another and with the troop at Malappuram.

Condition of the Mappillas before and at the time of the Great War.

Between 1898 and 1915 the district was free from fanatical outbreaks and it looked as if the influence referred to above had taken more or less permanent effect. Though, especially in the Ernad taluk, the pressure of an ever-increasing population on a limited area of land kept many at the bare subsistence level and therefore with their traditions liable to crime, the Mappilla had shown himself by no means slow to take advantage of some of the opportunities that were opening out to him. He enlisted in the army, took up the work in the rubber plantations and in the timber trade which flourished in the district, and also managed to get into his hands most of the petty retail business in the weekly markets. He emigrated to the Mysore goldfields, worked on the railways which were being constructed and even went as far afield as Ceylon, the Straits Settlements and the Dutch Indies to trade. But the outbreak of the Great War in 1914 and the embroilment of Turkey in it brought an outburst of rumours and among the Mappillas a widespread belief that the British Raj was coming to its end.

Outbreak of 1915.

As early as January 1915 there were signs of unrest in the "fanatical zone" manifested by an outbreak of both petty and grave crime. A Tiyya boy aged 10 or 12, apparently quite willingly, was taken into Islam. His brother who seems to have neglected him complained. The District Magistrate found the facts proved and fined the Mappilla responsible Rs. 50 on a technical charge of kidnapping. Outside the immediate area this was magnified into an apostasy forced by the District Magistrate and a plot seems to have been formed to murder both the Magistrate and the boy, commence dacoities and to collect arms and followers for an outbreak. The plot was discovered and the District Magistrate and District Superintendent of Police with a small force of police promptly went after the conspirators who "went out" in approved *Sahid* fashion. The District Magistrate (Mr. Innes) was ambushed on his way from Karuvarakundu to Pandikkad and narrowly escaped with his life. This was on 27th February. The reserve police special force and troops from Malappuram were brought into the threatened area (Manjeri-Pandalur-Pandikkad) and the five outlaws were eventually tracked down by a small party of police on 1st March and forced to take refuge in the Ayyappankavu temple at Alanallur. Police reinforcements with the District Magistrate and District Superintendent of Police arrived late that night. The necessary dispositions were made to prevent escape and the following morning the place was attacked. Four of the fanatics died fighting and one was captured severely wounded. Eight Mappillas including the wounded man were deported and kept either in jail or in other districts under Regulation II of 1819. Four Mappillas who had been arrested as a precautionary measure—among them being the afterwards notorious Variankunnath Kunhamad Haji and Potayil Ahamad Kutti Musaliyar—were released, their apparent implication in the outbreak being, it was decided, an elaborate concoction of evidence by their enemies. The local Mappillas seem on the whole to have behaved well and gave substantial assistance in tracking down the outlaws.

Outbreak of 1919.

Four years later in 1919 there was another small outbreak in the Malappuram area in which some youths led by Purapurath Valiachek Haji, a man of 65, who had previously been in the police, murdered several Hindus for no reason except Moslem fanaticism. The gang were rounded up by the police in a farm house and all shot.

The Mappilla Rebellion, 1921–22.

Though the Great European War had ended in 1918, the spirit of unrest created by it was accentuated very largely by the disrespect for orderly Government which was the outcome of the non-co-operation movement in 1920–21.

Propaganda against Government.

The Hindus of the Congress party had taken up the Khilafat agitation over the threatened break up of the Turkish empire and the alleged desecration of Moslem holy places with its appeal to Moslem prejudices. In August 1920 Gandhi and Shaukat Ali were allowed to visit Calicut and address meetings which

CHAP. II. MAPPILLA OUTBREAKS.

were attended by a number of Ernad Mappillas. They carried away with them advice, that if they were strong enough, they ought to fight, and, if too weak they should emigrate rather than continue under the British Raj. By February 1921 the results of almost unchecked agitation both by Hindus and Muhammadans were sufficiently disquieting; Khilafat volunteer corps were being formed with uniforms and even occasional wearing of swords. In Tirurangadi, a notoriously troublesome area, the volunteer movement and the carrying of arms was most pronounced. It was known that the Musaliyars and students at the mosques were taking considerable share in spreading the agitation. In Calicut itself there was intense excitement when the District Magistrate prohibited certain agitators from addressing meetings, and had them arrested, bound over and committed to jail before they could disobey the order under section 144, Cr.P.C., as it was definitely ascertained that they had decided to disobey the order. A very large crowd of Mappillas assembled on the sea shore and the streets leading thereto on 16th February; troops had to be called out, force was used and the mob dispersed but there was no shooting. There followed for a short time an outward appearance of quietness but agitation in Ernad still went on. The organization of "volunteers" especially under Ali Musaliyar of Tirurangadi grew bolder, and Hindu agitators along with Mappilla priests preached that the Amir of Afghanistan would come to overthrow the British Government, that the Mappillas should help Gandhi and the Ali Brothers and that Government officers should be done away with. The priests seem to have been in remarkably close touch with the developments of the Khilafat agitation throughout India and to have passed on at once anything calculated to inflame the feelings of their hearers. Counter-propaganda among the better class of Mappillas met with some success but with others was of little avail, and the district authorities found themselves facing a situation which grew steadily worse.

First signs of revolt.

Incidents significant of coming real trouble occurred at the end of July and the beginning of August. There had been a house-breaking in the Nilambur Kovilagam buildings and search of a suspected Mappilla's house was followed the next day (31st July) by a threatening demonstration by about 300 Mappillas led by the suspect. By the next day as many as 2,000 had collected at Pukkottur from the neighbouring amsams, mostly armed and accompanied by their women encouraging them and the young boys. The local police inspector by the exercise of considerable tact and courage managed to get them to disperse. At Tanur on 3rd August the police were prevented by a large crowd of Mappillas from arresting some of their people who have maltreated Tiyyans. There were signs also such as the making of special knives and the saying of special prayers at the burial place of *Sahids*, that the fanatical Mappilla spirit was superimposing itself on the imagined Khilafat grievance.

Outbreak of rebellion.

It was decided that, though the forces available were quite insufficient to deal with any strong resistance, an attempt should be made to nip the trouble in the bud by a surprise raid on Tirurangadi and its neighbourhood in order to effect the arrest of about 24 known ring-leaders. The raid was fixed for the 20th August, and was only partially successful. The news of the arrests and false rumours of desecration of the famous Mambram mosque near Tirurangadi brought great crowds of Mappillas and they were driven back with some difficulty. Mr. Rowley of the Police and Lt. Johnstone of the Leinsters were cut down while parleying with the crowd and apart from the fighting there were several deliberate murders of police-messengers, motor-drivers and a Special Force Inspector. The District Magistrate handed over control to the Senior Military Officer present. As if at a prearranged signal the railway lines were torn up, telegraph wires cut, stations attacked and attempts made to destroy bridges. Next day the column with great difficulty made its way back to Calicut by the railway line and met with rebel activity up to within six miles of Calicut. The district was for a time cut off from communication with the outside world, and with a large Mappilla population the situation at Calicut itself was far from reassuring. Ali Musaliyar had arrogated to himself the title of "King" at Tirurangadi and at Pandikkad the local Khilafat ring-leader divided the country into "Khilafat Kingdoms" and appointed "rulers". Disorder rapidly spread through Ernad, Walavanad, and Ponnani taluks and between 21st and 25th August most of the public offices were attcked, sub-treasuries robbed, police stations looted of their arms; many Hindu houses were dacoited and their inhabitants ill-treated or murdered, liquor shops were burnt, most of the main roads blocked with trees, and bridges and culverts broken down. The murders of Hindus for refusal to accept Islam were, however, more frequent from September onwards when troops were already operating against the various gangs into which the rebels broke up. In the earlier stages of rebellion a small number of Hindus mostly agitators had actually joined up with the Mappillas.

Engagements at Pukkottur.

A form of martial law was declared for the area, a military commander appointed with a special civil officer attached, and a moveable column sent from Bangalore. Meanwhile the officer commanding at Calicut determined with the force at his disposal to relieve Malappuram which had been cut off. Although motor transport was used the force of 100 Leinsters and 70 special police could only get as far as Kondotti 18 miles from Calicut on the first day owing to the damage done to the road

CHAP. II. MAPPILLA OUTBREAKS.

by the rebels. On the following day, 26th August, about six miles out of Malappuram at Pukkottur they were attacked by about 1,000 rebels at first with gun and rifle fire and then hand to hand fighting. The Mappillas came on determined to die, and no less then 400 were killed, before the relieving column could make its way to Malappuram. The casualties were one officer and two privates killed, four officers (including volunteers) and eight other ranks wounded.

On 25th August 1921 H.M.S. "Comus" arrived in the roads, having been sent from Ceylon by His Excellency the Commander-in-Chief, East India Squadron, at the request of the Government, and left after railway communication had been restored. Its presence in the roads was a strong influence for tranquillity deterring Mappilla sympathisers with the rebellion and local Mappilla rowdies from making trouble, and encouraging the Hindus at a time when the garrison and police had been heavily depleted by the departure of the relief column for Malappuram.

Arrival of reinforcements.

The Bangalore column consisting of the Dorsets, a troop of the Queen Bays and one section of Quarter Battery of Field Artillery (2 guns) had been held up by breaches on the railway and only reached Malappuram on the 28th. A second column of the Dorsets reached Tirur from Kuttipuram on the same date. These troops arrived at Tirurangadi on the 30th and found it deserted except for a gang under Ali Musaliyar which entrenched itself for its final battle in the Samath Mosque. After a sortie in which several were killed, the remainder including Ali Musaliyar, surrendered. Meanwhile a gang under V. Kunhamad Haji brutally murdered a Mappilla Head Constable Haidross at Mudikod and then proceeded to Annakayam, where they murdered the well-known retired Mappilla Police Inspector Khan Bahadur Chekkutti Sahib who had given shelter to a number of officials and neighbouring Nambudiris and other Hindus.

Rebel activities and measures taken against them.

Military posts were established at Wandur and Pandikkad while two moveable columns marched through the country trying to get into contact with the rebels, but without much effect, as the Mappillas instead of standing as of old to fight to the death had broken up into wandering gangs, which ambushed several convoys and caused some casualties and even made a midnight raid on Manjeri where a small garrison was maintained, and as often as not would descend from the jungle on a place after troops had passed through and take vengeance on any they suspected of giving help or information to the troops. The total strength of these armed gangs was approximately 10,000 and, as they got more desperate, dacoities, forced conversions and murders became more brutal and frequent. Also by the middle of October rebel activity in the west in the Ariakode area became more intense and developed into a *jehad* against the Hindus. It was about this time that the inland part of Calicut from Manjeri to Pudupadi went up, long after Ernad had burst into flames. The rebellion in this area was dealt with mainly by the Malabar Special Police (Fraser's and Charsley's Companies). It was marked by much more savagery than rebel activities elsewhere, Ariakode excepted, and Hindus refusing Islam were butchered wholesale. It was decided to bring additional troops into the area of a type accustomed to jungle fighting and the 3/70th Burma Rifles and 2/8th Gurkhas accompanied by a wireless section, a company of Sappers, half the 20th Draught Mule Corps and other transport details arrived in the middle of October. A section of a mule (mountain) battery of 2 guns and 4 armoured cars also came about this time. The section of mountain guns and the armoured cars took part in the fight at Melmuri. The 1/39th Garhwal Rifles and 2/9th Gurkhas arrived on 10th November. A Special Police Force of 350 local men also was raised.

Raid on Melmuri and defeat of rebels at Pandikkad.

There had been various minor skirmishes in which casualties were inflicted but it was not till 25th October when the Dorsets made a raid on Melmuri and accounted for 246 rebels that a really serious blow since Pandikkad and Pukkottur was struck. This success was followed by considerable offers of surrender from the less desperate among the rebels, but the tale of outrages continued and every military post was crowded with refugees. Offers to suspend military operations and overlook offences against Government property prior to 26th August on condition of surrender and active assistance in arresting wanted rebels and preventing the entry of gangs, were made to certain areas, but do not seem to have met with much response at first. It was decided to organize a drive by the troops in small parties right across the country and this lasted from 11th to 25th November. A surprise attack was made by 2,000 rebels on the camp of one company of the 2/8th at Pandikkad but after a severe struggle was beaten off by the small garrison. The Gurkha casualties were serious. The attack was just before dawn. A British Officer and 3 Gurkhas were killed, and 34 men wounded. Another part of the same regiment had a stand up fight with the rebels at Cheruvadi; but elsewhere the Mappilla was mainly on the run and the net results of the drive were moral rather than material.

Capture of leaders.

At the end of the drive the area system was reverted to and the constant pressure exercised on the rebel gangs which prevented them getting supplies, together with numerous small encounters, gradually broke their morale; surrenders and also information leading to capture of the ring-leaders became very frequent. Seethi Koya Thangal, an important leader, was captured on the 20th December. Chembrasseri Thangal surrendred on the 18th. A special party of Malabar Special Police was organized to round up V. Kunhamad Haji who had

CHAP. II. MAPILLA OUTBREAKS.

narrowly excaped from the troops searching for him on Pandalur hill on the 30th December. The police followed him up to Veetikundu on Chodad Hill where on 6th January he surrendered with the remnant of his gang to the police intelligence officer. From the end of January it was found possible gradually to remove the troops other than the regular Malappuram garrison and the regiment usually stationed at Cannanore, and the last regiment went in June 1922, leaving the Malabar Special Police on occupation of strategical posts in rebel area. Under the area system each military party had members of the local police attached to it for intelligence purposes; it was on information gathered by them from the local inhabitants that parties went out in pursuit of the Mappilla gangs as soon as they were heard of, and it was to the police generally that surrenders were made. Some of the rebels would even demand that their surrender be to a particular officer. It required practically two full brigades of infantry with transport and wireless details and detachments of Sappers and Pioneers and 700 Special Police to suppress the rebellion.

General features of the rebellion and after. Mappilla women.

The active part played by the Mappilla women especially in the early stages by inciting both men and boys deserves notice. Two are known to have been shot in actual fighting and 157 were known to have taken part in definite offences, chiefly dacoities and thefts.

Special Courts and offences.

To deal with the enormous number of criminal cases first a special tribunal of three judges followed by three courts of special judges and nine special magistrates with enhanced powers were appointed. Court martials were employed mainly in the case of rebel leaders captured or surrendered under arms: Martial Law Regulations and Summary Courts were, however, but sparingly used. As the number of prisoners increased special cages at selected points had to be constructed to accommodate them. For a number of offenders a scheme of suspended sentences and instalment fines was orginated. The total number of reported murders was 468, dacoities 5,941, arson 352. Three hundred and twenty Hindu temples were destroyed and in Ernad taluk alone 900 cases of forced conversions to Islam were reported. Owing to the difficulty of finding jail accommodation a number of those convicted were sent to the Andamans and a special jail was opened at Alipuram near Bellary. A most distressing occurrence which took place on the 10th November 1921 resulted in the death by asphyxiation of 70 Mappilla prisoners in the train, between Olavakkot and Podanur while they were being conveyed from the disturbed area to the Bellary Jail.

Distress and relief measures.

There was much distress among Hindu refugees from the affected areas and a Central Relief Committee which ran 22 camps was formed. In these camps some 20,000 refugees were given relief. In the affected area itself both to Hindus and Mappillas liberal grants for rebuilding of houses, food and clothing were given and in all over Rs. 2,72,000 were spent. State loans were also granted. The Mappillas recovered perhaps quicker than others. Large sums of money had to be spent in rebuilding public buildings and restoring communication to normal. The destruction of registration and private documents was considerable and presented a difficult problem, but the re-writing of revenue records was found less difficult than anticipated. Forests suffered less than might have been expected under the conditions. Special measures were adopted by general agreement in the Hindu community to make it easy for those forcibly converted to Islam to return to the Hindu fold. The Malabar Special Police raised in the rebellion was continued as a permanent force and its strength eventually fixed at 600 with the complement of officers and N.C.Os. It is divided into 6 companies each quartered at a post in the area and all connected with each other and Malappuram by wireless. The training is on military lines and the force has proved its usefulness also in other parts of the Presidency since.

Malabar Special Police made a permanent garrison.

CHAPTER III.

THE PEOPLE.

DISTRIBUTION OF POPULATION—Urban and rural—Movement of people. LANGUAGES—Malayalam—Tunjattu Ezhutacchan—Folksongs—Prose. RELIGIONS. THE HINDUS—The Malabar caste system. The *Marumakkattayam* system—The *Tarwad*—Origin of system—Early accounts of *Sambandham*—Present position—The *Tali kettu kalyanam*—Pollution—Ceremonial pollution—Birth and death pollution. CONSPECTUS OF CASTE SYSTEM. BRAHMANS—Nambudiris—Pattars and Embrandiris—Nambudiri subdivisions—Elayads and Mussads. ANTARALA JATHI—Ambalavasis—Kshattriyas and Samantans. NAYARS—High Caste Nayars—South Malabar—North Malabar—Non-military Nayars—Low Caste Nayars. POLLUTING CASTES—Tiyans and Izhuvans—Mukkuvans—Artizan, menial and devil dancing castes. ABORIGINAL CLASSES—Cherumans and Pulayans—Parayans—Nayadis—Jungle tribes. FOREIGN CASTES. VILLAGES AND DWELLINGS. DRESS—Hair—Ornaments. FOOD. AMUSEMENTS—*Kalaris*—*Kadhakalis*—Games. FESTIVALS. AGRICUTLURAL CEREMONIES. RELIGION—Temples—Religious life—Magic and superstitions. CEREMONIES—Nambudiri marriages—Other Nambudiri ceremonies—Death ceremonies—Ceremonies of Nayars and other castes — *Pulikudi* — Childbirth — *Pal-kudi* — *Chorunnu* — *Vidyarambham* — *Choulam* — *Kathukuttu* — *Tali kettu kalyanam*—*Tirandu kalyanam*—Marriage—Funeral and memorial ceremonies. MAPPILLAS—Origin—General characteristics—Houses — Dress — Food — Mosques—Religion—Saints—*Maulad*—Superstition — Ceremoneis — Childbirth — Circumcision — Marriage—Death. CHRISTIANS. SYRIAN CHRISTIANS—History—Characteristics—Churches — Clergy — Doctrines — Festivals—Social life—Marriage—Death. ROMAN CATHOLICS. BASEL MISSION.

CHAP. III. DISTRIBUTION OF POPULATION.

MALABAR is one of the most densely populated districts in the Madras Presidency, the average number of inhabitants to the sq. mile (481) being exceeded only in the Tanjore district, and being much above the average of the Presidency as a whole (270). But the district area includes large tracts of practically uninhabited hill country, as well as the sparsely populated plateau of the Wynaad, where the average density is less than 100 persons to the square mile; and the figures for Ponnani Taluk, in which the population at the census of 1901 averaged 1,123 persons to the square mile, may be taken as representing with fair accuracy the state of the country within 10 miles of the sea-board throughout the district.

Urban and rural population.

The houses of the people are not for the most part congregated in villages of the type common elsewhere in the Presidency; but are scattered on the cultivated lands, and along the foot of the hills surrounding the rice fields, each standing in its own garden. Only 8 per cent. of the people live in towns (the proportion for the Presidency is 11 per cent; and the major portion of these are to be found in five or six large towns, which include considerable areas more strictly rural than urban in character. For instance within the limits of Calicut, at once the largest and most densely populated town, there are large stretches of cultivation, and comparatively few streets; and the number of houses to the square mile is only 472, while in towns such as Madras, Madura and Salem the average ranges from two to three thousand to the square mile.

CHAP. III. DISTRIBUTION OF POPULATION.

Movement of population.

Details of the variations that have taken place in the periods between the last three censuses will be found in the separate volume of appendices. It will be seen that though the population increased by 12 per cent. in the decade between 1881 and 1891, the increase in the last decade only amounted to 5·6 per cent. It is not easy to assign a reason for this comparative decline; though it is partly attributable to the decay of the Wynaad industries. There is little emigration from Malabar, and bad seasons and plague are negligible factors. The tendency of the population to move to the towns, which was generally indicated by the results of the last census in other parts of the Presidency, was less noticeable in Malabar, but that it prevailed to some extent in the decade from 1891–1901 is shown by the fact that the populations of Calicut and Palghat increased by 11 and 13 per cent. respectively, while the general increase for the district was only 5·7 per cent.

LANGUAGES.

Malayalam is the language of 94 per cent. of the people; other languages are practically only spoken by foreigners. Tamil is the language of 4 per cent., made up mostly of East coast merchants (Chettis, Pillais and Ravuttans) and Pattar Brahmans in Palghat, of estate coolies in the Wynaad, and of the Goundan and other inhabitants of the Attapadi valley. On the coast there are a few merchants who speak Arabic, Hindustani, Guzarati and Maratti; and in the Wynaad, Canarese is spoken by many of the estate coolies. A few Goanese Eurasians returned Portuguese as their language at the last census; but it seems to be dying out. The dialects spoken by the more barbarous of the hill tribes differ considerably from Malayalam, but they hardly deserve to be regarded as separate languages; that of the Kurumbas of the Wynaad contains a considerable admixture of Canarese. In Minicoy, the language is Mahl, a dialect of Singhalese and belonging therefore to the Indo-European family.

The Malayalam language.

Malayalam is a Dravidian language closely akin to Tamil; but it is still a matter of dispute whether it should be regarded as an "old and much altered offshoot" of Tamil as Dr. Caldwell considered it, or as a sister language "both being dialects of the same member of the Dravidian family," as Dr. Gundert suggests in his dictionary. Modern Malayalam has a softer and less nasal sound than Tamil; but its main difference from the latter is that its verbs are not inflected to denote person,

CHAP. III. LANGUAGES.

number or gender. From the fact that verbal inflexions are found in the old copper plate deeds referred to on page 34; and in early poetry, it is argued that their disappearance is a comparatively late development; but if this were so we should expect some traces of such inflexions to survive in the colloquial language, as they do in English; and there are none. The language of the copper plate grants, which were made by a Perumal who according to tradition was a foreigner, is rather Tamil than Malayalam; and the early poets were no doubt much affected by influence of the early Tamil poets, who formed a literary school and developed a court language.[1] It is not impossible that colloquial Malayalam had already developed on different lines.

Tunjattu Ezhutacchan.

The classical epoch of modern Malayalam begins with Tunjattu Ezhuttacchan, who lived in the 17th century, and to whom is ascribed the invention of the existing Malayalam alphabet. The tradition is that he was a Nayar, who provoked the jealousy of the Brahmans by his genius and learning, and was by their magic seduced into the habit of drunkenness. To revenge himself he determined to exalt the Malayalam language to an equality with the sacred language of the gods and rishis; and accordingly proceeded to translate into it the principal Sanskrit epics such as the Ramayana, Mahabharata, Sivapurana and Bhagavatha, all of which he translated while under the immediate influence of intoxication. The result was, in the words of Dr. Burnell, that "there was perhaps no part of Southern India where Sanskrit literature was more studied by people of many castes during the 18th century"; and to this influence may perhaps be traced the number of Sanskrit words to be found now even in colloquial use, as well as the development of the Malayalam poetical diction, which has been described as "pure Sanskrit connected or concluded by a few Malayalam words."

Folk songs.

Altogether different is the language of the Malabar folksongs some of which have been reduced to writing. They celebrate exploits of popular heroes such as the Kunhali Marakkars and Taccholi Othenan (the Malabar Robin Hood), or historic occurrences such as Tipu's invasion, the Pychy rebellion, and famous Mappilla outbreaks; the language is the ordinary colloquial Malayalam, and there are no traces of verbal inflections, and few Sanskrit expressions.

Prose.

Of prose there is not much; the Keralolpatti, and similar historical and legal treatises of the seventeenth and eighteenth centuries, are the earliest examples, but they are mainly translations from Sanskrit, and full of Sanskrit words; and Dr. Gundert considered that the best early prose was to be found in the Tellicherry records. Modern prose has hardly yet a

[1] See *The Tamils Eighteen Hundred Years ago*, (Kanakasabhai Pillai).

LANGUAGES.

distinct and definite style. The labours of Dr. Gundert and his successors among the German Missionaries have done much to adapt the colloquial language to literary expression, though they have perhaps tended to assimilate it too much to Tamil; but in the most recent prose represented by the works of Mr. Chandu Menon, the influence of Sanskrit is still predominant.

RELIGIONS.

The education of the people is dealt within Chapter IX and their occupations in Chapter VI. The religion of the majority is Hinduism, but there is a far larger proportion of Muhammadans than is usual in the Madras Presidency. At the census of 1901, 68 per cent. of the people were classed as Hindus, 30 per cent. as Muhammadans and 2 per cent. as Christians. The bulk of the Christians, who are most numerous in the south of the Ponnani Taluk, belong to the Syrian Church. The Mappillas are most numerous in the Ernad and Ponnani taluks, and in the coast towns; unlike the East coast Labbais, the Mappillas belong almost entirely to the Sunni sect of Muhammadanism.

THE HINDUS. The Malabar caste system.

There is an entire heirarchy of castes peculiar to 'Malabar' in the wider sense of that term, that is, regarded as a geographical expression including the British district of that name and the adjoining Native States of Travancore and Cochin; and it is impossible within the limits of this chapter to give more than a brief outline of the system. The origin of the Hindu castes is a vexed question, which need not be discussed here; but it will be observed that Malabar affords excellent illustrations of the theories advanced by Sir H. Risley, in his treatment of the question in the report of the census of 1901. He suggested that the basis of fact underlying the idea of caste is the physiological instinct of race distinction, which encourages hypergamy, or the rule which forbids a woman to marry a man of an inferior race or group, and tends to separate the progeny of mixed marriages into distinct endogamous groups; and that the evolution of the elaborate modern systems of caste has been due largely to the influence of the fiction, that differences of religion, custom, locality, profession and the like, are analogous to race distinctions, and should be similarly stereotyped; a fiction characteristic of the Hindu genius, and popularized by the Brahman myth of the four Vedic castes. In Malabar, the primal race distinctions can readily be traced in the broad divisions of Brahman, Nayar, Tiyan, artizans, and the supposed aboriginal tribes; while the infinite variety of castes and subcastes well exemplifies the effect of hypergamy and the tendency to stereotype the most minute differences of custom, etc. There is for instance, little doubt that the Samantan is by race, a Nayar,[1]

[1] In 1888 the District Judge of South Malabar held in a suit between the Elaya Tirumulpad of Nilambur and the Collector, Mr. Logan, that there was no distinctive caste of Samantans, and that the plaintiff was a Nayar (*Vide* Moore's *Malabar Law and Custom*, p. 346).

CHAP. III. THE HNIDUS

differentiated by his social position and strict observance of hypergamy with Nambudiris; and that many at least of the intermediate temple-serving castes, are, as tradition relates, the result of violations of the rule of hypergamy by Brahmans. The Chembottis (copper-smiths), originally a class of Kammalans, who now claim to rank with Nayars, are an instance of a caste, which has been raised in the social scale by its profession; and the Veluttedans, a washerman subcaste of the Nayars, and the Kavuthiyans, a barber subdivision of the Veluttedans, are instances of classes which have been degraded by theirs. The influence of local residence may be seen in the differentiation of Izhuvan, Tandan, and Tiyan; as well as in the general rule that members of the same castes dwelling in North and South Malabar,[1] may not intermarry. But this is not all. In different parts of the country there are quite different sets of castes; where the same caste is common to two tracts, the subdivisions are often different; and sometimes subdivisions bearing the same name have a different social status in different places. Thus as a general rule, the subdivisions of Nayars in North Malabar, class for class, rank higher, or consider that they do, than the corresponding subdivisions in South Malabar. Again, ceremonies and customs vary even from desam to desam; and these differences extend to such minute or trivial matters, as the manner of discharging salvoes of *kadinas* (mortars) at festivals, and of slicing plantains for curry. Obviously a mere sketch of the system as a whole is all that can be offered here.

Before however proceeding to give a conspectus of the caste hierarchy, it is necessary to describe some remarkable peculiarities of Malabar society, which affect the system, and to which reference must constantly be made in explaining it.

The Marumakkattayam system.

The first is the system of inheritance, and of family organisation, known as *Marumakkattayam* or literally, "descent through sister's children"; bound up with which is the institution known as *Sambandham*, the loose form of "marriage" obtaining among the castes following *marumakkattayam*, which entails no responsibility or legal obligation whatever on the part of the "husband" towards his "wife" and children. According to this system, which is followed by the Kshattriyas, the Samantans, the Ambalavasis and the Nayars proper, and partially by some other castes, children belong to the same caste or subcaste and family as their mother, not to that of their father. The custom affects the caste system because, as has been remarked, the rule of hypergamy or *anulomam* (literally, "going with the heir"), which allows a woman, but not a man, to marry into a caste or subcaste superior to her own, is very widely observed in Malabar; and its violation, or

[1] The dividing line is the Korapuzha river, between the Calicut and Kurumbranad taluks.

prathilomam (" going against the heir ") is said to have given rise to some of the mixed castes. The Brahman castes follow the *Makkattayam* system, that is the system by which a child belongs to its father's family; and they contract within their own caste regular marriages, with all the ordinary legal and religious sanctions and incidents. But Brahman men are also in the habit of entering into *sambandham* unions with women of the lower castes.

The Tarwad.

The *marumakkattayam* joint family or *Tarwad*, as it is called, consists of all the descendants of a common ancestress, in the female line only. Neither party to a *sambandham* union becomes thereby a member of the others family; and the offspring of the union belong to their mother's *tarwad*, and have no sort of claim, so far as the law of *marumakkattayam* goes, to a share of their father's property, or to maintenance therefrom. The *tarwad* property is the joint property of all the members, and each member is entitled to maintenance from it, but is not entitled to claim partition. Partition may, of course, be effected by a mutual agreement between all the members; and when this is done there will remain between the branch *tarwads* only 'Community of pollution' (*pula sambandham*), which means that whenever a death or birth places one branch under ceremonial pollution, all the other branches are regarded as similarly affected. They have no further community of property (*muthal sambandham*) than is implied in the right of each, as reversionary (*attaladakam*) heirs, to succeed to the property of another branch should it become extinct.

Among the more influential families, and more especially those of the Rajas called *Kovilagams*, it is customary to set aside certain portions of the *tarwad* property for the life enjoyment only of the senior members. The separate estates thus created are called *Stanams*. The word means dignity and denotes the status of the senior members of the family, the theory being that the separate estates are assigned to enable them to maintain their position. The *Stanams* are enjoyed in succession by the several members of the family, as they succeed to the position to which they are attached. Thus the Zamorin's family is divided into three *Kovilagams* or palaces called the Pudiya, Padinnara, and Kizhakke, each with its separate estate under the management of its senior lady or *Tamburatti*; and there are five *Stanams* with separate properties set apart for the enjoyment of the five senior members of the whole family, who bear the titles of Zamorin, Eralpad, Munalpad, Edattaralpad, and Nediyiruppu Muttu Eradi. The *Stani* is in the position of a trustee with regard to this *Stanam* property; he has only a life estate, and cannot alienate except for the benefit of the *tarwad* as a whole.

CHAP. III. THE HINDUS.

Sometimes the husband, or the father of some of the members of a *tarwad*,[1] provides a separate house out of his self-acquired property for his wife and children, and the new household then becomes a separate branch *tavazhi* (*tay*, mother, and *vazhi*, way), of the original *tarwad*, but retains both community of pollution and community of property with it. In the *tavazhi*, as in the original *tarwad*, descent is traced in the female line in the manner already described. Every member of a *tarwad* is entitled to dispose of property acquired by himself as he wishes; but at death any property which may not have been disposed of by gift or otherwise *inter vivos*, or devised by testament, will lapse to the *tarwad*. The family property is usually managed by the eldest male member, termed the *Karnavan* who can only be removed for flagrant mismanagement or misfeasance, and then only by decree of a civil court (unless of course he and the other members of the *tarwad* consent that he shall resign his management to some other member); and until so removed he has practically absolute control over the family property. The younger members of the family are called *Anandiravans*; and their only rights as members of the *tarwad* are to succeed in order of seniority to the *karnavanship*, and to be maintained from the *tarwad* property. The words *anandiravan* and *karnavan* are also used in a relative sense; thus any member of a tarwad will call all the members elder than himself "my *karnavans*" and all those younger "my *anandiravans*".

Origin of System.

Various explanations of this curious system have been suggested. The traditional Brahman account is that it was ordained by Parasurama, who bade the women of the Samantan, and Sudra classes "put off chastity and the cloth that covered their breasts;" and declared that the duty of such women and the object for which they were created was to satisfy the desires of the Brahmans. It is no doubt an exceedingly convenient arrangement for the cadets of Nambudiri families whom it relieves from the life-long bachelorhood (*Brahmacharam*) to which they are supposed to devote themselves, without entailing any corresponding burden, whether in the form of more mouths to feed, or of more claimants to their ancestral property; and, combined with the rule of hypergamy, it of course ensures the higher race against contamination by the blood of the lower. But that it was ever deliberately introduced by the Nambudiris as a matter of policy it is difficult to believe; and it is to be remarked that it is more prevalent in North Malabar, where Nambudiri influence has always been less than in the South, and has there extended to Tiyans and Mappillas, and other castes who pollute Brahmans. Another theory connects it with the military organization

[1] Tarwad = Tara + vidu. Tara = Village unit.

CHAP. III. THE HINDUS

of the Nayar community. "Marriage is interdicted and all other recreations except warre," writes Montaigne, of "the nobility of Calicut;" and Mr. Warden, Collector of Malabar from 1804–1816, considered that "the profession of arms by birth, subjecting the males of a whole race to military service from the earliest youth to the decline of manhood, was a system of polity utterly incompatible with the existence among them of the marriage state," and that it was "obvious that, from the nature of their professional duties, their sexual intercourse could only have been fugitive and promiscuous, and their progeny could never under such circumstances have depended upon them for support." Others would regard it merely as a survival of a universal primitive state of sexual promiscuity, in which "the son inherits not after his father because a woman is allowed by custom to lye with several men, so that it cannot be known who is the father of the child she brings forth." But against this is the fact that the jungle tribes and the lowest castes, who are generally considered to represent the aborigines, have a regular system of marriage; while the fraternal polyandry practised by the Kammalans, Kanisans and some sections of the South Malabar Tiyans, is distinct from the *sambandham* system, and has its origin possibly in reasons of economy.

Early accounts of Sambandham.

Whatever the true explanation may be, there seems little doubt that the *sambandham* was, in its origin at all events, the simplest and loosest form of sexual union between man and woman. It depended for any permanence it might possess entirly on the free-will of the parties, either of which was at liberty at any moment and for any cause to terminate it by the simple expedient of discontinuing it, no sort of ceremony resembling divorce, whether legal or religious, being requisite for that purpose. The woman was at liberty to entertain in turn any number of lovers, and the latter were at liberty to share the favours of any number of women. So long as the woman observed the law of hypergamy, and did not contract an alliance within the exogamous group to which she belonged, no union and no number of unions could be regarded as illicit. An interesting account of the system is given by Duarte Barbosa, who travelled in Malabar in the beginning of the 16th century and whose narrative of his voyages shows that he was, as a rule, a careful and accurate observer :

"These (Nayars) are not married nor maintain women or children; their nephews, the sons of their sisters, are their heirs. The Nayar women are all accustomed to do with themselves what they please with Brahmans or Nayars, but not with other people of lower class under pain of death. After they are ten or twelve years old or more, their mothers perform a marriage ceremony for them in this manner. They advise the relations and friends that they may come to do honour to their daughters, and they beg some of their relations and friends to marry these daughters, and they do so. It

CHAP. III. THE HINDUS.

must be said they have some gold jewel made, which will contain half a ducat of gold, a little shorter than the tag of lace, with a hole in the middle passing through it, and they string it on a thread of white silk; and the mother of the girl stands with her daughter very much dressed out, and entertaining her with music and singing, and a number of people. And this relation or friend of hers comes with much earnestness, and there performs the ceremony of marriage, as though he married with her, and they throw a gold chain round the necks of both of them together, and he puts the above-mentioned jewel round her neck, which she always has to wear as a sign that she may now do what she pleases. And the bridegroom leaves her and goes away without touching her nor having more to say to her on account of being her relation; and if he is not so, he may remain with her if he wish it, but he is not bound to do so if he do not desire it. And from that time forward the mother goes begging some young men to deflower the girl, for amongst themselves they hold it an unclean thing and almost a disgrace to deflower women. And after she is already a woman, the mother goes about seeking who will take her daughter to live with him. But when she is pretty, three or four Nayars join together and agree to maintain her and to live with her; and the more she has the more highly is she esteemed, and each man has his appointed day from midday to the next day at the same hour when the other comes; and so she passes her life without any one thinking ill of it. And he who wishes to leave her does so whenever he pleases and goes to take another and, if she takes a dislike to any of them, she dismisses him. The children which she has remain at the expense of the mother and of the brothers of the mother, who bring them up because they do not know the fathers; and, even if they should appear to belong to any persons in particular, they are not recognized by them as sons, nor do they give anything for them; and it is said that the kings made this law in order that the Nayars should not be covetous and should not abandon the king's service."[1]

Present position.

This account is substantially corroborated by all the travellers and writers who have referred to the subject up to the beginning of the nineteenth century.[2] At the present day, the legal position is not changed, except in so far as it has been modified by the Malabar Marriage Act IV of 1896, which provides that when a *sambandham* has been registered in the manner therein laid down, it shall have the incidence of a legal marriage; that is to say, the wife and children shall be entitled to maintenance by the husband

---

[1] *The Coasts of East Africa and Malabar.* Duarte Barbosa. (Hakluyt Society), p. 124.

[2] Compare the accounts of Abdur Razzak, and Niccolo Conti in *India in the Fifteenth Century* (Hakluyt); of Castanheda (in Kerr's *Travels II*, p. 354), Ludovico di Varthema (*Travels*, Hakluyt, p. 145), and Linschoten (*Voyages* Hakluyt, I, p. 280) in the sixteenth century; of Pyrard de Laval (*Voyage of P. de L.* Hakluyt II, p. 384) and Pietro della Valle, *Travels* Hakluyt II, p. 379) in the seventeenth century; of Hamilton (*New Account of the East Indies*, I, p. 310) in the eighteenth century; and of Buchanan (*Journey through Mysore, Malabar and South Canara*, II, p. 411) in the nineteenth century.

or father, respectively, and to succeed to half his self-acquired property, if he dies intestate; while the parties to such a *sambandham* cannot register a second *sambandham* during its continuance, that is, until it is terminated by death or by a formal application for divorce in the Civil Courts. The total number of *sambandhams* registered under the Act has, however, been infinitesimal, and the reason for this is, admittedly, the reluctance of the men to fetter their liberty to terminate *sambandham* at will by such restrictions as the necessity for formal divorce, or to undertake the burdensome responsibility of a legal obligation to maintain their wife and offspring. If, as the evidence recorded by the Malabar Marriage Commission tended to show, "a marriage law in North Malabar and throughout the greater part of South Malabar would merely legalise what is the prevailing custom," it is hard to see why there has been such a disinclination to lend to that custom the dignity of legal sanction.

It is no doubt true, however, that polyandry amongst Nayars has practically disappeared; that polygamy is looked on with disfavour; that it is becoming more and more customary among the well-to-do for the husband to provide for his wife and children, often giving them a separate dwelling, which in due course becomes the nucleus of a fresh *tarwad*; and that among the more advanced Nayars it is the fashion to celebrate the commncement of a *sambandham* by the performance of a regular ceremony, such as the *Pudamuri*, in which the bridegroom presents a cloth to the bride and the relations are entertained at a feast. Nor can it be denied that the *sambandham* union, loose as it is, often lasts for a lifetime; while in the opinion of Mr. Logan "nowhere is the marriage tie, albeit informal, more jealously guarded, or its neglect more savagely avenged." In all these respects there is reason to believe that North Malabar is, and long has been, ahead of the South.

Nevertheless it is admittedly a defect of the *marumakkattayam* system that it gives rise to constant disputes between the members of the *tarwad*, owing to the irreconcilable conflict between the *karnavan's* duty to his *tarwad* and his affection for his wife and children; and it is doubtful whether an adequate compensation for those evils is to be found in the preservation of family property and the free play of the laws of natural selection which, it is claimed, are so fully secured and so beautifully exemplified in the system, in combination with the institution of *sambandham*.

The Malabar Marriage Act of 1896 providing for the optional registration of *sambandhams* has not been popular with the followers of the *Marumakkathayam* law. There has all the same been an ever-increasing demand with the advance of progressive ideas in the community for the legal recognition

CHAP. III. THE HINDUS.

of this customary marital union which the courts at present refuse to regard as a legal marriage. Protests against the management of *tarwads* have also been numerous. The law of marriage, succession and inheritance has been codified in the neighbouring States of Cochin and Travancore, and various enlightened members of the community in British Malabar have been attempting to get similar legislation enacted in regard to the Madras Presidency. Two Marumakkathayam Bills (Nos. 13 and 20 of 1931) were pending consideration in the Madras Legislative Council in 1932, which aimed at defining, regulating and amending the law of marriage, succession and inheritance and family management, partition and adoption among the followers of the *Marumakkathayam* law.

Talikettu-kalyanam.

Another institution found amongst all the classes following the *marumakkattayam* system, as well as amongst many of those who observe *makkattayam*, is that known as the *Tali-kettu-kalyanam* or "Tali tying wedding" which has been described as "the most peculiar, distinctive and unique" among Malayali marriage customs. Its essence is the tying of a *tali* (a small piece of gold or other metal, like a locket, on a string) on a girl's neck before she attains the age of puberty. This is done by a man of the same or of a higher caste (the usages of different classes differ), and it is only after it has been done that the girl is at liberty to contract a *sambandham*. It seems to be generally considered that the ceremony was intended to confer on the *tali*-tier or *manavalan* (bridegroom) a right to cohabit with the girl; and by some the origin of the ceremony is found in the claim of the *Bhu-devas* or "Earth Gods" (that is the Brahmans), and on a lower plain of the Kshatriyas or ruling classes, to the first-fruits of lower caste womanhood, a right akin to the mediaeval *droit de seigneurie*. This view is supported by the accounts of the ceremony given by Captain Alexander Hamilton[1]; but not by the earliest account quoted above, according to which the *tali* was not tied by a Brahman or a man of superior rank, and is merely described as "a token that the girl may do with herself as she pleases."

Nowadays at all events cohabitation by the *tali*-tier with the girl is certainly not essential, and is not even an usual sequel to the ceremony, at least amongst *marumakkattayam* castes; as will be evident from the facts that to reduce the expense of the feast which is an invariable accompaniment of the "wedding," it is becoming more and more usual for the *tali* to be tied simultaneouly on all the girls in a family who may be under the age of puberty, so that the rite is sometimes performed on mere

---

[1] *A New Account of the East Indies*, Vol. I, p. 310, Ed. 1744. Compare the account of Varthema (*Voyages*, Hakluyt, p. 141), who says that Brahmans had to deflower the kings' wives first.

babies; that it is not uncommon for one man to tie the *tali* for several girls at the same time, some of whom may be sisters; and lastly that the *tali*-tier is often a man of venerable age selected for his sanctity, who may have tied the *tali* of girl's mother, while in some castes, it is the custom for the *tali* to be tied by the girl's father or uncle, both of which cases would involve incest were any marital functions connected with the rite. In fact the ceremony is now little more than a meaningless survival, which has so far lost all real significance that the *tali* is in some cases, tied by the girl's mother. But a girl still becomes an outcaste, if she fails to have the *tali* tied before she attains the age of puberty. Mr. Fawcett's view "that the ceremony is . . . . analogous to that obtaining in the Bellary district and round and about it, through which women called Basavis, are, after an initiatory ceremony of devotion to a deity, compelled (under certain conditions) to follow no rule of chastity, but whose children are under no degradation" has been accepted by Mr. Justice Moore[1]; but it is to be observed that the ceremony is performed by the Tiyans and Izhuvans of South Malabar and other castes, who follow the *makkattayam* system, and have a regular form of marriage which is celebrated in addition to the *tali kettu*. In these cases the custom is perhaps merely an imitation of the practice of the higher castes.

Pollution

Bound up with the Malabar caste system are the strict theories with regard to pollution. Every man considers himself polluted by the touch of one of a lower caste; and there are castes low in the social scale which mutually convey pollution to each other. But in addition to this, at a certain point in the caste system, the taint is supposed to become so pronounced as actually to affect the atmosphere and carry pollution to persons, houses, and so on, within a radius of several yards from the person who is the centre of infection. Based on this theory there is a recognised scale of distances at which members of each of the polluting castes must stand from a man of higher caste or his house, the distance increasing as we descend the social scale. In ordinary conversation such expressions as a *Tiya-pad* or a *Cheruma-pad* (that is, the distance at which a Tiyan or a Cheruman has to keep) are commonly used. The distance is about 24 feet in the case of a Kammalan or member of one of the artisan classes, and in the case of the aboriginal Nayadis as much as 74. Under the Native Rajas Nayars thought nothing of cutting down on the spot a member of the lower castes who had approached within polluting distance of his person.[2] At the present day the higher casteman when

[1] Moore's *Malabar Law and Custom*, 3rd Ed., pp. 69 to 78. See also *Bellary District Gazetteer*, ch. III. and Thurston's *Ethnographic Notes in Southern India*, p. 121.

[2] Buchanan's *Journey through Mysore, Malabar and South Canara*, Vol. I p. 388.

CHAP. III. THE HINDUS.

walking along the road utters a warning grunt or hoot to persons of any lower castes, who thereupon retire to the necessary distance. The result is that a man of any of the very low castes may undergo considerable inconvenience and delay in getting from one place to another. Thus the Nayadis who were interviewed by Mr. Thurston of the Madras Museum in 1901 at Shoranur, "had by reason of the pollution which they traditionally carry with them, to avoid walking over the long bridge which spans the Bharatha Puzha (Ponnani river) and follow a circuitous route of many miles."[1] It is noteworthy that neither Jews, Christians or Muhammadans are considered to convey this "atmospheric pollution," and this is true even of converts to the two latter religions from the lowest castes. It is evident what an immense inducement is thus afforded to the latter to raise themselves in the social scale and rid themselves of so many vexations and degrading restrictions and disabilities by embracing Islam or Christianity. The pollution caused by the proximity or contact of a person of a lower caste can only be removed by plunging the whole body under water, which should however be done in a tank or stream in order to be efficacious.

Ceremonial pollution.

In addition to the pollution communicated by members of a lower caste to those of a higher, there is also what may be called "ceremonial pollution," which too may be either "contact pollution" or "distance pollution." A person ceremonially polluted conveys pollution even to members of the same caste. Women are regarded as so polluted and as conveying "Atmospheric pollution" during their monthly periods and after delivery. Till their purification, which cannot take place till after a certain number of days has elapsed, and has sometimes to be performed by members of a specified caste (other than their own), they have to live separately from the rest of the family in a room, or in the case of well-to-do a separate building, reserved for the purpose.

Birth and Death pollution.

A death or birth in a family entails pollution on all members of the *tarwad* and of those connected families which have community of pollution. This too lasts for a prescribed period the duration of which varies in the case of different castes increasing as we descend the scale; and has to be removed by prescribed ceremonies, which in most cases must be performed by a member of a certain prescribed class. The functions of the barber and washerman classes are, as will be seen, of special importance in connection with ceremonial pollution.

Food.

In the matter of food the general rule is that no one will eat anything cooked by a person whose touch would pollute him; but the rule is only applied strictly to the eating of cooked rice. In no case will a man eat rice cooked by a man substantially

[1] *Madras Government Museum Bulletin*, Vol. IV, No. 1, p. 73.

lower in the scale. Women may generally speaking only eat where they may marry, that is, with equals or superiors. Between the lines of classes separating those who cannot eat together, there are finer lines of distinction separating those, who though they may eat together, do not sit in the same row for the purpose.

CHAP. III. THE HINDUS.

CONSPECTUS OF CASTE SYSTEM.

It was realized at the census of 1901 that the only satisfactory basis of a classification of modern castes is that of social precedence, as recognized by public opinion and indicated by the practices observed with regard to inter-marriage and social intercourse. As has been said caste exclusively in Malabar manifests itself principally in the facts that the touch or approach of persons of substantially lower class carries pollution, and that women may marry only with equals or superiors, while men though for the most part restricted to their own caste or class, may in some cases form *sambandham* with inferiors. But the rules regulating endogamy and exogamy, the periods of pollution and the performance of purifactory ceremonies have been elaborated in an infinite variety of detail ; and it would be a hopeless, as well as an invidious task, to attempt any exact classification of the castes in order of social precedence. They fall into the following broad divisions (1) Brahmans, (2) Antarala-jathi or intermediate castes, including the Kshattriyas, Samantans, and Ambalavasis or Temple servants, (3) Sudras, divided into (*a*) Nayars proper, (*b*) caste now more or less generally recognized as Nayars, but probably not originally so regarded, and (*c*) low caste Sudras, (4) Tiyans, Kammalans or Artisans, and other polluting castes (*Pathita jathi*) said to be the result of mixed unions formed in violation of the rule of hypergamy, and (5) the depressed aboriginal classes, who are outcastes.

BRAHMANS. Nambudiris.

The generic name for the Malabar Brahman is Nambudiri. The origin of the word is disputed, but no derivation has ever been suggested which can be termed authoritative or convincing. It is sufficient to remark that the termination *tiri*, holy, is found in many other caste names and titles. Unnitiri and Embrandiri are examples of the former, and Nambiatiri a title given in old days to warrior chieftains (and still surviving in some places) is an instance of the latter class.

The Nambudiris, like other Brahmans, are divided into exogamous *gotrams*. They follow the *makkattayam* family system and the general rule is that only the eldest son is allowed to contract a regular marriage with a Nambudiri woman, the others being restricted to *sambandhams* with women of the castes below them. There have, however, been instances of young men, not the eldest of the family, getting wives from their own caste. *Parivedanams* (that is, a younger brother marrying before the elder brother is married) were prohibited. A spirit of reform has come over the younger members of the community who insist on the marriage of all male members, if so inclined, to girls of their own community and *Parivedanams* do occur. The first few marriages against the old custom created a stir, but they were soon accepted as *factum valet.* The young men do not take kindly to *sambandhams* with Nayar women, especially when their own sisters have to lead unmarried lives and die as old maids. Attempts are also being made to take their women out of the *purdah*, but so far without much success owing to the opposition of the Nambudiri women themselves. English education is slowly making progress in the community, which until recently was opposed to it. A Nambudiri from Travancore braving social ostracism went to England for higher studies, and another went to jail for a political offence and they were taken back into the community without much difficulty, the grumblers being outvoted. Attempts have also been made in recent years to amend the law relating to marriage, succession, inheritance, partition and maintenance among the Nambudiris so as to bring it more in accord with modern conditions of life (vide Bill No. 14 of 1931 of the Madras Legislative Council). The women marry after puberty; they may of course only marry Nambudiris and husbands are consequently at a premium. Nambudiri women are called *Anterjanams*, or *Agattammamar*, both of which terms mean "living inside" referring to the seclusion in which they are kept; and any one suspected of sexual irregularity is tried by a caste tribunal (*Smarta Vicharam*)[1] with an elaborate ceremonial, and if found guilty, outcasted. The Nambudiris are Vedic Brahmans and wear the *punul*; their pollution period is ten days. They are mostly landlords, and they claim that all the lands in Malabar were originally vested in them and them alone (see p. 302). They for the most part live quiet secluded lives in their family houses, which are called *illams*, occupied only with the mainfold ceremonial practices which their religion requires of them. A Nambudiri should rise very early at about 3 a.m. and immediately bathe in a tank; he should then proceed to his religious exercises in the temple. After that and till 11 o'clock he should read or recite the Vedas; then comes the principal meal followed by a period of rest, including the keeping of a solemn silence. At sunset he should bathe in oil and then again resort to the temple till 9 p.m.

Nambudiris are polluted by the touch of all castes below them, and by the approach of all lower than Nayars. A man of lower caste should uncover to the waist as a token of respect when approaching a Nambudiri, and must use special terms of respect when referring to anything belonging to him, while he debases everything of his own. As a class the Nambudiris may be described as less affected than any other

[1] See p. 380.

caste, except the very lowest, by Western influences of whatever nature. One Nambudiri is known to have accepted a clerical post in Government service; a good many are *Adhigaris* (village headmen); and one member of the caste possesses a Tile-works and is partner in a Cotton-mill. The bicycle now claims several votaries among the caste and photography at least one other. But these are exceptions, and exceptions which unimportant as they may seem to any one unacquainted with the remarkable conservatism of the caste, would certainly have caused considerable surprise to the author of the first "Malabar Manual." It may be indeed that they are the first indications of a ferment which will in another generation or two leaven the whole lump; but the Nambudiri, affluent and influential, lord of numberless broad acres, exercising in some cases much dreaded powers of social interdict or excommunication, courted by the flower of Nayar womanhood and reverenced as nothing less than divine, is secure from those pricks of necessity, which spur less (or more) favoured classes to progress.

Pattars and Embrandiris.

In addition to the Nambudiris, who may be termed "indigenous" though not, of course, in the sense in which the epithet applies to the low "aboriginal" castes, there are two classes of Brahmans who, though domiciled since pre-historic times in Malabar, are quite distinct in race, customs, and appearance from the Nambudiris and are looked down upon by them, as inferiors and foreigners. These are Pattars and Embrandiris; the former being immigrants from the East Coast with their headquarters at Palghat, while the latter are of Canarese or Tulu origin. The Pattars present no peculiarities distinguishing them from the ordinary East Coast Brahmans. Like the latter they engage in trade and business, and form a large proportion of the official, legal, and scholastic classes. With the exception of one class known as Chozhiya or Arya Pattars, they wear their *kudumi* (top knot) on the back of the head, in the East Coast fashion, and not on the top and hanging over the forehead, as is done by the genuine Malayali castes. They also live as a general rule in regular streets or *gramams*, on the East Coast plan. Few Pattars, except in the Palghat taluk, are large land-owners. As a class they have embraced modern educational facilities, eagerly, so far as they subserved their material prospects. Embrandiris are a peculiarly backward community, judged by Western standards; and are almost entirely engaged in priestly occupations. They sometimes usurp the title of Nambudiri. They are divided into six *desams*. Both Pattars and Embrandiris, but especially the latter, have adopted the custom of contracting *sambandhams* with Nayar women; but *sambandham* with the foreign Brahmans is not considered to be so respectable or desirable

CHAP. III. BRAHMANS.

as with Nambudiris, and except in the Palghat taluk (where the Nambudiri is rare) they are not allowed to consort with the women of aristocratic families.

Nambudiri subdivisions.

There are various subdivisions among Nambudiris ; but in the majority of cases at all events, they cannot be regarded as sub-castes, since marriage between them is not prohibited.

Tamburakkal.

The first of these is usually said to be the Tamburakkals ; but this appears to be a title merely, and not the name of a genuine subdivision, any more than Dukes are a subdivision of Englishmen from an ethnographic or anthropological point of view. There were originally two families with the title, but only one now remains, that of the Azhuvancheri Tamburakkal of Athavanad in Ponnani taluk. Such is the sanctity attached to this dignitary that the Maharajah of Travancore has to invite him once in six years to visit his court, and there performs *sashtanga namaskaram* (obeisance by touching the ground with six parts of the body, expressive of the utmost reverence) before him.

Adhyans.

Properly speaking the Tamburakkal is only the first of the Adhyans who form the highest class among Nambudiris. These have the title of Nambudiripad, the syllable *pad* being an honorific addition found in many other titles, such as Bhattatiripad, Velliichapad, etc. The title is usurped, it is true, by many who have no valid claim to it ; but this is merely another instance of what may be observed on all hands in Malabar at present. They are known as Ashtagrihattil Adhyanmar, or Adhyans of the eight *griham* or houses ; but it is not quite clear what the eight *houses* are or in what sense they are houses. According to one list the *grihams* are simply eight important Nambudiri *tarwads*, while the names given in another list are not those of *tarwads* or even of exogamous divisions.[1] The Adhyans are sometimes contrasted with the Asyans. The former are considered to be so holy that they are absolved from the necessity of observing two of the stages in the Brahman's life prescribed by the Vedas, namely, *Vanaprastha* (or dwelling in the jungle) and *Sanyasa* (or renunciation of all secular interest and occupations) ; a dispensation, which is somewhat superfluous in the present, whatever may have been its value in the past. They are also considered to have reached a stage at which *Yagams* (sacrifices) are unnecessary, and so never perform them. Asyans on the other hand do perform *Yagams*. Some Adhyans are *Tantris*, whose business it is to teach and to resolve difficulties connected with ritual. The position of *Tantri* is hereditary : but not all *Tantris* are Adhyans.

---

[1] The eight chief families or Ashtagrihattil Adhyans were Kalakkandam, Mathur, Mezhathur and Kulukkallur (in British Malabar) and Chemmangad, Vellangallur, Pazhur and Muringoth (in Travancore and Cochin). The various Adhyan *illams* scattered over Kerala are claimed to be the descendents of these eight *grihams*,

Visishta Nambudiris.

The next class are known as Visishta ('remarkable' or distinguished') Nambudiris. They are subdivided into Agni-hotris and Bhattatiris. The former perform the great *Yagams*, namely, *Adhanam* or Agnyadhana conferring the title of Akkittiripad, *Somayaga* conferring the title of Somayajipad, or Somattiripad, and *Agnichayanayaga* conferring the title of Adittiripad. The Bhattatiris are prohibited from performing *yagams*. Their business is to study philosophy, logic, etc. To this class belong the two heads or Presidents of Vedic Colleges (one in British Malabar at Tirunavayi, the other at Trichur in Cochin State), called Vadhyans; the six Vaidigans (one only is in British Malabar, Cherumukku Vaidigan in Walluvanad), or expounders of caste-law; and the six Smartas, whose duty it is to preside at the caste-tribunals or *Smarta vicharam*.

Samanya Nambudiris.

The next subdivision is termed Samanya or 'ordinary' Nambudiris, who are the Nambudiri proletariat. They are not entitled to perform *Yagams*, but they study the Vedas, and perform the duties of priests (*shantikaran*). Some are *Tantris*.

Jathimatrakar.

Next come the Jathimatrakar, or as it were, 'bare' Nambudiris. Amongst these are the Ashtavaidyans or eight families of hereditary physicians, considered as degraded because as surgeons they may have to shed blood, whose caste title is Mussad or Nambi (both these titles are used by a confusing variety of different classes); the Sastrangakars, who are said to be Brahmans who originally engaged in Military service and whose traditional occupation is a performance called *Yatrakali* consisting of songs and sword play;[1] and the Gramani Nambudiris who are said to have been degraded by undertaking the duty of administering the gramams. These are *Ottillattavar*, that is, they are not allowed to recite the Vedas, as opposed to the *Ottullavar*, those who are permitted to do so.

Sapthas and Papis.

Other classes of *Ottillattavar* are Sapthas or Sapagrastans whose degradation is due to their want of faith in Parasurama's power and impious attempt to test it; and Papis (sinners), including Urile-parisha Mussads who accepted gifts of land from Parasurama, and agreed to bear the sin which he had contracted by his massacres of the Kshattriyas, the Nambudiris of Panniyur Gramam, who are said to have been degraded on account of a sacrilegious act performed to a *Varaha murti*, or image of the Boar-incarnation of Vishnu, and those of Payyanur who are remarkable as following *marumakkattayam*.

Elayads and Mussads.

The Elayads are quasi-Brahmanical class of South Malabar, who act as *purohits* (priests) to Samantans and Nayars. It is sometimes said that Elayads are the lowest of the Brahmans, as

---

[1] An account of this will be found at p. 297 of the Travancore Census report of 1901.

CHAP. III. BRAHMANS.

the highest of the Ambalavasis are Muttads or Mussads. The names mean "youngest' and 'eldest,' respectively. The Mussads in question are not to be confused with the Urileparisha Mussads or with the Ashtavaidyans, already referred to. They appear to be identical with the caste called Agapothuval ('inside Pothuval' as distinguished from Purapothuval or 'outside Pothuval') in North Malabar. They are said to be the descendants of a Sivadwija Brahman man, and a pure Brahman girl to some extent a *prathiloma* union (*i.e.*, one violating the rule of hypergamy). According to another account, they lost status by eating rice offered to Siva, a practice prohibited by one of the *Anacharams*, or peculiar rules of conduct, obtaining in Malabar. They perform various duties in temples, their traditional duty being to escort the idol when it is carried in procession (*erunellikal*) on an arrangement called a (*tadambu*) a sort of wooden shield with a small shelf in the centre on which a miniature idol (*vigraham*) is placed. The Muttad's womenfolk have the title Manayamma.

Karuga Mussads and Kavil Mussads, or Pidarans.

There are at least two other classes bearing the title of Mussad. One class is known as Karuga Mussads in South Malabar. They wear the *punul*, and their exact position is disputed. The name is derived from *karuga*, a kind of grass used in ceremonies; and possibly they correspond to the Karuga Nambudiris in North Malabar who cook rice for *Sraddhas* and other ceremonies of Sudras, and are also called Nambidis.[1] The others are known as Tiruvalayanad or Kavil Mussads, and are a class of Ambalavasis. They appear to be identical with the class called Pidarans. They wear the *punul* but perform *puja* in Badrakali temples,[2] an incident of which is the shedding of blood and the use of intoxicating liquor. One class of Pidarans, however, wear no *punul* and cannot perform actual *puja*, but attend to miscellaneous matters connected therewith (*kazhagam*).

The Adigals are a similar class of Bhadrakali priests, who wear the *punul*; but they are said not to use liquor or flesh in their worship.

ANTARALA JATHI. Ambalavasis.

We have now reached the Ambalavasi or temple servant class, though no hard-and-fast boundary line can be drawn between them and the Brahmans or quasi-Brahmans. For convenience the remaining castes falling under this category will be mentioned before passing to the so-called Kshattriyas and Samantans, though the latter are higher both in the caste hierarchy and in the social scale. Speaking generally the Ambalavasis differ from the Brahmans in not wearing the *punul* and in observing pollution for 12 days instead of 10.

---

[1] The title Nambidi is also borne by a few military families (see Kshattriya); and by some Ambalavasis in the parts of Palghat which border on Cochin State.

[2] An account of a festival in such a temple will be found in Madras Government Museum Bulletin, Vol. III, No. 3, p. 263, *et seq.*

CHAP. III. ANTARALA JATHI

Pushpagans.

Amongst these may first be mentioned a group of castes between whom there seems to be little difference except in name, in fact some of the following are probably alternative titles for identical castes. These are Pushpagans (derived from *pushpam* a flower), Pu-Nambis (*pu*, flower), Nambissans, Pattarunnis or Unnis, and their traditional occupation is chiefly to provide flower garlands for the temples. The houses of some at least of these classes are known as *pu-madam* which like the class-names themselves contain obvious references to their duties. The women-folk of this class, known as Pushpinis, or Brahminis have to officiate at the *tali kettu* ceremony of Nayar girls. The traditional account of the origin of these classes traces their descent from a Brahman ancestress; their comparative degradation being variously ascribed to ceremonial impurity in her, or to a doubt as to her virtue. Apparently they follow *makkattayam* in some places and *marumakkattayam* in others; while, though their marriage ceremonies are similar to those of Brahmans, their widows are allowed to contract *sambandhams* either with Brahmans or with fellow caste men. They wear the *punul*, and observe ten days' pollution.

Chakkiyars.

Chakkiyars or Slaghyar-vakuvar are a caste following *makkattayam*, and wearing the *punul*. They are recruited from girls born to a Nambudiri woman found guilty of adultery, after the date at which such adultery is found to have commenced, and boys of similar origin, who have been already invested with the sacred thread. Boys who have not been invested with the *punul* when their mother is declared an adulteress, join the class known as Chakkiyar Nambiyars, who follow *marumakkattayam* and do not wear the thread. The girls join either caste indifferently. The women of the Chakkiyar caste are called Illottammas. The traditional occupation of the Chakkiyar is the delivery of a sort of combined recitation of, and commentary on, passages from the Puranas and Ittihasas, which performance is known as *Chakkiyarkuttu*.[1] It is interspersed with topical allusions to current events characterised, it is said, by a lively wit, and with criticisms of members of the audience, distinguished by a broadly personal tone. The Chakkiyar Nambiyar accompanies the performance on a curious sort of jar-shaped metal drum called *milavu*, while a female of the last-named caste (named Nangiyar) beats time with a cymbal. Chakkiyars may marry Nangiyars, but Chakkiyar Nambiyars may not marry Illottammamar.

Tiyyattu Nambiyar.

Tiyyattu Nambiars or Teyattunnis are a threaded caste who follow *makkattayam* as a rule, but apparently also follow *marumakkattayam* in some places. As in the case of Nambudiris the eldest son contracts a regular marriage with a woman

[1] A full account of such a performance will be found at pp. 261 and 262 of the Travancore Census report for 1901.

CHAP. III. ANTARALA JATHI

of his own caste, while the others contract *sambandhams* with Nayar girls, who are in this case of the lower subdivisions of Nayar (in South Malabar below Sudra Nayars). Polygamy is permitted and widow re-marriage prohibited. Their womenfolk are called *marumagalammar*. The occupation of this caste is the performance of a ceremony in Ayappan temples, in which they paint an image of the goddess on the ground and sing songs in her praise sitting before it. This is called *Teyattam*.

We now pass to the unthreaded classes, and from classes with a pollution period of 10 to those whose period is 12 days.

Pura-pothuvals.

Aga-pothuvals have already been referred to. Purapothuvals are of two classes Chenda-pothuvals, or drum-pothuvals, and Malapothuvals or garland-pothuvals, the names of course referring to the nature of the service which they have to render in the temple. The Chenda-pothuvals would appear to be closely connected with the Marars or Marayars who are also drummers. Mala-pothuvals follow *marumakkattayam*, their women having *sambandham* either with men of their own caste or with Brahmans, while the men can have *sambandham* in their own caste or with Nayar women of any of the subdivisions below Kiriyattil. Their women are called Pothuvarassiar or Pothuvattimar.

Pisharodis.

Pisharodis are a class of temple servants not wearing the *punul*. Their traditional occupation is the provision of flowers for the temple services. Some of them are now large land-owners of considerable wealth and influence. The traditional etymology of their name refers it to a Sannyasi novice, who deterred by the prospects of the hardship of life on which he was about to enter, ran away (*odi*) at the last moment, after he had been divested of the *punul*, but before he had performed the final ceremony of plunging thrice in a tank and of plucking out, one at each plunge, the last three hairs of his *kudumi* (the rest of which had been shaved off). But the termination "odi" is found in other caste titles such as Adiyodi and Vallodi; and the definition is obviously fanciful, while it does not explain the meaning of "Pishar." It is noticeable, however, that the burial-rites of this caste resemble those of Sannyasis, the body being buried in a sitting position and the grave filled with salt and paddy. And as in the case of Sannyasis, regular *Sraddhas* are not considered essential to the salvation of the departed.

Variyar.

The Variyars are a caste whose traditional duty is to sweep the temple precincts (*varuga*). At the present day some members of the caste are important land-owners or petty chieftains, occupying a very high social position. They generally follow the *marumakkattayam* principle: but they have also a form of marriage, called *kudivekkal*, similar to the Brahman *sarvasvadhanam*, by which the wife is adopted as a member of family into which she marries, and her children also belong to it. The Variyars' names and ceremonies indicate Sivaite proclivities, just as those of the Pisharodi are tinged with Vishnavism. His house is called a *Variyam* and his women-folk Varassiars. The Travancore Census Report for 1901 mentions eight subdivisions among Variyars, but these do not appear to exist in British Malabar. This class is perhaps the most progressive among the Ambalavasis, some of its members having received a Western education and entered the learned professions.

Marars and Marayans.

The Marars or Marayans are a caste whose exact position it is difficult to determine. It would appear that there are two subdivisions, or it may be separate castes. The highest subdivision Marars (or Marayars) are drummers, who beat a kind of a drum called *pani* in temples. In South Malabar they are either identical, or wish to identify themselves, with the Chenda-Pothuvals. The second subdivision, Marayans, who are found mainly, if not solely in North Malabar, have to perform certain duties, such as shaving, in connection with the funeral rites of Nayars and Brahmans, and seem to correspond with the Attikurrissi Nayars of South Malabar. One native authority specified no less than seven classes of Marayans in Chirakkal taluk none of which intermarry. They are generally speaking a backward class, but a few have entered Government service. Their period of pollution is 15 days, which seems to indicate that they properly belong to the Sudra rather than to the Ambalavasi caste. They follow the *makkattayam* family system.

Teyyambadi Kurup and Karo-Panikkar.

Here may also be mentioned as being temple servants, though not Ambalavasis in the generally accepted sense of the term, the *marumakkattayam* castes known as Teyyambadi or Teyyambadi Kurup, and Karo-Panikkar. The former appear to be peculiar to North Malabar ; while the latter is a very small caste in South Malabar ; in fact the member of it examined said that there was only one family of his castemen. The occupation of the Teyyambadi is the performance of a dance in Bhagavathi Temples, and also of a song called *Naga-pattu* (song in honour of serpents) in private houses which is supposed to be effective in procuring off-spring. The Karo-Panikkar is said to be descended from the union of Vettakoru-magan (the God of Hunting) and a Kiriyattil Nayar woman. His occupation is to act as Vellichapad, or oracle, in temples dedicated to his divine ancestor. His period of pollution is fifteen days.

KSHATTRIAS AND RULING CLASSES.

A few of the princely families of Malabar claim to be pure Kshattriyas ; but it is clear that, if the expression Kshattriya is to have any ethnological signification, it cannot be applied with any appropriateness to a class who practise hypergamy,

CHAP. III. ANTARALA JATHI.

and are therefore admittedly of hybrid race. Racially no doubt Kshattriyas and Samantans were originally Nayars ; and now indeed it is difficult to see what material difference in blood there can be between Nambudiris themselves and those lower castes, whether styling themselves Nayar, Samantan or Kshattriya, who follow the *marumakkattayam* family law and restrict their women folk to Nambudiri consorts. Among those who claim to be Kshattriyas are the Rajas of Beypore, Parappanad, Kottayam, Kurumbranad and Chirakkal. The Venganad Nambidi of Kollengod, who is of Samantan extraction, and enjoys several special privileges claims to be a Kshattriya by adoption ; and the Punnattur Nambidi, who wears the *punul* and observes ten days' pollution, and is traditionally a military chief, should presumably be included in the same class.

Samantan.

Samantan is the generic name of the group of castes forming the aristocracy of Malabar, and it includes the following divisions ; Nambiyar, Unnitiri, Adiyodi, all belonging to North Malabar ; and Nedungudi, Vallodi, Eradi and Tirumulpad, all belonging to South Malabar. There are also Nayars with the title of Nambiyar and Adiyodi. Nedungadi, Vallodi and Eradi are territorial names applied to the Samantans indigenous to Ernad, Walavanad and Nedunganad respectively ; or perhaps it may be more correct to say that the tracts in question take their names from the ruling classes who formerly bore sway there. Eradi is the caste to which belongs the Zamorin Raja of Calicut. It is also the name of a section of Kiriyattil Nayars. The Raja of Walavanad is a Vallodi. Tirumalpad is the title of a class of Samantans to which belong a number of petty chieftains, such as the Karnamulpad of Manjeri and the Tirumulpad of Nilambur in Ernad. The ladies of this class are called Kolpads or Koilammahs. Many Nambiyars in North Malabar claim to belong to the Samantan caste, but there is at least reason to suppose that they are properly Nayars and that the claim to the higher rank is of recent date. That such recruitment is going on is indicated by the difference between the number of persons returned as Samantans in the censuses of 1901 and 1891 (4,351 and 1,225, respectively), which is far above the normal percentage of increase of population.

Kshattriyas wear the *punul* ; Samantans as a rule do not. Most Kshattriyas eat with Brahmans and have a pollution period of 11 nights, indicating that their position in the caste hierarchy lies between the Brahmans with 10 days and the Ambalavasis proper with 12. Samantans as a rule observe fifteen days' pollution and may not eat with Brahmans. Both follow *marumakkattayam*, and their women as a rule have *sambandham* only with Brahmans or Kshattriyas. Those,

CHAP. III.

ANTARALA JATHI

who belong to the old "Royal" families, are styled Raja[1] or Tamburan (lord), their ladies Tamburattis, and their house *kovilagams* or palaces. Some Samantans have the caste titles of *Kartavu* and *Kaimal.* But it does not appear that there are really any material differences* between the various classes of Samantans other than purely social differences due to their relative wealth and influence.

NAYARS.

We now come to the Nayars, the most characteristic, perhaps, though not the most numerous of the communities in Malabar. The term in its widest sense includes a very large number of castes, which are now quite distinct; in fact all between the Ambalavasis on the one hand and the polluting castes on the other (excluding of course foreigners, *i.e.*, emigrants of comparative recent date, who are outside the Malabar system). Thus at the lower end of the scale we shall find castes whose traditional occupations are by no means military, though there is little doubt that the Nayars proper were primarily a military class, probably a sort of yeoman militia, who devoted themselves to agriculture in time of peace.

According to the Brahman tradition, the Nayar caste is the result of union between the Nambudiris with Deva, Gandharva and Rakshasa women introduced by Parasurama; and this tradition embodies the undoubted fact that the caste by its practice of hypergamy has had a very large infusion of Aryan blood. In origin the Nayars were probably a race of Dravidian immigrants, who were amongst the first invaders of Malabar, and, as conquerors assumed the position of the governing and land-owning class; and in the ethnological sense the term may be used to include the Samantan and Kshattriya castes. The large admixture of Aryan blood combined with the physical peculiarities of the country would go far to explain the very marked difference between the Nayar of the present day, and what may be considered the corresponding Dravidian races in the rest of the Presidency. The Nayars as a class are the best educated and most advanced of the communities in Malabar (excepting perhaps the Pattar Brahmans, who are not strictly a Malayalam class); and are intellectually the equals of the Brahmans of the East Coast. Many of them have risen to the highest posts in Government service, and the caste has supplied many of the leading men of the learned professions.

High caste Nayars.

[1] The distinction of Raja, as a title, is only recognised by Government as belonging to the heads of the old ruling families, the Zamorin, the Valiya Rajas of Chirakkal, Kadattanad, Kottayam, Kurumbranad, Parappanad, Beypore, Walavanad and Palghat, and the Eralpad or second member of the Zamorin's family. The recognised title of the others is Tamburan, though Raja is in many cases their family name. The present Venganad Valiya Nambidi of Kollengod has the personal title of Raja.

CHAP. III. NAYARS.

The Nayars proper or high caste Nayars, are the 'proud', 'martial' class so often described by early travellers. The best early description by a European is perhaps that of Duarte Barbosa.

"The Nairs are the gentry and have no other duty than to carry on war, and they continually carry their arms with them, which are swords, bows, arrows, buklers, and lances. They all live with the kings and some of them with other lords, relations of the kings, and lords of the country, and with the salaried governors; and with one another. They are very smart men, and much taken up with their nobility . . . These Nairs, besides being all of noble decent, have to be armed as knights by the hand of the king or lord with whom they live, and until they have been so equipped they cannot bear arms nor call themselves Nairs . . . In general when they are seven years of age they are immediately sent to school to learn all manner of feats of agility and gymnastics for the use of their weapons. First they learn to dance and then to tumble and for that purpose they render supple all their limbs from their childhood, so that they can bend them in any direction . . . These Nairs live outside the towns separate from other people on their estates which are fenced in. When thy go anywhere they shout to the peasants, that they may get out of the way where they have to pass; and the peasants do so, and if they did not do it, the Nayars might kill them without penalty. And if a peasant were by misfortune to touch a Nayar lady, her relations would immediately kill her and likewise the man that touched her and all his relations. This, they say, is done to avoid all opportunity of mixing the blood with that of the peasants . . . . These show much respect to their mothers and their elder sisters, whom they treat as mothers . . . They are very clean and well dressed women and they hold it in great honour to know how to please men. They have a belief amongst them that the woman who dies a virgin does not go to paradise.[1]"

Traces of their martial spirit survive, as will be noticed, in many of their titles, in the *Kalaris* (a sort of combined private chapel and gymnasium or fencing school) still attached to some of their houses, in their games, in the armed retinues of their chief men and in the sword play which is the invariable accompaniment of their more elaborate ceremonies; but they are now-a-days for the most part landowners and professional men. They follow the *marumakkattayam* family system; most of the women can enter into *sambandham* only with equal or higher castes or subdivisions, while in some of the subdivisions the men can form *sambandham* only with women of their own class. The North Malabar subdivisions rank as a rule higher than the corresponding subdivision in South Malabar, and hence a North Malabar Nayar woman cannot have *sambandham* with a South Malabar man; South Malabar Nayar women again seldom have *sambandham* with North

[1] *The Coasts of East Africa and Malabar*. (Hakluyt Society), Page 124.

Malabar men, as it is the rule for the wife in North Malabar to go to the husband's house and South Malabar Nayar women are prohibited from crossing the Korapuzha river, which is the dividing line. Their pollution period is fifteen days.

Kiriyam or Kiriyattil Nayars.

In South Malabar the highest class is that known as Kiriyam or Kiriyattil. The word is by some derived from the Sanskrit *Griham*, a house, but this does not seem very convincing. Kiriyam Nayars can cook for all others, and it is to this class that most of the old Naduvazhis and Deshavazhis, or rulers of '*nads*' and '*desams*', and most of the present *stanis* or titled persons belong. The nature of *stanams* has already been explained in treating of the *marumakkattayam* system (p. 96). In the case of Nayars the head of one of the great families will be styled the Muppil or Mutta (edler) or Valiya (great) Nayar preceded by the name of the place where he has his seat, as for instance the Mannarghat Muppil Nayar ; in some cases there is a second *stanam* of Elaya (or younger) Nayar, to which the second member of the family is entitled. Sometimes a *stanam* goes in turn to the eldest member of each of a group of *tarwads*, as in the case of the Nedunganad Pada Nayar (literally, Nedunganad General), an old military chieftain in Nedunganad. In one case the *stanam* name is *Acchan* (which is also the title of the Palghat Rajas). *Stanis* usually have a hereditary ceremonial personal name in addition to their title. The womenfolk of these aristocratic families are called Nettiyars.

Most Kiriyattil Nayars affix to their names the simple title Nayar ; but some use the titles Panikkar, Kurup and Nambiyar (the last two are not common in South Malabar). The two titles first mentioned have a reference to the profession of arms, and many families bearing these titles still maintain their *Kalari*. The title Menon, cheifly used by the three classes of Agattu and Purattu Charna and Sudra Nayars, should strictly speaking be conferred by the Zamorin or some other feudal lord ; but is now usurped at random. The appellation Nayar itself is probably in origin a title similarly conferred. There are a few other personal or family titles of rare occurrence such as Atti Nayar, Perimbra Nayar (feminine Amma Perimbrassiar), Arimbra Nayar, Karumiyar and Kuruvayil Nayar. Members of the lower castes term Nayars *Tamburan* or *Kammal*.

Agattu Charna and Purattu Charna Nayars.

The next class of Nayars in South Malabar is known as Charna or Charnavar, divided into Agattu Charnavar and Purattu Charnavar "inside" and "outside retainers" respectively. There are two explanations of the terms. According to one the Purattu Charnavar are the armed retainers of the various chieftains, while the Agattu Charnavar are the body and house servants. According to the other explanation the distinction refers to their position at *Yagams* (sacrifices)

CHAP. III. NAYARS.

during which it is said that various duties inside the *Yagayasala* or sacrificial *pandal* are to be performed by the Agattu Charna Nayars, while the Purattu Charna remain on guard outside. However this may be, the Purattu Charna are certainly considered to rank higher in the social scale. The ten thousand retainers, or *Purattu Charnavar*, of the Zamorin in Calicut taluk, including such families as the Manniledat Nayars, rank as Kiriyattil Nayars; the men form *sambandhams* with women of South Malabar Kiriyattil families and the women consort with Nambudiris or their own caste.

Sudra Nayars.

The last class of the high caste Nayars are known in South Malabar as Sudra Nayars. These are *par excellence* the attendants and retainers of the Nambudiris, as the Charnavar are those of the non-Brahman chieftain; and in consequence there is some dispute between these two classes as to precedence. Every Nambudiri woman must always be accompanied when out of doors by a maid-servant or *dasi*, who should belong to the Sudra Nayar class; and a woman of the class is indispensable for her various ceremonies. The classes of Charnavar and Sudras seem to correspond with those which are elsewhere termed Swarubakkar (from *swarubam*, a dignified term for a princely house) and Illakkar (from *Illam*, a Nambudiri dwelling).

Muttans.

Next come some castes most likely of foreign origin. This is certainly true of the Muttans, who are found only in the Palghat taluk and in the parts of Walavanad bordering on it, a part of the country where there is a large admixture of Tamils in the population. They now are advancing a claim to be Vaisyas, and some of them have adopted the title Gupta which is proper to that caste, while a few have the title Ezhutacchan. Some Muttans in Palghat are called Mannadiars, a title also apparently borne by some Taragans. The Muttans follow *makkattayam* and do not enter into the loose connections known as *sambandhams*; their women are called Chettichiars, clearly indicating their eastern origin; and their period of pollution is ten days, according to which test they would rank as high caste. On the other hand they may eat meat and drink liquor. Their purificatory ceremonies are performed by a class known as Chorttavans (literally, sprinklers), who are said to be identical with Kulangara Nayars, and not by Attikurrissi Nayars as is the case with Nambudiris, Ambalavasis and Nayars. There is considerable antagonism between the Palghat and Walavanad sections of the caste.

Taragans.

Another caste of traders which has now been practically incorporated in the Nayar body is the class known as Taragans (literally, brokers) found in Palghat and Walavanad, some of whom have considerable wealth and high social position. The Taragans of Angadippuram and the surrounding neighbourhood claim to be immigrants from Travancore, and to be descendants of Ettuvittil Pillamar of Quilon, who are high caste Nayars. They can marry Kiriyattil women, and their women occasionally have *sambandham* with Samantan Rajas. The Palghat Taragans on the other hand can marry only in their caste.[1]

Ravaris.

Vyabari or Ravari Nayars who are found further north are by some identified with the Taragans, and they also are according to tradition immigrants from Travancore. Their social position is somewhat lower than that of the Taragans; their men marry only within the caste, but their women have *sambandham* with Kiriyattil Nayars.

Ulumbans.

Another endogamous sub-caste of foreign origin is the Ulumbans or cowherds. According to one tradition they were originally immigrants from Dvaraka (Guzerat). Their original occupation still survives in the privileges of supplying ghee for the *abhishegam* or libation at the great annual festival at the jungle shrine of Kottiyur in Manatanna amsam, Kottayam taluk, and of supplying buttermilk to the Tiruvangad temple at Tellicherry, which are exercised by families of this caste; and in the general privilege of offering milk in any temple without previous ablution.

North Malabar Nayars.

In North Malabar a still more complicated and varied system obtains amongst the high caste Nayars. There are exogamous subdivisions (perhaps corresponding to original *tarwads*) called *kulams*, and these are grouped to form the sub-caste which are usually endogamous. It is quite impossible to attempt a complete account of the scheme, but to give some idea of its nature one example may be taken, and dealt with in some detail; and for this purpose the portion of Kurumbranad known as Payyanad will serve. This is the country between the Kottapuzha and Korapuzha rivers, and is said to have been given by a Raja of Kurumbranad to a certain Ambadi Kovilagam Tamburatti (the *stanam* or title of the senior lady of the Zamorin Raja's family). In this tract or *nad* there were originally six *stanis* or chieftains, who ruled, under the Raja, with the assistance, or subject to the constitutional control, of four assemblies of Nayars called *kuttams*. Each *kuttam* had its hereditary president. In this tract there are seven groups of *kulams*. The highest includes 12 *kulams*, Vengalat, Pattillat, Viyyur, Nelliot, Atunkudi, Amayangalat, Nelloli, Nilancheri, Rendillat, Pulliyani, Orkatteri and Venmeri. Of these the Pattillat and Rendillat ("members of the ten" and "members of the two *illams*" or houses) affix the title Adiyodi to their names, the last three affix the title Nambiyar and the rest affix Nayar. Of the six *stanis* already mentioned, three with the title of Adiyodi belong to the Vengalat

Payyanad.

[1] In Buchanan's time they were a despised class; see *Journey*, II, 409.

CHAP. III. NAYARS.

kulam, while two of the presidents of *kuttams* belonged to the Pattillat *kulam*. The younger members of the *stani* houses are called *Kidavu*. It is the duty of women of the Viyyur and Nelliot *kulams* to join in the bridal procession of members of the Vengalat *kulam*, the former carrying lamps and the latter salvers containing flowers ; while the Rendillat Adiyodis furnish cooks to the same class. Pattillat Adiyodis and Orkatteri Nambiyars observe twelve days' pollution ; while all the other *kulams* observe fifteen. The second group consists of six *kulams*, Eravattur, Ara-Eravattur (or "half Eravattur") and Attikodan Nayars, Tonderi Kidavus, Punnan Nambiyars and Menokkis. All these observe fifteen days' pollution. The third group consists of three *kulams*, Taccholi to which the remaining three *stanis* belong, Kotholi and Kuruvattancheri. All affix Nayar to their names, and observe fifteen days' pollution. The fourth group consists of three *kulams*, Peruvanian Nambiyars, Cholladan Nayars and Vennapalan Nayars. All three observe fifteen days' pollution. The name Peruvanian means "great" or "principal oil-man" ; and it is the duty of this caste to present the Kurumbranad Raja with oil on the occasion of his formal installation. The fifth group consists of the three *kulams*, Mannangazhi, Paranchela and Pallikara Nayars, all observing fifteen days' pollution. A member of the first-named class has to place an *amanapalaga* (the traditional seat of Nambudiris and other high castes) for the Kurumbranad Raja to sit on at the time of his installation, while a member of the second has to present him with a cloth on the same occasion. The sixth group consists of four *kiriyams* named Patam, Tulu, Manan and Ottu, respectively, and has the collective name of Ravari. The seventh group consists of six *kulams*, Kandon, Kannankodan, Kotta, Karumba, Kundakollavan and Panakadan Nayars. All observe fifteen days' pollution, and the women of these six *kulams* have certain duties to perform in connection with the purification of women of the Vengalat, Pattillat and Orkatteri *kulams*. Besides these seven groups there are a few other classes without internal subdivisions. One such class is known as Pappini Nayar. A woman of this class takes the part of the Brahmini woman (Nambissan) at the *tali-kettu kalyanam* of girls belonging to the *kulams* included in the third group. Another class called Palattavan take the place of the Attikurissi Nayar at the funeral ceremonies of the same three *kulams*.

Kurumbranad.

The caste system in the portions of Kurumbranad known as Kadattunad and Payyormala is constructed more or less on the same lines as that which has been just described, but there is considerable difference in the details.

Chirakkal and Kottayam.

In Chirakkal and Kottayam, on the other hand, we find two great groups of *kulams*, called Agattu and Purattu Charna.

The Purattu Charna claim to rank, not with the class of the same name in South Malabar, but with the superior Kiriyattil class; and affix to their names the titles Nayar, Nambiyar, Kurup or Adiyodi. The Agattu Charna Nayars are divided into several (in Chirakkal apparently eight) groups, each subdivided into exogamous classes called in this case Illams.

Non-military Nayars.

We now come to classes of a non-military character who rank as Nayars.

Andurans.

Andurans or Kusavans are potters; Ottatu Nayars, tilers (*Ottu* tile); Pallicchans or Parappur Nayars, palanquin-bearers.

Uralis.

Uralis, Ezhuttans, Kolayans, Muvaris and Erumans, who should perhaps all be considered as belonging to the same subcaste under the generic name of Urali, are mostly masons and were originally cow-herds. According to tradition, Uralis are immigrants from the Tulu country; the other four subdivisions are not found in South Malabar.

Chembottis.

The Chembukottis or Chembottis (copper-tappers) are copper-workers whose traditional business is the roofing of the *sri-kovil* or inner shrine of the temple with that metal. The latter are said to have originally formed part of the Kammalan or artisan community. When the great temple at Taliparamba was completed it was purified on a scale of unprecedented grandeur, no less than 1,000 Brahmans being employed. What was their dismay when the ceremony was well forward, to see a Chembotti coming from the *Sri Kovil*, where he had been putting finishing touches to the roof. This appeared to involve a recommencement of the whole tedious and costly ritual; and the Brahmans gave vent to their feelings of despair, when a vision from heaven reassured them. And thereafter the Chembottis have been raised in the social scale and are not regarded as a polluting caste.

Vattekadan Nayars.

Vattekadan or Chakkingal Nayars (*Chakku*, oil press) or Vanians are oil millers; and are said to be divided in some parts according as they work their mill by hand or by bullocks, and in others into the white (Vellutatu), and black (Karuttatu) subdivisions.[1]

Attikurissi Nayars.

Attikurrissi Nayars (*Asti*, human bones) or Chittigans have to perform certain purificatory ceremonies in connection with funerals and so forth for Nambudiris, Ambalavasis and Nayars. Some of them are also barbers.

Kulangara Nayars.

Kulangara Nayars are an endogamous caste who perform *puja* in temples of Bhagavathi, Ayappan, Sastavu, and certain minor deities such as Vettekkorumagan, Ariyambi, and Andimahagalan. They also officiate at the purificatory ceremonies of Taragans. Kallattakurups play a curious sort of shawm called Nandurini on such occasions and on others.

---

[1] *Madras Museum Bulletin*, Vol. III, No. 3, p. 203.

CHAP. III. NAYARS.

Edacheri Nayars are cowkeepers.

These castes all follow *marumakattayam*, and are entirely or almost entirely endogamous.

Low caste Nayars.

Below these come four classes which are considered as polluting other Nayars by touch, and may therefore be grouped together as low-caste Nayars. These are Vellutedans (those who make white) or Vannattans who are washermen; Vilakkataravans or barbers; Kadupattans who have the title of Ezhutacchan or "writing master," their ordinary occupation being that of school-masters or tutors; and Chaliyans or Teruvans (hut or street dwellers) who are weavers. These castes do not affix the title "Nayar" to their name (except perhaps some Vellutedans).

Vellutedans.

Vellutedans follow *marumakkattayam*. They follow Nayar customs generally speaking, but the place of the Attikurrissi is taken in their ceremonies by a subdivision of their own caste called Pothuvans, Talikkundavars or Kavuthiyans, who are also the caste barbers and are looked on as somewhat lower than the rest of the caste. The *tali* in their *tali-kettu kalyanam* is tied by a member of their own caste. Amongst the North Malabar Vannattans there are 8 exogamous *illams* Kolankada, Malakulangara, Malot, Mundayad, Chelora, and Trichambaram, being the names of six. They are divided in Ernad and possibly elsewhere into four subdivisions called Veluttedans proper or Kshettra Veluttedan, Vannattan, Mundapadan and Irankolli, the first named being endogamous and regarded as higher than the other three.

Vilakkataravans.

Vilakkataravans (*i.e.*, *tala velakkunnavan* or he who cleans the head ?) also follow Nayar customs except in the points just indicated. They are divided in North Malabar into Navithan, or Naviyan and Valinchian. They follow *makkattayam* in the south; while in the north the Navithans follow *makkattayam* and the Valinchians *marumakkattayam*. The Navithans are divided into exogamous illams the number of which has not been ascertained. The Valinchians are divided into 8 *illams*, which bear the same names as the Vannattan *illams*.

Kaduppattans.

Kaduppattans according to the traditional account of their origin were Pattars (Brahmans) of Kadu *gramam* and became degraded owing to their supporting the introduction of Buddhism. They follow *makkattayam*.

Chaliyans.

Chaliyans are almost certainly a class of immigrants from the East coast. They live in regular streets, a circumstance strongly supporting this view. The traditional account is to the same effect. It is said that they were originally of a high caste, and were imported by one of the Zamorins who wished to introduce the worship of Ganapathi, to which they are much addicted. The latter's minister, the Mangatt Acchan, who was entrusted with the entertainment of the new arrivals, and was nettled by their fastidiousness and constant complaints about his catering, managed to degrade them in a body by the trick of secretly mixing fish with their food. They do not, like their counterparts on the East coast, wear the thread (a parallel to this will be found later in the case of the artisan classes); but it is noticeable that their priests who belong to their own castes wear it over the right shoulder instead of over the left like the Brahman's *punul*, when performing certain *pujas*. In some parts the place of the regular *punul* is taken by a red scarf or sash worn in the same manner. They are remarkable for being the only caste in Malabar amongst whom any trace of the familiar East coast division into Right-hand and Left-hand factions is to be found. They are so divided; and those belonging to the righthand faction deem themselves polluted by the touch of those belonging to the left-hand sect which is numerically very weak. They are much addicted to devil-dancing, which rite is performed by certain of their numbers called *Komarams* in honour of Bhagavathi and the minor deities Vettekkorumagan and Gulikan (a demon). They appear to follow *makkattayam* in some places and *marumakkattayam* in others. Their pollution period is ten days and their purification is performed by the Talikunnavan (sprinkler), who belongs to a somewhat degraded section of the caste.

Yogi-gurukkals.

The Yogi-gurukkals of North Malabar are a caste which, though low in the social scale, is not regarded as conveying distance pollution. They follow *marumakkattayam*; but both men and women can form *sambandhams* only in their own caste. They perform *sakti puja* in their own houses, to which no one outside the caste is allowed to attend; they also perform it for Nayars and Tiyans. They are celebrated sorcerers and exorcists; and are also school-masters by profession. They are said to bury their dead in a sitting posture, like Sanyasis.

Wynaadan Chettis.

The Wynaadan Chettis are a small caste of cultivators in the Wynaad, who claim to be Sudras, and arein appearance and customs very similar to the Nayars. They are polluted by all castes below Nayars. Their marriage customs seem to be a mixture of East and West coast practices. They follow the *marumakkattayam* system and perform the *tali-kettu kalyanam*; but this is done on the tenth day *after puberty*, and *two talis* have to be tied on the girl, one by her maternal uncle and one by the senior female of her house. They also celebrate a regular marriage ceremony at which a bracelet is put on the bride's right arm, and bride and bridegroom garland each other; while next morning a *kanam* or bride-price has to be paid to the bride's *karnavan*. They are bold *shikaris*, and tiger spearing is a favourite pastime, closely associated with their religion. The tiger is encircled by a wall of netting six feet high which

CHAP. III. NAYARS.

is gradually closed up, and then speared; the carcass is not skinned, but is stretched on a pole and hung up as a sacrifice to their deity.[1]

POLLUTING CASTES.

We have now come to the castes which do not claim to be Sudras, and all of which, at all events in most parts of the country, are regarded as conveying 'distance pollution.' Their number is large and their subdivisions intricate; it is often impossible to say whether a particular class should be considered as a subdivision or as a caste by itself; and whether classes bearing different names, but performing the same functions in different parts of the country, should be treated as belonging to the same caste or not. No attempt will be made to determine in any detail their order of social precedence among themselves. Generally speaking, they follow the *makkattayam* system of inheritance, and many of them practice fraternal polyandry; but most of them perform the *tali kettu kalyanam* ceremony and in North Malabar many of them follow *marumakkattayam*. In their marriage ceremonies there are survivals of the practice of purchasing the bride; and as a rule they bury their dead, though many of them burn the older people. Their religion is more purely animistic than that of the castes above them, and included in their number are the devil-dancers, astrologers, and other representatives of the primitive 'medicine-man.'

Tiyans and Izhuvans.

First may be mentioned the great caste known as Izhuvans in the Palghat taluk, and elsewhere in the Malabar district as Tiyans. They form the most numerous Hindu community in Malabar, and are difficult to place in the social scale, since their status varies widely in different parts of the country. In North Malabar for instance the Tiyans claim to be a caste which does not convey distance pollution at all. There seems little doubt that the Izhuvans and Tiyans are racially the same, though the two communities now disclaim connection. According to tradition they are foreigners, who came from Ceylon; and the tradition is perhaps supported by their names, of which Izhuvan is usually connected with Simhala, the Sanskrit name of Ceylon, while Tiyan is said to be derived from *dwipam* (Mal. *tivu*) the Sanskrit word for "island". The tradition of their immigration is embodied in a well-known story which connects them with the Kammalan, or chief artizan caste. The legend relates that in order to get his washing done properly, one of the early Perumals promised to give his washerman in marriage to a girl of the carpenter class, who had given him some useful hints on the subject; to frustrate his intention, which they considered would degrade them, the Kammalans emigrated in a body to Ceylon, taking with them the razors of the barber caste, and leaving behind only a few of their number to attend to the necessary repairs to the eighteen Talli, or

[1] See *Indian Antiquary*, XXX, p. 400.

head, temples of Kerala. Finally at the request of the Perumal, whom his subjects pressed to terminate the inconvenient situation caused by this pre-historic boycott, the Kammalans returned; but the King of Ceylon sent with them, as a guard, against any possible treachery on the part of the Perumal, a number of his own subjects, who brought the cocoanut tree [1] with them and settled in the country, and became the ancestors of the Izhuvans and Tiyans.

Tiyans follow *marumakkattayam* in the north and *makkattayam* in the south; they are monogamous in the south, except in a few parts of Ponnani where fraternal polyandry is practised. Izhuvans on the other hand follow *makkattayam* and are monogamous, and among them it is very usualfor a man to marry his father's sister's daughter. Izhuvans and Tiyans will not intermarry; and it is opposed to custom for Tiyans of North Malabar to marry Tiyan women of the south, one reason against such a practice being no doubt the difficulties that would ensue in questions of inheritance owing to the different family systems followed by the two communities. North Malabar Tiyans are divided into eight exogamous groups, or *illams* called Koyikkal, Nellikkal, Vanmarikka, Pazhayar, Mankudi, Tenankudi, Padayankudi, and Villakudi. There are also 32 *kiriyams*, four to each *illam*. Among the Izhuvans there are no such subdivisions. The Tiyans consider themselves superior to the Izhuvans, and will not eat rice cooked by them; there are considerable differences between the dress and customs of the two communities, but more than hardly between those of the North and South Malabar Tiyans.

The traditional occupation of both Tiyans and Izhuvans is the planting and tapping of the cocoanut tree, which they are said to have brought with them from their island home; but many of them are now agriculturists, traders, shopkeepers, private servants and clerks, etc. They appear to have enjoyed several privileges in the old social organisation; and to this day their Tandans or hereditary headmen have to give their consent to marriages between artizans, and exercise control over the menial castes of washermen, barbers and the like. The latter function gives them considerable power, since by withholding the service of the Mannatti they can obstruct the purificatory ceremonies of the higher castes. By the end of the eighteenth century many Tiyans on the coast seem to have attained a considerable position as merchants, landowners, etc., and they further improved their position by the services which they rendered to the Company. These good traditions have been maintained; and the Tiyans as a whole are a most progressive community, especially in North Malabar where they form one of the most progressive classes in India. A large number

[1] The word for cocoanut, *tenga* is usually connected with *ten*, south. But the connection seems, to say the least, doubtful.

CHAP. III. POLLUTING CASTES.

of them have risen to the higher posts in the Government service, and many are vakils. Not a few families in North Malabar have in their veins a considerable admixture of European blood, as it used not to be considered that their women lost caste by living with Europeans; and there is no doubt that they have been benefited in physique, personal appearance, morale, and material prosperity by this infusion of Aryan blood, in the same way as the Nayars have been benefited by the relations between their womankind and the Nambudiris. But the custom has now fallen into disfavour with both parties.

Tandans.

The Tandans are a section of South Malabar Tiyans, found in the Ernad and Walavanad taluks, who consider themselves a separate caste. They are a *makkattayam* caste, and commonly practise fraternal polyandry; they will not marry either Tiyans or Izhuvans. The word Tandan is properly a title, and is applied to the headmen of the local caste groups of the Tiyans and Kammalans, who have to perform specified functions at marriages and other ceremonies.

Embron is a title given to certain Tiyans who perform priestly functions.

Mukkuvans.

Another caste, which according to a probably erroneous tradition came originally from Ceylon, is that of the Mukkuvans, a caste of fishermen, following *marumakkattayam* in the north and *makkattayam* in the south. Their traditional occupations also include chunam-making, and manchal-bearing. (A *manchal* is a kind of hammock slung on a pole and carried by four men, two at each end.) In the extreme south of the district, they are called Arayans, a term elsewhere used as a title of their headmen. North of Cannanore there are some fishermen known as Mugavans or Mugayans, who are presumably the same as the Mogayars of South Canara. Another account is that the Mugayans are properly river-fishers, and the Mukkuvans sea-fishers; but the distinction does not seem to hold good in fact.

The Mukkuvans rank below the Tiyans and the artizan classes; and it is creditable to the community that some of its members have recently risen to occupy such offices, as that of sub-magistrate and sub-registrar. The caste has supplied many converts to the ranks of Muhammadanism. In North Malabar the Mukkuvans are divided into four exogamous illams, called Ponillam (*pon*, gold), Chembillam (*chembu*, copper), Karillam, and Kacchillam, and are hence called Nalillakkar, or people of the four illams; while the South Malabar Mukkavans and Arayans have only the three latter *illams*, and are therefore called Munillakkar, people of the three *illams*. There is also a section of the caste called Kavuthiyans, who act as barbers to the others, and are sometimes called Panimagans (work-children). The Nalillakkar are regarded as superior to the Munillakkar and the Kavuthiyans, and exact various signs of respect from them. The three divisions are supposed not to intermarry. The Kavuthiyans, like other barber castes, have special functions to perform in connection with the removal of ceremonial pollution ; and it is interesting to note that sea water is used in the ritual sprinklings for this purpose.

CHAP. III. POLLUTING CASTES.

The old caste organization seems to have persisted to the present day among the Mukkuvans, to an extent which can be paralleled amongst few other castes. They have assemblies (*Rajiams*) of elders called Kadavans, or Kadakkodis, presided over by presidents called Arayans or Karnavans, who settle questions of caste etiquette, and also constitute a divorce court. The position of the Arayans like that of the Kadavans is hereditary. It is said to have been conferred by the different Rajas in their respective territories, with certain insignia, a painted cadjan umbrella, a stick, and a red silk sash. The Arayans are also entitled to the heads of porpoises captured in their jurisdictions ; and to presents of tobacco and *pan supari*, when a girl attains puberty or is married. Their consent is necessary to all regular marriages. The Mukkuvans have their oracles or seers called Ayittans, or Attans ; and when an Arayan dies these select his successor from among his *anundravans*, while under the influence of the divine afflatus, and also choose from among the younger members of the Kadavan families, priests called Manakkans, or Banakkans, to perform *puja* in their temples.

Valluvans.

A small inferior caste of fishermen and boatmen are the Valluvans, who follow *Makkattayam*.

The artizan, menial, and devil dancing castes.

We may next deal with the various artizan castes who with the menial servants, such as barbers, midwives, musicians, etc., occupied a position in the old social organization corresponding to the menials of an East coast village ; and were styled *Cherujanmakar* and entitled to certain hereditary rights and perquisites.

Kammalans.

The most important group of these has the collective name Kammalan, a word that is also used loosely of any artizan. They are divided into five castes, each with its appropriate craft to which it strictly adheres, which are said to owe their origin to the five faces of Visvakarma, the divine architect ; namely, Tattans or goldsmiths ; Perinkollans or blacksmiths ; Musaris or braziers ; Asaris or carpenters ; and Chembottis or copper-smiths. The last named, as has already been mentioned, have now raised themselves to the position of equality with the lower Sudra or non-polluting classes. The position of the four classes of Kammalans proper (*nangu varma*) is quite different from that occupied by their counterparts on the

CHAP. III. POLLUTING CASTES.

East coast, who wear the thread, and claim, on account of their mythical ancestry, equality with, if not superiority to, the very Brahmans.

Each of the four Kammalan castes forms an endogamous community, and each such community is itself divided into exogamous groups called *kiriyams.* The exact number of *kiriyams* is not known; but the names of ten have been recorded, namely, Mangat, Paliya, Velutha, Vazhayil, Nedumbra, Arimbra, Vykol, Chittini, Mezhum and Chinniyam. The same *kiriyams* seem to occur in all the four classes. Except for the purposes of marriage the four classes may be regarded as forming a single caste. They follow the *makkattayam* system of inheritance, and practise fraternal polyandry, the correct, if not the universal practice, being for several brothers to take a single wife between them.

Pathinettans.

Castes closely allied with the four main artizan castes are the Pathinettans, or "eighteen," who are carpenters and are said to be the descendants of the smiths who remained to attend to the repairs to the eighteen Talli temples, when the rest of the community fled to Ceylon, as related in the tradition of the origin of the Tiyans; the Poravannurkarans, also carpenters and apparently an offshoot of the Asari class, found in the Walavanad and Ponnani Taluks; the Puliakodans, another variety of carpenters whose traditional duty it is to construct oil mills; and the Kadacchikollans or cutlers.

Kolla-kurups.

The Kolla-kurups are another allied caste or sub-caste whose exact position it is difficult to define. They combine two professions which at first sight seem strangely incongruous, shampooing or massage, and the construction of the characteristic leather shields of Malabar. But the two arts are intimately connected with the system of combined physical training, as we should now call it, and exercise in arms, which formed the curriculum of the *kalari*, and the title Kurup is proper to castes connected with that institution.

Vil-Kurups.

A similar combination of functions is found in the Vil-Kurups (Bow-Kurups), whose traditional profession was to make bows and arrows and train the youth to use them; and who now shampoo, make umbrellas, and provide bows and arrows for some Nayar ceremonies.

Tol-Kollans.

Other classes closely connected and now not easily distinguishable, though their existence is a striking instance of the minuteness of the sub-divisions of ancient society, are the Kollans or Kurups distinguished by the prefixes Chaya (colour), Palissa (shield), and Tol (leather), all of whom are at present engaged in work in lacquer, wood and leather. Kidaran is a synonym for Tol-Kurup.

These castes all follow *makkattayam*, and practise fraternal polyandry; and they are apparently divided into exogamous *kiriyams*. They are called collectively with other inferior artizan classes the *pathinalu varma*, or fourteen castes.

Vadugans. Of the same social standing as the Kammalans are the Vadugans (northerners), a *makkattayam* caste of foreigners found in Palghat and the adjoining part of Walavanad. They are divided into two exogamous classes, one of which is regarded as inferior to the other, and performs purificatory ceremonies for the caste. They cut their hair close all over the head and have no *kudumis*.

Kancharans, etc. Other artizan castes are the Kancharans, a North Malabar caste whose occupation is the manufacture of brass vessels; the Kalkottis or Kallans, stone masons; the Neyttikkars, weavers of coir mats; and the Kundatons, chunam-makers, found in the Calicut Taluk. All of these are *makkattayam* castes.

Vettuvans. Vettans or Vettuvans [1] were once salt-makers, and are now masons, earth-workers and quarrymen; they are said to be divided into two classes, one *marumakkattayam* and regarded as indigenous to Malabar, and the other *makkattayam* and said to be immigrants from the south.

Paravans. The Paravans are an inferior caste whose principal occupation is chunam-making. The name, which seems to be connected with *paral*, shell, suggests that this is their proper caste function; but their women are also midwives, and they themselves gymnastic trainers.[2] On this account they are in some places called Parakurups and form a single community with the Kollakurups. Paravans apparently follow *marumakkattayam* in most parts.

Kanisans. The Kanisans, a *makkattayam* caste, are astrologers, and their services are indispensable on every important occasion in a Malayali's life. The tradition as to the origin of the caste makes them the offspring of a union between a Tiyan woman and a Brahman astrologer, which took place at Pazhur near Ernakulam in Cochin, the present home of the most celebrated members of the profession. They are also traditionally connected with the *kalari* institutions, as is indicated by the title Panikkar commonly given to them and the fact that many of them are now village school masters. The chief duty of the Kanisan is the casting of horoscopes and the choosing of lucky days for the celebration of marriages and other social ceremonies; he also supplies *yantrams*, or charms, consisting of a mystic arrangement of letters written on thin metal plates which are placed in cylindrical silver cases and worn on a string

[1] Not to be confused with the jungle tribe of Vettuvans, p. 137.

[2] *Vide* Madras Government Museum Bulletin, Vol. III, No. 3, p. 290.

CHAP. III. POLLUTING CASTES.

round the waist.[1] His astrology falls into three parts, *Ganitha*, *Sankitha* and *Hora*, dealing respectively with constellations and their origin, with that of earthquakes, comets and the like, and with the fate of man. For simple matters, such as foretelling lucky days, the astrologer has merely to consult his almanac, an abstruse document based on the *sastras* and unintelligible to those not learned in astrological lore. A horoscope is more difficult. Seated facing the sun, the astrologer draws a diagram with twelve *rasis* or compartments, one for each month in the year. He then pours his cowries on the ground, and after rolling them in the palm of his right hand, while repeating *mantrams*, he selects the seven largest and places them in a row outside the diagram at its right hand top corner. They represent the first seven planets, and he does obeisance to them, touching his forehead and the ground three times with both hands. The relative position of the nine planets (Suryan—the Sun ; Chandran—the Moon ; Chova—Mars ; Budhan—Mercury ; Vyazhan or Guru or Brahaspati—Jupiter ; Sukran—Venus ; Sani—Saturn and Rahu and Ketu) is then worked out and illustrated with cowries in the diagram. In Kottayam, the Kanisans are divided into four classes called Velumban, Peruvana, Nuchiladan, and Ambladan ; and similar divisions presumably exist elsewhere. The caste custom permits fraternal polyandry.

Mannans and Vannans.

The Mannans, a *makkattayam* caste of South Malabar, apparently identical with the *marumakkattayam* Vannans of the North, are a caste of washermen ; and their services are indispensable to the higher castes in certain purificatory ceremonies when they have to present clean cloths (*mattu*). They are also devil dancers, and tailors. They practise fraternal polyandry in the south, Mannans are divided into two endogamous classes, Perumannans (*peru*, great) and Tinda-mannans (*tinda*, pollution) ; and in Walavanad, into four endogamous classes called Choppan, Perumannan, Punnekadan, and Puliyakkodan. The Tinda-mannan and Puliyakkodan divisions perform the purificatory sprinklings for the others.

Velans.

Closely akin to the Mannans are the Velans, a small caste of physicians, who follow *marumakkattayam* in the extreme north and *makkattayam* elsewhere. They are also umbrella and basket makers. Their women are midwives and serve the higher castes. The Velan's art is mainly that of the sorcerer ; small-pox is cured by the muttering of *mantrams* or mystic

[1] An interesting account of some of these *yantrams* is given in the Madras Government Museum Bulletin, Vol. III, No. 3, p. 305 ; and a full description of the various lucky and unlucky omens is to be found in monograph No. 12 of the Ethnographical survey of the Cochin State.

invocations to Kali; devils are driven out by invoking Karinkutti. In South Malabar there is an inferior subdivision of the caste who act as Velicohappads, or oracles of Bhagavathi and inferior deities; while in the north the Velans are said to be divided into five classes called Anhuttan (five hundred), Munnuttan (three hundred), Elayanikkam (*elaya*, junior), Muttanikkam (*mutta*, elder) and Ramanikkam. The Munnuttans make winnowing-fans.

Kavuthiyans. The Kavuthiyans are barbers who serve the Tiyans and lower castes; they are also sometimes given the title Kurup. Their females act as midwives. There seem to be several sections, distinguished by the affix of the name of the castes which they serve, as for instance Tacchakavuthian (or Tacchakurup), and Kanisa Kavuthiyans, appropriated to the service of the Asaris and Kanisans respectively; while the barbers who serve the Izhuvans are known both as Aduttons, Vattis or Izhuva Kavuthiyans. But whether all these should be regarded as offshoots of one main barber caste, or as degraded sections of the castes which they serve, the Kavuthiyans proper being only barbers to the Tiyans, it is difficult to determine. The fact that the Naviyan or Kavuthiyan section of the Veluttedans, as well as the Kavuthiyan section of the Mukkuvans, are admittedly but degraded sections of those castes, makes the second the more probable view. It is also to be noticed that the Kavuthiyans, in the north at least, follow *Marumakkattayam*; while the Taccha and Kanisa Kavuthiyans follow the other principle of descent.

Panans. The Panans, who are also in some places called Malayans, are primarily musicians, exorcists, and devil dancers; but basket and umbrella making are also their traditional occupations. Their women are midwives; and one of the duties of the men is to convey news of births and deaths occurring in a Tiyan household to the relations. The name Panan is perhaps connected with *pan*, music; that of Malayan signifying as it does "hillman," points to their having been at one time a jungle tribe, but they have by no means the dark complexion and debased physiognomy which are characteristic of the classes which still occupy that position. The men do not shave any part of the head, but allow the hair to grow long; and either part in the middle and tie it behind like the people of the East coast, or tie it in a knot in front in the ordinary Malayali fashion. They follow the *makkattayam* family system and practise fraternal polyandry. The caste is endogamous; and in South Malabar at least there are said to be four subdivisions called Tirurengan, Kodaketti (umbrella tying), Minpidi (fish catching) and Pulluvan, of which the last named is inferior in status to the other three. They are also divided into exogamous *illams* or *kiriyams*.[1] They worship Kali and inferior deities such as Parakutti, Karinkutti, Gulikan and Kutti Chattan.

Their methods of exorcism are various. If any one is considered to be possessed by demons, it is usual after consulting the astrologer to ascertain what *murti* (lit. form) is causing the trouble, to call in Panans who perform a ceremony known as *Teyattam*, in which they wear masks and so attired sing, dance, tom-tom and play on rude and strident pipes. Other of their ceremonies for driving out devils called *Ucchaveli*, seem to be survivals or imitations of human sacrifice, or instances of sympathetic magic.[2] One of these consists of a mock living burial of the principal performer, who is placed in a pit which is covered with planks, on the top of which a sacrifice (*homam*) is performed with a fire kindled with jack branches. In another variety the Panan cuts his left fore-arm and smears his face with the blood thus drawn. Panans also take part with Mannans in various ceremonies at Badrakali and other temples, in which the performers impersonate in suitable costumes some of the minor deities or demons, and fowls are sacrificed, while a Velicchappad dances himself into a frenzy and pronounces oracles.[3]

Pulluvans. The Pulluvans are a low caste of physicians or rather herbalists; and it is their special function to assist at the performance of the *pamban tullal*, or snake dance; a ceremony to propitiate the serpent gods of the *nayattan kavus*, or serpent shrines, to be found in most Nayar compounds. A geometrical design of a snake is drawn on the ground, and a woman of the family sits by it holding a bunch of areca flowers, while a Pulluvan man and woman sing songs and dance. As the music proceeds, the Nayar woman becomes possessed and begins to quiver; and moving backwards and forwards rubs away the figure of the snake with the flowers. The Pulluvan accompanies the songs on a peculiar instrument which is called a *Pulluva-kudam* (Pulluva pot) and merits particular description. It consists of an earthenware chatty with its bottom removed, and entirely covered, except the mouth, with leather. The portion of the leather which is stretched over the bottom of the vessel thus forms a sort of drum, to the centre of which a string is attached. The other end of the string is fixed in the cleft end of a stick. The performer sits cross-legged holding the chatty mouth downwards with his right hand, on his right knee. The stick is held firmly under the right foot, resting on the left leg. The

---

[1] In Chirakkal there are said to be 9 illams, the names of five of which are Kodakudi, Velapa, Cheni, Palankudi, and Kalliat.

[2] A description is given in monograph No. 12 of the *Ethnographical Survey of the Cochin State*.

[3] For a description of such a ceremony see the *Madras Government Museum Bulletin*, Vol. III, No. 3, p. 261.

performer strums on the string, which is thus stretched tight, with a rude plectrum of horn, or any similar substance. The vibrations communicated by the string to the tympanum produce a curious sonorous note, the pitch of which can be varied by increasing or relaxing the tension of the string.

CHAP. III. POLLUTING CASTES.

The Pulluvans are a *makkattayam* caste; and a recent writer has shown reason for supposing that they were once in the habit of marrying their own sisters. They are subdivided into four exogamous *kiriyams*, called Kalliad, Palan, Cheni and Kondakutta. They live largely on alms.

ABORIGINAL CLASSES.

It only remains to deal with the depressed "aboriginal" classes of which those in the plains occupied till recently,[1] and indeed to some extent continue to occupy, the position of agrestic serfs, while those in the hills and forests are genuine "jungle tribes." It is extremely difficult to determine their relative positions, or to investigate their subdivisions, or customs, since they are entirely illiterate, while the more intelligent amongst them are apt to draw on their imagination and borrow from the manners of their superiors. They fall outside the proper caste system of Malabar. Generally speaking they follow the *makkattayam* system, in the sense that the father is the head of the family and the wife lives in her husband's house. They do not observe the custom of the *tali kettu kalyanam* and the main feature of their marriages is the payment of a bride-price. They bury their dead. Their religion is pure animism.

Cherumans and Pulayans.

The principal representatives of the agrestic serfs are the Cherumans or Pulayans. The names seem to be alternatives and both are probably generic terms applied to the aboriginal inhabitants of the country by their conquerors. Cheruman perhaps means "slave" (*cheru*; little, mean) and Pulayan, "polluters" or "polluted" (*pula*, pollution). They are said to be divided into 39 divisions, the more important of which are the Kanakka Cherumans or Kanakkans, the Pula Cherumans or Pulayas, the Era Cherumans or Eralans, the Roli Cherumans or Rolans, and the Kudans. Whether these subdivisions should be treated as separate castes or not, it is hardly possible to determine; some of them at least are endogamous groups, and some are still further subdivided. Thus the Pulayas of Chirakkal are said to be divided into one endogamous and 11 exogamous groups, called Mavadan, Elamanam, Tacchakudiyan, Kundaton, Cheruvulan, Mulattan, Talan, Vannattam, Eramalodiyan, Mullaviriyan, Egudan and Kundon. Some at least of these group names obviously denote differences of occupation. The Kundotti, or woman of the last group, acts as midwife; and in consequence the

[1] Buchanan gives an account of the ways in which they were bought and sold in his *Journey through Mysore, Malabar and South Canara*, Vol. II, p. 370.

CHAP. III. ABORIGINAL CLASSES.

group is considered to convey pollution by touch to members of the other groups, and they will neither eat nor marry with those belonging to it. Death or birth pollution is removed by a member of the Mavadan class called Maruttan, who sprinkles cow dung mixed with water on the feet, and milk on the head of the person to be purified. At weddings the Maruttan receives 32 fanams, the prescribed price of a bride, from the bridegroom, and gives it to the bride's people.

The Era Cherumans and Kanakkans, who are found only in the southern taluks of the district, appear to be divided into exogamous groups called *kuttams*, many of which seem to be named after the house name of the masters whom they serve ; in some marriage is forbidden between relations in the mother's side.

The Cherumans are almost solely employed as agricultural labourers and coolies ; but they also make mats and baskets. They pollute the high castes at a distance of 64 feet, and it is proper for them when addressing superiors to call themselves slaves (*adiyan*), and to refer to their rice as chaff, etc. They are wholly illiterate ; their dwellings are wretched huts (*chalas* or *madams*) and their dress of the scantiest and coarsest. The women usually wear a profusion of bead and shell necklaces, and brass or pewter bangles and rings. The men cut the hair close all over the head. Their chief deities are Kutti-chattan and Kuli.

Parayans.

The Malabar Parayans are a low class of basket-makers and agricultural labourers. They do not seem to be connected in any way with the East coast Paraiyans, though there are no doubt now many of the latter in Malabar with whom they are probably often confused. The name is perhaps connected with *para*, drum, as it is usually a Parayan who is the drummer at Cheruman funerals and puberty ceremonies. They do not seem to differ materially [1] from the other classes included in the generic term Cheruman, though the latter consider them inferior, and they are said to eat even cow's flesh. They are notorious sorcerers and practicers of black magic. Odi is the name of the principal cult, and Nili of Kalladikkod its patron goddess. With the aid of the magical oil called *pilla tilam* (child oil), the principal ingredient in which is derived from a human foetus of 6 or 7 months growth, the Odiyan can transform himself into any shape he likes, or render himself invisible, in order to accomplish his purpose of murder or maiming. To obtain his material the Odiyan chooses some woman in her first pregnancy, walks thrice round her house and charms her out ; she is stripped naked

[1] Buchanan includes "Parriar, Vullum, Canacoun, Erilay, etc." under the general term "Churrman." *Journey*, Vol. II, p. 370.

CHAP. III. ABORIGINAL CLASSES.

and the foetus removed.[1] Another form which the Parayan's magic takes is the well-known method of making a waxen image of the person whom he desires to harm and burning it with special rites.

Nayadis.

The Nayadis are the most degraded caste in Malabar. They live mostly by begging, and as they convey distance pollution to all castes they are accustomed to lay out their cloths on the roadside, and to retire themselves some way off and shout aloud for charity. Their name suggests that they were originally hunters; and their diet still includes such articles as pigs, hares, monkeys, and birds, which they shoot with slings; but their principal occupations now are the occasional collection of honey and gum, and the making of certain ropes, which custom requires them to offer to the Nambudiris and Nayars of the neighbourhood at the Onam and Vishu festivals. They make fire by friction with two twigs of *Litsaea sebifera*, in the shorter of which a cavity is scooped out. The Nayadis wear the *kudumi*; their women have plentiful strings of beads round their necks.[2]

Paniyans.

The Paniyans are the most numerous of the jungle-tribes. They are found in the Wynaad, where they are the chief agricultural coolies and in the foot-hills throughout the district except in the Palghat taluk. Like most of the hill-tribes, they cultivate hill rice in patches of forest which they clear by burning and shift from year to year; they are also employed as wood cutters and elephant *mahouts*, and are good *shikaris*. In physiognomy they are of an almost negroid type with black skin, curly hair and broad noses. In the Wynaad they wear, when working in the fields, a big basket-work hat made of split reeds and shaded like an inverted coal-scoop, called a *kontai*. Their headmen are called Kuttan and collectively Muppanmar (elders), whence the whole caste is often loosely spoken of as Muppans. The groups of their huts (*chala*) are called *padis*. Like most of the other hill-tribes, they worship animistic deities, of which the chief is Kuli, whom they worship on a raised plaftorm called *Kulitara*, offering cocoanuts but no blood. The Kuttan is the priest, and he is assisted by a *Komaram* or oracle.[3]

Kurumbans.

Another curly-haired and dark-skinned tribe are the Kurumbans or Kurumans, found in the Wynaad, Calicut and Ernad taluks. They are subdivided into Mullu (bamboo) Kurumbans. Ten (honey) Kurumbans also called Kadu or Shola

---

[1] The power of the Odiyan is still dreaded even by the high castes; and there are authenticated instances of the death of a woman being caused by the removal of a foetus for the purposes of black magic. See *Madras Government Museum Bulletin*, Vol. III, No. 3, p. 311.

[2] For a detailed account of the Nayadis, see the *Madras Government Museum Bulletin*, Vol. IV, No. 1, p. 66.

[3] A full description of the caste and its customs will be found in the *Madras Government Bulletin*, Vol. II, No. 1, p. 18.

CHAP. III. ABORIGINAL CLASSES.

Nayakkans, and Urali, or Bet Kurumbans ; of which the first-named class, who consider themselves superior to the others, are cultivators and hunters ; the second wood-cutters and collectors of honey ; and the third make baskets and implements of agriculture. The Mullu and Ten Kurumbans have headmen with titles of Muppan and Mudali respectively conferred by their janmis. The Kurumbans like many of the other hill-tribes use bows and arrows, with which they are expert. The caste deity of the Ten Kurumbans is called Masti. They do not seem to be in any way connected with the shepherd caste of Kurumban found in many of the East coast districts and supposed to be the representatives of the ancient Pallavas.[1] It is however perhaps worth remarking that the Urali Kurumbans of the Wynaad differ from the other two classes in having no headmen, observing a shorter period of pollution after a birth than any other Malabar tribe and none at all after a death, and in not worshipping any of the Malabar animistic deities.

Kuricchiyans.

The Kuricchiyans (*Kuricchi*, hill country) are a jungle tribe of *punam* cultivators and hunters, found in the Wynaad and the slopes of the ghats north of Calicut. They consider themselves polluted by the approach of the hill-tribes and by the touch of Tiyans and Kammalans ; and their women require water sanctified by a Brahman to purify them. They perform the *tali kettu* ceremony before puberty ; and say that they follow the *marumakkattayam* family system, though the wife usually goes to live with her husband in a new hut, and the husband has to pay a price for his bride. They act as oracles during the great festival at Kottiyur ; the performer becomes inspired after sitting for some time gazing into a vessel containing gingelly oil, and holding in his hand a curious-shaped wand of gold about a foot and a half long, and hollow.

Karimbalans.

The Karimbalans are *punam* cultivators, hewers of wood and collectors of wild pepper ; and are found in all the foot hills north of the Camel's Hump. They wear the *kudumi*, and are said to follow the *marumakkattayam* system ; but they do not perform the *tali kettu* ceremony. They are supposed to have the power of exercising the demon Karuvilli, possession by whom takes the form of fever.

Malakkars.

The Malakkars, also called Malamuttanmar and Malapanikkar, are a comparatively superior tribe of jungle cultivators and hunters found in the Calicut and Ernad hills. They follow the *marumakkattayam* system and observe pollution for 12 days. Some of them wear *kudumis*. They call their huts *illams* and, if they leave them to go down to the plains, must bathe before returning. They consider themselves polluted by all castes below Nayars. The name Muttan is

[1] See *Madras Government Museum Bulletin*, Vol. II, No. 1, p. 38.

properly a title, meaning elder, confirmed on their headman by their janmis. Their chief god is Maladevan. They are good forest watchers and elephant catchers.

Malayans.

Very similar are the Malayans of the Kottayam taluk and Kadans of North Malabar, both of whom pollute only by touch. The former have a tradition that they were originally Tiyans, and were transported to Gannaram amsam, where they now live, by the Kottayam Raja for some fault.

Malasars.

The castes having similar names in the hills south of the Palghat gap are to be distinguished from these. The Malasars or Malayars of Muthalamada amsam and Kollengod speak a patois which more nearly approximates to Tamil, and follow *makkattayam*, the proper practice being for a boy to marry a cousin on the mother's side. They observe only three days' pollution after a death, and worship chiefly deceased ancestors. They are employed in the forest to catch and train elephants, but also work as agricultural labourers. Their headmen are called Muppans. The Kadars of the Kollengode hills are a short broad nosed hill-tribe, who live mainly by hunting and collecting forest produce. They are excellent trackers of game and expert tree climbers, tackling the straight trees by driving in wooden pegs as they go up. They use a chain of loops of rattan to descend precipitous rocks in pursuit of the honey of the rock bee. Their marriage customs are similar to those of the Malasars, but they consider themselves superior to them. Their huts are called *cheris*. They eat roots and vermin and have a curious custom of chipping the incisor teeth to the shape of a sharp cone.[1]

Kadars.

Vettuvans.

The Vettuvans of Chirakkal taluk are a low caste of jungle cultivators and basket-makers, distinguished by the survival amongst their women of the custom of dressing in leaves, their only clothing being a kind of double fan-shaped apron of leaves tied round the waist with a rolled cloth. They live in huts made of split bamboo and thatched with elephant grass, called *kudumbus*. They say that they follow the *marumakkattayam* system, but the wife lives in her husband's hut. A girl cannot wear a necklace of beads till she is married.

The Vettuvans are divided into fourteen *illams*, which seem to be named after the house names of the *janmis*, whom they serve (Elayedath, Muttedath, Pungodan, etc.). Their headmen, who are appointed by their *janmis*, are called *Kiran*, or sometimes *Parakutti* (drummer).

Mavilons.

Another small tribe in Chirakkal are the Mavilons, divided into Tulu Mavilons and Eda Mavilons and subdivided into thirty *illams*. They are employed as mahouts and collect honey and other forest produce. Their headmen are called *Chingam* (*Simham*, lion) and their huts *mapura*.

---

[1] *Vide Madras Government Museum Bulletin*, Vol. II, No. 3, p. 142.

CHAP. III. ABORIGINAL CLASSES. — Arunadans.

In Ernad taluk there is a caste called Arunadans, who are perhaps the most primitive of all the hill-tribes north of the Palghat gap. They are a small black race with thick, bushy hair and broad noses. They eat roots and all sorts of vermin, being especially fond of pythons (*perupambu*). It is said to have been their custom, now abandoned, for a father to marry his eldest daughter.

FOREIGN CASTES.

The above sketch is confined to castes which properly belong to, or have been incorporated, in the Malabar caste system. There are also many foreign castes represented in a greater or less degree, which it is unnecessary to describe in detail. The chief are the Tamil and Canarese Chetties and Goundans, who are mainly merchants; the Kaikolans or Tamil weavers; the Vellalans or Tamil cultivators, all of whom are to be found mainly in the Palghat, Walavanad and Wynaad taluks; the various classes of beggars, gypsies and jugglers known as Kuravans, Andis and Pandarams; and amongst jungle tribes, the Irulas of the Attappadi valley and neighbouring hills.

Some account will now be given of the houses, dress, food, festivals, and religious and social ceremonies of the Malayali Hindus; and while an attempt will be made to describe in some detail what is most characteristic and striking, it must be remembered that only the broader features are, if at all, universal occurrence, and that the more minute the detail the more restricted will be its exact applicability.

VILLAGES AND DWELLINGS.

The true Malayali seems never to have lived in villages of the East coast type, that is, in houses built in streets. Each house, even the humblest, stands in its little compound or garden, which is usually thickly planted with areca and coconut palms, jack trees, plantains, betel and pepper-vines and the like. Flowering trees, such as the beautiful *Asogam* (*Saraca Indica*), are sometimes found; and shrubs, such as various sorts of shoe flowers (*Hibiscus*), single or double, crimson, rose, or buff, and of *Mandaram* (*Bauhinia*) with its curious "camel's foot" leaves and white or golden blossoms, are of common occurrence, their flowers being used for service in the temples. But the frugal Malayali finds no room for a merely ornamental flower garden.

The favourite situation for a Nayar house is in the strip of gardens fringing the broad expanse of green paddy fields, which occupies the centre of a typical Malabar valley. Such a position, though cool in the day time, is often stuffy at night in the hot weather, and damp and misty in the rains. But the Malayali's choice is determined by the necessity for a well and tank in every compound, and he likes too, no doubt, to live close to his fields.

At the entrance to the compound of a well-to-do *tarwad* stands a gate-house (*padippura*) approached from the paddy fields by steps or a ladder. The ground floor is usually occupied by two raised platforms, one on each side of the entrance, where no doubt in the old troublous times, sat armed sentries, but now affording a pleasant place for the master of the house to sit and chat and chew betel of an evening with his friends, or to transact business with any low caste neighbour whose approach to the main building would pollute it. The gate-house often has an upper storey reached by a ladder, originally no doubt a guard-room. Poorer people have merely a sort of thatched lych-gate, while *Kovilagams*, *Manas* and other aristocratic dwellings may have more pretentious gate-houses containing several rooms. The compound is enclosed by a laterite wall or by a fence of bamboo thorns often set on the top of a high mud bank; and the whole homestead is thus designed and fitted for defence against attack.

The compound being divided into four by imaginary lines running due north and south and east and west, the house should occupy the south-west angle of the north-east quarter. Thus it is practically in the centre of the garden. The south-east quarter is the proper position for the burning-ground. In the north-east square should be the bathing tank, and the *pamban kavu* or *nagattan kavu*, a little patch of jungle left undisturbed, and sacred to those holy reptiles, the snakes. The tank may be a mere pool, roughly revetted, prettily over-grown with lotus and other water plants; or it may be provided with sloping roofs of cadjan forming separate bathing sheds for men and women; or again it may be of a thoroughly substantial nature with regular laterite steps on all sides and solid sheds roofed with tiles. In the compound will also be found a byre (*tozhuttu* or *gosala*), and in some cases a *kottil*, a kind of platform, where grain can be thrashed in hot weather and ploughs and other agricultural implements are stored. The main front of the house should be on the east, though it may be on the west; and here is the *mittam* or yard which like the walk leading to it from the gate, is plastered with cow dung, bordered by low ridges and scrupulously clean. Here are spread to dry in the sun stores of golden paddy, its surface traced with intricate patterns so that any theft may be instantly detected. In the centre of the yard is the *tulasitara*, a sort of small altar or base, on which grows a plant of the sacred *tulasi* or basil (*Ocimum sanctum*).

The complete type of Malabar Hindu dwelling is that known as *Nalupura* (literally, four houses), which, like the ancient Roman villa, is built on four sides of a central court-yard open to the sky,—the classical *impluvium*, known in Malayalam as *nadumittam* or central yard. The buildings on the four sides are called *Vadakkini* or Northern house,

CHAP. III. VILLAGES AND DWELLINGS.

Tekkini or Southern house, *Kizakkini* or Eastern house, and *Padinnattini*, or Western house, respectively, with reference to their position relative to the central yard. Not every one can afford a complete *nalu pura* of course, but every house is regarded as forming part of an imaginary *nalu pura*, and this explains why in a house of the smaller type the main building though facing east is called the *padinnattini* or *padinnatta pura*, that being the principal block of the complete quadrangle. The following plan and description of a *nalu pura* will illustrate and explain what has been said :—

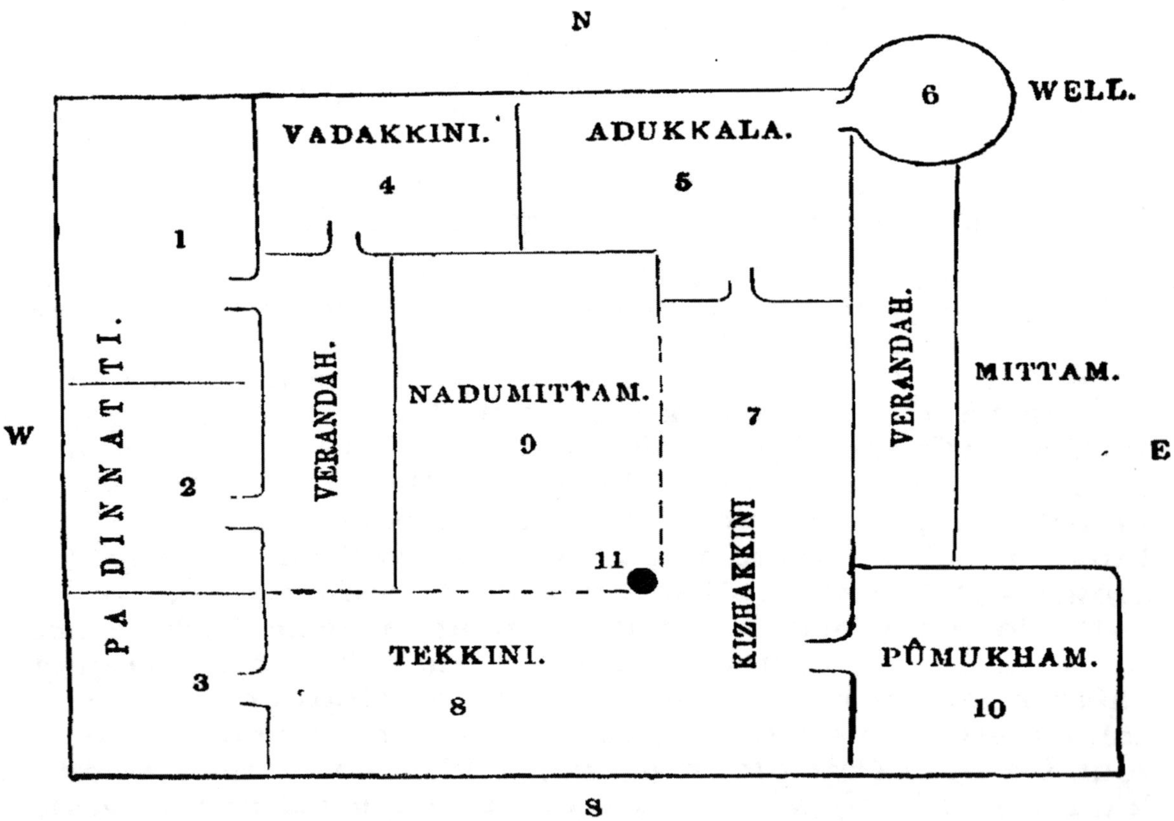

PLAN OF " NALU PURA " HOUSE.

Here it will be observed that there are three rooms in the *padinnattini*. Of these the northernmost (No. 1 in the plan) is the *pettu-kidakunna-muri* (lying-in room) where women are segregated during ceremonial impurity ; the central one (No. 2) is the *padinnatti-macchu*—a store-room where also household deities are sometimes kept. The southern one (3 in the plan), is a sleeping room or another store room. No. 5 is the *adukkala* or *veppu-pura*, the kitchen. Adjoining it is the well, and there is a window giving on to the latter, and usually projecting over it on corbels with a pulley above, so that water can be drawn from in-doors. The kitchen is sometimes however a separate building. No. 4, the *vadakkini* proper, is used as a dining room and for ceremonies. Nos. 7 and 8, the *kizhakkini* and *tekkini*, are open halls or verandahs, the dotted line bounding them indicating the beams, which support the court-yard walls of the upper storey, and are carried by a wooden pillar marked 11. There may be rooms opening off these halls. No. 10, the *pumukham* (or flower front), is a portico through which the main entrance is gained. It is used as a sort of drawing room. There are sometimes verandahs on all sides of the court-yard, and all round the exterior of the quadrangle as well, and these latter are sometimes enclosed with massive wooden bars having a reverse slope to that of the roof. The verandahs and *pumukham* are usually bounded by low dwarf walls or parapets carrying broad wooden seats (*padi*). In the upper storey there will usually be an open hall corresponding to the *tekkini* for the men to sleep in, and a series of small bed rooms for the women. There are separate stair cases to the former and the latter. The windows of the men's quarters open on to the compound only, that is there are none opening in the direction of the wings reserved for the women.

Of course the details vary considerably in different houses. A large house is made up of a series of such *nalupuras* ; while the Raja's palaces include temples within their precincts. The type of a smaller house is the *padinnatta-pura*, with or without wings, verandahs and *pumukham*.

The general design of the Nambudiri house is similar to that of the Nayar ; but the kitchen is at the south-east corner, the central room of the *kizhakkini* is appropriated to the ceremonies to the dead, the central room of the *tekkini* to the Penates, and room at the south-west corner to the performances of sacrifices.

The better houses are built of laterite set in mud (not as a rule in mortar), the walls being smoothly plastered with chunam and whitewashed. Others are simply built of mud (by no means lacking in durability), either whitewashed or coloured red. The roofs are either tiled or thatched with plaited cocoanut leaves and leaves of the palmyra (*borassus flabelliformis*). Under Native rule, tiled roofs were a prerogative (jealously reserved) of temples and of Nambudiri and other grandees. It was as a special favour that permission was given to the English merchants at Calicut by the Zamorin to tile their factory. The construction of a gate house also could not be undertaken without the permission of the local chieftain ; and even to this day the anger of some village tyrant may be aroused by the usurpation of such privileges without permission.

Distinct words are used to denote the houses of various classes : that of a Nambudirippad is called *mana*, of a Nambudiri, *illam*, of a Raja, *kovilagam* or *kottaram* or *edam*, of a Pisharodi, *pisharam*, of a Variyar, *variyam*, of a Nayar,

CHAP. III. VILLAGES AND DWELLINGS

bhavanam, or *vidu*, of the lower castes, *pura*. The lowest caste live in small windowless single-roomed mud huts (called *chala*) thatched with palmyra leaves; while the hill tribes as a rule construct their huts of split bamboo and thatch them with grass. A collection of such huts is usually known as a *padi*. Some of the hill tribes build their huts (*madam*) raised on clumps of bamboos cut level some height from the ground, as a protection against wild beasts.

DRESS.

The dress of the Malayali is extremely simple. The men wear a *konam*, a small strip of cloth passed between the legs and attached at the front and the back to a string tied round the waist, and a *mundu* or white cloth round the waist, tucked in on the right side, and hanging loose to the knees or ankles, not as in the East Coast twisted round the legs. They also sometimes carry a small upper cloth, *torttumundu*, thrown over the shoulder. The *mundu* of the high castes should reach to the ground, that of the lower castes should not go below the knee; but now-a-days the rule is not generally observed, and in the towns at least the general practice is for all but the lowest classes to have a cloth reaching to the ankles. Now-a-days, and especially in towns and amongst officials including village officers, and peons, the European shirt, worn with the ends hanging down over the *mundu*, is becoming common; as is the round cloth cap and dark short coat, and among the more advanced, trousers and collars. But in their houses it is still the custom for men as a rule to go bare above the waist.

For ceremonial purposes the Nambudiri wears his *mundu* in the fashion called *tattu*, that is wound tightly round the loins and then round each leg separately and tucked in at the back; and in this he is copied by some of the higher castes. The Nambudiri's *mundu* should be white like that of the other caste, but should have a gold border. Many castes in old days apparently used to wear blue cloths, but white is now practically universal except among the Pattar and Izhuvan women of Palghat, and the Tiyyattis and Mukkuvars of North Malabar, some of whom wear dark blue. Silk is never worn; but the higher castes have very fine semi-transparent cotton cloths. The only dress of the lowest classes and hill tribes is a short loin cloth worn loose.

Women wear a short cloth round the loins and a single long white cloth (*tuni*) tucked round the waist and hanging down to the ground. When going out they usually now-a-days wear a small cloth (*torttumundu*) thrown over the breasts and under the arms; but the old custom was for them to wear nothing above the waist, and it was considered immodest to cover the breast. Nambudiri *anterjanams* wear a single white cloth with a gold border about 10 cubits in length which is tucked round the loins and twisted round the legs reaching well below the knee and also covers the breast. Mukkuva women used to wear a black silk cloth somewhat similarly tied, but the custom is now dying out. In North Malabar the upper cloth (*torttumundu*) is now almost invariably worn, and the short bodice is becoming more and more common amongst the Tiyans.

Dress.

No turban is worn; it is in fact wrong for the higher castes to cover the head; but it is their universal practice to carry an umbrella. The umbrella of the country is made of leaves of the umbrella palm or the palmyra with a long bamboo handle, of which the length increases according to the dignity of person carrying it; it should be carried with the end of the handle in the palm of the hand and the arm stretched down at full length. But the ugly European black umbrella is becoming more and more common. The lower castes often twist a small cloth loosely round the head in the form of an embryo turban; but this should be removed in the presence of superiors, before whom custom demands that inferiors should always appear bare above the waist. Characteristic of the West Coast is the umbrella or mushroom-shaped hat made of palmyra leaves, which is invariably worn by fishermen and agricultural coolies, and serves as an admirable protection against sun and rain; such a hat with a crown too small for the head is often carried by Nayar women in their hands instead of an umbrella.

Hair.

The Malayali as a rule shaves head, face and body all over, leaving only a small oval patch of hair on the top of the head in front, called *kudumi*, which is allowed to grow long and is twisted to a knot, and hangs over the forehead in front or to one side, usually the left. This way of wearing the hair is universal and is distinctive of the West Coast Hindu. The few sub-castes who wear the East Coast chignon, as for example the Pattars, betray thereby their foreign origin. The latest fashion, however, amongst the younger generation of educated Nayars in South Malabar and Tiyan in the North appears to be to abandon the *kudumi* and wear the hair short in the European style. Some of the Cherumans and similar castes shave the head all over, and devil-dancers and the like wear the hair long; the ruder hill tribes also as a rule wear the hair long, but they are taking to the *kudumi* more and more as they are familiarised with civilization. The Nambudiri is often to be seen with a beard, but the reason is that he is not allowed to shav whene his wife is pregnant or when he is in mourning (*diksha*) or under pollution. Other castes also are forbidden to shave when in mourning.

Women wear their hair parted in the middle and either drawn tight to the ears and tied in a chignon or else twisted up in front in a sort of cone; the latter is the common custom in the south, except among Nambudiris; and the former in the north.

CHAP. III. Dress. Ornaments.

Men's ornaments consist of ear-rings, usually small gold oval rings (*kadukkans*) of which as many as four may be worn at a time; finger rings of gold, silver, bell metal or brass; and amulets, worn on a string round the waist usually as charms, but sometimes purely for ornament. Some of the Nayars as for instance, the Purattu Charnavar of Calicut, have their ears pierced but may not wear ear-rings; and among the more progressive ear-rings are going out of fashion. Bracelets are not worn, as a rule. The men of some of the hill tribes wear necklaces of beads.

Children wear gold necklaces, or a ring tied on a string round the waist (*pothumothiram*), which are discarded before the sixth year.

All women wear ear-rings. The *toda*, a boss-shaped hollow cylinder of gold or gilt, from an inch to an inch and a half or more in diameter, is the characteristic ornament of a Nayar woman, and it is the custom to dilate the lobe of the ear in childhood to enable it to be fitted in. It is also worn by Tiyan women and the lower castes. The *kathila* is a small ring of gold or gold beads worn in the outer edge of the ear, mainly by Tiyattis who sometimes have twenty or thirty of them in each ear. The *koradu* is another Tiyan ornament consisting of a kind of gold button fixed in the upper part of the ear; and there are many other varieties worn by the Mukkuvans and other castes. Gold necklaces of various kinds, often of coins, finger rings and bracelets, are also very generally worn by Nayar women and the richer women of the lower castes; and in the south nose pendants (*mukkutti*). The latter are also common now amongst North Malabar Tiyattis. Anklets are never worn.

A Nambudiri woman, in South Malabar at least, may not wear gold bangles, but wears instead many of brass or bell metal; she never pierces her nose. Some Nambudiri women wear circular gold plates over the chignon (*chudamani*), similar to the *mudis* worn by some North Malabar Nayars and Tiyans. Their necklaces and ear-rings which are of gold are of distinctive patterns. Cherumis and women of jungle castes wear a profusion of bead and shell necklaces, and many bracelets of brass or glass.

FOOD.

The staple food of the Malayali is rice. Nambudiris are forbidden liquor and flesh, and they observe the rule strictly. With their rice they eat various vegetable curries; there should be *pappadams*, round wafers made of the meal of the kidney bean, at every meal. The food is served on a plantain leaf or bell-metal plate; before eating, the Nambudiri must bathe and pray, and the meal starts with an offering of rice to the household fire and to the crows. Strictly speaking he should have only one meal of rice a day, other meals consisting only of fruit and sweets; but the rule is not observed. Tea and coffee are not permitted by the Sastras, but are sometimes taken. Nayars and lower castes will eat fish and meat, and drink toddy and spirits; and tea and coffee are becoming favourite beverages in the eating shops of the towns. Vegetables and fruit are eaten by all who can get them. The lowest classes live mainly on fish, kanji, and toddy; but the dietary of the Nayadi includes rats, monkeys, pigs, hares, crocodiles, shell fish, paddy birds and various roots. Most of the hill tribes eat roots and game of all sorts, and some of them snakes and carrion; but the Parayans are the only caste who are said to eat cows and are despised accordingly. All castes chew betel and some Tiyans and fishermen smoke cigarettes.

AMUSEMENTS. *Kalaris.*

Reference has already been made to the old *Kalaris* or gymnasia in which the Nayars were accustomed to go through a course of physical training and practice in the use of arms. Such physical exercises are still practised, and take the form of gymnastics and a kind of fencing with sticks representing swords and daggers (*Otta*, *cheruvadi* and *sarira vadi*). To begin with, the performers give a high kick in the air, sink slowly down on their haunches, leap up again and pirouette, all the time brandishing their sticks and twisting them about in every possible way. A similar display preludes the sword play, which is a usual feature at Nayar weddings and other ceremonies.

Kadhakalis.

Dramatic performances known as *kadhakali* are given by itinerant troupes of actors, who are usually Brahmans and Ambalavasis, and are supported by the chiefs and leading families. The plays celebrate the life and exploits of Krishna and Rama. A troop usually includes 12 actors, 4 singers and 4 drummers, who form the orchestra with drums (*maddalam* and *chenda*), gongs (*chengalam*) and cymbals (*elathalam*). There is no stage, but a cloth curtain separates the audience, who sit on mats on the ground, from the scene. The performers wear trousers and masks (*mudi*) painted in four or five stereo-typed modes known as red, green, black, etc., to represent different characters. The performance which is entirely in dumb show, 64 regular varieties of gesture being recognized, begins with a song (*todayam*) and a *vandana slogam* in praise of the God, followed by the *purapod* or entrance of the principal characters.[1]

The *kuttu* or mimes recited by the Chakkiyars have already been referred to on p. 111. The dancing girl is an institution practically unknown in Malabar; though there are occasionally to be met with small troops of girls, who go round the country

[1] *Vide Malabar and its Folk.* Mr. Gopal Panikkar (Natesan, Madras, 1906).

CHAP. III. AMUSEMENTS.

under the leadership of a *nattuvan* and perform a dance called the *mohiniyattam*. The performance is considered disreputable.

Games.

The principal village games are the *attakalam* a kind of prisoners' base played especially at the Onam festival and a ball game which consists on one side trying to throw a ball against a post guarded by the other side. Another game is called *eyttu* and consists in two sides shooting with bows and arrows at a single mark, and those who hit taking the arrows of those who miss. Cock fighting is also not uncommon. Amongst children swinging is a favourite pastime, and they have a game not unlike diavolo. Another popular amusement amongst girls is dancing ; they dance in a circle and one of them begins a song which is taken up by each in turn, while the whole join in the refrain.

FESTIVALS. Onam.

The principal Malayali festival is that of Onam, which is celebrated in Chingam (August-September) the time of the chief harvest, and commemorates the golden age of Mahabali (or Parasurama according to some), who is supposed to revisit Malabar on the Tiruvonam day. Houses are swept specially clean, the yard is carpeted with wild flowers [1] arranged in patterns on the floor, and *puja* is done to little clay images (*Trikkakurappan*) set up in the middle. The festival is an occasion of general rejoicing and giving of presents. The head of the family gives cloths, which must contain something of yellow about them, to his household and dependants ; and the latter bring presents of plantains (*nendra vazha*) which form an essential in the day's feast. After the midday meal come games and songs and dances.

Vishu.

Vishu, the Malayalam New Year's Day, which falls on the first of Medam (March-April), is the next most important festival. A man's prosperity for the year is considered to depend on his seeing something lucky on Vishu morning ; it is therefore the custom to prepare on Vishu eve what is known as a *kani*, that is, a bell-metal bowl in which are put a *grandham*, a gold ornament, a newly washed cloth, some coins, a bell-metal looking glass, a cucumber, a coconut cut in two, some mangoes, and jack fruit ; and over the whole some flower of the *konna* (*cassia fistula*). A lamp is left burning on each side of the *kani* throughout the night, and in the morning the members of the household are each taken with their eyes shut to the *kani* and seated in front of it on a grass mat facing east and then told to open their eyes and look at it. The *kani* is afterwards taken round from house to house for the benefit of the poor.

[1] These flower carpets are often very elaborate work of art. A description of one, and a translation of an onam song will be found in the Madras Government Museum Bulletin, Vol. III, p. 292.

The head of the family gives small presents of money to the children and servants and tenants; and field labourers bring their janmis presents of fruits and vegetables. CHAP. III. FESTIVALS.

Tiruvathira.

The third main festival is the Tiruvathira which comes in Dhanu (December-January). It is a festival observed by Nayar women in commemoration of Kama, the God of Love. In the early morning girls go to the tank and bathe together, and sing a song to Kama to the accompaniment of a curious noise made by holding the left hand slightly under the water and beating the surface above it with the right palm. The rest of the morning they spend in swinging (*uzhinjal*). Husbands should not fail to visit their wives' houses on Tiruvathira day.

Ayudha puja.

The Dasara is observed in Malabar under the name of Ayudha puja or Saraswati puja; it comes at the autumnal equinox, and every man should during it worship the implements of his craft and keep holiday. It is especially the festival of books and educational apparatus.

The Hindu festival of Sivarathri in Kumbham (February-March) is also observed by the higher castes.

Local festivals.

Of local festivals connected with particular temples the most popular is the Bharani or cock feast held at the Kali temple at Cranganore in the month of Meenam (March-April). Hundreds of pilgrims attend from all parts of Malabar, Nayars, Tiyans and lower castes alike. They march up to the shrine crying *Nada, Nada* (march, march), singing obscene songs and levelling all sorts of abuse at the Goddess; on arrival at the shrine they throw stones and filth at it, and continue their volleys of abuse. The chief of the Mukkuvan caste styled Kuli Muttatta Arayan has the privilege of beginning the work of polluting the shrine. The pilgrims make offerings of pepper, and in return are presented with turmeric powder (*manjal prasadam*) by girls attached to the temple; but the principal ceremony is the sacrifice of cocks which every pilgrim should perform. The day concludes with much drinking of arrack and toddy. The festival lasts seven days at the conclusion of which the temple is cleaned. A pilgrimage to Cranganore is said to be a safeguard against cholera and small-pox. The shrine was originally only a holy tree with a platform; and the construction of a temple with an image is said to have been a comparatively recent innovation. The priest belongs to the caste of Adigals. Other popular festivals are those at Kottiyur in Kottayam taluk, the Ekadasi feast at Guruvayur near Chowghat, the Kalpatti Car festival at Palghat, the Tiruchammaram festival at Taliparamba and the Kizhur festival in Kurumbranad. The Mahamakham festival at Tirunavayi is described at length in Chapter XV.

CHAP. III. AGRICULTURAL CEREMONIES.

Vishu.

Mention must also be made of the agricultural ceremonies which are an especially interesting feature of Malabar life. The agricultural year begins with Vishu day, the end of the hot weather. On the eve of that day the Kanisan (astrologer) of the desam is sent for to make a forecast of the agricultural prospects and the probable quantity of rain, which he estimates by astronomical calculations. The forecast called *Vishuphalam* is written on a cadjan. The Kanisan is also consulted in order to fix an auspicious day for the first ploughing. On the date fixed the master of the house, with his Cherumans, goes to the seed store and takes out some of each variety of seed, which he puts in a cup made of leaves of the *kanniram* (*strychnos nux-vomica*); and then places the cups in a basket near a lamp and a small heap of rice arranged in the yard. A new plough-share is fastened to a new plough, and a pair of cattle brought out. Plough, cattle and basket are all painted with rice water, and taken in procession to the field, on reaching which the head Cheruman makes a small mound of earth, on which is thrown a little manure and a handful of seed. The cattle are then yoked, and a square is ploughed by the head Cheruman. Inside it there must be at least seven furrows, and the plough must, at the end, be dropped to the right. An offering is then made to Ganapathi, the master throws some seed into a furrow, and the head Cheruman calls out "May the Gods on high and the deceased ancestors bless the seed which has been sown broadcast, and the cattle which are let loose, the mother and the children of the house, the master and his slaves; may they also vouchsafe us a good crop, good sunshine, and a good harvest." Next a coconut is cut on the ploughshare; if the hind portion is larger than the front one it augurs an excellent harvest; if the nut is cut into two equal portions the harvest will be moderate; if the cut passes through the eye of the nut or if no water is left in the cut portions misfortune is foreboded. The portions of the cocoanut are then picked up with the milk water inside them, and a leaf of *tulasi* plant (*ocimum sanctum*) dropped in; if the leaf turns to the right a prosperous harvest is assured; if to the left the contrary. The ceremonial concludes, with loud shouts and invocations to the Gods of husbandry; and the unused seeds are distributed among the workmen.

Nira.

The bringing in of the first fruits (*nira*) is celebrated at the beginning of Karkadagam. The house is thoroughly cleaned; the doors and windows are cleansed with the leaves of a tree called *paragam* (*ficus hispida*) and decorated with white rice; the walls are white-washed and the yard smeared with cowdung. Ten kinds of flowers (*desa pushpam*) [1] are collected and

[1] The flowers are Nilapana (*Curculigo orchoides*), Karuga (*Cynodon doctylon*), Erchupuli (*Aerua lanata*), Muyalchevi (*Emilia sonchifolia*), Puvam kuruntala (*Vernonia cinerea*), Ulinna (*Cardiospermum halicacabum*), Mukutti (*Biophytum ensitivum*), Tirutali (*Ipomaea sepiaria*), Kannanni (*Eclipta alba*) and Krishna Kananthi (*Evolvulus alsinoides*).

AGRICULTURAL CEREMONIES.

put in the gate house, together with leaves and branches of the following: *Atti* (*ficus glomerata*), *Itti* (*ficus infectoria*), *Arayal* (*ficus religiosa*), *Peral* (*ficus bengalensis*), *Illi* (young bamboo leaves), *Nelli* (*phyllanthus emblica*), Jack (*artocarpus integrifolia*) and Mango (*mangifera indica*). On the morning of the ceremony the priest of the local temple comes out preceded by a man blowing a conch shell. This is a signal for the whole village, and every house-holder sends out a man, duly purified by a bath and copiously smeared with sacred ashes, to the fields to gather some ears of rice. It is not necessary to pluck the rice from one's own fields; free permission is given to gather it from any field in which it may be ripe. The rice is brought to the gate of the house, where it is met by a woman with a lighted lamp, placed on the leaves already mentioned, and carried into the yard in procession, those assembled crying out "fill, fill, fill, increase, increase, increase, fill the house, fill the basket, fill the stomach of the children." It is carried three times round a small plank and then placed on it on a plantain leaf, the lighted lamp being put on the right. An offering of cocoanuts and sweets is made to Ganapathi; and the leaves and ears of paddy are stuck with cow-dung to various parts of the house, to the agricultural implements and even to the trees. A sumptuous meal brings the ceremony to a close.

Puthari.

The next ceremony is the formal cooking and eating of the new rice (*puthari*). In some places it takes place on the *Nira* day, but as a rule it is an independent festival. A day is fixed for it as soon as the first crop is harvested and threshed; it should be before Onam. The rice is cooked and eaten with a special curry consisting of *tagara* (Cassia tora), peas, the fruit of *puthari chundanga* (*swertia chirata*), brinjals (*solanum melongana*) and green pumpkin.

Uccharal.

At the end of Magaram (January-February) when the second uccharal crop has been harvested and the year's agriculture is over the Earth-mother, *Bhumi devi*, has rest during the hot weather until the first showers begin. At the beginning of this period, the Malayali observes a festival in honour of the Goddess' menstruations, which like the Roman Februaria are supposed to take place at this time. The festival is called *Uccharal* or *ucchal* and lasts three days, during which all granaries are closed, paddy is not sold and no implement of agriculture is touched. Even the rice to be eaten during the three days is pounded beforehand. On the first day towards the evening the granary is closed, some thorns and shrubs of broom being fixed to the door with cow-dung, and some ashes spread in front of it. The next two days are holidays for all; the house must not be swept nor the floors smeared with cow-dung and even the garden may not be watered. On the fourth day the granary is opened

CHAP. III. AGRICULTURAL CEREMONIES. *Uccharal.*

and a basketful of leaves is taken to the fields and burnt with a little manure, perhaps to indicate that the cultivator remains in possession. *Uccharal* is the date on which all agricultural leases should expire, and demands for surrender of property should not be made at any other time ; but by a liberal interpretation the Courts have extended the term up to the day of Vishu. Special *Ucharal* festivals are held at Cherpalcheri and at Kanayara near Shoranur, at which straw models of cattle are taken in procession to the temples of Bhagavati.

RELIGION.

The religion of the Malayali is a remarkable mixture of animism and Vedantism. The paramount influence of the Brahmans in religion as in social and legal matters is everywhere evident ; and yet Malabar is pre-eminently the home of witchcraft and magic and all that is indicated by the term animism. Animism as found in India has been described by Sir H. Risley as follows :—" It conceives of man passing through life surrounded by a ghastly company of powers, elements, tendencies, mostly impersonal in character, shapeless phantoms of which no image can be made and no definite idea can be formed. Some of these have departments or spheres of influence, of their own ; one presides over cholera, another over small-pox, another over cattle disease ; some dwell in rocks, others haunt trees, others again are associated with rivers, whirlpools and water-falls. All of them require to be diligently propitiated by reason of the ills which proceed from them, and the essence of all these practices is magic." In this sense it is obvious that the Malayali's religion is still largely animistic. Evidence of a widespread primitive worship of ancestors is to be seen in the kistvaens (*topikallus, kodakallus, nannangadis*), and rock caves containing sepulchral urns, which are found all over the district ; and the cult, which seems in origin to be based on fear of the spirits of the dead and a desire to deter such unwelcome guests from re-visiting the abodes of the living, survives in the present death ceremonies which require offerings to be made daily to the deceased in the yard of his house, until his ashes are cast into a river, or otherwise properly disposed of. Similar offerings are also made periodically afterwards, or when domestic calamities and the like suggest that the ghost is getting troublesome. Animistic again is the widespread worship of Badrakali, the Goddess who presides over small-pox and cholera, the worship of snakes and trees, and the common belief in exorcism and witchcraft, in which even the Brahmans share ; and it is not unusual for the horoscope even of a Nambudiri to mention the name of some bird, animal or tree which is to be regarded as his totem. On the other hand the Nambudiri is the strictest of all Southern Brahmans in the observance of the precepts of the

Vedas; while even the lowest castes and the hill tribes are inclined to give their deities Puranic names and strive to be incorporated in the Brahmanic system.

Temples.

Typical of the two elements in the Malayali religion are the two classes into which his shrines can be roughly divided. First there are the *Ambalams* or *Kshetrams*, which are temples dedicated to the superior deities of the Hindu pantheon, Siva and Vishnu, and their consorts and incarnations, and to Ganapathi or Vigneswara; and secondly the *kavus*, or temples and shrines, at which the inferior deities, such as Subramaniya, Ayyappan, Vettukorumagan, Bhagavathi or Badrakali, the goddess of small-pox; and malignant demons such as Kuttichattan, Mundian, Gulikan are propitiated with sacrifice, while their wishes are interpreted by oracles.

Ambalam.

The Malabar temples like the houses, are quite different from those of the east coast; and the stone pillars, massive pyramidal *gopurams*, and elaborate detail of Dravidian architecture are unknown. The principal shrine, or *srikovil*, containing the *lingam* or image, is usually a small rectangular building with a conical or pyramidal tiled roof; the sides consist of a peculiar kind of dense lattice-work of wood standing on a low laterite wall. The *srikovil* stands inside a quadrangle (*nalambalam*), enclosed by low verandahs or sheds with tiled or thatched roofs. Inside the *nalambalam* there may also be shrines of minor deities; and out-houses for cooking and feeding (*agrasala*) and a well, the whole called *chuttambalam*. The principal entrance to the *nalambalam* is at the east; and over the door is a small ornamental gable set on the slope of the roof, supported by two or more carved wooden pillars and decorated with carved barge-boards, finial and pendants. This ornamental gable is a peculiar characteristic of Malabar temple architecture. In front of the entrance is a *dipastambam*, a brass or bell-metal pillar for a lamp; close by is the bathing tank, and a little to the south the sacred peepul tree with a platform (*tara*) round it. In the bigger and more important temples, the roof of the *srikovil* is covered with copper sheeting and has a gilt knob at the top; the walls are of laterite, sometimes adorned inside with paintings, and the door-posts and cornices are of carved stone; while in front is a *mantapam* or stone platform, covered with a tiled canopy. The *nalambalam* itself is sometimes enclosed in an outer walled quadrangle, in the courtyard of which are the *agrasalas* and other buildings, and a *dwajastambam* or flagstaff; while at the entrances are *gopurams* or two-storied gate-houses. These *gopurams* have the characteristic ornamental gables over the porch and at the two ends of the upper storey, the wooden railings enclosing the verandahs and galleries have a peculiar slope outwards to meet the eaves, and the hips of the roofs have a slightly concave curve. The general

CHAP. III. RELIGION.

effect is distinctly Chinese or Mongolian, though there does not seem to be sufficient reason to attribute this to direct Chinese influence.[1]

The officiating priests (*shantikar*) in *ambalams* are Nambudiris or Embrandiris. Only Brahmans may enter the *srikovil* or *mantapam*; low caste Nayars may not go inside the *nalambalam*; while castes which pollute Brahmans by approach and not merely by contact may not go beyond the peepul tree. On festive occasions a miniature image of the deity is placed near the tree with a *bhandaram* or treasure box into which the votaries of the polluting castes drop their cash or jewel offerings.

Congregational worship is no feature of Hindu religion, and the ordinary services of washing the idol, offering food, etc., are conducted by the priest within closed doors to the music of drums, pipes and cymbals. The ordinary worshipper comes with or without offerings (flowers, ghee, rice, money or jewels, which are presented to the priest), enters the quadrangle, stands in front of the shrine, bows with joined palms and mutters a prayer which is usually the simple expression of a wish or request made in the colloquial vernacular and is not couched in set phrases. The educated few recite Sanskrit verses praising the deity. Having made his prayer, the worshipper performs *pradakshinam*, that is, he walks round the shrine keeping it on his right hand, or "withershins" to borrow a term from English folklore, once, thrice, seven times, or a hundred and one times, according to the fervour of his devotion; makes another bow before the idol muttering his prayer; receives *prasadam* (flowers and sandal powder, etc., which have been offered to the idol), from the priest and retires.

Kavus.

A Kavu is generally an unpretentious structure, mainly of wood with the characteristic tiled roofs and ornamental gables. In some cases the idol, a carved or uncarved piece of stone, stands in the open with no shelter except that afforded by the overspreading branches of some big tree such as an *Al* (*ficus religiosa*), *Pala* (*alstonia scholaris*) or *Kanniram* (*strychnos*). The priest is usually an inferior Brahman (Mussad, Elayad, Pidaran, Adigal), or one of the Sudra or polluting caste. In a few cases, where the employment is highly lucrative, Nambudiris or Embrandiris also officiate. The deities, as already observed, are the sons of Siva, the incarnations of his consort, Bhagavathi, or the innumerable host of his *bhuthams* or demons. The sons of Siva are propitiated by offerings similar to those

[1] Fergusson in his *History of Indian Architecture*, p. 307, argues a connection between Nepal and Malabar from the peculiarity of what he calls 'the reverse slope of the eaves above the verandah,' which is found in the temples of both countries. But the feature seems a not unnatural development of construction in wood. The photographs reproduced by Mr. Fawcett in the *Madras Government Museum Bulletin*, Vol. III, No. 1, p. 46, and No. 3, p. 272, illustrate the peculiarities referred to.

offered in *ambalams* ; but the other deities require the sacrifice of fowls and sometimes of goats. They have each their own oracles, who are usually members of the polluting castes and are called *Velicchappads*.

A good idea of the nature of the worship in a *Kavu* may be obtained from the detailed account of the seven days' festival at the Pishari Kavu at Quilandi, given by Mr. Fawcett in the Madras Government Museum Bulletin, Vol. III, 3, page 255. The temple priests there are Mussads, but Nambudiris purify the temple before and after the festival. The main features are the daily processions of the image round the temple with elephants and music, attended by the representatives of the Tiyan, Mukkuvan, Kammalan, Mannan, and other artizan and devil-dancing castes, each of whom has his appropriate caste function to perform in connection with the temple. On the last evening there is a grand procession, the goddess being represented by a sword wreathed in flowers carried by the chief Mussad, riding on an elephant ; a Mannan and Velan, painted and dressed up in elaborate masks to represent the demons Kutticchattan and Gulikhan, dance in front of it, and it is accompanied by a number of other devil-dancers of Velichappads, whose duty it is, as the procession moves on, to wring the necks of cocks offered in sacrifice by the bystanders in fulfilment of vows. After visiting the houses of the managers (*uralans*) of the temple the procession returns quickly ; the sword representing the goddess is placed on the sill of the door of the shrine by the chief Mussad, who prostrates himself before it ; and the chief Velicchappad, or oracle, with many contortions pronounces whether the goddess is pleased with the festival or not. Every one then leaves the temple precincts except the Mussads and a drummer and two temple servants, who finish the night by sacrificing goats and cocks in the shrine with the utmost secrecy. Before daybreak the temple is thoroughly cleansed.

Nagattan kavus.

Serpent shrines (*nagattan kavu* or *naga kotta*) are to be found in most house compounds, and their worship occupies a prominent place in the religious worship of the Nayar castes. The *Kavu* consists of a clump of jungle trees luxuriantly festooned with creepers, the whole being sacred and scrupulously reserved; in the middle are small snake-stones (*chittra-kuda-kallu*), or images of laterite. The snake is regarded as the tutelar deity of the house, and god and shrine are conveyed with the property and frequently specified in deeds of transfer. Snakes are also regarded as the gods of skin diseases. *Puja* is offered at least once a year, often by a Brahman ; and the serpents are periodically propitiated by songs and dances, called *nagam pattu* or *pamban thullal*, which have already been described in the account of the Pulluvan caste. The high priest of the serpent cult is the Pamban-makkad Nambudiri, who lives in Ponnani in a house full of cobras which are said to be harmless to his family.

Ancestor worship.

Ancestors are worshipped sometimes in special *kavus* and sometimes in small outhouses or special rooms in the house; generally there is no daily worship but there are periodical commemorations on the anniversary of the ancestors' death, or on the new moon days especially on Sivaratri or when the ghost proves troublesome. The ghosts are represented by stones or small images of gold or silver, kept usually in the middle room of the *padinnattim*; lamps are burnt throughout the night and offerings made of food and drink.

Religious life.

The Nambudiris are Vedic Brahmans and in the main worshippers of Siva, but throughout Malabar there is little sectarianism and no strict differentiation between the worship of Siva and of Vishnu. They perform the *Sandhyavandhanam* or daily worship of the sun; read portions of Ramayana or Maha Bharata or Bhagavata in the afternoon; and in the evening recite the invocation to Siva and Vishnu: "I adore thee, O Siva; I adore thee, O Narayana; I adore thee, O Achyutha; I adore thee, O Ananta; I adore thee, O Govinda; I adore thee, O Amrita; I adore thee, O Gopala; I adore thee, O Sri Krishna; I adore thee, O Vishnu." They observe the chief Vedic festivals and fasts (*vrathams*) and make the usual pilgrimage to holy places such as Benares, Srirangam, Perur and Rameswaram. They do not, as a rule, perform *puja* to any but Puranic gods; but they occasionally make offerings at serpent shrines; and they recognize the existence of evil spirits whom they exorcize by means of special *mantrams*. The peepul tree (*Ficus religiosa*), the Brahmani kite (*garudan*) and the *tulasi* plant or basil (*Ocimum Sanctum*) are sacred in their eyes.

High caste Nayars follow most of the religious practices of the Brahmans, but they are not permitted to read Vedas or perform Vedic rites; and serpent, tree, and ancestor worship occupy a more important place in their religion. The lower classes of Sudras and the polluting castes pay less attention to the Puranic gods. They recite the daily evening prayer, but worship in temples is confined to festive occasions. Fasts are seldom observed and pilgrimages seldom made outside the district. They assign most of the troubles of this life to the witchcraft of enemies, to the malignity of demons or ghosts, or to the evil eye. On the occurrence of any disease or calamity they consult the village astrologer who divines the evil spirit responsible, or the enemy who is at the bottom of the mischief, names the exorcist who can best deal with the case, and prescribes the mode of worship best suited to the occasion. The deities most adored are Subramaniyam, the small-pox goddess Kali, and Kutticchattan the most mischievous of the demons,

Religious life.

The outcastes and hill tribes sometimes make an annual offering to Brahmanic temples as an act of fealty, but their gods are the troublesome spirits of ancestors or demons; their medicine man, one of their own class, prescribes for diseases of both body and soul; he holds communion with the spirits world and can raise the devil as well as lay it.

Magic and superstition.

The Malayali is exceedingly superstitious. The witchcraft of several of the lower castes has already been referred to and it is remarkable how large a number of people make their livelihood by exorcism and magic. Velicchapads or oracles are to be found of nearly every caste below the Nayars. They visit private houses and declare their oracles when they have worked themselves up into a frenzy, dancing "withershins" round the yard, and slashing at their foreheads with a sword. The belief in the evil eye is universal; every new house has some grotesque wooden figure (*kanneru, drushti*) usually indecent, hung up, and every crop near a road some bogey struck up in a conspicuous place, to catch the evil eye. Spells and enchantments are implicitly believed in and have to be removed by incantations and special ceremonies. A common form of enchantment is to draw a figure representing your enemy on a small sheet of metal, preferably gold, add some mystic diagrams, and recite that on such and such a day the person in question shall die or be injured. The piece of metal is then enclosed in another metal sheet and buried in some place over which the person is likely to pass. Sometimes a live frog or a lizard is buried in a cocoanut shell with nails stuck into its eyes and stomach; and when it dies the enemy will also die. Of ceremonial to remove spells or possession the commonest is that known as *bali uzhiyuga* or *uzhicchal*. The *mantravadi* or magician draws diagrams on the floor of the verandah with charcoal, rice and saffron; and then makes an equilateral triangle or other geometrical figure, of the stem of a plantain leaf, with a bottom of flat pieces of plantain leaf placed crosswise, and fastened with plugs of bamboo, and small pieces of cocoanut leaves stuck on its upper sides. This is called the *pandibali* or *pandi*. It is placed on the diagram on the floor; and round it are put some beaten rice (*avil*), parched rice (*malar*), and bran (*tavitu*), a lighted lamp and two vessels, one containing water mixed with charcoal (*karutta kuruthi*), and the other water mixed with saffron and chunam (*chuvanna kuruthi*) to represent blood. The *mantravadi* performs *puja* with the rice and plantains, and repeats mantrams; while some one else waves pieces of plantain leaves, called *narukku*, and lighted wicks, *tiri*, round the patient's head and then throws them into the *pandi*. He then waves the *kuruthis* round the patient and lastly the *pandi* itself. Finally the *pandibali* which is supposed to contain the evil spirit is taken to a tank or field or some place remote from traffic and deposited there.

Bali.

CHAP. III. RELIGION.

There are a few Nambudiris who are celebrated *mantravadis*; but they are looked upon as degraded and strictly outcaste. They are Chela Nambudiris, that is the offspring of Nambudiris who were forcibly converted to Islam by Tipu. They are supposed to have complete control over the demon Kutticchattan.

Of omens, there is no end; and the most careful attentions is paid to them not only in embarking on important enterprises, but in the ordinary routine affairs of life. The Kanisans are the professional augurs. Crows flying left to right, jackals running right to left, and peacocks are amongst good omens; as are virgins, Rajas, elephants, white flowers, cows, swans; looking-glasses, and gold bracelets; evil omens are buffaloes, widows, salt, asses, broomsticks, cripples; cats mewing and owls hooting at night are unlucky and portend a death. To sneeze once is lucky, to sneeze twice is unlucky. The lizard (*gouli* or *palli*) has a whole science of augury attached to it; and it is the duty of the *Kanisan* on ceremonial occasions to interpret its prognostications.[1]

CEREMONIES. Nambudiris.

The Nambudiris are said to differ from other Brahmans in 64 *anacharams* or irregular customs, which are supposed to have been introduced by the great reformer Sankaracharya in the 9th or 10th century. A list of these is given by Mr. Fawcett in Madras Government Museum Bulletin, Vol. III, No. 1, p. 354, and by Mr. Logan in his Manual, Vol. I, p. 156; they include the rules already mentioned that only the eldest son should marry, that white only should be worn, and that women should not bore their noses, and many other minor details of ceremonial. Like other Brahmans, a Nambudiri should perform the sixteen ceremonies known collectively as the Shodasakriya; but the detailed ritual is in many of them peculiar. The most elaborate of the ceremonies are those performed at marriage (*vivaha*); and they deserve a detailed description.

Marriages.

The first preliminaries, in arranging a Nambudiri marriage are the inevitable comparison of horoscopes, and the settlement of the dowry.

When these have been satisfactorily concluded, an auspicious day for the wedding is selected in consultation with the astrologer. On that day, the bridegroom, before he starts from his illam, partakes with his relatives and friends of a sumptuous repast called the *ayani un*. A similar feast is held simultaneously at the bride's house. On leaving the *illam*, as he crosses the threshold, and indeed on all occasions of importance, the bridegroom must be careful to put his right foot first. He also mutters mantrams of an auspicious nature called *mangala-sutrangal*. As he passes out of the gate he is

[1] A list of deductions to be made from its behaviour may be found in the account of the Kanisan caste given in Monograph No. 12 of the *Cochin Ethnographical Survey*.

met by a bevy of Nayar ladies, carrying the eight lucky articles (*ashtamangalyam*).[1] On his journey to the bride's illam he is preceded by a noisy procession of Nayars, armed with swords and lacquered shields, who constitute his *agambadi* or body-guard, and by Nambudiri friends and relatives one of whom carries a lighted lamp. At the gate of the bride's illam he is met by a band of Nayar women, dressed like *antarjanams* and carrying the *ashtamangalyam*, and lighted lamps.

The bridegroom enters the inner court-yard (*nadumittam*), and takes his seat in the usual east-ward position. The bride's father comes and sits opposite him, and clasping his right hand formally invites him to bathe and wed his daughter, an invitation which he formally accepts. After his bath he returns clad in fresh clothes, and wearing a ring of *darbha* or *kusa* grass (*eragrostis cynosuroides*), and takes his seat in the room, adjoining the porch (*pumukham*), called *purattalam*. He then makes an offering of a few fanams to his family deities, performs Ganapathi-puja, and presents four or five Nambudiris with a few fanams each, and with betel-leaf and arecanut. This is called *asramapischetha prayaschittam*, and is in expiation of any sins into which he may have been betrayed during his bachelor days. Similar gifts are also made first to two Nambudiris of any gotra considered as representing the deities called Visvadevas, and then to two others of different gotras representing the deceased ancestors or Pitris. The last gift is called *nandimukham*.

Meanwhile, within the house the bride is conducted to the *Vadakkini* room, veiled in an old cloth and carrying a piece of bell-metal shaped like a hand-mirror (*val-kannadi*). Her father, after washing his feet and putting on a' darbha-ring, comes and performs Ganapathi-puja and repeats more or less the same ritual that has been performed without.

The bride is then sprinkled with holy water by her father and four other Nambudiris ; the *tali* or marriage symbol is brought in a small brass vessel containing holy water, and laid near the idol to which the daily domestic worship is paid ; and after further offerings to Ganapathi the bridegroom is summoned to enter the illam.

Before doing so he purifies himself taking off the *darbha* ring, making the " castemarks " with holy ashes (*bhasmam*), washing his feet, replacing the ring and being sprinkled with holy water by four Nambudiris—a form of ritual which recurs constantly in all ceremonies. He enters the *nadumittam*, preceded by a Nambudiri carrying a lighted lamp and takes his seat on a wooden stool (*pidam*) in the middle of the court where the

[1] The *ashtamangalyam* are a *grandha*, a washed cloth, a *cheppu* or rouge-box, some rice, a *val kannadi* or metal hand mirror, some *kankanum* (crimson), *chanthu* (ointment of sandal, camphor, musk and saffron), and *mashi* (bdellium or any eye salve).

CHAP. III. CEREMONIES.

bride's father makes obeisance to him, and is given four double lengths of cloth (*kaccha*), which the bridegroom has brought with him. They are taken to the bride, who puts on two of them and returns two for the bridegroom to wear.

The bridegroom then goes to the *kizhakkini* where he prepares what may be called the "altar." He smears part of the floor in front of him with cow-dung and then with a piece of jack-wood, called *sakalam*, draws a line at the western side of the place so prepared and at right angles to this line, five more, one at each end, but not actually touching it and three between these. He then places the piece of jack-wood on the altar and ignites it, with fire brought from the hearth of the bride's illam. He feeds the flame with chips of *plasu* or *chamatha* (*Butea frondosa*). This fire is the *aupasana agni*, regarded as the witness to the marriage-rite. It must be kept alight—not actually, but by a pious fiction [1]—till the parties to the marriage die, and their funeral pyre must be kindled from it.

Three pieces of *plasu* called *paridhi*, and eighteen pieces called *udhmam*, tied together by a string of *darbha*, are placed on the northern side of the altar on two pieces of jack-wood; and there are also brought and placed round the altar four blades of *darbha* grass, a small bell-metal vessel, an earthenware pot full of water, a pair of grindstones (*ammi* and *ammikuzha*), a small winnowing-fan, containing parched paddy (*malar*), and a copper vessel of ghee with a sacrificial ladle made of *plasu*.

Meanwhile the bride's father ties the tali round her neck in the *vadakkini*, and her mother gives her a garland of *tulasi* (*Ocimum sanctum*). She is conducted to the *kizhakkini*, preceded by a Nambudiri carrying a lamp called *ayyira-tiri* (thousand wicks) and is made to stand facing the bridegroom on the north or north-east of the altar. This is called *mukha-dharsanam* (face beholding). She gives the garland to the bridegroom.

Now comes the central rite of this elaborate ceremonial, the *udaga-purva-kannyaka-dhanam*, or gift of a maiden with water. The bride and her father stand facing west and the bridegroom facing them. All three stretch out their right hands, so that the bride's hand is between those of her father and the bridegroom, which are above and below hers respectively. A Nambudiri Othikkan or ritual expert pours water thrice into the father's hand. The latter each time pours it into his daughter's hand, and then grasping her hand pours it into the bridegroom's hand.

The dowry is then given to the bride who hands it over to the bridegroom. She then passes between him and the fire

[1] *i.e.*, by keeping a lamp lighted at the fire perpetually alight, or by heating a piece of *plasu* or *darbha* grass in the fire and putting it away carefully.

and sits on an *amanu-palaga* [1] on the east of the altar, while the bridegroom sits on another *palaga* on her left and burns the *idhmams* (except one piece of *plasu* and the *darbha* string used to tie the bundle), and makes an oblation of ghee called *agharam*.

The next rite is called *Panigrahanam*. The bridegroom rises from his seat, turns to the right and stands facing the bride, who remains seated holding the mirror in her left hand. She stretches out her right hand, palm upwards with the fingers closed and bent upwards. He grasps it and sits down again.

A brother of the bride now comes and takes the mirror from the bride, puts it on a *palaga* and professes to show her her own reflection in its surface. Then the bridegroom pours a little ghee into her joined hands ; to which the bride's brother adds two handfuls of paddy from the winnowing basket ; and the bridegroom then brushes the parched paddy from her hands into the fire. This is called the *Lajahomam*. At its conclusion bride and bridegroom perform a *pradakshinam* round the fire, passing outside the water-pot but not the grindstone and fan.

Next comes the important piece of ceremonial called *Asmarohanam* symbolising immutability. The bride and bridegroom stand west of the grindstones, and the bridegroom taking her feet one by one places them on the stones and then grasps her feet and the stones with both hands. *Lajahomam*, *pradhakshinam*, and *asmarohanam* are each repeated thrice.

Then comes the rite called the *Saptapadi* or seven paces. The bridegroom leads his bride seven steps towards the north-east, touching her right foot with his right hand as he does so. They then pass between the grindstones and the fire, and seat themselves on the west of the earthen pot facing east, the bride behind the bridegroom ; and the latter performs a somewhat acrobatic feat which it must be difficult to invest with any dignity. He bends backwards supporting himself by placing the palms of his hands on the ground behind him, until he can touch with the top of his head, that of the bride, who bends forward to facilitate the process. After this the bridegroom sprinkles himself and the bride with water from the earthen pot.

They then return to their seats west of the altar and face north, ostensibly looking at the pole-star (*Druvan*), the star Arundati, and the Seven Rishis (*Ursa Major*), which the bridegroom is supposed to point out to the bride, while he teaches her a short *mantram* invoking the blessing of long life on her husband.

---

[1] An *amanapalaga* or *amapalaga*, literally "tortoise plank" is a low wooden seat of *chamatha* wood, supposed to be shaped like a tortoise in outline.

CHAP. III. CEREMONIES.

The bridegroom then makes two oblations, pouring ghee on the sacred fire; the first called *Suishtakral homam* and the second *Darmmi homam.* He then places on the fire the *parudhis,* the remaining *idhmams* and *darbha* grass, and the rest of the ghee.

A start is then made for the bridegroom's illam, the bridegroom carrying the *chamatha* branch, used in making the *aupasana agni* in the bride's house. On arrival an altar is prepared in much the same manner as before, the *chamatha* branch is ignited and *darbha* and ghee are offered.

The bride and bridegroom next spend a few moments closeted in the same room, she lying on a skin spread over a new cloth on the floor and he sitting on an *amana palaga.* In the evening *aupasana homam* or offerings of *chamatha* in the sacred fire, and *vaisyadeva homam* or offerings of boiled rice are made. These which are known as a "second *homam*" may be postponed till next afternoon if there is no time for them on the actual wedding day. They have to be performed daily for ten months. The first three days on which these *homams* are performed (viz., the wedding day and the two days following it, or the three days after the wedding as the case may be) are regarded as days of mourning (*diksha*) and clothes are not changed.

On the fourth day the newly married couple have an oil bath, and the *diksha* is considered to be at an end. After the usual *homams* and worship of Ganapathi, the bride is led to the bridal chamber at an auspicious moment. Her husband joins her carrying two garlands of jasmine, one of which he puts on the lamp placed in the south-east corner of the room, and one round his wife's neck. He then smears the upper part of her body with the ointment known as *chanthu* and she herself smears the lower part. *Tum vir penem suum foeminae ad partes pudendas admovet, vestibus scilicet haud remotis.*

They then bathe and change their clothes and sit near each other, the wife screened behind an umbrella; her husband gives her water and after some further rites they eat from the same plantain leaf. Actual cohabitation commences from that night. The pair are conducted to the bridal chamber by the Vadhiyar. The nuptial couch is but a grass mat or a common country blanket covered with a white sheet, with a little ridge of rice and paddy signifying plenty around the edges.

The final ceremony is the *homam* called *stalipagam.* It is performed on the day after the first full moon day after the second *homam.* If the moon is at the full ¾ *nazhiga* before sunset or earlier, the ceremony may be performed on the full moon day itself.

CEREMONIES.

Mr. Fawcett, [1] M.R.Ry. Subrahmania Iyer Avargal [2] and Mr. Logan [3] mention one or two other ceremonies which are not referred to in the *grandhavari* from which the foregoing account is taken.

On the fifth day bride and bridegroom, it is said, "catch a fish about the size of minnow called in Malayalam *Manatt Kanni* (eyes looking upwards) in a tub of water using a cloth as a net"; on the same day they "anoint each other with oil and the bride combs the bridegroom's hair"; and in the evening "the bridegroom adorns his bride with flowers and makes her look into a mirror."

On the sixth or tenth day a few Brahmans are fed to please the deities, and the couple go to a jack tree under which some rice, curd and ghee are placed on some *kusa* grass and an offering is made of flower and sandalwood, or sandalwood powder. The *kanyanam*, the bamboo staff, the arrow and the mirror used during the ceremonies are given to the Vadhyayar and the wedding is over.

Pregnancy.

The chief ceremonies connected with pregnancy are *Pumsavanam* or rite to secure male offspring, at which the husband puts a grain of barley and two beans, to represent the male organ, into his wife's hand and pours some curds over them, which the wife then swallows, and also pours some juice of *karuga* grass into her right nostril: and *simantham*, a ceremony usually performed in the fourth month of pregnancy, at which the husband parts the wife's hair four times from back to front with a sprig of *atti* (*ficus glomerata*), a porcupine quill which must have three white marks on it, and three blades of *dharba* grass, all tied together; after which mantrams are sung to the accompaniment of *vinas*.

Jathakarmam.

The first ceremony to be performed on the birth of a child is called *jathakarmam*. A little gold-dust is mingled with ghee and honey; and the father takes up some of the mixture with a piece of gold and smears the child's lips with it, once with a mantram and twice in silence. He next washes the gold and touches the child's ears, shoulders and head with it, and finally makes a gift of the bit of gold and performs *nandimukham*.

Namakarmam.

The ceremony of naming the child *Namakarmam* takes place on the twelfth day. The father ties a string round the child's waist and marks its body with sacred ash (*bhasmam*). Then after the usual "gifts" he pronounces thrice in the child's right ear the words "*Devadatta Sarmmasi*" or if the child be a girl "*Nili dasi*." He then calls out the child's name thrice. Then taking the child from its mother he again

[1] Madras Government Museum Bulletin, Vol. III, No. 1.

[2] Travancore Census Report for 1901, p. 307.

[3] Malabar Manual, p. 128.

CHAP. III. CEREMONIES.

calls out the name thrice and finally gives the child back to its mother who in turn calls out the name thrice. Gifts and *nandimukham* complete the ceremony.

Nishkramana, etc.

In the fourth month the child is ceremonially taken out of doors (*Nishkramana* or *Vittil purapattu*) by the father, who carries it to a cocoanut tree round which he makes three *pradakshinams*. In the sixth month comes the *annaprasanam* or *chorunnu* ceremony when the child is given rice for the first time. The ear-boring (*kathu kuttu*) is generally done in the third year; and the *choulam* or tonsure in the fifth; and they are followed by the initiation into the alphabet (*vidyarambam*). The details of these ceremonies do not differ materially from those of the corresponding Nayar ceremonies, which are referred to in greater detail on p. 168.

Upanayanam.

The *upanayanam* or investiture with the thread is usually performed in a boy's eighth year. The thread is made of three fine threads spun into one: it must be white, sixteen feet long, and fastened in a special knot called *brahmagranthi*. After worship of Ganesha, the boy is dressed in new cloths and puts on a *darbha* ring; his father then invests him with the thread to which is attached a piece of blackbuck skin (*krishnajinam*) and with a belt (*mekhalam*) of *munda* grass. The boy is then given a stick, or *danda*, of *plasu* wood, which he holds in his hand, does obeisance to his father, and water is poured over his hands by his father and the priest. The boy then performs a *homam* himself. On the fourth day follows the boy's initiation into the vedas (*Ottu tudangal*), and thenceforward he must live the life of a *Brahmachari*, or celibate student of the vedas, seeing no one but his teacher or *guru* and wearing only the *Krishnajinam* and *mekhalam*, till he has performed the *Samavartanam* ceremony which marks the completion of his studies and his return to domestic life (*grihastiya*). It is performed usually in the sixteenth year; the boy bathes and throws the blackbuck skin belt and stick, which he was given at the *upanayanam*, into the water; he rubs himself with *chanthu*, puts an ear-ring in his right ear and a pearl necklace round his neck and garlands himself. He gives his upper cloth to his guru; and four days after is at liberty to marry.

Death.

When death is believed to be near, the dying man is taken to the west of the hearth of the sacred fire (*aupasana agni*) and laid with his head to the south on a bed of sand and *darbha* grass, while the *ottu mantram* is whispered in his ear. When life is extinct the body is washed and covered with a plantain leaf. The mourners dress themselves in *tattu* fashion and tear up a new cloth breadthwise into pieces called *sesham*, which they each wear round their waist. The body is then dressed in an undercloth; the forehead is smeared with the pounded root of the creeper *mettonni* (*Gloriosa superba*), and *tulasi* flowers are put on the head; the *kudumi* is untied, and the *punul* arranged to hang round the neck in front. The body is tied on to a bamboo ladder and covered with a new cloth, and then carried by four of the nearest relatives to the place of cremation within the compound of the *illam*; a trench is dug on the north-east of the pyre, and some water put into it, which is sprinkled on the pyre with twigs of *chamatha* and *darbha*. The body is then laid on the pyre with the head to the south and the fire is kindled. The ladder is thrown away and a *homam* performed of ghee and *darbha* grass made to represent the deceased, while *mantrams* are recited.

Then comes the ceremony called *kumbhapradakshinam*; the mourners go round the pyre three times, the eldest son leading the way carrying an earthen pot of water on his left shoulder: the water should run through the bottom of the pot, one hole being made for the first round, two for the second and three for the third, and the other mourners should sprinkle it on the pyre. At the end of the third round the pot is thrown on to the pyre, and all the mourners come away, the eldest son leaving last, and being careful not to look back. The *kumbhapradakshinam* is said to symbolize that the deceased has had his ablution in the water of the Ganges.

After bathing and shaving, the sons and other persons entitled to celebrate the obsequies each perform an oblation of water (*udagakriya*), to a piece of *karuga* grass stuck up to represent the spirit of the dead; concluding the ceremony by touching iron, granite, a firebrand, cowdung, paddy and gold three times, throwing away the *sesham*, and receiving a clean cloth (*mattu*). They then return to the *nadumittam* when they make offerings (*bali* or *veli*) of rice balls (*pindams*) to a piece of *karuga* grass. Both these ceremonies have to be repeated twice daily for ten days.

On the fourth day after death, provided it is not a Tuesday or Friday, the ceremony of collecting the bones, *Sanchayanam*, is performed. The eldest son goes to the pyre with a *pala* (pot made of the spathe of an areca palm) of milk, which he sprinkles on the pyre with a brush of *chamatha* tied with *karuga grass*; three *palas* are placed on the west of the pyre parallel to the places where the feet, waist and head of the corpse rested, and bones are removed from the feet, waist and head with tongs of *chamatha* and placed in the respective *palas*. The bones are then washed in milk, and all put into an earthen pot (*kudam*) with some *karuga* grass on the top; the pot is covered with a cloth, taken to a cocoanut tree and buried in a pit, the cloth being removed and the top filled with mud. A plantain is planted in the trench that was dug near the pyre.

CHAP. III. CEREMONIES.

On the eleventh day all the members of the family purify themselves and perform oblations of water and balls of rice. This constitutes the first *Sraddha*, which must be repeated on each anniversary of the eleventh day.

The funeral rites of Nambudiri women are similar; but if the woman is pregnant at the time of death, the body has first to be purified seven times with pounded *kusa* grass, cow-dung, cow's urine, ashes and gold, and to receive *mattu*; the belly is cut open four inches below the navel; and if the child is found alive, it is taken out and brought up; if dead, it is put back in the womb with a piece of gold and some ghee. Children not more than ten days old are buried with little ceremony, but all others are burnt.

In his account of Nambudiri funeral ceremonies in Madras Government Museum Bulletin, Vol. III, No. 1, Mr. Fawcett states that when the corpse is laid on the pyre it is uncovered, "rice is scattered over the face by all the blood relations present, and small pieces of gold are thrust into the nine openings of the body"; but this rite is not mentioned in the *grandhavari* from which the foregoing account is taken.

CEREMONIES OF NON-BRAHMAN CASTES.

It is impossible to deal fully with the manifold ceremonies of the various non-Brahman castes; and all that will be attempted is to describe in some detail a characteristic example of each ceremony, as it is performed by some caste or sub-division, noticing briefly distinctive differences in the observances of other castes. Generally speaking the ceremonies of the non-Brahman castes conform roughly to a uniform type, though there are of course vast differences in the degree of elaboration in the ritual and in the feasts that are the usual accompaniments of most ceremonies, corresponding to the wealth and social position of the family. The Nayar use has been taken as the type, as being the most distinctive, and the standard which the lower castes aim at imitating. The "degraded" classes and the hill tribes, of course, do not observe all the ceremonies referred to: and their marriage and death customs are in many respects peculiar. The more noticeable features are briefly alluded to in their place.

Pulikudi.

The first regular ceremony performed during pregnancy is known as *Pulikudi* or "drinking tamarind," which corresponds to the *Pumsavanam* of the Brahmans. But there are other observances of less importance which commonly, if not invariably, precede this, and may be considered as corresponding to the *Garbharakshana* (lit. embryo or womb-protection) ceremony sometimes performed by Brahmans, though not one of the obligatory sacraments. Sometimes the pregnant woman is made to consume daily a little ghee, which has been consecrated by a Nambudiri with appropriate *mantrams*. Sometimes exorcists of the lower castes, such as Panans, are called in and perform a ceremony called *Balikkala*, in which they draw magic patterns on the ground into which the girl throws lighted wicks, and sing rude songs to avert from the unborn babe the unwelcome attentions of evil spirits, accompanying them on a small drum called *tudi* or with bell-metal cymbals. The ceremony concludes with the sacrifice of a cock, if the woman is badly affected by the singing.

The *pulikudi* is variously performed in the fifth, seventh or ninth month. An auspicious hour (*muhurttam*) has to be selected by the village astrologer for this as for most ceremonies. A branch of a tamarind tree should be plucked by the pregnant woman's brother, who should go to the tree with a *kindi* (bell-metal vessel) of water followed by an *Enangatti* [1] carrying a hanging lamp with five wicks (*tukkuvilakku*), and before plucking it, perform three *pradakshinams* round it. In the room in which the ceremony is to be performed, usually the *vadakkini*, there is arranged a mat, the usual lamp (*nilavillakku*) with five wicks, and a *para* measure of rice (*niracchareppu*); also the materials necessary for the performance of Ganapathi *puja* (worship of the God Ganesa), consisting of plantains, brown sugar, leaves of the sacred basil or *tulasi* (*Ocimum sanctum*), sandal-paste, and the eight spices called *ashtagantham*.[2]

The woman's brother performs Ganapathi puja and then gives some of the tamarind leaves to the *Enangatti*, who expresses their juice and mixes it with that of four other plants.[3] The mixture is boiled with a little rice, and the brother takes a little of it in a jack-leaf folded like a spoon, and lets it run down the blade of a knife into his sister's mouth. He does this three times. Then the mixture is administered in the same manner by some woman of the husband's family, then by an *Ammayi* (wife of one of the members of the girl's tarwad). The branch is then planted in the *nadumittam* and watered, and feasting brings the ceremony to a close.

The above description was obtained from an Urali Nayar of Calicut taluk. In other localities and castes the details vary considerably. Sometimes the mixture is simply poured into the woman's mouth instead of being dripped off a knife.

---

[1] An *Enangan* or *Inangan* is a man of the same caste and subdivision or marriage group. It is usually translated "kinsman"; but is at once wider and narrower in its connotation. My *Enangans* are all who can marry the same people that I can. An *Enangatti* is a female member of an *Enangan's* family.

[2] The *ashtagantham* are *agil* (aloes), *kottagam* (*ocymum petiolare*), *murru* (myrrh), *manji* (spikenard), sandal, *gulguru* (bdellium), *iruveri* (*andropogon muricatum*), and *ramaccham* (kuskus grass).

[3] The *Aimpuli* or 'five tamarinds' are *Tamarindus Indica*, *Kodapuli*, or *Punarpuli* (*Garcinia Cambogia*), *Ambazham* (*Spondias magnifera*), *Narinnam* or *Arampuli* (*bauhinia racemosa*), and *Paricchagam* (*hibiscus hirtus*).

CHAP. III. CEREMONIES.

Some castes use a small spoon of gold or silver instead of the jack-leaves. In South Malabar there is not as a rule any procession to the tamarind tree.

Amongst Agattu Charna Nayars of South Malabar the ceremony takes place in the *nadumittam*, whither the tamarind branch is brought by a Tiyan. The girl carries a *valkannadi*, or bell-metal mirror, a *charakkol* or arrow and a *pisankatti*, knife. An *Enangatti* pours some oil on her head and lets it trickle down two or three hairs to her navel, where it is caught in a plate. Then the girl and her brother holding hands dig a hole with the *charakkol* and *pisankatti* and plant the tamarind branch in the *nadumittam* and water it. Then the juice is administered. Until she is confined the girl waters the tamarind branch and offers rice, flowers, and lighted wicks to it three times a day. When labour begins she uproots the branch.

Amongst the Izhuvans of Palghat the ceremony takes place in the *devapura* or the southern room of the *padinhatti*, in which the Lares and Penates are kept. Amongst the Calicut Tiyans three tamarind twigs are plucked by the woman's husband; the husband is thrice given some of the tamarind mixture by his wife's brother, while the husband's sister gives it to the wife.

Sometimes a kind of "lucky dip" forms part of the ceremony, either before the tamarind juice is administered or at the end. Six packets of gold, rice, saffron, charcoal, sandal and salt, are wrapped up in plantain leaves and put into a *kindi*; the girl has to pick out three at a time and give them to the *Enangatti*, who divines her future from the order in which the bags are picked out. This, or some similar method of divination, is a feature, which is introduced into many ceremonies.

The serf castes and the hill tribes do not seem to observe any regular ceremonies during pregnancy, though it is apparently the custom for some Cherumans to perform a *Balikkala* and to drink some tamarind juice, probably in imitation of their masters.

Child-birth.

As soon as a woman's delivery is imminent the midwife (Velatti) is called in. The astrologer is also called in to note the exact moment of birth, which it is necessary to ascertain in order to prepare the horoscope. The astrologer uses a sort of rude clepsydra for the purpose, consisting of a perforated cocoanut shell which gradually fills and sinks in a large vessel of water. Auspicious passages of the *puranas* are meanwhile read aloud by any one able to do so. The moment at which the child's head is presented is regarded for the purpose of horoscope as the time of birth. Amongst the Calicut Tiyans, a male child is greeted by the wife's brother with a cry of *Ku* thrice repeated, while he strikes the ground three times with a stick. The child as soon as born is bathed by the midwife in tepid water mixed with cocoanut milk.

CHAP. III. CEREMONIES.

On the fifth day after birth a woman of the Attikurissi or Marayan caste amongst Nayars, or of the barber caste in the lower classes, is called in, and purifies the mother, the other women of the household and the room in which the child was born, by lustration with milk and gingelly oil, using *karuga* (*Cynodon dactylon*) grass as a sprinkler. Her perquisites are the usual *niracchaveppu* (one edangazhi of paddy and one nazhi of uncooked rice) placed together with a lamp of five wicks in the room to be cleansed, and a small sum in cash. A similar purification ceremony on the 15th day concludes the pollution period. In some cases milk and cow's urine are sprinkled over the woman; and after she has bathed, the Marayan or Attikurissi waves over her and the child two vessels, one containing water stained red with turmeric and lime, and one water blackened with powdered charcoal.

Mattu.

During this and other periods of ceremonial pollution, a characteristic service called *mattu* (change) has to be rendered by people of the Mannan caste to Nayars, and to other castes by their proper washerman, who may or may not be Mannans. On the day of birth the Mannatti brings a clean *tuni* of her own and a *mundu*, which she places in the yard, in which she finds the accustomed perquisites of grain set out and a lamp. An Attikurissi Nayar woman takes the clean clothes and the Mannatti removes those previously worn by the mother. Every subsequent day during the pollution period the Mannatti brings a change of raiment; but it is only on the 7th and 15th days that any ceremonial is observed and that the Attikurissi woman is required. On those days a Mannan man attends with the Mannatti. He makes three *pradakshinams* round the clean clothes, the lamp and the *niracchaveppu*, and scatters a little of the grain forming the latter on the ground near it, with an obeisance, before the Attikurissi woman takes the clothes indoors.

This rite of *mattu* has far reaching importance. It affords a weapon by means of which the local tyrant can readily coerce his neighbours, whom he can subject to the disabilities of excommunication by forbidding the washerman to render them this service; while it contributes in no small degree to the reluctance of Malayali women to leave Kerala, since it is essential that the *mattu* should be furnished by the appropriate caste and no other.

Fifteen days is the period of pollution observed by Nayars and most of the polluting castes. Amongst Kshattriyas and Ambalavasis the period is eleven or twelve days. Amongst the degraded classes and the hill tribes the period varies; the

CHAP. III. CEREMONIES.

Cherumans are, according to Mr. Appadurai Aiyar,[1] considered to be under pollution for twenty-eight days in the South and forty-two in the North, during which time the husband has to do without rice; but according to other authorities pollution does not last beyond the purification on the seventh day. Nayadis and Paniyans are polluted for ten days, Kuricchiyans for twenty-eight, Malakkars for twelve and Kadars for four months. There is no ceremonial *mattu* among the lower castes, or the hill tribes, and the ingredients used in purification vary considerably; the Kuricchiyans and Malakkars who are the aristocracy of the hill tribes are said to require water drawn by a Brahman, as are also the Wynaad Chettis. Amongst *makkattayam* castes, and in *marumakkattayam* families where the wife lives with the husband, it is usual for her to be taken to her own *tarwad* house for the first child-birth; but the husband should pay the expenses. In the degraded castes and the hill tribes, the woman is either put in a separate hut or in a separate corner of the family hut. Amongst the Vettuvans when labour begins the woman is put in a hole dug in a corner of the hut and left there alone with some water till the cry of the child is heard.

Palu-kudi.

On the twenty-eighth day (including the day of birth) comes the *Pal-kudi* (milk drinking) ceremony, at which some women of the father's family must attend. Amongst castes in which the wife lives with the husband, the ceremony takes place in the husband's house, to which the wife and child return for the first time on this day. The usual lamp, *niracchaveppu* and *kindi* of water are set forth with a plate, if possible, of silver containing milk, honey and bits of a sort of plantain called *kunnan*, together with three jack leaves folded to serve as spoons. The mother brings the child newly bathed and places it in his *karnavan's* lap. The goldsmith is in attendance with a string of five beads (*mani* or *kuzhal*) made of the *panchaloham* or five metals, gold, silver, iron, copper and lead, which the father ties round the baby's waist. The *karnavan* or the mother then administers a spoonful of the contents of the plate to the child with each of the jack leaves in turn. The father's sister or other female relative also administers some, and the *karnavan* then whispers the child's name thrice in its right ear.

Chorunnu.

The name is not publicly announced till the *Chorunnu* or *Annaprasanam* (rice giving) which takes place generally in the sixth month and must be performed at an auspicious moment prescribed by an astrologer. The paraphernalia required are besides the five-wicked lamp, some plantain leaves on which are served rice and four kinds of curry called *kalan*, *olan*, *avil* and *ericchakari*, some *pappadams* (wafers of flour and

[1] See his article in the Calcutta Review for April 1900.

other ingredients), plantains and the sweetmeats called *upperi* (plantains fried in cocoanut oil). The mother brings the child, newly bathed and wearing a cloth for the first time, and places it in the *karnavan's* lap. The father then ties round the child's neck a gold ring, known as *muhurta mothiram* (auspicious moment ring); and the relatives present give the child other ornaments of gold or silver according to their means, usually a *nul* or neck thread adorned with one or more pendants, an *arannal* or girdle, a pair of bangles and a pair of anklets. The *karnavan* then, after an oblation to Ganapathi, gives the child some of the curry and whispers its name in its right ear three times. He then carries the child to a cocoanut tree near the house, round which he makes three *pradakshinams*, pouring water from a *kindi* round the foot of the tree as he does so. The procession then returns to the house, and on the way an old woman of the family proclaims the baby's name aloud for the first time in the form of a question asking it "Krishnan" (for instance) "dost thou see the sky?" In some cases the father simply calls out the name twice.

Amongst the lower castes the milk-drinking and rice-giving ceremonies are often combined. The child's name is sometimes fixed by a Velicchapad or oracle, called in to interpret the will of the gods: and magic rites with *balis* to avert evil spirits are often features of the ceremony. Amongst the serf castes, the name is often chosen by the janmi.

Vidyarambham.

The *Vidyarambham* ceremony to celebrate the beginning of the child's education takes place in the fifth or seventh year. In some places the child is first taken to the temple, where some water sanctified by *mantrams* is poured over his head by the *shantikaran* (officiating priest). The ceremony at the house is opened by Ganapathi *puja* performed by an Ezhuttacchan, or by a Nambudiri or another Nayar. The Ezhuttacchan writes on the child's tongue with a gold fanam the invocation to Ganapathi (Hari-Sri-Ganapathayi-nama), or sometimes the 51 letters of the Malayalam alphabet, and then grasps the middle finger of the child's right hand and with it traces the same letters in parched rice. He also gives the child an *ola* (strip of palm leaf) inscribed with them, and receives in return a small fee in cash. Next the child thrice touches first the Ezhuttacchan's feet and then his own forehead with his right hand, in token of that reverent submission to the teacher, which seems to have been the key note of the old Hindu system of education.

This and the next ceremonies are not observed by the lowest castes or hill tribes.

Choulam.

The Choulam, or tonsure ceremony, is performed usually in the fifth year, and takes place in the *pumukham*. The caste-barber sits opposite the boy, and shaves the whole of his head

CHAP. III. CEREMONIES.

except a patch on the top. He takes the boy's cloth, and the usual *nirachaveppu* as his remuneration, and is also paid a small fee in cash by the father.

Kathukuttu.

The *Kathukuttu* or ear-boring is performed either at the same time as the Palukudi or the *choulam* or at any time in the fifth or seventh year. The operator, who may be any one possessing the necessary skill, pierces first the right and then the left ear with two gold or silver wires brought by the goldsmith, or with *karamullu* thorns. The wires or thorns are left in the ears. In the case of girls the hole is subsequently gradually distended by the insertion of nine different kinds of thorns or plugs in succession, the last of which is a bamboo plug, till it is large enough to admit the characteristic Malayali ear ornament, the boss-shaped *toda*.

Tali kettu kalyanam.

We now come to the important ceremony known as *Tali kettu kalyanam*, the significance of which has been discussed already.

This must take place before a girl attains puberty and is usually performed in the ninth or eleventh year; but often to save expense, a regular "jail delivery," as it is humorously termed in the report of the Malabar Marriage Commission, takes place, the ceremony being performed simultaneously for all immature girls in a family whatever their age.

An auspicious time has to be selected for the purpose, and the preliminary consultation of the astrologer is itself the occasion of a family gathering. The *manavalan* or quasi-bridegroom is chosen at the same time.

For the actual *kalyanam* two pandals, a small one inside a large one, are erected in the court yard in front of the *padinhatta macchu* or central room of the western wing. They are decorated with cloth, garlands, lamps and palm leaves; and the pillars should be of areca palm cut by an Asari (carpenter) on Sunday, Monday or Wednesday.

The first day's ceremonies open with a morning visit to the temple, where the officiating Brahman pours water sanctified by mantrams and the addition of leaves of mango, peepul and darbha, over the girl's head. This rite is termed *kalasam maduga*.

The girl then goes home, and is taken to the *macchu* where a hanging lamp with five wicks is lighted; this should be kept alight during all the days of the *kalyanam*. The girl sits on a piece of *pala* wood (*alstonia scholaris*) which is called a *mana*. She is elaborately adorned, and some castes consider a coral neckalace as essential. In her right hand she holds a *valkannadi* (brass hand mirror), and in her left a *charakkel*, (a highly ornate arrow). In front of the girl are placed in addition to the five-wicked lamp and *nirachaveppu*, a metal dish or *talam* of parched rice, and the eight lucky things known as *ashtamangalyam* (p. 156). A woman termed Brahmini or Pushpini, usually of the Nambissan caste, sits facing her on a three-legged stool (*pidam*) and renders appropriate and lengthy songs, at the close of which she scatters rice over her. About midday there is a feast, and in the evening songs in the *macchu* are repeated.

Next morning the ceremonial in the *macchu* is repeated for the third time ; after which the paraphernalia are removed to the nearest tank or to the east of the household well, where the Pushpini sings once more, goes through the form of making the girl's toilet, and ties a cocoanut frond round each of her wrists (*kappola*). The girl then has to rise and jump twice over a *kindi* of water with an unhusked cocoanut placed on the top, overturning it the third time.

The party then proceed to the pandal, two men holding a scarlet cloth over the girl as a canopy, and a Chaliyan (weaver) brings two clothes (*kodi vastram*) which the girl puts on. In the evening the previous day's ceremonial is repeated in the *macchu*.

The third day is the most important, and it is then that the central act of the ceremony is performed. For this the girl sits in the inner pandal richly adorned. In some cases she is carried from the house to the pandal by her *karnavan* or brother, who makes a number of *pradakshinams* round the pandal (usually 3 or 7) before he places her in her seat. Before the girl are the various objects already specified, and the hymeneal ditties of the Pushpini open the proceedings. At the auspicious moment the *manavalan* arrives in rich attire. He is often preceded by a sort of bodyguard with sword and shield who utter a curious kind of cry, and is met at the gate of the girl's house by a bevy of matrons with lamps and salvers decorated with flowers and lights, called *talams*. A man of the girl's family washes his feet, and he takes his seat in the pandal on the girl's right. Sometimes the girl's father at this stage presents new clothes (*mantravadi* or *mantrakodi*) to the pair who at once done them. The girl's father takes the *tali*, a small round plate of gold about the size of a two-anna bit, with a hole at the top, from the goldsmith who is in waiting, pays him for it, and gives it to the *manavalan*. The *karnavan* or father of the girl asks the astrologer thrice if the moment has arrived ; and as he signifies his assent the third time, the *manavalan* ties the *tali* round the girl's neck amidst the shouts of those present. The *manavalan* carries the girl indoors to the *macchu*, and feasting brings the day to a close. Tom-toming and other music are of course incessant accompaniments throughout as on other festal occasions ; and the women in attendance keep up a curious kind of whistling, called *kurava*, beating their lips with their fingers.

CHAP. III. CEREMONIES.

On the fourth day, girl and *manavalan* go in procession to the temple richly dressed. The boy carrying some sort of sword and shield, heads the party. If the family be one of position he and the girl may be mounted on an elephant. Offerings are made to the deity and presents to the Brahmans. They then return home, and as they enter the house, the *manavalan* who brings up the rear is pelted by the boys of the party with plantains which he wards off with his shield. In other cases he is expected to make a pretence of forcing the door open. These two usages are no doubt to be classed with those marriage ceremonies which take the form of a contest between the bridegroom and the bride's relatives, and whcih are symbolic survivals of marriage by capture.

The *manavalan* and the girl next partake of food together in the inner pandal---a proceeding which obviously corresponds to the ceremonious first meal of a newly married couple. The assembled guests are of course lavishly entertained; the chief *Kovilagams* and big Nayar families will feed 1,000 Brahmans as well as their own relations, and spend anything up to ten or fifteen thousand rupees on the ceremony.

The foregoing account was in the main furnished by an Urali Nayar of Calicut. It has already been mentioned that the *tali* is sometimes tied by the girl's mother or aunt. The significance of this arrangement is seen, if we consider it in the light of the widespread custom which regards marriage between a man and his uncle's or aunt's daughter as the preferable union. Among the Calicut and North Malabar Tiyans, if real marriage and *tali kettu* are simultaneous, the husband ties the *tali*; if the girl is betrothed only, her betrothed's mother or sister ties it; and in other cases her maternal uncle's wife (regarded as the mother of her most natural partner) does so. Where a female relation ties the *tali*, a clay idol sometimes takes the place of a flesh and blood *manavalan*.

Whilst among many cases the *tali* tier must be of the same caste, and then there may be restrictions as to the section from which he may be taken, in other cases he must be of higher caste; for instance, a Brahman as amongst Samantans and Kshattriyas, Karo Panikkars and some Nayars, especially the families of local chieftains, or a Samantan, as amongst Agatt Charna Nayars. In North Malabar the *tali* is usually tied by a Nambudiri or an Embrandiri for Nayar girls. Amongst Vannattans it is tied by a Ravari woman. When the *manavalan* is a Brahman, Samantan or Kshattriya, one can tie the *tali* for several girls. Amongst the Marars of South Malabar the *tali* is tied at a temple by the mother, who receives it from the officiating Brahman. There is no *manavalan* properly speaking. Amongst Kiriyattil Nayars, and Nayars generally in North Malabar, the *tali* is tied on the first day instead of the third. In Palghat the *tali* is tied on the first day, the *manavalan* and the girl eat together on the fourth day and the procession to the temple on the fifth.

In some cases, for instance among Mala Pothuvals and Marars in South Malabar, a fictitious consummation is an incident of the *tali-kettu*; the girl and *manavalan* being made to lie on a bed together and left there alone for a few moments. Amongst the Mala Pothuvals this is done twice, once on the first and once on the last day, and they apparently also spend the three nights of the ceremony in the same bed chamber, but not alone, an *enangatti* sleeping there as chaperon. In these two castes, as in most if not all others, the ceremony also entails the pollution of the girl and her bridegroom. Amongst the Marars they are purified by a Nambudiri after they leave their quasi-nuptial couch. Amongst the Mala Pothuvals they are not allowed to bathe or to touch others during the wedding till the fourth day, when they are given *mattu* by the Veluttedan. Amongst Mukkuvans the girl's pollution lasts for six months at the end of which women of the Arayan or Kadavar families come, and in their presence the girl does obeisance to the four cardinal points, throwing rice towards each.

In the Palisa-kollan caste the girl and *manavalan* go to the tank on the last day of the ceremony. The girl standing in the tank ducks her whole body under water thrice. As she does so for the third time a *pandibali* or triangular platter made of cocoanut fronds and pieces of plantain stem and leaf plaited together, and adorned with five lighted wicks (see p. 155), is thrown over her into the water, and cut in half as it floats by an *enangan*, who sings a song called *Kalikkakam*. Lastly the girl chops in two a cocoanut placed on the bank. She aims two blows at it, and failure to sever it with a third is considered inauspicious. This *bali*, which is supposed to avert evil spirits, is a feature of the *tali-kettu* and other ceremonies amongst other castes also.

In some cases worship of the sun, sometimes performed on an elevated wooden platform, is an essential, while the planting of a jasmine (*jasminum angustiflora*) from which a branch is subsequently culled and carried in procession to the pandal, and similar rites are of widespread occurrence.

Amongst Palissa Kollans and some other castes the lucky dip ceremony described on p. 169 is performed on the last day (called *nalam kalyanam* or fourth marriage). An *enangan* drawing out the packets at random distributes them to the *manavalan*, the girl and himself in turn. It is lucky for the *manavalan* to get the gold and the girl the silver.

Lastly we are reminded of classical and other parallels by the importance attached in many castes to the principle in

CHAP. III. CEREMONIES.

this and other ceremonies of putting their right foot foremost when in the course of performing them they enter the house.

A significant finish to the ceremony in the form of a symbolical divorce is also not infrequent in South Malabar at all events. Thus amongst the Palisa Kollans the *manavalan* takes a piece of thread from his *mundu* and gives it saying "here is your sister's *accharam*" to the girl's brother, who breaks it in two and puffs it towards him. This is called *accharam tirka* and takes place at the gate. In other cases, the *manavalan* gives the girl a cloth on the first day and cuts it in two giving her one half on the last; or the *manavalan* and an *enangan* of the girl hold opposite ends of a cloth, which the *manavalan* cuts and tears in two and then gives both pieces to the girl.

The *tali* is worn for a varying period after the ceremony in different castes. The only permanent relation established between the *manavalan* and the girl is that obtaining in some castes in South Malabar, which requires her to observe death pollution should he die before her and belong to the same caste.

As has been remarked already, the *tali-kettu* ceremony is performed by most of the *makkattayam* castes except the very lowest. Though it is sometimes merged with the ordinary marriage ceremony proper, it is strictly independent of it and essentially different, since it does not in itself give the *manavalan* any right to cohabitation and must be performed before puberty, whereas the regular marriage is usually after puberty. Amongst the Cherumans, and the jungle tribes there is no *tali-kettu* ceremony, but the tying of a *tali* sometimes forms part of the ordinary marriage ritual; as indeed it does in some Mappilla and Syrian Christian marriages.

Tirandu kalyanam.

When a girl attains puberty, a ceremony called *Vayassariyikka* or *Tirandu kalyanam* (age indicating or puberty marriage) is generally performed. It lasts four days during which the girl is kept in a separate room under pollution. It should take place at her *tarwad* house whither she is taken at once if practicable, should she be living with her husband or father or elsewhere. The Mannatti gives her *mattu*, clad in which she goes to bathe in a tank, in the bed of which her brother has fixed an arrow to drive off the evil spirits. After bathing she attires herself in fresh cloths and returns to the house where she takes her seat in the court-yard, or the *nadumittam*.

Before her are arranged the same objects as figured in the opening ceremonies of the *tali-kettu*, and also the eight auspicious things called *ashtamangalyam*. An Attikuricchi woman wispers some formula in her ear and sprinkles parched rice over her head; and she is then made to lie down on a mattress in the *padinnatta vadakkini*, the floor of which has previously been decorated with arabesques in powdered chunam or rice.

CHAP. III. CEREMONIES.

The second and third days are devoted to the entertainment of near relatives. On the fourth day there is once more *mattu* ; and the ceremony closes with a feast at which the girl (whose pollution is now terminated) is present.

The *bali* ceremony described on p. 173 and the lucky dip rite described on p. 166 are also repeated among some castes. The girl should draw gold, rice and sandal ; the *enangan* silver, paddy and charcoal.

Amongst the Calicut Tiyans, gingelly oil is poured three times on the girl's head over a gold fanam ; and she sleeps with an iron knife under her mattress to protect her from evil spirits. *Mattu* is performed first on the third evening, and on the fourth day the *bali* rite is performed at the tank.

It is a traditional duty of the Panans to furnish a messenger to announce to an Izhuvan (or Tandan) girl's mother or husband (according to where she is staying) that she has attained puberty. The Izhuvas hold the *tirandu kalyanam* a week after that event in the house where it occurred.

Amongst Mukkuvans the Arayan and a Kadavan must lend the sanction of their presence to the *Tirandu kalyanam*. A song by Mannans is an essential to the girl's purification, but may take place any time up to a year after the ceremonial bath.

Amongst the Cherumans and the hill tribes, a girl is usually put in a separate hut, and considered under pollution for seven days when she attains puberty. Songs and devil dances (*malapattu*) often form part of the ritual of purification.

Marriage.

We now come to the actual commencement of marriage life in a practical sense. This may precede the attainment of puberty, but does not generally. It does not appear that any ceremonial on the occasion of first cohabitation is essential among the *marumakkattayan* castes ; but there seems to be a growing tendency to celebrate it with more or less elaborate rites for which western ideas are perhaps to some degree responsible, and into which even such alien features as bride-cake and wedding-ring have sometimes been introduced.[1]

Sambandham.

Many different names for this ceremony or occasion are in vogue in different places and among different castes, such as *pudamuri*, *vastradanam*, *uzhamporukkuka*, and *vidaram kayaruka*.[2] The most widely intelligible phrase is perhaps *Sambandham tudangal*, commencement of *sambandham* ; and the simplest form of rite, the presentation of a cloth by the bridegroom to the bride in the presence of relatives, to whom it is formally announced that "to-day X begins *sambandham* with Y."

[1] *See* Madras Museum Bulletin III, 3, p. 238.
[2] *Cf.* Malabar Marriage Commission's Report. para. 42.

CHAP. III. CEREMONIES.

It is usual for a man's first *sambandham* at all events to be arranged by his father or uncle. If the relatives of the girl selected agree to the match, and the astrologer is in favour of it after comparing the parties' horoscopes, an auspicious day is chosen for the wedding; and on the evening selected the bridegroom comes to the bride's house attended by fifteen or more relatives and *enangans*, but not by any of his immediate *karnavans* or *anandiravans*. He is received by the bride's brother who washes his feet. With him he brings a large quantity of chewing materials, which his party and the bride's male relatives proceed to discuss. The bridegroom then goes to the *padinnatta macchu*, where he presents the bride with four, eight or sixteen lengths of the ordinary white cotton cloth, and sometimes with betel leaf as well. He then rejoins the party outside. The men of both parties have a good dinner, after which the girl's aunt leads the man to the best room, which serves as nuptial chamber.

The bridegroom may go home either next morning or two or three days later. When he does so he sometimes leaves a small present of money under the girl's mattress. He also fixes the date of his *randam varavu* or second visit. On the latter occasion he is accompanied by three or four friends and brings a present of betel leaves for his wife's household, with whom he and his friends dine.

When the girl first visits her husband's *tarwad* she is met at the gate by his aunt or sister, carrying a lighted five-wicked lamp, and three or four other women. The aunt leads her to the *padinnatta macchu*, where she is fed to repletion with sweetmeats by the women of the house. In some cases a party of women go from the husband's house to the wife's *tarwad* to escort her. The occasion is termed *vettilakkettu*. In the North it is usual for her family to invite the wife to her old house for one night shortly after this. On her subsequent return to her husband the marriage is completed.

No formality is required to effect a divorce. Either party can break off the *sambandham*. The girl returns or is sent home (if she is at her husband's house) and the caste people are informed.

Vidaram kayaruka and *Uzhamporukkuka* are terms applied in North Malabar to marriage inaugurated by no ceremony at all. A wife so married does not live in her husband's house, as is usual in that part of the district, except for the wives of Rajas and Brahmans.

In the South there is generally speaking less ceremonial and the marriage tie is looser, while it is there usual for a woman to live at her *tarwad* house and not with her husband.

CHAP. III. CEREMONIES. — *Makkattayam marriage.*

Amongst those castes which follow *makkattayam*, the real marriage would appear generally to be accompanied by much the same ceremonies as the commencement of a *marumakkattayam Sambandham*.

Amongst Izhuvans a girl may be married before puberty, but the consummation is not supposed to be effected till after puberty, though the girl may live with her husband at once. If the marriage is performed before puberty, the ceremony is apparently combined with the *tali kettu kalyanam*. The bride is fetched from the *devapura* or family chapel with a silk veil over her head and holding a betel leaf in her right hand in front of her face. She stands in the pandal on a plank, on which there is some rice. On her right stand four *enangans* of the bridegroom, and on her left four of her own. The elder of the bridegroom's *enangans* hands one of the bride's *enangans* a bundle containing the *tali*, a *mundu*, a *ṛavu* (cloth), some rice, and betel leaves and a coin called the *meymel kanam*, which should be of gold and worth at least Re. 1. All these are provided by the bridegroom. He next hands the *tali* to the bridegroom's sister, who ties it on. After this all the *enangans* scatter rice and flowers over the bride. In this caste the claim of a man to the hand of his paternal aunt's daughter is recognised in the ceremony called *padikkal tada* (obstruction at the gate), which consists of a formal obstruction offered by 11 neighbours to the bride's removal, when she is not so related to her husband. They are bought off by a fee of 2 fanams and a packet of betel leaf. The girl is then taken to the bridegroom's house. If very young she is chaperoned by a female relative. On the fourth day there is a feast at the bridegroom's house called *nalam kalyanam*, and this concludes the ceremonies. Marriage after puberty is called *Pudamuri*. The ceremonial is the same, but there is no *padikkal tada*.

Amongst Tiyans, after the proposal and preliminary comparison of horoscopes, there is a regular betrothal ceremony called *kanhikudi* in Calicut, *kurikkal* in North Malabar and *accharam vekkuka* in South Malabar. It is attended by male relatives and friends of both parties and by the *Tandans* or headmen of their respective communities. Three men selected from those present sit facing east on a mat covered with a grass mat and a washed cloth, in the *padinnatta macchu*. Before them are a lighted lamp, a *kindi* of water and a plate (*talam*) of rice, and *kanji* is served to them. They repeat the terms of the proposed marriage contract, and a sum of 21 fanams (Rs. 5–4) and four pieces of new cloth are given by the bridegroom's party to the bride's uncle, after which the three men drink their *kanji*. The date of the wedding is then selected in consultation with the astrologer: the boy's *Tandan* gives some betel and two rupees to the girl's *Tandan*, and says "on such and such a date X (naming the bridegroom)

CHAP. III. CEREMONIES.

and friends and four women will come; you must give us the girl and prepare meals that day." To which the other replies "If you bring six clothes and 42 fanams as *kanam* and two fanams for the *machunan* (cousin), the girl will be sent with you." The business thus concluded, the company are feasted.

On the day of the wedding the bridegroom goes to the bride's house attended by his friends and relatives preceded by two Nayars and the *Tandan* or headman. The boy should carry a sword which the *Tandan* gives him. The procession sometimes includes a body of boys and men with swords and shields, who perform a dance. A party from the bride's house carrying lighted lamps meet them at a short distance from it, and sprinkling rice, lantana blossoms and rosewater over the bridegroom, escort him to the marriage pandal; where he takes his seat, in South Malabar, with a male companion (*changathi*) on either hand, and in North Malabar, with a single "best man." The girl is then led out dressed in new clothes brought by the bridegroom's sister and veiled with a silk veil; and is seated by the bridegroom, who puts on a stiff conical hat round which is tied a silk handkerchief. The girl's mother then places food (*ayani*) before the bridegroom and his best man or men, and they make a show of eating. A sum of 42 fánams (Rs. 10–8), the *kanam* or bride price, is then paid by the bridegroom's sister (in the north, his *karnavan*) to the bride's mother (also in the north to the *karnavan*). But another claim remains to be satisfied, that of the girl's maternal uncle's son, the rightful pretendant to her hand. He is accordingly bought off with a present of eight annas, and in acknowledgment that this account is settled in full, he gives betel leaf to his successful rival. The party then returns with the bride to the bridegroom's house, where they are received by the bridegroom's mother; the bride's party follows; betel and tobacco and sweets are distributed at the door (*vathil kanam*) and there is a general feast which concludes the ceremony.

Amongst the South Malabar Mukkuvans also, the first step is the proposal, which is made by the man's relatives. The selection of the wedding day (*pozhuttu kuri*) takes place in the girl's house in the presence of the Arayan and Kadavar of her village. The date selected is written by the astrologer on a palmyra leaf (*pozhutola*). On the evening before the wedding two men and a woman (usually his sister) are sent by the bridegroom to the bride's house with a *pudava* (woman's cloth), a piece of silk and a *kanam* of either 13 or 18 fanams tied in a cloth, according as it has been decided that the girl should or should not have a dowry. The headmen receive these and hand them over to the eldest woman in the bride's house. The bride is then attired in the *pudava* and silk, and taken to the bridegroom's house. She is met at the gate by a married woman of the house with a lighted lamp; preceded by whom, and amid showers of rice and flowers she enters the house taking care to put her right foot foremost. Next day there is a feast in the bridegroom's house, the dowry is paid, and the bride is formally handed over to the bridegroom's mother in the presence of witnesses (*Naduvanmar*) to the contract and with a prescribed formula of words.

Amongst Mukkuvans the *vidaram* marriage also obtains, but for this no ceremony is performed. The *vidaram* wife is not taken to her husband's house and her family pay no *stridhanam*. A *vidaram* marriage can at any time be completed, as it were, by the performance of the *kalyanam* ceremonies. Even if this be not done, however, a child by a *vidaram* wife has a claim to inherit to his father in South Malabar, if the latter recognises him by paying to the mother directly after her delivery a fee of 3 fanams, called *mukkapanam*. A curious custom is that which prescribes that if a girl be married after attaining puberty, she must remain for a period in the status of a *vidaram* wife, which may subsequently be raised by the performance of the regular *kalyanam*. A man can contract *vidaram* unions even if he is regularly married, but he can only enter into one regular marriage.

Amongst Kammalans the betrothal ceremony is similar to that of the Tiyans; if more than one brother is to be married to the same girl, her mother asks how many bridegrooms there are and replies that there are mats and planks for so many. Cohabitation sometimes begins from the night of the betrothal, the eldest brother having the priority and the rest following in order of seniority on introduction by the bride's brother. If the girl becomes pregnant, the formal marriage must be celebrated before the pregnancy has advanced six months. At the formal marriage, the bridegrooms are received by the bride's mother and brothers; two planks are placed before a lighted lamp, before which the bridegrooms and the bride's brothers prostrate themselves. The bride is dressed in a new cloth and brought downstairs by the bridegroom's sister and fed with sweetmeats. Next day all the bridegroom's party visit the *Tandan* of the bride's *desam*, who has to give them arrack and meat, receiving in his turn a present of two fanams. The next day the bride is again feasted in her house by the bridegrooms and is given her dowry, consisting of four metal plates, one spittoon, one *kindi* and a bell-metal lamp. The whole party then goes to the bridegroom's house, where the *Tandan* proclaims the titles of the parties and their *desam*; all the brothers who are to share in the marriage sit in a row on a mat with the bride on the extreme left, and all drink cocoanut milk. The presence

CHAP. III. CEREMONIES. of all the bridegrooms is essential at this final ceremony, though for the preceding formalities it is sufficient if the eldest is present.

Amongst Panans the principal features of the rite are that the husband makes a present of cloth and money to the girl and one cloth to her mother and he and the girl then feed together.

In the *makkattayam* castes various symbolical ceremonies are necessary to constitute a valid divorce. Amongst Mukkuvans the *vidaram* connection can be terminated without any such formality; but to break off a regular marriage the husband sends a piece of black cloth to the wife with the cognizance of the elders. Amongst Tandans the intention must be declared before four persons representing each party. Amongst Kolla Kurups the husband and the wife's brother stand east and west respectively of a lighted lamp placed in the yard of the woman's original home. The husband pulls a thread from his cloth and approaches the lamp and breaks the thread saying "here is your sister's *accharam.*" Amongst Panans the formality is practically the same. The husband gives the thread to the brother who puffs it away saying "your *parisham* is over."

Among the Cherumans and degraded castes, the payment of money and the presentation of a cloth to the bride are the principal features of the marriage ceremony. Monogamy is the rule, but divorce is easily obtained, provided that the marriage expenses are paid. Amongst the Pula Cherumans of the south an old custom, now dying out, is said to have been for the bridegroom's party to go to the bride's house, and bring her away with a procession headed by men who engage in a mock fight with sticks (*vadi tallu*); and for the bride on arrival at the bridegroom's house to weep and deplore her fate, and on entering to tread on the pestle placed across the threshold. In Ponnani the Pulayans are said to have no regular marriage observances, but to imitate the *sambandham* of their masters.

The Nayadis are monogamists, and it is the practice for a boy to marry his cousin. The dowry varies from one to five fanams, and a string of beads representing the *tali* is tied round the bride's neck by the bridegroom's sister on the day of the wedding. Bridegrooms are said to be selected sometimes by the following curious method; the girl is placed inside a hut made of leaves, and the eligible bachelors collected outside each with a stick in his hand; the girl's father beats a drum and sings songs, while the boys dance round the hut poking their sticks through the walls; the father says to the girl "Take whom fate gives you, if not whom you desire" and the girl catches hold of the end of one of the sticks. The boy whose stick she selects becomes the bridegroom, and the marriage is celebrated on the spot.

CHAP. III. CEREMONIES.

The marriage customs of the Paniyans are typical of those of the jungle tribes in general. The consent of the headman (*Kuttan*) has first to be obtained: and for thirty days the bridegroom has to bring rice and firewood to the bride's house. On the date of the wedding a sum of money, a cloth with four annas tied up in one corner and a string of beads are presented to the bride's father; the *Kuttan* washes the bridegroom's feet, and bride and bridegroom eat together in the bride's house. The relations are feasted separately with music and dancing. The bridegroom then takes the bride to his own house. He has also to make an annual present of rice to his wife's parents; and failure to do so entitles them to demand their daughter back.

Among the Malasars the bridegroom has to make presents of cloth and money to the bride and her parents, and a string on which is a brass ring is tied round the bride's neck by the bridegroom's mother. Divorce can be obtained by merely pronouncing the intention in the presence of ten persons; but the wife must pay back the price paid for her if she wishes for a divorce.

Amongst the Vettuvans of Chirakkal the bride-price in the form of paddy and toddy is given to the bride's uncle by the bridegroom's janmi, and he is also given a ring (*ari mothiram*) to put on the bride at her house. The bridegroom has to feed the relations at his house; husband and wife begin living together ten days after.

Amongst the Shola Nayakkars a feature of the marriage ceremony is said to be for the bride to roll a cheroot of tobacco leaves, which both parties must smoke in turn.

Funeral and memorial ceremonies.

Great importance is attached to the presence round his death bed of a man's *anandiravans* and sons; his elder relations should not take part in the funeral ceremonies. As the sad moment approaches each of the relatives present drops into his mouth with a jack leaf a little *kanji* or cocoanut milk, and obtains his last blessing. As soon as dead they carry the body to the *padinnatta macchu*, and lay it on a mat or plantain leaf spread on the floor. The body is then washed and the caste marks applied with sandal and ashes. The big toes and the thumbs are tied together. Paddy and rice are sprinkled all round: a lamp with one wick is lighted and placed at the feet with a *niracchaveppu*: a cocoanut is cleft and one half is placed at the feet and the other at the head, and in each is put a lighted wick. Each of those present then drops a little water into the dead man's mouth over a *tulasi* leaf and a bit of gold. If the family can afford it, the gold

CHAP. III. CEREMONIES.

(preferably a fanam) is placed in the mouth and left there. The corpse is then covered with clean cloths and with kerchiefs of scarlet silk. These serve as a shroud and most of them afterwards become perquisites of the Attikurrissi Nayar, who performs the purification and directs the funeral ceremonies.

Meanwhile the pyre is being prepared, a duty which is performed in the case of North Malabar Nayars by the *Tandan* or Tiyan headman of the neighbourhood. A pit is dug 7 or 8 feet long, 3 or 4 feet deep and 3 feet broad running north and south and the pyre built over it with mango billets, and if possible some sandalwood, in a framework of cocoanut planks. When the pyre is ready, the *anandiravans* and sons of the deceased who are to act as bearers, make three *pradakshinams* round the body sprinkling rice on it as they go. They then carry it to the pyre, on which after making three *pradakshinams*, they place it with the head south. The senior *anandiravan* then half tears a strip from the cloth covering the deceased's face, and sets fire to pyre at the feet. The others assist, and as soon as the pyre is alight the senior *anandiravan* tears the strip of cloth right off and tucks it into his waist. It is called the *sesham*.

The Attikurrisi Nayar then gives the senior *anandiravan* an earthenware pot full of water. Bearing this on his right shoulder he makes three *pradashinams* round the fire followed by the Attikurrissi, who as he goes chips several small holes in the vessel and by the *anandiravans* who catch the spouting water in their hands and sprinkle it and parched rice on the fire. Finally the senior *anandiravan* drops the pot behind him smashing it on the southern end of the pyre. This is called *kumbhapradakṣhinam*.

The *anandiravans* and sons then come to the northern end of the pyre and prostrate themselves; after which the Attikurrissi sprinkles them with milk and gingelly oil, and they go to bathe.

At the tank the mourners make an oblation of water (*udagakriya*) to the spirit of the dead man; and on their return perform in the courtyard the ceremony known as *bali*. The celebrant dressed *tattu*-wise and wearing the *sesham*, a *darbha* ring and a *pishankatti*, sits facing east on an *amana palaga* with a lamp, a *niracchaveppu*, a cocoanut and a piece of palmyra leaf (*patta*) before him; also a bunch of *darbha* grass, on which he places some flowers of the *cherula*, sprinkling over it sandal wood paste, gingelly and saffron. He first performs Ganapathi *puja*. He then makes a hole in the ground and plants the palmyra leaf in it putting round it sandalwood paste, gingelly and *cherula* blossoms. He then cuts open the cocoanut and pours the milk over the *patta*, which is supposed to represent the spirit of the deceased. He then makes a big rice ball (*pindam*) with parched rice, gingelly, saffron and ghee

This he first holds close to his heart and then puts down on the *darbha* and sprinkles with water, *cherula* flowers, sandal paste, saffron and gingelly, each three times. Then he covers it with the plantain leaf, and joins his hands over it in the attitude of prayer. He next tears the leaf down the mid rib and placing both hands on the ground he bows low over the *pindam*. He then puts it in another plantain leaf; and after covering the *patta* with a basket, takes the *pindam* to the southern courtyard, where he lays it down and the crows are supposed to come and devour it.

This ceremony is performed daily for ten days. On the tenth he plucks up the *patta* and throws it into a flowing stream; on the 11th and 12th days he performs a similar ceremony without a palmyra leaf in the courtyard, and on the 13th in the *vadakkini*. On this day ten *enangans* must be present, to each of whom he gives betel leaf and one fanam. He and they then receive *mattu* and go to bathe; and he throws the *sesham*, which he has worn continuously up till now, into the tank. After the bath the entire household is purified by lustration with holy water by five Brahmans. After this the *bali* ceremony is performed once more in the *vadakkini*, and presents are given to eight more *enangans*. The men and boys of the family all make a *pradakshinam* round the *pindam*, and prostrate themselves, and the *pindam* is disposed of as usual. They then put on their caste marks which they have been hitherto prohibited from doing during the mourning. The man who led the *bali* ceremony must be shaved on the day of the death, and on the next day; after that he may not shave till the 13th day, or if he is to continue to perform the subsequent memorial ceremonies (*sraddha*) for a year; but on the 13th day he can appoint a deputy to perform them and in that case the latter alone need grow a beard. The ceremony is to be performed daily for a year in the *vadakkini*.

On the fifth or seventh day of the mourning the ceremony of collecting the bones (*sanchayanam*) takes place. All the pieces of bone that can be found in the ashes of the pyre are collected in an areca pot (*pala*) and carried to the sea or a river into which they are thrown; unless indeed the family be able to afford a journey to the Ganges, or any of the other *tirthams* (sacred waters) held in special reverence by the Hindus, in order to dispose of them.

The above account refers specially to the Mala Pothuvals. The Nayar use is generally on the same lines. The pollution period of course differs in different sections; one or two tender cocoanuts are sometimes planted instead of a palmyra leaf to represent the deceased, while *karuga* grass takes the place of *darbha*. On the night before pollution terminates, *puja* is performed by an Attikurrissi Nayar in the death chamber before a figure of Bhadrakali made of rice flour, beaten rice, parched rice, saffron and bran.

CHAP. III. CEREMONIES.

Amongst Tiyans, who usually burn old people and head of families and bury others, the ceremony of dropping water into the mouth of the corpse is performed at the pyre, or burial place (always in the compound of the house); and the barber cuts a hole in the cloth which covers the body, over the mouth, for the purpose. The *sesham* cloth is tied round the mourner's forehead instead of the waist. The pyre is watched by Panans beating drums for the first four nights. On the night before the *Sanchayanam*, a vigil before a lighted lamp is kept by the deceased's niece, or daughter if the deceased is a woman. Each mourner performs *bali* with three rice *pindams*. Pollution ends on the eleventh, thirteenth or fifteenth day (usually on the eleventh) when there is a special purificatory ceremony (*Pulakuli*). The barber draws a figure of the deceased on the ground with rice flour, on which he places two plantain leaves, a new cloth and a basket of three measures of paddy. The chief mourner measures out the paddy with his hands into two portions, and puts it in separate folds of a clean cloth (*mattu*), in the four corners of which are tied a piece of charcoal, a little salt, some chillies and a gold fanam. He places the cloth on his head and then touches with it his forehead, his ears, shoulders, loins, knees and toes. He then bows over the figure on the floor three times, with his legs crossed and holding the left ear with the right hand and the right ear with the left hand and touching the ground with his elbows. After the bones are cast into the river or sea, there is a further purificatory ceremony, and the barber is given various perquisites. *Diksha* is observed for forty-one days or a year, *bali* being performed each day. A year after the funeral, a ceremony somewhat similar to *Balikkala* described on p. 164 is performed, one of the young girls of the house acting as oracle of the ghost. Amongst North Malabar Tiyans on the last day of pollution an image of the deceased is sometimes made in rice, and carried in procession to a river or sea in which it is thrown.

Amongst Mukkuvans, who also bury, the corpse is borne three times round the grave, while the chief mourner stands at the head or southern end with a pot of water, supported by a barber who holds a winnowing basket (*murram*) of paddy. Each of the persons present then takes a handful of rice, dips it in the water and throws it in the grave. When the grave is filled up there is the usual *kumbha pradashinam*, and the chief mourner plants a branch of *tulasi* at the northern end. The first purificatory ceremony is performed on the fifth day, and the pollution ends on the 15th.

The Era Cherumans and Kanakkans bury as a rule; but the Pula Cherumans in Ernad are said to burn their dead. Offerings of cocoanuts and rice balls are made over the grave till the period of pollution is over, usually fourteen days. A curious device is said to be resorted to in order to minimise the inconvenience to which the death pollution necessarily subjects the Cheruman by interrupting the labour on which he is dependent for his daily bread. A ball of cowdung and paddy is placed in an earthen chatty, the mouth of which is stopped with clay. The pollution remains in abeyance so long as the pot is closed. When it will cost least inconvenience the pot is opened; but the pollution which then begins lasts for forty days.

Amongst the Nayadis the dead are buried in special burial grounds; and on the tenth day after death *bali* is performed. water being sprinkled thrice by each of the mourners over a small heap of rice and *karuga* grass. In the seventh month the bones are dug up and partially burnt, and then placed in a new pot which is tied to a tree near the deceased's hut; finally the pot is buried near a stream and the place marked by a heap of sand. Stones are also set up in the burial grounds in a circle to represent deceased's ancestors, and worshipped with offerings of rice and toddy at the chief festivals.

The Paniyans also bury their dead. On the seventh day after burial a ceremony is performed, at which the mourners dance to a dirge sung to the accompaniment of beads shaken in a *murram* or winnowing basket. This ceremony is repeated every Magaram (January) for three years; and the third year's performance is preceded by the delivery of an oracle by a *Komaran* who has a cloth tied round his head, and beads round his feet, and dances himself into a frenzy shaking the *murram*.

MUHAMMADANS.

The Muhammadans in Malabar number 850,000 or 30 per cent of the total population. In Palghat there are some 20,000 Ravuttans or Labbais and a few Pathans, and in the bigger coast towns a few pure Arabs; but the bulk of the Muhammadans are Mappillas, a race peculiar to the West Coast. They are spread over the whole of the district, and are most numerous on the coast and in the interior of the taluks of Ernad and Walavanad.

MAPPILLAS. Origin.

The tradition of the origin of the Mappillas, which connects them with the conversion of a Perumal to Islam in the ninth century, and the subsequent mission of the four apostles, Malik Ibn Dinar, Habib Ibn Malik, Sherif Ibn Malik and Malik Ibn Habib who are said to have founded the nine original mosques, has already been referred to in the last chapter. The name Mappilla has been variously interpreted to mean "mother's son" or "bridegroom", in allusion to the supposed union between the early Arab traders with women of the country; but it is perhaps merely a title (*ma*, great and *pilla*, child), which was given to foreigners whether Musalman (Chonaka Mappilla) or Christian (Nasrani Mappilla). As has been stated there was considerable trade between Arabia and Malabar in the eighth and ninth centuries, and no doubt many of the traders gradually settled in the country. As traders they would come

CHAP. III. MAPPILLAS.

without their women and as Muhammadans would not fail to proselytise; and the result would be the rise of a hybrid community composed of the offspring of mixed unions and of converts from the lower classes of the Hindus. The Zamorin of Calicut, who was one of the chief patrons of Arab trade, definitely encouraged conversion in order to man the Arab ships on which he depended for his aggrandisement; and he is said to have directed that in every family of fishermen in his dominion one or more of the male members should be brought up as Muhammadans. The practice has continued to the present day and it is not uncommon to find Mukkuvan boys being trained in the Koran. Numbers of recruits come also from time to time from the ranks of the Tiyans, and from the Cherumans and serf castes to whom "the honour of Islam" brings enfranchisement from all the disabilities of an outcaste.[1] Occasionally but not often, converts are drawn from amongst the Nayars and Native Christians. During the time of Tipu there was of course wholesale conversion of all castes; but most of the Brahmans and Nayars who were forcibly converted subsequently disowned Muhammadanism, and their descendants now belong to their original castes, though they are looked upon to some extent as polluted, and are known as Chela Nambudiris, or Chela Nayars. The mixed nature of the race may be traced to-day in its varied physiognomy; those of old family and social position are often extremely fair with fine features, sometimes of a distinctly Semitic type; while those at the other end of the scale are indistinguishable from the low castes from which they are constantly reinforced.

Characteristics.

The Mappillas are as a rule frugal, industrious and enterprising. They conduct the bulk of the trade of all descriptions, and many of them have amassed considerable wealth; all who can afford it invest money in land, and most of the new garden cultivation on the margin of the jungle in the interior is being opened up by them. The lower classes are fishermen, labourers of every description, and petty cultivators. The physique of the Mappilla is on the whole remarkably good, and the race has supplied the most satisfactory coolies for railway work and the like. Many enterprising Mappilla traders are also to be found in Ceylon, the Straits Settlements and Burma.

The outrages referred to in the last chapter have given the Mappillas a reputation for turbulence and fanaticism, which perhaps they hardly deserve. A respect for authority is one of the chief virtues inculcated in the Koran, and the child-like reverence with which Mappillas regard their own leaders, or

[1] The average number of converts received annually from all parts of the district during the last three years in the *Mannat-ul-islam Sabha* at Ponnani—an institution where converts are circumcised and instructed in the rudiments of the Faith—was 750.

Tangals, is remarkable. The religion of Islam preaches fraternity, and the Mappillas present a striking contrast to the Hindus in their capacity of standing by one another ; they are faithful and can be relied upon in emergencies. It is no doubt true that the experiment of enlisting them for the Indian Army has not been a success, and the two regiments recruited in the last few years have recently been disbanded ; but those best competent to judge do not consider that the Mappilla has been thereby proved unfit for military service. The recruits were drawn principally from Ernad and Walavanad, where as has been noticed in the last chapter special conditions conduce to keep the Mappilla poor, ignorant and fanatical ; and they were not infrequently taken from the criminal classes. In Calicut, and the north, poverty is far less common, and the Mappilla is as a rule prosperous and law abiding.

Dwellings. The Mappilla dwelling varies in size and material from the mud hut, roofed with cadjans or straw, of the lower classes, to the large and airy buildings of one or more stories constructed of stones and roofed with tiles, occupied by the wealthy. There are no peculiarities in architecture or design which call for special comment. The Mappilla trader does not, like the Hindu, object to living in streets, and is content with a very minute back garden, if he has one at all, surrounded by a high wall to protect his women from the public gaze. The typical Mappilla street is picturesque, but dirty.

Dress. The ordinary dress of the men is a *mundu* or cloth, generally white with a purple border, but sometimes orange or green or plain white. It is tied on the left (Hindus tie them on the right) and kept in position by a *nul* or waist string, to which are attached one or more *elassus* (small cylinders) of gold, silver or baser metal, containing texts from the Koran or magic *yantrams*. A small knife is usually worn in the waist. Persons of importance wear in addition a long flowing white garment of fine cotton (a kind of burnoos) ; and over this again may be worn a short waistcoat-like jacket, though this is uncommon in South Malabar, and (in the case of Tangals, etc.) a cloak of some rich coloured silk. The European shirt, and short coat are also coming into fashion in the towns. A small cap of white or white and black is very commonly worn, and round this an ordinary turban or some bright coloured scarf may be tied. Mappillas shave their heads clean. Beards are frequently worn especially by old people and Tangals. Hajis or men who have made their pilgrimage to Mecca, and other holy men often dye the beard red.

Women wear a *mundu* of some coloured cloth (dark blue is most usual) ; a white loose bodice, more or less embroidered ; and a veil or scarf on the head. In the case of the wealthy, the *mundu* may be of silk of some light colour. Women of the

CHAP. III. MAPPILLAS.

higher classes are kept secluded and hide their faces when they go abroad; but the lower classes are not particular in this respect.

Men wear no jewellery except the *elassus* already mentioned and in some cases rings on the fingers, but these should not be of pure gold. Women's jewellery is of considerable variety and is sometimes very costly. It takes the form of necklaces, ear-rings, zones, bracelets and anklets. As amongst Tiyans and Mukkuvans a great number of ear-rings are worn; the rim of the ear is bored into as many as ten or a dozen holes in addition to the one in the lobe. Nose-rings are not worn.

Food.

Rice and fish are the Mappilla's staple food. Those who can afford it eat meat, but it must have been properly killed (*halal*) by having its throat cut. All Mappillas will eat together. Alcohol is strictly forbidden to followers of the Prophet; and the prohibition is generally respected, except by some of the fishermen.

Religion.

The Mappillas belong to the Shafi school of the Sunni sect of Muhammadans, that is they acknowledge besides the Koran, the authority of the Sunneh, or customary law of Arab theology, as interpreted by Shafi. In South Malabar they are divided into two divisions, preferring allegiance to the Valiya Jaratingal Tangal of Ponnani and the Kundotti Tangal respectively. The followers of the latter are said by those of the former to be Shiahs, but they themselves claim to be Sunnis.[1] The differences between the two parties sometimes become acute and lead to disturbances, but intermarriage between them is not prohibited and persons often forsake one sect for the other to suit the convenience or caprice of the moment. The division between the two is born in fact of party spirit rather than based on any essential doctrinal difference. The Mappillas acknowledge the spiritual supremacy of the Sultan of Constantinople. The Tangals[2] are their religious leaders; they are regarded with a high degree of reverence, but are not as a class distinguished by learning. The principal authority on religious subjects is the Makhdum Tangal of Ponnani. He is the head of the Ponnani religious college and confers the title of *Musaliyar* (*moulvi* or elder) on *Mullas* who have qualified themselves to interpret the Koran and the commentaries (*Kitab*). The office of *Kazi* is sometimes held by a Tangal.

---

[1] Sunnis accept Abu Bakr Muhammad's father-in-law, the first Calif, as the rightful successor to Muhammad: Shias disown him and declare that succession should have gone direct to Ali, Muhammad's adopted son, and the father of Hussain. The latter refused to subscribe to the Sunneh or traditions of Arab theology. The Sunnis when praying cross their arms over the heart Shiahs keep the arms straight.

[2] The title is merely the honorific plural of the personal pronoun, commonly used in addressing superiors. It should, strictly speaking, be confined to the descendants of the Prophet, who are distinguished by the title Sayid.

CHAP. III. MAPPILLAS.

Mosques.

Mappilla mosques (*palli*) are rectangular buildings with sloping tiled roofs and ornamental gables in front like those of the Hindu temples ; some of them have gate houses, and a few of the oldest have circular towers attached. They are built with the main entrance to the west so that the congregation faces east towards Mecca. There is often a small tank close by. A *Mulla* who can read, but not necessarily understand, Arabic is attached to every mosque to lead the services. He is appointed by the congregation, though the *Kazi* as a rule nominates him. The *Kazi* is the head of the *Jamat* (lit. assembly), or Friday mosque, which corresponds to the parish church. His functions include the reading of the Friday sermon (*kutba*), the registration of marriages, and general arbitration in civil and religious matters. His jurisdiction may extend over more than one *desam*, or over only a part of a *desam* ; and may include several minor mosques. *Musaliyars* are not necessarily attached to any mosque, but travel about preaching and teaching.

Religious observances.

Mappillas strictly observe the five essentials of the Muhammadan religion, viz., the recital of the *kalima* or creed, the five daily prayers (*niskaram*), the Ramazan fast, the duty of alms (*zakkath, tithe*), and the haj or pilgrimage to Mecca.

The daily prayers should be said at daybreak, at midday, before sunset, after sunset and at about 8-30 or 9 p.m. ; ablution of hands and feet should precede each ; the first *niskaram* should consist of 2 *rakayats* or forms of prayer, comprising the *fateha* or recital of the first chapter of the Koran, and the usual genuflexions and prostrations (*sujud*) ; the second, third and fifth *niskarams* should consist of four *rakayats*, and the fourth of three. All prayers are in Arabic, a language which few even of the Tangals understand. On Fridays, prayers should be said in the mosque. The call to prayer (*azan, vanku*) is made by the *mulla* or *mukri* [1] ; it begins with the *Thakbir*, 'Allahu Akbar,' and ends with the *kalima*, 'La illaha illa-l-lah.'

The Ramazan is a thirty days' fast corresponding to the Christian Lent, which begins as soon as the Ramazan new moon is seen and ends with the appearance of the next new moon. It is supposed to be a relic of the old Kaaba worship at Mecca. The fast is strictly observed, a good Mappilla refraining even from swallowing his spittle, from sunrise till sunset ; after which he may take food. The last *niskaram* should during Ramazan be said at the mosque and consist of 20 *rakayats*. At the Friday service there is a general congregational confession. The 27th night is the most holy time,

---

[1] In most parts of Malabar *mulla* and *mukri* are alternative titles for the person in charge of the mosque, who leads the prayers, etc. ; but in some parts of South Malabar the *mukri* is a distinct official, who calls to prayers, lights the lamps, digs graves, etc.

CHAP. III. MAPPILLAS.

since it is on that night that the Koran is said to have been sent down from heaven; and prayers said on that night secure pardon for all sin. On the 27th also the pious Mappilla should not fail to give alms (*zakkath*) to the poor amounting to 2½ per cent on his money, cattle and merchandise. The fast concludes with a big feast called *cheriya perunal* (little big day), as soon as the new moon has appeared, accompanied as are all Mappilla festivals by many fireworks, etc.

The *Haj* should be performed by all who can afford it; it may be done by proxy after a man's death.

Festivals.

The main festival celebrated by Mappillas is the Bakrid, or *valiya perunal*, in the third month after Ramazan. The festival is said to commemorate Abraham's offering of Isaac, and every Mappilla who can afford it must sacrifice a he-goat or a bullock, and distribute the flesh amongst his friends and relations and the poor.

The Mappillas only observe the ninth and tenth days of Muharram; they do not make *taboots*.

The Shabi Barat, or "night of record" on the 14th of Shaban, the month before Ramazan, is celebrated amongst the rich by the distribution of alms.

Saints.

The religion of the Koran is a pure monotheism, but the Mappilla worships many saints (*ouliyakanmar*) and martyrs (*Sayids* or *Sahidis*); and his religion betrays not a few traces of primitive animism and ancestor worship. Celebrated Tangals such as the Tangals of Mambram and men of holy and austere life are freely canonized, and their tombs (*mukham, jaram*) become holy shrines and popular places of pilgrimage (*ziyarat*). Canonization is often easily obtained, for it is both honourable and profitable to be the guardian of such a shrine; and an unknown beggar who dies of starvation on the roadside may be endowed with all sorts of virtues after death, and worshipped as a saint and miracle-worker. The *Sahids* are celebrated in hymns and popular songs, which have served to inspire the fanatics of many of the Mappilla outbreaks.[1] Annual festivals called *Nercha* (lit. vow) are celebrated in commemoration of these saints, the most important being those at Malapuram and Kondotti.

Maulads.

A common religious observance is the celebration of what is called a *mavulad* or *maulad*. A *maulad* is a tract or short treatise in Arabic celebrating the birth, life, works and sayings of the prophet, or some saint such as Shaik Mohiuddin, eleventh descendant of the prophet, expounder of the Koran, and worker of miracles, or the Mambram Tangal, father of Sayid Fasl.[2] For the ceremony a *Mulla* is called in to read the book, parts of which are in verse, and the congregation is required to make

---

1 Some of these songs are translated in the Indian Antiquary, XXX, p. 499.

2 See p. 77.

responses and join in the singing. The ceremony which usually takes place in the evening concludes with, or is preceded by, a feast to which the friends and relations are invited. Those who can afford it should perform a *maulad* in honour of Sheik Mohiuddin on the eleventh of every month, and one in honour of the prophet on the 12th. A *maulad* should also be performed on the third day after a death. It is also a common practice to celebrate a *maulad* before any important undertaking on which it is desired to invoke a blessing, or in fulfilment of some vow; hence the custom of *maulads* preluding outbreaks.

Every Mappilla family that can afford it has a *Nattu Mulla* or chaplain who attends the house daily to read one of the thirty sections into which the Koran is divided so that the whole can be read each month; he also officiates at the family *maulads*, and reads the Koran over the dead and over the graves.

Superstition.

Though magic is condemned by the Koran, the Mappilla is very superstitious, and witchcraft is not by any means unknown. Many Tangals pretend to cure diseases by writing selections from the Koran on a plate with ink or on a coating of ashes, and then giving the ink or ashes mixed with water to the patient to swallow. They also dispense scrolls for *elassus*, and small flags inscribed with sacred verses which are set up to avert pestilence or misfortune. The Mappilla *jins* and *shaitans* correspond to the Hindu demons and are propitiated in much the same way. One of their methods of witchcraft is to make a wooden figure to represent the enemy, drive nails into all the vital points and throw it into the sea, after curses in due form. A belief in love philtres and talismans is very common, and precautions against the evil eye (*kanneru*, *drishti*) are universal.

Ceremonies.

A brief description of the principal social ceremonies must suffice. In the details there are often traces of Hindu ritual and sometimes amongst the lower classes, at least, performances of *bali*, as already described, to drive away evil spirits; but the more orthodox do not admit such practices. The music of the tom-tom, and the distribution of betel are almost universal features of all their ceremonies, though not prescribed by the Koran.

Birth.

As soon as a child is born it is bathed in cold water, a *Mulla* is called in and he lifts the child up and recites in its ear the formulas of the call to prayer. Then the child is given a little gold dust mixed with some honey or date juice. The midwife should be a Velatti; but this custom is dying out, and in South Malabar at any rate it is now more usual for a Mappilla woman to be employed. The mother should bathe on the fifteenth and twenty-eighth and fortieth days after birth; and her pollution does not cease till the last bath, which is followed by a feast.

CHAP. III. MAPPILLAS.

The child should properly be named and shaved on the seventh day, but the ceremony more often takes place in the second or third month after birth. A goat or cow should in any case be killed on the seventh day and the flesh distributed amongst the relations. The orthodox method of selecting the name is for a Mulla to draw a *sors vergiliana* from the Koran. A feast follows the ceremony and money is given to the poor.

Circumcision.

A boy should be taught to pronounce the name of God, and to recite the *kalima* at the age of four. Circumcision should be performed between the ages of seven and fourteen years ; it is usually done in the tenth or twelfth year in North Malabar. A *Mulla* offers prayers and *fatehas* before the operation, which is performed by the barber with a sharp razor. The barber sits opposite to the boy, who has his cloth tied up over his shoulders ; and a by-stander should hold a lighted lamp, even if the operation is performed in the day time ; the proper time is just before high tide. The ceremony which is the outward sign of the boy's admission into the fold of Islam is made the occasion of much feasting and rejoicing, and large sums of money are often distributed to the poor. The boy should go to the mosque on the first Friday on which he is able to go out.

Marriage.

Boys are married at the age of 18 or 20 as a rule in North Malabar and girls at 14 or 15 : in South Malabar early marriages are more common, boys being married between 14 and 18 and girls between 8 and 12. In exceptional cases, girls have been known to be married at the age of 2½ ; but this only happens when the girl's father is *in extremis*, since an orphan must remain unmarried till puberty. The first thing is the betrothal, or settlement of the dowry which is arranged by the parents or in North Malabar by the *karnavans*. Large dowries are expected, especially in North Malabar where, in spite of polygamy, husbands are at a premium and a father with many daughters needs to be a rich man. The only religious ceremony necessary is the *nikka*, which consists in the formal conclusion of the contract before two witnesses and the *Kazi*, who then registers it. The *nikka* may be performed either on the day of the nuptials or before it, sometimes months or years before. In the latter case the father of the bride and the bridegroom go to the bride's family mosque and repeat the necessary formula, which consists in the recital of the *kalima* and a formal acceptance of the conditions of the match, thrice repeated. In the former case the *Kazi* as a rule comes to the bride's house where the ceremony is performed, or else the parties go to the *Kazi's* house. In North Malabar the former is the rule ; but in Calicut the *Kazi* will only go to the houses of four specially privileged families. After the performance of the *nikka* there is a feast in the bride's house. Then the bridegroom and his attendants are shown to a room specially prepared, with a curtain over the door; the bridegroom is left there alone and the bride is introduced into the room by her mother or sister. In North Malabar she brings dowry with her wrapped in a cloth. She is left with the bridegroom for a few minutes, and then comes out, and the bridegroom takes his departure. In some cases the bride and bridegroom are allowed to spend the whole night together. In some parts of South Malabar it is the bride who is first conducted to the nuptial chamber, where she is made to lie down on a sofa; and the bridegroom is then introduced and left with her for a few minutes.[1] Cohabitation as a rule begins at once unless the bride is too young.

In North Malabar and Calicut the bride lives in her own house with her mother and sisters, unless her husband is rich enough to build her a house of her own. In South Malabar the wife is taken to the husband's house as soon as she is old enough for cohabitation, and lives there. Polygamy is the rule; and it is estimated that in South Malabar 80 per cent. of the husbands have two wives or more, and 20 per cent. three or four. In North Malabar it is not usual for a man to have more than two wives. The early age at which girls are married in South Malabar no doubt encourages polygamy. It also encourages divorce (*mozhi, talak*) which in South Malabar is common; while in the North it is comparatively rare and looked upon with disfavour. All that is required is for the husband to say in the presence of the wife's relations, or before her *Kazi*, that he has "untied the tie and does not want the wife any more"; and to give back the *stridhanam* or dowry. Divorce by the wife (*faskh*) is rare and can be had only for definite reasons, such as that the husband is incapable of maintaining her or is incurably diseased or impotent. Widows may remarry without limit; but the dearth of husbands makes it difficult for them to do so.

In North Malabar Mappillas as a rule follow the *marumakkattayam* system of inheritance, though it is opposed to the precepts of the Koran; but a man's self-acquisitions usually descend to his wife and family in accordance with the Muhammadan law of property. The combination of the two systems of law often leads to great complications. In the South the *makkattayam* system is usually followed, but it is remarkable that succession to religious *stanams*, such as that of the Valiya Tangal of Ponnani, usually goes according to the *marumakkattayam* system. There seems to be a growing discontent with the *marumakkattayam* system; but, on the other hand, there is no doubt that the minute subdivision

[1] In Thurston's *Ethnographic Notes in Southern India*, p. 20, it is stated that a *tali* is tied round the bride's neck, and that the bridegroom lifts her up and runs off with her to bridal chamber. But according to my information this is not a Mappilla custom.

CHAP. III. MAPPILLAS.

of property between a man's heirs, which the Koran prescribes, tends to foster poverty, especially amongst petty cultivators such as those of the taluks of Ernad and Walavanad.

Funerals.

When a man dies his body (*mayyat*) is undressed and arranged so that the legs point to Mecca ; the two big toes are tied together and the hands crossed on the chest, the right over the left ; the arms are also tied with a cloth. *Mullas* are called in to read the Koran over the corpse, and this has to be continued until it is removed to the cemetery. When the relatives have arrived the body is washed and laid on the floor on mats over which a clean cloth has been spread. Cotton wool is placed in the ears and nostrils and between the lips, the fingers and the toes ; and the body is shrouded in white cloths. It is then placed on a bier which is brought from the mosque, and borne to the mosque. In the mosque the bier is placed near the western wall ; the mourners arrange themselves in lines and offer prayers (*niskaram*) standing. The bier is then taken to the grave which is dug north and south ; the body is lowered, the winding sheets loosened and the body turned so as to lie on its right side facing Mecca. A handful of earth is placed below the right cheek. The grave is then covered with laterite stones over which each of the mourners throws a handful of earth reciting the *kalima*, and passages from the Koran. Laterite stones are placed at the head and foot of the grave ; and some *mailanji* is planted at the side. A *Mulla* then seats himself at the head of the grave, and reads certain passages of the Koran called the *tilku* or teaching, intended to instruct the dead man how to answer the questions about his faith, which it is supposed that the angels are then asking him. The funeral concludes with distribution of money and rice to the poor.

For three days, a week or 40 days, according to the circumstances of the deceased, *Mullas* should read the Koran over the grave without ceasing day and night. The Koran must also be read at home for at least three days. On the third day a visit is made to the tomb ; after which a *maulad* is performed, the *Mullas* are paid, alms are distributed and a feast is given to the relations, including the deceased's relations by marriage who should come to his house that day. A similar ceremony is performed on the 40th day which concludes the mourning ; and by the rich on anniversaries. Widows should keep secluded in their own houses for three months and ten days without seeing any of the male sex. After that period they are at liberty to remarry.

Christians.

The Christians in Malabar number slightly over fifty thousand, of whom 4 per cent. are Anglicans, 12 per cent. Lutherans, and the rest Roman Catholics and Syrians.

CHAP. III. SYRIAN CHRISTIANS.

The Syrian[1] Christians, who are the most numerous, are found mainly in the south of Ponnani taluk, and in the parts of Palghat taluk which border on Cochin State. They are at present divided into three main bodies; the Romo Syrians who are in communion with Rome, but follow the Syriac rite; the Jacobite Syrians who adhere to the Jacobite Patriarch of Antioch; and the Reformed or St. Thomas Syrians, whose ritual conforms more or less to that of the Anglican church and who consider their church independent and its metropolitan their spiritual head.

History.

The history of the Native Syrian Christian church is complicated, and has been the subject of much controversy. The facts will be stated here as briefly as possible. Fuller accounts will be found in the chapter on Christianity in the *Travancore State Manual* by Mr. J. T. Mackenzie, who deals with the question from the point of view of a Roman Catholic; and in *The Syrian Church in India* by Mr. G. Milne Rae, who presents the Anglican side.[2]

St. Thomas.

According to a widespread tradition which is believed by most of its members, the church was originally established in the year 52 by the Apostle St. Thomas, who landed at Malankara near Cranganore, or Muziris, converted some Brahmans and others and founded seven churches, six in the Native States of Travancore and Cochin, and one at Palayur near Chavakkad in Malabar. The apostle subsequently went to Mailapur and thence to China, and on his return to Mailapur he suffered martyrdom, or was accidentally killed, on St. Thomas' Mount. His grave is shown in the present Roman Catholic cathedral at St. Thome, and at the Little Mount is a cave, with a cross and Pahlavi inscription, where he is said to have sought refuge from his enemies.

There is no inherent improbability in the tradition, since as has been seen, there was considerable trade between Cranganore and the Roman Empire in the early centuries A.D.; but it is usually discredited as there is no reliable evidence to support it. The *Acta Thomae* (third century A.D.), which contains the earliest detailed account of St. Thomas' apostolic labours, connects his mission to India with an application from a King Gondophares, whom coins prove to have been an Indo-Parthian king reigning at Kabul,[3] and

[1] The term 'Syrian' is of course not used in a local or ethnological sense; but in the same way as 'Roman' in 'Roman Catholic'. Its use is comparatively recent, the old appellation of the Christians in Malabar being 'Nazrani Mappilla.'

[2] Other authorities are Geddes', *History of the Church of Malabar*; *Hough's, History of Christianity in India*, Vol. III.; La Croze, *Christianisme dans les Indes*, tom. i; Assemannus, *Bibliotheca Orientalis*, tom. iv.; Gibbon, *Decline and Fall of the Roman Empire*, ch. XLVII.; Whitehouse, *Lingerings of Light in a dark land*.

[3] *The Syrian Church in India*, p. 54. See also Asiatic Journal, VI, 10, and *Bishop Medlycott's St. Thomas in India*.

CHAP. III. SYRIAN CHRISTIANS.

leaves no room for a journey to Southern India. Eusebius [1] (264—340) also makes St. Thomas the Evangelist of Parthia; Dorotheus, Bishop of Tyre at the end of the third century, says that he preached to the Parthians, Medes and Persians and died at Calamina;[2] and Rufinus (371 A.D.) says that St. Thomas' bones were brought to Edessa from India, meaning evidently India Minor, as the country west of the Indus was called by mediæval geographers. If Parthia and India Minor were the scenes of the apostle's labours, it is improbable that he came by sea to Cranganore.

St. Bartholomew.

Another theory is to connect the origin of the Syrian church with St. Bartholomew, on the authority of Eusebius,[3] Clement and Jerome,[4] who refer to the mission of Pantaenus of Alexandria at the end of the second century to India "where he found his own arrival anticipated by some who were acquainted with the gospel of Matthew, to whom Bartholomew one of the apostles, had preached and had left the gospel of Matthew in the Hebrew, which was also preserved until this time." The converts are assumed to have been some of the early Jewish settlers in Cranganore; but there is nothing to support this theory, and it is very doubtful whether there were any Jewish settlers in Malabar in apostolic times. Moreover Clement goes on to describe in some detail the Indian philosophers, and gymnosophists with whom Pantaenus came into contact, and mentions Brahmans and "Sarmanae some of whom are also called Hylobii; and neither inhabit cities nor have roofs over their heads, and know not marriage nor the begetting of children," referring no doubt to the Sanyasis; and it is improbable that there were Brahmans in Malabar in the second century A.D.[5] On the other hand Aramaic had no doubt penetrated to Parthia; and it was probably to the valley of the Indus that Pantaenus went.

Nor is there any reason to believe that Bishop John who attended the Nicene Council as Bishop of Persia and Maxima India represented a church in Peninsular India. The term India was used very vaguely in early times and the distinction of India Minor and India Major, the India of the Indus Valley and Peninsular India, is hardly found till the middle ages.

Manichaeans.

Another theory connects the Syrian church in Malabar with a Manichaean named Thomas who is said to have come to Cranganore in 277 A.D.; and in support of this it is argued that the Manigramam referred to in the Syrian copper plate grant means the village of the Manichaeans.

---

[1] *Hist. Eccles.*, I. 13.

[2] Possibly Calama, a town mentioned by Nearchus, on the seaboard of Gedrosia, which was under the rule of Gondophares; but the identification is disputed. In any case there is no good ground for identifying it with any place in Southern India. (See *The Syrian Church in India*, p. 59.)

[3] *Hist. Eccles.*, V. 10.

[4] *Liber de viris illustribus*, XXXVI.

[5] See Rae, *The Syrian Church in India*, p. 37.

CHAP. III. SYRIAN CHRISTIANS.

This theory had the support of Dr. Burnell ;[1] but there seems to be nothing to recommend it. The Syrian Christians themselves have a tradition that the Manigramakars were converts, who were reconverted to Hinduism by a magician named Manika Vachakar, and their descendants are said to be still known in Travancore by the name of Manigramakars[2].

Manichæans

Nestorian origin.

The first indisputable reference to Christians in Malabar is that of Cosmas Indicopleustes,[3] a Nestorian Christian who travelled to Ceylon in the sixth century and reported that there were churches there "and in Malo where the pepper grows ; and at Kalliana there is a bishop usually ordained in Persia." It is therefore not improbable that the church was founded in the fifth century by Nestorian Missionaries from Babylon, for we know that, notwithstanding the decision of the Council of Ephesus in 431 A.D., the Nestorians flourished in the East and that the patriarch of Babylon sent missionaries as far as Tibet and China between the sixth and eleventh centuries.[4]

Thomas of Cana.

Whatever the true origin of the church, it appears to have been strengthened, and brought into more direct communication with the Nestorians in the eighth or ninth century by the arrival of a merchant known as Thomas of Cana, or Cananeo, who is said to have come to Cranganore with a colony of 400 Christians from Bagdad, Nineveh and Jerusalem including several priests and deacons and a bishop named Joseph.

Thomas of Cana is also said to have built a church in Mahadevapattanam and to have obtained the grant of the privileges specified in the copper-plate grant given by Vira Raghava Chakravarti to Iravi Cortan. As has been noticed (p. 35) there is nothing in the grant itself to connect it with Thomas of Cana ; but it seems to be a fact that privileges such as are described were enjoyed by some of the Christians of Cranganore, and traces of them indeed survive to this day. It is not improbable that the grant was made to a Christian trading community, and if so it testifies to their social and commercial importance at this time ; and this is corroborated by the story of the Embassy sent by King Alfred in A.D. 883 to the shrine of St. Thomas in India, which returned with a rich load of spices and pepper.[5]

---

1 *Madras Journal*, XIII, 146.

2 Whitehouse, *Lingerings of Light*, p. 47.

3 *Topographia Christiana*, xi, p. 337. Kalliana is sometimes identified with Quilon, but is more probably Kalyan, north of Bombay.

4 *The Syrian Church in India*, ch. viii; Gibbon, *Decline and Fall*, ch. XLVII.

5 According to a Jesuit MSS. of the 17th century in the British Museum the date of the arrival of Thomas Cananeo was 346 A.D. ; and the same manuscript contains a Portuguese version of a grant made by a Perumal "Cocurangan" to Thomas, similar to the Manigramam grant. *Travancore State Manual*, p. 189.

CHAP. III. SYRIAN CHRISTIANS.

Northerners and Southerners.

From this time is said to date the division into Southerners (*Tekkumbhagar*) and Northerners (*Vadakkumbhagar*), the former being the new immigrants who settled in the south street in Cranganore, and the latter the old indigenous Christians. Another account is that the Southerners and Northerners are respectively the descendants of Thomas of Cana by two native wives, a Nayar and a Mukkuvan.[1] The Northerners are also further subdivided into Kurakkenikollamites, said to be the descendants of the church at Quilon which was founded or re-established by the arrival of a party of Persians in 822 A.D., amongst whom was Mar Sapor who has been identified with the Maruvan Sapir Iso of the Kottayam copper-plate grant; and Mahadevapattanamites or the representatives of Thomas of Cana and his church at Cranganore.[2]

The Southerners are fairer in complexion and have finer features than the Northerners; they are endogamous, observe more of the old Hindu customs than the Northerners and 'walk after the way of the mother.'

Latin Missionaries.

From this time down to the arrival of the Portuguese the church in India seems to have been in more or less regular communion with the Nestorian patriarch of Babylon from whom it obtained bishops from time to time. At the beginning of the fourteenth century three Latin Missionaries, John of Monte Corvino, Friar Jordanus, and John de Marignole, visited Malabar and made some converts; but until the arrival of the Portuguese the Malabar Christians practically all belonged to the Nestorian church.

The Portuguese.

The Portuguese at first welcomed the Syrians as brother Christians, and made no attempt to interfere with their doctrines; but with the consolidation of their power and the establishment of a headquarters at Goa they soon entered on a policy of proselytism and took steps to cut off the Syrian Christians from communion with the Eastern Patriarch. Franciscan and Dominican friars and Jesuits all worked to win the Malabar church over to Rome; the Inquisition was established at Goa in 1560; a Jesuit church and seminary were founded at Vaippacotta near Cranganore in 1584; and finally at the Synod of Diamper (Udiamperur) in 1599 Menezes, Archbishop of Goa, backed by the terrors of the Inquisition succeeded in inducing practically the whole of the Syrian church to acknowledge the supremacy of Rome, subscribe to the Latin doctrines and ritual, and disown the patriarch of

[1] In their own *Brief History* (referred to by Whitehouse, *Lingerings of Light*, p. 62), the Syrians say that the Northerners are the descendants of four hundred superior families formed of mixed unions between Thomas' immigrants and the people of the country; and the Southerners the descendants of seventy-two inferior families; but the facts are opposed to this.

[2] *Travancore State Manual*, p. 127. *The Syrian Church in India*, p. 164. The Persian cross with the Pahlavi inscription at Kottayam is generally referred to this time.

Babylon and his Nestorian heresies. They were incorporated with the Roman Catholic converts of the Jesuits in one community under the government of the Archbishop of Goa. But the victory was shortlived. The rule of the Jesuit Archbishop soon proved distasteful to the bulk of the Syrian Christians and they sent to the Patriarchs of Babylon and Antioch for a bishop. A man named Ahatalla was sent, apparently from Antioch, but was intercepted by the Portuguese and taken to Goa, where he was made away with. Enraged at this a large body of Syrian Christians assembled before the Coonen Cross at Mattancheri in 1653, and renounced their allegiance to Rome. Out of 200,000 persons only 400 are said to have adhered to the Portuguese Jesuit Archbishop.

Pazhayakuru and Puttankuru.

From this date is traced the division of the church into Romo Syrian or *Pazhayakuru*, the section that adhered to the communion with Rome entered into at the Synod of Diamper; and the Jacobite Syrians or *Puttankuru*, the section which after the oath at Coonen Cross obtained a bishop, Mar Gregory, from Antioch, and now follows the Jacobite ritual.

Carmelites.

After the failure of the Jesuits a body of Carmelites was sent out to win back the Syrians to the Roman fold; and they succeeded in doing this to a considerable extent under Father Joseph, whom the Pope appointed in 1659, without the knowledge of the King of Portugal, as Vicar Apostolic of Malabar.

For the next two centuries the Carmelite Vicars Apostolic continued practically to govern the Roman Catholics and Romo-Syrian communities in Malabar. The King of Portugal in virtue of his *Jus Patronale* still appointed Archbishops of Cranganore and Bishops of Cochin; but their jurisdiction was confined to the actual limits of the Portuguese territories, and with the rise of the Dutch power it virtually ceased. With the British supremacy the struggle between the Portuguese and Jesuit Archbishops of Cranganore, and the Carmelite Vicars Apostolic of Verapoly broke out again; and it was brought to a head by the Papal Bull *Multa Praeclare* of 1838, which abolished the Sees of Cranganore and Cochin and placed them under the jurisdiction of the Archbishop of Verapoly. Matters were finally settled by the Concordat of 1886, which defined the limits of the jurisdiction of the rival priests, and gave the rule of the Romo-Syrian community in Malabar to the Archbishop of Verapoly.

In 1868 a coadjutor to the Vicar Apostolic of Verapoly had been appointed to have immediate charge of the Romo-Syrians as distinct from the Roman Catholics, and he was replaced in 1892 by two separate European Vicars Apostolic. These again were replaced in 1896 by three Native Syrian priests, who were consecrated as Vicars Apostolic of Trichur, Ernakulam and Tangasseri in 1896.

CHAP. III. SYRIAN CHRISTIANS.

Jacobite Syrians.

The Jacobite Syrians who seceded from the Romo-Syrians in 1653, chose as their bishop Mar Thomas of the Pakalomattam family, which was according to tradition one of the original Brahman converts of St. Thomas; and he was consecrated in 1665 by Mar Gregory, who was sent out by the Patriarch of Antioch. This section of the church continued to acknowledge the Patriarch of Antioch; and its history is uneventful until the beginning of the nineteenth century, when the Church Missionary Society came on the field and entered into friendly relations with it on the advice of Dr. Claudius Buchanan and Colonel Munro, the British Resident. When, however, the mission established a college for the instruction of Syrian priests, the conservative party began to fear that the Syrian church would be brought under Protestant control. In 1825 some of them appealed to the Patriarch of Antioch and Mar Athanasius was sent out to replace Mar Dionysius, who was supposed to be too much inclined to Protestantism. The dispute was settled finally in 1840 by the withdrawal of the Church Missionary Society from all connection with Syrian church. But the influence of the teaching of the Society made itself felt in the rise of a party of reform, which succeeded in getting a new bishop, Mathew Athanasius, consecrated by the Patriarch of Antioch. Mar Dionysius refused to give way and reported that Mathew Athanasius was the friend of Protestantism; whereupon the Patriarch sent out another bishop to supersede him. The dispute was finally brought to the Travancore High Court, the main point at issue being whether consecration by the Patriarch of Antioch was essential to constitute a valid title to a bishopric over the Syrian Christians. The decision was ultimately given in 1889 in favour of Dionysius and the anti-reform party.

Reformed Syrians.

From that date begins the separation of the Jacobite Syrians, who owe allegiance to the Patriarch of Antioch, and the Reformed Syrians or St. Thomas Syrians who consider their own *Metran* as their spiritual head, and claim that the church of St. Thomas is apostolic and independent.

Chaldæan sect.

In addition to the three main divisions of Romo-Syrians, Jacobites, and St. Thomas Syrians, there is a small section called Chaldæan or Nestorian Syrians, who first separated themselves from the Romo-Syrians in 1856, on account of the refusal of the Archbishop of the Verapoly to ordain candidates for holy orders, who had been trained in the smaller seminaries by native *Malpans* instead of in the chief Romo-Syrian seminaries. They are now presided over by a Chorepiscopous ordained by the Patriarch of Babylon. They are to be found mainly in and round Trichur in Native Cochin.

Bishop of Annur.

Finally there remain to be noticed the adherents of the Bishop of Annur or Tozhiyur, near Chavakkad, a small see founded in the middle of the 18th century by Mar Cyril, who quarrelled with the Jacobite Bishop Mar Thomas and got himself consecrated by one of the three bishops whom the Patriarch of Antioch had sent out to validate the consecration of Mar Thomas. The church is practically a branch of the present Jacobite Syrian sect ; but its bishops ordain their own successors, and do not recognize the necessity of ordination by the Patriarch of Antioch. Most of the members of this subdivision are to be found in Malabar proper.

General characteristics.

The Syrian Christian community in Malabar proper is small and of no great importance. Its members are for the most part small cultivators, fishermen and petty traders ; and though a few of the priestly families are of Syrian blood, and some trace descent from members of the Brahmans and Nayar castes, the bulk of the community are converts from the Izhuvan and Mukkuvan castes, from whom they do not differ materially in appearance, dress and general mode of life. They do not however wear the *kudumi* nor do the men wear ear-rings ; while the women usually wear bodices. The men are also to be distinguished by the small cross worn round the neck ; and the women by their *tali*, which has 21 beads on it set in the form of a cross.

Churches.

Their churches are ugly rectangular buildings with flat or arched wooden roofs and whitewashed facades ; they have no spire, but the chancel which is at the east end is usually somewhat higher than the nave. Between the chancel and the body of the church is a curtain which is drawn while the priest consecrates the elements at the mass. Right and left of the chancel are two rooms, the vestry and the sacristy. At the west end is a gallery, in which the unmarried priests sometimes live. Most churches contain three altars ; one in the chancel and the other two at its western end on each side. There are no images in Jacobite or Reformed churches, but there are sometimes pictures ; crucifixes are placed on the altars and in other parts of the churches. The clergy and men of influence are buried in the nave just outside the chancel.

Clergy.

The Syrian bishops are called *Metrans*. They are celibates and live on the contributions of their churches. They wear purple robes and black silk cowls figured with golden crosses, a big gold cross round the neck and a ring on the fourth finger of the right hand. Bishops are nominated by their predecessors from the body of *Rambans*, who are men selected by the priests and elders in advance to fill the episcopate. *Metrans* are buried in their robes in a sitting posture. Their priests are called *Cattanars*. They should strictly pass through the seven offices of ostiary, reader, exorcist, acolyte, sub-deacon and deacon before becoming priests ; but the first three offices

CHAP. III. SYRIAN CHRISTIANS.

practically no longer exist. The priestly office is often hereditary, descending by the *marumakkattayam* system. Jacobite and St. Thomas Syrian priests are paid by contributions from their parishioners, fees at weddings and the like. Their ordinary dress consists of white trousers and a kind of long white shirt with short sleeves and a flap hanging down behind, supposed to be in the form of a cross. Over this the Jacobites now wear a black coat. Priests are allowed to marry except in the Romo-Syrian community; but among the Jacobites a priest may not marry after he has once been ordained, nor may he re-marry or marry a widow. Jacobites also now shave clean, while other Syrian priests wear the tonsure. *Malpans*, or teachers, are the heads of the religious colleges, where priests are trained.

Every church has not more than four *Kaikkars* or church wardens, who are elected from the body of parishioners; they are the trustees of the church property, and with the priest constitute a disciplinary body which exercises considerable powers in religious and social matters over the members of the congregation.

Doctrines.

The Romo-Syrians follow the doctrines and ritual of the Roman Catholics, but they use a Syriac [1] version of the Latin liturgy. Jacobites and St. Thomas Christians use the Syriac liturgy of St. James; but few even of the priests understand Syriac; and in the Reformed Syrian Churches, a Malayalam translation of the Syriac liturgy has now been generally adopted. The Jacobites say masses for the dead, but do not believe in purgatory; they invoke the Virgin Mary, venerate the cross and relics of saints; they recognize only three sacraments, baptism, marriage (which they always celebrate on Sundays) and the mass; they prescribe auricular confession before mass, and at mass administer the bread dipped in the wine; they recite the eastern form of the Nicene creed, and discourage laymen from studying the Bible. The Reformed Syrians differ from them in most of these points.

Festivals.

The Jacobites observe the ordinary festivals of the church; the day of the patron saint of each church is celebrated with special pomp, and on the offerings made on that day the priests largely depend for their income. They keep Lent, which they call 'the fifty days fast', strictly from the Sunday before Ash Wednesday, abjuring all meat, fish, milk, ghee and toddy. On Maundy Thursday, they eat a special kind of unsweetened cake, marked with a cross in the centre of which the karnavan of the family should drive a nail, and drink a kanji of rice and

[1] The Syriac is not a modern Syrian dialect, but is very like the ancient Aramaic.

cocoanut milk (the meal is said to symbolize the Passover and the Last Supper, and the nail is supposed to be driven into the eye of Judas Iscariot).

Amongst the Syrian Christians as amongst the Mappillas, there are many survivals of Hindu customs and superstitions; and caste prejudices have by no means disappeared amongst the various sections of the community. Southerners and Northerners will not intermarry; and families who trace their descent from Brahmans and Nayars will in many cases not admit lower classes to their houses, much less allow them to cook for them or touch them. Most of the Syrians observe the Onam and Vishu festivals; the astrologer is frequently consulted to cast horoscopes and tell omens; while it is a common custom for persons suffering from diseases to seek a cure by buying silver or tin images of the diseased limb, which their priest has blessed.

Social ceremonies.

Similar survivals are to be noticed in their social ceremonies. A *pulikudi* ceremony similar to that of the Hindus was commonly performed till recently, though it has now fallen out of use. Immediately on the birth of a child three drops of honey in which gold has been rubbed are poured into his mouth by his father; and the mother is considered to be under pollution till the tenth day. Baptism takes place on the fourteenth day amongst the southern Jacobites and amongst other divisions on the fifty-sixth day. A rice giving ceremony similar to the Hindu *Chorunnu* is still sometimes performed in the fifth or sixth month, when the child is presented by the mother with a gold cross, if a boy, or a small gold coin or *taluvam* if a girl, to be worn round the neck.

Marriage.

Among the Jacobites early marriage was the rule, until comparatively recently, boys being married at ten or twelve years of age and girls at six or seven; now the more usual age for marriage is sixteen in the case of boys and twelve in the case of girls. Weddings take place on Sundays and amongst the Northerners may be celebrated in either the bride's or the bridegroom's parish church. On the two Sundays before the wedding, the banns have to be called in the two churches and the marriage agreements concluded in the presence of the parish priests (*Ottu Kalyanam*). The dowry, which is an essential feature of Syrian weddings, is usually paid on the Sunday before the wedding. It should consist of an odd number of rupees and should be tied up in a cloth. On the Thursday before the wedding day, the house is decorated with rice flour, and on the Saturday the marriage pandal is built. The first ceremonial takes place on Saturday night when bride and bridegroom both bathe, and the latter is shaved. Next morning both bride and bridegroom attend the ordinary mass, the bridegroom being careful to enter the church before the bride. Now-a-days both are often dressed more or less in European fashion, and it is essential that the bride should wear as many jewels as she has got, or can borrow for the occasion. Before leaving his house, the bridegroom is blessed by his *guru* to whom he gives a present (*dakshina*) of clothes and money; he is accompanied by a bestman, usually his sister's husband, who brings the *tali*. After mass, a tithe (*pathuvaram*) of the bride's dowry is paid to the church as the marriage fee, a further fee to the priest (*kaikasturi*) and a fee called *kaimuttupanam* for the bishop. The marriage service is then read; and, at its conclusion the bridegroom ties the *tali* round the bride's neck with threads taken from her veil, making a special kind of knot, while the priest holds the *tali* in front. The priest and the bridegroom then put a veil (*mantravadi*) over the bride's head. The *tali* should not be removed so long as the girl is married and should be buried with her. The veil should also be kept for her funeral.

The bridal party then returns home in state, special umbrellas being held over bride and bridegroom. At the gate, they are met by the bride's sister carrying a lighted lamp and she washes the bridegroom's feet. The married couple then go to the pandal where they are ceremonially fed with sweets and plantains by the priest and by representatives of their two families to the accompaniment of the women's *kurava* (p. 171) and in the presence of the guests, who are seated in order of precedence, the chief persons having seats of honour covered with black rugs and white cloths (*vellayum karimbadavum*), traditionally a regal honour. The bride and bridegroom are then led into the house by the bestman and bride's uncle, the bride being careful to enter it right foot first; and the guests are feasted in order of rank. It is a peculiar custom of the Syrian Christians at these feasts to double up the ends of the plantain leaves which serve them as plates, and this is supposed to be symbolical of the royal privilege of eating off a double plate. Until the following Wednesday, the bestman sleeps with the bridegroom in the bridal chamber, the bride occupying another room.

On Wednesday evening comes the ceremony called *nalam kuli*, or fourth day bath. The bridegroom and the bestman who are in the bridal chamber lock the door; the bride's mother knocks and begs the bridegroom to come out, which he at last does after she has sung a song (*vathilturapattu*) celebrating the virtues and attractions of the bride. The bridegroom and bride then bathe, dress in new clothes and go to the pandal where they perform *pradakshinams* round a lighted lamp, and the bridegroom gives cloths to the bride's uncle, mother and grand parents. The married couple are then escorted to the bridal chamber, which has in the interval been cleaned and prepared for them.

The next morning they have to go to the bridegroom's or bride's house as the case may be, and there eat together and go through a ceremonial similar to that which they performed on the wedding day in the other house. This concludes the marriage ceremonies; but on Sunday the bridegroom and bride should attend mass together in the bride's parish church, if they were married in the bridegroom's, and *vice versa*.

Amongst the Southern Jacobites the ceremonies are very similar; but the dowry is not paid till the marriage day, or till the girl's first confinement, half the *pathuvaram* is paid to the priest instead of a *kaikasturi* and the bridegroom puts a ring on the bride's finger during the marriage service. After the church service the couple go to the bridegroom's house, where they are fed ceremonially by the bride's mother, and the subsequent feast is at the expense of the bride's people. On Monday morning the bridegroom is ceremonially fed by the bride's mother in the bridal chamber (*manavalan choru*); and in the evening there is a ceremony called *manavalan tazhukkal* in which the bride and bridegroom are embraced in turn by their respective parents and relations, after which there is a feast with singing of hymns. Before the couple leave for the bride's house on Thursday, there is a big feast called *kudivirunnu* given by the bridegroom to the bride's people, followed by a ceremony called *vilakku toduga*, in which men and women sing hymns and dance round a lighted lamp which they touch at intervals.

Amongst the Romo-Syrians and the Reformed Sect the marriage ceremonies have less trace of Hindu ritual; they do not celebrate weddings on Sunday and have no *ṅalam kuli* ceremony but a *tali* is usally tied in addition to the giving of a ring.

Funerals.

At funerals (except amongst the Reformed Sect) it is usual for each of the dead man's connections to bring a cloth to serve as a shroud. Before the body is lowered into the grave, holy oil is poured into the eyes, nostrils and ears. The mourners are under pollution and fast till the day of the second funeral or *pula kuli* (purification), and till then masses should be said daily for the dead. The *pula kuli* is celebrated usually on the 11th day, but may be deferred till the 15th, 17th or 21st or sometimes to the 41st. The mourners are censed, while hymns are sung and prayers offered; each then gives a contribution of money to the priest, and receives in return a pinch of cummin. A feast is then given to the neighbours and the poor. On the 40th day there is another feast at which meat is eaten by the mourners for the first time. A requiem

CHAP. III. SYRIAN CHRISTIANS.

mass should be said each month on the day of death for twelve months; and on the first anniversary the mourning concludes with a feast.

ROMAN CATHOLICS.

The Roman Catholic community consists of the converts made by the Jesuit and Carmelite missionaries beginning practically with the arrival of Francis de Xavier in 1852. Their history has already been alluded to in dealing with the Romo-Syrians. According to the Concordat of 1886 the Roman Catholics in Malabar proper are divided as follows: the Portuguese Bishop of Cochin, a Suffragan of the Archbishop of Goa who has the title of Primate of the East and Patriarch of the East Indies, has a diocese along the sea coast of Cochin and Travancore which includes British Cochin; the Carmelite Archbishop of Verapoly is the head of the Roman Catholics and Romo-Syrians elsewhere south of Ponnani; north of Ponnani the Roman Catholics are under the Bishop of Mangalore; and in Palghat taluk under the Carmelite Bishop of Coimbatore, a Suffragan of the Archbishop of Pondicherry.

The Roman Catholics are scattered all over the district in the chief towns, but are most numerous in Cochin and in the strip of coast which forms the southern half of the Ponnani taluk, where the converts are mostly of the lower castes. These latter are divided into Munnuttikkar (or three hundred), Annuttikkar (or five hundred) and Ezhunuttikkar (or seven hundred), traditionally said to be the descendants of 300 Pulayans, 500 Mukkuvans and 700 Izhuvans, who were given by the Raja to the Portuguese as servants of their community.

BASEL MISSION.

The only Protestant Mission at work in Malabar is the Basel German Evangelical Mission.[1] The Mission was founded by Dr. H. Gundert, the author of the Standard Malayalam English Dictionary and First Government Inspector of Schools for Malabar and South Canara. The sixty-seventh report of the Mission shows that on the 1st January 1907 the Society had in Malabar 6,804 church members and 195 adherents, distributed over Mission stations at Tellicherry (founded in 1839), Calicut (founded in 1842), Chombala (founded in 1849) in Kurumbranad taluk, Kodakkal (founded in 1857) in Ponnani taluk, Palghat (founded in 1858), and Vaniamkulam (founded in 1886) in Walavanad. A new station is being opened at Manjeri in Ernad.

The Basel Missionaries were the pioneers of Western education in Malabar and the Mission schools, which number fifty and educate over five thousand pupils, continue to hold a foremost position. There are four high schools for boys at Nittur, Tellicherry, Calicut and Palghat, and one for girls at Calicut; one theological school and one training school at

---

[1] For the following brief account of the Mission I am indebted to the kindness of the Rev. Mr. Bader of Nittur.

Nittur; and two orphanages, one at Chombala for girls and one at Paraperi for boys. Education up to the IV standard is compulsory for all children belonging to the Mission.

The industrial establishments, which are worked by a separate fund and managed by a separate board, form a characteristic feature of the Basel Mission. They are maintained for the purpose of providing a means of livelihood for converts and of training them in handicrafts. They comprise weaving establishments at Cannanore and Calicut, with branches at Nittur, Chombala and Kodakkal, and tile factories at Calicut, Ferok, Kodakkal and Palghat. The number of persons employed in them in 1907 was 2,209, of whom 1,755 were Christians. The Mission maintains a hospital at Calicut founded in 1886, and two dispensaries at Kodakkal and Vaniamkulam; and it manages the Leper Asylum at Calicut which it took over from the municipality in 1894.

CHAPTER IV.

AGRICULTURE AND IRRIGATION.

AGRICULTURAL PRACTICE. IRRIGATION-PROJECTS. WET LANDS—Wet cultivation—Punjakol cultivation—Kaipad cultivation—Plantains and vegetables—Methods of wet cultivation—Standard of cultivation—Agricultural improvements—Agricultural cattle. DRY CULTIVATION—Punam—Modan, gingelly and samai—Ginger. GARDENS—The cocoanut—The jack tree—The areca palm—Pepper—Betel. SPECIAL PRODUCTS—Coffee—Cinchona—Tea—Rubber. ECONOMIC POSITION OF RYOTS—Signs of material prosperity—Relations of landlord and tenant—Mr. Logan's report—Rack-renting—Renewal fees—Improvement rates—Evictions—Social tyranny of janmis—The kariyastans or land agents—Mr. Logan's proposals— Criticism—Tenants Improvements Act—Effect of the settlement—The Malabar Tenancy Act, 1929—Conclusion.

CHAP IV. AGRICULTURAL PRACTICE.

ARABLE lands in Malabar are divided into wet, dry and garden. The first are devoted almost exclusively to the cultivation of paddy and in the last cocoanut, arecanut and jack-trees are grown. Dry lands are of two kinds, occupied and unoccupied. The distinction between the former and garden lands is largely conventional, as explained in Chapter XI below ; and on the latter (which are assessed only when they are cultivated) crops of hill-rice, samai, gingelly and ginger are raised every few years. The following table gives the area of each class of land in the plain taluks in thousands of acres :—

Taluks.	Wet.	Garden.	Occupied dry.	Unoccupied dry.
Chirakkal ..	53	50	35	275
Kottayam ..	21	45	29	82
Kurumbranad ..	43	98	33	88
Calicut	25	48	26	76
Ernad	65	53	49	222
Walavanad ..	83	20	65	190
Palghat	117	12	55	112
Ponnani	89	73	44	45
Total ..	496	399	336	1,090

The great preponderance of unoccupied dry lands would at first sight seem to imply that an immense field is available for the extension of cultivation; but among such lands are included large blocks of uncultivable hill, rock and lantana jungle, which are so intermingled with the *parambas* or fields on which cereals and other crops are grown, that it would be impossible to demarcate them separately except at great cost. Palghat contains the greatest proportion of wet lands ; but the most fertile flats occur in the old Cheranad taluk corresponding to parts of the Walavanad, Ernad and Ponnani taluks.

CHAP. IV. AGRICULTURAL PRACTICE.

Cocoanuts thrive in the alluvial soils of the coast, and are found in the greatest profusion in the Ponnani, Kurumbranad and Cochin taluks. Ernad boasts the finest ginger lands, and the pepper vine flourishes best in the interior of Kottayam and Chirakkal.

IRRIGATION.

Paddy, the staple crop on wet lands, grows luxuriantly in the deep valleys which wind in and out of the numberless laterite hills of Malabar ; and so heavy is the rainfall that in some taluks, notably Walavanad, wet cultivation is carried on on terraces, *palliyals,* as they are called, high up on the hill sides. There are no Government irrigation works ; but at Enamakkal and Viyyattil in the Ponnani taluk dams are maintained by Government to keep out the salt water and enable crops to be raised in the beds of the shallow lakes thus formed. Similar dams, but on a smaller scale, are maintained by the ryots at various places in the Cochin, Ponnani and Kurumbranad taluks, all with the same object of protecting the crops from the inrush of salt water. Especially along the banks of the Ponnani river, the water-supply for the second crop is often eked out by baling from wells and rivers ; and in the Palghat taluk, where the rainfall is less than in the rest of the district, tanks for the storage of water and anicuts over jungle streams are not uncommon. Punja or hot weather paddy crops, and arecanut and betel gardens are very frequently irrigated from wells. Such wells are private property dug with private money, and no advantage is taken in the district of the Land Improvement Loans Act (XIX of 1883) or of the Agriculturists' Loans Act (XII of 1884).

Projects.

The Malampuzha Reservoir Project in the Palghat taluk was intended to irrigate 40,000 acres (20,000 acres double crop land, 10,000 acres single crop land and 10,000 dry crop land) for fifteen days after the south-west monsoon and for forty-five days after the north-east monsoon to enable the crops to mature after the cessation of the rains, but its investigation was, in 1926, postponed till the requirements of the Ceded districts have been attended to.

WET LANDS.

Wet lands are divided into *orupugil, irupugil* or *muppugil* according as they bear one, two or three crops. Three-crop lands are rare. The crops are on the ground for ten months in the year leaving but two months for the preparation of the soil. Double-crop lands are more common, and of nearly 500,000 acres of land classed as wet at settlement nearly half were registered as double crop. The *kanni* or first crop is sown in April or May, as soon as the surface soil has been moistened by the thunder showers which break over Malabar in those months.

Wet cultivation.

A form of *kanni* crop is North Malabar called Nuri in Malayalam consists in sowing the seed in small groups

CHAP. IV. WET LANDS.

by hand, the sowers following close behind the plough as it turns the furrows. It costs less seed and less manure than in the usual haphazard broadcasting but it yields better. The crop is reaped three or four months later, in September or at the beginning of October, according to the variety of seed sown; and on double crop lands preparations begin forthwith for the second or *magaram* crop, harvested at the end of January. On some lands, where owing to their clayey soil or low situation the ground is water-logged in the first heavy burst of the monsoon, one long *karinkara* crop takes the place of the usual two. Seedlings for the *magaram* crop are raised when the *kanni* crop is on the ground on selected loamy plots called Palliyals and they are left in their beds much longer than is the case in the Cauvery delta. Seedlings are planted out in August and January is the harvest month. The *kanni* crop is reaped with the water on the ground; and, being cut near the ears, yields, unlike the *magaram* crop, only a little straw. On some exceptional lands, where the water supply is perennial, a *medha punja* or hot weather crop succeeds the first two. More usually this crop is grown on lands which lie so low that they are flooded save in the months immediately preceding the monsoon. *Meda punja* crops are also raised by baling on double crop lands in Walavanad and north Ponnani taluks. Artificial irrigation is indispensable, and the cost of cultivation is high.

Punjakol cultivation.

The wet cultivation in the bed of the Trichur or Enamakkal lake, which lies partly in Venkidanga amsam of Ponnani taluk and partly in Cochin territory and measures about 20 square miles, demands special notice, if only for the singular struggle between human industry and the forces of nature which it entails. At the close of the rains, the water which in the monsoon is ten or twelve feet deep is drained off the portions to be cultivated into the numerous channels which, separated from the fields or *kolas* by substantial fences of wattles and mud, intersect the lake, by means of mechanically operated pumps. Agricultural operations begin in November, and the fences are repaired and strengthened. The water is then drained off, until the fields are ready for the plough and seedlings can be planted out. As the season advances and the sun grows hotter, water has to be pumped back from the channels into the fields to save the crops from withering; but with the first thunder-showers in April, harbingers of the south-west monsoon, the struggle with the rising floods begins again; and it is only by ceaseless labour day and night that the water can be kept under control and the crops saved. The soil in the bed of the lake is largely silt brought down by rivers and streams from the surrounding high country and splendid crops not seldom reward this remarkable industry. But the cost of the cultivation is very high, and the crop is extremely precarious. At times the fences are breached by an early burst of the monsoon, and the ripening crop is drowned, and often a large area is reaped simply by heading the stalks from boats. Remissions of assessment are the rule and not the exception, and in the fifty years ending 1879 there were only six in which remissions amounting in some cases to over Rs. 4,000 had not been granted. The lake is protected from tidal influences by a dam maintained at the joint expense of the British and Cochin Governments. Locally this cultivation is known as *punjakol*. It is also carried on in the Viyyattil lake, and on a smaller scale in the numerous *kayals* or shallow lagoons of the Ponnani taluk.

Kaipad cultivation.

A peculiar feature of Chirakkal, Kottayam and Cochin taluks is *kaipad* cultivation. This method of wet cultivation is largely practised on the low-lying lands near the coast subject to inundation from backwaters. Its peculiarity is that in the hot weather the soil is heaped in small mounds which are levelled after the monsoon has burst. The soil and the seedlings planted on the tops of the mounds thus get the benefit of passing showers without being damaged by the salt water, which overflows from the backwaters in these months. When the monsoon bursts, continuous rain keeps the water in the fields comparatively fresh, and the seedlings can be planted out. The cultivation is precarious, as an unusually high-tide may destroy the seedlings, and the crop is more dependent than ordinary cultivation upon seasonable rains. The cultivation expenses are also high.

Plantains and vegetables.

Cucumbers, pumpkins, bitter gourds, brinjals, water-melons, chillies and other vegetables are often raised on *kanni* crop wet lands in the hot weather with the aid of artificial irrigation. This cultivation is common all along the coast north of Calicut, more especially in the sandy soils near Tellicherry and Cannanore. Horsegram, sweet potatoes and occasionally ragi are cultivated as a second crop on *palliyals* in the Ernad and Walavanad taluks, and plots of plantains among the growing paddy are a frequent sight all the district over. The cultivation of one variety, known in Malayalam as *nendra* plantains, is so extensive as to deserve remark. The fruit is large and coarse, and is used chiefly for curries and for frying. A peculiarity of the plant, which is also grown in forest clearings and on dry lands generally, is that it comes to maturity, bears fruit and perishes all in one year. One thousand *nendra* plantains sell, according to season, at from five to ten rupees, and the cultivation is highly profitable. Plantains, including *nendran*, cannot be grown more than once in four or five years on the same land, but the profits from them when they are grown are considerable. In several cases cultivation with plantains is a preliminary to the conversion of high-lying wet lands into garden lands.

CHAP. IV. WET LANDS.

Methods of wet cultivation.

The Malabar ryot is a practical agriculturist whose methods are traditional and are not progressive. His implements are few in number and rude in construction, but they have the advantage of being light and cheap, and answer his purposes sufficiently well. A common wooden plough, two hoes (*kaikots* or *mamottis*); a rake and a levelling instrument of the usual South Indian pattern are the most important. Deep ploughing is not in vogue. The initial cost of an iron plough is great, and for the puddle cultivation of the *magaram* crop its weight is prohibitive. In preparing for the *kanni* crop it might be of use, but the fine tilth to which the surface soil is reduced by frequent ploughings with a native plough probably absorbs the light showers that fall at the time of sowing more readily than would the deep furrow turned up by an iron plough, which the fierce heat of the sun would soon bake to brick-like consistency. Another objection to their use is that the *kandams* or plots are too small to admit of rapid working with a plough drawn by several yoke of oxen. Manure is plentiful and the ryot is not driven by lack of fuel to divert cowdung from its natural use and to utilise it as fuel. Wood ashes are cheap, a fair sized basketful generally costing less than an anna, and green manure grows in abundance on most of the laterite hills. But the ryot does not take full advantage of the resources at his command. Poudrette is sparingly used in the vicinity of Cannanore, but the prejudice against night-soil has yet to be overcome. Goats (the climate does not suit sheep) are not penned on the fields for the sake of their manure, and, as the practice of bedding cattle on leaves and branches is unknown, the whole of their urine is lost. Chemical manures are manufactured in a factory at Calicut, but the planters of the Wynaad are the only customers in Malabar. Perhaps the best feature of the wet land cultivation is the frequent ploughings that precede the sowing. No sooner is the last crop of the season off the ground than preparations begin for next year's *kanni* crop. Sun baked clods are reduced to powder by clubs, locally known as *katta-kols*, and by all rules of agricultural practice the land should be ploughed not less than seven or eight times before the seed is sown. Upwards of 150 varieties of paddy seed are known, but probably the same kinds are called by different names in different parts of the district. The seed is sown dry or sprouting, but transplantation is the method adopted whenever there is prospect of sufficient rain for the nurseries. Generally speaking the *kanni* crop is sown broadcast, and seedlings are planted out for the *magaram* and *karinkara* crops. To induce germination the seed is soaked in water for twenty-four hours, then wrapped in plantain leaves and covered with a mat. On the third day it sprouts. Nurseries for seedlings are prepared with peculiar care. The plots are usually on high level, and the soil should be a good loam free from stones or gravel. They are ploughed many times and are liberally manured with ashes, leaves and liquid cowdung. For the rest the cultivation is of the ordinary puddle kind. The *kanni* crop is weeded once, the *magaram* not at all. After reaping the grain is beaten out with sticks or trodden under foot by labourers; bullocks are not used for the purpose, except in the Wynaad and parts of Palghat. It is winnowed by being poured out from a basket on to the threshing floor when a wind is blowing. In the absence of a wind fans are used: Until a few years ago paddy in Malabar was comparatively free from pests but in 1903–04 the well-known rice hispa (*Hispa aenescens*) made its appearance in the Ponnani and Ernad taluks as well as another fly now identified as *Leptispa pygmoea* B. Other major pests of paddy are *spod optera*, rice-bug and paddy stem-borer. These pests have not been eredicated but their life histories have been studied and remedial measures suggested for controlling them. Notwithstanding the efforts of the Agricultural department to popularise chemical manures among the farmers in Malabar there has been no great demand for them in this district, and fish manure, bone-meal and oilcake are largely exported, though the first is used to some extent in the coastal villages; and few attempts have been made to conserve cattle manure.

Standard of cultivation.

In the North Arcot district, according to the District Manual, crop experiments continued over a period of eight years showed the average outturn of paddy per acre to be 1,346 Madras measures in one taluk, 1,192 in another and 846 in a third, and Mr. H. A. Stuart concludes that "800 measures is a very fair average outturn for all wet lands." In the margin are tabulated the results of 901 experiments conducted in Malabar by the Revenue and Settlement Departments during the past sixteen years. The average outturn is only 535 Madras measures per acre. The soil of the ordinary flat in Malabar is probably not so rich as that in the ayacuts of many East Coast tanks. The *kanni* crop, the principal crop in Malabar, is rarely on the ground more than four months; and poor crops of paddy are often raised at a minimum cost on terraces high up above the double crop lands. These are partial, but only partial,

Taluks.	Number of experiments.	Outturn per acre in Madras measures.
Chirakkal ..	33	570
Kottayam ..	37	560
Kurumbranad.	73	494
Calicut	68	448
Ernad	31	661
Walavanad ..	196	595
Palghat ..	157	673
Ponnani ..	258	362
Cochin	16	1,006
Wynaad ..	31	839
District	901	535

CHAP. IV. WET LANDS.

explanations of the low average; and the real reason probably is that the standard of wet cultivation is lower than on the east coast. Under the influence of the unfailing rains the soil responds too readily with moderate crops to inefficient cultivation, and the ryot's wits are not sharpened by a constant struggle with the forces of nature. The fields are over-cropped and are given no rest, and wastage is not repaired by sufficient manure. The grain land cultivator, moreover, is too often a pauper tenant with no capital. He is often rack rented, and he has little inducement towards intensive cultivation. The Agricultural Associations that have recently been formed are wisely devoting a large share of their attention to the possibility of improving the rice cultivation.

Agricultural improvements.

The Agricultural department is attempting by propaganda and demonstration in private lands various improvements in agricultural practice in the district. Among such improvements may be mentioned the conservation of cattle manure in such a way as to minimise the loss of fertilising matter from it; the raising of green manure crops; and a judicious use of concentrated manures like oil-cakes, bone-meal, fish-guano and such chemicals as superphosphates, and ammonium sulphate in conjunction with bulky organic manures. The smallest variety of improved plough of the Meston type has been advocated especially for dry ploughing, also the Guntaka or harrow of the Ceded districts, to save labour charges and to ensure a thorough working of the soil. As a result of their propaganda improved seeds, well-manured nurseries and economic transplantation of paddy are becoming popular. Ryots are taking up the cultivation of industrial crops like sugar-cane, groundnut and chillies. The spread of sugar-cane cultivation has been handicapped by the inexperience of the ryot in preparing jaggery and the trouble and expense which it involves. Cotton and onion growing are attempted in a few places, and the growing of pepper on a plantation scale in the southern taluks has been somewhat of a success. The growing of cashewnut and cocoanut cultivation has been encouraged and superior varieties of tapioca, pine-apple, mango grafts, sapota and other fruit trees have also been encouraged.

In response to representations from the Wynaad planters an agricultural experimental station was opened in 1905 at Taliparamba to study pepper in all its aspects and to control pests on that crop. Both wet and dry land are included in the estate. Though the work done on pepper made but slow progress, that done on paddy and sugar-cane has attracted public attention. In 1922 an agricultural middle school was attached to the station, where tuition in the vernacular on the best methods of agriculture suited to the West Coast was given, in addition to geography, arithmetic and civics. The

Tavalakannan and *Kayama* varieties of paddy were grown on the estate and continual seed selection has improved the strains considerably. Seed is now being distributed from this station to the West Coast ryots, as the yield from them is at least 20 per cent higher than that from locally produced seed. *Punam* cultivation being considered very unscientific, attempts are being made to substitute for it systematic dry land cultivation with an appropriate rotation of crops. In 1926 a farm was started at Pattambi mainly for paddy breeding work. There is a Deputy Director of Agriculture at Tellicherry with jurisdiction over Malabar and South Kanara and each taluk (except Wynaad) has an Agricultural Demonstrator who is engaged in propaganda work amongst ryots for the betterment of agricultural methods.

Agricultural cattle.

Agricultural cattle in Malabar are a much-neglected lot. They are underfed and practically starved during the dry season when they can hardly get a bite of grass by way of grazing. This is specially marked in the localities where the hillslopes are covered with plantation crops like the cocoanut. In September-October there is an abundant growth of hill grass and the grasses are in full bloom in October and November. On the advice of the officers of the Agricultural department they are now cut and preserved as silage in pits underground and serve as fodder during summer. Where the supply of grass is limited and the lands are under cocoanut, a fodder crop like cholam is raised under the shade of the palms and converted into silage or preserved as stalks. The use of oil-cakes and cotton seed as feed for milch cows and calves is slowly becoming popular. An improvement in the breed is effected by keeping bulls with good milching pedigree for stud purposes in important villages or by subsidizing the keeping of such bulls by private owners.

DRY CULTIVATION

A well-established rotation of crops is a noticeable feature of dry cultivation in Malabar, and after two, three or at the most four crops are taken off the ground the land is allowed to lie fallow for two or three years. The cultivation is shifting, and hence the distinction referred to in Chapter XI below between occupied and unoccupied dry lands. The most important dry crops are *punam* and *modan*, both a species of hill rice, gingelly (*Sesamum indicum*), samai or millet (*Panicum miliare*) and ginger (*Zinziber officinale*). Ragi is the staple dry crop of Wynaad, and in the drier parts of Palghat cholam (*Sorghum vulgare*), cumbu (*Pennisetum typhoideum*), castor and other crops characteristic of the east coast are cultivated. Experiments are now being made with ground-nut and jute, for both of which the conditions seem suitable ; and it is hoped that in them may be found a valuable crop for the better dry

CHAP. IV. DRY CULTIVATION

lands. In the eastern *desams* of the Palghat taluk, that adjoin Coimbatore district every variety of grain grown in the latter district is found, groundnut, varagu, ragi, blackgram, chama, cholam, horsegram and even cotton. The cultivation of the first is extremely profitable and blackgram is a valuable crop in South Palghat.

Punam.

The term *punam* is applied to cultivation on the forest-clad hills at the foot of the ghats, and on the ghat slopes themselves. It is a most destructive form of cultivation, with ruinous effects upon forest growth. A patch of forest is cleared and burnt, trees too big to be burnt being girdled and left to die. A crop of hill rice, mixed with which dholl, millet and plantains are often grown, is raised, and the ground is then left fallow for some years, the cultivators, generally hillmen, moving on to another patch to repeat the process. The seed is sown in April and beyond an occasional weeding the crop, which is reaped in September, requires little attention. The crop, however, has to be watched or fences have to be erected to keep away wild beasts. The virgin soil is wonderfully rich, and the small amount of seed that is sown yields a bountiful harvest. The best land experimented on by the Settlement Department in Chirakkal taluk gave an outturn of 900 Madras measures to the acre, and the average of 20 experiments was 557 measures. *Punam* cultivation is especially common in the two northern taluks.

Modan, gingelly and samai.

Modan is grown on the low hills which abound in the plains of Malabar ' or near the coast in among the young cocoanut plants in new plantations and is of a coarse kind. The rotation is usually modan, gingelly and samai, but on the best lands a ginger crop frequently precedes the modan. Preparations for modan begin in August and between that month and the sowing of the crop in the following April the land is ploughed twelve times. The seed is sown with ten times its own weight in ashes and cowdung, and the crop, which is weeded once, is reaped in September. Gingelly is then put down and harvested in December or January. The samai crop, which is not of great value, is raised in the following May and June; and the land is then allowed to lie fallow for two, three or four years according to its fertility.

inger.

One of the distinctive features of agriculture in Malabar is the cultivation of ginger, a very valuable crop. Its cultivation in almost every taluk is extending yearly, but the Ernad taluk produces the most and the best ginger. The methods of its cultivation are simple in the extreme, and the chief factors in the success of the crop are a good soil and a timely rainfall. Operations begin in the first week in May. The ground is cleared of stones, stubble and the rank growth of the previous monsoon, and is then ploughed six times. Towards the end of the month the tubers are planted out in raised beds twelve feet long by two broad, separated one from another by shallow trenches. In these beds shallow pits, about four inches square, are made at intervals of a foot, and in each pit a tuber is placed on a small quantity of cattle manure. The tubers are then covered lightly with earth, and are protected from the sun by a covering of leaves and branches. Chembu (*calladium esculentum*) is often grown as a mixed crop. Six weeks later fresh leaves and branches are put down, and the opportunity is taken to weed the beds, and, by heaping up the mud round the edges, to repair the ravages made on them by the heavy rains of the first monsoon. After another six weeks, in September, the process is repeated and the covering of leaves and branches renewed. The tubers mature in the month of Dhanu (December-January), and are hoed up much in the same way as potatoes in England.

Ginger is sold either green or dry. Dry ginger is four or five times as expensive as green, but the difference in price is accounted for not only by the cost of drying but also by the shrinkage that ensues in the process. Before drying the rhizomes are pared with a knife, and the outer skin is removed. The crop is then spread out on a rock, and is left for at least a week exposed to the sun by day and the dew by night. It is then sent to Calicut to be cured and bleached.

Upon the bleaching the flavour of the ginger largely depends. The ginger is first dried once more in the sun, washed in lime-water and dried again : it is then placed in racks or baskets in the upper part of a kiln through which the smoke of a sulphur fire slowly filters for some three hours. The process, including the drying and washing, is repeated three times ; but in the final bleaching the rhizomes are left ten or twelve hours in the kiln. One final drying ensues, and the ginger is packed up ready for export in mango wood boxes, the insides of which have been steeped in lime-water. Commercially the ginger is divided into four qualities according to the size of the rhizomes and the number of eyes or nodules. The best is exported to England and other European countries, the poorer qualities to Bombay and a certain amount is retained for sale locally, as ginger enters largely into the native physician's pharmacopoeia.

Ginger is a very valuable crop. Thirty tulams of 25 lbs. each are sown to the acre, and an ordinary crop yields sixfold or 180 tulams of green ginger. At As. 12 the tulam, the average price of green ginger, this represents in money a gross return of Rs. 135. But the cultivator's stake in the crop is a very high one. Cultivation expenses are heavy and the crop precarious. A late monsoon and an unusually heavy one

CHAP. IV. DRY CULTIVATION

are alike disastrous, and a parasite not infrequently does great damage. The charges for cultivating an acre of land have been estimated as follows :—

	RS.	A.	P.
Cost of bullocks for ploughing 1 acre	2	0	0
30 tulams of seed at Re. 1 per tulam	30	0	0
150 baskets of cattle manure at 6 pies each ..	4	11	0
300 bundles of leaves at 6 pies the bundle ..	9	6	0
Cost of labour, implements, etc.	8	15	0
	55	0	0

The net return to the cultivator is thus Rs. 80 per acre, but out of this he has to defray the charges of paring the rhizomes before the preliminary drying. The old women, to whom this task is allotted, are paid at the rate of As. 1-6 per tulam, and the cost for the whole crop thus amounts to Rs. 17. The Rs. 63 that remain have to be divided between the cultivator, the janmi, and Government; but, as the janmi's share is usually nominal and the assessment never exceeds Rs. 2 per acre, the bulk of the profits go to the cultivator. The cultivator's actual outlay in money is probably small, and his return in money much greater. Ginger is usually cultivated in small patches, not more than half an acre in extent, and the labour expended on it is generally that of the cultivator and his family. The implements and bullocks are those used in the cultivation of his wet lands, the manure he gets from his cattle, the leaves are generally to be had close at hand for the cost of carriage, and the seed he has saved from his last year's crop.

Tubers for seed are selected on the day that the crop is dug up, those with the most pronounced eyes or nodules being selected. They are at once buried in a hole in the ground, and the aperture is covered with planks. Eight or nine days later the planks are removed and the tubers are exposed to the air for two days. The hole is then covered up again, until the tubers are required for planting.

GARDENS.

Gardens are as a rule cultivated with more care than wetlands for the reason that the cultivator has greater fixity of tenure and consequently more inducement to improve them. They are usually demised on *kanam* for a period of not less than twelve years, and full value has to be paid for improvements on redemption. The characteristic garden products are the cocoa and areca palms, the jack tree and the pepper vine. These four are known *par excellence* as the *nal bhogam*, the four improvements. Betel vines, talipot and sago palms, bread fruit, mango and tamarind trees, plantains, pine apples, saffron and wild arrowroot (*Curcuma angustifolia*) are also grown in gardens in addition to many species of vegetables.

The cocoanut

Historically the most interesting of these is pepper, the magnet which drew first the Moors and then the Portuguese to Malabar; but economically the most important is the cocoanut. Its importance can be partially exhibited in figures. Products of the cocoanut—cocoanut oil, copra, coir yarn, rope and *poonac*, to mention the most important—accounted for about half the total exports from Malabar in 1903–04, valued at close upon 500 lakhs of rupees. But apart from these products, every bit of the tree is of value. It is tapped for toddy, and from the toddy jaggery is prepared, and arrack is distilled. Its leaves are used for thatching, their stems and the hard shells of the kernels for fuel; the unripe nut or *elanir* is full of the most refreshing liquid; and in the last resort the tree is cut down, and its trunk utilized in building.

The cocoanut thrives best on the alluvial deposits of silt and sand found on the coast in the vicinity of estuaries and backwaters; but it also flourishes with careful cultivation on the lower slopes of the laterite hills of the interior which dominate the paddy flats. These two classes of land are distinguished in Malabar by the names *attu veppu* and *kara veppu*, 'river' lands, and 'bank' or high lands. On the latter cultivation is more difficult and more expensive, and the initial cost of planting is especially high. The rainfall of the district is heavy, and the position of the gardens is such that much drainage water passes through them. To prevent the soil being washed away, deep trenches are dug round the garden; and, with the earth thus obtained, mud-walls are raised. Each garden is thus separated from its neighbour by a double embankment with a deep trench between. These trenches or *edavazhis* are often in the case of older gardens perpendicular cuttings ten or fifteen feet deep, and serve as water courses in the monsoon and also as foot paths for man and beast. In such gardens too, where the soil is laterite, the pits in which the seedlings are planted out are wider and deeper, more manure is required, and the trees begin to bear later than in *attu veppu* gardens.

For propagation fully matured nuts from old trees are selected. They are left in the sun for some days, until the liquid within the kernel has nearly dried up, and are then soaked in water for periods varying in different parts of the district from ten days to a month. They are then buried in good, loamy soil with only the tops left showing. At this state almost daily watering is required, except during the monsoon. Three months after being put down the nuts begin to sprout; and three, nine or even twelve months later, according to the quality of the soil, the seedlings are

CHAP. IV. GARDENS.

planted out in pits just before the burst of the south-west monsoon. The size of the pit varies. On alluvial soils they are not more than two feet deep and two feet in diameter; but in rocky *parambas*, where space has to be given for the roots of the tree to spread, they are occasionally six feet deep and nine in diameter. The pits should be forty men's feet apart; but this is a counsel of perfection rarely followed, and over-planting is one of the commonest defects of garden cultivation in Malabar. Ashes are put down with the seedlings, and, to keep away white ants, a handful of salt is often added. The young plants are watered in the hot weather for the next three years; and the pit is gradually filled up, partly with soil washed in by the rains, partly with leaf, ash and cattle manure. A mature garden is ploughed up every year, and a shallow trench is dug round the roots of each tree and filled up with manure.

The age at which the cocoanut palm comes into bearing varies with the species of the tree and the soil in which it is grown. Some varieties—thirty different species are well known—grow more rapidly and perish sooner than others, and in alluvial soils the tree bears sooner than in *kara veppu* lands. On an average the cocoanut comes into full bearing about its tenth year, bears vigorously for the next forty years and less and less in the last thirty years of its life. The number of nuts it bears is another vexed question. The cautious calculations of the Settlement Department, based on the saying that the trees should be forty men's feet or thirty-two linear feet apart, allow forty trees to an acre, and an average of fifty-five nuts for 'best' trees. This estimate of 2,200 nuts a year as the produce of an acre of the best cocoanut land is very moderate. In the Ponnani and Cochin taluks, especially in a year when sardines (the finest of all manures for cocoanuts) are plentiful, a yield of 100 nuts per tree is not uncommon; and 60, 80 and even 100 trees are planted to the acre. The standard in Cochin State is 60 trees per acre, in Ceylon 64, and in Travancore 100. The nuts take between eight and ten months to mature, and are plucked six or eight times in the year by coolies who are paid at the rate of one nut for every five trees plucked.

The cocoanut has many enemies. In the Laccadive islands and on the mainland rats do great damage by gnawing holes in the tender nuts. In some parts they are kept away by small shields of plaited cocoanut leaves placed above each bunch of growing nuts. The rats are scared by the plaits, and the device is said to be not so ineffectual as it would appear. Toddy cats are also destructive and are kept at bay by thorns bound round the trunk of the tree. Worms destroy the roots and burrow into the trunk, and the leaves are devoured by a species of beetle known as 'chela.' White ants attack the seedlings. The black headed caterpillar (*Nephantis serinopa*) is a serious pest on cocoanut trees in the coastal areas. A small caterpillar about 1½ inches long striped with pale purple, living on the undersurface of cocoanut leaflets eats up the green matter from behind galleries made of the chewed leaf and excreta. The pest is kept under control by cutting and burning the infested leaflets or by liberating a few of their natural enemies. There is a staff at work in the district for eradicating this pest.

The jack tree.

The jack tree, another valuable tree, flourishes best in clayey soils, its growth on sand being poor and stunted. The tree covers twice as much ground as a cocoanut, and the saying is that jack trees should be planted so far apart that a monkey cannot jump from one to another. Gardens planted with jack trees only are, however, almost unknown, and they are generally scattered here and there in cocoanut and arecanut gardens. In North Malabar there is a superstition that jack trees planted at the four corners of a garden flourish better than elsewhere, and higher rates of compensation were at one time allowed by the courts for such trees. An average tree begins to bear in its eighth year and yields 20 or 30 fruits in the year. They are said to live for 400 years and to bear for 100 years. The fruit is not always sold, unless it is grown within easy distance of a bazaar or market. It is eaten green or ripe by all classes, and in the hot weather, when grain is getting scarce and dear, it is the staple food of the poor. The timber is valuable for carpentry and furniture. When freshly cut the heart wood is yellow; but on long exposure to the air it gradually darkens, finally becoming of a mahogany colour. The wood contains colouring matter useful in dyeing.

The areca palm.

The areca palm, like the jack, does not thrive on sandy soil and is at its best on the banks of rivers in the interior of the district. It is cultivated in much the same way as the cocoanut. Ripe nuts from an old tree are plucked in December or January; and, after being covered with cowdung and left in the sun for two or three days, are planted out a few inches apart in carefully prepared beds. The beds are covered with leaves to protect them from the sun, and watered almost daily. The nuts begin to sprout two months later, and in the following year the seedlings are planted out in pits at the beginning of the monsoon. Three handfuls of cowdung are put down at the same time, and leaf manure and more cowdung are applied three months later. The gardens are ploughed every year, and the trees are manured in the same way as cocoanuts, but require more watering. Betel vines are often trained up the palms. Areca trees come into bearing in the seventh or eighth year and are in full vigour for the next 30 years. The Settlement Department allowed 480 trees to the acre for a fully planted garden, but double that number

CHAP. IV. GARDENS.

are often planted. The trees produce from 150 to 500 nuts a year, 200 nuts being a fair average. A good fully planted garden measuring an acre thus produces nearly 100,000 nuts a year, worth about Rs. 100, and the cultivation is very profitable. The nuts are plucked three times a year, in the months of January, February and March. The nut is chewed with the betel-leaf, but is also a useful purgative for dogs and other animals.

Mahali is the local name of a pest that affects tender arecanuts; and can be recognized when the tender arecanuts dry up with an ashy bloom on their surface. It is a fungoid disease caused by *Phytophthera omnivora* and spreads very fast the spores of the fungus being carried from tree to tree by rain and moist wind. Spraying the trees with bordeaux mixture is the only effective remedy; and the gardens should be well drained. The disease is said to have been introduced by a villager of Mullasseri bringing an affected nut from outside the district and throwing it into his own garden. Since 1924, the Co-operative and Agricultural departments have combined in a campaign for spraying areca gardens and checking the spread of this pest.

Pepper.

Pepper is indigenous in Malabar. It is grown chiefly in the three northern taluks of the district. The best comes from the north of Chirakkal, and is known commercially as Taliparamba pepper. Vines are scattered here and there in the gardens of the other taluks, but south of Kurumbranad regular plantations are almost unknown. Twenty years ago, hard hit by leaf disease in coffee, the planters of the Wynaad turned their attention to pepper. For years it throve and its cultivation yielded larger profits; but recently a mysterious disease, seemingly of a fungoid origin, has made its appearance in the taluk, and the outlook of the industry is gloomy. The symptoms are a whitling of the vine and loss of foliage due to diminished supply of sap, and its worst feature is that the soil of an infected plantation becomes so poisoned that the planting of cuttings from healthy vines is quite useless. The disease prevails also on the plains, but in a milder form. To study its history and combat it, Government have started an experimental garden near Taliparamba.

The disease referred to as "Wilt of Pepper" is caused by a fungus of the *Rosellinia* variety, which originates from rotting stumps of jungle or shade trees. It attacks the roots or the base of the pepper vine just below ground and cuts off nourishment from the growing points, with the result that the leaves turn yellow and drop down and the whole vine soon dries up. As the infection starts under-ground, and the disease is usually detected just before the death of the vine, its treatment consists in preventing the spread of the disease to the neighbouring vines through the soil. The infected vine or vines are isolated by a trench about 2 feet deep and the soil from the trench is thrown into the infected area. The diseased vines are then carefully collected with their roots and burnt. Sprinkling lime in the trenches and over the infected area to form a layer about ½ an inch thick on the surface and raking the same into the soil is also recommended but it is expensive on a large scale.

The disease was noticed on a few vines at the Taliparamba Agricultural Research Station, but did not spread on the methods described above being adopted. It is not a common disease in the low-lying pepper plantations. Another serious disease of the pepper vine now being investigated at Taliparamba is what is locally known as "Pollu". The outward sign of the disease is an excessive number of hollow pepper berries or the spikes dropping off altogether. The grub of a small beetle called "*Langitarsus nigripenus*" is responsible in some cases for the hollow berries, but the full causation of the disease has not yet been satisfactorily traced.

The initial cost of forming a plantation is heavy, but the garden is not expensive to keep up. The vine is trained to a standard, and flourishes best in loamy soils near the foot of the Western Ghats. A rainfall of 100 inches or more is required. Copious rain is essential in the blossoming season between June 20th and July 5th, but in the three months before picking a heavy downpour injures the soft pulpy berries. On the coast, where pepper is grown incidentally in cocoanut and other gardens, umbrageous trees such as jacks and mangoes are used as standards; but in the regular plantations of the interior *murikku* trees (*Erythrina Indica*), which grow quickly and can be planted close together, are preferred. *Murikku* seeds are sown with hill rice and pulses, and in three years when they are six feet high and five inches in girth the trees are cut down at the roots in Dhanu (December-January) and stacked in some convenient spot till the monsoon. The *paramba* selected for the plantation is in the meantime terraced, levelled and cleared of all jungle and forest growth. Just before the monsoon bursts, the *murikku* trees are planted out about six feet apart; and three weeks later, when they have struck root, cuttings from healthy mature vines are planted at their feet. The roots of the *murikku* tree do not go deep; and, to prevent the tree from offering too much resistance to the wind and being blown down, its branches are lopped off every year. In Malabar pepper is propagated from cuttings, and the other two methods of layering and growing from germinated seed are rarely adopted. The cuttings are about two and a half feet long and are planted two feet deep, five or six being trained to a single prop. No manure is put down at this stage. In Karkkidagam (July-August) and again in Tulam (October-November), the soil of the garden is turned up with a hoe,

CHAP. IV GARDENS.

and plantains are cultivated between the props to provide shade for the growing vine. Subsequently the garden requires little attention. The soil is dug up twice a year, and the shoots of the vines (which grow rapidly and ultimately attain a height of twenty feet), are tied with fibre to the prop, and their roots are covered with leaves in the hot weather. The vine begins to bear fruit in its third or fourth year. It yields for twenty years and then fails gradually. Blossoms form at the end of June, berries in August and September. The gathering season is from January to March. The flowers and fruit are delicate, and readily damaged by rough handling. Bamboo ladders are therefore used in tying up the vines and plucking the berries. The clusters (known as *chittal* in Malabar) are picked by hand and placed in a basket slung round the picker's neck. There are several varieties of the pepper vine, the best on the plains being *kalluvalli*, *valankotta* and *uthirankotta*. The first named is the best, its berries being heavier and bigger than those of other varieties. The produce of a vine varies. In good years the best varieties planted in suitable soil yield as much as ten Tellicherry seers of green pepper, but the average yield is about three or four seers. Very little manure is put down in the pepper gardens of the plains of Malabar. In North Canara, where the vines are trained up areca palms, quantities of leaf mould manure are used by the growers of the spice.

Betel.

Betel (*Piper betile*) is the most important bye-product of a Malabar garden. The vine is usually trained on artificial standards; but in Nannambra amsam of the Ernad taluk, where the soil is a sandy loam and the finest betel is grown, the stems of areca palms are utilized as props. The advantage of this practice is that one watering suffices both for the vine and its prop; and, as watering is necessary for six months in the year, and in the hot weather is repeated every four days, the saving of expense is considerable. The vine also shares the benefit of the manure put down for the areca palm. In October the old vine is taken down, rolled up and buried once more at the foot of the palm with only the top showing. By the end of February it is eight or ten feet high, and the young leaves are ready to be plucked. They are picked twice a month till October, and in the monsoon months the vine is fruitful. Estimates of the yield vary greatly. Near Malappuram, where the betel is not so good and the leaves are less carefully selected for the market, a vine is said to produce 2,000 leaves a year. In Nannambra the estimate is much lower, but the betel fetches two or three times the price of other varieties in the Calicut bazaar. In the hot weather a bundle of 100 leaves of Nannambra betel fetches from eight to ten pies.

It remains to deal briefly with the chief special products of the Wynaad plantations, coffee, cinchona, tea and rubber.

CHAP. IV. SPECIAL PRODUCTS.

Coffee.

The cultivation of the coffee plant was introduced into Malabar by Mr. Murdock Brown in his plantation at Anjarakandi at the end of the 18th century, and thence appears to have found its way up to Manantoddy, where a few bushes were planted in the Mess compound by the officers of the detachment then stationed there. Between 1830 and 1840 their luxuriant growth attracted the attention of two members of the firm of Messrs. Parry & Co., who were travelling up to their estates on the Baba Budan hills in Mysore; and at their suggestion the 'Pew Estate' was opened on the hill where the Forest office now stands. The venture prospered, and gradually soon estates sprang up all over the taluk. Their success was immediate; half a ton an acre was an ordinary crop, and the possession of an estate was looked upon as a short cut to a furtune.

The first serious check to the industry was given by the borer, *Xylotrechus quadrupes*, which in 1865 destroyed whole estates; and soon after a remedy for its ravages had been discovered in the planting of quick-growing trees to shade the coffee, the fungus, *Hemeleia Vastatrix*, commonly known as leaf disease, made its appearance, and by 1875 had devastated the whole district. The decline of the industry was accelerated by the fall of prices due to increased production in other countries, and the low water mark was reached at the end of the century when the competition with Brazil drove prices down to £2-7-0 per cwt. There has been some improvement since, and coffee is still the staple product of the Wynaad plantations; but it pays only on the most favourably situated estates and only with the most careful cultivation. In the ten years from 1893 to 1903 the acreage under it decreased from 20,096 to 5,477, and it is gradually being supplanted by tea.

The two principal species grown, are *Coffea Arabica* and *Coffea Liberica*. The latter produces a coarser-flavoured coffee, and the former is the plant usually cultivated:

"Its foliage resembles that of the Portuguese laurel; the small white blossom is not unlike that of the jessamine in form and scent; the berries are at first dark green, changing as they mature to yellow red and finally deep crimson. Beneath the skin of the ripe berry, or 'cherry' as it is called, is a mucilaginous, saccharine, glutinous pulp, closely enveloping the 'beans' . . . these beans are coated with a cartilagineous membrane known as 'parchment,' and beneath this by a very delicate semi-transparent jacket, termed the silver-skin."

There is a considerable literature regarding the cultivation of coffee, and it is unnecessary to discuss here the various methods advocated. Manures are almost universally employed in large quantities.

CHAP. IV. SPECIAL PRODUCTS.

The processes of manufacture are briefly as follows: the 'cherry' is picked when it is quite ripe; the 'pulp' is removed and the bean now known as 'parchment' coffee is dried. When thoroughly dried the parchment is sent down to the coast to be cured. The processes are more easily effected in a dry and warm atmosphere, and require special machinery. The bean is left in the parchment for some weeks, and is then 'hulled' or 'peeled' by being warmed in the sun and passed through a machine similar to that used for mortar. Finally the beans are sorted and the different grades are 'garbled' by women with native winnowing fans.

The labour on the estates is nearly all imported; and in 1903, on the motion of some of the planters in this and other districts who considered that the existing Act XIII of 1859 was inadequate to secure control over defaulting labour contractors and absconding coolies, the Madras Planters Labour Act I of 1903 was passed into law; but it has not found favour with employers of labour, and its amendment is already under consideration. The Planters' Labour Act has since been repealed.

Cinchona.

Cinchona was one of the remedies to which the planter had recourse when coffee began to fail, and between 1880 and 1890 was largely grown. Unfortunately for the Wynaad, Ceylon entered the field about the same time; the drug was poured upon the market and in ten years time prices dropped from one pound per ounce to ten pence. Very little cinchona is now grown in Malabar. The cinchonas, of which there are numerous species, are natives of South America. Quinine is a corruption of the word "Quina quina" or "bark of barks" and its virtues were probably known to the American Indians, before the arrival of the Spanish; but Europe and the East Indies are indebted to the Countess of Chinchon, the wife of a Viceroy of Peru, and her Jesuit friends for the introduction of the drug into Europe in 1640; and it was long known as "Countess' Powder" or "Jesuits' bark." The usual method of harvesting the bark is the coppice system; the tree is cut down close to the ground in about its fifteenth year, and the bark is sliced off and dried in the sun or by artificial heat. Quinine is not manufactured in the district, and all the bark is either sent to the Nilgiri factory or to Europe.

Tea.

Tea was first introduced into the Wynaad by Messrs. Parry & Co., who grew it for many years on their Perindotti Estate. The failure of cinchona gave an impetus to its cultivation, and since 1892 many coffee estates have been converted into tea gardens. Extensions are still going on, for tea does well in many parts of the Wynaad, and it may yet prove the salvation of the planting industry there. Prices show a tendency to rise and efforts are being made to create a market among

CHAP. IV
SPECIAL PRODUCTS.

natives of India. From the 1st April 1903, a customs cess of one quarter of a pie per pound on all tea exported from India was imposed by law, and the proceeds are handed over to a committee to be expended in increasing the consumption of tea outside the United Kingdom; the results so far seem to have been satisfactory. The tea planter however requires more capital than the coffee planter, since the tea must be manufactured on or close to the estate where it is picked, and considerable outlay is necessary on machinery and buildings. Picking and manufacture also goes on all the year round, whereas the coffee planter has only one crop to deal with.

The tea plant is a *Camelia*, and its blossom closely resembles that of the ordinary single white Camelia and has a similar scent. Three varieties are grown, the pure China tea, the indigenous Assam sort and the hybrid between these two, which is the most useful and generally grown of the three. It produces twice as much leaf as the pure China and yet possesses a great deal of the latter's hardiness.

Each of the leaves of the shoot of a tea plant is known by a technical name. The bud at the extreme end is called the tip or the "flowery pekoe"; the two next to it "orange pekoe"; the two next "souchong"; and the next two, the largest of the series, "congou." When a 'flush' or 'burst' of young green leaf occurs on the estate, all these leaves are all plucked together and taken to the factory, where they are spread out on shelves and left to wither, until they can be rolled between the fingers without breaking. The leaves are then rolled by machine, and laid out in a thin layer in a darkened and moist room and left to ferment. When the required stage of fermentation is reached, the tea is roasted or 'fired' in a machine called a "sirocco," which drives hot air between trays on which the leaves are spread. Finally, the fired tea is sifted by machinery, the grades usually distinguished being orange pekoe, broken pekoe, pekoe, pekoe souchong, broken souchong and congou.

Rubber.

Rubber is a product which is now attracting considerable attention. The three principal rubber trees are *Hevea Braziliensis*, called Para, from the district round one of the mouths of the Amazon in which it abounds, *Manihot glaziovii*, or Ceara so called after a province in Brazil where it flourishes, and *Castilloa elastica*, also a South American tree. The first trees planted in South India were some Ceara plants sent from Kew to the Nilambur teak plantations in 1878. Some Para and Castilloa plants were received in the next year, and at plantation house in Calicut are some specimens of the three trees which were put down in the same year. In 1882, an attempt was made to open an experimental plantation of *Castilloa* at Ingapuzha at the foot of the Tamarasseri ghat, but

CHAP. IV
SPECIAL PRODUCTS.

the undertaking was abandoned owing to difficulties about the title to the land. About the same time, some of the Wynaad planters following the lead of Ceylon tried *Ceara* in small plots or as shade amongst coffee : but it was found that the tree killed any coffee growing under it, and ignorance of the best methods of tapping the trees combined with unfavourable results in Ceylon gradually led to the neglect of the experiment. Recently, interest in rubber has revived ; many coffee planters have put down small patches of Para in their estates, and special plantations of rubber are being opened out in the Nilambur valley, on the slopes of the neighbouring hills, and near Puthupadi in the Calicut taluk. The whole subject of rubber cultivation is yet in its infancy ;[1] but the soil and climatic conditions of the new plantations seem eminently suitable to the tree.

To extract the latex, which occurs chiefly in the bark of the tree, regular incisions, in the form of spirals round the tree and so on, are made in the outer layers of the bark ; and the latex is collected as it drips from the incisions. It is then left to coagulate in shallow pans, and the caoutchouc globules rise to the surface and form a thin sheet of rubber, which is known as 'biscuit' or sheet rubber. 'Scrap' rubber is that which dries round the incisions and fails to fall into the collecting tins. In this district, there were in 1930, 61 planters' estates with 12,355 acres under tea, 2,776 under coffee, 9,247 under rubber, 1,923 under pepper and 443 acres under cardamoms, with an uncultivated reserve acreage of 50,345 acres.

ECONOMIC POSITION.

Economic position of ryots.

The economic position of the agricultural classes in Malabar, which number two-thirds of the total population, can hardly be judged by the ordinary standards adopted elsewhere. The ryotwari districts on the east coast were in most cases surveyed and settled many years ago, and their material progress can be gauged by comparing the increase of occupied area with the increase of population ; they are mainly grain-producing districts, and the average production of food per head of population now and many years ago can be estimated with some accuracy. In Malabar, all that is known is that prices rose steadily in the nineteenth century. The district is largely a horticultural one, and as its area was ascertained only a few years ago by professional survey, it is impossible to say whether its production of food is keeping pace with the increase of population. The statistics given in the separate appendix are also apt to mislead. Thousands of acres are shown as cultivable waste, and the inference is that there is room for a great extension of cultivation ; but a large part of the "cultivable waste" is really uncultivable, and much of the rest is modan and punam land cultivated once in two or three years and

[1] The latest hand-book on Para rubber is "*Hevea Braziliensis*, Para rubber" by Herbert Wright (Ferguson, Colombo, 1906).

CHAP. IV. ECONOMIC POSITION.

then left fallow, but treated as unoccupied for settlement purposes. Again, in Malabar excluding the Wynaad, the average agricultural holding measures 6·43 acres, compared with 7·35 in the rest of the Presidency; and 75 per cent of the pattadars pay an assessment of ten rupees or less, and together pay less than twelve per cent of the land revenue of the district, while for the rest of the Presidency the figures are 66 and 19, respectively. But it is not to be inferred from this that there are more petty proprietors in Malabar than elsewhere; the value of an acre of occupied land is higher than the average, and the number of pattas includes many issued for house-sites, to persons who do not belong to the agricultural class. Moreover, the desam, which is the unit for the issue of pattas, is usually smaller than the east coast village, and even small pattadars often hold lands in more than one desam.

Signs of material prosperity.

The general prosperity of the country is obvious. The rainfall is unfailing and famine is unknown. The soil is naturally fertile, and no one who travels by the South Indian Railway through the Palghat Gap can fail to be struck by the contrast between the arid plains and treeless wastes of the Carnatic and the rich paddy fields and luxuriant gardens of Malabar. The revenue is collected without difficulty, and the general standard of comfort is comparatively high. But a large proportion of the land is concentrated in the hands of a small class, and the welfare of the agricultural community depends largely upon the relations between landlord and tenant.

Landlord and tenant—Mr. Logan's report.

The subject was dealt with exhaustively by Mr. Logan in 1883,[1] and his report though it deals with the state of affairs fifty years ago is still valuable. It is a strong indictment of the janmi based on a detailed study of the revenue history of the district and upon enquiries made in every part of Malabar and extended over sixteen months. The financial position of 7,994 cultivators was examined, and it was found that 4,401 were in debt to an aggregate amount of nearly 17½ lakhs of rupees, while 1,406 had 7½ lakhs out at interest. Thus there was a balance of debt amounting to nearly 10 lakhs against the cultivators examined, and the interest on this huge sum went for the most part into the hands of the money lender. Mr. Logan concluded that the cultivators must be rapidly degenerating into a state of insolvent cottierism, a result which he attributed mainly to three crying evils, rack-renting, extortionate renewal fees, and inadequate compensation for improvements.

Rack-renting

He found that wet lands were rack-rented more often than gardens; the reason being that a garden requires an initial

[1] Report of the Malabar Special Commission, 1881–82, Volume I.

CHAP. IV. ECONOMIC POSITION.

outlay of capital and constant attention subsequently, and the janmi is therefore more or less in the power of his tenant. On the other hand, the cultivation of wet lands requires comparatively little labour and capital, and Mr. Logan found that the competition for such lands was very keen and rents proportionately high. At the beginning of the 19th century when rents were settled not by competition but immemorial custom, one-third of the net produce was reserved as *Kozhu labham* or the cultivator's share.[1] In 1881 in only two or at the most three of the 98 estates in the low country elaborately examined by Mr. Logan were the cultivators receiving their fair share. They held generally on *verumpattam* or simple lease, and in extreme cases the rent was the whole of the estimated produce after deducting the bare cost of seed and cultivation. Often again, the *verumpattakar* did not hold directly under the janmi, but under a *kanamdar* or other intermediary. To pay the ruinous renewal fees demanded by his janmi, the *kanamdar* had, in many cases, to borrow at interest varying from 12 to 36 per cent, and to relieve his position he had retained possession only of the best lands and sub-let at an extreme rack-rent the worst portions of his holding. Tenants ready to take up wet lands on any terms were not wanting, and the result was that the pressure was often the heaviest on the lands least able to bear it.

Renewal fees.

Renewal fees are the fees payable for the renewal of a *kanam* tenancy. Mr. Logan was of opinion that the practice of demanding such fees had its origin in an old custom, by which a tenant was bound, whenever a new janmi succeeded to the estate, to remit a portion of the advance which he had originally made to the janmi on entry; and he held that the evidence of old custom proved that the fine or premium on renewal ought not to exceed 20 or 25 per cent of the advance, or one year's rent at the janmi's option. But he found that in practice the renewal fee was fixed at any sum which the *kanamdar* could be brought by the threat of eviction to pay. The custom had in fact developed into an 'outrageous system of forehand renting,' the tenant often having to pay in a lump sum the greater part of the rent for the whole period of 12 years. The result was that the tenant and the sub-tenant, if there was one, were alike impoverished, and the land deteriorated for lack of cultivation.

Improvement rates.

In theory the Malabar law as to improvements secured to the tenant, even though he were a trespasser, 'the right of being paid for all kinds of improvements irrespective of the period during which he had been in possession of the land improved.' But the law failed in its application. The improvement rates for trees, shrubs and the like, were rates

[1] Rickards's proclamation, dated 29th June 1803.

fixed by old custom, and varied enormously throughout the district. For the coconut alone there were 74 rates varying from 10 pies to Rs. 14; and in North Malabar and the Calicut taluk the highest rate allowed for a coconut in full bearing was As. 8, or about half a year's rent for a good tree. For the areca palm there were 28 rates, ranging from 1 pie to Rs. 4–8–0, and for the jack tree 45 rates varying between 1 pie and Rs. 40. The tender of the value of improvements by janmis before filing a plaint was the merest farce, the sum offered being invariably grossly inadequate. The practice therefore was to depute Commissioners to assess the improvements at the rates of the locality and the door was opened to the most monstrous injustice. The Commissioners were men with no special qualifications for the task; their sympathies were usually rather with the janmi, often a Nambudiri with a high reputation for sanctity, than with the tenant who was not seldom a Mappilla; and their estimates were never checked except by another Commissioner with no better qualifications.

Evictions.

The practice of eviction Mr. Logan traced to the break up of the feudal system, which had preserved the balance of power between the janmis and the *kanamdars* who were their armed retainers, before the Muhammadan invasion. Rents came to be fixed by competition instead of by custom, and an unscrupulous class of janmis gradually appreciated the significance of the change, and the power of the weapon which the inadequacy of the improvement rates and the faulty methods of assessing the value of improvements placed in their hands. As a result evictions had increased with alarming rapidity, especially between 1860 and 1889. The average annual number of suits for eviction had risen from 2,039 in the five years ending 1866 to 4,983 in the four years ending 1880. The average annual number of persons against whom decrees for eviction were annually passed had increased from 1,891 to 8,355 in the same period. A suit for eviction was a common device for raising rents, and the decree was often executed only if the tenant refused to come to terms. Frequently a tenant was evicted just when the garden which he had planted up with the sweat of his brow and the outlay of all his capital was beginning to repay him for what he had spent on it; and after twelve or more years of hard labour he found himself homeless, with his capital exhausted and the scanty sum allowed for improvements swallowed up in the cost of the inevitable suit.

Social tyranny of janmis.

A further grievance was alleged to exist in the social rights and dignities, which had from time immemorial been attached to the title of janmi. The smallest show of independence by the tenant was resented as an affront. The Hindu tenants were the worst sufferers, and the penalty for offending a Nambudiri landlord was ex-communication. They were not allowed

CHAP. IV. ECONOMIC POSITION.

to be shaved; they were forbidden access to temples and tanks; and their women were refused purification after confinement. They were required to contribute to the expenses of wedding and other ceremonies in their janmi's house, and to make presents on asking permission to celebrate weddings in their own families. Resistance to the janmi and refusal to meet his illegal demands meant eviction and ruin.

The kariyastans or land agents.

Between the janmi and the tenant, moreover, there stood in many cases a still more unscrupulous tyrant in the person of the *kariyastan* or land agent. The estates of the bigger janmis are often immense; and instead of being concentrated in one or two large blocks, as in England, are scattered in small patches all over Malabar. The Zamorin, for instance, has lands in five taluks and 520 desams; the Kizhakke Kovilagam in four taluks and 263 desams; the Kadattanad Raja in 116 desams, and five other janmis in 80 or more desams. For their management many *kariyastans* were required and they were as a rule poorly paid and beyond the reach of effective control; and the nature of their duties, which were to collect rents and renewal fees and to grant receipts, placed immense power in their unscrupulous hands. A common compliant was that unless he was bribed the *kariyastan* refused receipts for rent; and, as the alleged arrears were deducted from the *kanam* amount on eviction, this was a hardship which pressed with peculiar severity on the tenant.

Mr. Logan's proposals.

Such was the position of the agricultural tenants fifty years ago according to Mr. Logan; and he considered that the only effective remedy would be to create a statutory class of peasant proprietors with permanent rights of occupancy, and to provide by law for adequate compensation to be paid for tenants' improvements. But there is little doubt that the picture was overdrawn. Mr. Logan was prejudiced in favour of the tenants who, he considered, had been deprived of their rights by the interpretation which the early British administrator had put on the meaning of *janmam* and *kanam* tenures; and the janmis' side of the question was insufficiently considered in his enquiry. The petitions which he received, in response to his request for evidence of particular terms of tenancy and particular grievances, were mainly from Mappillas of Ernad and Walavanad, and showed that many of the complaints of high rent were unfounded and many of the threatened evictions justified.

Criticism.

Mr. Logan's report was subjected to elaborate criticism by two Commissions;[1] his theories of the origin of the *kanam* tenure, and of the customary sharing of the produce of all land between janmi, *kanamdars* and cultivator were not generally

[1] See the report of the Malabar Land Tenures Committee, 1887.

accepted; and though it was agreed that there was much rack-renting and that the practice of the courts tended to deprive tenants of the value of their improvements, it was doubted whether on the whole the position of the Malabar cultivating tenant compared unfavourably with that of tenants in other districts, and it was held that there was no justification for legislation which would destroy rights long recognized and interfere with freedom of contract in fixing rents. There is considerable evidence to justify the conclusion of the earlier writers that before the Mysore invasion the incidents of the various tenures of landed property had become more or less fixed on a basis of contract; and the effect of the invasion must have been to strengthen the position of the moneyed *kanamdars* and enable them to obtain unduly favourable terms from their janmis. Between 1818 and 1822 the Special Commissioner, Mr. Farmer, reported that in many cases the *kanamdar*, after deducting the assessment which he paid to Government and the interest on the *kanam* amount, was paying the janmi only 20 per cent of the *pattam* and in other cases nothing at all. In 1831–32 prices began to rise and the rise continued for many years; and the subsequent attempt of the janmis to redeem *kanams* or renew them on terms more advantageous to themselves was a natural result of settled government and a rise of prices, and cannot be condemned wholesale as unscrupulous rack-renting.

The Tenants Improvements Act.

The ultimate result of Mr. Logan's enquiries was the enactment of the Malabar Compensation for Tenants Improvements Act (I of 1887, since superseded by Act I of 1900) which the Commissioners of 1885 believed "would remove a most prominent grievance of the tenant in Malabar" and was "calculated to exercise a beneficial effect on the relations of all agrarian classes in the district." As the law now stands the full market value of his improvements is secured to the tenant, and the landlord cannot contract himself out of the obligation to pay for them. The janmi is no longer tempted to evict to secure the value of the improvements, and he has been shorn of much of his power to demand exorbitant renewal fees. No doubt the value of improvements in wet lands can seldom be more than trifling; but a large number of tenants hold both wet lands and *parambas* on the same lease, and the amount of the *kanam* is usually greater in the case of wet lands than in the case of *parambas*. It may be said therefore that the Improvements Act has placed "a powerful weapon of defence—not to say defiance—in the hands of the tenants.[1]"

[1] See the Settlement Officer's report in G.O. No. 245, Revenue, dated 15th March 1905.

CHAP. IV. ECONOMIC POSITION.

The full effect of the enactment can hardly yet be gauged, but it is significant that since 1892 the annual number of suits for eviction has steadily declined, as the following figures for South Malabar show :—

——	Five years ending 1896.	Five years ending 1901.	Five years ending 1904.
Average annual number of suits for eviction ..	3,178	2,951	2,601
Decrees passed ..	2,352	2,175	1,707

Effect of the settlement.

At the recent settlement the old assessment was enhanced by nearly 80 per cent. and the pattas were issued to the janmis. The increase was justified and the new demand will not be collected in full for some years ; but the introduction of a settlement with the janmi, accompanied by an enhancement of the assessment which must obviously reduce the share of the produce available for distribution between the landlords and tenants, could hardly have failed to exaggerate the evil plight of the tenants, if the janmis were all powerful and everywhere oppressive. No such result has been apparent ; indeed the complaints are largely from the janmis, who object with some reason to having to pay the assessment on gardens and house-sites, where, as a rule the improvements belong to the tenant, and the janmi often gets only a nominal rent, a mere fraction it may be of the assessment. Section 14 of the Janmam Registration Act (III of 1896) makes some provision for this, by declaring that, if both consent, janmi and tenant may, under certain conditions, be registered jointly as pattadars and the tenant be then held responsible for the assessment in the first instance ; but comparatively little use has as yet been made of the section. The experience of the Court of Wards in managing the Kavalappara and Punnattur Estates may also be quoted in illustration of the difficulties of the janmi's position. The Collector and Agent to the Court finds that his tenants are in many cases scheming to acquire janmam rights by adverse possession and decline to pay rent or renewal fees ; he has not powers of distraint under Act VIII of 1865, and he is debarred from evicting on a large scale by lack of ready money ; the estate's wealth for the most part consists in land, its rents are paid in kind, and to sell its janmam right would be considered dishonourable.

The Malabar Tenancy Act, 1929.

An enquiry into the working of the Malabar Compensation for Tenants' Improvements Act (Act I of 1900) was held by the Government in 1911. Opinion as to its success varied and the question of a comprehensive tenancy legislation again assumed importance. Mr. (now Sir Charles) Innes, the then Collector of Malabar was deputed to report on the desirability and practicability of legislation. He was in favour of legislative interference. His report was referred to Mr. Evans, his successor, who took a totally different view, the Board of Revenue supporting his views and the matter was dropped by the Government. But the cry for legislation from certain quarters did not abate and a bill conferring occupancy rights on all *kanam* tenants and on all actual cultivators of six years' standing and prohibiting *melcharths* altogether was introduced as a private Bill by Diwan Bahadur (now the Hon'ble Sir) M. Krishnan Nayar in 1924 and was passed by the Legislative Council in 1926 with certain alterations such as the abolition of renewal fee. His Excellency the Governor, however, withheld his assent to it on account of certain grave defects in the Act. Soon afterwards a Committee under the presidency of Diwan Bahadur T. Raghavayya was appointed for a thorough re-examination of the question. The Committee recommended legislation for grant of qualified fixity of tenure to cultivating *verumpattamdars*, customary *verumpattamdars*, *kanamdars*, and *kuzhikanamdars*. The Government accordingly introduced a Bill on the lines of the proposals contained in the Report of the Raghavayya Committee and, with certain modifications made by the Legislative Council, it became the Malabar Tenancy Act, 1929 (Act XIV of 1930). During its passage through the Council, the tenants supported it generally as a measure of compromise, while the *janmis* opposed it vehemently. The Act came into force on the 1st December 1930. It is too soon to say anything about its probable effect. It introduced changes of importance in the relations of cultivating *verumpattamdars*, customary *verumpattamdars*, *kanamdars* and *kuzhikanamdars* with their landlords. Cultivating *verumpattamdars* were given fixity of tenure on condition of regular payment of "fair rent." The others were empowered to apply for and obtain renewals through Court, enuring for periods of 12 years, on the termination of their tenancies on payment of the prescribed renewal fees. The Act contains provisions for determining "fair rent" and "renewal fee." The landlord is given power to evict if he *bona fide* requires the land for cultivation by himself or the members of his family. His right of eviction for waste, denial of title or collusion in encroachment is also preserved while arrears of rent and renewal fee are made a charge on the tenants' interests in the holding. The holder of a decree for the eviction of a *kuzhikanamdar* is permitted to enforce it by sale of the holding. A *kudiyiruppu* which exclusively comprises a holding as well as one which is capable of convenient severance from a holding are specially protected by enabling tenants of ten years' standing to purchase them through Court at the market price in suits for eviction relating to them. The rights newly created in favour of the tenants

CHAP. IV. ECONOMIC POSITION.

are of great value and are calculated to confer a considerable measure of permanency on those who are prepared to conform to the requirements of the Act. The Act thus substantially strengthens the position of the tenants and materially improves their condition socially and economically without prejudicing the inherent rights of the landlords. It has been passed in the hope that it would bring about better relations between them. The Act applies to the entire district of Malabar and generally does not make any difference between North and South Malabar. *Kanams* which are essentially in the nature of mortgages, as is often the case in North Malabar, are, however, expressly excluded from its scope.

CHAPTER V.

FORESTS.

FORESTS—Denudation of ghat slopes—Zones of forest growth—Deciduous forests of the plains—Evergreen forests of the ghat slopes—Evergreen shola forests—Bamboo forests of the Wynaad—Deciduous forests of the Wynaad and Attapadi valley. STATE FORESTS—Development of conservancy—North Malabar—Teak forests of the Wynaad—The Tirunelli forests and the Kanoth range—Elephant catching—Forests of South Malabar—New Amarambalam reserve—Palghat range—Silent and Attapadi valley reserves—Nilambur teak plantations—Defoliation of teak trees—Mahogany and rubbers—Forest crime.

CHAP. V. FORESTS.

Denudation of ghat slopes.

ALLUSION has already been made in Chapter I above to the wonderfully varied and interesting flora of Malabar. Most of the forests belong to private janmis; and unhappily, unscientific forestry, the ravages of the timber thief and the destructive *punam* cultivation are slowly but surely denuding the ghat slopes of all valuable timber, and the paddy flats below have already been injured by the wash of sand and gravel. The average janmi is anxious to turn his trees into money with the least possible delay, and in this, perhaps, he is hardly to blame; for, if he hesitates, others will not be slow to take advantage of his procrastination. He has not the means adequately to conserve his forests, and of late years the timber thief has been bolder and more ubiquitous than ever. Generally a Mappilla, he gets from the janmi in the guise of an honest merchant permission to fell and remove a certain number of trees on payment of a *kuttikanam* or stump fee. Usually he fells ten times as many trees as he has paid for, nor is he particular on whose land they stand. The cultivation of *punam* which involves the clearance of all timber from the land cultivated is fatal to tree growth, but it is unrestricted in private forests.

Zones of forest growth.

The forest growth of the district falls naturally into five well marked zones, differing in climate, soil and rainfall, and the resultant forest flora.

Deciduous forests of the plains.

The deciduous forests of the plains and the lower ghat slopes stretch in a continuous belt along the foot of the ghats from the northern extremity of the district to the Palghat Gap, and in

CHAP. V. FORESTS.

places extend up the hill sides for some 1,500 feet. Formerly they must have been very valuable; but, being easy of access, they have long been worked out by their native owners, and now are almost destitute of good timber. Most of the trees are deciduous, but evergreen trees are found along the river banks. Commercially the most valuable trees in this zone are teak (*Tectona grandis*); Bombay blackwood or East India rosewood (*Dalbergia latifolia*); ventek (*Lagerstroemia microcarpa*); irul (*Xylia dolabriformis*); karumarudu or matti (*Terminalia tomentosa*); and pumarudu (*Terminalia paniculata*).

Evergreen forests of the ghat slopes.

The moist evergreen forests of the ghat slopes climb from their foot to an elevation of 4,000 feet above sea level, and are found both on their western and eastern faces. The rainfall is very heavy, in places exceeding 300 inches, and the forest growth is magnificent. The trees grow to an immense size, and sometimes attain a diameter of ten feet at the base and a height of more than 200 feet. They are all evergreen, and with their variety of foliage and colour, especially when the leaves are flushing—some pure white, some crimson, others all possible tints of brown, yellow, red and green—are beautiful in the extreme. Their trunks are often covered with epiphytic orchids, ferns and mosses, which add to the beauty, but detract from the commercial value of the tree; and there is a glorious profusion of rattans, tree ferns, climbing ferns and creepers. The more accessible portions of the zone have been worked out of late years, but there are still to be found a few tracts of virgin forest where the axeman has not yet penetrated. The trees which yield the most valuable timber are irumbogam or urupu (*Hopea parviflora*); white cedar (*Dysoxylon Malabaricum*); red cedar (*Acrocarpus frazinifolia*); poonspar (*Calophyllum elatum*); ebony (*Diospyros ebenum*); aini (*Artocarpus hirsuta*); jack (*Artocarpus integrifolia*); ironwood (*Mesua ferrea*); pali (*Dichopsis elliptica*); and white dammer (*Vateria Indica*). The palm *Caryota urens* and the wild areca tree are conspicuous, as also are several species of rattan, and two fine reed bamboos, *Oxytenanthera Thwaitesii* and *Teinostachyum Wightii*.

Evergreen shola forests.

The evergreen shola forests are found on all the higher slopes of the ghats, as well as on the Brahmagiri range and in the higher parts of the Attapadi valley. The forests, especially on the Brahmagiri and other hills east of the ghats, where the rainfall is less, are usually interspersed with stretches of open grass land. Apart from the fact that owing to the altitude their growth is smaller and less vigorous than in the second zone, the forests are so inaccessible that their timber is of little commercial value. All the trees are evergreen, and the tints of their leaves are at certain seasons very beautiful. Ferns and mosses abound, but orchids are poorly represented. The orders chiefly represented are myrtaceae, lauraceæ and styraceæ. *Asophila latebrosa*, a tree fern, is abundant and there is one species of reed bamboo, *Arundinaria Wightiana*.

Bamboo forests of the Wynaad.

The bamboo forests of the Wynaad plateau cover a narrow belt of country lying east of the ghats, stretching from the foot of the Nilgiris on the south to the Brahmagiris on the north. The rainfall ranges from 60 to 100 inches, and the landscape consists of low rounded hills and ridges, intersected with innumerable, branching valleys. The forest is of little value. Timber trees no doubt once abounded; but the tract is comparatively thickly populated, and, as the land for the most part belongs to private janmis, almost all trees of value have long disappeared. The most characteristic feature is the growth of the common bamboo (*Bambusa arundinacea*), which covers the sides and many of the summits of the hills. Lantana, too, is common, and is fast spreading over the open grass lands. With the bamboo is associated a sprinkling of timber trees of stunted growth such as jack, aini and blackwood, and there is a considerable quantity of small scrubby evergreen growth. Noticeable features of the uncultivated swampy lands are screw-pine (*Pandanus odoratissimus*), *Melastoma Malabaricum* and *Ligodium*.

Deciduous forests of the Wynaad and Attapadi valley.

The deciduous forests of the Wynaad plateau and the Attapadi valley are found in the eastern border of the Walavanad taluk where the country is fairly flat and in the lower portions of Attapadi valley. The rainfall is less than is usual in Malabar, and varies between 40 and 80 inches. With the exception of a few swamps, these tracts are covered with heavy forest. Most of the trees are deciduous, and the general character of the forest growth resembles that of the deciduous forests of the plains, the most noticeable difference being the absence of irul and pumarudu, characteristic trees below the ghats. Teak grows luxuriantly in the Wynaad and, thanks to the level nature of the country and the comparatively light rainfall, is easily transported eastwards through Mysore territory. The forests are in consequence a very valuable asset to Government to whom fortunately they belong. After teak the principal timber trees are:—Vengai or honne *Pterocarpus marsupium*), matti or karumarudu (*Terminalia tomentosa*), ventek (*Lagerstrœmia microcarpa*), bejal or dinduga (*Anogeissus batifolia*), jal (*Shorea baccifera*), and kadambu (*Adina cordifolia*).

STATE FORESTS.

Development of conservancy.

Although, as has been pointed out above, most of the forest lands are the property of private owners, the State owns large tracts in the Wynaad, Kottayam, Calicut, Ernad, Walavanad and Palghat taluks, some leased, others acquired by purchase or escheat. At first no distinction was made between private and Government forests, and the first essay

CHAP. V. FORESTS.

at conservancy was the introduction in 1807 of a state royalty on teak and other valuable trees. This measure, which soon assumed the form of a Government monopoly, led to such discontent among the landholders and inhabitants that Sir Thomas Munro decreed its abolition in 1822. The public forests continued to be worked by the Collector on the stump fee system, till in 1847 the Executive Engineer brought to the notice of Government that trees of value were rapidly disappearing. A special officer was appointed to explore, work and conserve the forests, but work was limited to the extraction of timber required by the Engineering Department and the Bombay Marine. The importance of protection and reproduction of forest growth was gradually recognised, and by 1860 both the Forest and the Jungle Conservancy departments had been organised, the former independent of the Revenue authorities, the latter designed for the protection of village forests under their supervision. The two departments were merged in one as a branch of the Revenue department in 1882, and for purposes of administration the district is now divided into three divisions each under a district forest officer with headquarters at Nilambur, Manantoddy and Palghat.

North Malabar.

The forests of North Malabar are divided into the Begur, Chedleth and Kanoth ranges, and comprise in all an area of 164,928 acres, or nearly 259 square miles. The first two ranges lie in the Wynaad taluk and are composed of the evergreen and deciduous forests of the Tirunelli valley in the north of the taluk, and the valuable belt of deciduous teak forest on its eastern border. All these form part of the Pazhassi or Pychy escheat. The Kanoth range includes the Kanoth reserve in the Kottayam taluk, originally the property of Kannavad Nambiyar, one of the principal adherents of the Pazhassi Raja; the Kottiyur and Chinkanni valleys, purchased from a private syndicate in 1903; and the evergreen forests near Periya in the west of the Wynaad taluk, also part of the Pazhassi escheat. At the forest settlement a Mappilla claimant to portions of both the Periya and Kanoth reserves had to be bought out at Rs. 2 per acre.

Teak forests of the Wynaad.

Before 1859 when a Forest Officer was appointed, the teak forests of the Begur and Chedleth ranges were worked by the Collector on the stump fee system. From that year onwards felling was done departmentally and the logs were conveyed by road and river to various places in Mysore for sale. From 1878 till 1895 the felling of live trees was stopped and removals were confined to dead or windblown trees, and the system of sale at forest depots seems to have been introduced about the same time. Working plans for these forests were made in 1902, and fellings were prescribed in certain areas for the next ten years. Up to a fixed maximum in each area, all trees of valuable species which measure not less than two feet in diameter at five feet from the ground are now felled. After the trees have been sawn into logs, and the logs have been roughly squared, the timber is dragged by elephants to the nearest depot and sold there. In 1925 a sale depot was opened at Nanjangud in Mysore, and timber from the Chedleth and Sultan's Battery Ranges was carted there for sale. In 1924 a sale depot was opened in Mysore City for the timber of Begur Range. In 1921 the system of working was changed, and clear felling of annual coupes followed by artificial regeneration, with teak as the main species, was begun. In 1926 a saw mill was erected in Chedleth. A considerable area is now being clear-felled and planted up annually, and the forests generally brought under more extensive management.

The Tirunelli forests and the Kanoth range.

Little work has been done in the other reserves of North Malabar. Beyond demarcation and building a bungalow on the Brahmagiri hills, Government have as yet undertaken no work in the Tirunelli forests. The Periya and Kottiyur reserves and the eastern portion of Kanoth reserve contain valuable timber of evergreen species. In the more accessible parts of these areas, and in Kanoth Reserve, mature trees of the more valuable species are now being felled and converted into sleepers. Experimental plantations of teak were formed about the year 1875 by the old Jungle Conservancy Department in the Kanoth reserve, but the soil proved too poor in organic matter, and planting has since been abandoned. The bamboo plantations and natural bamboo forest cover a considerable area. The Kuricchiyans, who from time immemorial have lived in large numbers in the forest, were until quite recently permitted to make clearings for *punam* cultivation where they pleased, but they are now confined to prescribed areas. A few permits for the removal of individual trees have been from time to time granted, but the forest has not yet been regularly worked. The small experimental plantations are protected from fire, but protection is unnecessary for the major portion of the reserve as fires are almost unknown. A road has been built up the Kottiyur valley to Kottiyur but little timber has yet been extracted from that area. The forest growth is magnificent ; but, thanks to its inaccessibility, it has been spared the usual fate of most private forests. Floating is possible at a point about seven miles below the reserve, where the two small streams which drain the forest unite in an arm of the Valarpattanam river. It is proposed to construct a road to this point, and the extraction of timber and its conveyance for sale at Valarpattanam will then be an easy matter.

Elephant catching.

Elephants have been captured in pitfalls in Malabar from time immemorial, but it was not till 1896 that their capture was systematically taken up in the Government forests in the

CHAP. V. FORESTS.

Wynaad. In that year Mr. Marshall, the District Forest Officer, had a number of pits dug, and succeeded in capturing seventeen elephants. Since then, except in 1901, operations have been carried on every year with most satisfactory results. Between 1896 and 1903 eighty-three elephants were captured, and seventy-one brought to the kraals and trained. The system of capture is a comparatively simple one to manage, and, if care be exercised, the percentage of casualties is probably smaller than in keddah operations. A small special establishment is maintained to conduct the operations, and the pits are examined every morning. On one occasion in 1898 no less than four elephants, two cows and two calves, were found in one pit. Both cows moreover were in calf; and, though one calf was still-born, the other was safely dropped, so that practically five elephants were captured at the same time in a single pit. One or two elephants are caught annually in the new Amarambalam reserve in South Malabar, but operations are not carried on on so large a scale as in North Malabar, and no special establishment is maintained. Elephants are of course also still regularly caught in private forests by private janmis, and in many cases, as for instance in the Kollangod forests, form a valuable source of income to the landowner.

Forests of South Malabar.

Commercially the forests of South Malabar are at present far more important than those of North Malabar and unlike the latter they have more than paid for their upkeep.

The South Malabar forest division is now known as the Nilambur Division and consists of two ranges Nilambur and Amarambalam covering an area of 81,198 acres or about 127 square miles. The Palghat forest division includes three ranges of which two (Mannarghat and Palghat) are in this district and the third (Bolampatti) is in Coimbatore. The forests of Ernad and Walavanad taluks form the Mannarghat range, with the exception of a block in the Attapadi reserve (Block VI) which, for convenience of administration, is made part of the Bolampatti range. The total area of reserve forest in the Palghat division is 112,140 acres.

New Amarambalam reserve.

The New Amarambalam reserve situated on the western slopes of the Kundahs and including the broken country at their foot, is about 97 square miles in extent. The tract formerly belonged to the Amarambalam Tirumalpad but was purchased by Government at a court sale in 1887. Under its former owner most of the accessible timber was cut, but the higher ranges which probably contained valuable timber could not be exploited. The soil in the low ground is for the most part very good and is a fine field for the extension of the Nilambur teak plantations. Up to 1926 an extension of only 243 acres of teak plantations had been made in this reserve as the department was planting areas round the existing teak area in Nedungayam. The tracing of road and paths into the Amarambalam reserve is under consideration with a view to opening up this area for reconnoitering parties and to take up some sylvicultural method of working it.

Palghat range.

In the Palghat taluk the most important reserve from a financial point of a view is the Chenat Nayar escheat reserve. This and the adjoining Dhoni reserve, which were handed over to the Forest department in 1883, are now attached to the South Coimbatore forest division. They are situated on the slopes of a range of hills running westward from the south-west corner of the Attapadi valley. Only six miles from the railway, the forest has been overworked in the past, large quantities of timber having been removed by the department and its contractors. Nor have timber thieves been slow to take advantage of its accessibility and its distance from the head-quarters of the District Forest Officer. In 1903 the Forest department commenced to supply fuel to the Madras Railway Company from these two reserves, and the enterprise is still being carried on successfully. In 1919 a scheme was prepared for exploiting the evergreen forests in the Chenat Nayar reserve. Teak logs had till then been supplied to the Kolar Gold Fields. The scheme was primarily launched with a view to exploit the inferior species of timber and make them economically useful instead of allowing them to rot on the forests. This proved unprofitable and it was decided to try to sell wood in the form of scantlings. Thereupon an up-to-date saw mill was installed very near the Olavakkot railway station and kilns were constructed in which the sawn timber was scientifically seasoned. The exploitation of these forests was done under the district forest officer till 1922 when it was placed in charge of a special officer. The saw mills were, however, found to be unprofitable and so abandoned and sale of timber in logs has been resumed. Walayar forests in this range are also commercially important and contain many valuable teak and other trees. The department has taken up regeneration work and is stump-planting teak plants in the coupes. The Attapadi reserve block I is not exploited at present, and the chief items of revenue from it are sale of fuel, bamboo coupes and grazing fees. The Bolampatti Valley contains many villages and organized timber smugglers which render the protection of the forests a difficult affair.

Silent and Attapadi valley reserves.

Large tracts of forests are also owned by Government in the Silent and Attapadi valleys. The timber in these forests is excellent, but the difficulties of transport are so great that it is under present conditions impossible to extract it except at a loss. Previoulsy Government confined themselves to selling the right to collect minor produce in the Silent Valley and to granting concessions for the extraction of small quantities of

CHAP. V. FORESTS.

timber. Such licences are no longer granted. The reserves lie in a highly malarial zone, the only inhabitants of which are the Malasars; and they are useful on forest works and in protecting forests from fire and have been given lands free for cultivation. The forests are still unexploited, but many bridle paths and inspection bungalows have recently been constructed. Their inaccessibility mainly accounts for the absence of timber theft. The Bhavani and Kundipuzha rivers rise respectively in the Attapadi and Silent Valley reserves where herds of wild elephants roam at will at all seasons of the year.

Nilambur teak plantations.

The forests of South Malabar, however, owe their commercial importance and their financial success almost entirely to the famous Nilambur teak plantations, which were started in 1840 by Mr. Conolly, Collector of Malabar, with the object of 'replacing those forests which have vanished from private carelessness and rapacity— a work too new, too extensive and too barren of early return to be ever taken up by the native proprietor.' By a fortunate coincidence the Trikkalayur Devasvam, which owns in the Nilambur valley many of the best sites for planting, happened to be in want of funds; and, in return for a royalty upon fellings and an advance of Rs. 8,000 without interest, the temple authorities consented to lease their lands for as many years as Government wished to retain possession. Somewhat similar leases were arranged with the Zamorin for the Nellikkut block in 1841, with the Wandur Nambudiripad for the Chattamborayi block in 1871, and with the Amarambalam Tirumulpad for the Amarambalam and Karimpuzha blocks in 1878. The janmam right of the last two blocks was purchased by Government at a court sale in 1892.

No better site for planting could have been chosen. The Nilambur valley is of the shape of a horse shoe and lies some 400 feet above sea-level beneath the shadow of an amphitheatre of hills. The Wynaad plateau on the north and north-east does not attain an elevation of more than 3,000 feet, but the Camel's Hump range on the north-west and the towering Kundahs on the east and south-east rise into peaks upwards of 8,000 feet high. The soil of the valley, especially on the banks of its many streams, is an alluvial deposit of immense depth and wonderful fertility. The rainfall is about 130 inches; the temperature ranges from 80° to 90° Fahr. throughout the year. Gales are experienced in April to July and in October, often accompanied by whirlwinds originating in the river beds. Their course is easily marked by the destruction which follows in their wake and is confined to the banks of the river. The Chaliyar, Ponpuzha, and Karimpuzha, fed by innumerable smaller streams, unite in the heart of the plantations, and thence, as the Beypore river, flow into the sea only six miles south of Calicut. Four miles from its mouth a canal leads to the great timber mart at Kallayi, and thousands of logs are placed annually on the market at a minimum cost. The river is navigable for rafts from June to January and below Mambad navigation is so easy that the largest raft can be managed by a single man.

An initial difficulty was experienced in getting the seed to germinate, and it was not till 1843 that Dr. Roxburgh suggested the true method, which subsequent experience has only slightly modified, of sowing the seed at the beginning of the rains in shaded beds lightly covered with earth and straw. Planting commenced in 1842, and, with the exception of 1843, 1877–1885, 1895 and 1896, has been continued every year up to the present time. For the first ten years operations were restricted to the good alluvial soil on the river bank west of Nilambur; but, when this was exhausted, a move was made up the river, and, with a view no doubt to concentration, from 1854 onwards the planting of each year was confined to one large block. Thus for many years the mistake was made of including in the planted area laterite hills on which teak is an utter failure. The young plantations are weeded every year until the trees get their heads above the weeds, but the former practice of weeding the older plantations has long been given up as a contravention of all principles of sylviculture. The teak trees are attacked by a parasite belonging to the Loranthus family, and this is periodically cleared. Almost every year too the trees are stripped bare of their leaves by the larvae of *Hyblaea puera* and *Pyrausta Machairalis*, pests for which no effective remedy has yet been discovered. Some of the latter larvae hibernate in the fallen leaves during the time that the teak is leafless. The plantations which are divided into thirteen blocks cover in all about 15,000 acres. Of this nearly 5,400 acres have now been planted up.

Defoliation of teak trees.

The Forest Research Institute at Dehra Dun has been investigating this since April 1924. A number of species of insects have been identified and their life histories studied on the spot by research workers sent from Dehra Dun. Several species of parasites besides *Hyblaea puera* and *Pyrausta Machairalis* have been identified, but no effective remedy has yet been evolved to combat them except to encourage crows and mynas of which there are large numbers now in these plantations.

The fully stocked teak plantations in the Nilambur valley now cover only an area of 4,764·8 acres, as the teak planted in about 235 acres failed to develop satisfactorily.

Thinning was commenced in 1852; and by 1859 most of the plantations more than six years of age had been thinned twice,

CHAP. V. FORESTS.

but only by the removal of dominated saplings. Subsequently more scientific methods were employed, and a system introduced by which at 63 years of age each plantation would have been thinned ten times, and the number of trees reduced from 1,040 to 74 per acre. Regular working plans were made out in 1885, and revised five years later. The plantations are at present worked on plans, drawn up in 1895 by Mr. P. M. Lushington, and recently revised. They are rigorously protected from fire. In 1918, a new working plan was sanctioned for the forests of the Nilambur valley. This plan provides for the felling of mature crops in the plantations in a rotation of 60 years tentatively (this may possibly be raised to 70 years later), extension of plantations by felling and planting suitable blocks of natural forests, and the thinning and tending of the young woods.

The growth of teak on the better classes of soil is magnificent, some of the 60 year old trees being as much as 120 feet high and 7 feet in girth. Thinnings have practically repaid the outlay on the plantations at this early stage, and the capital stored in the forest in the shape of big trees insures a splendid ultimate return for the money invested. Prices at Calicut are high, having touched as much as Rs. 3 per cubic foot, and the cost of placing the timber on the market is very small. The age of exploitability is calculated at 105 years on first-class soils and 140 years on those of the second class, and Mr. Lushington estimates that the final yield will be 3,000 cubic feet per acre on the former soils, and 2,000 cubic feet on the latter. The total receipts from the plantations since they were started amount to Rs. 17,41,739 and the expenditure on them to Rs. 15,32,308, but, if compound interest at 4 per cent. be added, there is a balance of rather less than two lakhs against the plantations.

Mahogany and rubber.

Experiments have also been tried at Nilambur with mahogany and rubber, and small plots of these are planted out every year. The soil and climate seem to suit the former, and both *Swietenia mahogani* and *Swietenia macrophylla* apparently thrive on soil which is too poor for teak. They suffer in early life from the attacks of boring beetles and caterpillars, but appear to recover later on. The trees however have only a short bole, and, if wood cut from young trees can be taken as a criterion, the timber is wanting both in colour and figure.

Among rubbers experiments with Para (*Hevea Braziliensis*) have been successful over a small area; and some promising private plantations are now being opened up in the Nilambur valley and the slopes of the ghats to the south.

Forest crime.

The State forests cover such a small proportion of the forest land of the district that there is little or no friction with the people, who can as a rule graze their cattle and gather fuel in the private forests free of cost. The people living in or near the large tracts of reserved forest in the Wynaad are allowed to remove fuel, bamboos and timber of the less valuable species free of charge. A small fee is charged for grazing. Minor forest offences are rare, but of late years there have been considerable thefts of timber from the Silent valley and Panakkadan blocks. The blocks are surrounded by large private forests; and, it is extremely difficult to bring the offenders to justice unless they are caught in the act.

CHAPTER VI.

OCCUPATIONS AND TRADE.

OCCUPATIONS—Census statistics—Influence of caste. INDUSTRIES—Cocoanut-oil—Gingelly and other oils—Lemon grass oil—The soap industry—The coir industry—Timber trade–Preparation of coffee, pepper and ginger for export–Tile works—Weaving—Weaving mills—Tailors—Cap-making—Fishing—Toddy-drawing—Jaggery—Leaf umbrellas, huts, mats and baskets—Steel umbrellas—Palghat grass mats—Grass and bamboo mats and baskets—Iron smelting—Goldwashing—Bell-metal work—Metal-works—Minor industries—Cocoanut shell carving—Beedies—Knives and locks—Safety matches. PROFESSIONS—Transport and storage. TRADE—Volume of trade—Ports—Exports—Their distribution—Imports—Rail-borne trade. WEIGHTS AND MEASURES—Weights—Grain measures—Liquid measures. CO-OPERATIVE SOCIETIES—Their origin—Management—Working capital and membership—Non-credit societies.

CHAP. VI. OCCUPATIONS

Census statistics.

THE elaborate statistics of occupations and trades collected at the census of 1901 confirm the popular impression that Malabar is a comparatively wealthy and prosperous district, and reveal its manifold natural resources. It is true that, as in India generally, so in Malabar, the margin between a modest competence and extreme poverty is exceeding small. Few but the very old and the very young can afford to eat the bread of idleness, and women and even children are impressed into labour. But less so in Malabar than in the average district. In the presidency, as a whole, 54 per cent. of the population work for their living, and 42·5 per cent. of the workers are women. In Malabar the percentages are 47 and 39 respectively. In the presidency again more than 70 per cent. are supported by agriculture, and less than 18 per cent. by industrial occupations. In Malabar the corresponding figures are 62½ and 24½ respectively. Thus agriculture, though the predominant profession, does not exhaust the resources of the district. The sea that washes its coasts teems with fish, and provides upwards of 80,000 persons with their daily occupation, and the whole community with an almost inexhaustible supply of cheap and wholesome food. The forests that clothe the Western Ghats from head to foot, and cover a great part of the Wynaad plateau, besides making Calicut one of the most important timber marts in India, support thousands of carpenters, sawyers and woodcutters and their numerous progeny. On the many rivers of the district and the backwaters into which they discharge, an immense fleet of boats plies for hire, and numbers earn their living by propelling them. More important still industrially are the palmyra, the sago and above all the cocoanut palm. Toddy-drawing alone supports 50,000 people; coir rope-making nearly 40,000; and oil-pressing, jaggery-making and the manufacture of palm leaf hats, umbrellas, baskets and mats are all important trades. Trade statistics

CHAP. VI. OCCUPATIONS.

show moreover that products of the cocoanut more than pay for the grain imported into Malabar, and thus indirectly they support the numerous dealers who distribute the grain all the district over. The standard of comfort is comparatively high. Houses built of laterite and roofed with tiles meet one at evey turn. Tea in the cup is sold in every petty bazaar, and is being drunk more and more every year. The native is also acquiring a taste and creating a demand for soda water and various syrups. Malabar has more cooks, barbers, household servants, tailors, cap-makers, stone-workers and knife-grinders than any other district, and the learned professions are strongly represented. Manufactures, however, are still scanty and one might almost write to-day as the Joint Commissioners did in 1793 'its manufactures, unless vegetable oils and coir fall under that denomination, there are hardly any other.'

Influence o caste.

At a very remote period of history, Malayalam society appears to have been organized into castes or guilds, each with its own function in the body politic; and in Malabar behind the shelter of its mountain wall the system has survived with less modifications than in any other district. Most of the castes described by Durate Barbosa 400 years ago are still practising the same trades.[1] Many of them, the Chaliyans or weavers especially, have been hard hit by the introduction of machine-made goods from Europe; but they still struggle on without thought of improving their time-honoured methods, or of deserting their hereditary trades for more remunerative employment. Barbosa was impressed more with the customs than with the handiwork of the artisans of Malabar, and they are still more interesting from an ethnological than from an industrial point of view. Their work, moreover, does not differ materially from that turned out elsewhere, and with rare exceptions they require little notice here. Agriculture has been dealt with in a separate chapter, and it remains only to mention those industries which are of importance either because of their economic value, or because they are out of the common.

INDUSTRIES. Cocoanut-oil trade and oil pressing.

The value of the cocoanut-oil shipped from Cochin in the commercial year 1903–04 was more than 87 lakhs; and, though a great part of this was made in Native Cochin and Travancore, the oil trade takes the first place among the industries of Malabar. Copra, the dried kernel of the cocoanut, from which the oil is extracted, and the refuse or poonac are also exported in large quantities. Copra is of two qualities, white and black. The former is the more valuable, and the oil expressed from it is reserved for export to Europe; the oil made from black copra is sold locally, and used for lighting, cooking and for the hair. Oil-pressing is the hereditary

[1] *The Coasts of East Africa and Malabar*, 124–148.

CHAP. VI. INDUSTRIES.

calling of the Chakkans or Vaniyans, as they are also called, and of the less numerous Vattakadans, low Nayar classes or sub-castes. Their mills are of the usual pattern ; but mills on the same principle, worked by steam and far more efficient and economical, have sprung up of late years in Cochin and its vicinty and in Calicut. The Chakkan is in a bad way in consequence. Working all day he cannot extract in his mill more than a maund or two of oil, whereas with steam power a single *çhakka* in a mill, which possibly contains thirty or forty, will turn out fifteen maunds. Poonac is shipped to Hamburg to be made into oil-cake for cattle, and is used locally both as cattle food and as manure.

Gingelly and other oils.

Other oils made in Malabar are gingelly, castor, *iruppa*, *ungu*, *puvam*, *niretti*, and *veppu*. The last five are substitutes for cocoanut-oil in the interior taluks where the palm does not thrive, and are used for lighting. The last is also used medicinally for external application as a cure for rheumatism. Castor is an insignificant crop in Malabar, but gingelly is one of the chief dry crops, and its oil is extracted in much the same way as cocoanut-oil, and is used for cooking and for the oil bath. Oil is also pressed from groundnuts and *morati* seeds. Groundnut is generally imported from Pollachi, Coimbatore and other places and *morati* seeds are available locally. These oils are also used in the manufacture of soaps and the *poonac* or cake is used for manure and bought up by Messrs. Peirce, Leslie & Co.

Lemon grass oil.

The demand in Europe for lemon grass oil, which is an ingredient in many perfumes, is considerable and prices have recently ruled high. The grass grows wild in the neighbourhood of Pandikkad and Angadipuram in the Ernad and Walavanad taluks. It is boiled with water in a huge copper cauldron ; the resulting liquid drips into a flat open vessel from a pipe at the bottom of the cauldron, which is regulated by a tap, and the oil is skimmed off with a spoon. The industry is mainly in the hands of Mappillas. The oil is taken to Cochin for export. Lemon grass oil is also made in Anjengo from grass grown in Travancore.

The soap industry.

Of recent years the manufacture of soap in the district has been developed. There are two processes one by boiling, and the other a cold process. The former being more elaborate and efficient is adopted in large factories worked by mechanical power, like the Government Kerala Soap Factory at Calicut. In the cold process neither much capital nor skilled labour is needed, and a great many people are employed in making soap in this way. Cocoanut oil, the oil *par excellence* for soaps, is largely used, sometimes mixed with groundnut, cotton seed, *morati* seed and other oils. The only implements required are a small tank for dissolving caustic soda, a pan for mixing the oil, and a frame or box for cooling the soap, all these (costing about Rs. 50) being made of iron to resist the corrosive action of caustic soda. The trade suffers from the adulteration practised by some manufacturers.

CHAP. VI.
INDUSTRIES.

The Kerala Soap Institute owes its origin to the disinterested labours of Sir Frederick Nicholson. Attempts at soap manufacture were made at the Tanur Fisheries Experimental Station in 1914–15 where fish-oil soap was first made in the course of refining and purifying fish-oil at the factory. This soap which is in great demand among planters and other agriculturists as a valuable and cheap insecticide continues to be made at the institute. Household and toilet soaps are manufactured on a fairly large scale and they are well known throughout India for their pure quality and low price. The institute also trains young men in the art of soap making to enable them to open or manage soap factories on a commercial scale in various parts of India and Burma, and since 1927 several batches of students have been trained and sent out. The gross profit earned by the institute up to 31st March 1929 was about Rs. 8 lakhs and the net profit about Rs. 1 lakh, but as Sir Frederick stated "the profit of this institute is not to be gauged by its cash profits but by the profits of private factories which it can stimulate into existence." Another factory was opened at Calicut by one of the old pupils of the institute, and it is said to be working well.

The coir industry.

The manufacture of coir yarn, rope and matting is another great and expanding industry, 62 lakhs' worth of coir in various forms having been exported from Cochin in 1904 against 31 lakhs' worth in 1894. The further south one goes the more the industry flourishes. Aleppy yarn is the best and that from Anjengo is very good. The best yarn in Malabar proper comes from Vadanapalli and Venkidanga amsams in Ponnani taluk. The husks of the cocoanuts are buried in pits as near as possible to the water line of rivers, backwaters and creeks, and are left to soak for six months, a year or even eighteen months, the longer the better. The colour of the yarn, and thereby the quality, depends very much on the water in which the husks are steeped. It should be running water and, if possible, fresh. If the water be salt, the yarn may at first be almost white, but in a damp climate it soon becomes discoloured and blotchy. As soon as the husks are taken out of the pits, the fibre is beaten out with short sticks by Tiyattis and women of the Vettuvan[1] caste. It is dried in the sun for twelve hours and is then ready for sale to native merchants at Calicut and Cochin, who in their turn deal with the European firms. The fibre is twisted into yarn by Tiyattis and other women, and in that form the greater part of the coir made in Malabar is exported from Cochin to all parts of the world, but chiefly to the United Kingdom and Germany. Excellent ropes

[1] The mason caste not the jungle tribe; see p. 129.

CHAP. VI. INDUSTRIES.

and mats, however, are made in Cochin, and a coarser quality in Calicut. Fibre is also extracted from the stalks of the leaves of palmyra palms in the neighbourhood of Ottapalam and some parts of Palghat, and sent to the coast for export to Ceylon and elsewhere. During the five years ending 1925–26, coir and rope exported from Calicut and Cochin were worth Rs. 26 lakhs and Rs. 114 lakhs, respectively. The chief centres where cocoanut husk is converted into fibre are Beypore, Parappanangadi, Ponnani, Tirurangadi, Tikkoti, Quilandy and several villages along the coast. In British Cochin and Alleppey certain European firms manufacture rugs, matting, belting and brush mats, but the bulk of the coir industry consists in extracting the fibre and in making it into thin yarn for export to Europe and America. The export trade is in the hands of European firms who have branches at Cochin, Calicut and Alleppy. These get their supply from Indian merchants who collect the yarn from middlemen or direct from spinners. Prices vary according to colour and quality of the yarn ; and between the owner who wishes to get the highest price for his husks and the merchants who are unwilling to reduce their profits, the sufferers are the actual spinners, and it is said that the Tiyatti or the Vettuvathi who beats the husks into fibre and spins the yarn is hardly able to earn more than an anna and a half a day. Germany, among the European countries, continues to be the largest buyer of coir yarn.

Timber trade.

The timber trade of Malabar is of great economic importance. The forests of the district (*vide* Chapter V) produce immense quantities of magnificent timber, and the majority of them are so placed that their exploitation is comparatively easy. The Government forests are worked departmentally ; in private forests trees are felled by Mappilla merchants on payment of *kuttikanam* or stump fee to the owner, and after being roughly squared are dragged by elephants to the nearest road or river to be carried or floated to the depots of the timber merchants on the coast. The former is an expensive method of conveyance, and is resorted to only where floating is impossible. The Beypore river, which taps the forests of the Nilambur valley and the adjacent hills and is connected by canal with Kallayi the great timber mart of Malabar, is the main artery of the timber traffic ; but quantities of timber are floated down the Kotta river to Kottakkal and through the Payyoli canal and Agalapuzha to Kallayi, and down the Valarpattanam river to the port of that name. In the season, the river at Kallayi is a wonderful sight, the water being scarcely visible for the thousands of logs floating on its surface. The logs are left in the water until they are sold, and eventually are exported by sea and rail to Bombay, Madras, Kolar and other parts of India. Three steam sawmills are working at Kallayi and a fourth in British Cochin.

In Cochin, casks and barrels are made of such excellent quality that the European merchants allow only two per cent. for wastage on cocoanut oil taken to New York.

Timber industry.

Next to Madras City, Calicut has the largest business in furniture-making in the presidency; every important town in the district has its furniture shop where tables, chairs, almirahs, shelves and cots are made and sold. Malabar woodwork is known favourably throughout southern India.

Coffee-curing, etc.

At Tellicherry and Calicut, large quantities of pepper, coffee and ginger are garbled, cured or bleached, as the case may be. Bonemeal and other manures are also made in a factory at Kallayi.

Tile works.

Tiles are extensively manufactured in Malabar and South Canara, and in both districts the Basel Mission establishments lead the industry. The first factory was opened at Pudiyarakallu near Calicut in 1874, and others were founded in 1891 and 1892 by the Mission at Kodakkal in the Ponnani taluk and at Olavakkod near Palghat, and by Messrs. Henke & Co. at Ferok. Since then, natives have begun manufacturing tiles on a small scale at Calicut, at Shoranur in Walavanad, and at Parali and two other places in the Palghat taluk. Messrs. Henke & Co.'s factory is the largest in Malabar and in the presidency. Their tiles and those of the Basel Mission are famous all over India, under the generic name of 'Mangalore Tiles', and are exported to Rangoon, Colombo, Singapore and even to Australia. Clay is obtained from paddy flats near river banks and stored for a year. It is then moistened with water and mixed with river sand. The tile factories owned by the late Basel Mission have been acquired by the Commonwealth Trust, Ltd., whose headquarters are in London. The tile works in the district are managed by local agents and continue to make and export large quantities of what are now called "Calicut tiles". Some Indian firms have also started tile factories at Feroke, Kallayi, Palghat, Shoranur, Ottapalam, Baliapatam, Cannanore, Ponnani, Parli and Olavakkod. They are all doing well, excellent clay and sand being available near those factories.

Weaving.

In spite of the fact that calico takes its name from Calicut weaving is not an industry of very great importance in Malabar. There were about 12,000 looms in actual operation in the district in 1931 of which about a third were fitted with fly shuttles. Side by side with handloom weaving, there are in the district a few well-organized factories where weaving is done by power. The cotton handloom weavers are chiefly Chaliyans, colonies of whom are found scattered over every taluk except Wynaad. Among Kaikolas, Tamil Devanga Chettis and a section of the Rowthens in the Palghat and Walavanad taluks, weaving is the hereditary occupation. Each amsam, however, has its group of weavers, while large colonies of them are found at Punniangara and Kacheri (suburbs of Calicut), Kizhaketara, hamlet of Kollengode, Palapuram in Walavanad and at Taliparamba, Chirakkal and Tellicherry. The handloom weaver is a very conservative person and refuses to benefit by the recent improvements in handloom weaving, although by working with his wife and children long hours at his loom he is hardly able to earn more than six annas a day.

Hindus (men and women) in Malabar clothe themselves in white and the coloured saris in common use by women in districts to the east of the Ghats are not worn by Malayali women. White Manchester mulls are fashionable among the Nayars and the Mappilla imports coloured cloths for his womenkind from Madras and gets his own cloths from Tiruppur, Vaniyambadi, Salem, Kumbakonam and Kulasekharapatnam, while the locally-woven mundus and thundus (long and short towels) are used by the generality of the people, the coarser ones by the lower castes. A few coloured saris woven by the Kaikolas are sold to the women of the Tamilian or Kanarese castes who have settled in this district. Locally woven cloths have narrow coloured borders at their ends and the yarn is mostly Indian mill-made purchased from the Mappilla merchants. Taliparamba towels have attained some local celebrity, so have also the *Karimpuzhapavu* woven by the Tamil Devangas of Karimpuzha in the Walavanad taluk and *lungis* for Muhammadans woven by the Rowthens of Palghat. There is very little weaving of silk cloths in the district.

Weaving mills.

More important than the handloom industry are the weaving mills and factories of which there were 13 in 1931 (nine at Calicut and four at Cannanore) having a total of 1,500 looms at work in them. The Commonwealth Trust, M. N. Nayar & Co., and the Standard Cotton and Silk Weaving Company owned the more important of the factories. They do not compete with the local handloom weavers and avoid weaving the kind of *mundus* and *thundus* made by them and confine their attention to the manufacture of sheets, towels, table-cloths, shirtings, trouserings, ginghams and mercerised silks. There are also a few knitting factories at Feroke and Calicut where banyans are made. The yarn for all the factories is obtained from Madura, Tinnevelly or Kallayi. The oldest factories were started by the Basel Mission at Cannanore and Calicut with branches at Nittur and Chombala and at Kodakkal, hamlet of Calicut. For finer varieties of goods, foreign (chiefly English) yarn is used and some dyeing is also done in these factories. During the Great War of 1914–19, the mission's industrial concerns were sold to the Commonwealth Trust who are now in management of them. Their checks and cotton shirtings are distributed all over India. The chief spinning mill in the district, the Malabar Spinning and Weaving

Mills, is now under the management of Nattukottai Chettis and their yarn is popular in Malabar and several other districts of the presidency. Cotton rugs and carpets are woven in the Central Jail at Cannanore. CHAP. VI. INDUSTRIES.

Tailors.

The tailors of Malabar deserve a passing mention, if only for their numbers, the district supplying one-quarter of all the followers of these trades in the presidency. Attached to the Basel Mission weaving establishments at Cannanore and Calicut are tailoring departments, where practical and theoretical instruction is imparted under European supervision to youthful Native Christians.

Cap-making.

The manufacture of Mappilla skull caps which when embroidered were comparatively expensive articles is now practically dead in Malabar and has shifted to Talangeri, two miles from Kasaragod in South Kanara where it flourishes as a cottage industry. With the introduction of sewing machines, the caps can be made quicker and at less cost. Boys stitch the design and the women fill up the interspace with black yarn. Cannanore supplies the yarn and about 150,000 caps are made in a year and exported to Arabia, Basra, Colombo and the Straits Settlements and to Madras and Bombay. Each cap costs about 12 annas.

Fishing.

Fishing (combined curiously enough in former times with palanquin bearing) is the hereditary occupation of the Mukkuvans, a caste which has given many converts to Islam. Their boats, made of aini (*Artocarpus hirsuta*) or mango wood, and fitted with a mat sail, cost from Rs. 200 to Rs. 500 and carry a crew of 5 or 8 men according to size. Their nets are of all shapes and sizes, ranging from a fine net with a $\frac{3}{8}''$ mesh for sardines and such small fry to a stout *valiya śravuvala* or shark net with a $6\frac{1}{2}''$ or $7''$ mesh; and for a big Badagara boat a complete equipment is said to cost as much as Rs. 1,000. They are generally made of fibre, cotton thread being used only for nets with the finest mesh. Salt is not usually carried in the boats, and the fish decompose so rapidly in the tropical sun that the usual fishing grounds are comparatively close to the shore; but boats sometimes venture out 10, 15 or even 20 miles. Shoals of the migratory sardine which are pursued by predaceous sharks, *kora* and cat fish yield the richest harvest of fishes great and small to the Mukkuvan; but, whether it be owing to steamer traffic, the absence of grey ooze on which they feed, or to the wickedness of the people, all of which reasons have been assigned, the shoals are said to be less frequent than in former days.[1] Huge quantities of mackerel or *aila* are also caught, and seir, white and black pomfret, prawns, whiting and soles are other common fish. The arrival of the boats is the great event of the day in a fishing

[1] In the last two years, they have, however, been abundant, and this year (1907) has been a record one.

CHAP. VI. INDUSTRIES.

village. Willing hands help to drag them up the beach, and an eager crowd gathers round each boat, discussing the catch and haggling over the price. The pile of fish soon melts away and a string of coolies, each with a basket of fish on his head, starts off at a sling trot into the interior, and soon distributes the catch over a large area. Relays of runners convey fresh fish from Badagara and Tellicherry even as far as the Wynaad. All that is left unsold is taken from the boats to the yards to be cured under the supervision of the Salt department with Tuticorin salt supplied at the rate of 10 annas per maund. The fisherman is sometimes also the curer; but usually the two are distinct and the former disposes of the fish to the latter 'on fixed terms to a fixed customer' and looks to him 'for support during the slack season, the rainy and stormy south-west monsoon.' Salt for the fish curing yards is being supplied at Rs. 1–4–0 per maund from 1st April 1924. Under the rules, fishermen can take salt out to sea in their boats free of charge, but this concession is not generally availed of by them. Efforts have frequently been made to induce the curers to improve their methods, and a gradual improvement has been noticeable since the curing yards came under the Fisheries department. The salt fish is conveyed by coasting steamers to Ceylon, and by the S. Indian Railway to Coimbatore, Salem and the East Coast generally. Sardines are the most popular fish and are known as *kudumbam pulartti* or the family blessing. In a good year, 200 sardines can be had for a single pie; sun-dried, they form valuable manure for the coffee planter and cocoanut grower and are exported to Ceylon, the Straits Settlements and occasionally to China and Japan; and boiled with a little water they yield quantities of fish oil for export to Europe and Indian ports. Salted shark is esteemed a delicacy peculiarly good for a nursing woman. Shark's fins find a ready sale, and are exported to China by way of Bombay. The maws or sounds of kora and cat fishes are dried and shipped off to China and Europe for the preparation of isinglass.

Fish-oil.

Oil is also pressed from fish on a fairly large scale in and around Badagara, Tellicherry, Quilandy and other places on the coast. The fish are first boiled in large cauldrons, the water is drawn off and the fish put into coir nets and placed under flat screw-gear presses. The oil which has some admixture of water flows into a cistern and may or may not be boiled again. When the brew settles the oil rises to the top and the water below is drawn off by a tap at the bottom of the receptacle. The residue of the fish is sold as guano. Fish oil is used largely in the manufacture of soaps and the guano is valuable as manure. Deodorized oil sells at Rs. 500 and crude oil at Rs. 150 per ton and guano at Rs. 140 per ton, if pure.

CHAP. VI. INDUSTRIES.

Toddy drawing.

The cocoanut is the tree most commonly tapped for toddy. The sago palm is more productive, but is comparatively scarce; and the palmyra is rare except in Palghat and Walavanad. The tapper and the toddy shopkeeper are generally partners, the former renting the trees paying the tree-tax and selling the toddy at fixed prices to the latter. Sometimes the shopkeeper pays both rent and tax, and the tapper is his servant paid by the bottle. The trees are rented half-yearly, and the rent varies between Re. 1 and Re. 1–8–0 per tree. They are fit for tapping as soon as they come into bearing, but four years later and in the succeeding decade are most productive. They are seldom tapped for more than six months in the year, and the process, though it shortens the life of the tree, improves the yield of nuts in the rest of the year. The tapper's outfit is neither costly nor elaborate. A knife in a wooden case, a bone weighted with lead (the leg bone of a sambhur for choice), a few pots and two small rings of rope with which to climb complete the tale. Operations begin when the spathe is still enclosed by its sheath. Once a day the sheath is gently bruised on either side with the bone, and on the third and following days a thin slice is cut off the end twice a day. On the fifteenth day drawing begins, and the bruising ceases. Sheath and spathe are swathed for the greater part of their length in a thick covering of leaves or fibre; the ends are still cut off twice or three times a day, but, after each operation, are smeared with a paste made of leaves and water with the object, it is said, of keeping the sap from oozing through the wound and rotting the spathe. The leaves used for this purpose are called *ecchil* and are taken from a tree called *vetti*, which is apparently akin to *Wrightia tinctoria*; but in British Cochin, where the tree does not grow, backwater mud is utilized. Round the space between the end of the sheath and the thick covering of leaves a single leaf is bound and through this the sap bleeds into a pot fastened below. The pot is emptied once a day in the morning. The yield of sap varies with the quality of the tree and the season of the year. In the hot months the trees give on an average about a bottle a day, in the monsoon and succeeding months sometimes as much as three bottles. In the gardens along the backwaters south of Chettuvayi Messrs. Parry & Co. consider that in a good year they should get a daily average of three bottles or half a gallon of toddy per tree. A bottle of toddy sells for three or four pies.

Jaggery.

The methods employed in making jaggery are simple in the extreme. The trees are treated in precisely the same way, but to prevent fermentation the pots are slightly coated with lime. The freshly drawn juice is heated in an iron pot over a wood fire, and as soon as it boils a small portion is removed in a vessel made from the sheath of a cocoanut spathe and left to cool on a plank of wood. As it cools, it hardens into a cake, and this cake is rubbed with half a cocoanut shell till it is reduced to powder. The powder is added to the rest of the juice, and the mixture is stirred till it thickens. It is then poured off into halves of cocoanut shells, and rapidly dried in the wind, after which it is ready for the market. Two bottles of toddy make one *kudu* of jaggery and a *kudu* sells for four pies. It must be remembered that no tax has to be paid on trees tapped for sweet toddy. The pattam is not usually paid in money. In South Ponnani most of the cocoanut growers make jaggery on their own account, and in return for tapping the tappers are allowed to keep the sap for themselves on alternate days. Sugar is not made from sugarcane in Malabar.

Leaf umbrellas, hats, mats and baskets.

The manufacture of palm leaf umbrellas, palm leaf hats, mats, winnowing fans and baskets is carried on in almost every taluk of the district. The first two, which are peculiar to the West Coast, are made by Panans, who are also exorcists and devil dancers. The quaint umbrella hat serves to protect the field labourer from sun and rain, and palm leaf umbrellas are still carried by the conservative; but the present day Malayali of the towns has long discarded them in favour of the ugly if more convenient articles of English make. The frame work and 'leg,' as it is called, of the umbrella are made usually of bamboo, the covering of the leaves of the palmyra. By caste custom a Panan can make only the frame-work; the covering of the umbrella is the work of his womankind, and, if he be so unfortunate as to lack female relatives, he must seek the aid of the women of other Panan families. It is not a remunerative occupation; ordinary umbrellas and umbrella hats sell at prices varying between six pies and two annas which do not leave much margin for profit. Dyed grasses are woven into the framework of the more expensive umbrellas, and the best varieties with painted handles are imported from Trichur. Kanisan women and Parayans also manufacture umbrellas and umbrella hats. Coarse mats are very cheap and in every household, however humble, take the place of carpets. They are made by Cheruman and Pulayan women of bamboo, cocoanut, sago or date leaves and of screw pine (*Pandanus odoratissimus*). The best baskets are made in Chirakkal by Vettuvans and Malayans; good baskets of reeds, bamboo, and rattans are also made by low caste people, such as Cherumans and Parayans, in all parts of the district. They are sold very cheap, and are used for domestic purposes and in the fields for carrying seed, manure and the like. Fans are made in Palghat.

Steel umbrellas.

There are now three factories in Calicut engaged in the manufacture of cloth umbrellas and the biggest of them owned by Nagji Purushotham is run by power. The iron ribs of the umbrella and the cloth are imported from Germany or England and the factories only make the sticks and handles from thin bamboos obtained from the local forests, and the ribs and cloths are fitted to them. Calicut supplies umbrellas to several other districts in the presidency. The extensive use of cloth umbrellas has hit the Panan and the Parayan owing to the lesser demand for their products.

CHAP. VI. INDUSTRIES.

Palghat grass mats.

Excellent grass mats, some of a quality so fine that they can be rolled up into a very small bundle, are made by Kuruvans in Palghat. The grass is gathered from river banks. Each blade is split into four, and the pith is carefully removed. The grass is dried for six days, then steeped in water, then dried again for a day. It is then boiled in water with dye of the required quality and woven into mats. The prices of these mats vary according to their size or quality. The finest fetch Rs. 10 and more, coarser kinds between Re. 1 and Rs. 3.

Grass and bamboo mats and baskets.

The Palghat kora grass mats are exported largely to Madras, Singapore, Bombay and other places. The grass is also obtained from the hills and grows in abundance (and sometimes to as high as six feet) in the rainy season when it is collected by Ezhavas and Mappillas and sold to the mat-makers or their principals.

In parts of Ernad and Walavanad small quantities of iron are still smelted by the rude process described by Dr. Buchanan [1] more than 100 years ago.

Iron smelting.

"The ore is dug out with a pick-axe, and broken into powder with the same instrument. It is then washed in a wooden trough, about four feet in length, open at both ends, and placed in the current of a rivulet; so that a gentle stream of water runs constantly through it. The powdered ore is placed in the upper end of this trough; and as the water passes through the heap, a man continually stirs it about with his hand. The metallic sand remains in the upper end of the trough, the quartz is carried to the lower end and the clay is suspended, and washed entirely away . . . . . The furnaces are excavated out of the front of a mound of clay. . . . . From behind opposite to each furnace, an arched cavity is dug into the mound, so as to leave a thin partition between the two excavations. For allowing the vitrified matter to run off, there is in this partition a hole one foot in diameter. Above the furnace is erected a chimney of clay, built with four plain sides, which in two different places is strengthened by four bamboos, lashed together at the angles. The front of the furnace is quite open.

"Early in the morning when going to smelt, the workmen put wet sand mixed with powdered charcoal into the bottom of the furnace; so as to fill it up as far as the hole in its back part, through which the vitrified matter is to run out. The sand and charcoal are well beaten, and formed so as to slope from the outer and upper edge, both toward the hole and toward the ground in front of the

[1] *Journey through Mysore, Malabar and South Canara*, Vol. II, p. 436.

CHAP. VI. INDUSTRIES.

furnace. The hole is then well stopped with clay; and clay pipes are inserted at each corner of the furnace, for the reception of the muzzles of the bellows. A row of clay pipes, eight or ten in number, is then laid on the surface of the sand, at right angles to the back of the furnace. Their outer ends project a little beyond the front, and their inner ends reach about half way to the back. The front of the furnace is then shut up with moist clay; and stoppers of the same are put in the outermouths of the pipes. By removing these stoppers, and looking through the pipes the workmen judge how the operation is going forward. Ten baskets of charcoal, each weighing 63 lb. are then poured in by the chimney; and this having been kindled, the bellows are set to work. Then 16 porays of prepared ore, weighing 2,160 lb. and 20 baskets more of charcoal, as the fire makes room for them, are gradually added. The operation lasts 24 hours, two sets of men relieving each other at the bellows, and keeping up a constant blast. The principal workman who attends the fire adds the fuel and ore, and stops up the breaches; and, when mass of iron has formed, breaks the clay that shuts up the hole in the back part of the furnace, and lets out much vitrified matter, that strongly resembles brown hæmatites, and no doubt contains much iron; which this imperfect operation is unable to reduce. The bellows are then removed, and the front of the furnace is broken down. A great part of the charcoal which has not been consumed is then pulled out with sticks or forks and extinguished by water. The mass of iron is allowed to remain on the sand 24 hours, and to cool gradually. According to the success of the operation it weighs from 8 to 12 tolams, or from 256 to 384 lb. The mass, when cool, is broken in pieces with a large hammer, and sold for use it being then malleable, although somewhat brittle. The mass is extremely porous, and irregular in its shape and has never formed what chemists call a button; that is to say, the liquefaction produced on the iron has only been partial, sufficient to cause the particles to adhere in a mass but not adequate to form a fluid that expels all matters of a different specific gravity."

Gold washing.

The defunct gold mining industry in the Wynaad has been described in Chapter I, but there is still a little washing for gold in the rivers at Nilambur by the Kudans, a hill tribe who work for the Nilambur Tirumulpad. The process is still apparently much the same as it was in 1831, when the Collector described it as follows:—

"The earth is put into a pautty, a kind of wooden tray hollowed in the centre and not unlike a turtle's shell, the soil is immediately submerged in water just enough to overflow it, and no more, and kept in an undulating motion by the washer with one hand; while the earth is stirred up with the other until all the earthy particles are washed entirely out of it, and a sediment is left in the hollow, consisting chiefly of a mixture of black sand particles of iron and gold. The pautty is then taken out of the water, and one end of it being somewhat elevated, water is gently poured upon its contents until the gold distinctly appears on the border quite divided from the principal mass. The golden particles are separated with a grain or two of quicksilver which is rubbed into them, and then put in a piece of tobacco leaf, which being placed in a crucible, or more generally between two pieces of lighted charcoal, the heat causes the quicksilver to evaporate, and the gold is then taken out in a pure state."

CHAP. VI. INDUSTRIES.

Bell-metal work.

Every amsam has its potters, goldsmiths, carpenters and blacksmiths ; but bell-metal work is the only craft that calls for special mention. The Musaris or bell-metal workers are not very numerous, but they supply all the richer families with their cooking pots. They have no fear of the competition of aluminium, for a vessel made of bell-metal has the great advantage that when it begins to wear out, the Musari buys it back at a slightly reduced price, and utilises the metal again. Moulds are made of bees-wax with a core of clay, and a thick covering of the same material. In the kiln the wax runs out through a hole in the covering of clay left for the purpose, and through the same hole the molten metal is poured into the mould. The best bell-metal work is said to come from Kunnimangalam in the Chirakkal taluk.

Metal works.

Kannans, Mussaries and Goanese Christians are the chief metal workers, the first two working in brass and bell-metal and the last in copper. Dish plates or *thalams* of bell-metal which are largely used by the people are made at various places ; the metal is an alloy of copper and tin in the proportion of 100 : 28. Kujas, Kindis, tumblers and lamp-stands are also made chiefly in Palghat and in a few villages of Ernad and Walavanad taluks. The copper workers throughout the district (except Peruntalmanna) are Roman Catholic Christians from Goa. These are a very hard-working class of people who have acquired special skill in this work.

Minor industries cocoanut shell carving.

A few Musaris of Quilandy make fine artistic wares of brass carvings inlaid with cocoanut shells, samples of which can be seen at the Victoria Technical Institute at Madras. The articles made by them are hooka pots (which are exported from Calicut to Arabia and Persia), lamp-stands in brass and cocoanut shell, candle sticks of various designs, flower vases, ash trays, finger bowls, photo frames, cigarette and cigar cases all of rosewood and cocoanut shell inlaid in brass with shellac ; also paper weights of brass representing scorpions, frogs, lizards, etc., and caskets for presentation.

Beedies

A minor industry in Malabar is the making of beedies. The tobacco and the dry leaf for wrapping it in, come from other districts, but the supply of cheap labour indoors during the long rainy season has been responsible for the starting of this industry in several towns and villages. There is a large export trade in beedies with Ceylon.

Knives and locks.

Knives and locks are made in large numbers for local needs and some are even exported to the east coast districts where they are known as Palghat knives and Palghat locks. The knives are strong and well made.

---

[1] See *Correspondence on gold mines in Wynaad*—Mad. Govt. Press, 1874

CHAP. VI. INDUSTRIES. Safety matches.

Several species of timber suitable for matches are available in the forests of Malabar and supplies of veneers, boxes and sticks for several match factories in the presidency are obtained from a firm at Palghat which owns also a safety match factory. The factory produces daily materials for about 300 gross of match sticks and for about 50 gross of boxes.

PROFESSIONS.

A curious side light is thrown upon Malayalam society by the census returns relating to the learned, artistic and other porfessions. In Malabar extremes meet; it is one of the most literate districts in the presidency, and the best provided with exponents of law, medicine and letters: but as has been noticed in Chapter III it is also pre-eminently the home of priestcraft, astrology, necromancy and black magic and at the recent census nearly 2,000 persons claimed to be witches, wizards and cow poisoners.

Transport and storage.

The number of porters (22,052) in Malabar is noteworthy. They are partly the product of the heavy shipping trade of the district, and partly a relic of the times when, as Ibn Batuta says, 'there were no beasts of burden in Malabar, and goods were all carried on the backs of men.'

TRADE. Volume of trade.

The trade of Malabar is chiefly sea-borne, and for a Madras district its volume is immense, as the following statistics in lakhs of rupees of the average trade in the presidency and in Malabar between the years 1899 and 1903 show :—

—	Presidency.			Malabar.		
	Imports.	Exports.	Total.	Imports.	Exports.	Total.
Foreign ..	806	1,290	2,096	22	254	276
Coasting ..	615	506	1,121	275	212	487
Total ..	1,421	1,796	3,217	297	456	763

From this table ports with a trade aggregating in value less than two lakhs annually are excluded, and the average annual trade of the district must therefore be worth nearly $7\frac{3}{4}$ crores or very nearly one-fourth of the value of all the sea-borne trade of the presidency.

Ports.

In British Cochin, Malabar possesses the third port in the presidency, with a coasting trade which even exceeds that of Madras and Tuticorin. Calicut, the fourth port in the presidency, follows next in importance, and after Calicut come Tellicherry, Cannanore, Badagara and Beypore in the order named. Ponnani, Azhikkal and Kallayi are minor ports, and there are numerous sub-ports in the district. None of these unfortunately are provided with proper harbours, or with any shelter for big vessels in the monsoon gales, and in the monsoon months trade is in consequence almost at a standstill.

Exports.

The balance of trade is much in favour of the exports, but only a small proportion of the produce shipped from Malabar is actually grown in the district. Tea and coffee find their way by road and rail to Malabar ports for shipment from Coorg, the Nilgiris and Anamalais as well as from the Malabar-Wynaad, and of the oil and yarn exported from Cochin a great part comes from Travancore and Native Cochin. Oil, coir, copra and other products of the cocoanut are rapidly out-distancing all their competitors as articles of export, their value in Cochin alone, where the trade is chiefly concentrated, having increased from less than 80 lakhs in 1891 to upwards of 160 lakhs in 1904. Next in importance is coffee which is exported in about equal quantities from Calicut and Tellicherry. Tellicherry is the headquarters of the pepper trade ; Calicut of that in ginger and nux vomica seeds, the Malabar variety of which is of very high quality. Cochin takes the lead again in tea, mostly of Travancore origin.

Their distribution.

Malabar has customers all the world over, and distributes its exports in almost equal proportions between foreign countries and Indian ports. Calcutta takes the greatest share of the cocoanut oil, closely followed by Bombay, America, Germany, the United Kingdom and Burma. Coir goes chiefly to England and Germany, poonac to Hamburg and Bombay, and lemon grass oil to France. London is the market for tea and coffee, though large quantities of coffee go to France ; ginger and pepper are almost monopolized by European countries, though a certain amount goes in the first instance to Bombay.

Imports.

In return for these heavy exports, Malabar imports very little direct from foreign countries, kerosene oil, metals and machinery being Europe's only contributions of importance. From other Indian ports, on the other hand, the imports into the district are very considerable. Immense quantities of grain, pulses and paddy come to all Malabar ports from Burma, Bengal, Madras and Bombay, Cochin taking the bulk, probably for distribution in Travancore and Cochin. Bombay supplies Cochin and Calicut with many lakhs' worth of raw cotton, cotton twist, yarn and piece-goods and Calicut, Ponnani and other ports with salt not only for local consumption, but for export by rail to the east coast. Sugar is the only other import of importance.

Rail-borne trade.

Compared with that by sea, rail-borne trade is insignificant. Grains and pulses are the principal imports, and timber, salt and salt-fish the chief exports. Calicut, Palghat and Kallayi are the stations where most traffic is done, the last owing its position entirely to its timber trade.

CHAP. VI. WEIGHTS AND MEASURES. Weights.

A standard table of weights and measures is one of the crying needs of Malabar. Throughout the district, except in Cochin ($42\frac{1}{2}$ tolas), 40 tolas are the accepted equivalent of 1 lb. avoirdupois, and 20 *tulams* make a *baram* or candy. But the multiples and sub-multiples of the *tulam* differ so widely as to make it impossible to enter into all the local variations. Complexity is carried so far that in some places the weight of the *tulam* varies with the nature of the goods sold. In Cannanore, for instance, pepper, coffee and cardamoms are all sold by different weights, and in Chavakkad the *tulam* weighs variously 25, 30 and $37\frac{1}{2}$ lbs.

In the bazaars of **North Malabar and North Wynaad** the following table is in fairly general use :—

10 tolas	=	1 pallam.
4 pallams	=	1 lb. avoir.
32 lbs.	=	1 tulam.
20 tulams	=	1 baram or candy.

In **South Malabar** the commonest tables perhaps are those in use in Palghat and South Walavanad, which differ from the above only in that the *tulam* weighs 25 lb. or 100 *pallams*, and that current in Ernad, North Ponnani and Perintalmanna wherein the *tulam* = 35 lb. = 100 *pallams* = 1,400 tolas.

In commercial circles the *tulam* is the accepted equivalent of the maund, and the *baram* of the candy, but in business transactions the weight of the candy is invariably specified in lb. avoirdupois. The weights used in wholesale transactions with the European firms seem to differ in many cases from those in retail use in the bazaar. The following is a list of the most important candies :—

Cannanore	(coffee) ..	=	$680\frac{5}{8}$	lb.	
Do.	(pepper) ..	=	$618\frac{3}{4}$	,,	
Do.	(cardamoms)	=	660	,,	
Cochin	(yarn) ..	=	672	,,	
Do.	(oil)	=	656	,,	
Calicut ..	.. ..	=	700	,,	
Do. ..	.. ..	=	560	,,	(for Government salt and coir yarn).
Palghat ..	.. ..	..	500	,,	
Tellicherry	.. ..	..	660	,,	
Quilandi ..	.. ..	..	773	,,	
Badagara	.. ..	..	660	,,	

Grain measures.

Grain measures are equally bewildering. The Macleod seer, introduced in 1802 by the Principal Collector of that name, is the standard grain measure in Palghat, Walavanad and North Malabar, and in Calicut and Ponnani the half seer is used. Liberally heaped as is the practice, its normal contents are 130 tolas of rice. In Cochin a *nali* of 43 tolas, and in Manjeri and Manantoddy local seers containing 92 and 90 tolas respectively

CHAP. VI. Weights and Measures.

are in use. The multiples and sub-multiples of the seer are *nalis, uris, olaks and alaks*, and throughout Malabar the *nali* = 2 *uris* = 4 *olaks* = 8 *alaks*. But the capacity of the nali varies greatly in different towns. Expressed in tolas of rice, in Ponnani and Pudiyangadi it contains 43⅓ tolas, in Cochin 43 tolas, in North Malabar, Chavakkad and Tirurangadi 32½, in Manantoddy 22½, in Calicut 26, in Palghat and South Walavanad 21⅜, in Manjeri 18 and in Perintalmanna 16¼. In South Malabar the *para* is more commonly used in selling paddy and other grains. The Palghat and Calicut *paras* contain 10 *edangalis* or 40 *nalis*, the Perintalmanna *para* 60 *nalis* and the Ponnani *para* 30 *nalis*. In North Malabar the *para* is not often used, but the *edangali* contains 4 *nalis*, and is the equivalent of the Macleod seer.

Liquid measures.

Liquid measures are still more complex, and it is impossible to reduce them to a common denominator. As in grain measures, the *nali* = 2 *uris* = 4 *olaks* = 8 *alaks*, but there all uniformity ends. In Calicut and North Malabar bigger measures are called *kuttis* and *padams*, and the commonest table is as follows :—

4 nalis or 1½ Macleod seers	1 kutti.
16 kuttis..	1 padam.
8 padams	1 candy.

But the *kutti* is the equivalent in some places of 1¾ Macleod seers, in others of 2½. In South Malabar the *chodana*, measuring variously 16, 20, 24 and 30 *nalis*, is the multiple of the *padam*. In Cochin the headquarters of the oil trade, a candy of oil contains 656 lb. avoirdupois.

Co-operative societies. Their origin.

In Malabar it was comparatively late when the first co-operative society was organized. The idea had been prevalent that the soil of Malabar was not congenial to the growth of co-operation owing to the special system of inheritance (*Marumakkatayam*) prevalent and to the peculiar system of land tenure. The first co-operative credit society was registered in 1910 and started work at Kannambra. In 1913–14 there were only nineteen societies, but in 1930 there were 630 affiliated to 24 supervising unions.

Management.

The District Central Co-operative Bank was started in 1917–18 and became the chief financing bank. With the increase in the number of societies, the need for non-official supervision began to be increasingly felt, and supervising unions began to be formed to which a number of societies were affiliated. A few years later the District Co-operative Union was started at Calicut. The district is now in charge of a Deputy Registrar who is assisted by 21 Inspectors in the auditing of the accounts and in supervision of the activities of the various classes of societies.

CHAP. VI. CO-OPERATIVE SOCIETIES.

Working capital and membership.

The District Bank had a share capital of Rs. 1·14 lakhs in 1929–30, a membership of 145 individual members and 556 societies, and secured deposits to the extent of Rs. 32 lakhs and a total working capital of Rs. 27 lakhs. The bank continues to finance adequately the increasing needs of the societies affiliated to it. The statistics of 1929–30 show that 56,000 people were members of co-operative societies, of whom 2,000 were Brahmans, 37,500 Non-Brahman Hindus, 14,000 Muhammadans and 4,000 Christians and Adi-Dravidas. Rs. 12·9 lakhs were due from them on account of loans advanced.

Non-credit societies.

Of the non-credit societies the following deserve special reference. For the coir workers of Kallayi a society was started in 1920, and in 1925 an enquiry was made into the possibilities of improving the coir industry in which many of the Tiyas of the Coast were engaged ; as a result of that enquiry four more societies were started in Calicut ; three more were formed in 1927 and a central society was started to co-ordinate their work and to act as their agent for joint purchase of coir and sale of finished products. These societies are a source of immense help to the workers. Societies for fish-curers and sellers have been started and they provide fishing materials to the poorer fishermen and enable them to realize the whole profit of their catches. Weavers have their own societies and the first two of them were organized by the Devadhar Malabar Reconstruction Trust in 1922 and have been working satisfactorily. There are now three societies of this class : similar societies for wholesale purchase and retail sale have been organized for school students, for irrigation, for building houses, and for mat-makers with considerable benefit to their members. There were 28 societies solely for the depressed classes (excluding fishermen) and their membership was 1,266 on 30th June 1931, and working capital Rs. 6,259.

CHAPTER VII.

MEANS OF COMMUNICATION.

WATERWAYS—Rivers, backwaters and canals—Their commercial importance. ROADS—Tipu's gun roads—Roads in the first years of the British supremacy—Retrogression in the first half of nineteenth century—Existing roads—Their condition—Avenues. TRAVELLERS' BUNGALOWS. FERRIES. RAILWAYS—Pollachi—Palghat railway—Proposed lines.

CHAP. VII. WATERWAYS.

Rivers, backwaters and canals.

THE climate and the nature of Malabar are alike unfavourable to road-making, and, up to the time of the Mysorean invasion, the rivers and backwaters of the district were the main channel of trade. Through every taluk, as stated more at length in Chapter I, one or more big rivers find their way from the Western Ghats to the coast, and deprived of outlets to the sea by the littoral sand banks, discharge into a long line of backwaters running parallel with the shore. Connecting links are supplied in many places by canals, and, with slight interruptions, there is communication by inland water from Kavvayi in the extreme north of Malabar to Trivandrum in Travancore. With the exception of the Sultan's canal between the Mount Deli river and the backwaters of the Taliparamba and Valarpattanam rivers, which was dug in 1766 by the Ali Raja of Cannanore, these artificial cuttings all date from the middle of the nineteenth century. Designed as far back as 1822 by Special Commissioner Mr. Græme, they were not carried out till twenty years later when Mr. Conolly was Collector. The Payyoli, Conolly, Ponnani and Badagara canals were all completed between 1840 and 1860; and the unsuccessful attempts to unite the Kadalundi and Ponnani rivers were continued down to 1857. The canals were in charge of the District Board till 1906, but as little was done to maintain them in proper order they were transferred to the Public Works Department for maintenance.

Their commercial importance.

The commercial importance of these inland waterways was not lost upon the foreigners who centuries ago came to Malabar in quest of spices. The Mappilla towns at the mouths and on the banks of nearly every river are relics of old Moorish settlements. The English factory at Tellicherry with its outworks on Darmadam island secured to the Honourable Company the lion's share of the pepper produced in the territories of the Randattara Achanmar, the Kottayam Raja and Iruvalinad Nambiyars, tapped by the rivers converging on Darmadam. The French settlement at Mahe on the river of that name

CHAP. VII. WATERWAYS.

attracted the trade of Kadattanad. Chettuvayi at the mouth of a widespread system of backwaters was held by the Portuguese, Dutch and English in turn, and was often hotly contended for. Cochin, the headquarters first of the Portuguese, then of the Dutch, owed its importance then, as now, to its splendid situation at the chief outlet of an immense system of backwaters as well as to its fine natural harbour. From Tangasseri the Dutch commanded the many navigable rivers which there find their way into the sea; and finally at Anjengo the English settled on a spit of sand with the sea on one side and a river on the other solely for the advantages afforded for trade by this river and its neighbouring creeks.

ROADS.

Tipu's gun roads.

If Tipu did his best to ruin the trade of South Malabar by destroying the pepper vines, he conferred at least one great economic boon upon the country. He was the pioneer of its roads. Before his time wheeled traffic was unknown, and even pack bullocks were not used until comparatively recent times. 'No one travels in these parts', wrote Ibn Batuta in the fourteenth century, 'upon beasts of burden; nor is there any horse found except with the king. When, however, any merchant has to buy or sell goods, they are carried upon the backs of men who are always ready to do so (for hire).' Narrow footpaths 'running at random through paddy lands without any regard to convenience of travelling' took the place of highways, and it was not until Tipu brought his artillery into Malabar that the need of proper roads was felt. 'He projected and in great part finished,' in the words of Major Dow, one of the Joint Commissioners,[1] 'an extensive chain of roads that connected all the principal places of Malabar and pervaded the wildest parts of the country.' He invaded the district both from Mysore by way of the passes through the Western Ghats and from the Carnatic through the Palghat Gap; and, while Seringapatam was 'the grand termination of these inter-communications,' and many of the roads converged upon the Tamarasseri and other passes into the Wynaad, Palghat was also an important road centre. Not much is known of his roads in North Malabar save that the majority started from Mount Deli, and had for 'their general direction' the Tamarasseri and Periya ghats; but full details are on record of his road system in the south of the district. The Tamarasseri ghat, up which a steep gun road ran, was the meeting place of no less than four roads. Two led by different routes from Malappuram and two from Calicut, one following more or less the line of the present Mysore road, and the other passing through Ferok and Chattamangalam. Ferok, Tipu's capital in Malabar, was connected with the Karkkur ghat by a road which run through Kondotti, Edavanna and Nilambur, and

[1] See the report of the Joint Commissioners, 1793.

with Coimbatore by two alternative routes. A road led *via* Tirurangadi to Venkatakotta (the modern Kottakkal) in the Ernad taluk, and then bifurcated, one branch going to Coimbatore by Angadippuram, Mannarghat and the Attapadi valley, and the other by Kavalappara, Mankara and Valayar. The coast road from Beypore to Cranganore *via* Tanur, Ponnani, Veliyangod and Chettuvayi was another gun road, as was also the existing road from Tanur to Palghat by way of Pudiyangadi, Trittala and Lakkidi. Palghat was also connected with Dindigul and Kollangod by lines of communication.

Roads in the first years of the British supremacy.

In a hilly district blessed with a heavy rainfall, like Malabar, roads require unremitting attention; and Tipu's hastily-improvised roads, which, although they were cleverly traced so as to keep on the watersheds and avoid paddyfields, were neither well made nor properly drained, soon fell into disrepair. In 1796 a Captain-lieutenant of Engineers was deputed to report on the state of the gun roads, and in 1797 a new trace from Palghat to Dindigul was taken in hand. The Collectors of the small districts, into which Malabar was divided in 1800, were encouraged to pay special attention to the roads; and Mr. Wye of Angadippuram was permitted in 1801 to devote to roads and bridges the proceeds of ferry farms and magisterial fines. In North Malabar the Pychy rebellion gave a great impulse to road-making, and the interior of Kottayam and Kurumbranad taluks was opened up by military roads which for the most part still exist. Dr. Buchanan, who travelled through Malabar, in 1800 and 1801, was constrained to condemn the majority of roads as very bad; but in 1807 Mr. Thackeray,[1] a less impartial witness, felt justified in reporting to the Board that 'Malabar was intersected by better roads perhaps than any other province in India.' At this time the main roads were the coast road, and those from Palghat to the sea, from Palghat to Kuttiyadi *via* Tamarasseri, from Kuttiyadi to Calicut, and from Calicut to Tamarasseri.

Retrogression in first half of nineteenth century.

A long period of stagnation ensued. All interest in communications was in a state of suspended animation, and the roads steadily deteriorated, till in 1848 Mr. Conolly reported that there were only 'two carriage roads in Malabar, one from the borders of Coimbatore to the sea, and one by the Periya pass from the Mysore frontier to Cannanore and Tellicherry.' The coast road was also 'generally available, though in parts very difficult for carts,' and there were important bullock tracks up the Perambadi, Kuttiyadi, Tamarasseri and Sispara ghats; but of the 'vast number of secondary roads intersecting the district' few if any were practicable for wheeled traffic.[2] The deterioration of the roads in this period is hardly

[1] An uncle of the novelist. Extracts from his report are printed in the Fifth report.

[2] Report of the Public Works Commission of 1852, I, 369, and Mr. Conolly's report to the Board, dated January 21st, 1848.

CHAP. VII. ROADS.

surprising, for in 1831 Government formally renounced all attempts to maintain them in good order. The *maramut* department which had charge of them was devoid of professional skill, being in fact the revenue department under another name, and had only the Military Engineer of Malabar and South Canara and subsequently the Civil Engineer appointed for those districts to look to for guidance. Under the Collector the Tahsildars, assisted by taluk maistries, were the executive officers; and for a time they were entrusted even with the preparation of estimates. The department was also supplied with insufficient funds. In accordance with the terms of the despatch of the Honourable Court in 1817, the whole of the net proceeds from ferries, which averaged not less than Rs. 30,000 a year, should have been devoted to roads, but in the twenty-five years from 1826 to 1850 the average expenditure was not more than Rs. 18,000. Between 1810 and 1830 some companies of the Madras Pioneers worked in the district, and among others constructed the road from Cannanore to Nedumpoyil *via* Kottayam and Kuttaparamba, and the Periya ghat road. But they were officered from regiments of the line by 'men who not only had no knowledge of engineering but did not affect to understand surveying or levelling or even the use of a plan or section,' and much of their work was mere waste of time and labour. Their trace up the Periya ghat was too direct and steep, and the road, which was only three miles long instead of eight as at present, was abandoned as soon as the Perambadi ghat was opened to cart traffic. The construction of the road from Cannanore to Coorg by way of this ghat, which was sanctioned in 1848 and completed three years later, was the chief benefit conferred on Malabar by the road department created in 1845 for the maintenance of trunk roads in the presidency.

Existing roads.

The last half century has witnessed an immense extension of roads, and great changes in their relative importance. The Sispara ghat road is no longer the shortest and most direct route to Ootacamund, and Ariyakkod in the Ernad taluk is no longer the centre of a widespread system of roads. With the advent of the railway to Malabar the Valayar-Ponnani road ceased to be the main artery of traffic between the Carnatic and Kerala; and with the extension of the line to Mangalore the coast road from Calicut to Cannanore has lost much of its former importance. With few exceptions, the roads are now, as they should be, mere feeders to the railway; but among the exceptions are the great highways of the district. First and foremost are the Perambadi and Tamarasseri ghat roads which tap the planting districts of Coorg and Malabar-Wynaad, and convey to the sea at Tellicherry and Calicut heavy consignments of coffee, pepper and tea. The Tamarasseri ghat, which fifty years ago resembled a ruined staircase formed of huge blocks of stone with a gradient varying from 1 in 1 to 1 in 4, was provided with a new trace in 1858 and a new road between 1860 and 1870 constructed by the Madras Sappers and Miners. The failure of coffee in North Wynaad has diminished the importance of the Periya ghat up which a new and easier road has been traced; but the traffic on the Karkkur ghat road from the Nilgiri-Wynaad to Calicut is very heavy in the shipping season.

Their condition.

The extension of the road system is due partly to the restoration of the secondary roads mentioned by Mr. Conolly, partly to the formation of new roads in the Mappilla zone with the proceeds of Mappilla fines. In 1846 the made roads of Malabar measured 138 miles; they now measure more than 1,700 miles. But this great increase, however desirable in itself, has raised in an acute form the problem of maintenance, which, as pointed out in Chapter XIV, presents peculiar difficulties in Malabar. The two great highways from Tellicherry and Calicut to Coorg and Mysore are kept in good order by the Public Works Department, and the 170 miles of municipal road are usually in fair condition. But the state of those Local Fund roads, on which traffic is at all heavy, leaves much to be desired, especially in the monsoon, and the ruins of great bridges over many rivers attest the chronic impecuniosity of the Local Boards. A gradual improvement has, however, manifested itself of late years.

There were about two thousand miles of roads in 1931, of which about 1,525 were maintained by local boards, 200 by municipal councils and 100 by the Public Works Department. In 1920 the following roads were designated as trunk roads and Government undertook to provide grants for their maintenance —the Madras-Calicut road (94 miles), Gudalur-Calicut road (40 miles) and Gudalur-Vayittiri road (19 miles). They paid the district board at the rate of Rs. 500 a mile, but after repeated requests they have increased the grant by Rs. 70 a mile. Towards the maintenance of all other roads Government contribute half the cost subject to a maximum of Rs. 1,57,200, but the District Board with its other engagements for education, etc., finds it difficult to increase its share of the expense and improve the condition of these roads sufficiently to cope with modern traffic.

Very little progress has been made in opening up new roads in North Malabar. Attempts are, however, being made to connect South Kanara with Malabar by road. Most of the existing rivers in North Malabar are not bridged.

Considerable damage was caused to roads and bridges in the Mappilla rebellion of 1921 and in the floods of 1923 and 1924, including huge land-slips on the Karkkur Ghat along one of the trunk roads. Repairs to damages to the trunk roads

CHAP. VII. ROADS.

were made entirely from provincial funds and those to other roads partly from provincial funds and partly from local funds.

The district still stands in need of many bridges. Six on important roads costing between Rs. 1½ to 2 lakhs each have been built during the last ten years. The cost of two of them, over the Naragampalli and Nellipuzha rivers on the road from Palghat to Calicut was met entirely by Government. The other four bridges span the Yakkara river on the road from Palghat to Kollengode and Alathur, the Pulamanthole river on the road from Pattambi to Perintalmanna, the Mahe and Koodakadavu rivers on the Calicut-Cannanore road and the Government contributed half their net cost. For the bridge over the Mahe river the French Government contributed Rs. 25,000. A bridge near Tirurangady over the Panampuzha river was under construction in 1932, the estimated cost being Rs. 3·06 lakhs.

AVENUES.

"Elegant avenues" as Dr. Buchanan called them, have always been a feature of the Malabar roads and their trees are often the sole remaining guide to ancient lines of traffic. Jacks, mangoes and banyans are the trees generally planted. When the Collector and the Revenue Divisional Officers were in charge of District and Taluk boards, village officers were entrusted with the duty of replacing windfallen trees and were also paid a small sum for every sapling planted in the monsoon, which was found alive at the close of the official year. This system has been discontinued since these boards became entirely non-official with elected presidents and the work to be done for them by the Revenue officials has been strictly defined. Wherever necessary regular programmes for planting avenues are now drawn up for a series of years on various roads and the saplings are looked after by the local fund engineering establishments. Planting of avenues on Public Works Department roads is done by that department.

TRAVELLERS' BUNGALOWS.

A list of travellers' bungalows with details of accommodation will be found in the separate Appendix. In this direction marked progress has been made in the last half century, the 130 bungalows and rest-houses maintained by the various departments being a great improvement on the 44 which existed in 1846. They are a great convenience in a district, where tents are useless for a great part of the year, and are always expensive to carry about. There were in 1905, 37 choultries and the number went down in 1932 to 23 choultries, of which eleven were endowed, the endowment consisting of certain inam lands in the Ernad taluk. The choultry at Nadugani in the Nilgiri district is also supported by this endowment.

FERRIES.

The importance to the Local Fund revenues of the 298 ferry farms in Malabar is alluded to in Chapter XIV. The system of

CHAP. VII. TRAVELLERS' BUNGALOWS.

farming was introduced in 1801–02. 'Under the Rajas and Mysore Government boats were kept up by private owners for ferrying passengers over rivers, and slight contributions were levied for their trouble according to the circumstances of the passengers. In some places individuals maintained boats as a charity for the gratuitous passage of travellers.'[1] For the carriage of carts and horses *jangadams*, railed platforms placed on two dug-outs tied together, are used on the plains, *pandis* or rafts of bamboos and brushwood in Wynaad.

There were in 1931, 304 ferries managed by the district board. They included 22 ferries on the Cochin Frontier, the income from which is shared equally between the Durbar and the district board. Twenty more ferries on the same frontier are managed by the Durbar, on the same terms as to division of profits. The District Board owns two ferries on the French border (Mahe) and pays the French authorities half the income.

RAILWAYS.

The South Indian Railway[2] (standard gauge) enters the district through the Palghat Gap just before Valayar station, and, following the windings of the Ponnani river as far as Edakkulam, gradually approaches the coast. From Tirur the line runs parallel with the shore to Mangalore, often in sight of the sea and never more than a mile or two from it. It leaves the district at Kavvayi, a few miles beyond Payyanur station. The total length in Malabar of the main line is about 174 miles; and a small branch line, three miles long, connects Palghat with Olavakkod junction. From 1861 to 1888 the terminus was at Chaliam on the southern bank of the Beypore river. The line was extended to Calicut in the latter year. In 1901 and the two following years it was opened for traffic as far as Badagara, Tellicherry and Cannanore, respectively; and in 1907 it reached Mangalore. Beyond Kadalundi construction was difficult and expensive. Considerable rivers were encountered every few miles, and the swamps at Elattur, Tellicherry and Azhikkal caused much delay. At the last place a bank, twenty or thirty feet high, often sank five or six feet in a single night, till now the original earthwork is all below ground level. At Chala, in a cutting a few miles south of Cannanore, a bed of kaolin was met with below the laterite which necessitated heavy and expensive retaining walls connected underneath the line by inverts. The bridge consisting of twelve spans of 100 feet each over the river at Valarpattanam or Baliapatam is the most important engineering work on the Malabar section of the line. Other big bridges are the iron girder bridge of twelve spans each of 64 feet over the Kadalundi river, the bridge of six spans of 130 feet over the

[1] *Vide* Graeme's Report on the District of Malabar, dated 14th January 1822.

[2] Formerly, till February 1908, the Madras Railway.

CHAP. VII. RAILWAYS.

Beypore river at Ferok and the bridge of twelve spans of 60 feet over the Kotta river. At Shoranur the Cochin State Railway branches off to Trichur and Ernakulam.

There is a proposal to change the gauge of the Shoranur-Ernakulam railway to the broad gauge. The South Indian Railway has constructed at a cost of Rs. 70 lakhs a new line, on this gauge, from Shoranur to Nilambur *via* Angadipuram—a distance of 41·5 miles. The section from Shoranur to Angadipuram was first opened for traffic in February and the rest in October 1927. The line runs through the Walavanad and Ernad taluks, the main centres of the Mappilla rebellion of 1921, and is of considerable political and administrative value. The tract traversed is undulating low plain country and differs considerably in physical formation from the plains in other districts. The line cuts at right angles the natural drainage of the district which flows from east to west. The richly cultivated and densely peopled country through which the line passes is broken by a succession of low laterite ridges with sinuous valleys winding in and out which added considerably to the cost of construction. There are six important bridges (costing Rs. 5·32 lakhs), of which the largest spanning the Kudiraipuzha near Nilambur cost Rs. 1½ lakhs. The line should help the development of parts of the district which are at present in a partial state of cultivation and much hampered by want of transport facilities.

Pollachi-Palghat Railway.

The Pollachi-Palghat Railway, 33·45 miles (cost Rs. 52 lakhs), was under construction in 1930–32 and was opened for traffic in April 1932. About twenty miles of this railway runs through the Palghat taluk with stations at Mudalamada, Kollengode, Pudunagaram and Palghat. The largest bridge is across the Kannadi river and cost about two lakhs of rupees. The line forms part of a new feeder railway connecting the broad and metre gauges and gives more direct communication between Dindigul on the main southern line and Palghat; and passing as it does through a populous and rich country and important mercantile centres, should afford great facilities for development of trade.

Proposed lines.

A detailed survey was made in 1923–24 for a line from Tellicherry to Nanjangode in Mysore territory with a branch from Peravur to Makkat in Coorg; but owing to the prohibitive cost the proposal has for the present at least been dropped.

APPENDIX.

TRUNK AND BRANCH ROADS.

I.—TRUNK ROADS.

NOTE.—The abbreviations used in this section are—

r.s. = railway station; R. 1 = one room; R. 2 = two rooms; B. 1 = one bath room; B. 2 = two bath rooms; H. 1 = one hall; F. = furnished; S. 1 = one stable; 4·5 m. = 4 miles 5 furlongs.

The amount noted within brackets is the charge for a single person for a day.

* Asterisks on names of towns indicate the existence of petrol depots in them.

1. *Gudalur-Calicut Trunk Road.*—The road is metalled and bridged. Ghat begins 57 m., motorable. Mileage is calculated from Calicut. Gudalur 77·1 m., district limit 64·3 m.

Edakara (R. 1, B. 1, S. 1, F., As. 8) 53 m.; Nilambur (R. 2, B. 2, S. 1, F.,As. 8) 45 m.; Manjeri (R. 2, S. 1,B.2,F., As. 8) 29·4 m.; Nediyiruppu 23·7 m.; Kondotti (R. 2, B. 2, S. 1, F., As. 8) 16·3 m., cross the Beypore river by road bridge; Feroke 7 m.; Calicut.*

2. *Gudalur-Vayittiri-Calicut Road.*—83·5 m., metalled and bridged throughout and motorable.

As far as Vayittiri it passes through undulating hilly ground and there is hardly any portion perfectly level. Up to Choladi the mileage is calculated from Gudalur and in the rest of the section from Calicut. Choladi bridge 24·6 m.

Meppadi (R. 2, F., As. 8) 36·5 m.; Vayittiri* (H. 1, R. 2, B. 2, F., As. 8) 40 m.; Lakkiti * (R. 2, B. 2, S. 1, F., As. 8) 34·5 m.; Tamarasseri * (R. 3, B. 2, F., As. 8) 18·4 m.; Makkuttam 10·7 m.; Calicut * (r.s., R. 4, B. 4, S. 1, F., Re. 1). The portion from Vayittiri to Gudalur is maintained by the P.W.D.

3. *Madras-Calicut Trunk Road.*—454 m., Metalled and bridged throughout. Enters district at 343·5 m. Kanjikod (r.s.) 351 m.; Palghat * (r.s., R. 3, F., Re. 1) 354 m.; Thuppanad bridge 372·4 m; Nellipuzha bridge 381·6 m.; Kumarambuthur 382·2 m.; Nattukal (R. 1, B. 1, S. 1, F., As. 8) 390 m.; Angadipuram (R. 2, B. 2, S. 1, F., Re. 1) 403 m.; Malappuram 412 m.; The Calicut-Gudalur road branches off at 420·4 m. at Mongam. Kondotti (R. 2, B. 2, S. 1, F., As. 8) 428 m., cross Beypore river by road bridge; Feroke 438·2 m.; Calicut * (r.s., R. 4, B. 4, S. 1, F., Re. 1) 444·3 m.

II.—BRANCH ROADS.

Angadipuram to Melattur 9 m. Bridged and metalled throughout, practicable at all seasons.

2. Badagara (r.s., R. 2, B. 2, S. 1, F., As. 8) to Kuttippuram 9 m. Good road. Practicable at all seasons.

3. Cannanore to Kannoth 30·4 m. The road is metalled and bridged and fit for motors. Cannanore * (r.s., R. 2, B. 2, S. 2, F., Re. 1); Kudali 10·1 m.; Chavasseri 20·5 m.; Kannoth * 30·4 m.

4. Cannanore to Kakkat 56·3 m. From Kuttur to Pullur there is only a track across the frontiers of Malabar. Cannanore* (r.s., R. 2, B. 2, S. 2, F., Re. 1); Taliparamba (R. 2, B. 2, S. 2, F.,

CHAP. VII. RAILWAYS.

As. 8) 14 m., cross the Taliparamba river provided with a ferry boat ; cross Vannathikadavu ; Kuttur 29·5 m. ; Puliyanur 43·1 m.; Kakkat 56·3 ; Pullur (South Kanara district) 62·5 m.

5. Chavakkad (R. 1, B. 2, S. 2, As. 8) to Enamakkal (R. 1, B. 1, F., As. 8) 8·5 m. Unfit for motors.

6. Chavakkad to Nilambur 60·5 m. Road metalled and bridged except over Orampuram river, and fit for motors. Chavakkad (R. 1, B. 2, S. 2. As. 8), Kunnamkulam 6 m. (Cochin State) ; Tritala (R. 2, B. 2, S. 3, F., As. 8) 17·1 m., cross the ferry ; Pattambi (r.s., R. 2, B. 2, S. 1, F., As. 8) 20·1 m. ; cross the Pulamanthol river now bridged ; Angadipuram 35·1 m., cross the Orampuram river, unbridged ; Pandikkad (R. 2, B. 2, S. 1, F., As. 8) 44·5 m. ; Wandur (R. 2, B. 2, S. 1, F., As. 8) 52·5m. ; Nilambur (R. 2, B. 2, S. 1, F., As. 8) 60·5 m.

7. Edappal to Betathpudiyangadi 13 m. Metalled and practicable at all seasons ; Edappal, cross the Kuttipuram river, unbridged ; Kuttipuram (r.s.) 5·4 m. ; Betathpudiyangudi 13 m.

8. Kalpatta to Cherambadi 39·5 m. The road is metalled and bridged up to Sultan's Battery. From there to Cherambadi, road unmetalled, partly unbridged. Kalpatta* (R. 2, B. 2, S. 2, F., As. 8) ; Sultan's Battery* (R. 2, F., As. 8) 15 m. ; Yeddadurai 23·1 m. ; Cherambadi 39·5 m.

9. Kolinjampara to Manjeri 70 m. The road is metalled, fit for motors and is also bridged with the exception of the river Thutha and Anakayam ; Kolinjampara ; Palghat* (r.s., R. 3, F., Re. 1) 14 m. ; Lakkiti* (R. 2, B. 2, S. 1, F., As. 8) 29 m. ; Ottapalam (r.s., R. 2, B. 2, S. 1, F., As. 8) 35 miles ; Cherpalacheri (R. 1, B. 1, F., As. 8) 46 m., cross the Thutha river, unbridged ; Angadipuram 56 m., cross the Anakayam river, fordable ; Manjeri (R. 2, B. 2, S. 1, F., As. 8) 70 m.

10. Kollengode to Lakkiti 28·4 m. Road metalled and partly bridged. Kollengode (R. 2, B. 2, S. 2, F., As. 8) ; Kunisseri, 7·4 miles ; Alathur* (H. 2, B. 2, S. 2, F., As. 8) 12·4 miles, cross the Mingara and the Ponnani rivers, unbridged ; Lakkiti (r.s., R. 2, B. 2, S. 2, F., As. 8) 28·4 m.

11. Kollengode to Palghat 14 m. Road metalled and bridged. Practicable at all seasons. Kollengode * (R. 2, B. 2, S. 2, F., As. 8) ; Tattamangalam 10 m. ; Palghat * (r.s., R. 3, F., Re. 1) 14 m.

12. Kunisseri to Koduvayur* (H. 1, B. 1, S. 3, F., As. 8) 6 m. Partly metalled and bridged, practicable at all seasons.

13. Kunisseri to Palghat* (r.s., R. 3, F., Re. 1) 11 m. Cross the Palghat river, bridged. Metalled and practicable at all seasons.

14. Kottaparamba to Kavvayi 159·6 m. To Chaliyam the road is a mere track running along the sea coast with a great number of unbridged backwaters to be crossed and composed entirely of heavy sand and impracticable for carts. From Chaliyam to Payyanur the road is good and practicable at all seasons, the unbridged rivers being crossed in boats ; it is fit for motors between Chaliyam and Payyanur. Kottaparamba* (R. 2, B. 2, S. 1, F., As. 8) at 4·1 m., pass Madilagam ; Perinnanam 6 m. ; Valapad (R. 1, B. 1, S. 1, As. 8) 14·6 m., cross a backwater and the Chetuvayi

river, unbridged ; Chetuvayi* (R. 2, B., 2) 22·5 m., cross the Chetuvayi river, unbridged ; Chavakkad (R. 1, B. 2, S. 2, F., As. 8) 29·1 m., cross a backwater ; Manalkunam 35·6 m., cross the Veliyangod river, unbridged ; Ponnani (R. 2, B. 2, S. 2, F., As. 8) 44·2 m., cross the Ponnani river, unbridged ; Kuttayi 49 m. ; Tanur (r.s., R. 2, B. 2, S. 2, F., As. 8) 58·2 m. ; Chaliyam 71 m., cross the Beypore river, unbridged ; Calicut* (r.s., R. 4, B. 4, S. 1, F., Re. 1) 78 m. ; Elattur (Korapoya) (r.s.), 85·7 m., cross the Korapoya river, unbridged ; Panthalayini (r.s., R. 2, B. 2, S. 1, F., As. 8) 93·5 m. ; Tikkodi (r.s., R. 1, B. 1, As. 8) 99·4 m., cross the Moorat river, unbridged ; Badagara (r.s., R. 2, B. 2, S. 1, F., As. 8) 107·3 m. ; Chombal 112·3 m. ; Tellicherry* (r.s., R. 2, B. 2, S. 1, F., Re. 1) 121·7 m. ; Cannanore* (r.s., R. 2, B. 2, S. 2, F., Re. 1) 135·7 m. ; cross the Baliyapatam river, unbridged ; Pazhayangadi (R. 2, B. 2, S. 2, F., As. 8) 149·4 m. ; Kavvayi 159·6 m., cross the Kavvayi river Chandare (South Kanara district) 170·6 m.

15. Kottaparamba to Palghat 62·5 m. To the backwater beyond Kottaparamba this is a mere track over heavy sand and never used by carts. At Karupadana, the landing place on the east of the backwater the main road begins and thence to Palghat is metalled and partially bridged ; from Pattikad, the road is fit for motors. Kottaparamba, cross a backwater by ferry (Cochin State) ; Vadakkancheri (H. 2, B. 2, F., As. 8) 42·5 m. ; Alattur* (H. 2, B. 2, S. 2, F., As. 8) 49·5 m. ; Palghat*(r.s., R. 3, F., Re. 1) 62·5 m.

16. Kunnimangalam to Kuttur 8 m. ; cross the Vannathikadavu river, unbridged, a fair-weather track, practicable in the dry season only.

17. Lakkiti to Ponnani 38·4 m. This road is metalled throughout and fit for motors and bridged with the exception of two rivers (the Pattambi and the Ponnani), which are provided with ferries. Lakkiti* (R. 2, B. 2, S. 2, F., As. 8) ; Vaniyamkulam 8 m. ; Tritala (R. 2, B. 2, S. 3, F., As. 8) 22·4 m. Ponnani (R. 2, B. 2, S. 2, F., As. 8) 38·4 m.

18. Malappuram to Chaliyam 27·1 m. Road is partly metalled and bridged, practicable beyond Parappanangadi only in the dry season ; Malappuram, cross the Panampuzha river, bridge under construction ; Chaliyam 27·1 m.

19. Manjeri to Quilandi 50 m. Road metalled, practicable at all seasons, except for ten miles beyond Arriakod where it is a mere track ; Manjeri (R. 2, B. 2, S. 1, F., As. 8) ; Arriakod 12 m., cross the Kodathay, Iruvunji and Arriakod rivers, unbridged ; Tamarasseri* (R. 3, B. 2, F., As. 8) 31 m. ; Ulliyari 39 m., cross the Kaniyangod river, unbridged, by a ferry ; Quilandi (r.s.) 50 m.

20. Manjeri (R. 2, B. 2, S. 1, F., As. 8) to Wandur (R. 2, B. 2, S. 1, F., As. 8) 12·4 m. Metalled and fit for motors.

21. Mannarghat to Pandikkad 29 m. Metalled and bridged, practicable at all seasons and fit for motors ; Mannarghat (R. 2, B. 2, S. 1, F., As. 8) ; Alanallur 11 m. ; Pandikkad (R. 2, B. 2, S. 1, F., As. 8) 29 m.

CHAP. VII. RAILWAYS.

22. Mundur to Cherpulcheri (R. 1, B. 1, S. 1, F., As. 8) 19·4 m. Metalled and bridged and fit for motors.

23. Nedumpoyil to Kunnimangalam. The road is metalled as far as Srikandapuram, about five miles beyond Irukkur, thence to near Talipparamba it is a mere track impassable in the rains; the remainder of the road is metalled. Metalled portions practicable at all seasons; Iritty* 12·4 m.; Irukkur* (R. 1, B. 1, S. 1, F., As. 8) 23 m., cross two rivers, unbridged; Talipparamba (R. 2, B. 2, S. 2, F., As. 8) 41 m., cross the Talipparamba river by ferry; Kunnimangalam.

24. Palghat* to Kondotti 72·3 m. The road is metalled and fit for motors. Palghat (r.s., R. 3, F., Re. 1), cross Paliampal and several streams, all bridged. Thuppanad 13 m.; Mannarghat (R. 2, B. 2, S. 1, F., As. 8) 34·7 m.: Angadipuram (R. 2, B. 2, S. 1, F., As. 8) 44·7 m.; Malappuram 58·3; Kondotti (R. 2, B. 2, S. 1, F., As. 8) 72·3 m.

25. Panur to Kathirur 5 m. Gravelled and practicable at all seasons.

26. Parli (r.s.) to Mundur 3·4 m. Road metalled and bridged throughout, practicable at all seasons.

27. Pattambi (r.s., R. 2, B. 2, S. 1, F., As. 8) to Cherpulcheri (R. 1, B. 1, S. 1, F., As. 8) 11·4 m. This road is practicable for carts at all seasons and fit for motors.

28. Perinkulam to Kottaparamba 9·1 m. Well gravelled and practicable at all seasons; Panur 3·3 m.; Kottaparamba* (R. 4, B. 2, S. 1, F., As. 8) 9·1 m.

29. Ponnani to Manjeri 32·2 m. The road is metalled and bridged and fit for motors, practicable at all seasons. Betatpudiyangadi 3·2 m.; Tirur (r.s.) R. 2, B. 2, S. 2, F., As. 8) 82 m.; Malappuram 25·2 m.; Manjeri (R. 2, S. 1, F., As 8) 32·2 m.

30. Sultan's Battery to Cannanore 85·1 m. Up till Manantoddy the road is bridged throughout and metalled, practicable at all seasons; thence to Cannanore the road is metalled throughout and all streams but the Mambaram river to backwater are bridged; road fit for motors. Sultan's Battery * (R. 2, F., As. 8); Panamarathukota 17 m.; Manantoddy * (H. 1, R. 2, S. 2, F., As. 8) 27·2 m.; Periya* 43·6 m.; Nedumpoyil* 54·6 m.; Kannoth 61·3 m.; Kottaparamba* (R. 4, B. 2, S. 1, F., As. 8) 69·1 m.; Cannanore* (r.s., R. 2, B. 2, S. 2, F., Re. 1) 85·1 m.

31. Tellicherry to Chavasseri 22 m. Road well gravelled practicable at all seasons and fit for motors. Tellicherry (r.s., R. 2, B. 2, S. 1, F., As. 8), Kathirur; Kottaparamba (R. 4, B. 2, F., As. 8) 8·4 m.; Muttanur, 16 m., cross the Merumpoya river; Chavasseri.*

32. Tellicherry to Manantoddy 48·5 m. Tellicherry (r.s., R. 2, B. 2, S. 1, F., Re. 1) cross the Perinkolam river, unbridged, by ferry; Kuttipuram 15·6 m.; Kuttiyadi (R. 2, B. 2, S. 1, F., As. 8) 21·2 m.; Koroth (R. 2, S. 1, F., As. 8) 34·2 m., cross two

large streams, bridged ; Tharavanna 42·2 m., cross the Manantoddy river, unbridged ; Manantoddy* (R. 2, H. 1, S. 2, F., As. 8) 48·5 m.

33. Tritala to Tanur 25 m. Road metalled and passable. Tritala (R. 2, B. 2, S. 3, F., As. 8) ; Kuttipuram (r.s., R. 2, B. 1, S. 1, F., As. 8) 8 m. ; Tirur (r.s., R. 2, B. 2, S. 2, F., As. 8) 19 m. ; Tanur, (r.s., R. 2, B. 2, S. 2, F., As. 8) 25 m.

34. Trichur to Tritala, 32·4 m. Metalled and bridged, practicable at all seasons ; Trichur to Vadakkancheri 11·5 m. ; Shoranur (r.s.) 20·4 p.m. ; Vattolikavu 27·4 m. ; Tritala 32·4 m.

35. Vadakkancheri to Kollengode 13 m. Metalled and bridged, practicable at all seasons and fit for motors, Vadakkancheri (H. 2, B. 2, F., As. 8) ; Vallangi 7 m. ; Kollengode* (R. 2, B. 2, S. 2, F., As. 8) 13 m.

36. Vayittiri to Manantoddy 27·2 m. Road bridged and metalled, practicable at all seasons and fit for motors ; Vayittiri* (H. 1, R. 2, B. 2, As. 8), at 6 miles pass Chundale ; Kalpatta (R. 2, B. 2, S. 2, F., As. 8) 6 m., Panamaram 17 m. ; Manantoddy* (R. 2, B. 2, S. 1, F., As. 8) 27·2 m. Two ferries fordable at all seasons at Panamaram and Kingsferry.

37. Vattolikavu to Pattambi (r.s.) 3·2 m. Metalled and bridged, practicable at all seasons. Cross the Ponnani river.

CHAPTER VIII.

RAINFALL AND SEASONS.

RAINFALL. THE SEASONS—Liability to famine—Early scarcities—Famine of 1865–66—Famine of 1876–1878—Scarcity in 1890–91. FLOODS—The Tamarasseri landslip—Floods of 1923 and 1924. STORMS—The hurricane of 1848—Cyclones in 1925 and 1932. EARTHQUAKES.

CHAP. VIII. RAINFALL.

THE rainfall of Malabar is very heavy, and the district average for the last 34 years is nearly 117 inches. As recorded officially, it ranges from nearly 78 inches at Palghat to 169 at Vayittiri; but in many parts of the Wynaad on the slopes of the ghats a fall of 300 inches in the year is not uncommon. More than 360 inches of rain fell in the year 1904–05 at Tagarapadi on the Tamarasseri ghat, and of this 300 inches were collected in June, July and August. Statistics of the rainfall at the majority of the recording stations in the district are given below. Kottayam was a recording station between 1870 and 1883, and Chevayur between 1870 and 1891; and in these years the average fall at these two places was 123·72 and 101·96 respectively. Rain gauges have lately been set up at Mankara, Ottapalam, Cherpalcheri, Mannarakkad, Irrikkur, Payyanur, Kuttiyadi and Triprangod; but the statistics are too recent to be trustworthy, and these places have therefore been omitted from the table.

Station.	Years recorded.	January to March.	April and May.	June to September.	October to December.	Total.
Palghat ..	1870—03	1·27	8·04	55·52	13·04	77·88
Angadipuram.	1870—03	1·41	11·45	75·32	18·17	106·35
Manjeri ..	1870—03	1·03	10·29	81·19	18·03	110·54
Nilambur ..	1871—03	·85	8·19	84·87	14·60	168·51
Vayittiri ..	1870—03	1·98	10·82	140·16	16·36	169·32
Manantoddy.	1870—03	1·76	7·94	87·56	9·17	106·43
Taliparamba.	1879—03	·27	8·56	104·03	13·54	126·70
Cannanore ..	1870—03	·77	10·05	99·50	11·41	121·73
Tellicherry.	1870—03	·80	12·49	105·63	12·31	131·23
Badagara ..	1870—03	1·23	11·39	97·97	12·46	123·05
Quilandi ..	1894—03	·82	11·24	102·55	11·47	126·08
Calicut ..	1870—03	1·14	12·80	89·02	15·49	118·45
Tirurangadi.	1870—03	·79	12·71	81·78	15·63	110·91
Ponnani ..	1870—03	1·77	15·00	71·08	15·79	103·64
Chevvakkad.	1894—03	1·18	13·65	75·51	16·65	147·00
Cochin ..	1870—03	3·77	17·36	73·05	21·03	115·02
District average		1·30	11·39	89·05	14·70	116·44

CHAP. VIII. SEASONS.

The climate is remarkable for the orderly march of the seasons and the regularity of seed-time and harvest. January, February and March are the dry months, when burning land winds blow and the heat is tempered only by the cool evening breeze off the sea. Early in April the first distant mutterings of thunder are heard on the ghats, and the husbandman knows that the time of sowing is at hand. Almost every evening storms break over the interior, sometimes extending as far as the coast; and towards the end of May their greater violence and a bank of blue-black clouds gathering in the south-west herald the onset of the monsoon. In some seasons the electrical disturbance at this period is terrific; the roll of thunder is continuous for minutes together and the blaze of lightning incessant. With the burst of the monsoon, generally about the second week of June, the thunder-storms cease, the floodgates of heaven are opened, and the clouds descend in rain. In August the rains slacken, and at the end of September they die away. The land winds assert themselves once more, and, though the north-east monsoon brings frequent showers, by the end of December the dry weather has usually set in.

Liability to famine.

The north-east monsoon sometimes fails, the south-west never; and, as the latter brings three-quarters of the rainfall of the district, it is perhaps unnecessary to add that real famine is unknown in the land. Malabar, it is true, does not grow sufficient foodgrain for its own consumption, and has to make up the deficiency by importation. Artificial famines are therefore always possible, and at one time, when Mangalore was the granary of Malabar and pirates infested the sea, were fairly common. But of real famine due to widespread failure of crops there is little or no record, and no special programme of relief works is drawn up yearly, as in other districts.

Early scarcities.

In August 1727 factors of Tellicherry recorded in their diary that there was an 'extraordinary scarcity of rice.' The factory stock was reduced to barely a month's supply. There was none to be had at Mangalore, where parents were selling their children to obtain food, and the factory doors were daily besieged by crowds of starving men and women; no further entries on the subject appear, and probably with the reaping of the *kanni* crop in September the worst symptoms disappeared. It is always in the months that just precede the harvest of this crop that the pinch of poverty makes itself most severely felt. In July and August the paddy crops have been planted out and require but little labour, and the poorer classes, whose scanty stock of grain saved from the previous season's crop is exhausted, have a hard struggle to make both ends meet.

Famine of 1865–66.

The severe famine which raged throughout the presidency in 1865 and 1866 made its effects felt in Malabar. A daily average

CHAP. VIII. SEASONS.

of 6,353 people were relieved during the five months from July to November 1866, of whom 6,198 were relieved gratuitously and 155 employed on wages. The maximum number relieved in any one month was 24,206 in August 1866. An unprecedented outbreak of dacoity and violent crime was a marked feature of these two years.

Famine of 1876 to 1878.

In 1876 to 1878, the terrible years in which the whole of South India was stricken with famine, Malabar suffered in common with the rest of the presidency, but to a far less degree. The north-east monsoon of 1876 failed with the result that the *magaram* crops on the plains perished, and the coffee crop in the Wynaad was short. In ordinary years prices would have risen slightly, and supplies of rice would have poured in from Burma and Bengal. Some distress would have been felt among the poor, but not so much as to call for the interference of Government. But, with famine raging in Mysore and the rest of the presidency, and no grain available for import except at famine prices, actual famine threatened Malabar in general and the Wynaad taluk in particular. Into this taluk at that time more than 30,000 coolies flocked every year from Mysore for the picking season. Ordinarily they found ample work on the coffee estates till the middle of February, and were then able to return home with money saved. But in 1876, with ragi, the staple food of the coolies, at three times its usual price, and the coffee all picked by the end of December, the authorities were confronted with the prospect of having thousands of destitute coolies thrown on their hands with no money saved and no inducement to return to Mysore, where famine was far worse. A sum of Rs. 5,000 was therefore allotted by the Board for relief in the Wynaad early in 1877, and the Mysore Government agreed to depute an officer to deport the coolies to their homes.

As usual, however, it was only in the monsoon months that real distress was experienced. Relief camps were opened in May at Vayittiri and Manantoddy, and in July at Palghat, where emaciated and destitute coolies were beginning to arrive in large numbers from Coimbatore and Salem. The average number relieved daily at these camps is given below :—

——	Manantoddy.	Vayittiri.	Palghat.	Total.
June	10	55	..	65
July	21	98	6	125
August	16	71	80	167
September ..	15	60	27	102
October ..	9	72	..	81

In August the severity of the distress began to tell on the local population ; but the richer classes generously stepped in and in nearly every taluk opened relief houses where one meal

CHAP. VIII. SEASONS.

of rice-kanji was distributed daily to all comers. The numbers thus relieved weekly will surprise even those well acquainted with the district. It will be noticed that in September the numbers on relief fell away rapidly :—

Week ending.	Number relieved.	Week ending.	Number relieved.	Week ending.	Number relieved.
August 11	14,200	September 8	39,157	October 6	2,577
,, 18	35,715	,, 15	15,484	,, 13	1,084
,, 25	44,002	,, 22	4,969	,, 20	403
September 1	40,383	,, 29	2,298	,, 27	407

Preparations were made for opening relief works in the plain taluks in 1877, and in June the tracing of a road from Mannarakkad to Cherpalcheri in the Walavanad taluk was commenced. Nothing further was done, however, as the opening up with roads of the country round Kolattur with fines collected from the amsams implicated in the Mappilla outrage of 1873 at that place, provided sufficient work for the poorer classes all through the period of scarcity. Early in 1878 relief works were opened in the Wynaad. The Governments of Madras and Mysore each subscribed Rs. 2 for every rupee subscribed by the planters, and with the Rs. 9,138 thus raised several roads were put in order.

Between 1876 and 1878, with the exception of the failure of the north-east monsoon in the first year, there was no deficiency of rain in the district, and the crops were also good. The scarcity therefore, for it can hardly be called a famine, was merely sympathetic with the famine raging all round Malabar. The great famine of 1876 to 1878 cost the State 690 lakhs in direct expenditure ; but of this only Rs. 11,063, an infinitesimal fraction, were spent in Malabar, and that largely on refugees from other districts.

Scarcity in 1890–91.

At the end of 1890 there was a very general failure of the *magaram* rice crop on the plains and of the coffee crop in the Wynaad. The collection of arrears of kist in the Ernad, Walavanad and Ponnani taluks was postponed till the following October ; but a programme of relief works proposed by the Collector was not sanctioned by Government for the reason that the ordinary local fund works, for which a provision of Rs. 63,000 had been made in the budget, would probably provide sufficient work for the poorer classes nearer their homes. Partial scarcity prevailed again in 1899, and a certain amount of private relief was dispensed at Tellicherry and other places.

FLOODS.

Excessive falls of rain are common, and floods by no means infrequent. On the 19th and 20th May 1882 between 18 and 22

CHAP. VIII. FLOODS.

inches of rain fell in the 24 hours in different parts of Calicut; and in the monsoon of 1871 the rain gauge at the Collector's office registered over six inches a day for six consecutive days. During almost every monsoon the small *todus* or water-courses that feed the rivers overflow their banks, and convert into placid lakes the green paddy flats through which they run. But the rivers themselves have in the course of long ages worn out for themselves deep beds, and rarely overflow their banks to any serious extent. In the monsoon of 1902, however, which burst almost unprecedentedly late with tremendous rain on the ghats, several of the big rivers overspread the country side. Many hundred native huts collapsed in the district, and the Nuradi bridge at Malappuram which is 30 feet above the bed of the Kadalundi river was submerged. Similar floods recurred in Ernad and Walavanad in the monsoon of 1907.

The Tamarasseri landslip.

In 1900 an exceptionally heavy monsoon culminated on the early morning of August 4th in a perfect deluge of rain on the Tamarasseri ghat. Only 14·28 inches of rain, collected in two measurements at 7 p.m. and 4 a.m. respectively, were registered at Lakkidi near the head of the ghat; but the gauge which held only 10½ inches must have overflowed the greater part of the night, and the actual rainfall was probably at least double the amount recorded. The effect on the upper six miles of the ghat road was disastrous. Numerous landslips, great and small, took place. The road was breached in several places, and in some disappeared altogether, not a vestige of the trace remaining. The worst damage was done where a deep nullah crossed the road several times in a very short distance, as it went zig-zag down the mountain side. 'At four such points', wrote the Chief Engineer [1], who inspected the damage, 'the torrent rushing down the nullah evidently rose to a depth of 25 to 30 feet, and carried every thing before it, huge trees and rocks, boulders, vegetation and of course the road, its culverts and revetments. Such devastation caused by water I never saw before, and it seems as if the flood could only have been caused by a water spout.' Nine human bodies and some dead bullocks were discovered, but the exact loss of life and property can never be ascertained. To show the magnitude of the disaster, it was estimated that 1,200,000 cubic feet of earth, rocks, trees and debris had to be removed, the whole surface of the road re-made and re-metalled, a large number of culverts and revetments re-built and a quarter of mile of new road made. These repairs were effected at a cost of considerably more than a lakh of rupees.

Floods of 1923.

Heavy rains in July and August 1923 flooded the whole district causing much damage and loss. The rainfall in the taluks of Wynaad, Chirakkal, Kottayam and Kurumbranad was heavier than any recorded during the previous sixty years,

[1] G.O. No. 2584 W, dated 19th September 1900.

CHAP. VIII. FLOODS.

and in Walavanad it was 19 inches between 1st and 11th August as against 4 inches in the previous year. Between 1st July and 15th August, there were 97 inches of rain in the Wynaad as against an average of 73 inches in July and August during the previous thirteen years. North Malabar suffered more than South and in Chirakkal taluk, especially the country between Iritty bridge and Azhikode on the Valarapattanam river, 3,000 houses and huts worth two lakhs of rupees and the crops on 2,000 acres were ruined, and timber stored in the river worth a lakh of rupees was lost. There were numerous landslips on the ghats, those on the Ayilliar-Kavumala covering an area of two square miles and engulfing the famous Kottiyur temple and the sheds around it (all since restored). In Calicut town itself the portions lying close to the Conolly canal and the Kallayi river were under water and about 170 houses and huts worth Rs. 14,000 were lost. The railway line was little affected, except for the submersion of the main line for a short distance between Pantalayini and Tikkotti. On the roads damage was but slight.

Floods of 1924.

While the floods of 1923 affected only North Malabar, those of 1924 which were even greater affected the south of the district more than the north. There was steady rain for a week from about the 12th July and by the 18th rivers were in full flood. A heavy downpour on the 20th and 21st drove the water still higher. In the Wynaad and in the taluks below the ghats the rainfall was heavier than on the coast. Vayittiri recorded 103·54 inches between 12th to 24th July (13·30 inches on the 16th July alone) while Manantoddy had 44·80 inches in the week ending 17th, 21 inches of it falling on the 16th and 17th alone. The result was that all the rivers running west to the sea carried more water than their usually high banks could hold and flooded the country around for many days. In several places people had to be rescued from the tops of houses and cocoanut trees whereto they had been driven for safety. Warned by their experiences in the previous year's floods, the people in threatened areas betook themselves early to any available high ground and there were only 25 deaths ascribable to the floods. The high floods in the Baliapatam and the Panamaram rivers resulted in the collapse of about 4,000 houses and damage to crops on about 2,000 acres in the northern taluks. In the south 25,840 houses (including some substantial buildings) were reported to have been destroyed and crops on about 30,000 acres damaged and 3,200 acres of land rendered unfit for cultivation by land-slides or by deposit of silt. Serious damage was also caused to railways and roads. A number of bridges were washed away and there were several serious breaches in the roads. In North Malabar the Kuttupuzha bridge was on 24th July partially destroyed by the floods and the slipping of the hill on the Tellicherry side of the river on to the bridge and

CHAP. VIII. FLOODS.

the bed of the river completed the destruction, the water rising to 18 feet over the roadway. A new bridge has since been built. The Iritty bridge was also seriously damaged, the 5th and 6th spans being washed away, water having risen 5·25 feet over the top level of the decking. The road from Iritty to Kuttupuzha was badly cut up and scoured, water having overflowed it to a depth of 10 to 14 feet in several places.

The Calicut-Mysore Frontier road was badly damaged by lansdlips, erosion of the margins and washaways at the culverts. Timber valued at three lakhs of rupees stored in Kallayi river was washed into the sea. Water was running above the railway line in several places and breaches on 16th July extended throughout the line from Olavakkote to Tirur, a distance of 55 miles. Nearer Calicut one span of the girder bridge across the Pooraparamba river and a 20 feet girder bridge between Feroke and Kallayi were washed away, these two bridges not being permanently replaced and extended until two years later. On most of the district roads water was running several feet deep and washed away all the metal, and a huge landslip, about 300 feet long settled down on the 8th mile of the Ottapalam-Cherpulcheri road ; a similar landslip happened at Pandikkad. Numerous landslips occurred on the ghat roads, the Peria Tamarasseri and Nadugani ghats were blocked and the Karkur ghat had 300 landslips and took three years to repair at a cost of Rs. 1½ lakhs. Landslides in Chirakkal, Ernad, Wynaad and Walavanad taluks damaged the wet lands and blocked the roads near them. Among the bridges that were washed away may be mentioned the Mahe bridge (between Mahe and Tellicherry), the Nellipuzha bridge (between Mannarghat and Thuppanad), the Naicutty bridge (between Wynaad and Coorg) and the Bavali bridge (between Wynaad and Mysore) ; one of the piers of the Yakkara bridge in Palghat taluk sank. The collapse of these bridges, and the landslips and breaches on the roads rendered communication with the neighbouring districts difficult and trade was paralysed for a time. Postal and telegraphic communication was interrupted for ten days (17th to 26th July), Rs. 4·35 lakhs were distributed by Government under the Loan Acts besides free gifts of money (Rs. 15,000) and timber to the poorer people to rebuild their houses. Repairs to the roads and bridges cost about Rs. 10 lakhs in all.

STORMS.

The squalls that usher in the south-west monsoon are often terrific in their violence, and work havoc among any hapless *pattamars* that have lingered too long on the inhospitable coast. But the sheltering ghats protect Malabar from the cyclones which periodically devastate the Coromandel coast, and great storms are rare.

The hurricane of 1848.

The hurricane of the 16th, 17th and 18th of April 1848 is one of the few of which details are on record. Originating somewhere south of the Laccadives, the storm swept across the islands of Kalpeni and Androth, and of 90,000 cocoanut trees in each island left only 700 standing in the former and 1,000 in the latter. Kalpeni was partially submerged by a tidal wave, and of a population of 1,600 only 450 remained, the rest having escaped from the island or perished in the storm. The population of Androth was reduced from 2,500 to 900, and a boat from Agatti containing 96 men and some women was caught in the storm and never heard of again. The storm wave then dashed on the main land, and its effects were felt from Cannanore to Chettuvayi. The Cannanore Customs House was destroyed. The Palayad dam in the Veliyangod backwater was breached and the wave forced a new and deep opening in the Chavakkad backwater.

Cyclone in 1925.

The district experienced a severe cyclonic storm on 11th November 1925. It began in the small hours of the morning and lasted till 8 a.m. and blew along the coast from Badagara to Cannanore and for a distance of 20 miles inland. On the coast a number of trees were uprooted or smashed and thatched roofs were blown away. Tellicherry was the worst sufferer; here fallen trees completely disorganized traffic and interrupted telegraph communication for two days. In the inland, plantain cultivation suffered serious damage and communication with Coorg was interrupted by the washing away of the temporary bridge at Iritti. At sea the effect was more serious and the storm centre was somewhere off the port of Tellicherry and extended from Cochin to Cannanore. The force of the wind was terrific at sea and survivors from wrecks reported that their boats were bodily lifted from the water and then dashed against the waves. Ninety-four fishing boats with 223 men were reported lost, and 21 "pattamars" of this district with about 50 men and cargo worth about Rs. 50,000 were sunk.

Cyclone in 1932.

South Malabar was visited by another severe cyclonic storm on the night of May 24th, 1932. There was rain throughout the district and a strong wind, mainly from the west, blew over portions of the Calicut, Kurumbranad, Ernad and Ponnani taluks, chiefly along the coast to a depth of 20 miles inland from Quilandy in the north to Ponnani in the south. Trees were blown down in large numbers all over this area, many houses collapsed and about one house in four was appreciably damaged. Telegraph and telephone wires were cut, and roads blocked by fallen trees, seriously interrupting communications. A rainfall of 10·75 inches was recorded at Calicut between 8 a.m. on 24th to 8 a.m. on 25th.

No serious floods, however, occurred and the rain abated on the 25th. Water in the rivers subsided though precautions had

CHAP. VIII. STORMS. to be taken to evacuate people from certain low-lying places along their banks. Sixteen deaths were reported, mostly of children, due to the collapse of houses or the falling of trees. Among the buildings damaged in Calicut was the Malabar Club on the sea front, portions of its roof being blown off and furniture shattered.

EARTHQUAKES. Earthquakes are not infrequent, but the shocks are mild and have never done any serious damage. Tremors have been felt in 1881, twice in 1882, in 1899 and 1904.

CHAPTER IX.

PUBLIC HEALTH.

MEDICAL INSTITUTIONS—INDIGENOUS MEDICINE. VITAL STATISTICS—Sanitation. GENERAL HEALTH—Characteristic diseases—Cholera—Small-pox—Vaccination—Plague—Malarial fever—Infirmities—Leper and lunatic asylums.

CHAP. IX. MEDICAL INSTITUTIONS.

Civil hospitals were first opened in Malabar in the middle of last century. Government had already been maintaining the Palliport Leper Asylum bequeathed by the Dutch, and primarily for the benefit of officials, troops and jails, stationed zillah surgeons in North and South Malabar (at Tellicherry and Calicut) and assistant surgeons in one or two other places. But it was not till October 1845 that the first public hospital was opened at Calicut. Then came those at Palghat and Cochin. Twenty years later, when municipalities were first constituted, all the municipal towns were provided with similar institutions, and the hospitals at Calicut, Tellicherry, Palghat and Cochin were handed over to the respective municipalities, Government paying the salaries of the medical officers out of provincial funds. The local boards which began to function about the same time also opened hospitals or dispensaries gradually at all taluk centres and at important villages like Chowghat and Angadipuram.

The Palliport Leper Asylum was abolished in the year 1920 and the patients were transferred partly to the Leper Asylum at Chevayur and partly to Trivandrum. With a view to improve the facilities for medical relief at district headquarters, Government took over the management of the hospitals at Calicut and Tellicherry in 1920, and two years later offered to pay the salaries of the medical officers employed in certain local fund and municipal hospitals at taluk headquarters, so that there might be at least one efficiently managed medical institution in each taluk. This scheme was developed subsequently by the assumption by Government during 1928 of the management of the hospitals at Palghat, Cochin, Cannanore, Ponnani, Manjeri, Chowghat and Manantoddy. Government also pay the salary of the assistant surgeon in charge of the local fund hospital at Angadipuram. The other hospitals, for the upkeep of which Government are now directly responsible, are the Women and Children's hospital at Calicut (which owes its

CHAP. IX. MEDICAL INSTITUTIONS.

inception in great part to the generosity of Raja Sir Ramaswami Mudaliyar of Madras), the mental hospital at Calicut, the two Police hospitals at Malappuram and Cannanore and the two island dispensaries at Minicoy and Androth.

The mental hospital opened on 28th May 1872 is at Pudiyara, a suburb of Calicut, and receives civil mental patients from Malabar, South Kanara, Coimbatore and the Nilgiris. It has accommodation for 200 male and 62 female patients. The island dispensaries were opened in October and November 1925.

Exclusive of mission, police and railway medical institutions, there are 65 hospitals and dispensaries or one to every 89·2 square miles. The Mission Trust of Southern India maintains a hospital at Calicut and outlying dispensaries at Kodakkal and Chombala. The "Mission to Lepers" maintains the Leper Asylum at Chevayur which has accommodation for 82 men and 32 women, and towards the maintenance of this Asylum Government pay a capitation grant of Rs. 4–8–0 per patient per mensem. There are besides three railway dispensaries at Calicut, Cannanore and Shoranur. There were in the district in 1931, thirteen hospitals entirely run by Government, thirty dispensaries belonging to the local boards in sixteen of which there was accommodation for in-patients, and twenty-two subsidized dispenaries in rural areas (an experiment started in 1925). Seven lakhs and three thousand persons were treated in them for some ailment or other at a total cost of 4·47 lakhs of rupees.

INDIGENOUS MEDICINE.

The district is also noted for the great advance it has made in the teaching and practice of certain indigenous systems of medicine, especially Ayurvedic. There are three colleges attached to vaidyasalas (or hospitals) in this district and in the neighbouring States of Cochin and Travancore, where students are taught the theory and practice of Ayurveda as followed in India from a remote past; and such of those scholars as have not ventured out and settled in other parts of the Presidency as "Malabar" Vydyans, carry on the practice of medicine in their own villages or towns and earn a decent living. There is a great demand for their services among all classes of people. The local boards and municipalities are now establishing Ayurvedic dispensaries in charge of men trained in the Malabar colleges or at the School of Indian Medicine, Madras.

VITAL STATISTICS.

In municipal towns, births and deaths are registered by a special agency; elsewhere the work forms part of the duty of the *adhigari*. The registration is naturally defective. The vital statistics tabulated in the separate Appendix show that between 1893 and 1902 the average annual excess of births over deaths was 4·2 per 1,000. At this rate the population should have increased by 111,407 between 1891 and 1901, but the actual increase recorded by the census was 147,990.

CHAP. IX. VITAL STATISTICS.

The table of vital statistics for the district between 1916–25 showed an average increase of 7·7 of births over deaths which should have given an increase of 23,908 in population in 1921 over that in 1911, but the actual figure was 84,118 which is an indication of defective registration. With the establishment of the Public Health Department in 1925 registration of vital statistics has improved.

Madras Act III of 1899 has been enforced in the three union towns in the district, and Pantalayani amsam in Kurumbranad taluk. Even in these areas, the *adhigaris* continue to be registrars.

Sanitation.

Sanitation in the true sense of the term may be said to be non-existent in Malabar. In the municipal towns, a certain proportion of the council's income has always been set apart for sanitary purposes, but the real reforms which are so urgently required are at present far beyond their limited financial resources. Conservancy systems have been established, and a staff of qualified Inspectors entertained, but the towns are still without effective systems of drainage and water-supply, and their sanitary establishments are usually inadequate. In Calicut, for instance, each sweeper has to attend to seventy houses, a number far beyond his ability to cope with. In the smaller towns, there is no attempt at systematic sanitation except in Kollengode in the Palghat taluk and Beypore in the Calicut taluk, where the private scavenging system has been introduced by the taluk boards. Only in municipal towns are public latrines provided, and even there they are not always used. Elsewhere, domestic sanitary conveniences are non-existent, and the people resort for the purposes of nature to their gardens and hedges or to the banks of channels and rivers. The taluk boards do their best to provide masonry wells with proper platforms where necessary, but the majority of the people live in scattered houses, and are dependent for their water-supply on unprotected wells. No municipality can as yet boast of a protected water-supply or an effective system of drainage. They now employ Health Officers and have provided public latrines in the crowded localities and facilities for the disposal of night soil by trenching and for the sanitary disposal of rubbish.

In the three other towns, Beypore, Kollengode and Ponnani, public latrines have been provided so far as their limited resources permit, but private scavenging exists only on a very limited scale. The only other places where public latrines have been provided are Manantoddy, Vayittiri and Meppady in Wynaad taluk. All taluk boards, except Ernad, maintain a staff of sweepers in the more important villages and bazaars.

GENERAL HEALTH.

The general health of the district is on the whole good, and compares favourably with that of other districts. The rainfall

CHAP. IX. GENERAL HEALTH.

is heavy, and the climate hot and damp. The unhealthy months of the year are those of June, July, August and September, when the south-west monsoon prevails, and the heavy rains bring in their train rheumatism, bronchial affections, diarrhœa and dysentery and other diseases associated with chill and damp.

Charactoristic diseases.

Among the characteristic diseases of Malabar may be mentioned elephantiasis (or, as it is sometimes called from its predilection for the town, Cochin leg), ankylostomiasis (a disease caused by the presence of nematode parasite, *ankylostomium* or *dochmius duodenalis*, in the small intestines), enteric fever and worms. The first two are undoubtedly filarial in origin, and all are most commonly found in the crowded Mappilla towns on the coast in the south of the district, where the shallow wells in the sand are easily polluted by the infiltration of sewage and other poisonous matter. Other common diseases are hydrocele, epithelioma of the cheek and tongue, Malabar itch or ringworm of the body, tubercular affections of the lung and granular ophthalmia.

Cholera.

Outbreaks of cholera are frequent and often assume a severe epidemic form. Mappillas with their filthy habits, their contempt for the most elementary laws of sanitation, and their reluctance to submit to rational methods of treatment, are the chief sufferers, and, when once the disease has obtained a footing in a densely crowded dirty Mappilla town like Ponnani, the difficulty with which it is eradicated is easily imagined. In most municipalities, the Mappilla quarter is, for this reason, a standing menace to the health of the town. Chalil in Tellicherry, the Old Town in Cannanore and Kalvetti in Cochin are cases in point. Cholera usually makes its appearance in the hot months of March, April and May, and dies away with the onset of the rains in June. There does not appear to be any endemic area in the district, infection being usually introduced from the adjoining Cochin State and from Coimbatore district, but when once the disease obtains a footing in the taluks of Ernad, Walavanad and Ponnani, it readily spreads and can only be eradicated with the greatest difficulty. The custom of performing the Maulud ceremony in the house of the deceased immediately after the funeral, and the preservation of the mats used for carrying the dead body to the mosque are two important factors that influence the spread of the disease in this community.

Small-pox.

A yet more frequent visitor is small-pox, which is more prevalent in Malabar than in any other district. This is no doubt due to the backward condition of vaccination. The disease breaks out periodically, and is stamped out only by congregating vaccinators in the infected area.

Vaccination.

Statistics as to vaccination are given in the separate Appendix. As early as 1801, rewards were offered to natives who successfully practised inoculation for small-pox, and in 1803 the Sub-Collectors were directed to exert themselves 'personally to the utmost in persuading the principal inhabitants of the country, who have not had small-pox' to submit to the operation. For a variety of reasons, however, Malabar, in the matter of vaccination, is still the most backward district in the presidency. The vaccinators, as a class, are most indifferent, and their work is harder than on the east coast. There are no villages where the children can be readily collected, and a dozen operations performed in as many minutes. Houses are scattered, and to make up the prescribed tale of work, the vaccinator has often to tramp over large areas. Progress is, however, being made, and in the last ten years a gradual improvement has shown itself.

Vaccination was made compulsory in all the municipalities and in the district exclusive of Wynaad taluk and Attapadi village in 1914, and in 1925 it was extended to a few selected villages in Wynaad taluk also. The municipalities have their own vaccinators who work either under the immediate supervision of their Health Officers or the Civil Surgeons. The rural parts of the district are divided into fifteen ranges each under the supervision of a Health Inspector, who themselves are controlled by the District Health Officer. There are 35 vaccinators in the district, including two reserve men appointed by the District Board. Lymph obtained from the King Institute in Madras is employed.

Plague. In spite of the fact that its frontier touches South Canara, Coorg, Mysore, the Nilgiris and Coimbatore, all of which have at one time or another been infected, plague has never become indigenous in Malabar except in Tellicherry,[1] where it first obtained a footing in March 1906. It is difficult to assign a reason for this immunity. The climate and physical characteristics of the district may be in part responsible, and the establishment of passport stations and observation circles, and other precautionary measures taken by the authorities, have no doubt contributed to the result. Special measures have also been taken in the seaport towns to guard against the introduction of the disease by sea. Up to the end of September 1907 there were in all 213 reported seizures and 173 deaths, of which about 180 cases were considered to be indigenous. It is interesting to note that there was a plague scare in the district more than a century ago. In August 1800, strict quarantine rules were imposed on vessels arriving from 'the Gulf, Red Sea and Arabian Coasts,' lest the plague then raging in Baghdad should be imported into India. Vessels from these ports were required to anchor as far from the shore as possible, and to be inspected by 'a confidential person'

[1] It has since become indigenous in Calicut and Cannanore.

CHAP. IX. GENERAL HEALTH.

before communication with the shore was permitted. Since 1906, the largest number of deaths from plague in any year was 595 (1908). Four localised outbreaks of pneumonic plague have occurred since 1922.

Malarial fever.

Malarial fever prevails in the interior of the district all along the foot of the ghats, and throughout the Wynaad taluk in certain seasons of the year. On the sea-board, it is not at all common. Instituted in 1895, the system of selling quinine through the medium of postal authorities is growing more popular every year. The sales have increased from 104 packets in that year to 825 in 1901–02 and the receipts from Rs. 100–4–0 to Rs. 799–6–0.

Infirmities.

In the census of 1901, the afflicted population of Malabar was returned as 6,610. In other words, of every 10,000 persons nearly 24 were insane, blind, deaf-mutes, or lepers, the presidency average being nearly 21. Blindness is especially common, Anantapur being the only district with a higher percentage. Cherumans and Mukkuvans (fishermen) seem peculiarly prone to the affliction ; the reason in the latter case is probably the constant exposure to the glare of the sun on water. In the census of 1921, the afflicted population of Malabar was returned as 8,048. The number of insanes (1,289) is the largest in any district in the presidency, but so is the population : 3,816 were returned as blind. Only 1,109 persons were reported to be afflicted with leprosy, but this number, although high compared with other districts, is probably a gross underestimate.

Leper and lunatic asylums.

The leper asylums at Palliport and Chevayur have already been alluded to. The former has accommodation for 48 patients, the latter for 40. A lunatic asylum, opened in May 1872, is maintained by Government at Pudiyara near Calicut. The institution, which is intended for natives only, is built on the block system, and has accommodation for 107 males and 36 females. Since 1892, criminal lunatics have been sent to the asylum at Madras.

CHAPTER X.

EDUCATION.

LITERACY—Literacy by castes, religions and taluks. EDUCATIONAL INSTITUTIONS—Colleges—Malabar Christian college—Brennen college—Victoria college, Palghat—The Zamorin's college—High schools—Middle schools—Elementary schools—Female education—Labour Department schools—Panchama schools—Mappilla schools—Training schools—European schools—Industrial schools—Adult schools and rural reconstruction work—Indigenous education—Indigenous school.

CHAP. X. LITERACY.

EDUCATION has made marked progress in Malabar during the last half a century and has more than kept pace with the growth of population. The general percentage of literacy increased from 7 in 1881 to 15 in 1931 and the number of literate women per thousand from 8 to 64. Another feature is the growth of secondary education, and the progress is specially marked during the last fifteen years. The natural aptitude of the higher castes for education and the increased grants given by Government since 1919 for elementary education have been responsible for a great increase in the number of schools and scholars. Elementary schools more than doubled themselves during this period and the secondary schools in the district had the largest number of pupils of any district in the presidency, with 58 schools and 18,000 pupils.

One in every five Malayali men can read and write and six in every hundred women. These proportions are nothing to boast about, but the district continues to occupy the foremost place in the presidency in point of literacy among its people of both sexes. In female education, both elementary and secondary, Malabar takes the highest place, Madras and the Nilgiris being excluded from the calculation for obvious reasons. The urban population of Malabar is remarkably small which makes the prominence of the district in literacy all the more noteworthy.

Literacy in English has also shown great progress, two in every hundred persons being literate in that language.

Literacy by castes, religions, and taluks.

The percentage of literacy would be far higher, were it not for the backwardness of the Mappilla and Cheruman castes. 945 Mappillas and 999 Cherumans out of every 1,000 are illiterate; and, as these two castes between them number more than 37 per cent of the total population, it may almost be said that literacy varies in different parts of the district in inverse ratio with the Mappilla and Cheruman population. For this reason, North

CHAP. X. LITERACY.

Malabar is better educated than South Malabar, and Ernad, the only taluk where Mappillas outnumber Hindus, shares with the Wynaad, a backward tract for special reasons, the unenviable distinction of being the most illiterate taluk in the district. Calicut too owes its low position educationally among the great towns of the presidency chiefly to its swarming Mappilla quarter. But the statement is only partially true, for Palghat, where Mappillas are scarce, is one of the ignorant taluks. As usual, the Christians are more literate than those of other faiths, but it is contrary to the ordinary rule to find in Malabar the Hindus better educated than the Mussalmans. The Eurasians, Nambudiris and Nayars are the most literate castes, and the census figures bring out in strong relief the superiority in education of the Malayalis over their corresponding Tamil castes. The Nambudiri takes the lead of all Brahmans, the Tiyan excels the Shanan, and the Nayars are proportionately seven times as well educated as the Vellalas. After the Eurasians, the Nambudiris and Nayars are the most enlightened castes in the matter of female education in all the presidency, and the Tiyans are surpassed only by Native Christians and by Brahmans of other districts. In Cochin, which is more a town than a taluk and is better educated even than Madras, and in Kottayam, Kurumbranad and Calicut, Malabar has four out of the ten best educated taluks of the presidency. Ernad with 15 per cent literates among males and 3·3 per cent among women and the Wynaad with 15 and 2·2 per cent are still the two most illiterate taluks; and Walavanad and Palghat taluks in the south showed a better record, but North Malabar is more advanced educationally than the South. The Mussalmans who include the large Mappilla population are less educated than the Hindus, which is not the case in other parts of the presidency.

EDUCATIONAL INSTITUTIONS. Colleges.

The four principal educational institutions in the district are the Government Victoria College, Palghat, the Government Brennen College, Tellicherry and the Zamorin's and the Malabar Christian College at Calicut. The first is a first-grade college and the others are second-grade colleges with secondary schools attached to them. The first two are maintained by Government, the third was founded and endowed by the Zamorin of Calicut, and has been handed over to a committee of management. The last which was until recently being managed by the Christian College at Madras has been taken over by the Basel Mission at Calicut.

Malabar Christian Colle

The Basel Evangelical Mission opened a primary school at Kallayi in 1848, which was transferred ten years later to a more spacious building in Calicut, and in 1872 raised to a middle and in 1878 to a high school. The high school developed into a second grade college in 1907. On the breaking out of the Great War of 1914–18, the German missionaries had to give up the work and leave the country; and the college was then being managed by the local Christians, under great financial difficulties, until 1919 when the Madras Christian College took it over. In April 1927 the management of the college was handed back to the Basel Mission.

Brennen College.

The Brennen College, the smallest of the three, is also the oldest. It owes its inception to Mr. Brennen, Master attendant at Tellicherry, who died in 1859 leaving Rs. 12,000 for the foundation of a school to be called the Brennen School, wherein 'persons of all creeds and denominations might receive a sound English education.' Since its opening in 1862, the school has passed through many vicissitudes. Under the Basel German Mission, to which it was first entrusted it was not a success, and in 1872 it became a Zilla School under the direct control of Government. In 1883 and 1884 the middle and high school departments were made over to the municipality for management. The institution was affiliated to the Madras University as a second grade college in 1891, and since then has done very well. The endowment of the college amounts to Rs. 8,900. Its trustees are the Collector and Sub-Collector of Malabar and the Inspector of Schools, Western Circle. The college and the school departments were taken over by Government in June 1919 and the Secondary Training School for masters was amalgamated with it in 1925. A branch school teaching up to the third form has been opened at Tiruvangad.

Victoria College, Palghat.

The Victoria College, Palghat, started life in 1866 as a rate school, but in 1871 was transformed into a local fund high school. In 1877 Government took over charge for some years, but in 1884 they made it over to the municipality. Four years later the school was raised to the rank of a college, and since then it has never looked back. Under Mr. C. M. Barrow, headmaster from 1890 to 1903, it made rapid progress, and became the largest and most successful institution of its kind in Malabar, a position which it still holds. In 1905, Government found the College self-supporting and discontinued their grant. In response to the Palghat municipality's request Government took over the institution in April 1919 and six years later raised it to the first grade, handing over the classes below Form IV to the municipality. In the high school forms attached to the college manual training in wood work and metal work is compulsory and commercial subjects are also taught. The students of the college started a night school in 1926 for the depressed classes, the expenses being met by voluntary subscriptions.

The Zamorin's College.

The Zamorin's College was founded in 1877 as a school for young Rajas under the headmastership of Mr. C. M. Barrow. In the following year it was thrown open to all caste boys, and, in recognition of the 'enlightened and liberal action' of the

CHAP. X. EDUCATIONAL INSTITUTIONS.

Zamorin, the Government of Madras presented the institution with the nucleus of a library and scientific apparatus at a cost of upwards of Rs. 2,000. In 1879 the school was affiliated to the University of Madras as a second-grade college, and as such it has done on the whole excellent work. Till recently the Zamorin or one of the Rajas of the family held the office of manager, but at the beginning of 1904 the management of the college was vested in a board of control. The Zamorin's family now contributes annually to the college, which receives no aid from Government, a sum of Rs. 5,000. In 1915 the college was taken over by the Court of Wards along with the Zamorin's estate; and on its rendition in 1921, its management has been entrusted as before to a committee.

High schools.

High school education in Malabar is primarily a matter of local board and private enterprise. There are two Government secondary schools for boys which are adjuncts of the Brennen and Victoria Colleges and the only municipal high school is maintained by the Cannanore municipality. Local private effort is responsible for thirteen, the District Board for fifteen and Christian Missions for six high schools for boys. All these institutions are in receipt of Government aid. The local board schools were mostly started during the last decade, but some of the mission and private schools can boast of some antiquity. Among the non-mission aided schools are those started by the Venganad Nambidi at Kollengod, the Kudiravattath Prabhakaran Thamban at Ottapalam, the Valia Thambratti of Kizhakke Kovilagam at Kottakkal, the Muthedath Mallisseri Kuberan Nambudiri at Taliparamba, and Kulapathi V. V. Parameswara Ayyar at Palghat. The Raja's High School at Palghat was abolished in 1905 and its place was appropriately taken by the Nellikal Edom school which was started early next year by the senior member of a branch of the Palghat Raja's family (Nellikal Edom, Vendazhi). The Nurni High School at Palghat is another important high school under private management.

The Basel Mission has three high schools, at Palghat, Tellicherry and Badagara and the Roman Catholic Missions have two at Cochin (Santa Cruz) and at Pavartti (St. Joseph's).

Middle schools.

Many of these high schools were originally middle schools and were raised to high school grade to meet the demand for increased facilities for high school education in the respective localities. This has been especially so in the case of local board schools, some of which were first opened as middle schools in these centres where private enterprise had not led to the opening of schools above the elementary grade. Of the existing middle schools one belongs to the local fund, one each to the Palghat and Cannanore municipalities, two to the Basel Mission, two to the Roman Catholic Mission; and three schools are the result of private effort. There were two secondary schools for

Mappillas in Calicut one of which was last year reduced to the higher elementary grade. The expenditure on secondary education in 1930–31 was over Rs. 8 lakhs, of which over Rs. 4·51 lakhs were realized from fees and nearly Rs. 2 lakhs from Government grants.

Elementary schools.

There were in 1931 over 4,126 elementary schools for boys and girls in the district with a strength of 342,000 pupils, the largest for any district in the presidency, Tanjore following with 2,374 schools with 111,098 pupils. Here again private enterprise was responsible for 65 per cent of the schools, and local and municipal effort for 33 per cent. The expenditure on primary education was about Rs. 30 lakhs of which Rs. 4·56 lakhs were met from the public revenues. About 104,790 of the pupils were Muhammadans, mostly Mappillas.

Statistics of upper and lower secondary schools and of primary schools will be found in the separate Appendix. Malabar bids fair to maintain its prominent position in the field of education among the districts of Madras. In the latest year for which statistics are available nearly a quarter of the boys of 'school age' were in the primary stage of instruction, a proportion exceeded , outside of Madras and the Nilgiris, only in Tinnevelly ; and Tanjore was the only district in the mofussal with more boys undergoing secondary education.

Female Education.

Secondary education for girls is largely in the hands of missionaries. But in Malabar a number of girls attended secondary schools for boys, their number in 1931 being 1,207, of whom 81 were attending the school at Ottapalam. The Government Girls' Secondary School at Cannanore has the largest number of pupils and is followed by the Sacred Heart's Girls' School at Tellicherry and the Basel Mission School at Calicut. There is a mission girls' secondary school at Calicut (Roman Catholic), the municipalities of Cochin and Calicut have each a girl's middle school and the district board has two (at Palghat and Badagara) and has opened a third at Ottapalam. Malabar has 566 elementary schools for girls, more than half of which are private aided schools. The total expenditure on secondary and elementary education for girls in 1929 was Rs. 1·05 and 3·76 lakhs, respectively.

Labour Department schools.

The Labour Department of Government had, in 1930–31, 39 elementary schools for the depressed classes in the taluks of Calicut, Palghat, Chirakkal and Kurumbranad in which their activities were concentrated since April 1929. They also maintain a small boarding establishment for the benefit of the poor students of these classes.

Panchama schools.

Cherumans, Parayans, Pulayans, Kuravans, Nayadis, Paniyans and Kuricchiyans have been registered as backward castes in Malabar, but very little is being done for their education. No schools have been opened for aboriginal and

CHAP. X. EDUCATIONAL INSTITUTIONS.

hill tribes such as the two last, and in 1903–04 less than 2½ per cent of Panchamas of 'school age' were under instruction. In this respect Malabar lags behind all other districts except South Canara. The chief difficulties in the way of Panchama education are the almost insurmountable ignorance of castes like the Cherumans, and the reluctance of higher castes to allow them to elevate themselves out of their position of serfs.

Mappilla schools.

The education of the Mappillas, who number a third of the population, is the most difficult problem which the educational authorities have to deal with in Malabar. It has long been recognised that in the long run the best safeguard against the recurrence of Mappilla outbreaks will be the spread of education in the caste, and special efforts, now continued for more than thirty years, have been made to secure this end. In 1871–72 a plan was devised for improving the education imparted to Mappilla children in the small schools then, as now, attached to almost every mosque. At these schools the children received no education worth the name, being taught merely to repeat by rote passages from the Koran. Inducements were held out to the *mullas* to combine with religious training elementary instruction in the vernacular, and took the form of small salaries and grants for each child successful at an inspection held annually by two Muhammadan Inspectors specially appointed for the purpose. Progress was for long exceedingly slow, and as late as 1898 the President of the District Board expressed his conviction that the results were not commensurate with the outlay. The *mullas* were generally incompetent to impart even the small amount of instruction in the vernacular insisted upon. Religious scruples had to be overcome, and in North Malabar, where an alphabet in which Malayalam and Arabic characters were freely and illogically mixed had hitherto been in use, a change to the vernacular was not altogether welcome. But the greatest obstacle of all was and is now the supreme indifference of the Mappilla to secular education. For a time the scheme was worked under the auspices of the local boards; but since 1886 results grants to Mappilla schools have been paid from provincial funds, the distribution being left to the local boards on the understanding that they contribute towards Mappilla education a sum of not less than Rs. 10,000. A gradual improvement then manifested itself; but Mappilla outbreaks still continued, and after that of 1894 the Mappillas of Ernad and Walavanad were officially recognized as a backward caste, and grants at a rate 75 per cent higher than those of the standard scale were provided for them in the Grant-in-Aid Code. Aided schools have been separated as fas as possible from the mosques, and freed from the reactionary influence of the *mullas*. There are now upwards of 280 public schools with pupils numbering more than 16,000 but the census figures quoted above show how little impression has been made upon the dense mass of Mappilla ignorance. It is most unfortunate that Mappillas will not attend primary schools opened for Hindus. There is no language difficulty as in other parts of the presidency; but rightly or wrongly they consider that they are looked down upon by the Hindu castes, and special schools have to be maintained for Mappillas throughout the primary stage of instruction at least. If they could only be induced to attend Hindu schools, not only would they benefit educationally by association with the more eager Hindu youths, but it would be feasible to open schools common to all castes in many places where it is now impossible for financial reasons to maintain separate schools for Hindus and Muhammadans. To give an impetus to the education of the Mappillas a special assistant to the district educational officer was appointed in 1926 and he held office till April 1929, when the district was bifurcated * for educational purposes. Twelve deputy inspectors are working in connexion with Mappilla education, eight of whom are employed in Ernad and Ponnani taluks which have a large number of elementary schools for this community. There were one middle school and one higher elementary school for them in Calicut in 1931 with a strength of 320. The number of elementary schools for Mappillas in 1931 was 1,410 and their total strength 102, 639, and that of the schools for Muslim girls 87 and the number of girls in them and in boys' schools was 4,000. There were besides several night schools for adult Mappillas.

The schools for Mappillas are naturally most numerous in the Ernad, Walavanad and Ponnani taluks. Schemes of compulsory education have been introduced in selected places in them. Government also opened in 1931 a special sessional school to train religious instructors for Mappilla elementary schools. An orphanage and a boarding house have been opened in Calicut by private effort for Mappilla children. Special scholarships in secondary and elementary schools have been increased chiefly to help the poor pupils in the fanatical zones. The indifference to education among the poorer classes of Mappillas still continues though it is steadily being combated by the efforts of the education department.

Training schools. There are eleven training schools for teachers: two of these are at Calicut, two at Tellicherry, two at Cannanore, two at Palghat, one in Malappuram and one at Badagara and one aided school at Nettur maintained by the Basel Evangelical Mission. The schools for men-teachers at Calicut and Tellicherry train teachers of the secondary grade; the former, with the

* The whole district was, however, placed under one Educational Officer, from 1st December 1932 (G.O. No. 1581, Law and Education, dated 29th October 1932).

CHAP. X. EDUCATIONAL INSTITUTIONS.

School of Commerce, is the direct descendant of the provincial school founded at Calicut in 1854, and the latter is attached to the Brennen College. Other Government training schools train teachers of the elementary grade, higher and lower. The Malappuram school is specially intended to train Mappilla teachers, though teachers of that community seek admission in other training schools as well. The mission training school at Nettur trains men for elementary higher-grade teacherships. There are four training schools for school mistresses, all maintained by Government, at Calicut, Tellicherry, Palghat and Cannanore, the last for secondary and the first three for elementary higher and lower grade teachers.

European schools.

The St. Joseph's school at Calicut is the only high school for European boys in the district; it also admits students of other communities. There were 190 European and Anglo-Indian boys in it in 1929 out of a total strength of 260. The same mission has a middle school for them at Cannanore. There are two secondary schools for European and Anglo-Indian girls at Calicut and Cochin, a middle school for girls at Cannanore and a primary school at Cochin, all these schools being run by Roman Catholic nuns.

Industrial schools.

The district continues to be badly off in respect of industrial and technical education. The only two aided industrial schools are the Ariacode Y.M.C.A. Rattan Work School and the Calicut Commonwealth Trust Embroidery School. Manual training classes are attached to the Victoria and Brennen Colleges and to all the Government training schools and to some aided secondary and elementary schools. The Government School* of Commerce is the largest institution of the kind in the presidency and teaches commercial and technical subjects and has several of its old boys holding positions of trust and responsibility in public offices and firms in important towns all over India and even outside it, in Ceylon, Burma, Federated Malay States, Mesopotamia and East Africa. There is an agricultural middle school at Taliparamba in which, in addition to the subjects ordinarily taught in middle schools, instruction in practical agriculture is given. This school is under the agricultural department. The department of fisheries has opened 26 schools for the benefit of the children of fishermen and in these are taught, besides the usual subjects, the technique of their ancestral calling and co-operation and allied subjects.

Adult schools and rural reconstruction work.

A considerable number of night schools for boys and adults have come into existence in recent years. The Servants of India Society is principally responsible for adult education work in Ernad and Ponnani. The Devadhar Malabar Reconstruction Trust, which was started for relief work after the rebel-

* The school was closed in May 1932—Vide G.O. Mis. No. 722 (7-8) Law (Education), dated 14th May 1932.

lion, has been continued as an agency for rural reconstruction and uplift work. Government affords special encouragement to such voluntary effort in the field of adult education.

Indigenous education.

Indigenous education is fast being superseded by education on western lines. There are still a few Arabic schools, and the Muhammadan college attached to the Jamat mosque at Ponnani attracts students from all parts of Malabar. Many Nambudiris too still spend a great part of their youth at the Ottanmar Madam near the Tirunavayi temple. But the village school is yielding place to the primary school, and the *Ezhuttacchan* or village school master is losing his occupation. Among Malayalis education is still connected intimately with religion, and an important ceremony, *Vidyarambham* (p. 169), marks initiation into the mysteries of letters. The education given at village schools is very simple. Boys and girls are taught first to write the letters of the alphabet in sand on the floor of the school, and are then promoted to writing on cadjans. Elementary *slogas* are next committed to memory, and finally from the Amaram, a collection of verses giving the names of all things in heaven and earth. The study of the Puranas, especially the Ramayana, follows; but few get beyond the Amaram.

Indigenous school.

There were in 1929 two colleges and eight recognized schools teaching Sanskrit, with a strength of 52 and 640, respectively; and six of the scholars were girls and in the largest school at Pavaratti a third of the students were Christians. Of Arabic schools there were 172 with a strength of 6,754, all Muhammadans.

CHAPTER XI.

LAND REVENUE ADMINISTRATION.

THE LAND REVENUE SYSTEM. LAND TENURES—Traditional accounts. The Keralolpatti—Early British authorities—Mr. Farmer—Dr. Buchanan—Major Walker—Mr. Thackeray—Mr. Warden—Mr. Logan's theories—Sir W. Robinson's criticisms—Views of Commission of 1884—Sir Charles Turner's minute —Mr. Baden Powell's account—Criticism—Possible Course of evolution—Actual tenures at beginning of 19th century—Waste-lands—Changes between 1793 and 1884—Legal incidents of tenures to day. REVENUE ADMINISTRATION—Sources of revenue of Rajas—First instance of land revenue—Malayali mode of stating extent of lands. EARLY SETTLEMENTS—Mysorean settlement—South Malabar—Palghat taluk—North Malabar—Results of different systems in North and South Malabar—British rule—Quinquennial leases—Smee's Pymash—Macleod's revision of assessments—Mr. Rickards' proposed settlement—The janmi pymash and Hinduvi pymash—Munro's report—Graeme's report—Garden settlement—Abortive wet settlement—*Pugil vivaram* pymash—Reversion to jama of 1800–1—Pre-settlement dry rates. THE SURVEY AND SETTLEMENT—Scheme reports—Delay in introduction—Settlement with janmi—Janmam registration—The garden difficulty—Introduction of the settlement—Principles—Grouping—Wet rates—Dry rates—Garden rates—Average money rates—Financial results—Remission and relinquishment—Re-settlement, 1931–34—Special features—Objections answered—Financial results—WYNAAD—Warden's wet settlement—Its subsequent development—Dry lands—Estates—Wynaad escheat settlement—Principles of revenue settlement—Sanctioned rates—Average rates—Financial results—Settlement with tenant declared illegal—Working of settlement—Relinquishments—Pepper. The Wynaad Resettlement, 1926–27—Special features—Wet lands—Dry lands—Estate lands—General. COCHIN—Early revenue history—Mr. Conolly's settlement—Escheat settlement—Re-settlement. MALABAR ESCHEAT SETTLEMENT—Sale of janmam right—Discontent in Cochin—Mr. Logan's proposals—Escheat quit-rent—Janmabhogam. INAMS. VILLAGE SYSTEM—The Malabar revenue village—The Mysorean system—The amsam system—Its redistribution. DIVISIONAL CHARGES.

CHAP. XI. THE LAND REVENUE SYSTEM.

THE land revenue settlement of Malabar differs from the ordinary ryotwari settlements of the Madras Presidency, in that the existence of a landlord between the State and the actual cultivator has been recognised in the theoretical distribution of the produce, on which the rates of assessment are based. As elsewhere the State claims a share of every crop, and that share commuted to money and called assessment, is a first charge on the land, and is recoverable by the usual processes, including in the last resort the attachment and sale of the land itself. But in fixing the share of the State, account has been taken of the landlord as well as the cultivator.

The reason for this divergence from the ordinary rule can only be explained by an examination of the history of the principal land tenures in the district. Their origin has been

CHAP. XI. THE LAND TENURES.

much debated, and it is impossible to deal with the subject exhaustively within the limits of this book; but it will be desirable to state briefly the different theories which have been put forward.

Traditional accounts.

The traditional accounts are to be found in the vernacular treatises, which, though full of inconsistencies and Brahman bias, seem, as has been remarked in Chapter II [1], to embody to some extent a plausible history of early political development; and in the matter of law are not the less valuable as authorities, because they reflect the theories of the Brahmans, who were the chief makers of the law.

Keralolpatti.

Of the origin of the *janmam* and *kanam* rights, the Keralolpatti says—

"Parasurama created Malayalam, the Keralabhumi, and gave it as a gift to the Brahmans of the 64 *gramams*. The gift of flower and water given to the sixty-four gramams together for their enjoyment is called janmam. That gift was given to the *tarawads* of a *gramam* together and called *Egodagam*. Afterwards he gave the right called Rajamsam to 3,600 Brahmans of ten *gramams* by pouring water on the sword. They can put their finger in water and say this is my *janmam*; but the others may not put their finger in water and say 'this is my *janmam*'; they have only enjoyment.

"Parasurama having sent for Sudras from various countries made them settle and prescribed various rules of conduct for them. He created *adima* and *kudima* in the *desam*, protected *adiyans* and *kudiyans*, established *taras* and *sankethams*, separated the Nayars into *taras* and ordered that to them was to belong the duties of supervising (lit: the eye), executing (lit: the hand) and giving orders, in such a manner that rights should not be curtailed or suffered to fall into disuse. To the *kudiyans* the *kizhkur* (inferior share), to the Brahmans the *melkur* (the superior share); to the former the *kanam*, and to the latter *janmam*; and so the law of *kanam* and *janmam* and the rules of conduct for the Brahmans and custom for the Sudras were ordained."

On these texts the Brahmans support their claim, that they and they alone have always enjoyed the full janmam or proprietary right in the land; and as Brahmans are expressly exempted by Manu from payment of taxes, the tradition is offered as a simple and satisfactory explanation of the absence of any general land revenue in Malabar at the time of the first Mysorean invasion.

Early British authorities—Mr. Farmer.

The Brahman tradition was accepted generally by the early British administration, but they were more concerned with giving an accurate account of the land tenures as they found them, than with speculating about their origin. Mr. Farmer [2],

[1] *Vide* p. 40.

[2] Mr. Farmer's report (Voucher No. 39) to the Bombay Presidency, dated 25th February 1793.

CHAP. XI. THE LAND TENURES.

one of the first "Commissioners for inspecting the countries ceded by Tippu Sultan," reported in 1793 that the possessors of land were said to be of two descriptions—

"1st *Jelm-kaars* or free holders who hold their lands either by purchase or by hereditary descent.

"2nd *Kanoom-kaars* or mortgagees, to whom an actual delivery of the land appeared to be made, although the money taken upon it was not at all proportioned to the value of the land . . . . .

"Many of the Raja's principal Nayars and Nambudiris holding estates at a distance from their residence, or holding more land than they chose to attend to the cultivation of, were necessitated to farm them out to others, at a certain fixed rent settled between the parties, and for the security of the land-lord, or Jelm-kaar, the following regulation seems generally to have been observed in the Malleam."

"The farmer, called Kanoom-kaar, deposited with the landlord a certain sum to remain with him as a pledge for the due payment of the stipulated rent; on this sum an interest was allowed to the Kanoom-kaar or farmer, who might perhaps frequently be obliged to borrow the money on other pledges; after deducting the amount of this interest from the *pattom* or rent agreed on, the difference was paid to the Jelm-kaar or landlord."

Dr. Buchanan.

Dr. Buchanan,[1] a most careful enquirer, wrote in 1800:—'

"I have already mentioned that the Nambudiris pretend to have been possessed of all the landed property of Malayala ever since its creation; and in fact it is well known that before the conquest by Hyder, they were the actual lords of the whole soil, except some small parts appropriated to the support of religious ceremonies, and called Devastanam, and other portions called Cherical, which were appropriate for supporting the families of the Rajas. All the remainder, forming by far the greater part, was the janm or property of the Numbudiri Brahmans; and this right was, and by them is, still considered as unalienable; nor will they allow that any other person can with propriety be called a Janmcar or proprietor of land. As, however, both duty and inclination prevented the Numbudiris from attending to the management of their lands, they took various means of obtaining an income from the Sudras, to whom they granted a temporary right of occupancy."

He proceeded to give the details of the various tenures, showing that, at the time he wrote, their incidents had become more or less definitely settled, and that the terms of the contracts in each case were usually reduced to writing.

Major Walker.

In 1801 an elaborate treatise on the several forms of conveyance and lease then in use was prepared by Major Walker. He derived his information mainly from Brahmans, and drew largely from the Vyavahara Mala, a Sanskrit legal manual; but

[1] Buchanan's *Journey through Mysore, Malabar and Canara*, Vol. II, p. 360.

CHAP. XI. THE LAND TENURES.

that does not diminish the value of the details, which he collected, of the practice of the day. He concludes his treatise [1] as follows :—

"The jenma-karan possesses entire right to the soil and no earthly authority can with justice deprive him of it. But his right is confined to the property, and he possesses neither judicial nor political authority . . . ."

"In no country in the world is the nature of this species of property better understood than in Malabar, nor its rights more tenaciously maintained. It is probable that the possession of jenmam land was originally unalienable and confined to one or two castes. At present, however, any person possessed of money may become a purchaser of jenmam. It is still more probable that this possession was exempt from any direct burden except military service. There seems to have been no regular tax anterior to the Mahommedan invasion. The Rajas were supported by the produce of their own lands and by certain fugitive forfeits or immunities which were more singular than advantageous. In cases of public necessity, they might have recourse to the voluntary or constrained assistance of their subjects ; but their power was very limited, and it was seldom that they could more from a jealous and discordant aristocracy than a short personal service . . ."

"It is obvious from the tenor of the deeds that considerable provision has been made in Malabar for the security of landed property . . . In all the stages of conveyance, the most watchful jealousy is observed, to prevent the possession being loaded with additional engagements, and to save it from total alienation. The conditions of each step are the subject of a new writing in which they are recorded with precision . . . . . . In the inferior tenures, which only convey a temporary possession, there appears an equal attention to the interests of the proprietor and of the tenant . . . . . . Few or none of these tenures are simple. They unite almost in every case the consideration of mortgage and rent, and in this they discover that distrust and want of confidence peculiar to infant societies, when a pledge is the most natural security for property ; another proof of the great antiquity of these institutions."

Mr. Thackeray.

The accounts of Mr. Thackeray, who reported on the land tenure in 1807, and Mr. Warden, who was Collector of Malabar for twelve years from 1804 to 1816, are to the same effect.

"Almost the whole of the land in Malabar, cultivated and uncultivated, is private property and held by jenmam right, which conveys full absolute property in the soil. We find the land occupied by a set of men, who have had possession, time out of mind ; we find that they have enjoyed a landlord's rent, that they have pledged it for large sums, which they borrowed on the security of the land, and that it has been taken as good security; so that at this day, a very large sum is due to creditors to whom the land is mortgaged . . . The deeds which serve to record these transactions are drawn out in apeculiar character, which may be termed the black letter of Malabar . . . . There is no proof that

[1] Major Walker's *Report on the Land Tenures of Malabar*, 1801,

CHAP. XI. THE LAND TENURES.

any land-tax existed in Malabar before Hyder's invasion. The proprietors were bound to render military service and were liable to contribute 2 per cent in case of invasion. The pagodas and Rajas had lands of their own; the Rajas had other sources of revenue from fines, imports, personal taxes and plunder which were sufficient to support them."[1]

Mr. Warden.

"The *jenm* right of Malabar vests in the holder an absolute property in the soil. *Kanamkar* is a mortgagee, or one who has land pledged to him in security for the interest of money advanced to the jenmkar, which advance is the kanam that is ever incumbent on the land until it be redeemed. . . . The peculiarity of the kanam or Malabar mortgage is that it is never foreclosed, but is redeemable after the lapse of any number of years. The quantum of money lent characterises the different gradations of the kanam tenure. Their variety and numbers till they reach the deed which for ever alienates the jenm afford the most conclusive evidence that can be adduced of the tenacity with which the ancient land holders cling to their jenm right . . . It was a prerogative (and is still claimed), inherent in the jenm right, that the kanamkar should renew his kanam deed after the lapse of a certain number of years. The renewal entitled the jenmkar to a remission of a fixed percentage on his original debt. . . There is no such thing as an established division of the produce in shares between jenmkar and tenant."[2]

On these reports the Government acted in considering the principles on which the land revenue should be settled; and the Civil Courts similarly, accepting the position that the janmi was the *dominus* or the landlord in the English sense, proceeded gradually to define the legal incidents of the various tenancies.

Mr. Logan's theories.

The first serious attempt to question the correctness of the position was made by Mr. Logan in his report on the land tenures of Malabar, which he prepared, when appointed in 1884 as Special Commissioner, to enquire into tenant right in connection with Mappilla disturbances. He refused to accept the theory of a Brahman theocracy and monopoly of land; but emphasizing the importance of the function assigned by the Keralolpatti to the Nayars, and relying on some doubtful interpretations of the Syrian copper-plate grants and other documents which he had collected,[3] developed a theory, which, briefly stated, is that *janmam* and *kanam* were originally political offices, conveying each a right to a definite customary share of the produce; and that rights of property in the soil were imperfectly developed even at the time of the Mysorean invasion.

Early social system.

"The unit of the Hindu social system was the family, not the individual. An association of families formed a body corporate, as, for example, the *gramam* (village) among the Brahmans, the *tara* (foundation street, village) among the Nayars, the *cheri* (assemblage, village, street) among the Tiyar (Cingalese, islanders) and

---

[1] Mr. Thackeray's report to the Board of Revenue, dated 4th August 1807.

[2] Mr. Warden's report to the Board of Revenue, dated 12th September 1815.

[3] See Logan's *Malabar Manual*, Vol. II, Appendix XII.

other foreigners . . . These guilds or corporate bodies had each distinct functions to perform in the body politic, and those functions were in old times strictly hereditary. . . . The Nayars were, as the Keralolpatti expressly says, the people of 'the eye,' 'the hand' and 'the order' and it was their duty 'to prevent the rights from being curtailed or suffered to fall into disuse. The word *kanam* comes from the Dravidian verb *kanuka* (= to see or to be seen) and the root from which that verb is derived is kan (= the eye) . . . . so that *kanam* in its original sense seems to have denoted this function of theirs in the body politic . . . . But what was this supervision right (kanam)? The *kon* (shepherd, King) and the *pati* (Lord, Master) had shares of the produce due to them as the persons of authority in the land. And the specific words used in the ninth century A.D. to denote these shares have probably survived to the present day and are still in common use in a contracted form as pattom. For pattom seems to be a compound word signifying the *padu* (= authority's) *varam* (share) . . . . The Nayars were no doubt spread over the whole face of the country (as they still are) protecting all rights, suffering none to fall into disus, and at the same time supervising the cultivation of the land and collecting the kon or king's share of the produce, the public land revenue in fact. . . .

"In order to understand the Malayali land tenures aright it is therefore first of all necessary to realise the fundamental idea that certain castes or classes in the State were told off to the work of cultivation and the land was made over to them in trust for that purpose, and in trust that the shares of produce due to the persons in authority should be faithfully surrendered.

"The next most important point to keep in remembrance in regard to Malayali tenures is the fact that from the earliest times grants of land by the ruling power were customary, and what those grants conveyed requires to be examined attentively.

Early grants system.

"In the first place the grants were of a hereditary character. This is fully borne out by the earliest deeds. The distinctive phrase used was *peru*. It occurs in various combinations—Viduper, Attiperu, Attipettola, Perumarthan, Epperpettattu, etc. *Peru* itself is the verbal noun of the verb *peruka* (= to bring forth) and it means birth. The word has fallen into disuse of recent years and it has been supplanted by its Sanskrit equivalent *janmam*, which coming from the root *jan* also signifies birth. Both words when applied in speaking of land tenures conveyed the idea of hereditary grants. . . ."

"In regard to the next and perhaps the most important point of all, the sharing of the produce in these hereditary holdings, much has already been said, and it is needless to say more here than that all the State functionaries employed had well-defined shares of the produce set apart for them. The *kon* or king had his share. The *pati* or overlord (the hereditary grantee apparently if there chanced to be one) had likewise a share. And if there was no such *pati* or hereditary grantee, then it seems his share went to the general body of protectors and supervisors—the 'six hundred,' the Nayar guild the kanakar. . . .

"But when the right of the Perumals came suddenly to an end, their (the kon's) share of the produce was, in Malabar at least, certainly not passed on to the chieftains who in some measure supplied the Perumal's place. . . . These chieftains certainly had revenues from their demesne lands, but from the lands of the bulk of those subject to them they certainly levied nothing. The chieftains were hereditary holders (janmis) of the lands from which they derived a share of the produce, and on the other hand the bulk of their subjects—the headmen of the Nayar protector guild—had likewise become hereditary holders (janmis) of their own lands by usurping the kon's share of the produce. This is the only explanation which accounts for the state of the facts at the time of the conquest of Malabar, and moreover it is a very natural explanation . . . .

"In Malabar the hereditary property (janman) was freely bought and sold, long before the Mysorean invasion took place. And it was this buying and selling, and in particular the wording of the deeds in which such transactions were recorded, that misled the early British Administrators and caused them to form erroneous views on the general subject of the Malayali land tenures. . . . The things enumerated (stones, thorns, snakes, holes, treasure, wells, skies, streams, forests, paths, lower world, etc.) seem at first sight to have been named purposely to express, with exaggerated force, the completeness of the relinquishment of the seller's right in the soil. But with these material objects were conveyed such things as 'authority in the Desam,' 'Battle wager' and 'Rank' and 'Customs' which are clearly outside the idea of *dominium* as understood by Roman lawyers. . . The idea of property in the soil—the Western or European idea—was evidently not the idea uppermost in the minds of the persons who executed these deeds. What in fact they were buying and selling was not the soil, but a position with emoluments (in Malayalam) *Stanam Manam*) conferring authority of different kinds and of varying degrees ŏver the classes resident within the limits specially laid down in the deeds . . . If the fundamental idea of the Malayali land tenures is borne in mind, namely, that the land was made over in trust to certain classes for cultivation, the above will be seen to be a most natural out-come of the Hindu system.

The Kanam.

"While on the one hand therefore it is erroneous to suppose that the janmi was the dominus, it is equally inaccurate, on the other hand, to say of the kanakkar or supervisors that they were the real proprietors of the soil . . . The Nayar kanakkar collected the share of the produce due to the janmi. But janmis were at times hard pressed for coin and it became customary for them to borrow what money they wanted from the kanakkar. In proportion to the sum borrowed the kanakkaran deducted, from the pattam (*i.e.*, the *padu* or authority's, *varam* or share) collected by him for the janmil a quantity of produce sufficient to meet the interest on the sum lent. The interest was calculated at certain customary rates and the balance of produce alone went to the janmi. . . . What he pledged was evidently not the soil itself but only his share of its produce so far as that went, and after that his other income and emoluments attaching to his status as janmi of the land. But the Civil Courts, acting on the idea that the janmi was a dominus and as such entitled to take what he could get out of the land, viewed his pledges as pledges of the soil itself, and in this way they have almost completely upset the native system of customary sharing of the produce.

CHAP. XI. THE LAND TENURES.

"Under that system of customary sharing of the produce, the kanakkaran's advance to the janmi used to be periodically revised in one or other of two ways, namely :—

"(a) A deduction of about thirteen per cent of the advance was made, and a renewal deed showing the loan diminished by this percentage was prepared, or

"(b) No deduction was made, but instead of it the kanakkaran made to the janmi a payment equivalent to the customary deduction described in (a) and the renewed deed showed the full original sum advanced. . . . .

"The latter method (b) is that which has generally been adopted, and the periodical renewal fees—now however extravagantly enhanced, amounting in the most favourable cases to about twenty-five per cent of the mortgage advance—form one of the regular sources of a janmi's income. The idea at the root of this system of renewals was that in due course of time the janmi's customary share of the produce should be freed from the mortgage with mutual advantage both to the janmi and to the kanakkaran. If, on the other hand, it was to their mutual advantage to maintain the existing relations, the payment made in lieu of the customary deduction was of advantage to both of them. The system was admirably conceived for binding the two classes together in harmonious interdependence. . . . . . . When after a series of renewals by the method (a) described above, the Janmam holding had been freed from mortgage, the parties (janmi and kanakkaran) simply resumed their original stations. The kanakkaran began to yield up again to the janmi the whole of the janmi's customary share, as he had been in the habit of doing before the loan had been made, and remained on the holding in his capacity as supervisor (kanakkaran)."[1]

Sir W. Robinson.

Sir W. Robinson criticised Mr. Logan's history and etymology; and argued that in Malabar private property in land was an old established institution quite distinct from political office, and that proprietary rights were, before the Mysorean invasion, distributed among *janmis, kanandars* and *verumpattamdars,* all of whom paid land revenue (*pattam*). The term *janmi* did not, he considered, in itself connote any rights of property in land; but was properly a title attaching to certain families, and indicative of many social, territorial and taxationary privileges.

"The organization of the country for agrarian, civil, social and administrative purposes, was the ordinary Hindu type, and intimately allied to that of Tamul nationalities, the cradle of its races, languages and institutions. It rested on the village system in its truest and least disturbed form. There were the *tara* and *che·i* (Tamul) and later the *deshom* and *uldeshom* (village and hamlet), with its institutions of headman (*pati, Deshadhepati,*

[1] Logan's *Malabar Manual,* Vol. I, pp. 506–606.

CHAP. XI. THE LAND TENURES.

Deswali, etc.), hereditary village servants (*Cheri-janmakar* and village *Panchayet* or *Kuttam*); there were the *vattoms* or village circles of Tamul countries, possibly with their official organization, for revenue registration and record; there probably existed—in many parts of the country at least—the *kaveli* system of police and watch and ward, common to all South Indian populations, with its *kavelgars* of many grades down to the village watch, and its grain fees, etc., etc., there were the ordinary village pious uses, and wider religious orders and personages (Nambudiris, etc.) and institutions with their usual privileges. And finally there were the independent native princes, with their large private properties and usual sources of public income and taxation—with their occasional and latterly (during the last and probably the previous century, at least) very active levies of the inhabitants for aggressive and defensive purposes amongst themselves and against external menace. With these probably rested, in the main, the guidance of the revenue system and assessment (*pattam*) of the properties of their subjects, such as it was from time to time within their respective territories, and the exercise of the usual functions which belonged to the position under ordinary Hindu conditions.

"All land was private property, with all the legal incidents of inheritance, sale, etc.; and it was distributed amongst a multitude of prescriptive ryotwari landholders and 'proprietors' of various classes and conditions from the native ruler, noble and religious institution, with their large estates tilled by their predial slaves and under-tenants (*Kudian*), down to the *Verumpattakar* or hereditary occupant (the *Mulguenigar* of Canara and *Ulkudi* of Tamil countries), who were more or less directly in account (*warg* of Canara) with the State in respect of their fixed and moderate revenue demand. These paid what was equivalent to a prescriptive and more or less fixed land revenue (*pattom*, *janmi-pattom*, *kanom-pattom*, *nigudi-pattom* or the like) assessed on fixed, moderate and mutually recognized principles on their holdings, to the State for the time being or to some assignee or representative of the ruler's rights. At the same time there were under the native rulers privileged classes, institutions and persons whose properties remained—for pious reasons, exigencies of warlike calls on them, such as became heavy during later centuries and other causes—unassessed and untaxed until the Muhammadan conquest supervened, and placed all on equal footing in this respect . . . . . Practically what we have to do with in Malabar is the dethroned native 'ruler and others who had possessed rights of taxing their fellow-subjects' private properties, self-constituted as Zamindars."[1]

The Commission of 1884. The Commission appointed to consider Mr. Logan's report did not accept all his theories; but they agreed with him in holding that the *kanamdars* had, before the British Courts interfered, permanent rights of occupancy. They assigned to the *kudian*, or occupant, the hereditary rights of the ryot who first clears the land; and to the *janmi*, the rights of the ruler who claims a share in the produce.

---

[1] Report of the Malabar Land Tenures Committee, pp. 85 to 87. (Madras Government Press, 1887.)

CHAP. XI. THE LAND TENURES.

"Both the *pattam* and the *kanam* were, we believe, originally revenue and not rent—revenue paid to the public purse by the hereditary raiyat or *kudian*. In the political history of Malabar, one fact at least is supported by a considerable amount of evidence, *viz.*, that lands were originally held free of rent and taxes, and that in times of public exigency the Rajas levied a tax of one-fifth of the produce on all lands except those appertaining to the temples. This then was the *pattam* or share of the *pad*, *i.e.*, the paramount authority. It may perhaps be said that the lands were held free of rent or taxes on condition of performing military service; but so far as the evidence goes, this liability to military service was purely a personal liability, and had nothing to do with the land.

"The *kanam* (money secured on the land) may not improbably have originally been the contribution levied on extraordinary occasions by the Rajas, which was treated not as a land-tax but as a loan.

"The practice of levying a periodical fine for the renewal of a *kanam* was really in the nature of a succession duty (*Purushantaram*). The fine was payable at the death of janmi and at the death of the kanamdar, or once in twelve years at the feast of Mahamakam at Tirunavayi, when, the parties having met together, the old document was torn up and a new document substituted (*policheluttu*). That the janmi had, however, the power to refuse the renewal at his own caprice is a proposition to which we are unable to assent.

"Non-payment of the janmi's customary share, non-payment of renewal fees, neglect to cultivate, and perhaps the inability of the kudian to advance further sums of money to his janmi, may have been considered adequate grounds of forfeiture, but not a simple desire on the part of the janmi to favour another kudian.

"So long as he behaved himself and acted up to the unwritten law of custom, the *pattamkar*, whether he held on *kanam-pattam* or *verum-pattam*, was practically the settled occupant of the land having as much right to the customary share of the produce, as the janmi had to his. . . .

"It is possible that the relations of the two classes were slowly but steadily tending towards the independence of the janmi and the dependence of the kudian. The janmi may have had full *dominium* over some lands either because there was no settled kudian, and he cultivated them by means of his slaves; or because as kudian he has purchased the janmam, and the two rights became merged into one. All that we maintain is, that at no period had the relations of the janmi and the kudian reached that stage of development, that it was proper to apply to them literally the terms landlord and tenant, and that at all events as regards the bulk of the old Nayar kudians, the ancient custom had never been lost sight of."[1]

Sir Charles Turner.

The theories put forward by Mr. Logan and the Commission were subjected to a trenchant criticism by Sir Charles Turner, then Chief Justice, who pointed out the slender basis on which they rested and emphasized the authority due to the early

[1] Report on Malabar Land Tenures, p. 122. (G.O. No. 500, Political, dated 29th July 1884.)

CHAP. XI
THE LAND TENURES.

reports. Many of his arguments are conclusive, and his minute deserves to be quoted at some length. After referring to the early organization of Malabar society and alluding to the predominant influence of Brahmanism, as evidenced to-day by the Nayar marriage customs, the strict regard paid to caste, and the very large endowments of religious institutious, he proceeded :

Property in land.

"Mr. Logan not only denies that there was any such thing as absolute property in land in Malabar . . . but goes so far as to assert that while 'the Europeans look to the soil, the soil and nothing but the soil, the Hindus on the other hand, at any rate in Malabar, look to the people, the people and nothing but the people located in the soil.'

"Whatever may have been the case in Malabar there is no doubt that Hindu (*i.e.*, Brahminical) law recognized the private ownership of land . . . The Hindu law exhibited so much regard for this form of property that it imposed more than ordinary restraints on the power of the manager of the family to alienate it, and every sale of the whole ownership of land in ancient times took the form of gift . . . It was also required or recommended that the sale should be attested by the heir, kinsmen, neighbours, an officer of the sovereign, and the scribe . . . The Hindu law also recognized a multiplicity of forms of mortgage, some extending to the usufruct of land, others to the actual ownership . . .

"Mr. Logan admits that some of the deeds which he has collected 'express with exaggerated force, the completeness of the relinquishment and of the acquisition of the rights conveyed' . . . and that 'at first sight it looks as if the soil and all above and below it (the soil), from the highest point of heaven to the lowest depths of the earth, were the objects conveyed, and that the parties had purposely employed words to show how complete the dominion was that has thus been bought and sold.' I do not understand on what principle we are to repudiate the expressions which the parties have themselves used in these deeds as indicative of the interests with which they intended to deal. They proposed to sell not only the surface of the soil within defined boundaries but stones good or bad, stumps of nux-vomica, thorns, roots, pits, mounds, treasure, low earth, water, ores, boundaries, field ridges, canals, washing places, foot paths, streams, deer forests, shady places for honey, etc., and in some cases rights which may be termed manorial . . . Now if these words had any meaning, and we may presume they had, they point to an ownership of the soil as complete as was ever enjoyed by a free-holder in England. Private property in the soil is not inconsistent with payment of a land tax to the Government, nor is it inconsistent with the existence on the soil of persons who may have subordinate rights, or of village artificers who receive for the services they render a customary dole at the time of harvest or a rent-free holding . . .

"It appears to me impossible to resist the conclusion that whatever the origin of the title, the janmis were, and for centuries before Britishrule had been, the owners of the soil in full proprietary right; and that their rights were recognized even by the class that would have been most hostile to them, the Mappillas, who owing to the persecution of Tippu, had for some years been the masters of the situation. Indeed this seems to be admitted by Mr. Logan; for he notices that when the janmis fled the country, they received considerable advances in money from their Mappilla tenants.

"I have, I hope, established that Hindu law allowed almost as complete a property in land as is recognised in England and that although in many parts of India this right had become practically valueless when the country passed under our rule, it subsisted in full vigour in Malabar prior to the Muhammadan invasion, probably for the reason that revenue was raised if at all only occasionally by an assessment of the produce."

Absence of land revenue.

On the question of the absence of a general land revenue he wrote as follows :—

"The absence of land revenue, which appeared to the early enquirers and to the Court of Directors so extraordinary, is explained on the hypothesis that the Brahmin whom the Hindu law declared free from tax was the owner of the soil. I do not, of course, intend to assert that the janmam right had at any time been enjoyed in all the land by the Brahmin. It is probable that some of the land was held throughout by Nayars, but these and the Mappillas who were in possession as janmis when the District was ceded by Tippu claimed the same completeness of ownership as was claimed by the Brahmins.

"So far as I can understand Mr. Logan's theory, he regards the pattom received by the janmi as the land revenue, and this is also the view supported by the Committee and by Sir William Robinson. If this were so, it would point to the existence at some time or other of a Brahminical oligarchy which had constituted itself the sovereign of the soil and had retained the land revenue after it had lost other rights of sovereignty or, to a very general dedication of the land revenue as an inam to the Brahmins; but I cannot say that I find any sufficient evidence to support either suggestion. The earliest instance we have of the payment of a land tax in Malabar occurs in 1731 to 1732 when the dominions of the Raja of Kolateri were invaded by the Bednur Raja's forces, and the Kolateri Raja in consequence imposed a tax of 20 per cent on the pattoms of all rice lands. It will be noticed that the tax was not the pattom, but was taken out of the pattom; and it could be taken from no other source, for the cultivator received little more from the land than would induce a tenant to cultivate it . . .

"I am satisfied that for some hundreds of years the term pattom has been used in Malabar as meaning neither more nor less than rent, while the land revenue is invariably termed Nigadi, and this is a further argument as to its origin, for Nigadi is a corruption of Muhammadan term Nakel."

The Kanam.

He then discussed the *Kanam* tenure at length :—

"I now come to the kanam. Mr. Logan observes that the term kanam applied to this tenure is comparatively recent. If by comparatively he means within the last 300 or 400 years he is possibly right. But the tenure itself was known antecedently to that period under the more ancient but analogous names of Abhayya, Abhayya Pattola Karmam or simply Pattola Karmam.

"The term Abhayya (literally without fear) means an assurance of safety, security, thus Abhayya Patra is a safe conduct and Pattola Karmam is a written deed of lease. From these names we may, I think, form a pretty accurate opinion both of the antiquity and of the nature of the tenure . . . .

"It may well be imagined that in Malabar where the central authority was certainly for many centuries weak, and each division of the country from time to time involved in war with the other, the landlord felt it necessary to obtain some security from his tenant. A tenant could escape without much difficulty into a neighbouring jurisdiction where it would be difficult if not impossible, for the landlord to follow him and exact his dues; and the view that the kanam was a security for the rent, so far from being as Mr. Logan suggests, a modern one, is supported not only by the opinions of the earliest enquirers but by the ancient name of the instrument by which the tenure was created, and by the purpose which it is represented as serving in the Malayalam treatises . . . .

"The conclusions which I draw from the Malayalam text-books and the information acquired by the English officers, is that originally the kanam tenure was a tenure with a payment of rent in advance,but that advantage was taken of it for the purpose of raising money on loan . . . .

"That the kanam was periodically renewed is admitted by the Committee. . . The renewal entitled the janmkar to a remission of a fixed percentage on the original debt. . . The renewal fee was devised to meet this result . . . If the landlord had no desire to reduce the charge or the tenant wished to continue the security which the indebtedness of his landlord assured to him, the obvious course was that tenant should pay an amount equal to the reduction o which the landlord was entitled.

"The right to insist upon a renewal does not of course necessarily involve the absolute right of resumption. The practice of renewals might have been introduced only that the parties might readjust their rights at certain definite periods, but there is abundant evidence to show that the janmi also possessed the right to resume. It is shown by the Proclamation of the Joint Commissioners in 1793 and asserted by Dr. Buchanan and Mr. Warden . . . .

"Much difference was found to exist, probably owing to varying local usage, as to the length of the term for which the kanam was granted. According to Mr. Walker, it endured for from 3 to 6 years. Mr. Farmer mentions that such leases were in general for from 3 to 5 years, and that it was only when the owners of land wanted to borrow a considerable sum of money that longer leases were granted from 20 to 25 years or for life. Mr. Graeme states that in North Malabar the kanam was renewed every 3 or 4 years. If, as I believe to be the case, the kanam was resumable the court conferred a great boon on the kanamkar when they held that the term of a kanam in the absence of special contract was 12 years. . . . ."

He concluded:

"I have not entered on a discussion of the deeds collected by Mr. Logan, because on those points on which he bases his arguments there is very much reason to doubt whether Mr. Logan's translations are accurate. So far as the construction of these deeds is undisputed, they entirely coincide with what was for more than 80 years the unanimous opinion regarding land tenures in Malabar. I have only to observe that we find a marked difference between deeds which purport to deal with janm or full proprietary rights and deeds which create inferior interests. We find the janmis when they profess to sell their janm rights, describe it in terms which would apply only to the most complete interest in the soil. We find a recognition of various tenures, some for terms of years and others in perpetuity, and the conversion of one tenure into the other. We find an inam created by a Rajah of the rent reserved on a plough right in perpetuity (Arikaraima), and of his right to levy taxes and percentages on the transfer of janmam property. And we find deeds which are identical in their substance with the kanam deeds of the present day."[1]

Mr. Bad Powell

It remains to notice the account of the Malabar land tenures given by Mr. Baden Powell in his *Land Systems of British India*. Though he does not accept Mr. Logan's etymologies, he relies to a large extent on his history, and endeavours to show that the claim to *janmam* right is an instance of the phenomenon common in India, of Rajas or chiefs who were originally rulers and claimed only revenue, without interfering with the proprietary title of the original soil occupants, gradually, as their rule is weakened by invasion or conquest, assuming the rights of landlords and demanding rent. The early organization into *taras* and *nads*, as described by Mr. Logan, is, he considers, typically Dravidian ; and the next stage, the introduction of a King (Kon, Perumal), to whom a land revenue is assigned, is in accordance with the custom common to Dravidians and Aryans. The petty chiefs, who succeeded to the Perumal, claimed no general land revenue, and were content with demesnes, feudal services and miscellaneous revenues ; but with the Mysorean conquest, a general land revenue was reintroduced, and the petty chiefs became landlords or zamindars, in their turn paying revenue.

"The whole process of the growth of the landlord right then reduces itself to an evolutionary process, which is in all essentials the same as that taken place in other parts of India. The Dravidian adopting Aryan ideas, and perhaps, in return, suggesting his own ideas to the Aryan, establishes a kingdom in which the rulers and chiefs are military castemen, the advisers Brahmans. The inferior castes who are above the status of slaves or serfs are first settled in their localities, holding undisturbed (as proprietors if it please us to say so) the cultivated plots which they cleared from the jungle, but paying a part of the produce to the king or to some local chief or immediate overlord. As long as there is a powerful sovereign or overlord he keeps the subordinate military in feudal subjection ; they were content with their places in council, the privileges of rank,

[1] Chapters II and III of Sir Charles Turner's *Minute on the draft bill relating to the Land Tenures of Malabar.*

CHAP. XI. THE LAND TENURES.

the right to special dues from estates granted to them or the perquisites of headship over the Governmental groups of territory, the desam and the Nad. In time the supreme ruler ceases to exist and the country is then held in small groups or estates by the chief Nayars, while the smaller men are content to hold lands under the chiefs as privileged tenants or on terms of the kanam ; inferior castemen are reduced to being tenants. In this stage there is no one to collect any general revenue. Each chief lives on the produce or grain-share of his own demesne and on the payments of the smaller landholders whom he has now made his subjects. . . . .

"Then comes the Mysore conquest and the disruption of the ruling chiefships. As many of the Nayars as can do so cling to their ancestral lands, no longer as rulers or as official heads of districts and subdivisions, but as landlords inventing terms to signify their claim to the soil . . . .

"Lastly comes the British power, and finding the landholders making such claims, and misled by names into supposing these rights to be something really ancient and exceptional, not only recognises the proprietorship (which as it was practically established, was the obviously right thing to do), but further accepts totally unfounded theories about the perfection and antiquity and exceptional character of the right, whereby the claim of the State to the forest and unoccupied waste which has elsewhere been properly asserted has been lost."[1]

Criticism.

The objection to Mr. Baden Powell's theory is that it is based largely on incorrect and doubtful assertions. It rests in the first place on the position that there was a general land revenue and an organized system for its collection in the time of the Perumals. There is no proof that this was so. Nor is there any evidence that the landlords, who claimed *janmam* rights at the time of the Mysorean invasion, based their claims on the fact that they represented the chiefs, who succeeded the Perumals as rulers. The deeds of the fifteenth and sixteenth centuries collected by Mr. Logan[2] go to show that, at that time, the "perquisites of headship" might be held by Nambudiri Brahmans ; that property in land pure and simple, unconnected with any political office, might vest in persons who were not Brahmans or Rajas or officials in any sense ; and that Rajas, Nambudiris, and private persons were all equally competent to grant leases of their private lands on definite rents and for definite periods set out in written documents. But they show no trace of the existence of a State land revenue.

Nor is it inconceivable that such a system of land-holding should have been evolved from what is supposed to be the type of primitive Aryo-Dravidian tribal organization—an aggregate of villages under a chief, each village being an aggregate of the family holdings of the original cultivators, with special allotments for the priest and temple and for the chief. The normal development from this to the village of ryotwari holdings, each

---

[1] Baden Powell, *The Land Systems of British India*, pp. 157 *et seq.*

[2] See Logan's *Malabar Manual*, Vol. II, Appendix XII.

CHAP. XI. THE LAND TENURES.

paying a share of the produce to the king, would naturally be arrested by the peculiar conditions of Malabar. The physical features of the country would in themselves go far to prevent the formation of village communities; the martial spirit and organization of the Nayars would militate against the establishment of any strong central Government or system of land revenue; and the matriarchal family system and supreme influence of the Nambudiris would tend both to the preservation of large family estates, and to the accumulation of land in the hands of Brahmans and temple trustees. On the other hand, with a Government organized on a military basis, it would be natural for the Nayar janmi to hold his lands free of State revenue on condition of supplying his Raja with men; and the prevalence of the *kanam* tenancy may well be explained by the fact that, while it provided the janmi with some security for his rent, it would attract retainers by offering them a larger interest than that of an ordinary tenant at will.

But whatever the true history of the tenures may be, it can hardly be denied that the early British administrators were right in treating the janmis, who then included Mappillas, Tiyans and Mukkuvans in their number as well as Nayars and Brahmans [1], as being in fact in the position of landlords and the kanamdars in the position of tenants, in the English sense of the words.

Waste lands.

It is perhaps unfortunate that instead of asserting the State's right to waste lands, they adopted the presumption that every acre of land was the private property of some janmi; but the position was difficult. Cultivable and uncultivable lands are inextricably mingled in Malabar, and few of the low hills which surround the paddy flats are altogether valueless for cultivation; and the existence of special forms of lease for the reclamation of jungle, and even for shifting cultivation in forest, goes to show that private rights had been claimed and acknowledged over most of the "waste" lands in the less remote desams. It is also probable that private rights had become defined in the more accessible timber forests. But there must have been "wide stretches of primeval forests, unreclaimed wastes and sandy tracts, and hills and waste lands used from time immemorial as common grazing grounds and places where the people at large cut grass and fuel" over which the Rajas and their officials claimed at most the prerogatives of sovereignty; and these prerogatives should have passed to the Honourable Company. In respect of these, what Sir Henry Winterbotham called "the pestilential legal fiction that all waste land must have a private owner" has operated as "a direct standing invitation for the preferment of unfounded preprosterous individual claims."

[1] See Logan's *Collection of Treaties*, etc., Part II, No. XXXIX.

CHAP. XI. THE LAND TENURES.

Development between 1793 and 1884.

In settling the proportion of the State's share leviable as land revenue, provision was accordingly made for the landlord's interest separately from the interest of the cultivator; but the tenants, whether *kanamdars* or *verumpattakars*, were not regarded as having a permanent right of occupancy. No doubt the *kanamdars* held a powerful position before the Mysorean invasion, as the fighting material on whom the janmis depended to perform their military service to the Rajas, and were seldom evicted; their position was still further strengthened by the general flight of the bigger janmis before the terrors of Tipu's rule; and many of the Mappilla *kanamdars* apparently proceeded to claim the *janmam* rights of the lands of which they were left in possession. On the return of the janmis in 1793, the Joint Commissioners in arranging for a settlement with them, considered it desirable to effect a compromise; and published a proclamation declaring that Mappilla *kanamdars* who had been in possession of lands for over six years should be left undisturbed in full rights, but that janmis who had been absent for only five or six years might claim their old rights, and should if necessary sue for possession of their lands. The janmis apparently in most cases came to terms with their *kanamdars*; but they were still heavily in their debt; and when subsequently the collection of the revenue was taken over by the British officials, the *kanamdars* in most cases paid it, and there was often little left for the janmis after the assessment and the interest on the *kanam* had been deducted from the rent. With a settled Government prices gradually rose, and the janmis in course of time naturally endeavoured to improve their position and get better rents from their lands. The result was a disturbance of the hitherto quiescent relations between the landlords and tenants, and a more frequent resort to the Courts in proceedings for eviction; and to this amongst other causes was attributed the recurrence of Mappilla outbreaks in the middle of the nineteenth century. An elaborate enquiry was held into the system of land tenures, and proposals (to which allusion has already been made in Chapter IV) were considered, to give certain of the tenants a statutory right of permanent occupancy; but no change was actually effected.

Legal incidents of present tenures.

The legal incidents of the various tenures, as they have been gradually defined by the Civil Courts, are now briefly as follows:—

Janmam [1] is the full proprietary right in the soil, subject only to the payment of the Government revenue.

---

[1] *Janmam* means birth. In connection with landed property it first appears in a Nambudiri deed, dated 1681, in the collocations "*Tarwad Janmam Land*" and "*Janmam water*" (ജന്മനീരക്കം). The collocations *Janmabhumi, Janmakhandam*, for "hereditary property" are also found. The use of the word *janmam* alone for "ancestral property," "hereditary right" is not a more violent transference than the use of "*nir*" and "*udagam*" (water), or *attiperu* ("obtaining in a lump" or "a parcel of rights") for "conveyance of landed property" or "property conveyed."

Kanam [1] is a tenure partaking of the nature of both a mortgage and a lease ; the tenant pays a lump sum (*kanam*) to the janmi ; an annual rent (*pattam* [2]) is fixed according to the capacity of the land, and from it the tenant is entitled to deduct the interest due to him on the amount of the *kanam* ; the net balance payable to the janmi annually is called the *purappad* ; the *kanamdar* is entitled to twelve years enjoyment, unless another term is definitely fixed, and on its expiry to the value of improvements effected by him, if the tenancy is not renewed. If at the expiry of the twelve years the parties desire renewal, the tenant must pay a renewal fee, which is fixed by the janmi. The *kanamdar* is at liberty to transfer his interest during his tenancy, or to submortgage it. Denial of the janmi's title, and wilful waste by the *kanamdar* entitle the janmi to compensation before the expiry of the usual term.

Akin to the *kanam* are several varieties of tenure carrying similar incidents, and differing chiefly in the amount and nature of the sum advanced to the janmi.

In the *Kuzhikanam* lease the sum to be expended on improvements is considered the advance made ; the tenant is entitled to enjoy the land rent free, or on a merely nominal rent for twelve years. At the end of that period he must get an ordinary *kanam* or *verumpattam* lease from the janmi, or must surrender on receiving the value of his improvements.

The *Otti* differs from the *kanam* only in that, (1) the amount advanced is sufficient to make the interest on it equal to the *pattam* so that the janmi gets no *purappad*, and (2) the *Ottidar* has the right of pre-emption, if the janmi wishes to sell.

The Kaividuga-otti, Otti kumpuram, Nirmudal, and Janma Panayam are further species of mortgage, in which the janmi surrenders all his rights retaining nothing but the mere name. Whether all or any of these are redeemable is a disputed point, but the forms of deed are now practically obsolete.

The *Panayam* is a simple mortgage, with or without possession. The terms may be similar to those of a *kanam*, but there are no implied covenants for twelve years enjoyment, or for compensation for improvements. The *undaruthi panayam* is a mortgage of which the amount is such that both principal and interest will be extinguished by the usufruct within a definite period, and the land then reverts free of encumbrance to the mortgagor.

---

[1] "*Kanam*" is probably from *kanu* to see, appear ; and Gundert gives its first meaning as "possession, goods." In its legal usage, the underlying idea seems to be that of a "fee" or "cash down" ; as in *Oppukanam* and *Tushikanam*, the sum paid to the witnesses and the writer of the deed : compare "*Kanam*" the price paid for the bride in Tiyan and Mukkuvan marriages. (*Vide* pp. 176–177.)

[2] *Pattam* from root *padu*, "fall," seems to mean primarily "share." A common collocation in the old deeds is "the object of this lease is that such and such a land is a *pattam* on a *pattam* of so much (പാട്ടമായി പാട്ടമാന)."

CHAP. XI. THE LAND TENURES.

The *Verumpattam* is a simple lease from year to year; the rent is often the whole of the net produce after deducting the bare cost of the seed and cultivation, in which case the tenant is practically a labourer on subsistence wages; but the older custom is for one-third of the net produce, after deducting cost of seed and cultivation, to be reserved for the tenant, and the remaining two-thirds paid to the janmi. The lease may continue in force for years and the tenant is entitled to compensation for proper improvement effected with the express or implied consent of the janmi.

Finally there are grants of land *pro servitis impensis vel impendendis*, which generally take the form of perpetual leases; if made to a Brahman, the grant is called *Santathi Brahmasvam*; if to a non-Brahman of caste equal to or higher than the grantor, it is called *anubhavam*, or *sasvatham*; if to a person of inferior caste, *adima* or *kudima janmam*. A nominal fee is payable ordinarily to the janmi, in acknowledgment of his title. Similar grants of temple lands on service tenure are termed *karaima*. None of these grants are redeemable so long as the land remains in the grantor's family; and it is doubtful whether the Courts would now in any case refuse to recognise alienation by the grantee.[1]

Most of the ancient systems of landholding in Malabar have, however, been materially affected by the Malabar Tenancy Act of 1929 (Act IV of 1930). Reference has already been made to its history and material provisions in Chapter IV. The tenures which it principally deals with are cultivating *verumpattams*, customary *verumpattams*, *kanams* and *kuzhikanams*.

LAND REVENUE ADMINISTRATION.

In describing the land revenue administration of Malabar, it is impossible to deal with the district as one homogeneous whole. Different systems have at various times prevailed in different parts. After a brief notice, therefore, of the revenues collected in the days before the Mysorean invasion the revenue history of the eight plain taluks of Malabar will be described, and tracts like the Wynaad and Cochin taluks, which for special reasons require separate treatment, will be dealt with separately.

Sources of revenue of Rajas.

Allusion has already been made to the taxes upon which, as well as upon their *cherikkal* lands, the Hindu Rajas depended for their revenues between the date of the departure of the last of the Perumals and the Mysorean invasion. Many of them were not so much taxes as feudal rights and prerogatives. The Raja levied customs duties upon imports and exports, and taxes upon the houses of fishermen, tradesmen and professional men. Criminal fines went to fill his coffers, and succession duties were

[1] For a full account of the land tenures, see Mr. Justice Moore's *Malabar Law and Custom*, Part II. (Higginbotham, 1905.)

levied upon the estates of deceased persons, especially those who held offices or rights over land. Outcaste women were a two-fold source of profit. They were made over to the Raja with a premium as compensation for the trouble of looking after them, and they were sold by him as slaves or wives to Chettis. The estates of persons who died without heirs were escheated; nor could an heir be adopted without the Raja's consent, given of course at a price. Protection fees under various names were levied from dependants and strangers, and customary presents were his due on occasions of feast or funeral. Wrecks were his perquisite, and various animals his monopoly. Among such animals may be mentioned cows with three or five dugs, cattle that had killed a man or other animals, cattle with a white spot near the corner of the eye, buffaloes with white tips to their tails, wild elephants caught in traps and wild hogs that had fallen into wells.[1]

First instance of land revenue.

The first recorded instance of the levy of land revenue in Malabar licensed in historical times was in 1731–32 A.D., when the Kolattiri Raja, hard pressed by the invasion of the Bednur Raja, imposed a tax of 20 per cent of the pattam on all rice and garden lands in Kolattanad. When the invaders retreated, the tax was probably discontinued, and the district was not assessed again till the Mysorean invasion. In 1757 the Zamorin, who had previously possessed himself of the *nad* of Naduvattam, overran the remaining territory of the Palghat Raja, and to meet the expenses of the force required as a defence against the Mysoreans, who were then threatening an invasion by way of the Palghat Gap, imposed a land tax called *kaval-phalam*. This tax was levied at the rate of an anna on every piece of land which required for a single crop one local *para* (10 seers) of seed.

Malayali mode of stating extent of grain and garden lands.

Before proceeding to consider the land assessments of the Mysoreans, it is essential to point out that no system of survey at this time obtained in Malabar, and that the Malayali had no means of determining correctly the extent of his cultivated land. On the other hand the same amount of seed was sown with little variation each year in a given field; its yield, at any rate for the first crop, was fairly constant, and on this was based the share of the produce paid to the janmi. With regard to each paddy field therefore three particulars were well known then, as they are now, to the most illiterate cultivator, viz., its seed capacity, its outturn multiple, and the *pattam* or share paid to the janmi. The produce of gardens was shared in similar customary fashion, and to estimate the produce available for

[1] For a complete list, *see* Mr. Graeme's "Report to the Board of Revenue on the District of Malabar," dated 15th January 1822 (paragraphs 79 to 93).

CHAP. XI. EARLY SETTLEMENTS.

distribution, the custom arose of taking into account only bearing trees. Thus in the *pattam* paid to the janmi the Mysorean found the simplest and most expeditious way of assessing the land revenue.

The Mysorean settlement.

Another point is to be noticed. The Mysorean settlement did not proceed upon any definite plan or any fixed principles. It was in this that the Joint Commissioners in 1792–93 made their mistake. They obtained from Jinnea, a Brahman formerly in the employ of the Mysoreans, a statement purporting to give details of Arshad Beg Khan's settlement of South Malabar in the year 1784–85. This statement gave the number of *paras* of seed sown in South Malabar in that year, the outturn multiple, the gross produce and the assessment thereon. It also showed the number of productive trees of each kind (cocoanut, arecanut, jack and pepper trees), and the gross assessment on them. The Joint Commissioners therefore divided the gross assessment on wet lands and on each kind of garden produce by the total number of *paras* of seed and the total number of productive trees respectively, and therefrom deduced a fixed money rate for each *para* of seed and each kind of bearing tree, and assumed that the Mysorean assessments had proceeded on fixed principles. As to wet lands they wrote : " The settlement of Arshad Beg Khan supposes that one purrah of seed sown will on a medium produce in each year (whether from one or more harvests) give 10 purrahs, whereof 5½ will go to the cultivator and 4½ remain to be divided between the jenmkar or landholder and Government, on which 4½ remaining purrahs of produce, 1 fanam was fixed as the payable jama, or money value per purrah, 1½ of which went to the jenmkar and 3 to Government."

Mr. Graeme, however, Special Commissioner in 1822, had no difficulty in showing that Jinnea's details as to the measures of seed sown and the number of productive trees were utterly false, and that the rates deduced therefrom by the Joint Commissioners had been applied to " a fictitious seed of assessment " and " an artificial tree of account."

Considerations of space forbid any detailed examination of the assessments as they varied from *nad* to *nad*. It will be sufficient however to indicate the lines on which they were imposed in North and South Malabar, the Kotta river being taken as the dividing line.

South Malabar.

In South Malabar, except in Palghat taluk, wet and garden lands were assessed on what is known as the ' Huzzur Niguthi ' system. For the first few years after his invasion Haidar Ali contented himself with occasional and irregular nuzzers and that only in a few *nads*. But in A.D. 1776–77 Sirdar Khan, Civil and Military Governor of the province of Malabar, prepared accounts, and sent them to Haidar's Darbar at Seringapatam. They were there revised, and upon them an assessment was founded, known from the fact that it was fixed at headquarters as 'the Huzzur Niguthi'. Sirdar Khan's accounts gave the information specified above for each wet land and garden, and a certain proportion of the *pattam*, known in the case of wet lands as the 'Niguthi Vittu' or assessed seed, was fixed as the share due to Government. But what share of the *pattam* Haidar Ali intended to take is not known. Probably he merely fixed the demand on each *nad*, and left it to his officials in Malabar to distribute the assessments on individual lands. In any case his calculations were vitiated by the fact that the *pattam* was afterwards proved to have been grossly underestimated in Sirdar Khan's accounts.

Mr. Graeme, by enquiries made among the principal inhabitants of each taluk, found that the share of the *pattam* actually levied by Haidar Ali's officials in South Malabar ranged from one-tenth to one-third. These seeming discrepancies however were partially equalized by the commutation rates at which the Government share was converted into money. As a rule these rates varied in inverse ratio with the proportion taken of the *pattam*. In Cheranad, for instance, where only one-tenth of the *pattam* was exacted by Haidar Ali, the commutation rate was in some desams Rs. 125 per 1,000 Macleod seers, in others Rs. 250. In South Parappanad, where one-third of the *pattam* was taken as the Government share, the commutation rate was only Rs. 62–8–0 per 1,000 Macleod seers.

On garden lands a tree-tax was nominally fixed upon each kind of tree, usually at the rate of As. 2 for every bearing cocoanut, As. 4 for every bearing jack, 8 pies for every bearing arecanut, and As. 12 for every pepper vine estimated to produce 15 seers of green pepper. But these rates were never applied in practice. Haidar Ali's intention was apparently to claim the whole *pattam* upon gardens; and, in order to exact this and at the same time to preserve some uniformity in the method of taxation, the Mysorean officials assessed only the number of bearing tree required to make the specified *pattam*. All other trees whether bearing or not were classed as unproductive, and left unassessed. For example, a garden, the *pattam* on which had been specified at Rs. 2–8–0, might contain 50 bearing cocoanut trees, but of these only 20 would be assessed at the above rates, and the other 30 would be entered in the accounts as unfruitful. The *pattam* had of course been generally understated ; but even where the whole of it was exacted, the commutation rates were so much below market prices as not to leave the janmi altogether destitute. For the purpose of fixing the assessments, cocoanuts were converted at Rs. 7-8-0 per 1,000 nuts, arecanuts at As. 4 per 1,000 nuts, jacks at As. 4 per tree. In some *nads*, such as Parappanad and Vettanad, where Mappillas were very numerous, a deduction of one-fifth was made from the *pattam* as the proprietor's share. Complaints against these assessments were widespread, and

CHAP. XI. EARLY SETTLEMENTS.

Arshad Beg Khan, Haidar's Governor in 1782–83, ordered a general reduction of 20 per cent on the wet and garden demand in each *nad* of South Malabar. How far these orders were carried out, there is no evidence to show ; and in any case the distribution of the reduction on individual lands was left to subordinate officials. 'As regards individual estates', Mr. Graeme wrote, 'the reduction was very irregularly applied, some having received a greater remission than they were entitled to, others not having benefited in the smallest degree'. Bribery and corruption came into play, and the rich got off lightly at the expense of the poor. The effect of the reduction, moreover, was practically neutralised by the substitution in 1786–87 of the Sultani fanam for the old Viray fanam. The old Viray fanam had been worth As. 4, but the rate of exchange of the new coin was in 1788–89, 3½ to the rupee. The assessments were thus automatically enhanced by 12½ per cent.

Miscellaneous crops were not assessed on any uniform principles in South Malabar. In some *nads* modan was unassessed ; but in the majority one-fifth of the gross produce, converted into money at current market rates, was taken as the Government demand. In Kavalappara, the wet assessments were enhanced by one-sixth to cover the assessment on modan lands. Gingelly and *punam* were not as a rule assessed, but in some *nads* the former was charged only when it was grown instead of modan.

Palghat taluk.

The treatment of Palghat was exceptional. Gardens, which are few and far between in the taluk, were not interfered with ; and modan and gingelly were taxed only in Temmalapuram, where the assessment took the form of a tax of As. 8 upon each individual paying wet assessment. On wet lands the *kavalphalam*, which the Zamorin had imposed at the rate of one anna, or one quarter of the old Viray fanam per local para of seed land, was raised to four annas or one fanam in 1766. In 1773–74, the assessments were raised again to 1½ fanams ; but, on complaint of their oppressiveness, they were lowered in Palghat and Temmalapuram. Probably, for fear of Haidar Ali, the rates were not reduced ; but, where the *pattam* was less than five times the seed sown, the accounts were falsified and the quantity of seed understated. For instance, in the marginally-noted table, column 1 shows the quantity of seed actually sown in local *paras*, column 2 the *pattam* in kind and column 3 the quantity of seed entered in the Mysorean accounts for purposes of assessment at the specified rate of 1½ fanams. Thus in Palghat the seed of assessment was just as fictitious as elsewhere in South Malabar.

Col. 1.	Col. 2.	Col. 3.
10	50	10
10	40	8
10	30	6
10	20	4

North Malabar.

North Malabar was assessed on different principles. It was never so thoroughly subjugated as the land south of the Kotta river, and was tributary rather than subject to the Mysore

Government. Till 1789, when they fled the country for fear of conversion, the Rajas were left almost in the position of Zamindars, paying the revenue due from their *nads* in a lump sum, and distributing it individually at their discretion. The assessments were thus fixed more in accordance with Malabar customs, and took the form of a proportion either of the *verumpattam* or share of the produce reserved for the janmi, or of the *vilacchal meni pattam*, or the balance of the gross produce available for distribution between Government and the janmi after deductions had been methodically made for seed, cultivation expenses and the cultivator's profits. The proportion of the *pattam* exacted on the wet lands was as a rule one-half. This was a higher proportion than was taken anywhere in South Malabar ; but to compensate for this, the commutation rate rarely exceeded Rs. 41–8–0 per 1,000 Macleod seers. The garden assessments varied from *nad* to *nad*. In Kolattanad and Cotiote half the *pattam* was usually taken. In Iruvalinad a tree-tax was levied. In Kadattanad contributions in money varying from Rs. 5 to Rs. 10 were exacted upon each garden till 1778, the whole or part of the *pattam* then being taken for a few years, and a tree-tax being finally introduced in 1788. Modan and *punam* were very highly assessed, as much as 40 per cent of the gross produce being demanded in some *nads*. The rates indeed were so high that it is impossible to suppose that they were rigorously exacted, and it is probable that a great part of the cultivation of grain crops was concealed.

The different systems of assessment adopted in North and South Malabar naturally had different results. The North Malabar chieftains were not easily deceived as to the capability of the land ; and moreover naturally so distributed the gross revenue demand upon their *nads* as to make the assessments heavy on all lands except their own. But the assessments, though heavy, were on the whole evenly distributed, being based on fixed proportions of the gross or net produce. In South Malabar, the assessment was the work of Mysore officials, who as strangers in the land were easily imposed upon, and were perhaps ready to be complacent or severe as inducements were held out or refused to them, and was undoubtedly lighter, especially on wet and modan lands. But the Huzzur Niguthi represented no fixed share of the gross or net produce, and individual assessments were very unequal. In one instance Mr. Graeme found the garden assessment to be 4,055 per cent of the *pattam*, in two instances over 2,000 per cent, and in three instances over 1,000 per cent.

British rule.

In 1792 by the Treaties of Seringapatam, Malabar was ceded to the Honourable Company ; and the Joint Commissioners appointed from Bombay and Bengal at once proceeded to make careful enquiries into the Mysorean land revenue system. The principles upon which they conceived it to rest have already

CHAP. XI. EARLY SETTLEMENTS.

been explained. They made no attempt to introduce any new settlement; but, in spite of the inequalities of the assessments and the imperfections of the existing system, made it their aim to realise as much as possible of the Mysorean demand, leaving it to the Rajas to collect the revenue from individuals in their respective *nads*. In South Malabar, Arshad Beg Khan's jama of 1784 continued to be the standard to which all partial revisions of assessment approximated, and on wet lands at least the assessments remained in force up to the time of the late settlement. In North Malabar, the system, though differing in details, was understood to lead to much the same result, and continued to influence the wet assessments until their recent revision by the Settlement Department. In this part of the district, however, the share of the *pattam* reserved for Government was, during the first ten years of the British occupation, increased from 50 to 60 per cent in some *nads* and in Iruvalinad to 72 per cent, but, on the other hand, the Mysorean jama was not enhanced by 10 per cent for collection charges, as in South Malabar.

Quinquennial leases.

The system of leasing the *nads* to their respective chieftains for a lump sum approximating to the Mysorean demand was not a success; and, as arrears accumulated, the quinquennial leases made with the Rajas were gradually cancelled by the Company between 1796 and 1801. To compensate the Rajas, one-fifth of the revenues of their districts in 1800–1 was set apart for their maintenance; and a sum of Rs 2,57,290–15–9 is still paid to the families of the old rulers of Malabar. The Zamorin's family alone receives more than 1·30 lakhs per annum, and the Chirakkal and Kadattanad families Rs. 22,000 and Rs. 21,000 respectively. These allowances, or *malikhanas*, are 'perpetual during good conduct', but are 'subject to revocation on proof established of flagrant misbehaviour or rebellious conduct.'

Smee's pymash.

In 1798–9, Mr. Smee, a member of the Commission appointed in 1796 to execute the office of Supravisor and Chief Magistrate of the Province of Malabar, made a pymash or survey of the district. His pymash was never acted upon and the accounts are of little value. They were probably compiled by village officers.

Macleod's revision of assessments.

In 1802 Major Macleod, first Principal Collector of Malabar, considering the assessments of the district unduly low, made an ill-advised attempt to impose on them a high percentage increase. On modan lands, in the *nads* where they had not been assessed by the Mysoreans, he claimed a share of the produce, generally one-fifth, for Government; and, dividing the assessments by three, increased the permanent *jama* of each *nad* by that amount. On wet lands, he estimated that as much as 35 or 40 per cent of the gross produce might fairly be claimed by Government; and he estimated the annual produce of a cocoanut and arecanut tree at the high average of 48 and

CHAP. XI. EARLY SETTLEMENTS.

200 nuts respectively. Starting with these initial errors, he endeavoured with the help of the parbutties or village officers to make a survey of the district within 40 days. The time allowed for the purpose was ludicrously small : the parbutties were as corrupt as they were incompetent ; and the resulting accounts were ridiculously false. Actual produce was over-estimated ; produce was assessed that existed only in the imagination of the parbutties ; and assessments were imposed on the wrong man. But his mistakes did not end here. Not content with revising the assessments, he revised also the rates of exchange ; and the unfortunate cultivator, when he paid into the treasury his heavy assessments in fanams, found that owing to the revised table of exchange a balance was still due from him. An insurrection followed, and in the beginning of 1803 the province rose *en masse*. To allay the storm which he was powerless to quell, Major Macleod summarily resigned his position to Mr. Rickards, Principal Judge of the Court of Adalat, and left the district.

Mr. Rickards' proposed settlement.

On the very day that he took over charge, Mr. Rickards issued a proclamation cancelling the new rates of exchange and restoring the demand of 1801–2. But complaints of the inequalities of the Mysorean assessments, especially in South Malabar, were still general ; and after careful enquiries, among the chief landholders of Malabar, Mr Rickards set himself seriously to the task of fixing the principles which would serve as a basis for a new pymash. On June 17th, 1803, he submitted to the Board of Revenue his proposals for assessing wet and garden lands, and requested permission to grant patta fixing the assessment for a period of twelve years. On June 29th, he circulated a paper among 'the Rajas, Nambudiris, Mookistens and principal landholders' of the district containing the principles which, subject to the approbation of the Board, he proposed to adopt in the new pymash. Headed by the Zamorin more than one hundred of the chief janmis of Malabar expressed their willingness to accept the principles. They were also approved by Government ; and Mr Warden, who in 1804 had succeeded Mr Rickards as Principal Collector, embodied them in his famous proclamation of 1805 [1] :—

"The Government of Fort St. George having received information through various channels that great inequalities exist in the present revenue jamabundy of the province of Malabar, transmitted orders sometime back to the Principal Collector to frame by survey and assessment a new jamabundy upon improved principles ; founded on a liberal consideration of the relative rights of the Sirkar, of the proprietor and cultivator. Those orders the Principal Collector has now determined to carry into immediate and due execution.

---

[1] Logan's *Treaties*, etc., ii. CCLXII–CCLXIII.

CHAP. XI. EARLY SETTLEMENTS.

"It is well known to be considered a just system of assessment for the Government to derive its land revenue from the *pattam* (or net rent) payable by the cultivator's tenant to his proprietor.

"To establish a fixed rule by which the *pattam* shall be calculated and ascertained, it must be in the recollection of every one that the principal Malabar Rajas, Head Nambudiris and Mukyastans in each district were some months ago assembled by summons at Calicut; and, after the most patient enquiry into the mode by which the *pattam* was usually rated, it was found that a variety of systems prevailed, which might chiefly be ascribed to the existing inequalities in the revenue in the different districts in the province.

"In order to rectify such errors and establish a permanent revenue, by which one ryot shall neither be more heavily nor more favourably assessed than another, it became obviously convincing and desirable to all parties that one uniform system should obtain, in estimating the *pattam* on which the Sirkar revenue was to be fixed.

"Having fully and deliberately discussed the many points connected with so material a question, and pretty accurately ascertained the customs which in former times regulated the *pattam* on lands and gardens generally throughout the province, the aforesaid Rajas, Head Nambudiris and Mukyastans at length unanimously concurred in certain fixed principles whereby to determine the Sirkar revenue, which they recorded and authenticated by their several signatures.

"Those being the very principles which the Right Honourable the Governor in Council had formally and finally confirmed and ordered to be adopted in framing the new assessment of Malabar, they are now hereunder written and hereby published for the information of all its inhabitants.

"*First.*—On wet or rice grounds, after deducting from the gross produce, the seed and exactly the same quantity for expenses of cultivation and then allotting one-third of what remains as *kolulabham* (or plough profit) to the *kudiyan*, the residue or *pattam* is to be divided in the proportion of six-tenths to the Sirkar and four-tenths to the janmakar;

"*Secondly.*—On *parambu* or orchard lands one-third of cocoanut, supary and jack tree produce being deemed sufficient for the *kudiyan*, the remainder or *pattam* is to be equally divided between the Sirkar and janmakar; and

"*Thirdly.*—On dry grain lands (which are very scantily cultivated in Malabar) the Sirkar's share is to be half of the janmakar's *varam* on what is actually cultivated during the year.

"The assessment in the pepper produce will be fixed upon hereafter.

"The new pymash on the preceding principles has, in the first instance, been entrusted to the execution of the several Subordinate Collectors, to whom the necessary orders have been issued.

"As the present mode of assessment has been acknowledged to be fair and moderate, it is expected that the janmakars will render a true and faithful account of the pattam of their estates at the cutcherries of the Subordinate Collectors, who on their parts will take care that every assistance shall be given by the local revenue servants in each district, as the janmakars belonging to it might want to obtain information from their tenants relative to the existing state of their landed property. A form will be likewise given to the several janmakars by order of the Sub-Collectors, agreeably to which the required accounts are to be drawn out.

"After these accounts are all delivered in, a rigid scrutiny will be made and the fullest means devised to ascertain their accuracy. The true result will then be submitted for the approbation of the Board of Revenue and Government, under whose sanction the principal Collector will visit each district for the purpose of granting sealed and signed *pattas*, or assess notes, to the several janmakars and other inhabitants, specifying the correct annual revenue they are to pay to the Company's Government.

"The principal Collector therefore confidently expects that, without making themselves liable to punishment by any act of palpable fraud or deception, the inhabitants will willingly and readily render exact accounts of their property, in order that all their apprehensions might be dissipated by the early establishment of an unalterable assessment."

This phrase "unalterable assessment" long gave rise to the misapprehension that the assessments in Malabar were permanent and unchangeable. It is well, therefore, to clear away this idea by pointing out that, from the history of the proclamation, it is plain that there was to be a new survey and settlement, and that the rates imposed at the settlement were to be unalterable for a period of 12 years. It is also clear that what Government bound themselves to was not, as Mr. Conolly subsequently put it, 'a permanency of aggregate amount of tax,' but a 'permanency of the proportion of the Government demand to the produce.' Finally, as will be shown below, whatever interpretation be put upon the proclamation of 1805, there never was a settlement on the principles fixed therein.

The Janmi pymash and Hinduvi pymash.

As a preliminary to the new settlement, Mr. Warden carried out in 1805–06, what is called the janmi pymash; and obtained from each landed proprietor under his signature a detailed statement of his landed property. These accounts, to which was subjoined the written declaration of the proprietor that he had rendered a true and faithful statement of his property, and would willingly forfeit to Government any land which might be found thereafter to have been omitted, showed for each janmi the number of rice fields in his possession, their names, extent and net rent, and the number of gardens, specifying the trees in each both fruitful and, whether from age or immaturity, unfruitful. Mr. Warden then proceeded with the aid of surveyors from Coimbatore to survey all the wet lands; and the accounts they prepared between 1806 and 1810 are known as the Hinduvi or *alavu* pymash. In spite of many inaccuracies, these accounts, under the name both of the janmi pymash and *alavu* pymash, remained up to the

CHAP. XI. EARLY SETTLEMENTS.

introduction of the settlement the most valuable revenue records extant in the district; but no attempt was made to make use of the survey. In some nads of South Malabar, the jama of 1800–01 was enhanced in 1804 by one-fourth of the increase ordered by Major Macleod; and in parts of North Malabar, on the conclusion of the janmi pymash, assessments, which fell short of the proper proportion of the rent laid down by Mr. Rickards as due to Government, were raised. But no general settlement founded on the principles formulated in the proclamations of 1803 and 1805 was introduced. As Mr. Warden explained in a letter to the Board of Revenue, dated 16th June 1813:—

> "The several changes which afterwards took place brought with them such an accumulation of duty and trouble upon me, with diminished means of getting through them, being left almost entirely to native assistance, that the new assessment, with every thing connected with it, has for some time back been laid aside, and the revenues of the province have been continued to be collected on the Commissioner's jama of 976 (A.D. 1801)."

unro's port.

With the exception that in 1806 the tax on the pepper vine was abolished, matters remained in this state till 1817, when Sir Thomas Munro, then a member of the Commission for revising establishments, paid a visit to Malabar; and, notwithstanding the fact that he spent only a month in the district, wrote a valuable report (*Revenue Selections*, Vol. 1, p. 838). He received many complaints regarding the assessments of garden and wet lands, not so much however directed against the general oppressiveness of the assessments which were 'in general very moderate,' but against the continuance of assessment on lands which had deteriorated or been destroyed by natural causes. The landholders, unable to pay such assessments, had had their holdings sold for arrears of revenue, an innovation in Malabar which was looked upon with great disfavour.

Graeme's report.

Sir Thomas Munro's report resulted in 1818 in the deputation to Malabar of Mr. Graeme, one of the Judges of the Southern Court of Circuit, with a special commission to introduce the new system of police and magistracy, and to consider what improvements might be introduced into the revenue administration of the district. The fruit of his labours which lasted for four years was a report, submitted in 1822, which Sir Thomas Munro considered to be 'on the whole the fullest and the most comprehensive report ever received of any province under this Government.'

In his proposals for the revision of assessments Mr. Graeme departed in two points from the letter of the proclamation of 1805. Apparently for the reason that his enquiries had shown that by adopting the *Vilacchal meni pattam*, as calculated by Mr. Rickards, the Rajas and other janmis had made it appear that they were enjoying a much larger share of the produce than really accrued to them, he proposed (and the proposal was approved by Sir Thomas Munro), to discard the *Vilacchal meni pattam* altogether, and to assess the revenue on wet lands at 65 per cent of the *verumpattam*, or actual rent, as ascertained from deeds and by actual enquiry. This proposal he estimated would result in a loss of revenue of Rs. 1,39,922 or about 13 per cent.

In respect of garden lands Mr. Rickards' plan of taking 50 per cent of the *pattam* was adhered to. But, whereas Mr. Rickards (who, owing to the Pychy rebellion then raging in the north of the district, had confined his enquiries almost entirely to the janmis of South Malabar) had estimated the *pattam* to be two-thirds of the gross produce, and had based thereon his calculations of the assessment, Mr. Graeme found janmis of North Malabar to be in enjoyment of four-fifths of the gross produce. While, therefore, in South Malabar he followed Mr. Rickards in exacting one-third of the gross produce as the share due to Government, in North Malabar he assessed that share at two-fifths of the gross produce.

The details of his plan were then worked out as follows. The janmi pymash accounts showed the total number of trees existing in 1805–06. From this number Mr. Græme deducted one-fifth of the trees entered in these accounts as productive, to allow for those which had gone out of bearing, and all the trees reported to have been past bearing or too young to bear fruit in 1805–06. He then assumed that 75 per cent of the young trees had in the interval come into bearing, and thus he arrived at the total number of trees both productive and unproductive. Deducting from the latter one-fifth, on the presumption that when the rates came to be applied they would be cut down, and adding the remainder to the productive trees, he determined what would be the total number of full-grown trees standing when the assessment came to be made. After this, to obtain the gross produce of the cocoa and areca trees in the district, all that Mr. Græme had to do was to multiply the number of productive trees of either kind by the number of nuts which on an average they produced every year according to the janmi pymash accounts, and of this gross produce, converted into money at locally ascertained prices, one-third in South Malabar and two-fifths in North Malabar represented the Government share. In respect of jack trees the procedure was even simpler. The janmi pymash accounts stated the *pattam*, not as any prescribed share of the gross or net produce, but in money. By multiplying the number of productive trees by these money rates, he obtained the customary *pattam* due on all the jack trees of the district ; and of this one-half went to Government. Finally, dividing the total money demand due to

CHAP. XI. EARLY SETTLEMENTS.

Government on each kind of tree by the number of productive and unproductive trees, Mr. Græme was able to fix certain rates per tree which he proposed to impose on all standing cocoa, areca and jack trees, except those too young to bear. These rates, he proposed, were to remain unaltered for twelve years. The result of the settlement Mr. Græme expected would be a loss of ·7 per cent of the revenue then collected.

Mr. Græme made no specific proposals as to *punam* and *ellu* crops ; but on modan he recommended the continuance of the prevailing system of taking not more than 20 per cent of the gross produce, in the case of all new assessments to be spread over the period of years when the lands are alternately cultivated and left fallow.

This scheme for the revision of the assessments was in all important particulars approved by Government ; and Mr. Græme was sent back to Malabar to carry it into effect. He was directed to revise first the revenue establishments, then the garden assessments and finally those on wet lands, this being considered the order in which the subjects required attention. The first of these tasks was completed, and the second begun. But unfortunately, before he had time to do more than fix the total garden assessment on each hobali of one taluk, Calicut, Mr. Græme left the district, resigning to the Collector, Mr. Vaughan, the task of completing the revision of the garden settlement, and carrying through that of the wet assessments.

From this time forward different principles prevailed in the treatment of wet, garden and dry lands and it will make for clearness if their further history up to the introduction of the settlement be traced separately.

The garden settlement.

Before leaving Malabar, Mr. Græme sketched out a plan of operations to be followed by the Collector in his revision of the garden assessments. In his report of 1822, he had explained his general principles ; and, by fixing on the basis of the janmi pymash accounts a fair average tax for each kind of tree, had attempted to forecast what would be the financial results of his scheme. But in introducing the settlement into Calicut he discarded the janmi pymash account, and obtained in their stead returns from each cultivator in each hobali, showing the total number of trees of each kind in his garden and their gross produce in nuts. From these returns, verified by local inspection where necessary, he obtained the gross produce of the hobali in cocoanuts, arecanuts and jack fruits ; and one-third of this, converted into money at rates locally ascertained to be correct, he exacted as the share due to Government. He thus arrived at the total garden assessment to be imposed on each hobali, and an average rate of tax for each kind of garden tree. But recognizing that cocoanut gardens vary in quality according to their soil and situation, and that they flourish more on the sandy soils of the coast than upon the slopes of the laterite hills of the interior, he divided them into *attuveppu* (low lying gardens) and *karaveppu* [1] (bank or high lying gardens), and subdivided the former into two and the latter into three classes. He provided, also, that while the gross demand on coconut trees in the hobali remained unchanged, the tax on individual trees should be graduated according to the class of garden in which they grew, the tax on *attuveppu* and the best *karaveppu* trees being slightly higher, and that on the two inferior classes of *karaveppu* trees slightly lower than the average hobali rate. The gross garden assessment thus fixed was to be communicated to the inhabitants of the hobali, and its distribution on these lines left in their hands. The advantage of the system of course was that nothing was left 'to the difficult and uncertain judgment of the gross produce of each garden' ; but a very obvious objection was the extreme multiplicity of the rates of tree-tax. They varied from amsam to amsam ; and in 1889, 30, 15 and 20 different tree rates prevailed in the district for cocoanuts, arecanut, and jacks respectively. In the case of cocoanuts they ranged from As. 2–6 to 5¼ pies per tree, for arecanuts from 9 pies to 2½ pies, and for jack trees from As. 5 to A. 1–4.

Mr. Græme's principles were followed by Mr. Vaughan and his successors ; but in practice some details were modified, and at Sir Thomas Munro's advice all trees past bearing were exempted from tax. Mr. Vaughan completed the garden survey, and introduced the rates without orders in 1824–25 ; but Government condemned the settlement, and directed that no further collection should be made until a more correct survey had been effected and the accounts had received the sanction of the Board of Revenue and of Government. Mr. Sheffield, who succeeded Mr. Vaughan as Collector in 1826, next took up the task, and till 1840 revision was in continuous progress. The final result was a small increase of Rs. 18,849 instead of the loss of revenue anticipated by Mr. Græme.

Periodical revisions every twelve years had been a part of Mr. Græme's scheme ; and in 1842 and again in 1850 the Board brought up the question. But the Collector, Mr. Conolly, discouraged all such ideas. The rates had just been introduced with enormous difficulty and after twelve years' hard labour ; and, as a subsequent Collector pointed out, revisions were too invidious and unpopular undertakings to be undertaken lightly. Between 1850 and 1852 indeed, owing to complaints of over-assessment, the gardens of the old Kurumbranad taluk were re-inspected, and the demand reduced by Rs. 336. Trees too young to be assessed when the original survey was made were also brought to assessment, or supposed

[1] See p. 219.

CHAP. XI. EARLY SETTLEMENTS.

to be brought to assessment; and the rule was formulated, that any one claiming remission of assessment on one of his gardens must submit them all for inspection. But practically up to the time of the Settlement there had been no interference with, and no revision of, the assessments fixed on Mr. Græme's principles, and those assessments had in course of time come to be regarded not as tree, but as land assessments. Time had naturally wrought many changes. Gardens once flourishing and highly assessed had decayed, but their assessment continued to be paid without a murmur. Other gardens, poor at the time of the pymash and therefore let off lightly, had become va'uable properties; but, the revenue on them, if any, had not been increased. Many good gardens, Mr. Ballard reported in 1864, were paying fewer annas than their poorer neighbours were paying rupees; and he quoted instances of excellent gardens paying no more than As. 8 and As. 10 per acre, while others paid as much as Rs. 65. The assessments, in other words, had ceased to bear intelligible relation to the gardens on which they were paid.

Abortive wet settlement.

Mr. Græme's scheme for the revision of the wet land assessments proved a failure. Its weak point was that it depended on obtaining through the village officers correct returns of the *pattam* received by proprietors on their wet lands.

"'He left the district in 1823', wrote Mr. (afterwards Sir William) Robinson in a letter to the Board, dated 5th August 1857, 'directing Mr. Vaughan to continue the survey of the province hitherto carried on under his own control. He had himself, however, experienced that the account of the survey returns of gardens were so understated and suspicious as to require the greatest caution in accepting them, and that the accounts of rice-land which had hitherto been rendered by the proprietors seemed by no means entitled to credit. Mr. Græme did not indicate how this plague spot in his proposed scheme of survey was to be remedied."

"The correspondence noted in the margin kept the Board of Revenue acquainted with the failure of this almost ridiculous attempt. 'The Desadhikaris are excessively backward in the survey of the rice-lands and pay not the least attention to orders, demeaning themselves in such a way as evidently to prove their lukewarmness in the cause'; that he (the Principal Collector) had been unable to make the least impression on them (the Desadhikaris); that the accounts they give are 'grossly false beyond description; and that they sedulously conceal the deeds making it next to impossible to ascertain the resources of the country.' In his letter, 3rd June, paragraph 10, Mr. Vaughan speaks of his 'utter despair of being able to prepare any returns within reasonable time' and of the 'hopelessness of the chance of getting any true deeds' through the Desadhikaris.

In the original, 16 letters which passed between the Board and the Collector during the years 1823–25 are quoted.

"The ryots, too, naturally had recourse to every expedient to secure the easy defeat of the proposed settlement. Desadhikaris

CHAP. XI. EARLY SETTLEMENTS.

made large fortunes, the country 'teemed with ficticious deeds,' 'temporary deeds and agreements were executed to suit present purposes, and were prepared with a view of corresponding with a survey notoriously fallacious.' A number of returns was eventually obtained, 'but the great majority was of the most grossly fraudulent description. Special and singular legislative provisions were proposed, penalties and rewards to informants were suggested, forfeiture of concealed lands was threatened, and assessment to the full amount of the rental in cases of fraud was actually authorized by the Board but all in vain. In paragraph 5 of his letter, dated 12th October 1824, to the Board, Mr. Vaughan boldly calls on the Board to reflect on the effects of 'these collusions on the morals of the people in giving rise to innumerable disputes and feuds, as well as suits beyond calculation in the Civil Courts'; adding that 'it is full time to adopt measures to check the pending evil.' A variety of futile endeavours to induce the Desadhikaris and ryots to return faithful statements were made, but on the 9th June 1825, after two years' struggle to carry out Mr. Graeme's pymash, Mr. Vaughan reported the 'total failure in the promises made by the inhabitants to revise and give in true and correct accounts.'

"Such is the history of another period of five or six years wasted in futile exertion to get reliable revenue accounts from parties most interested in concealing the information, which was sought for through the corruptest, most suspicious and equally interested channels, viz., the Desadhikaris of Mr. Graeme's appointment. The Utopian scheme of Desadhikari's pymash and azmaish died of its own corruption, and infinitesimal authority is attached to the bundles of imperfect returns which load our records under the name 'Desadhikari Pymash.'"

It[1] is unnecessary to follow up in detail the steps which were taken subsequently and which eventually led to nothing. It will be sufficient to say that the wet land survey was postponed till after the completion of the garden survey as suggested by Sir Thomas Munro, and that meanwhile prices of produce had increased so much as to enable the collections to be made with a facility hitherto unknown. The necessity for a revision, therefore, did not force itself into notice.

Pugit vivaram pymash.

Nevertheless an important change was made in consequence of the want of accounts to show the particulars of the holding of each individual tax-payer. The want of such accounts began to be seriously felt in the year 1832–33. Holdings had been enlarged, had been diminished in size, had been thrown together, and had been parcelled out afresh; and simultaneously the distribution of items of assessment had been tampered with, without any regard to the principles of the assessment by which they are at first fixed. A holder with good and bad land in his occupation and under some ordinary obligation to part with a piece of it to meet his necessities, naturally enough parted with the bad land first; and,

[1] This and the next two paragraphs are taken *verbatim* from Mr. Logan's Manual.

there being no control over him (owing to a want of any accounts to show what he was doing), he naturally also assigned with the bad land an obligation to pay as much of the revenue assessed on the good and bad land together, as he could get his assignee to accept. The principles of the assessment thus became completely changed: the good land was in future assessed with less and the bad land with more, of the land revenue than they respectively ought to have borne; and to remedy them a pymash was instituted by Mr. Clemenston in 1833 and the succeeding years, the result of which was what are generally known as the *Pugil vivaram* accounts.

As if no experience had been gained of the value to be set upon accounts prepared by the interested heads of villages, the old mistake was again made, and these officials were again entrusted with the duty of preparing returns of the lands within their respective limits. No measurements, no accurate description, nor classification of soils were called for. In fact it was, as Mr. Robinson described it, in his letter to the Board of Revenue of 5th August 1857, a repetition of the Desadhikari's pymash, with fewer guarantees for fidelity or accuracy; and it was more carelessly conducted and supervised. The Tahsildars were to check the accounts and send them to the Huzzur; but after repeated reminders, the accounts came in driblets and without verification by the Tahsildars. In 1843 a small quantity having been received, a small establishment was entertained, and about half of them were copied hastily into a form of Kulawar Chitta (individual account); but directly it was sought to verify or use them, their worthlessness was seen, and Mr. Conolly at once stopped further expenditure. Mr. Robinson's opinion of these *Pugil vivaram* accounts was expressed in his letter to the Board above quoted; he considered that they were not worth examining, as they recorded imperfectly certain particulars of the land as it existed in 1833–43.

Reversion to Jama of 1800–01.

The upshot of the matter was that Mr. Robinson determined that the only escape from the confusion was to face the question determinedly and to bring back the deranged revenue demand to the only certain and common basis that the land revenue accounts admitted of, viz., the pymash accounts of 1806–1810. These accounts showed the assessment on the wet land as it existed in those years, in other words the demand fixed by the Commission in 1800–1801 modified in parts of South Malabar by the addition of one-fourth of the increase ordered by Major Macleod, and in North Malabar by the enhancements made by Mr. Warden, on receipt of the janmi pymash accounts on those lands where the assessment fell short of 60 per cent of the *pattam*. The *jama* of 1800–1801 was in its turn practically the Mysorean demand, the main differences being that in South Malabar it had been increased by 10 per cent for expenses of collection, and that in North Malabar the share of the *pattam* exacted by Government had in some nads been raised. Mr. Robinson's proposals were sanctioned by Government, and carried out by his successors Messrs. Grant and Ballard. It is therefore clear that, although they had been considerably modified, the wet assessments prevailing in the district at the time of the late settlement were at bottom those of the Mysoreans. From these statements wet lands brought under wet cultivation subsequently to 1822, must be excluded. On those lands, under orders issued by Mr. Clemenston in 1833, 65 per cent of the *pattam* was levied, and converted into money at local commutation rates.

The inequalities of the Mysorean assessments, especially in South Malabar, where the Huzzur Niguthi system was enforced, have been already alluded to. A few figures compiled by a Settlement officer in 1894, which showed the rates then existing in 165 desams taken at random in the four taluks of Palghat, Walavanad, Ponnani and Kurumbranad, bring these inequalities into stronger relief. More than 7,000 acres of wet lands in these desams were assessed at less than As. 8 per acre, the lowest possible settlement rate being As. 12; and upwards of 4,000 acres at rates varying between Rs. 6, the highest settlement rate, and Rs. 40.

Pre-settlement dry rates.

Up till 1870 the only dry crops in Malabar liable to assessment were modan, *ellu* or gingelly and *punam*. The difficulty with lands on which these crops are raised has always been that the cultivation is shifting, the same plot of ground being cultivated only once in every three or four years. Every year therefore, before the crops can be assessed, the extent under cultivation has to be measured up. Mr. Græme, following Major Macleod, proposed to obviate these difficulties by taking one-fifth of the gross produce of modan lands in the year of settlement as the Government share, and by spreading the demand over three years. But the latter of these proposals was rejected by Mr. Sheffield, whose revision of the modan and ellu assessments remained in force till 1861. He divided the lands into three classes according to their estimated outturn multiple, and assumed for every 100 *perukkams* [1] a 'fair and moderate' quantity of seed. The land under cultivation was measured every year with a six-foot *kol*; and the gross produce ascertained by multiplying together its extent in *perukkams*, the quantity of seed sown and the outturn multiple. The assessment was fixed at one-fifth of the gross produce, converted at rates fixed annually, at any rate up to 1845, in accordance with

[1] A perukkam = one square six-foot kol.

CHAP. XI. EARLY SETTLEMENTS.

market prices. *Punam* seems to have been overlooked, and there is no record of any revision of the principles on which it was assessed till 1861.

In that year Government obviated the necessity of the intricate calculation of gross produce and assessment by imposing uniform acreage rates. *Punam* was assessed at As. 12, As. 10 and As. 8 according to the taluk in which it was grown, modan and ellu at As. 12 and As. 9 respectively throughout the district. This facilitated the calculation of the assessment, but did not get rid of the yearly inspection and yearly measurement of a cultivation that was essentially casual and always shifting. To obviate this and to encourage the permanent occupation of such lands, Government directed that the rate for the permanent occupation of modan and *ellu* lands should be As. 6 per acre. Little advantage was taken of the concession, and in 1889 only 16,500 acres had been taken up on these terms.

In the taluk of Palghat the following crops, when grown on modan lands, were after 1870 charged at the rate of As. 12 per acre on the area cultivated :—

(1) Cholam.
(2) Ragi.
(3) Chama.
(4) *Kambu*.
(5) Horsegram.
(6) Pulses.
(7) Tobacco.
(8) *Tuvara* (dholl).
(9) *Amarhay*.
(10) Castor-oil seeds.

In 1871 the Board proposed to extend these assessments to other parts of the district, and to include other crops such as ginger and pepper among the taxable products ; but on the representation of the Collector the scheme was abandoned in 1875. As has been explained above the tax on the pepper vine had been abolished in May 1806 ; and in 1827 Government 'authorized the Collector to declare that Government adhered to its proclamation of 1806, and would not renew the tax on the growing vine'. Between 1806 and 1874–75 an export duty was levied on the spice at varying rates. It may be noted that, what Government pledged themselves to in 1827, was never again to impose a tree-tax on the growing vine. Opponents to the settlement have ingeniously construed the proclamation into a pledge never again to assess either the vine or the land upon which it was grown.

THE SURVEY AND SETTLEMENT.

In the meantime the necessity of a scientific survey and settlement of Malabar had gradually been forcing itself upon the notice of the authorities. In 1859 the Board had expressed the hope that it would 'be found practicable to extend the operations of the Revenue Survey to this province before long,' and in 1864 Government had actually called upon the Superintendent of Survey to report when he could take up Malabar. No increase of revenue was expected at this time to

CHAP. XI. THE SURVEY AND SETTLEMENT.

accrue from a revision of the assessments ; but their redistribution was considered essential, and Collector after Collector pointed out how sore was the need in Malabar for proper accounts. There was no land register, and therefore no check upon cultivation and no means of protecting Government lands from encroachment.

The question was, however, allowed to rest till 1880, when the Government of India asked for information about the land revenue system of the district. The old superstition that "Malabar is a district of private estates assessed by Haidar Ali on a rent charge system which is unchangeable" and that neither was relief necessary nor enhancement practicable, prevailed at this time in high quarters ; but the Collector Mr. McWatters had no difficulty in exposing the falsity of this idea and once more he took the opportunity of urging the necessity of surveying and settling the district. "We have no land register", he wrote, "we have no regular register of gardens, and we have no register of dry lands. In fact we have nothing whatever reliable about the land revenues, and we know next to nothing about them. The rice fields cannot generally be identified by means of the only register we have got, and we have consequently no control over the apportionment of the revenues. It is believed that the poor man with the worst land pays the highest assessment". Government accepted the Collector's views, which were supported by the Board and the Advocate-General, and directed that the survey which had already been begun in the Wynaad should be extended in due course to Malabar.[1] The bogey of the permanency of the Mysorean settlement was finally laid to rest by the Secretary of State's despatch No. 35, Revenue, dated 13th December 1883, though opponents of the new settlement strove hard to resuscitate it in 1894, and again in 1901 when His Excellency Lord Ampthill visited Malabar.

Scheme reports.

The survey of the Wynaad taluk was hampered by many difficulties and made slow progress, and it was not for some years that operations could be commenced in the plain taluks. Mr. Castlestuart Stuart, the Special Settlement Officer, was able however to begin the classification of Palghat in 1889 ; and three years later he submitted a scheme for the settlement of the taluk. A revised scheme founded on the classification of the four typical taluks of Palghat, Walavanad, Kurumbranad and Ponnani, was prepared in 1894 by Mr. Moberly. Schemes for Kottayam and Calicut followed in 1896 and 1899 respectively ; but it was not till almost exactly eleven years had elapsed since Mr. Stuart had begun work in Palghat, that on August 29th, 1900, Government finally

[1] G.O. No. 459, Revenue, dated 18th April 1883.

CHAP. XI. THE SURVEY AND SETTLEMENT.

decided on the principles and rates to be adopted in the new settlement of the plain taluks of Malabar.[1]

Delay in introduction.

The explanation of the long delay of almost exactly eleven years between the beginning of the classification of Palghat on September 2nd, 1889, and the final decision of the Government on August 29th, 1900 as to the principles and rates to be adopted in the new settlement, is that two difficulties of long-standing and great complexity had in the mean time to be solved. Government had to decide in the first place whether the settlement was to be with the janmi or the tenant, in the second how garden lands were to be assessed.

Settlement with the janmi.

The Mysoreans had settled with the tenant, but from accident rather than design. Their methods were not such as to inspire confidence. The Nayars were continually in revolt, and both Brahman and Nayar landholders were afraid to trust their persons at the Muhammadan cutcherries. Finally, when Tipu entered on his campaign of proselytism to Islam, so many of them fled the country that the Mysorean officials had no choice but to settle with the actual cultivator. The system worked well, being peculiarly suited to a district where the janmi is often a proprietor only in name; and, in spite of the fact that the proclamation of 1805 contemplated a settlement with the janmi, it was accepted almost without question by the British authorities, till its fundamental irregularity was pointed out by High Court in Second Appeal No. 78 of 1888. The High Court held that the Malabar pattadar was not a landholder within the meaning of the Revenue Recovery Act, unless he were also the janmi. Not one in twenty of the 185,000 pattadars of the district, in Mr. (now Sir Henry) Winterbotham's opinion, fulfilled this condition; and the decision placed the greater part of the land revenue in jeopardy. A simple solution of the difficulty would have been to amend the definition of 'landholder' in Act II of 1864 so as to include a Malabar pattadar, and to amend section 42 by adding a proviso that the phrase 'free of all encumbrances' included in Malabar the janmi's interest. But Government preferred to institute an organised registration of janmam titles under the provisions of Regulation XXVI of 1802.[2]

Janmam registration.

The immediate result was that all the Wynaad settlement registers, which had been prepared on the old system, had to be revised; and no work could be undertaken in the low country till this revision had been carried through. It was not till 1895 therefore that registration was begun in earnest in the Palghat and Walavanad taluks by two Special Deputy Collectors appointed for the purpose. A year later to give legal force

---

[1] G.O. No. 883, Revenue, dated 29th August 1900.

[2] G.O. No. 1152, Revenue, dated 3rd December 1891.

CHAP. XI. THE SURVEY AND SETTLEMENT.

to their decisions, and to provide some assurance that sales of land for arrears of revenue would not be set aside by the courts on the ground that the real janmi had not been registered, the Malabar Janmam Registration Act (Act III of 1896) was passed.

But the work of the registrars proceeded with unexpected slowness. The janmi apparently had no wish to be registered, and by a 'strange apathy' put off the evil day of the new settlement as long as he could. Two more Deputy Collectors were accordingly appointed in 1898 for work in Ponnani and Kurumbranad. All work was stopped in the former taluk, however, in September 1900 when only 37 desams had been dealt with; and by the middle of the following year registration was brought to completion in the other taluks, but only after the janmam registration establishments had been merged in the Settlement department. In the rest of the district the registration of proprietors was carried out by the Settlement Officers simultaneously with the introduction of the new rates. The preliminary registry was in the main that of the Survey department. The rough patta gave each proprietor particulars of the lands registered in his name, and appeals against the registry were heard at the same time as objections to the revised assessments. The work that this procedure entailed was enormous, upwards of 170,000 claims having to be heard and decided by the Settlement Officers. But the janmis, now that they saw that the settlement was being introduced in earnest, were as eager to be registered as they had previously been apathetic; and the officers of the department managed to complete their enquiries into janmam titles in the same year as they introduced the rates into the taluks not dealt with by the Special Deputy Collectors.

The garden difficulty.

The difficulty of assessing gardens is obvious and need not be laboured. A patch of sand on the sea coast yields nothing, and *ex nihilo nihil fit*; the same patch covered with cocoanut palms pays a tax of Rs. 7 per acre with ease; but the process of conversion takes time and money, and, while it is going on, an assessment in any way commensurate with the future value of the garden is out of the question. The tree-tax hitherto in force had proved unsatisfactory; but the difficulties in the way of discarding it for acreage rates, which, without pressing unduly on thinly planted gardens, would secure to Government a fair share of the produce of those fully planted up, long seemed insuperable. A committee appointed in 1889 unanimously declared for the abolition of the tree-tax and proposed acreage rates ranging from Rs. 5 to Re. 1. The Government at first rejected these proposals on the ground that the rates, not being based on any fixed proportion of the money value of the produce, could not be revised at a resettlement with reference to prices, and despaired of being

CHAP. XI. THE SURVEY AND SETTLEMENT.

able to dispense with tree counting altogether. Various schemes were weighed in the balance and found wanting;[1] but in 1894 it was recognised that no scheme could be devised which would not involve a reclassification of gardens at resettlement; and in 1900, after trees had been counted and the gardens classified in six taluks and part of a seventh, it was decided to apply[2] a system of acreage rates varying from Rs. 7 to Re. 1 according to the quality of the garden, regard being had both to the number and quality of the trees.

Introduction of the settlement.

By the new settlement, which was introduced into the eight plain taluks between September 1900 and June 1904, the revenue system of the district has been brought into line with that of the rest of the Presidency, due allowance being made for special local conditions. Apart from the settlement with the janmis, and the abolition of the tree-tax, the chief departure from the old system is that on dry lands the practice of charging only certain specified crops has been abandoned. The principle of charging occupation has, with the important exception mentioned below, taken the place of the principle of charging cultivation.

Principles.

Cultivable lands have been classified according to their soil in the red ferruginous or arenacious series of soils, 84 per cent being classed as red ferruginous loam (class VII) and the bulk of the rest as red ferruginous sand (class VIII), and have been divided into wet, garden and dry lands. Lands levelled, bunded, and adapted for wet cultivation are treated as wet. To constitute a garden, a minimum of ten cocoanut trees to the acre, or the equivalent in arecas or jacks,[3] is necessary; and, following the ancient custom, these trees alone are recognised as garden products. Other cultivable lands are classed as dry and are divided into two kinds, occupied and unoccupied. Occupied dry lands are lands which are under permanent occupation continued from year to year, and are charged assessment each year. Unoccupied dry lands are waste lands or lands cultivated intermittently with fugitive crops. Assessment is levied only on the extent cultivated in each year, no charge being made for fallows. The building of a house, the planting of fruit trees, the erection of a permanent fence, the conversion of land into wet, or the cultivation of a dry crop for three years in succession, are the criteria of permanent occupation for the purpose of the registry of land as occupied dry.

---

[1] Reference may be made to G.O. No. 883, Revenue, dated 29th August 1900 and B.P. No. 477, dated 27th December 1904.

[2] G.O. No. No. 144, Revenue, dated 20th February 1900.

[3] Cocoanut = 12 arecanuts = ½ jack.

Grouping.

For the purposes of wet and dry assessment, desams were divided into three groups on a consideration of the following conditions :—

(*a*) Proximity to markets.
(*b*) Facilities of communication.
(*c*) Similarity and productive capabilities of soils.
(*d*) Local features affecting relative fertility.
(*e*) Unhealthiness or otherwise of localities.
(*f*) Liability to ravages by wild animals.

Wet rates.

In order to fix the money rates on wet lands paddy was of course taken to be the standard wet crop, and after numerous experiments the outturn was estimated to vary from 900 to 200 Madras measures per acre. The outturn thus determined for each class and sort of soil was converted into money, at a rate calculated upon an average of the prices of the 20 normal years, ending with 1892–93, reduced by 15 per cent to allow for cartage and merchants' profits. A commutation price of Rs. 125 per garce of 3,200 Madras measures or Rs. 42·5 per thousand Macleod seers was thus arrived at. Reductions (*a*) of 15 per cent for vicissitudes of season and unprofitable areas, (*b*) of cultivation expenses and (*c*) of one-third of the remainder for the cultivator's share, were made from the gross value ; and six-tenths of the remainder was taken as the share due to Government. This share was still further reduced, as will be seen from the marginal table. The extreme leniency of these rates and the wide margin allowed for error are apparent. The proclamation of 1805, in which no allowance had been made for vicissitudes of seasons or unprofitable areas, was adhered to in so far as it provided for the division of the wet produce between the Government, the landlord and the cultivator ; and the Government demand was thereby reduced from the normal one-half of the net produce nominally to two-fifths thereof, but in practice to an even smaller proportion. On land regularly yielding two crops, the charge for the second is consolidated at the lenient rate of one quarter of the first crop charge. For occasional second crop on single crop lands, the charge is one-half the first crop assessment. Inducement is thus held out to cultivators to compound.

Taram.	$\frac{8}{10}$ of net value on account of Government share.			Sanctioned rate.		
	RS.	A.	P.	RS.	A.	P.
1	6	15	3	6	0	0
2	5	13	2	5	0	0
3	4	14	4	4	0	0
4	4	4	10	3	0	0
5	3	3	10	2	0	0
6	2	8	2	1	8	0
7	1	12	7	1	0	0
8	1	0	11	0	12	0

Dry rates.

Dry rates were calculated in similar fashion ; but are even more moderate, as the Government share works out at only one-third of the net produce. Modan or upland rice was taken as the standard crop, and its outturn was estimated

CHAP. XI. THE SURVEY AND SETTLEMENT.

to vary from 400 to 150 measures according to soil Rs. 120 per garce was adopted as the commutation price; one-fifth of the gross value was deducted for vicissitudes of season; and cultivation expenses were calculated at sums varying from Rs. 6 to Rs. 3 per acre. One-third of the net produce being deducted for the cultivator's share, the balance was divided in equal proportions between Government and the janmis. The resulting rates rise from As. 4 to As. 12 by increments of As. 2 and thence to Re. 1, Re. 1–8–0 and Rs. 2 per acre.

Garden rates.

In assessing gardens, seven acreage rates varying between Rs. 7 and Re. 1 were imposed, according as the garden was 'best,' 'superior,' 'good,' 'ordinary,' 'inferior,' 'bad', or 'worst.' In applying these rates, the classifier first had to decide by which of these adjectives the garden could appropriately be described, on a consideration of the quality of the trees and soil, and then to estimate whether the garden was fully, three-quarters, half or quarter planted. To take a simple example, a fully planted garden estimated to contain not less than 40 'ordinary' trees to the acre, a three-quarter planted garden of 'good' trees, a half planted 'superior' and a quarter planted 'best' garden, were all placed in the fourth taram and assessed as an 'ordinary' garden at Rs. 4 per acre. To work the system successfully a large staff of well-trained subordinates and constant supervision were essential. Both conditions were fulfilled in the Malabar Settlement Party, which at one time included no less than thirty-five Special Inspectors on Rs. 50 a month and eight Gazetted Officers. The rates are extremely lenient, and would have been greatly enhanced had Government thought fit to claim the full share to which they were entitled. Mr. Moberly after cautious and elaborate calculations, estimated the average annual produce of a best cocoanut tree at 55 nuts, and converting this into money at a very low commutation rate of Rs. 20 per 1,000 nuts, deducting 25 per cent for vicissitudes of season and making allowance for cultivation expenses, he proposed a tax of As. 3–6, representing one-third of the net produce of a best tree. At these rates the assessment on a fully planted best garden would have been Rs. 8–12–0. The usual *pattam* or rent on a best tree, moreover, is Re. 1 per annum; and in many gardens there is in addition to the taxable trees much miscellaneous produce grown, such as pepper, betel, mangoes and vegetables of all kinds, of which no special account is taken.

Average money rates.

Thirty-four per cent of the total wet area has been assessed at rates varying from As. 12 to Rs. 2, and 53 per cent from Rs. 3 to Rs. 4 per acre. About four-fifths of the garden lands have been assessed at the four lowest rates, and only 8 per cent at Rs. 6 or more. Nearly 28 per cent of the occupied dry land has been assessed at between As. 4 and As. 10 per acre, 39 per

CHAP. XI. THE SURVEY AND SETTLEMENT.

cent at As. 12, and nearly 24 per cent at Re. 1. The percentage increase or decrease in the area of wet and garden lands, revealed by the first scientific survey of Malabar, and that of assessment due to the settlement, are exhibited in the following table [1] :—

Taluks.	Wet land. Percentage increase of		Garden land. Percentage difference in	
	EXTENT.	ASST.	EXTENT.	ASST.
Chirakkal	22	36	+ 34	+ 69
Kottayam	29	27	+ 45	+ 96
Kurumbranad ..	36	38	+ 34	+109
Calicut	35	26	+277	+ 71
Ernad	39	62	+ 45	+ 97
Walavanad	33	75	— 16	+ 37
Palghat	38	76	— 14	+156
Ponnani	24	42	+ 46	+112
District	34	56	+ 43	+ 94

The table, it will be noticed, confirms the old impression that the wet assessments in North Malabar were heavier than those in South Malabar.

The average rates per acre in each taluk on wet, garden, occupied and unoccupied dry land are shown below :—

Taluks.	Wet.	Garden.	Occupied dry.	Unoccupied dry.
	RS. A. P.	RS. A. P.	RS. A. P.	RS. A. P.
Chirakkal	3 3 10	2 14 4	0 11 5	0 10 10
Kottayam	2 14 2	2 15 6	0 12 0	0 10 5
Kurumbranad ..	2 15 8	2 15 10	0 11 4	0 9 2
Calicut	3 0 6	2 8 11	0 12 2	0 9 10
Ernad	3 7 4	2 8 2	0 14 1	0 11 3
Walavanad	4 6 6	1 15 2	1 0 11	0 12 4
Palghat	3 14 10	2 3 0	0 14 0	0 11 7
Ponnani	3 1 9	3 14 10	0 9 11	0 9 3
District average ..	3 8 11	2 15 3	0 13 2	0 10 10

Financial results.

The financial result of the new settlement was an increase of Rs. 13,53,890, or 77 per cent in the total revenue. Before the settlement Malabar had paid far less than its fair share of the public revenue. This inequality has now been partially rectified ; but had Government deemed it expedient to exact what they might have claimed with justice, the increase would

[1] Occupied dry lands have been excluded as the area permanently assessed prior to the settlement was trifling.

CHAP. XI. THE SURVEY AND SETTLEMENT.

have been much greater. By the Increment Remission rules, which in Malabar are worked on peculiar principles, [1] it will be many years before the full settlement demand is collected.

With the introduction of the settlement, the general rules as to remission, which hitherto had not been in force in the district, were extended to Malabar [2].

Re-settlement. 1931–34.

[3] The term of thirty years for which the existing rates of land assessment were sanctioned for the eight plain taluks having expired between 1929–30 and 1932–33 as shown below, a revision of the rates and the conditions of assessment was carried out on the basis of the proposals made by Mr. A. R. MacEwen, I.C.S., Special Settlement Officer :—

Taluk.	Last settlement expired in	New settlement from
Palghat and 94 desams of Calicut.	1929–30	1931–32
Walavanad and rest of Calicut.	1930–31	1931–32
Kurumbranad	1930–31	1932–33
Chirakkal, Kottayam, Ernad and Ponnani.	1932–33	1933–34

In the isolated lands in the Cochin State attached to certain desams in Palghat taluk, isolated bits attached to the main desam of Manathana of Kottayam taluk and the Cannanore *Karar* lands of the Chirakkal taluk, where the re-settlement would expire in a few years later, it has been proposed to introduce the new rates in the same fasli along with other lands in the taluks to which they are now attached. As regards the Laccadives no survey or re-settlement was considered necessary as the coir monopoly from which Government revenue was derived was working satisfactorily.

At the last settlement paddy was taken as the standard crop for wet lands, modan or hill paddy for dry lands and cocoanut for garden lands. Since then the prices of these standard crops have increased considerably. While the price per garce of paddy was found to be Rs. 125 at the last settlement after making the usual deductions, the price on the basis of the average of the last twenty non-famine years was even during the ryots' selling months Rs. 346 and after making the usual deductions Rs. 294 or an increase of 135 per cent. The price of modan paddy was taken as 7½ per cent less than that of second sort paddy and its price was found to be 133 per cent in excess of the commutation rate of Rs. 120 per garce at the last settlement. As regards cocoanuts, the commutation rate

[1] G.O. Nos. 857, 857-A, Revenue, dated 20th September 1902.
[2] B. P. (Settlement), No. 477, dated 22nd December 1904.
[3] B.P. No. 80, Press, dated 17th October 1930, for Scheme Report and the Board's resolution thereon. Also G.O. No. 2717, Revenue, dated 23rd December 1931, for orders passed on them.

worked out to an increase of 113 per cent over the rate which formed the basis of taxation in 1904. The prices adopted at the previous settlement were extremely liberal and the recommendation of the Special Settlement Officer which the Board of Revenue and Government approved allowed an increase of three annas per rupee in the current rate of assessment or 18¾ per cent (which is the maximum percentage of enhancement to which the Government have committed themselves). The rate for the eight tarams thus varied from Rs. 7–2–0 to 14 annas an acre as against the original rates which ranged from Rs. 6 to 12 annas. The rates for dry lands were increased by 12½ per cent or by two annas in the rupee, the original rates of the tarams from Rs. 2 to 4 annas being altered to rates ranging from Rs. 2–4–0 to 5 annas. The garden rates were, like the wet rates, increased by 18¾ per cent.

Special features.

There were a few special features of the re-settlement. The terms "janmabhogam" and "private janmam" were replaced by "new holdings" and "old holdings" respectively, and as in the case of the Wynaad re-settlement the practice of levying two rates, one for the taram assessment and the other for janmabhogam was abandoned in favour of a consolidated assessment. The classification and grouping of wet lands in the district had been based on the productivity of the best lands in Palghat and Walavanad taluks, and this led to lands in other taluks being graded low and charged lower rates than their productivity would warrant. But Government decided not to have a reclassification of soils made in view of the labour and expense involved. The grouping and classification of dry and garden lands were also not disturbed. Power was, however, reserved to the Special Settlement Officer to transfer to the appropriate head occupied dry lands converted into wet or garden and unoccupied dry lands converted into occupied dry, wet or garden. He was also authorized on the ryot's application to transfer garden or wet lands to dry provided the change was necessitated by causes beyond the control of the ryot. The question was considered whether for occasional second crop raised on single crop wet lands, some method might not be devised by which the second crop charge could be consolidated so as to minimise the extensive inspections by revenue officers; but in view of the financial loss involved and the absence of any possibility of saving in establishment charges, the matter was dropped. Fugitive cultivation on unoccupied assessed dry lands was paid for only in years in which there was cultivation, and no flat rate was levied on such lands as in Wynaad; and the concession allowed to ryots of using unoccupied dry lands for seed beds was continued as the privilege had not led to any abuse. Escheat quit-rent, that is an annual charge

CHAP. XI. The Survey and Settlement.

levied on lands which holders of escheated property from Government were asked to pay instead of lump sums in return for janmam right which Government gave up in them being fixed and unalterable was continued unaffected. For miscellaneous rents bearing " an amazing assortment of names " taram assessment was substituted except where the original grants showed that the rents were unalterable. Patches of cultivation in several thousand acres of unsurveyed jungle land were proposed for survey, if need be as independent units, for assessment at taram rates. Fugitive dry cultivation in unsurveyed lands used to be paid for at rates which varied for each crop, but a flat rate of 10 annas per acre was levied on them ; and on such lands where garden and wet cultivation was going on taram assessment was ordered to be levied. Survey was ordered to be made of lands growing such special products as coffee, tea, cardamoms and rubber so that appropriate dry taram rates may be levied on them. The methods of assessment in the Attapadi valley were found to be inequitable, as the lands were rarely visited by the revenue inspector or tahsildar and the menon could not even identify the various plots and his demands were arbitrary, wet rates for instance varying from Rs. 4–3–7 to As. 7–4 an acre. The Settlement Officer's proposals to abolish the distinction between permanent and fugitive cultivation and to enforce a uniform rate of 8 annas an acre for dry lands and Rs. 1–8–0 for wet lands under cultivation was accepted. Areas grown with estate crops were ordered to be surveyed and suitably classified and assessed at dry rates. Dry lands under wet crop in the Vandithode anicut system were allowed to be transferred to wet in cases where the lands were irrigable with the water from this channel.

Objections answered.

No objections or representations had been made within the three months allowed in the resettlement notification of January 1931, but a deputation of some janmis waited on the Hon'ble the Revenue Member and urged that the first settlement in the district was a permanent one, that pending legislation fixing the future policy of Government on the settlement of land revenue, no resettlement should be made and that in any case the prevailing economic condition cannot warrant the imposition of enhanced rates. A resolution was moved and carried in the Legislative Council asking for the postponement of the proposed enhancement. The theory that the original settlement was a permanent one was based on the words " unalterable assessment " used by Mr. Warden who was Collector of Malabar in his proclamation of 1805. What was meant was that " the principles on which the Government's share was to be based were to be permanent." These principles had never formed the basis of a settlement in the district and as early as 1883 Government had made it clear that there was nothing in the proclamation to show that they were in any way pledged to maintain the settlement unaltered; and as observed at the time of the last settlement and again in the proposals for the present settlement Government were in fact making a concession by abandoning a strict adhesion to the formula laid down in Mr. Warden's proclamation.

As regards the argument that resettlement should not be introduced pending legislation on resettlement policy, Government had already explained their position more than once in the Logislative Council. Attempts at such legislation were made but were unsuccessful and in view of the pending constitutional changes they did not propose to take further steps towards legislation on the settlement of land revenue, and saw no reason to postpone introduction of the new settlement. In regard to the argument that the economic condition of the people had not materially improved since the last settlement, the report of the Settlement Officer clearly showed that there was an obvious and substantial increase in the prosperity of the ryots, that notwithstanding the general fall in prices a comparison of the prices of the standard crops in the months of July to November 1931 with those prevailing at the time of the previous settlement showed that they were higher by 50 to 71 per cent, whereas the maximum increase in the rates was only 18¾ per cent. One of the objects of resettlement is to ensure as far as practicable an equitable distribution of the incidence of land revenue throughout the Presidency. The recent fall in prices was general and the effect of the continuance of the existing rates in this district would be to perpetuate the advantage which it is enjoying and has for some years enjoyed at the expense of the other districts for which there can be no justification. In view of the recent fall in prices Government as a matter of grace allowed for this district, as for the two Godavaries and Kistna, the grant of increment remission in respect of the percentage increase of the rates of assessment in the fasli in which the new rates were introduced and the following two faslis.

Financial results.

Roughly speaking the resettlement is expected to bring in an increase of 18·48 per cent over the present revenue demand. Subject to certain conditions the new settlement will remain in force for a period of 30 years from the year of its introduction.

WYNAAD Warden's Wet settlement.

Owing to the constant disturbances which convulsed the Wynaad, no attempt was made to introduce any settlement, until in 1806, after the suppression of the Pychy rebellion, Mr. Baber proposed to fix the assessment upon the basis of a *pattam* estimated at twice the seed sown. Mr. Warden, the Collector, however adopted a more elaborate scheme, and one peculiar to the Wynaad. The gross produce of each wet holding was ascertained by multiplying the seed sown by the outturn multiple; and, a deduction of twice the seed being

CHAP. XI. THE WYNAAD SETTLEMENT.

made for cultivation expenses, the balance was divided in equal shares between Government, the janmi and the cultivator. The intricate enquiries into actual yield, entailed by this scheme, were obviated by fixing, after numerous crop experiments, standard outturn multiples varying from one to fifteen fold for each amsam.

This labour-saving device proved ultimately the ruin of a settlement unobjectionable in theory, save for the necessity of ascertaining annually the seed sown. Wet lands differ enormously in soil, situation, and productive powers even in a single amsam; and in fixing the outturn multiples, no allowance had been made for these differences. To make the scheme workable therefore and to preserve some apparent uniformity in the method of assessment, precisely the same fiction was resorted to, as had been utilised by the Mysorean officials in Palghat. Assessing officers were allowed to use their discretion to prevent over-assessments upon inferior lands, by fixing the Government share on a calculation based not upon the actual quantity of seed sown, but upon such quantity as they might deem advisable. This measure was known as *niguthi vittu* or seed of assessment.

A further modification of the scheme was found necessary in practice. Mr. Warden had provided for the conversion into money of the Government share at prices locally prevalent. As can easily be imagined, the result was immense diversity of rates with no guarantee for their equity; and to remedy the evil, commutation rates were fixed for each amsam. For the sake of convenience, the rates were calculated upon each *pothi* [1] of *niguthi vittu* by the simple method of dividing, in a sufficient number of cases in each amsam, the average money value of the Government share by the average number of *pothis* of seed actually sown. On these lines a 'riwaz' or table of rates was drawn up by Mr. Baber. In Mr. Græme's time they varied from As. 15 to Rs. 2–10–0 per pothi; in 1884 from Re. 1–4–0 to Rs. 2–5–7.

This amsam settlement was adhered to by Mr. Vaughan under instructions from Mr. Græme. Modified in some ways, but always to the disadvantage of Government, it subsisted till 1888.

Its subsequent developments.

The annual ascertainment of the amount of seed annually sown was left to the village officers, themselves cultivators; and in their hands the system gradually developed into organised fraud. Originally the *niguthi vittu* had been only in exceptional cases less than the real quantity sown. But the exception became the rule, and in 1884 it was only a fraction thereof, sometimes one-half, generally a quarter. The

[1] Pothi = 30 local measures = 26 Macleod seers = 22½ Madras measures.

village officers were of course interested in making the fraction as small as possible; and the remoteness of the taluk from central authority and the consequent laxity of supervision facilitated the fraud. At best the old system had been a tax on cultivation. In its later form it became a tax on such cultivation as the ill-paid amsam officials thought fit to bring to account.

Its subsequent development.

But the loss to Government did not end here. The *niguthi vittu* system made no provision for the numerous cases in which Government were also the proprietors of the holding, and entitled to rent as well as assessment therefrom. Accordingly, between 1822 and 1860 Government had levied *janmabhogam* at various rates, in addition to assessment on lands over which it exercised proprietary rights; and in the latter year had fixed it at a uniform charge of As. 8 per acre upon all lands occupied for whatever purpose. In theory *janmabhogam*, as opposed to assessment, had always been a tax on occupation; but in the general demoralization of the land revenue system it had degenerated, like assessment, into a tax on supposed cultivation, and was calculated on the *niguthi vittu*.

A single instance of the way Government were defrauded of their dues will suffice. In 1884 the average wet rate in Ganapathivattam amsam, where the riwaz was highest, was As. 9–5 per acre, *plus* As. 2–7 *janmabhogam*. By Mr. Warden's settlement, it should have been Rs. 2–15–0, *plus* As. 8 *janmabhogam*.

Dry lands.

Dry grain lands were not charged till 1862, when acreage rates of Re. 1–4–0 upon land inspected annually, and As. 10 upon that in permanent occupation, were sanctioned. On Government janmam lands these rates were enhanced by the usual *janmabhogam*. The rules for the sale of Government waste lands were introduced in the same year; and the assessment reserved on them was Rs. 2 for forest, and Re. 1 (reduced in 1871 to As. 8) for grass lands.

Estates.

Coffee estates were taxed in 1860 at a uniform rate of Rs. 2 per acre from the third year after planting, plus the usual *janmabhogam* if the land belonged to Government. Cinchona was similarly assessed; but no charge was made for the 'garden' products of the plains. Subsequently, Government waste lands sold under the above rules, were taken up almost exclusively for coffee and cinchona cultivation. In 1883 the assessment on coffee was remitted for an extra year; but the concession was limited to lands sold under these rules. The same year, cinchona lands held on patta, whether as private janman or under Government, were exempted temporarily from assessment for four full years after planting.

The revision of the Wynaad settlement had its own difficulties, but they were different from those which afterwards had to be faced in the low country. There were no garden lands, and the problem of assessing estates devoted to the cultivation of special products had already been solved in the manner related in the preceding paragraph. A settlement with the tenant had not as yet been pronounced illegal; but for reasons which will now be explained an investigation of titles, similar to that carried out below under Act III of 1896, but on a more limited scale, was a necessary prelude to, and in its way the direct cause of, the settlement of the taluk.

Wynaad escheat settlement.

By a proclamation issued in 1805, the estates of the Pychy rebel and those of his principal adherents had been confiscated; but the sentence had only partially been carried into effect, and only paddy flats then under cultivation had been actually escheated. Hills, forests and unoccupied tracts, which in the Wynaad made up the greater portion of the escheated property, remained undefined; and in course of time, as coffee cultivation expanded and the land became valuable, they were encroached upon by private persons, who set up vague claims to janmam right. The subject came up for the consideration of Government in 1859 in connection with the conservancy of forests throughout the presidency; and the necessity of a survey was at once realized, to define not only the boundaries of Government escheats, but also those of private estates. A survey was accordingly undertaken; but for various reasons, mainly connected with the difficult nature of the country and its extreme unhealthiness, it dragged along in so fitful and desultory a manner, that by 1882 only about a third of the taluk had been mapped. In 1880 the 'boom' in gold mining once more raised the question in an acute form; and it was decided that the investigation of titles, contemplated in 1859, should be taken in hand without further delay; and, as a necessary sequence to this resolution, that the survey should be expedited.[1] In 1883, Mr. A. E. C. Stuart, I.C.S., was deputed to the Wynaad, at first with definite instructions to restrict his operations to the enquiry into titles. But in the following year, holding that the results of his investigations could not be permanently secured until regular and complete land registers of the usual type were prepared, Government resolved upon a revenue settlement of the taluk.

Principles of revenue settlement.

A scheme was submitted in 1885, and the methods and principles to be adopted were defined in the following year.[2] As afterwards in the plains, the principle of taxing cultivation was abandoned in favour of an assessment of occupation; but in view of the peculiar circumstances of the taluk, it was resolved that the settlement, like that of the Nilgiri hills, should be an entirely special one, the soils being roughly

[1] G.O. No. 471, Revenue, dated 6th May 1882.

[2] G.O. No. 611, Revenue, dated 22nd July 1886.

CHAP. XI. THE WYNAAD SETTLEMENT

arranged in classes or tarams and a scale of rates applied thereto. The patta was to be a mere note of the revenue payable, and was to be ssued in the name of the person, whether janmi or not, who in virtue of occupation paid the tax. With the settlement, the ordinary system of darkhast and relinquishment was to be introduced; but, the rate of janmabhogham fixed in 1860 was to remain unchanged.

Sanctioned rates.

In fixing the rates no attempt was made to estimate actual yield or cultivation expenses, or to base the assessment upon any definite proportion of the net produce. Cultivable lands were divided into wet, comprising swamps and paddy flats, and dry, including all other lands whether cultivated with modan, *punam* or special products. For wet lands, a scale of rates rising from As. 8 to Rs. 2–8–0, by increments of As. 4 was adopted; and the soils were classified and arranged in classes, sorts and tarams to correspond with the money rates. Dry lands were not classified, but were arranged in four classes, and assessed at rates ranging from As. 8 per acre by increments of As. 8 to Rs. 2 per acre. The highest class included forest lands and coffee and cinchona cultivation, the second class the better kind of scrub, the third inferior scrub and best grass lands, and the fourth inferior grass lands. Estates held under the waste land rules were not interfered with by the settlement; and all concessions exempting tea, coffee and cinchona lands from assessment for certain periods after planting, were confirmed.

Special rates were fixed for estates held under private janmis or acquired in good faith from private janmis, who had been ousted by Government at the escheat settlement. Land under actual cultivation was charged at the ordinary Rs. 2 rate, but only a pepper corn charge of 6 pies per acre was levied on the unplanted portion. Estates held on Government patta were charged the proper rate per acre on the whole area occupied, whether cultivated or not, in addition to the usual *janmabhogam*. House-sites were allowed free up to an extent of 25 cents. Shifting cultivation of all kinds was prohibited upon forest lands of the first class (which may not be given on darkhast and may be sold only under the waste land rules) and is now allowed only in the inferior classes of dry lands.

The settlement on these lines was introduced by Mr. Stuart into the three amsams of South-East Wynaad, Nambalakod, Munnanad and Cherankod in 1886–87, in the following year, into eight amsams of North Wynaad, Ganapathivattam, Pudadi, Kuppatod, Ellornad, Nallurnad, Etavara, Periya and Thondarnad, in 1888–89 into the remaining five amsams of Malabar-Wynaad, and in 1889 into the Ouchterlony valley. The first and last tracts are now part of the Nilgiri district and may be passed over in silence.

CHAP. XI. THE WYNAAD SETTLEMENT.

Average rates.

The wet lands were classified either in the regar and the red ferruginous series, the latter being in enormous preponderance and comprising nearly 96 per cent of the total wet area. In assessing them little use was made of the first two and the last two tarams, nearly 47 per cent of the wet lands being assessed at Rs. 1–12–0, 26 per cent at Rs. 1–8–0, 16 per cent at Rs. 2 and the bulk of the remainder at Rs. 1–4–0. Of the dry lands, exclusive of unassessed forest and estates held on the Rs. 2 *plus* 6 pies rate and lands sold under the waste land rules, 41 per cent were classed as forest at Rs. 2 per acre, 34 per cent as superior scrub, 19 per cent as inferior scrub, and only 5 per cent as grass land. The average wet and dry rates are shown below :—

——	Wet.		Dry.	
	Occupied.	Unoccupied.	Occupied.	Unoccupied.
	RS. A. P.	RS. A. P.	RS. A. P.	RS. A. P.
North Wynaad ..	1 11 0	1 11 3	1 13 8	1 8 6
South Wynaad ..	1 6 2	1 8 5	1 13 9	1 8 2

Financial results.

Considering the system or rather the want of system hitherto in vogue, it is not surprising that the financial result of the new settlement was an enormous increase of revenue. But the increase by survey was even greater. In North Wynaad the assessment had been increased by 154 per cent and the occupied area by 289 per cent. In South Wynaad the percentages were 120 and 226, respectively. Details are given in the appended statement :—

	Wet lands. Percentage difference in		Dry lands. Percentage increase of	
	Extent.	Assessment.	Extent.	Assessment.
North Wynaad ..	+ 269	+ 135	309	185
South Wynaad ..	— 8	+ 148	616	105

There was also a large increase of *janmabhogam*. The As. 8 rate was not enhanced ; but the escheat enquiries had added largely to the number of Government janmam lands in the taluk, and the occupied area of those previously charged with *janmabhogam* had been much underestimated. In Wynaad, unlike the rest of Malabar, the proprietary right of such land has not been parted with, except under the waste land rules, and the escheat settlement, inaugurated by Mr. Conolly in 1852, was not enforced in the taluk. The increase of assessment, when it exceeded 25 per cent, was collected by annual increments of 25 per cent.

Settlement with tenant declared illegal.

No sooner had the new rates been introduced than the revised revenue was endangered by the decision of the High Court, already referred to, that a settlement in Malabar with any one but the janmi was illegal. In 1891, therefore, at the same time that it resolved upon janmam registration in Malabar proper, Government decided that the registration of private lands in the Wynaad must be revised; and that the system of darkhast and relinquishments introduced with the new settlement, must be abandoned as incompatible with janmam right, and unsuited to the country and its peculiar tenures. The settlement notification of the Wynaad was accordingly amended by a proclamation issued in 1893, but without interfering in any way with the classification of land, the rates of assessments or the settled demand.

Once more surveyors had to be sent to the Wynaad, and a Special Deputy Collector was deputed to find out janmis and their lands. Private janmam lands had to be identified, demarcated and surveyed. Mistakes in the former survey had to be corrected; escheat lands, included in the same block with unoccupied waste or private janmam lands, had to be separated; and the claims of private persons to unoccupied lands, not declared escheat, but registered as Government janmam, had to be investigated. The transfer of the pattas to the janmis was completed by the end of fasli 1304 (1894–95); but the land registers re-written and revised in accordance with the revision survey were not issued for some years.

Working of settlement.

In substituting the system of payment on occupation for payment on cultivation, Government were well aware that the result must be the abandonment of a large extent of land assessed as occupied. The country was covered with squatters at the time of the settlement; and most of the squatters, who had no acknowledged janmi, though fully warned of the consequences, claimed to be in occupation of as large extents as they thought they would be suffered to hold without challenge. On the other hand, those who had secured leases from a landlord, had taken up the greatest possible area for the least possible rent. Thus both classes were in occupation of far larger areas than they could possibly cultivate; and, in spite of the moderation of the rates, the total tax on the holding was often more than the occupant could pay. For the three years following the settlement moreover, the Wynaad was visited by a disastrous outbreak of rinderpest which swept away large numbers of cattle, and the seasons were exceptionally bad. Under these circumstances the consequences which had been foreseen ensued. By 1895–96, 19,420 acres of occupied land had been relinquished and 18,826 acres sold for arrears of revenue, 13,076 acres being bought in by Government. Of the total area relinquished and bought in by Government, only 6,561 acres had been taken up again for cultivation. [1]

[1] G.O. No. 738, Revenue, dated 3rd December 1898, and B.P. No. 671, dated 16th October 1897.

CHAP. XI. THE WYNAAD SETTLEMENT.

Relinquishments.

As a concession to the peculiar conditions of the Wynaad, where the population is steadily decreasing and much good land is going out of cultivation simply for lack of labour, special rules as to the relinquishment of private janmam land were introduced in 1896.[1] Such land is now not charged with assessment if left waste, provided that notice of relinquishment for the ensuing revenue year is given before July 1st.[2] No remission however is given for fallows, and the remission is cancelled, unless the land is left waste for two consecutive faslis ; nor are relinquishments of land, which is in the possession actual or constructive of tenants, allowed.

In 1904 pepper was classed as a special product in the Malabar-Wynaad and was exempted from assessment for three years after planting.[3] A similar concession has been extended to rubber.

The Wynaad Re-settlement, 1926–27.

The term of thirty years for which the rates of land assessment sanctioned at the original settlement for Wynaad having expired, a revision of the rates and conditions of assessment was carried into effect from fasli 1336 (1926–27). The taluk was resurveyed before Mr. A. H. A. Todd, I.C.S., the officer appointed to carry out the resettlement, started operations. The following are some of the important features of the resettlement.

Special features.

Lands known as "Government janmam" and "private janmam" at the original settlement were classified as "new holdings" and "old holdings", and on all lands on which *janmabogam* was collected and on all Government assessed waste lands, the *taram* assessment and *janmabhogam* were amalgamated and a consolidated assessment was fixed, and all future assignments of Government waste lands were to be at these rates.

Wet lands.

In regard to wet lands the soil classification was left unaltered, except in the case of lands transferred from dry to wet. Private *janmam* wet lands (which were under cultivation in three out of five years) and Government *janmam* wet lands were registered as "permanent wet" ; and failure to cultivate such lands could not create any right to remission of assessment on them unless their registered holders had relinquished before the prescribed date all their rights in them. The provision of the Board's Standing Order concerning seasonal remissions was however allowed to apply to all "permanent wet" lands. Other wet lands were registered as "fugitive wet" and were liable to be assessed only when cultivated ; and Government reserved the right to transfer lands registered as "fugitive

---

[1] G.O. No. 250, Revenue, dated 11th June 1896.

[2] G.O. No. 1181, Revenue, dated 29th October 1906.

[3] G.O. No. 797, Revenue, dated 25th July 1904.

CHAP. XI. THE WYNAAD SETTLEMENT.

wet" to the head "permanent wet" and *vice versa* at any time during the currency of the resettlement. The rates of land revenue on all wet lands were enhanced by $18\frac{3}{4}$ per cent.

Dry lands.

With reference to dry lands private *janmam* lands under regular occupation from year to year and Government *janmam* lands were classed as "developed" and all other lands as "undeveloped". All "developed" lands were inspected with a view to their classification being revised if necessary, and except in the case of dry lands hitherto known as Government dry land, the taram and rates of assessment adopted at the original settlement were retained. A consolidated rate of assessment took the place of the charges separately made under the heads "taram assessment" and *janmabhogam* where they occurred in the assessment of individual fields, as a result of reclassification or alteration in area.

Fugitive cultivation on "undeveloped" lands (commonly kown as *punam*) was not separately assessed but to cover all such fugitive cultivation "undeveloped" lands were charged a flat rate of six pies an acre. "Developed" or "undeveloped" lands were not entitled to any remission unless the registered holders of the lands relinquished to Government all their rights before a certain date. Government reserved the right to transfer dry land registered as "undeveloped" to the head "developed" and to assess it at the appropriate *taram* rate in lieu of the composition rates during the currency of the resettlement.

Estate lands.

Small plots of land cultivated with special crops were at the discretion of the settlement officer excluded from the definition of "estate lands" of which there were two classes "estate developed" and "estate undeveloped". Under the former came all lands within estates planted with tea, coffee, rubber, cinchona or any other special crop or occupied by buildings required for or auxiliary to the cultivation of these crops or their preparation for the market. All other estate lands were "estate undeveloped" lands. "Estate developed" lands were assessed at a flat rate of Rs. 3 and "estate undeveloped" lands at ten annas an acre, but lower rates of Rs. 2-6-0 and six pies were allowed in the case of those estate lands on which *janmabhogam* was not previously paid to Government. Right to re-survey and re-assess when necessary "estate developed" lands at intervals of not less than five years during the currency of the settlement was reserved to Government. ***Punam*** cultivations on "estate undeveloped" lands were not, however, subject to any separate assessment besides the composition rate ten annas or six pies as the case may be.

General.

All lands not relinquished to Government before 30th April in any fasli were liable to assessment for the following fasli, and applications for remissions of assessment on permanent wet

CHAP. XI. THE WYNAAD SETTLEMENT

lands for any fasli must be made before the 31st July. The rates of assessment were to be current during a period of thirty years.

Pepper.

COCHIN. Early revenue history.

Cochin with its outlying *pattams* was acquired from the Dutch by right of conquest in 1795. The proprietary right of the soil vested in the Dutch; but gardens and house-sites belonging to Christian residents of whatever nationality, which lay for the most part within the precincts of the fort or in Vypeen, were not taxed. Other lands were leased for periods of twenty years, on the expiry of which they reverted absolutely to Government, no occupancy right or claims to compensation being admitted. All the rights of the Dutch passed to the British; and thus in Cochin, unlike the rest of Malabar, there was no body of janmis to complicate a ryotwari settlement. But no settlement was introduced for many years, and the system of periodical leases was continued. Mr. Conolly revised the system in 1847, when a number of leases fell in. He had the estates surveyed and assessed in conformity with the usages of the district; and made them over as far as possible to the former lessees. The assessments were liable to revision every twenty years, and by 1858 all but three estates had been settled in this manner.

Mr. Conolly's settlement.

On wet lands the gross outturn was fixed in the usual way by multiplying together the extent of the holding, the seed and the outturn multiple, and, after making deductions for seed and cultivation expenses, one-third of the balance was reserved for the cultivator, and the remainder was claimed as the Government share. Of this 65 per cent was shown in the accounts as assessment, and 35 per cent as *janmabhogam*. Government in fact in its capacity of jenmi as well as sovereign claimed two-thirds, instead of the normal half, of the net produce. But the extreme moderation of the commutation rate (Rs. 25 per 1,000 Macleod seers) secured to the cultivator a much higher share of the produce than at first sight appears. Nevertheless the prevailing wet rate in Cochin (Rs. 4-3 per acre) was much higher than the average rate in the rest of Malabar.

In respect of gardens Mr. Conolly was even more severe. He treated all trees as *attuveppu*, and divided them into three classes, estimated to bear respectively 56, 42 and 24 nuts per annum. The trees were then classified, and the gross produce of the holding ascertained and converted into money at Rs. 10 per 1,000 nuts. From this money value was deducted the assessment, at rates fixed at 60, 52 and 44 reas [1] respectively per tree of each class; and the balance was charged as *janmabhogam*. At these rates, the Government share of the gross produce was rather less than one-third in the case of trees

[1] 2 reas = 1 pie. 25 reas = 1 anna. 400 reas = Re. 1.

of the first two classes, and nearly a half in the case of the third class. But as janmi, Government took the whole of the balance of the gross produce, leaving nothing for the cultivator. Here again however the extremely low commutation rate saved the settlement from undue severity; and the average garden rate, viz., Rs. 5–5 per acre, though high as compared with the rest of Malabar, was not excessive considering the magnificent gardens of Cochin.

Escheat settlement.

The revenue settlement had been barely completed when another—the so-called 'Escheat settlement'—was begun in 1864. The history of this ill-fated enterprise is described in detail below. The janmam values were calculated on different principles from those adopted by Mr. Conolly, and were so exorbitant that, after wasting twenty years in fruitless efforts to force them upon occupants who would have none of them, Government were forced to discard them altogether and to revolutionize their methods. It was resolved to fix the valuation on the basis of the existing *janmabhogam*. The escheat quit-rent was to be redeemable at twenty years' purchase, and its payment to be secured by the issue of janmam deeds. In carrying out these orders, however, the quit-rent in the case of wet lands was calculated at two-thirds of the assessment, and in gardens was taken to be the *janmabhogam* or assessment, whichever was greater. In the case of building sites, the escheat quit-rent was to be fixed at the existing ground-rent.[1] The right of redemption was subsequently withdrawn with effect from November 12th, 1896. 739·59 acres of land were dealt with by the escheat department. 47·02 acres have been sold outright and the remaining 692·57 acres pay escheat quit-rent amounting in all to Rs. 8,980–3–5. In other words Government have sold the janmam right of the greater part of Cochin at the very light rate of Rs. 260 per acre.

Re-settlement.

In revising Mr. Conolly's settlement, it was considered whether a special scale of rates should be drawn up for Cochin. The deduction made elsewhere in Malabar for cartage and merchants' profits was hardly necessary in a market town of the commercial importance of Cochin, and the value of land in the town, which is the third port of the Presidency, and contains 19,000 inhabitants cramped into an area of less than two square miles, is very high. But Cochin, which in one way and another had paid a revenue of Rs. 16,000 on an occupied extent of not more than 1,000 acres, was the one part of the district which had hitherto borne its fair share of the financial burden, and sufficient allowance had been made for the value

---

[1] Ground-rent at Cochin is levied at 6 rates, viz., As. 4, As. 8, As. 12, Re. 1, Re. 1–8–0 and Rs. 2 per 100 carpenter's kolu perukkams. seventy-eight of these perukkams make 1 cent and the average rates are, therefore, Rs. 19¾, Rs. 39½, Rs. 58¾, Rs. 78½, Rs. 117½ and Rs. 156. The high rates are due to the enormous value of land in the town.

CHAP. XI. THE COCHIN SETTLEMENT.

of land in fixing the escheat quit-rent. The settlement was therefore introduced in 1904–05 on the same principles, and with the same rates, as had been adopted in the rest of Malabar. A small decrease of revenue (4 per cent) was the result. The average wet rates were reduced to Rs. 3–10–0 per acre, and the average garden rates were fixed at Rs. 6–9–8. The question of the lands held tax-free by Christian residents had been brought to the notice of Government as early as 1848, but the order[1] confirming them as the personal inams of Christians then in possession had never been properly carried out. Such lands as were found at settlement to be still in the occupation of descendants of the original grantees, have been confirmed as inam.

MALABAR ESCHEAT SETTLEMENT.

One of the prerogatives inherited from the former rulers of Malabar by the Honourable Company in 1792 was the right to assume the estates of private persons dying without heirs ; and on the death of the Vettatnad Raja in 1793, they had immediate occasion to exercise the privilege. The confiscation of the properties of the Pychy rebel and his principal adherents followed in 1805 ; and by the middle of the nineteenth century, when the question how to deal with escheated properties was first comprehensively considered by Government, other important escheats were the Chenat Nayar escheat in Palghat, and the estates of certain Mappillas in Ernad and Walavanad confiscated for complicity in various outbreaks.

Sale of janmam right.

The Wynaad escheats were not included in the escheat settlement and have been dealt with separately. The Vettatnad estates were surveyed by 1843, and proposals were submitted to the Board to charge *janmabhogam* on the lands. But in 1852 Mr. Conolly, the Collector, recommended the sale of the janmam right of the escheated lands, on the ground that it would be difficult to induce the tenants to pay a reasonable rent or *janmabhogam* without great delay and trouble. The recommendation was accepted by Government on the express condition that the janmam right should be transferred to the existing holders, whose occupancy right was under no plea to be disturbed.

In 1862 Mr. Grant proposed that all escheat lands in the district should be disposed of in the same way ; and in supporting the proposal, the Board expressed the opinion that Government should divest itself of all its janmam rights in Malabar, 'involving as they do landlord's duties which Government cannot adequately fulfil,' and the measure being 'highly desirable in order to set at rest the minds of present occupants and thus encourage enterprise and capital'. Government concurred, and the escheat settlement was extended not only

[1] G.O. No. 1322, dated 5th December 1848.

THE ESCHEAT SETTLEMENT.

to escheats proper but to Government lands in Cochin, Tangasseri, Manapuram and Anjengo. These lands were not escheats at all; proprietary rights in the first three places had been a legacy from the Dutch, and in the last had always belonged to the British since the settlement had first been founded in 1684.

Government at first had no conception of the magnitude of the undertaking on which they had embarked. The sales of the Vettatnad lands began in 1854, the tenants who had the right of pre-emption, being offered the janmam right of their holdings at a 'fair valuation,' and being allowed to pay either in a lump-sum or in instalments. These lands were expected to realize about Rs. 60,000, and the value of all escheats in Malabar was estimated roughly at four lakhs. But by 1871 actual payments amounted to Rs. 22,20,301, and the arrears to another 12 lakhs. The settlement was becoming a drain upon the resources of the district, and was withdrawing capital which might otherwise have been invested in the improvement of the soil.

Discontent in Cochin.

No articulate complaint however made itself heard except from Cochin. In Cochin taluk and in the island of Manapuram (Chettuvayi) not only were the occupants offered an alternative of buying the janmam right themselves, or seeing it pass from Government into the hands of some janmi less scrupulous about evictions, but the valuations fixed by the escheat department were, as they were afterwards admitted to be, 'enormously excessive'. They were not based in Cochin upon the *janmabhogam* but upon the market value of the properties. The *janmabhogam* paid annually on wet lands amounted at that time to Rs. 869–4–2, and on gardens to Rs. 4,963–2–2, though according to the proclamation of 1805 it should not have exceeded the assessment which was only Rs. 2,622. But the janmam right of wet lands was valued by the escheat department at Rs. 1,40,652 or at 160 years' purchase of the *janmabhogam*, and of the gardens at Rs. 3,42,533–4–0, or at 70 years' purchase. It mattered little that the valuations were below the price which the occupants would have had to pay in open market for their lands. The valuations were excessive seeing that the sales were forced, and that so much land was thrown at once upon a contracted market. Similarly in Manapuram, the escheat valuation varied from 133 to 324 years' purchase of the *janmabhogam*.

Many years elapsed, however, before Government would admit that the valuations required revision. They were deterred from doing so by the apprehension 'that any departure from the present method of settling the remaining cases should in fairness, be followed by a re-adjustment of the settlement already made not only in Cochin but in the rest

CHAP. XI. THE ESCHEAT SETTLEMENT.

of the district, that the task of revision would be gigantic, and that it would entail the refund of vast sums with interest'.[1] In 1871 however, at the suggestion of the Secretary of State, they relieved the occupants of the necessity of paying up the capitalized janmam value of their holdings; and allowed them to take over the right after executing interest bonds, binding them to pay interest at 5 per cent on the valuation, redeemable at 20 years' purchase.[2] The expedient had little effect, especially in Cochin taluk and Manapuram. The valuations, which were the chief ground of complaint, had not been reduced; and the tenants stubbornly declined to come to terms or to execute interest bonds.

Mr. Logan's proposals.

Collector after Collector in the meantime beginning with Mr. Ballard in 1866, had criticized the valuations; but it was left for Mr. Logan in 1884, not only to expose their absurdity in Cochin taluk and Manapuram, but to demonstrate to the satisfaction of Government that they were on a plane by themselves, and could be revised without arousing discontent elsewhere in Malabar, and without necessitating any readjustment of settlements already made. In North Malabar, Vettatnad and other parts of the district, he decided that a reduction of the interest on the valuation amount from 5 per cent to 4 per cent would be a sufficient inducement to recalcitrant tenants to come to terms. In Cochin, Tangasseri, Anjengo and Manapuram, he proposed to cancel existing valuations altogether, and to sell the janmam right at 20 years' purchase of the *janmabhogam*, giving credit for payments already made against the new valuations, and charging 5 per cent interest on the balance as a permanent charge in the pattas. The interest bonds were to be cancelled, and janmam deeds issued in their stead without payment of any description.

Escheat quit-rent.

These proposals were accepted by Government with two modifications suggested by the Board, viz., that the payment secured by the janmam deeds should be called quit-rent instead of '*palisa*' (interest), as suggested by Mr. Logan, and that the quit-rent instead of being made a permanent charge should be made redeemable at 20 years' purchase.[3] This latter concession was subsequently withdrawn with effect from November 12th, 1896,[4] and is not enjoyed by those who have come to terms since that date No further modification has been made, and since 1886 the settlement has proceeded without much difficulty.

[1] G.O. No. 264, Revenue, dated 6th April 1886.

[2] G.O. No. 1434, Revenue, dated 17th October 1872.

[3] G.O. No. 264, Revenue, dated 6th April 1886.

[4] The date on which G.O. No. 459, Revenue, dated 2nd September 1896, was received in the Malabar Collector's Office.

Escheat quit-rent. Escheat quit-rent, therefore, is the interest on the janmam value of lands over which Government once exercised proprietary rights. It differs from janmabhogam in that it is fixed and unalterable, and in certain cases may be redeemed. Escheat quit-rent lands are registered as private janmam.

Janmabhogam. *Janmabhogam* is the share of the net produce due to Government as landlord on lands, the janmam right of which belongs to Government. In accordance with Mr. Warden's proclamation of 1805 it is fixed at two-thirds of the assessment on wet lands, and at the same rate as the assessment on gardens. On dry lands it is also equal to the assessment. *Janmabhogam* is liable to revision with the assessment.

INAMS. Generally speaking, inams in Malabar are either personal or subsistence grants, or endowments for the support of religious and charitable institutions or for the maintenance of service therein They are not very numerous, and their total extent is less than 13,300 acres, or rather more than one per cent of the occupied area of the district. Inams are assignments of the whole or a portion of the rights of the Government in lands; and since, as a rule in Malabar lands are private property, the majority of the Malabar inams consist of the assignment of the Government assessment. Where, as is occasionally the case, the inamdar and the janmi are distinct persons, the former collect. from the latter the Government assessment on the land. More commonly inamdar and janmi are identical; in which case, the inam is merely a remission of assessment, so long as the conditions of the grant are fulfilled. There are no village service inams; and perhaps the only exceptions to the rule that the inam consists of the grant of the Government assessment are the lands granted to the Quilandi Tangal for the upkeep of the Quilandi mosque and caravansari. In this case, at Mr. Conolly's suggestion, the full rights of Government in certain escheat lands in Ernad, the assessment and *janmabhogam* of which amounted to Rs. 1,800, were made over in lieu of a money grant of that sum.

THE VILLAGE SYSTEM.

The Malabar revenue village. The village communities of the East Coast have no exact counterpart in Malabar, where there are no villages in the usual sense. The earliest social organization was apparently based upon the family group, into which the various tribes or castes divided on their settlement in the country, each with more or less defined territorial limits The Brahmans were grouped in *gramams*, the Nayars and other castes in *taras* and *cheris*; and the affairs of the groups were under the management of the headmen or elders (Gramini, Karnavan, Mudalal, Thandan). To deal with wider questions, to try offences against caste, etc., there seem to have been periodical assemblies, or *kuttams*, of the heads or elders of the various family groups in a single nad; and these *kuttams* of the Nayar

CHAP. XI. THE VILLAGE SYSTEM.

tarawad karnavans appear to have gradually acquired considerable political influence; and to have acted as a wholesome check upon the power of the Raja and his ministers. "These Nayars" writes a representative of the Honourable Company at Calicut in 1746 "being heads of the Calicut people resemble the parliament and do not obey the king's dictates in all things, but chastise his ministers when they do unwarrantable acts." Caste *sabhas*, representing perhaps the old *kuttams*, still meet to deal with caste questions, and *gramams* and *taras* still exist as local social units.[1] But it is doubtful whether the original *tara* was ever, as Mr. Logan maintained, an administrative unit or a territorial division;[2] and the genesis of the present revenue village is to be traced in the organization of the several petty kingdoms of Malabar into *desams* and *nads*. This organization is usually said to have been primarily a military one; but, though it may have become so by the eighteenth century, it can hardly have been so originally, as the distinctive functions of the head of the desam were religious and social, and he might be a Nambudiri. A full account of the system is to be found in the report written by Sir Thomas Munro in July 1817.

"All lands except those set apart for religious purposes were held [so far as the state was concerned] on military tenure, . . . every little subdivision of territory instead of being called a district of so many thousand pagodas, being called one of the so many thousand men . . . The districts (nads) were divided into villages (desams) under hereditary chiefs, whose duties making allowance for the military nature of the Government did not essentially differ from those of the district village officials of other countries. The Headman of the desam was called the desavazhi or the jenmiwar (janmi) according as he enjoyed the whole or only a part of the rights which were supposed necessary to the constituting the complete chief of the desam. These rights were as follows:—

"1. The Ambalapathi or the direction of the religious ceremonies of the village pagodas.

"2. The Urayma or the management of the pagoda lands and servants.

"3. Desam or the control of marriages and all village ceremonies, none of which could be performed without his leave.

"4. Desadipathi or the general superintendence of all offences of the Desmi or village.

"When the head of the village possessed all these rights he was the Desavazhi; when he wanted the ambalapathi and the

---

[1] The *Thandan* of the *tara*, or headman of a local aggregate of families, still plays an important part in Tiyan marriage ceremonies in Calicut and North Malabar (*vide* pp. 177 78). In Palghat taluk, the word *tara* is used of a collection of Nayar houses round the 'fort' of an ancient chief. The word means literally 'mound,' 'site of house'; hence *tarawad*, house, family.

[2] In the deeds collected by Mr. Logan the lands and the parties to the deed are always described as being in, or of, such and such a *desam* or *ur*.

Urayma, but had the other two, he was the janmi of the village. These rights where they existed could not be separated. The direction of the civil, religious and military affairs of the village were always vested in the same person.

"There was a Desavazhi to every village, except where the village was the private property of the chief of the district called the Naduvazhi, or of the Raja, when the rights of the head of the village belonged to the Naduvazhi or the Raja; but in most of the villages which the Rajas had acquired the property of by purchase, the old desavazhis still retained their office. Where there was no desavazhi, the Raja employed an officer called Pravarthikar as the manager of one or more villages according to their size.

"The Desavazhi had the direction of all the affairs of the village; all orders regarding them were sent to him to be carried into effect. Where there was no regular land rent, he could not have much employment as a Revenue Officer; but he assisted in the collection of occasional contributions as well as of fines, forfeitures and other dues of Government. He was the military chief of the village and marched at the head of its quota when ordered to the field, and he had the direction of the Police, and the power of deciding petty suits. In police and judicial matters he was aided by two or three respectable inhabitants who were called Pramanis.

"There were usually from one to five or six Pramanis to a Desam or village, but in some villages none. They had no regular appointment, nor were they hereditary. They were of all the superior castes—Nambudiris, Nayars, Tiyars, Chettis and Mapillas—but chiefly Nayars; any respectable man in the village who was considered as more intelligent than his neighbours, and who was on that account resorted to by the inhabitants for the adjustment of their little differences, gradually acquired among them the title of Pramani. . . . The Desavazhi had no village curnam, the nature of the revenue did not require an officer of that kind. The accounts of the collections were kept by District servants, employed by the Naduvazhi or acting immediately under the Raja. He had none of the inferior village servants, such as Peons, Thottis and Taliaris, so common in the other provinces. The office next above the Desavazhi, and placed between him and the Raja, was the Naduvazhi or the chief of the Nad or District. He was a kind of District Desavazhi in the village. He claimed to hold his office by a tenure as ancient as that of any of the present Rajas, and to have derived it from the Nambudiri Brahmans or from the same former conqueror, from whom they derived their rights. He was sometimes the Desavazhi of every village in his district, and sometimes of only one or two, the rest being held by Desavazhis or by the Rajah as part of his domains.

"The Naduvazhi collected the ordinary and extra revenue, and in this duty he was assisted by one, two or more accountants called Putwallis. The Naduvazhi was the military chief of his district and was bound to attend the Raja in the field, or march wherever he was directed, with all the fighting men of his district under the desavazhis or heads of their respective villages."

CHAP. XI. THE VILLAGE SYSTEM.

The Mysorean system.

A village system was necessary to the Mysoreans for the collection of their land revenue, but for many reasons the quasi-military organization of *desams* and *nads* was unsuitable. The Military tenures were abolished and a regular land assessment imposed. Subahdars and Faujdars took the place of Rajas and Naduvazhis, and the village system was reorganized.

"Small villages yielding a revenue of only ten to twenty or fifty pagodas, when lying contiguous, were joined together to make a sum of two hundred pagodas, and the whole was called a tarrah (tara) which took the name of the principal village. From forty to eighty tarrahs were joined into a Nad or District. To each tarrah a Parbutti and menwa (menon) or curnam was appointed, and to each district a Tahsildar and two Sheristadars. In each village it was ascertained who were the leading men exclusive of the former Desavazhis, and one of these was appointed head of the village and called the Mookhyist."[1]

Subsequently as the men first appointed as Mookhyists died, the *desavazhis* being the most influential men in the villages gradually regained their former position, and became Mookhyists. The collection of the revenue was the duty of the Parbutti; the Mookhyist only assisted and advised him.

The amsams.

Under the Company's Government, the Mookhyist was continued as the head of the village: but the revenue unit was enlarged to the hobali and the number of Parbuttis reduced, and one Parbutti had to collect the revenue of ten to twenty villages. Sir Thomas Munro pointed out the defects of the system; it was in fact not a village system at all, and instead of bringing the collector more in touch with the people only served to lengthen the chain already too long of officials between them. The result was the institution of the existing amsam system by Mr. Graeme in 1822. The 2,212 old desams, which were considered too small to have each its own village establishment, were grouped into 429 amsams, or parishes, each under a head man or *adhigari*; and as many of the old *desavazhis* as possible were appointed as adhigaris. To assist the *adhigari* a *menon* or accountant, and a small staff of *kolkarans* or peons, were appointed to each amsam.

Their redistribution.

The large increase of revenue resulting from the settlement has necessitated the redistribution of village establishments, and the number of amsams is now 736, divided into 2,222 desams. Unfortunately perhaps, the desam instead of the amsam was taken as the unit of survey and settlement; and, separate revenue accounts have to be maintained for each one,

---

[1] If this account is correct, the Mysorean *tara* was an artificial administrative unit in no way connected with the old Nayar *taras*. Possibly, the Mysoreans adopted the name as the verbal equivalent of *taraf*(?). In the sanads granted by Tipu to the Bibi of Cannanore (Logan, *Treaties*, Pt. i, CLI and CLII) *tarrah* is used of a division of a hobali apparently smaller than a *desam*.

CHAP. XI. THE VILLAGE SYSTEM.

the clerical work that has devolved upon the village and taluk establishments is enormous. The village officers are paid fixed salaries, those of the *adhigaris* and *menons* varying in accordance with the amsam demand. A peculiarity of Malabar is that security bonds are furnished by the *adhigaris*.

The existing divisional charges.

The revenue administration of the district is controlled by the Collector who is aided by assistants of the standing of sub-collectors or deputy collectors at Tellicherry, Palghat, Malappuram, Calicut and Cochin. The Wynaad division was abolished in the year 1924 and the Wynaad taluk was added on to the Tellicherry division from which Kurumbranad taluk was detached and added on to Calicut. As usual there is a tahsildar in each taluk except Cochin and each tahsildar is assisted by a deputy tahsildar. In Ponnani taluk, there are two deputy tahsildars.

APPENDIX.

Succession List of Commissioners, Supervisors, Principal Collectors and Collectors of Malabar.

I. Commissioners for inspecting the countries ceded by Tippu Sultan—

Names.	Year.
William Gamull Farmer (senior merchant).	1792–93.
Major Alexander Dow (Military Commandant of Tellicherry).	
William Page	
J. Duncan	

II. Supervisors of the Province of Malabar—

William Gamull Farmer ..	1793–94.
James Stevens	1794–95.
A. W. Handley	1794–96.

III. Commissioners for executing the office of Supervisors and Chief Magistrate of the Province of Malabar—

T. Wilkinson	1796, 1797.
Lieut.-Col. A. Dow	Do.
Robert Rickards	Do.
James Rivett	1797.
Richard Torffin	Do.
John Spencer	1797–1801.
Major-General Hartley ..	Do.
J. Smee	Do.
Joshua Uthoff	1798–1799.
Lieut. Joshua Watson	1800.
Major A. Walker	1800–1801.

Names.	Date of taking charge.
IV. Principal Collectors of Malabar—	
Major William Macleod	1st October 1801.
Robert Rickards	11th March 1803.
Thomas Warden	March 1804.
James Vaughan	2nd November 1816.
William Sheffield	15th April 1826.
A. F. Huddleston	15th March 1831.
F. F. Clementson	17th August 1832.
E. P. Thompson	1st October 1839.
V. Collectors of the Malabar District—	
H. V. Conolly	21st January 1840.
T. Clark	25th September 1855.
W. Robinson	9th September 1856.
P. Grant	18th May 1858.
G. A. Ballard	2nd May 1862.
J. C. Hannyngton	26th February 1867.
E. C. G. Thomas	26th March 1869.
Alexander Mc Callum Webster.	17th August 1869.
William Logan	2nd April 1870.
A. MacGregor	8th April 1870.
William Logan	3rd February 1871.
D. Buick	6th April 1875.
W. Logan	6th June 1875.
D. Buick	7th February 1878.
W. Logan	9th May 1878.
C. W. W. Martin	22nd April 1879.
E. N. Overbury	5th May 1879.
G. MacWatters	11th June 1879.
W. Logan	23rd November 1880.
G. MacWatters	4th February 1881.
C. L. B. Cumming	2nd April 1881.
W. Logan	24th June 1882.
L. R. Burrows	12th November 1882.
W. Logan	23rd January 1883.
C. A. Galton	28th April 1883.
V. A. Brodie	12th October 1884.
W. Logan	22nd November 1884.
C. A. Galton	8th January 1885.
H. M. Winterbotham	16th April 1886.
W. Logan	2nd November 1886.
H. M. Winterbotham	2nd December 1887.
J. W. F. Dumergue	2nd August 1888.
H. Bradley	7th July 1892.
H. Moberly	17th August 1894.
J. Hewetson	17th September 1895.
G. W. Dance	21st July 1896.
A. F. Pinhey	17th January 1901.
A. R. Loftus-Tottenham	25th May 1903.
A. F. Pinhey	6th July 1903.
A. R. Knapp	8th November 1904.
L. G. Moore	25th April 1905.
A. R. Knapp	6th June 1905.

Names.	Date of taking charge.

V. Collectors of the Malabar District—*cont.*

Names.	Date of taking charge.
C. A. Innes	6th August 1906.
A. R. Knapp	20th August 1906.
W. Francis	15th April 1907.
F. C. Parsons	20th January 1909.
R. B. Wood	3rd April 1909.
C. A. Innes	31st January 1911.
J. F. Hall	16th September 1915.
F. B. Evans	19th October 1915.
J. F. Hall	1st February 1919.
E. F. Thomas	16th September 1919.
M. McGilligan	15th May 1920.
E. F. Thomas	25th June 1920.
T. H. Hill	22nd November 1921.
R. H. Ellis	26th January 1922.
J. A. Thorne	12th December 1922.
C. H. Brown	23rd April 1924.
J. A. Thorne	19th May 1924.
H. R. Pate	11th November 1925.
E. M. Gawne	25th March 1928.
C. G. Herbert	9th July 1929.
E. M. Gawne	7th November 1929.
E. C. Wood	28th October 1930.
D. W. Dodwell	1st February 1932.
T. B. Russell	9th February 1932.

CHAPTER XII.

SALT, ABKARI AND MISCELLANEOUS REVENUE.

SALT—The monopoly system—Present system—Arrangements with Mahe—Arrangements with Cochin and Travancore—Manufacture of earth salt—Fish-curing—Fishery investigations. ABKARI—The joint renting system—Arrack—Jaggery or molasses arrack—Existing system—Special tracts—Foreign liquor—Toddy—Sweet toddy—Opium and hemp drugs. CUSTOMS. INCOME TAX—SUPER TAX.

CHAP. XII.
SALT.

The monopoly system.

In 1807, by Regulation II of that year, the salt monopoly, which two years before had been introduced into the rest of the presidency, was extended with slight modifications to the two West Coast districts. Previously there had been no restriction upon the manufacture and sale of salt, but a light land tax was levied upon the pans, which in 1800 Dr. Buchanan found all along the coast.[1] With the introduction of the monopoly, private manufacture was not absolutely forbidden, as in the other districts, but the sale of salt except to Government was prohibited. From this time forward, however, the industry declined. The climate, soil and brine of Malabar are not suited to the production of salt of good quality, and at the monopoly price local salt could not compete with that imported from Bombay, though the latter was sold at far higher prices. The manufacture of salt was therefore abandoned in 1823, and for the next half century Malabar was supplied with salt imported from Bombay by Government contractors. In 1856, an effort was made to withdraw from importation on behalf of Government; but, with the monopoly price at Re. 1 per maund and the excise duty only two annas less, private enterprise could not compete with Government, and the principle was therefore formulated that the monopoly price should always exceed the excise duty by the original cost of the salt plus the cost of carriage.

Present system.

The monopoly system was abolished in 1877, and since that time the revenue has been realised by an excise duty paid at Bombay on each maund of salt issued for consumption. The importation is left entirely to private enterprise. The duty was reduced from Rs. 2–8–0 to Rs. 2 per maund in March 1903, and by another As. 8 in 1905. It is too early to estimate the full effect of these reductions. Prices have fallen, but consumption has not appreciably increased.

[1] *A Journey through Mysore, Malabar and South Kanara.* II, 460.

Bombay salt still holds the market, and imports from Madras are small. The local practice of selling salt by measure and not by weight is undoubtedly favourable to the lighter salt of Bombay, and the cost of freight in the native *pattamars* is very small.

Arrangements with Mahe.

A certain quantity of salt is annually supplied to the French settlement at Mahe at cost price under an old convention with the French Government. The convention of 1818, renewed in 1837, stipulates that the British Government shall deliver such quantity of salt as shall be requisite for the domestic use and consumption of the inhabitants; the purchase, delivery and subsequent sale of the said quantity being regulated according to the stipulations contained in the convention of the 7th March 1815. By the 4th article of this convention the French Government agrees to charge nearly the same price for salt as obtains in British territory in the vicinity of the settlement. Under these conventions, and at the instance of the French authorities, Bombay salt is supplied to Mahe for human consumption and Madras salt for fish-curing purposes.

Arrangements with Cochin and Travancore.

Up to May 1865 the two Native States of Cochin and Travancore had monopolies of salt; and, their selling price being lower than that of Malabar, smuggling was rife, and the loss to British revenue by the introduction of Cochin salt was estimated in 1860 at 1½ lakhs per annum. Inland depots along the Cochin frontier where salt was sold at specially low rates were established between the years 1852 and 1856, but the experiment was soon abandoned. By the convention of 1865 both States agreed to adopt the British selling price, and to raise the rates at inland depots so as to place the salt of Cochin, Travancore and British India on the same footing in the market. The two States were to import salt on the same terms as those on which it was imported into British-Indian ports, and since then their selling prices have nominally followed the successive changes in the rate of duty in British territory. Under the revised arrangements made in consultation, with the Indian States of Travancore and Cochin in 1920, Madras (Tinnevelly district) salt is supplied to the two States duty-free, single duty at the rate in force in British India being levied on all short deliveries by the contractor and credited to the Durbar concerned. No allowance however is made for wastage of salt in transit. The States also get a portion of their requirements of salt from Bombay.

Manufacture of earth salt.

As stated above, Malabar salt is of such poor quality that its manufacture for sale to Government was given up in 1823. But there was always a market for country salt at prices much below those fixed by Government, and its manufacture which was not in itself illegal, had at the time of the Salt Commission of 1876 become so extensive as seriously to affect the revenue. There were salt pans all along the coast in which salt was made

CHAP. XII. SALT.

by lixiviating salt earth with backwater brine; and in the Ponnani and Chirakkal taluks especially operations were carried on on a large scale. In the former taluk alone the extent of land under salt cultivation at this time was estimated to be capable of producing 1,17,000 maunds per annum. The sale of this salt was of course illegal, but detection was difficult, and most of the salt so made was sold in the bazaars at As. 4 per maund. On the recommendation of the Commission of 1876 the law on the subject was amended, and the possession of contraband salt earth, swamp salt, or earth salt is now an offence under the Salt Act. Crime of this kind was fairly common a few years ago, but in the last few years has been almost stamped out. Since 1899 the practice has been introduced of inducing landowners to plough up dangerous tracts at the beginning of each season; and in the northern taluks the Mappillas, who are the worst offenders, have been made by their *tangals* to take oaths in their mosques to abstain from salt crime. "Salt earth" has been declared "contraband salt" in the Chirakkal, Kottayam, Calicut, Kurumbranad, Ponnani and Cochin taluks of the district. The saline soils are being patrolled by special preventive parties, as experience has shown that salt crime is still prevalent in the district.

Fish-curing.

The fish-curing industry which is of great economic importance in Malabar has for the last 25 years been supervised by the Salt Department. Before the suppression of its use, earth salt manufactured locally had been used for curing, and the industry would have been ruined had the curers been compelled to pay duty on the salt they used in their business. Curing yards were therefore opened all along the coast in 1877–78, in which salt imported from the Government factories at Tuticorin is sold to curers at exceptionally low rates. In Malabar alone there are now thirty-two yards at an average distance of five miles apart. The industry has become firmly established, and its great economic importance is illustrated by the following statistics relating to the year 1903–04:—

		Calicut subdivision.		Eight East Coast subdvisions.
Number of yards ..		43		89
Weight of fish brought in for curing.	Mds.	1,073,331	Mds.	376,812
Value of salt sold ..	Rs.	1,32,595	Rs.	24,220
Weight of salt sold ..	Mds.	148,320	Mds.	44,406

These figures speak for themselves. The quantity of fish cured in the Calicut subdivision, which includes Malabar and South Canara, was nearly treble that dealt with in the eight subdivisions of the East Coast of the presidency. To promote the development of the industry the price of the salt issued from the yards has recently been reduced from one rupee to ten annas, and salt is allowed to be taken to sea in the fishing boats free of charge under certain conditions. The Madras Salt department continued to supervise the industry till 1924. On the introduction of the Montford Reforms the department became a central subject and the fish-curing yards were transferred to the Fisheries department under the Local Government. The issue price of salt was increased from As. 10 to Re. 1–4–0 a maund from 1st April 1924 as the Government of India were unwilling to bear any portion of the loss sustained by the maintenance of these yards. The position of the industry in 1929–30 was as follows :—

	West Coast.	East Coast.
Number of yards ..	60	53
Weight of fish bought for curing.	770,966 mds.	249,660 mds.
Weight of salt sold ..	128,261 ,,	40,652 ,,
Value of salt sold ..	Rs. 1,60,327	Rs. 50,815

It will be seen that the quantity cured in the West Coast is just over thrice that dealt with in the four districts of the East Coast.

Desultory efforts have been made from time to time to induce curers to improve their methods, and 262 maunds of fish cured departmentally in the Calicut circle in 1884 realized in the bazaar As. 8 per maund more than fish cured in the ordinary way. These experiments, which were discontinued in 1893, were not without result and a gradual improvement in curing has been noticed since the yards were opened.

Fishery investigations.

From 1884 the Salt Department kept a record of the quantity of the most common species brought into the yards ; but the statistics thus collected proved useless owing to the lack of an uniform method of classifying and naming fish, and in 1898 the scope of the investigations was narrowed, and a less ambitious but more accurate system was introduced under the superintendence of the Curator of the Government Museum at Madras. The statistics now collected by the department are confined to a few of the most valuable fish, such as the sardine, pomfret, seir and mackerel[1]. Recently the development of the fishing industry has formed the subject of a special investigation, which is being undertaken by Sir F. Nicholson K.C.I.E. ; and it is proposed to open a Government Experimental Fishery Station at Tellicherry.

ABKARI.

Unlike that upon salt, a tax upon intoxicating liquors is one sanctioned by the traditions of Malabar. The Hindu Rajas and after them the Muhammadans levied a sort of profession tax upon drawers of toddy and distillers of arrack. This tax under the name of *Katti Chatti*, the knife and still tax, was continued by the British Government, and long survived in parts of the

[1] An account of the sea fisheries of Malabar and South Canara will be found in Bulletin, Vol. iii, No. 2, of the Madras Government Museum.

CHAP. XII. ABKARI.

district. The tax was enhanced by Major Macleod, Principal Collector in 1801–02, but after his time no further increase was made. The *Katti*, the tax on the toddy knife, varied throughout the district from Re. 1 to Rs. 2–8–0; and the *Chatti*, that on the still, from Re. 1–8–0 to Rs. 3. Only knives and stills stamped with the Government mark were allowed to be used; but, owing to difficulties of detection, illicit tapping and distillation were rampant. The defects of the system were glaring; and farming was gradually introduced, first into the principal towns and the Wynaad and Cochin taluks, and finally by 1860 throughout the district. The effect on the revenue was magical. Between 1810 and 1860 the revenue had been almost stationary and had never exceeded Rs. 70,000; but in 1869 the rents rose to Rs. 2,28,000, and in 1872 they were sold for three years for an annual sum of Rs. 2,77,950.

The joint-renting system.

This system by which the privileges of manufacture and sale of toddy and arrack were farmed out conjointly remained in force in the district for several years. Its short-comings were pointed out by the Committee of 1884; but it was considered that in Malabar, where toddy arrack alone was then drunk and the toddy shopkeeper had the materials for distillation always ready to hand, the concentration of manufacture which is essential to the successful working of an excise system was impossible. Experience has shown that these fears were unfounded, and except in the seventeen outlying *pattams* attached to British Cochin the joint renting system has long been abandoned.

Arrack.

A beginning was made in 1886. In that year a modified excise system was introduced into the five municipal towns of the district. The privilege of the manufacture and vend of arrack, subject only to a duty upon each gallon issued from the distillery, was assigned to a contractor on payment of a lump sum determined by competition. A modified form of the contract distillery system was introduced in the year 1888–89 into the four taluks of Chirakkal, Kottayam, Calicut and Palghat, and in 1891–92 the system was extended practically throughout the district. Arrack was distilled from toddy drawn from marked trees upon which tax had been paid, and was supplied at fixed prices to licensed vendors. Exclusive privileges of retail sale were sold by auction for small areas, except in the municipal towns where shops were sold separately. Two years later the independent sale of arrack shops was extended; in 1895–96 it was introduced throughout the district with the exception of the Wynaad and Cochin taluks and the Attapadi Valley, and in 1901–02 it was extended to the Wynaad.

Jaggery or molasses arrack.

In 1898–99 an important innovation was made. To avert a threatened failure of supply, permission to sell jaggery or molasses arrack was accorded to outside distillers, and Messrs.

Parry & Co. at once opened depots. Contrary to all expectations, the experiment met with entire success. Nearly 6,000 proof gallons were sold in 1899–1900 and more than 14,000 gallons in the following year, and the consumption increased so rapidly in the succeeding year that it was found possible to prohibit the consumption of toddy arrack or country spirit from 1st October 1906.

Existing system.

In 1899–1900, Government, dissatisfied with the working of the toddy arrack contractor, bought up all his distilleries, and in the following year gave the contract for the two West Coast districts to Messrs. Parry & Co. Their contract was renewed in 1903 for three years. By its terms, they were bound to manufacture a minimum quantity of toddy arrack at the Government distillery at Chavakkad, and sell it at fixed prices to the arrack shopkeeper. The toddy was drawn from coconut trees in the Chavakkad Deputy Tahsildar's division, in which the contractors then held exclusive privileges of manufacture and sale of toddy and arrack. The contract expired at the end of September 1906, and from October of that year the sale of toddy arrack as country liquor has been prohibited, and the exclusive privilege of manufacturing and supplying molasses arrack has been renewed to the same contractors for a period of three and a half years. Messrs. Parry & Co. have ever since continued to be the contract suppliers for the district, the contract being renewed every year.

Special tracts.

With the exception of a few exempted areas, the contract distillery system combined with the separate sale of shops obtains throughout the district. The combined arrack and toddy renting system prevails in the seventeen outlying *pattams* of Cochin, and in Cochin itself the renter is allowed the option of manufacturing spirits from toddy drawn from trees which have paid tax or of importing them from Native Cochin or Travancore free of duty. In the isolated settlements of Anjengo and Tangasseri, the management of abkari revenue is leased to the Travancore Government. In the Wynaad taluk and the Attapadi Valley, no toddy revenue is raised. In the former, arrack shops are sold separately under the contract distillery system, and the arrack is supplied by Messrs. Parry & Co., under a separate contract. In the Attapadi Valley, the exclusive privilege of manufacture and sale of country spirits is disposed of under the renting system. This renting system was in force till 1st April 1919 in the Attapadi valley, which was then brought under the contract distillery system and included in the supply area of the Coimbatore distillery. These shops were assigned on fixed fees and the shop-keepers obliged to observe certain special conditions, one of which was that they should issue only arrack of 40° u.p., the sale strength in other parts of the district being 35°

CHAP. XII. ABKARI.

u.p. In 1923-24, one of the shops was closed and the two remaining shops were sold on tender. These shops also ceased to work from April 1925.

Foreign liquor.

The exclusive privilege of manufacturing and supplying coconut toddy arrack to foreign liquor dealers throughout the Presidency has been granted to Messrs. Parry & Co. The arrack is distilled in the Government supervised distillery at Chowghat, the toddy required being drawn from trees on which tree-tax has been paid and which are marked for the purpose. The Company are allowed a refund of tree-tax according to the total outturn of arrack. Though coconut toddy arrack is excised at a lower rate of duty than the tariff rate, viz., at Rs. 17-8-0 per proof gallon since 1st April 1923, it is for all practical purposes considered as foreign liquor, as its sale is permitted under the foreign liquor licences only.

Toddy.

The toddy revenue is raised on the tree-tax system, by which a tax is levied upon each tree tapped, and the right to open shops is sold annually by auction. The system was first introduced, as an experimental measure, into the five municipal towns and the Calicut taluk in 1886. In 1889, it was extended to the rest of the district, except the special tracts mentioned above, and has been in force since, except in the Deputy Tahsildari of Chavakkad which during the period from 1899 to 1906 was worked under the combined arrack and toddy renting system. Toddy is drawn from coconut, sago and palmyra trees. Licences to tap the first two trees are issued half yearly at a cost of Re. 1-8-0 and Rs. 3, respectively. The tax on palmyras is Re. 1 per annum. The current rates of tree-tax on coconut and sago palm trees are Rs. 4-8-0 and Rs. 9 a tree, respectively, per half-year and that on palmyra is Rs. 3 per tree per annum.

Sweet toddy.

Since 1892 tapping for sweet toddy in Malabar has been controlled by the Abkari department with the object of safeguarding the revenue from fermented toddy. No tax is levied on trees so tapped, nor have the trees been marked since 1900; but licences for which no fee is charged must be taken out for tapping, and the toddy must be drawn in pots freshly coated with lime to prevent fermentation. As is inevitable, the system opens the door to many offences against the abkari laws. Much of the toddy drawn under the cloak of these rules is allowed to ferment, and the sale of the sweet juice mixed with fermented toddy is becoming increasingly common. The latter is the more serious offence, beacuse the more difficult to detect, but attempts are being made to check it by evaporating suspected toddy in shops and analysing the residue.

Opium and hemp drugs.

The sale of preparations of hemp and opium is controlled in the usual way, the right to open shops being sold annually by auction. Before 1897, the hemp plant (*Cannabis Sativa*

CHAP. XII. ABKARI.

Opium and hemp drugs.

or *Indica*) was freely cultivated in the Wynaad taluk, and supplied the demand for Malabar. The cultivation of the plant was, however, prohibited in 1897, and now no hemp is grown in the district. The shops get their supply of hemp drugs from one of the two storehouses, Vetapalam or Santavasal and that of opium from the taluk cutcheries. The sale of opium and hemp drugs is controlled in the usual way, the right to open shops being sold annually by auction. Before 1897 the hemp plant (*Cannabis satira* or *indica*) was freely cultivated in the Wynaad taluk and supplied the demand for Malabar. The cultivation of the plant was however prohibited in 1897 and now no hemp is grown in the district.

CUSTOMS.

Before the Muhammadan invasion, land in Malabar was free from assessment, and for the expenses of Government, which were not heavy, the Rajahs were dependent upon certain traditionary sources of income. Among them were *chungam* or customs duties upon all imports and exports by land and sea, and as early as 1723 Hamilton records that all vessels unloading at Tellicherry paid a royalty of two bales of rice to 'the Nayar that was lord of the manor.' These duties were levied at rates variously estimated at from 23 to 1½ per cent *ad valorem*, and the right to collect them was usually farmed out. Apparently, they were not a very fruitful source of revenue, for in 1761 'the King Badalameur', the regent of the kingdom of the Kolattiri, granted to the Honourable Company 'the whole right of collecting customs' throughout his dominions for an annual sum of 21,000 silver fanams.[1] In addition, however, to the duties levied on imports and exports, the *nadvazhis* seem to have been entitled to levy tolls or transit duties on goods passing through their *nads*. The Muhammadans were more exacting in their demands, and their annual revenue from customs was estimated by the Joint Commissioners to have been not less than two and half or three lakhs of rupees.[2] In their time too the inland chowkis or tolls multiplied so enormously as seriously to hamper trade and agriculture. In 1793, they were 'established almost in every village,' and the exactions to which traders and travellers were subject from them were endless. The tariffs were arbitrary, and not infrequently 'the poor merchant is forced out of his direct road, to make a circuit of many miles till he has run the gauntlet through almost every Customs House of the Province.'[3] One of the first acts of the Joint Commissioners was to put a stop to these exactions; and by the 10th article of their regulation of March 11th, 1793, they provided, with the assent of the Governor of Bombay, for the abolition of all

[1] Græme's report, para. 81.

[2] Joint Commissioners' report, para. 433.

[3] *Ibid*, para. 428.

CHAP. XII. CUSTOMS.

interior tolls. They continued the duties on imports and exports by land and sea but revised the tariff. Statistics of sea customs are given in the separate Appendix. In the district, there are nine ports, of which six are open to foreign trade and the remaining three to coasting trade only. Since April 1924, the Government of India have taken the Customs Department under their direct control and the Central Board of Revenue has been constituted the chief Customs Authority.

Income-tax and super-tax.

Income tax is levied in the usual manner, but the difficulties of working the tax are greater in Malabar than in most districts. A large proportion of the tax is paid by the mercantile classes in sea port towns, whose incomes vary from year to year. They trade chiefly in coffee, pepper and copra, and their profits depend not only upon local conditions, such as good or bad crops, but also upon fluctuations in the European markets. Variations between the original and the final demands are therefore inevitable; and the percentage reduction on appeal not only of the number of assessees, but also of the amount of tax, is more than usually high. Since 1917, an addition to the usual income-tax called the super-tax is being levied on incomes above Rs. 50,000. The rates for both taxes are fixed yearly by the Finance Act, the maximum in 1931 being 6 annas per rupee for income-tax and 6 annas 3 pies for super-tax.

The district has been divided into two circles for the collection of these two taxes, with headquarters at Calicut and Palghat. There were (in 1930–31) 1,908 assessees in both circles and the demand was Rs. 6·53 lakhs. Excluding Madras, Malabar was the seventh district as regards the number of assessees and fourth in regard to the amount of the demand, Ramnad, Madura and Coimbatore being the only three districts where the demand was higher. The proportion of assessees to the total population is, however, low and the incidence of the tax per head of the population was As. 2–10 as against As. 3–8 for the whole presidency excluding Madras. The average tax paid by each assessee in Malabar was Rs. 342–8–3 as against Rs. 238–6–7 per assessee for the whole presidency. Statistics relating to the tax will be found in Table XXXIII of this book.

CHAPTER XIII.

ADMINISTRATION OF JUSTICE.

HISTORICAL—Justice in ancient times—Trials by ordeal—Procedure against debtors—Smarta Vicharam. CIVIL JUSTICE—Early British Courts—Existing Civil Courts—Village Courts—Volume of litigation. REGISTRATION—Malabar Wills Act and Marriage Act. CRIMINAL JUSTICE—The various courts—Grave crime—Criminal castes—Mappilla outbreaks—Dacoity—Other forms of crime. POLICE—Police force—Malappuram special force—Malabar Special Police. JAILS. ARMS ACT.

CHAP. XIII. HISTORICAL.

Justice in ancient times.

As early as the 14th century civilization had reached a high level in Malabar, and private property was as secure as it is to-day. 'They put a thief to death,' says Shaikh Ibn Batuta of Tangiers who travelled through Malabar in the middle of the century, 'for stealing a single nut or even a grain of seed of any fruit, hence thieves are unknown among them.' A hundred years later Abdur-razak visited Calicut, and bore witness that 'security and justice were firmly established in the town.' Varthema was impressed with the honesty of its merchants, and the favourable testimony of previous writers was confirmed by Pyrard De Laval, the Frenchman, who came to Calicut in 1607 : 'As for justice it proceeds from the king and throughout the kingdom there is no other judge but he. For all that justice is well administered and is awarded to all gratuitously.'[1] The most detailed account, however, of the 'Fashion of Justice in the Kingdom of Malabar' is given by Duarte Barbosa,[2] the Portuguese, who spent sixteen years in India in the beginning of the 16th century, and the system described by him seems to have undergone little change in the succeeding three centuries. There is a striking similarity between his account and those of the Rajas, who at the request of the Joint Commissioners in 1792 described the mode in which justice had hitherto been administered in their dominions.

The systems differed of course in details in the various nads, but in all essentials they were the same. The Rajas were the fount of justice, but were assisted by their *kariakars* and the Brahmans. Caste offences were left to the caste assemblies to deal with, and civil disputes were referred to arbitration either by the caste assemblies or by three or four 'creditable persons'. There was no written code, but the punishment assigned by tradition usually fitted the crime. The penalty of death was

---

[1] *Voyage of Pyrard De Laval.* Translated by Gray and Bell, Hakluyt series, 1887. Vol. I, p. 407.

[2] *A description of the Coasts of East Africa and Malabar,* by Duarte Barbosa. Printed for the Hakluyt Society, 1866, p. 116.

CHAP. XIII. HISTORICAL.

reserved for the more heinous offences such as sacrilege, wilful murder and slaying or wounding a Brahman or a cow, but was enforced more freely against men of low caste. Mutilation and fines were more common forms of punishment. There was not one law for all, but justice was dispensed 'according to the qualities of persons because there are diverse sects and races among them.' Nobles enjoyed the privilege of being exempt from being put in irons. Brahmans and women were never put to death. The former were punished for grave crimes by loss of caste and banishment, the latter by being sold as slaves. Torture was not unknown, at any rate in Barbosa's time. The life of the accused person who refused to plead guilty was, to use his euphemism, 'made uncomfortable for eight days,' and, if he still remained obdurate, recourse was had to trial by ordeal. No criminal was put to death until he admitted his justice of the sentence; but, if he deliberated too long on the subject, torture was employed to convince him. Capital sentences were usually carried out with a sword, but in earlier times more barbarous methods were employed. Criminals were occasionally cut in two and exposed on a cross bar, and as late as 1795 the Pychy rebel had a man impaled alive after a mock trial for robbery. This form of punishment was known as the *kazhu* or eagle, and the impaling stake seems to have been so named from its resemblance to that bird. Great criminals were at times wrapped in green palm leaves and torn asunder by elephants. Hanging was introduced by the Muhammadans.

Trials by ordeal.

Trials by ordeal were an essential feature of the system, and some forms were in use in comparatively recent times. The Zamorin in 1710 entered into an agreement with the Tellicherry factors to subject contentious merchants to the oil ordeal. The engagement stands recorded in the factory diary for May 6th, 1728, as 'a grant that any Malabare having accounts with us must put his hand in oil to prove the verity thereof, given anno 1710.' The ordeal was to pick a coin out of a pot of boiling oil. The hand was then swathed in bandages and sealed up, and its condition three days later when the bandages were removed, determined the matter. In later times, at any rate in criminal cases, the oil ordeal was reserved for Brahmans and men of higher caste, Mappillas, Tiyans and others being required to handle or lick a red hot hatchet. In other places, notably at Palliport seventeen miles north of Cochin, criminals who refused to admit their guilt had to prove their innocence by wading across a piece of water swarming with crocodiles.

Procedure against debtors.

A curious custom, which seems to have prevailed all over Southern India, is thus described [1] by Varthema :—

"Let us suppose the case that some one has to pay me twenty-five ducats, and the debtor promises me to pay them many times,

[1] *The travels of Ludovico di Varthema* (Hakluyt Society), p. 147.

and does not pay them. I, not being willing to wait any longer, nor to give him any indulgence, shall take a green branch in my hand, shall go softly behind the debtor, and with the said branch shall draw a circle on the ground surrounding him, and if I can enclose him in the circle shall say to him these words three times: 'I command you by the head of the Brahmans and the king that you do not depart hence until you have paid me and satisfied me as much as I ought to have from thee' and he will satisfy me, or truly he will die there without any other guard and should he quit the said circle the king would put him to death."

Smartha Vicharams.

An interesting example of the form of trial by caste tribunals is to be found in the *Smartha Vicharams*, or enquiries into charges of immorality brought against Nambudiri women, which are still held in the ancient form. The suspected woman, who is thereafter referred to as the *sadhanam*, or thing, is relegated to an outhouse (*anjampura*), and her family is temporarily excommunicated. The husband has to apply to the Raja, in whose (ancient) jurisdiction the offence was committed, to appoint a *panchayat* to conduct the *vicharam*, and to issue summons (*tittu*) to them. The *panchayat* consists of the Smartha or President (see p. 109), two or more *mimamsakars*, or Nambudiris versed in caste law, the Agakoyma or local head of the community, and the Purakoyma or representative of the Raja, whose duty it is to stand with a drawn sword during the trial and keep order. The proceedings open with Iswara *puja* at the temple, after which the trial begins with an examination of the accused's *dasi* or maid servant, who incriminates her. The Smartha, Agakoyma and Purakoyma then go to the *anjampura* and question the accused through the *dasi*. The woman remains all the time in a separate room or behind a curtain. The object is to make her confess her guilt, and until she does so the proceedings drag on with a short daily examination by the Smartha. In the old days various methods of persuasion are said to have been used such as the introduction of rats and snakes into the woman's room. When once she has admitted her guilt, the *sadhanam* is brought out and subjected to a minute cross-examination before all the members of the court, with the purpose of eliciting the names of all the persons who have had a share in her offence. At the close of the trial the names of the guilty parties are proclaimed by a Pattar; the *sadhanam* is deprived of her umbrella, her funeral rites are performed, and she is driven out of the house. The husband has to perform elaborate purificatory and expiatory rites (*prayaschittam*), concluding with a *sudhabhojanam*, or feast to celebrate his re-admission into caste, after he has obtained the Raja's permission. The outcaste woman sometimes continues to be maintained by her husband; but more often becomes a prostitute, or finds a refuge in an institution such as that of the Aramanakkal Mannannar in Chirakkal, said to have been founded by a Tiyan who had had intercourse with an *anterjanam* and was given a

CHAP. XIII. HISTORICAL.

grant of land by the Chirakkal Raja on condition of his receiving and maintaining outcaste Nambudiri women. All persons implicated by the woman at the trial are also outcasted. In the old days they are said to have had the right to challenge trial by the oil ordeal, but nowadays their resort is a civil suit for defamation. At a recent *cause celebre* in Ponnani the number of persons implicated amounted to over sixty. *Smartha vicharams* are often very protracted and necessarily very costly, the husband having to feed and house the members of the court, in addition to paying various fees and to the expense of the prescribed purificatory ceremonies. These Smartha Vicharams are now constituted only very rarely. There was one in 1929, the offending parties coming from the same *illam* Kothamangalam near Tirur. The parties admitting their guilt, they were outcasted without the usual costly and protracted enquiry and feasts and they are now being maintained by the estate.

CIVIL JUSTICE. Early British Courts.

In 1792 when they took over Malabar, the British first conceived the idea of leaving the administration of justice in the hands of the Rajas. But the plan was doomed to failure from the first, and in December 1792 a temporary Court of Justice, presided over by each of the Joint Commissioners in turn was established in Calicut. Three months later when Mr. Farmer was appointed Supravisor of Malabar this court was abolished. Subject to the appellate authority of the Supravisor, his assistant was vested with civil and criminal jurisdiction in Calicut and its vicinity, and the Northern and Southern Superintendents with like powers in their respective divisions. Seven local Darogas were established on July 1st, 1793, in Cannanore, Quilandi, Tanur, Tirurangadi, Ponnani, Chettuvayi and Palghat. In 1802 an important step in advance was made in the separation of the judicial from the executive administration. A Provincial Court was established at Tellicherry, presided over by three judges, two of whom went periodically on circuit. Zillah Courts were established at Tellicherry and Calicut, and a Registrar's Court at the latter town. In 1812 an auxilliary Zillah Court was set up in Cochin, and in 1816 District Munsiff's Court was instituted. All these courts save the last were abolished in 1845, and their places were taken by the Civil and Sessions Courts of Tellicherry and Calicut, the Subordinate Court of Calicut, and the principal Sudr Amins' Courts at Tellicherry and Cochin. In 1875 the designation of the courts was changed. The Civil and Sessions Judges became the District and Sessions Judges of North and South Malabar, and the Principal Sudr Amins became Subordinate Judges.

Existing Civil Courts.

The district is divided into two district judgeships of North and South Malabar with headquarters at Tellicherry and Calicut. In theNorth district there are a Subordinate Judge's

CHAP. XIII. CIVIL JUSTICE.

court at Tellicherry and district munsifs' courts at Badagara, Cannanore, Kuthuparamaba, Nadapuram, Payyoli, Quilandi, Taliparamba and Tellicherry. In the South district there are sub-courts at Calicut, Palghat and Ottapalam and district munsifs' courts at these stations and at Alattur, Chowghat, Manjeri, Parappanangadi, Pattambi, Ponnani, Tirur, and at Perintalmanna. Under the Civil Courts' Act as last amended an additional sub-judge has been appointed to the sub-court at Calicut and one or more additional munsifs for the courts at Badagara, Calicut, Palghat and Tellicherry. A third district munsif at Calicut was given jurisdiction over the Wynaad taluk but that court was abolished in 1932 and the jurisdiction taken over by another munsif at the same station. There were, in 1931, 30 superior civil courts working in the district,* far more than in any other district of the presidency, the next largest district Tanjore containing only 20 civil judges.

Village courts.

Village headmen (*adhigaris*) are empowered under the Village Courts Act of 1889 to try petty suits where the value of the cause of action does not exceed Rs. 20; and the system of trial by Bench Courts under section 9 of the same Act is in force in certain areas. But the village courts are not popular, and do not appreciably lighten the burden of the civil courts. More than a quarter of the total number of suits launched in the presidency in 1903 were filed in the village courts; but in Malabar the proportion was only one-eleventh.

Volume of litigation.

The volume of litigation in the district is immense. In the last twenty years Malabar has contributed one-eighth of the total litigation of the presidency, exclusive of Madras, and, if suits filed before village courts be excluded, the proportion rises to one-sixth. North Malabar is a worse offender in this respect than South, and shares with Tanjore the dubious distinction of being the most litigious district in the presidency. In the last ten years an average of one in every 56 persons in North Malabar has been engaged in litigation, and one in every 99 persons in South Malabar.

Litigation is a luxury of the rich in India, and the accepted explanation of the constant report to the courts in Malabar is the general prosperity of the district and it, immunity from famine. Other causes are the complexity of its land tenures, and the inevitable dispute as to the value of improvements on the termination of *kanam* or other demises. Since 1885, the worst year on record in point of litigation, litigation has not increased, and in the last two or three years it has been less than in any of the preceding eighteen.

REGISTRATION.

Intimately connected with the civil courts, the Registration department has equally heavy work, and of all the documents

* The additional sub-judge's Court at Calicut and the district munsifs' Courts of Pattambi, Vayittiri (at Calicut), Palghat (additional) and Badagara (additional) were abolished in 1931 and 1932.

CHAP. XIII. REGISTRATION.

presented for registration in the presidency in the latest year for which figures are available no less than one-sixth were registered in Malabar. Registration was inaugurated in 1799 when a proclamation was issued that 'all writings in evidence of the transfer of landed property. . . shall be registered either in the Provincial or local adawlets.' There are now two District Registrars, with jurisdictions corresponding to those of the District Judges of North and South Malabar, and forty-nine Sub-Registrars. Doubtless owing to the operation of the *marumakkattayam* system of inheritance, and to the rooted objection of the Malabar landlord to divest himself of the title of janmi, sales and absolute alienations of property are rare; but Malabar accounts for the greater portion of the leases registered in the presidency. The value of registration as conferring security of title has long been recognised in the district, and more than half the registrations affecting immoveable property effected in Malabar in 1902 were optional. Between 1919 and 1932, Malabar was divided into three districts for registation purposes, Tellicherry, Calicut and Palghat, and the last district was abolished in the latter year. Each district registrar is assisted by one or more joint sub-registrars in his own or separate offices to exercise concurrent jurisdiction with the registrar in original registration in his sub-district. There were, in 1932, 55 offices on the whole in the district and the work in them was managed on the same lines as elsewhere.

Malabar Wills Act and Marriage Act.

The effect of the Malabar Wills Act (Act V of 1898), which placed the testamentary disposition of self-acquired property by persons subject to *marumakkattayam* law on a secure basis, is beginning to make itself felt, the number of wills registered in 1901–02 being more than double those registered three years before. The Malabar Marriage Act (Act IV of 1896) for the registration of *sombandhams* is on the other hand almost a dead letter, (see p. 100), and since the passing of Act V of 1898 husbands have been able to make provision for their wives and children without registering their *sambandhams*. Sixty applications for registry were received in Malabar in the first fourteen months after the Act was put in force, nineteen in the next three years but only six in the triennium ending 1903–04. All registering officers have been appointed marriage registrars.

CRIMINAL JUSTICE. The various courts.

All village magistrates have the usual powers in petty cases arising in their jurisdictions but rarely exercise them. Panchayat courts which have been established in several villages under the Madras Village Courts Act I of 1888 are sometimes also invested with criminal powers. Such panchayat courts replace the court of the village magistrate and election to the court is by open vote and the members elect their own president. The sub-registrars of Mannarghat, Irikkur, Wandur and Kondotti are special magistrates empowered to try offences triable

CHAP. XIII. CRIMINAL JUSTICE.

by the panchayat courts and there are at Calicut, Palghat, Tellicherry, Badagara, Kollengode, Ponnani, Ottapalam and Cannanore benches of magistrates who are authorized to try petty cases arising within those areas. All tahsildars have second-class powers and some have also first-class powers, but they try only cases which are transferred to them for disposal by the district and divisional magistrates. A stationary magistrate with second-class powers is sanctioned in each taluk, except Wynaad and Cochin where their places are taken by sharistadar-magistrates, and the various deputy tahsildars of the district are also subordinate magistrates with second-class powers. The number of these subordinate magistrates including stationary sub-magistrates and sharistadar-magistrates is 20. The district magistrate, the five divisional magistrates and the treasury deputy collector have the usual first-class powers. The two courts of sessions of North and South Malabar sit at Tellicherry and Calicut, respectively.

The various courts.

Grave crime.

Mappilla outbreaks have given Malabar a bad name as a turbulent and lawless district; but the ratio of grave crime to population is comparatively small, and the reputation is not deserved. Malabar is protected from famine by the unfailing south-west monsoon, and the prices of foodstuffs, a natural barometer of crime, do not fluctuate so much as in other less fortunate districts. Agrarian depression, due to rack-renting, evictions and the oppression of the janmi, has occasionally in the past led to outbreaks of violent crime; but on the whole labour is plentiful, wages are high, and actual want drives fewer people to crime than is the case elsewhere. The bitter faction feuds of the Ceded Tracts and the criminal tribes of the southern districts of the presidency are alike absent, and comparatively little use has hitherto been made of the security sections of the Criminal Procedure Code. But the fanatic Mappilla requires careful watching, and the large body of police maintained in the district chiefly on his account has helped to keep down crime. Burglary and dacoity are comparatively rare, a sure test of successful preventive work and the percentage of cases detected and stolen property recovered has been in the last five years much above the average.

Criminal castes.

The backward Mappilla caste, which has a preference for town life, strong caste sympathies, and a natural talent for organisation, supplies most of the professional criminals. The majority of Mappillas are peaceful and law-abiding citizens, but those who take to a life of crime find a safe asylum in the crowded Mappilla quarters of the big towns, and combine readily into gangs. Most of these gangs are well known to the police, and are carefully watched. Two of the worst long made Panur in Kurumbranad and Minchanda in Calicut the

CHAP. XIII. CRIMINAL JUSTICE.

headquarters of crime in North and South Malabar respectively but they have recently been broken up and many of their members are serving long terms of imprisonment.

Mappilla outbreaks.

The Mappilla outbreaks, which have periodically disturbed the peace of the district since 1836, are peculiar to Malabar and its most distinctive form of crime. They differ from ordinary crime in many essentials, and are referred to at length in Chapter II.

Dacoity.

Dacoity is not a common crime in Malabar. It was however very prevalent between the years 1865 and 1878, a period of agricultural depression and Mappilla unrest. In 1866 and again between 1876 and 1878 foodgrains were at famine prices, and there were Mappilla outrages in 1864, 1865 and 1873, and an abortive attempt in 1877. Between 1874 and 1877 a vigorous campaign was instituted against the dacoits, and, no less than 408 being convicted, the crime was stamped out in the district for many years. There was a recrudescence in Ernad and Walavanad in 1896 after the serious outrage of that year; but energetic measures were taken, and the taluks were cleared of the worst characters. Since 1897 dacoity has been of comparatively rare occurrence in Malabar except as a precursor to, or a concomitant of, a fanatical outbreak and the occurrence of a series of dacoities should always be taken as a warning of an impending outrage. In December 1914 the entry of Turkey into the great war as an ally of the Central Powers had an unsettling effect on the Mapplillas and the occurrence of a series of dacoities in Ernad and Walavanad gave grounds for believing that an outbreak of some kind was being prepared. The early detection of some of these dacoities resulted in a premature explosion of the plot and the unsuccessful attempt made on the life of the district magistrate. Dacoities in 1919, when the district was badly disturbed as a result of the non-co-operation movement and Khilafat campaign, were followed by the serious rebellion in 1921. This was followed by wholesale dacoity and rapine. A large number of the offenders were either killed or sentenced to long terms of imprisonment and the district has again assumed its normal freedom from this form of crime.

Other forms of crime.

House-breaking, theft and cattle-lifting are the favourite forms of grave crime. The last named is peculiarly common in the Ponnani taluk near the Cochin frontier and in the Angadipuram division. In Ponnani the thieves have a safe asylum close at hand in the Cochin State, and the system of *tuppukuli* or blackmail is firmly established. In the Angadipuram division more ingenious methods are employed. Buffaloes are usually stolen, and, after being rapidly driven long distances, are kept in close confinement for some days. Their appearances is cleverly altered by branding and by docking their ears and tails, and oil rubbed daily into their skins makes them change colour. An accomplice is then secured to impound the cattle for alleged trespass, and the thieves by releasing them on payment of feeding and other charges obtain documentary evidence of title. House-breaking and cattle theft have always been the main form of grave crime in the district, but have never attained any serious proportions. A general rise of crime was noticeable in common with the other parts of the Presidency during the period of high food prices prior to 1920. Since 1921 as a result of the elimination, during the rebellion, of a large proportion of the criminal classes, crime has shown a large decrease.

POLICE.

In ancient times the *nadvazhis* and the *desavazhis* supported by their armed Nayar retainers maintained law and order. With the Muhammadan invasion the system broke down. Tipu's brutal methods of obtaining converts to Islam, which drove the Rajas and thousands of their principal adherents out of their country broke up the social organism, and engendered a fierce and abiding hatred between Hindu and Muhammadan; and in 1792, when the British took over Malabar, this animosity had reached a dangerous height, and the foundations of law and order had been undermined. South Malabar was in particular terrorised by bands of marauding Mappillas who found a secure retreat in the jungles of Ernad and Walavanad. The military held the country for a time; but were gradually drafted out of Malabar to prosecute the campaign against Tippu, which ended with the fall of Seringapatam, and their departure rendered necessary the organisation of police. To overawe the jungle Mappillas, Nayar *sibbandi* corps were raised to serve under their native chieftains, and by the end of the eighteenth century a more regular police force had been established in each of the collectorates into which the district was then divided. In the collectorate of Angadipuram, to take a single instance, which included Vellatiri, Cheranad, Vettatnad and Parappanad, the establishment of police in 1800 consisted of two jemadars, 8 daffadars and 277 kolkars, besides detachments of sibbandi corps stations at various places in the division. In 1801 the irrugular and undisciplined *sibbandi* corps were disbanded, and their place was taken by a force of 500 armed police raised by Captain Watson, mainly for the purpose of collecting the revenue. In the troublous times of the Pychy rebellion this force, which then numbered 1,200, did conspicuous service. Not only did they clear the low country of the small bands of rebels which infested it, but under Mr. Baber they were mainly instrumental in bringing the Raja to bay and in stamping out the rebellion. This force was disbanded about 1810, and since that date the Malabar police has followed normal lines of development. The existing establishment of 'police daroghas and tanahdars'

CHAP. XIII. POLICE.

was abolished by Regulation II of 1816, and a system was introduced piously believed to be founded upon the 'ancient usages of the country.' Under the general control of the Zillah Magistrate and his assistants, the *adhigari* was the head of the village police, the Tahsildar of the taluk police, and amins were appointed to discharge police duties in important towns. A curious feature of the system was that no special establishment of constables existed. Police duties were discharged by the ordinary revenue peon, and about 1823 a very common response to a request for an escort for prisoners was that the peons were 'too busy with the revenue survey to be spared.' The Mappilla outbreaks which began in 1856 soon revealed the inadequacy of the system. The establishment of a local police corps consisting of 31 native officers, 2 buglers and 150 men under the command of two military officers was sanctioned by the Government of India in 1854,[1] but the murder of Mr. Conolly (see p. 80) in 1855 once more exposed the 'utter inefficiency of the police.' The assassins after their escape from jail wandered about the district for some weeks, and though it was a matter of common knowledge that they were contemplating some crime, the Tahsildars took no notice of them, and made no effort to inform one another of their movements. The ease with which the Collector of Malabar had been murdered was a strong argument for the reform of the police, which was then under discussion; and a few years later the present police force was organised under Act XXIV of 1859.

Police Force. The district is divided for police purposes into North and South Malabar, the taluks of Chirakkal, Kottayam, Kurumbranad, and Wynaad forming the northern division, and those of Calicut, Ernad, Walavanad, Palghat and Cochin the southern. Tellicherry is the headquarters of the former, and Calicut that of the latter. The Superintendent of the South Malabar division district is assisted by Assistant Superintendents at Malappuram and Palghat. The force in the two districts consisted in 1906 of 188 officers and 1,278 men. In the same year there were 106 police stations, an average of one to every 55 square miles,[2] the average for the Presidency being one to 85 square miles. Recruiting presents no difficulties, and men are enlisted in Malabar for Madura, Tinnevelly and South Canara. Any number of Nayars of good physique are available, but literate Mappillas and Tiyans are not so plentiful, and care has to be taken to avoid an undue preponderance of the first-named caste.

The Mappilla rebellion of 1921 showed that the district Superintendent of Police, South Malabar, with his subdivisions

---

[1] Correspondence on Moplah outrages in Malabar II, 623.

[2] Under the re-allocation scheme the number of stations in this district will be reduced to 39 with 27 out posts.

of Malappuram and Palghat had too heavy a charge to devote adequate attention to the Mappilla country. The entire Mappilla area of Ernad and Walavanad taluks and a portion of Ponnani taluk was therefore constituted as a separate police district under the charge of a special District Superintendent of Police with headquarters at Malappuram assisted by a Subdivisional Officer at Manjeri. The rest of the Malabar district is in charge of the District Superintendent of Police, Malabar, who is assisted by Subdivisional Officers at Cannanore and Palghat. The taluks of Anjengo and Tangasseri have been transferred from Malabar to Tinnevelly district, but for police purposes it has been found convenient to include the taluks in the Government railway police district of Trichinopoly. The present strength of the ordinary force under both the District Superintendents of Police is 1,454 officers and men inclusive of one Inspector, two sergeants and 113 men for the armed reserve at Calicut and one sergeant and 61 men for the armed reserve detachment at Cannanore. There are 53 stations and 25 out-posts and recruiting presents no difficulty.

Police Force.

Malappuram Special Force.

All the finest recruits are drafted into the Special Force, established as a punitive force in the Mappilla zone temporarily in 1885 and made permanent in 1897. The force which is quartered in permanent lines at Malappuram consists of 80 constables, 4 native head constables, 4 sergeants, a bugler and a European Inspector. It is a fine body of men holding its own with European troops in drill and signalling, and rendered a good account of itself in the outbreak of 1896. During each Ramzan the Special Force and Calicut reserves are mobilised and distributed into parties stationed at Pandalur, Pandikkad, Tuvvur, Manjeri and Malappuram. The parties are kept in touch with one another by elaborate signalling arrangements.

Malabar Special Police.

The Mappilla Rebellion showed that the Malappuram Special Force was too small and ill-equipped to quell armed disorder of a serious and widespread character. The Special Force was disbanded in 1921 and the Malabar Special Police, six companies strong, and organized and trained on military lines was constituted. The Special Police is armed with 303 magazine rifles, lewis guns and grenades and is equipped with motor transport and hospital arrangements. Pending adequate housing arrangements, the companies are now located at Angadipuram, Areakode, Nilambur, Karuvarakundu, Malappuram and Tirurangadi (Klari) but eventually the three posts at Angadipuram, Nilambur and Karuvarakundu will be concentrated at Pandikkad. The special District Superintendent of Police, Malappuram, is the Commandant of the Malabar Special Police. There are two Assistant Commandants of the rank of Assistant District Superintendent of Police each in charge of three companies, the senior of them being the Adjutant of the force. The strength of the force is 32

CHAP. XIII. POLICE.

Indian officers and 742 Indian other ranks. Companies of the Special Police are also deputed on duties outside the district to meet emergencies when it is possible to do so. Recruitment to the force is confined to Hindus and Christians of the West Coast.

There is a wireless station in each camp and at the district Police Office, Calicut.

JAILS.

Imprisonment was not a common form of punishment in olden days, and jails are a British innovation. In the early part of the 19th century the principal towns of the district, Palghat Cochin, Calicut, Tellicherry and Cannanore, each had its own prison, and work was found for the convicts on the roads. In the middle of the century the death rate among the prisoners was terribly high, and in particular the old jail near the French *loge* at Calicut was notoriously unhealthy. Epidemics of cholera and small-pox were frequent, and in 1859, 153 convicts out of a daily average strength of 382 died in prison. The jail at Palghat was abolished in 1868 and those at Tellicherry, Cochin and Calicut in the order named between 1885 and 1892. The Central Jail at Cannanore, built in 1869 on the association block system with accommodation for 1,062 prisoners, is now the only one in Malabar. A printing press has lately been set up, but the chief industries are furniture carving, wood and cocoanut shell carving, and the weaving of coarse rugs and blankets. This jail which receives long-term convicts from South Kanara also has now been considerably enlarged and provides accommodation for 1,684 prisoners. There are special wards for juveniles and women and an up-to-date hospital and a school for youthful offenders. Everything possible is done to teach prisoners a trade that will be useful to them on release, and a Discharged Prisoners' Aid Society finds suitable occupation for ex-convicts. The jail stands on the top of Pallikunnu hill and commands a good position on the Baliapatam road, about three miles from Cannanore town and the railway station.

The special sub-jail at Calicut is under the direct control of the Inspector-General of Prisons and has accommodation for 114 prisoners. There are twenty other sub-jails in the district.

ARMS ACT.

The Arms Act is worked in the usual manner, the only special feature being that as Malabar is a partially disarmed district licensed muzzle loading guns pay double fees. There are 5,200 licences to possess arms for the protection of cultivation and 3,900 licences to possess arms for sport, protection or display. A large number of sword licences are issued and these are used for ceremonial purposes in temples, the weapons being decorative rather than useful. The number seems immense, but the jungles are so vast, and deer and pig do such damage to the crops, that if agriculture is to be

Arms Act.

carried on at all on the margin of cultivation, the game must suffer. Carrying arms was forbidden under pain of death by a proclamation issued in 1802[1]. The possession of the Mappilla war knife was declared illegal by Act XXIV of 1854. Finally in 1885, the four taluks of Calicut, Ernad, Walavanad and Ponnani were disarmed.

APPENDIX.

LIST OF ZILLA JUDGES, CIVIL AND SESSIONS JUDGES* AND DISTRICT AND SESSIONS JUDGES IN THE MALABAR DISTRICT.

A.—Zilla Judges (1802—1843).

Northern Division of Malabar at Tellicherry.

Name.	Date of taking charge.
H. Clephane †	1802.
T. H. Baber †	7th December 1808.
A. Wilson	13th December 1814.

Southern Division of Malabar first at Angadipuram and then at Calicut.

Name.	Date of taking charge.
G. W. Gillio †	14th May 1806.
J. H. Pearson †	10th December 1813.
J. Forbes	8th May 1818.

There was a temporary Zilla Judge's division at Cochin between 1812 and 1817.

Name.	Date of taking charge.
J. H. Pearson †	9th June 1812.
S. Money	10th December 1813.

The first two divisions (North and South) were combined into one in 1823 and Mr. A. Wilson was the first Judge of the combined Zilla Courts and continued as such till succeeded by Mr. F. Holland.

Name.	Date of taking charge.
A. Wilson	1823.
F. Holland	24th December 1824.
T. Gahagan	26th April 1828.
S. Smith	14th May 1830.
R. Nelson	11th January 1833.
M. D. Cockburn	1st November 1836.
E. B. Thomas	14th November 1840.
T. L. Strange	12th August 1842.

From 15th August 1843, the district was split up into two Civil and Sessions Judgeships with headquarters at Tellicherry and Calicut.

B.—Civil and Sessions Judges, North Malabar (*from* 1843).

Name.	Date of taking charge.
G. J. Waters	15th August 1843.
W. A. Forsyth	18th October 1845.

[1] Logan's *Treaties*—CCXXXIV.

* The lists were compiled from the Madras Record Office.

† These were Bombay Civil servants employed in the Presidency of Madras.

B.—*Civil and Sessions Judges, North Malabar (from* 1843)—cont.

Name.	Date of taking charge.
H. Frere	13th June 1851.
R. W. Chatfield	24th December 1855.
H. Frere	24th October 1857.
W. Holloway	17th November 1859.
J. G. Thompson	23rd December 1862.
A. W. Sullivan	8th June 1863.
J. C. Hannyngton	11th August 1868.
G. D. Leman	21st September 1868.
J. W. Reid	9th August 1869.
W. Logan	10th June 1873.
J. W. Reid	23rd October 1873.

C.—*District and Sessions Judges (from* 1875).

Name.	Date of taking charge.
G. A. Parker	31st May 1876.
F. H. Woodroffe	20th October 1878.
S. T. McCarthy	15th April 1879.
E. N. Overbury	27th August 1879.
G. D. Irvine	19th September 1879.
T. V. D. Hardinge	21st October 1882.
W. P. Austin	2nd October 1884.
H. T. Ross	5th November 1884.
L. Moore	29th July 1885.
W. P. Austin	10th November 1885.
C. S. Crole	10th September 1886.
H. Sewell	22nd October 1886.
S. H. Wynne	8th June 1887.
A. Thompson	24th June 1887.
J. H. Nelson	16th August 1887.
A. F. Cox	6th November 1887.
J. H. A. Tremenheere	8th October 1888.
A. F. Cox	23rd December 1888.
J. P. Fiddian	9th June 1889.
A. Thompson	18th March 1891.
M. D. Bell	27th May 1895.
B. Macleod	6th December 1895.
A. Thompson	21st January 1897.
E. L. Vaughan	4th June 1900.
M. J. Murphy	14th September 1900.
N. S. Brodie	12th November 1900.
M. J. Murphy	18th July 1901.
N. S. Brodie	30th September 1901.
A. M. Slight	17th December 1901.
A. Venkataramana Pai	23rd September 1902.
L. G. Moore	24th July 1905.
R. D. Broadfoot	25th November 1905.
W. W. Philips	23rd December 1906.
M. J. Murphy	10th January 1910.
A. Edgington	3rd January 1911.
M. J. Murphy	4th February 1911.
F. B. Evans	12th October 1911.
S. G. Roberts	16th January 1912.
A. Narayanan Nambiyar	1st October 1915.

Name.	Date of taking charge.

C.—District and Sessions Judges (*from* 1875)—cont.

H. D. C. Reilly	18th November 1915.
T. V. Narayanan Nayar	3rd September 1918.
H. D. C. Reilly	15th October 1918.
V. Panduranga Rao	13th February 1920.
T. V. Narayanan Nayar	26th April 1924.
M. McGilligan	15th June 1924.
A. V. Govinda Menon	31st May 1926.
P. C. Lobo	23rd June 1930.
Mir Zyn-ud-din	15th June 1931.

B.—Civil and Sessions Judges, South Malabar (*from* 1843).

Henry Morris	15th August 1843.
C. R. Baynes	9th December 1845.
T. W. Goodwyn	30th October 1846.
Henry Morris	22nd February 1848.
R. W. Chatfield	21st October 1851.
S. N. Ward	1st July 1852.
G. A. Harris	1st January 1854.
H. D. Cook	19th February 1856.
G. R. Sharpe	25th July 1866.
E. C. G. Thomas	27th July 1868.
J. C. Hannyngton	5th October 1868.
J. W. Reid	8th June 1869.
C. R. Pelly	7th August 1869.
G. R. Sharpe	11th January 1870.
W. Logan	12th December 1874.

C.—District and Sessions Judges (*from* 1875).

A. J. Stuart	17th June 1875.
D. Buick	14th October 1875.
R. Wigram	6th December 1875.
W. A. Happell	2nd March 1881.
R. Wigram	6th June 1881.
G. Turner	11th June 1882.
E. N. Overbury	4th December 1882.
F. H. Wilkinson	31st March 1883.
H. T. Ross	1st August 1884.
F. H. Wilkinson	1st November 1884.
H. J. Stokes	24th January 1885.
H. M. Winterbotham	4th January 1886.
F. H. Wilkinson	23rd February 1886.
L. Moore	22nd November 1886.
J. W. F. Dumergue	26th June 1889.
L. Moore	8th August 1889.
A. Thompson	9th May 1890.
L. Moore	6th February 1891.
R. S. Benson	11th March 1892.
J. A. Davies	29th March 1895.
H. H. O'Farrell	4th November 1895.
W. H. Welsh	27th January 1898.

Name.	Date of taking charge.
C.—District and Sessions Judges (from 1875)*—cont.*	
M. J. Murphy	3rd February 1900.
W. H. Welsh	20th March 1900.
S. Russell	28th September 1900.
A. Venkataramana Pai	26th July 1901.
N. S. Brodie	24th December 1901.
J. P. Bedford	10th June 1903.
L. C. Miller	24th August 1903.
A. T. Forbes	5th April 1904.
L. G. Moore	19th June 1904.
J. H. Munro	21st January 1905.
L. G. Moore	19th June 1905.
J. H. Munro	17th July 1905.
R. B. Wood	29th May 1907.
J. H. Munro	30th June 1907.
L. G. Moore	5th November 1907.
A. C. Dutt	6th June 1910.
A. Edgington	4th February 1911.
K. Imbichunni Nayar	30th June 1913.
A. Edgington	30th July 1913.
H. D. C. Reilly	31st October 1914.
A. Edgington	13th December 1914.
G. H. B. Jackson	29th July 1915.
H. R. Bardswell	23rd April 1917.
G. H. B. Jackson	25th June 1917.
T. V. Narayanan Nayar	12th November 1918.
G. H. B. Jackson	22nd December 1918.
V. Panduranga Rao	7th July 1919.
G. H. B. Jackson	8th February 1920.
A. J. King	1st July 1921.
G. H. B. Jackson	13th August 1921.
C. G. Austin	10th June 1922.
G. H. B. Jackson	19th February 1923.
M. McGilligan	12th January 1924.
T. V. Narayanan Nayar	16th June 1924.
C. G. Austin	27th November 1924.
T. V. Narayanan Nayar	27th June 1925.
J. K. Lancashire	10th July 1926.
M. McGilligan	25th June 1926.
J. C. Stodart	16th June 1930.
M. Narasinga Rao	28th June 1930.
J. C. Stodart	28th July 1930.
B. Venkat Rao	10th December 1931.
J. C. Stodart	15th December 1931.
A. J. King	6th November 1932.

CHAPTER XIV.

LOCAL SELF-GOVERNMENT.

LOCAL BOARDS—Receipts—Expenditure—Difficulties. MUNICIPALITIES—Calicut municipality—Palghat municipality—Cochin municipality—Tellicherry municipality—Cannanore municipality.

OUTSIDE the five municipalities of Calicut, Palghat, Tellicherry, Cannanore and Cochin, local affairs are managed by the District Board, taluk boards and panchayats. Originally there were five taluk boards - Tellicherry, Calicut, Malappuram, Palghat and Wynaad, corresponding to the revenue divisions of the same name. On the passing of the Local Boards' Act of 1920, seven taluk boards were constituted for the revenue taluks of Calicut with Kurumbranad, Ernad, Walavanad, Wynaad, Palghat, Ponnani, Chirakkal with Kottayam, but owing to mismanagement of their finances the administration of the latter area had to be taken over by the District Board.* The outlying pattoms of Cochin originally directly under the District Board have been included in the taluk board of Ponnani. The Wynaad taluk has been under the direct control of the District Board since 1924. CHAP. XIV. LOCAL BOARDS.

The enclaves of Anjengo and Tangasseri, which were originally directly under the District Board, have now been transferred to the jurisdiction of the Tinnevelly District Board. The three unions at Badagara, Ponnani and Chowghat have now become panchayats under the amended Local Boards Act of 1930. The District Board and the taluk and union boards have elected unofficial presidents.

Statistics of the income and expenditure of the local boards are given in the separate Appendix. As in other districts, they derive the greater portion of their income from the land-cess. The cess was originally levied under Act III of 1866 at the rate of 6 pies in the rupee of assessment; but when the Local Funds Act (Act IV of 1871) was introduced, the rate was raised, as in other parts of the presidency, to one anna in the rupee. In Malabar however the assessment was so light that the revenue thus raised proved wholly inadequate for the purposes of the Act. By 1877 entire insolvency had been reached under most heads of local fund expenditure, and financial difficulties Receipts.

* By a notification in the *Fort St. George Gazette.*, dated 21st June 1932, page 583, a taluk board has been constituted for each taluk except Wynaad.

were staved off only by large annual grants from provincial funds, varying from Rs. 2,38,030 to Rs. 1,78,630. The rate was accordingly doubled by the Malabar Cess Act (Act I of 1878), and the cess was collected till 1902 at the rate of two annas in the rupee. In that year the Government of India expressed the opinion that the reasons for the specially high local rate would disappear with the introduction of the settlement, and suggested that the rates might be lowered to 1 anna 3 pies per rupee of the new assessment without sacrificing any portion of the revenue hitherto raised for local funds. The suggestion was adopted by the Government of Madras with some modifications necessitated by the working of the increment remission rules. As the actual land revenue demand for each fasli, on which the cess is calculated, is the settlement demand less the increment remission, the rate for each taluk is fixed so as to continue the income derived by the local funds before the settlement, and is being gradually lowered till the rate of 1 anna 3 pies fixed by the Government of India is reached. These arrangements are not in force in the Wynaad taluk, where the cess is still levied at the rate of two annas in the rupee. Tolls follow next in importance as a source of income. There are 42 toll-gates in the district at all of which, except two, full rates are imposed. Ferries also yield a large revenue but the income from markets, many of which are owned by private persons, is comparatively small. The incidence of local fund taxation per head of population was in 1903-04 As. 2–2 including and As. 1–8 excluding tolls. The average for the presidency for the preceding year was As. 3–3 and As. 2–10 respectively.

The important item of receipt continues to be the land-cess which under the Madras Local Boards Act, 1920, as amended in 1930, is levied throughout the district at one anna six pies in the rupee of assessment. Half of the cess is credited to the District Board (one-third under District Funds and one-sixth under the Village Development Fund) and one-third to the taluk boards and one-sixth of the cess raised in their areas to the panchayat boards. In areas where there is no taluk board the taluk board share is credited to the District Board and similarly where there are no panchayats the one-sixth due to panchayats is credited to the taluk board. Next to land-cess come tolls. There were 54 gates at which tolls were levied at the maximum rates allowed by the Madras Local Boards Act, 1920. Tolls on all vehicles were abolished by the Motor Vehicles Taxation Act of 1931, the loss to District Board being made good by a contribution from Government out of the Motor Vehicles Tax. Ferries yield to the District Board about a lakh of rupees a year. Taxes on companies and professions at maximum rates are levied by the local boards which also issue licences for dangerous and offensive trades under the provisions of the Act and collect licence fees. The most important source of income to the panchayats is house-tax.

Expenditure.

Schools, sanitation, medical institutions and vaccination are some of the objects upon which the boards spend their money, but as usual the greater part of their income is devoted to communications. The prescribed minimum to be spent on communications in the district is one-half the land cess plus the net receipts from tolls and ferries, Government in 1902 having ordered that the net receipts from ferries should be expended on roads in general and bridges in particular. Bridging is an expensive item in Malabar. In one year alone, for instance, (1902–03) 114 bridges were built or rebuilt and 162 repaired at an outlay of nearly half a lakh. The boards are fortunate however in deriving an income of more than Rs. 60,000 annually from ferries, an unimportant source of revenue in most districts. The District Board maintains nineteen secondary schools, of which two are for girls. Elementary education has made marked progress, as the number of schools at the end of each of the following years would show: —

1923–24	466
1925–26	774
1927–28	1,045
1928–29	3,336
1930–31	4,134

The schools were opened mostly with the aid of provincial grants, and some of the taluk boards notably Chirakkal, opened more schools than they could properly maintain. A cess is levied under the Elementary Education Act by all the local boards and it is utilized for the improvement of elementary education; and compulsory elementary education has been introduced in select areas under the Ponnani, Ernad and Walavanad taluk boards. There are still many secondary and elementary schools which stand in need of suitable buildings.

Difficulties.

The struggle to make both ends meet is in Malabar more than usually hard and the difficulties with which the District and taluk boards have to contend are many. The fact that the houses are not as a rule collected in villages increases the difficulty and expense of supervising such matters as sanitation and vaccination; and in spite of the many navigable rivers and canals the conditions of the country necessitate an immense system of roads, which owing to the heavy rainfall it is impossible to keep in order except at a great cost. On the East Coast village roads and tracks fit for bandy traffic can easily be improvised over the dry wastes which intervene between the ayacuts of the different tanks. In Malabar with its broken laterite surface and deep closely cultivated valleys, where in the

CHAP. XIV. LOCAL BOARDS.

words of Ibn Batuta, as true to-day as when they were written 'every one has a garden, and his house is placed in the middle of it and round the whole is a fence of wood,' it is difficult to ride across country for any distance, and usually impossible to make even a short road without undertaking much expensive earthwork, constructing innumerable culverts, and building one or two bridges of considerable span. The Wynaad taluk, where the expenditure invariably exceeds the income by nearly half a lakh, is a constant drain upon the resources of the District Board, which for lack of funds has had to hand over to the Public Works Department of Government the maintenance of the two most important roads in the district, the Calicut-Mysore and Tellicherry-Coorg roads, and many ruins are to be seen of important bridges which the Boards cannot afford to rebuild. Nevertheless in the last half century the mileage of made roads has increased from 133 miles to more than 1,700, and of late their condition has steadily improved. In the same period the number of travellers' bungalows has been trebled; medical relief has been brought within comparatively easy reach of every part of the district: and the local boards are in part responsible for the proud position which Malabar holds in education among the districts of the presidency.

MUNICIPALITIES.

All the five municipalities which were originally constituted under the Town Improvements Act of 1865 are now governed by the District Municipalities Act of 1920, as amended by Act X of 1930. (Statistics of their income and expenditure will be found in the separate appendix.)

Calicut municipality.

The largest and most important municipality in Malabar is that of Calicut, the headquarters town. With an income amounting to upwards of two and a half lakhs of rupees, derived mainly from taxes, the municipality administers an area of about 13 square miles with a population of nearly a lakh and maintains 70 miles of road.

The municipality has had a chequered career. In 1882 the rate-payers were allowed for the first time to elect one-half of the councillors, and in 1886-87 the full complement of elected councillors, viz., 18 out of 24, was secured, and the privilege of electing its chairman was conferred upon the council. The experiment, however, was not a success, and the administration of the municipality, never good, went from bad to worse, till in 1890, in view of the 'discreditable and unsatisfactory' administration of the previous year, both privileges were withdrawn. A paid chairman held office for two years, and subsequently the Revenue Divisional Officer was *ex-officio* chairman till 1901. The privilege of electing one-half of the councillors was restored in 1896–97, and since 1901 the council has once more been permitted to elect its own chairman. Subsequently, the council became entitled to elect three-fourths of its members, the remaining one-fourth being appointed by Government. The official element in the strength of the council was gradually withdrawn and with the coming into force of Act V of 1920, the nomination of Government officials was completely stopped and the strength of the council rose from 24 to 32, composed entirely of non-officials. The council continues to elect its own chairman and vice-chairman. Under Act X of 1930 now in force the nomination by Government of one-fourth of the total strength of the council has ceased altogether and the council is composed of purely elected members. In recent years there has been considerable improvement in the administration.

This brief history of the constitution of the council is a commentary upon its work. Till the year 1890 its administration was condemned by Government with unfailing regularity, but in the last ten years there has been a gradual improvement, and in the latest municipal review Calicut was one of the towns selected for honourable mention. The municipality's record, however, during its 38 years' work has been characterized by apathy and lack of enterprise, and compares unfavourably with that of Palghat. For a municipal town the roads are bad. The town is still without a regular system of water-supply or drainage, and owes to its municipality few public improvements. A few wells, the new buildings for its civil hospital, the new Mappilla and Christian burial grounds, the æromotor and reservoirs erected to preserve the water of the Mananchira tank from pollution and the footpath over the Kallayi railway bridge are its most important additions to the town. The incidence of municipal taxation per head of the population has averaged Rs. 1–12–6 in the last five years. Most of the roads are metalled and are in fair condition in spite of the heavy monsoons. The town is still without a protected water-supply or modern system of drainage. The water-supply schemes suggested were too costly to be taken up. The Mananchira tank continues to supply drinking-water to a large part of the town, almost throughout the year. Public wells have also been sunk in many places. The headquarters hospital which was originally maintained by the municipality has been taken over by Government. One Ayurvedic and three allopathic dispensaries are maintained by the council. Elementary education for boys is compulsory in the municipality from 1925 and there are now 42 elementary schools maintained by the council which has also opened a free reading room and public library. Electric lighting under private licence has been introduced in the town. Of the markets belonging to the council, the most important one is the central market on the Court road. The small French settlement (called the French *loge*) in the heart of the town is amenable to the municipal laws. The incidence of taxation in 1929–30 was Rs. 2–6–3.

CHAP. XIV. MUNICIPALITIES.

Palghat municipality.

Next in importance comes the municipality of Palghat with an area of 10 square miles, a population of 44,177, and an income only slightly less than that of Calicut. Here the experiment of local self-government has proved a decided success, and in its annual review Government have rarely had occasion to find fault with the general administration of the municipality. No doubt the conditions of the town are favourable to the growth of municipal insitutions. Its situation on the railway in the middle of a rich taluk, with roads converging upon it from every direction, enables the municipality to levy contributions in the shape of tolls upon a large volume of trade passing through the town, and in spite of the share of the receipts paid to the local boards, the council's income from this source is nearly double that of Calicut where so much of the trade is sea-borne. Continuity of administration however has also contributed to the success of the municipality which for the past fourteen years has been presided over by the same chairman. The chairman is nominated by Government and of 20 councillors 15 are elected. The council was given the privilege of electing its chairman in 1912 and under the Act of 1930 councillors will all be elected. The bridge over the Kannadi river at Yakkara known as the Cardew bridge (costing 1·32 lakhs of rupees) has rendered communication with the rural parts of the taluk easy.

The council has been peculiarly successful in its educational policy, and for many years under the administration of Mr. C. M. Barrow, the Victoria College, which is referred to in Chapter X above, yielded a handsome profit to the municipality. The college was provided with new buildings in 1890 at a cost of Rs. 15,169 and further additions were made in 1894 and 1902 at a total outlay of Rs. 7,000. Among the many other improvements in Palghat, which are due to municipal enterprise, may be mentioned the Dance Market opened in 1897, the new municipal office and slaughter house, and two branch dispensaries, and it is to large contributions towards the expenses of construction made by the municipality and local boards, that the public owe the convenience of using for passenger and wheeled traffic the Kalpati railway bridge between Olavakkod and Palghat. The Sanitary Commissioner however has condemned the water-supply of the town as unsatisfactory and its drainage as deficient. The council maintains upwards of 60 miles of roads. The Victoria College has since been taken over by Government and raised to a first-grade college. Water-supply and drainage continue to be unsatisfactory.

Cochin Municipality.

In Cochin municipal administration has always been fairly satisfactory considering the small income at the council's disposal and the difficulties with which it has to contend.

The conditions of the place are, as Government pointed out in its review of the administration report of 1872, favourable to the working of municipal institutions. The town is compact, and the population largely of a class to be reached by taxation. But the very compactness of the town renders the problems of water-supply and sanitation peculiarly difficult. This is inevitable in a crowded eastern town with a population of 19,274 and 2,639 occupied houses, cramped into a strip of sand between the back water and the sea measuring barely a square mile. The wells which are used by the poorer classes are polluted by infiltration of sewage and drainage water and the health of the town is usually bad. Water for the better classes is conveyed in casks from the Alwaye river; but the supply is in the hands of private contractors, and its purity cannot be depended on. Various schemes for the improvement of the water-supply have been taken up by the municipality. Iron tanks for the storage of rain water were imported in 1882, and in 1893 an unsuccessful attempt was made to bore an artesian well at a cost of nearly Rs. 5,000. Another proposal, broached in 1895, to convey water to the town from the Hill Bungalow of the Cochin Raja at a cost of 8 lakhs also fell through. The drainage problem is also still unsolved. There are nearly 21,000 feet of masonry drains in the town, but the Sanitary Commissioner has condemned them as practically useless. The crowded and insanitary Mappilla quarter of Kalvetti is a standing menace to the health of the town, and the cholera and small-pox epidemics that periodically ravage Cochin all originate here. The council's income is small and barely suffices for the ordinary objects of municipal expenditure. Notable improvements to the town effected by the municipality are therefore few. Among them may be mentioned the reclamation of the Kalvetti swamp and the revetment with granite of the canal. Fires are a danger that has to be specially guarded against in Cochin; and since the last great fire of 1889 thatched houses have been forbidden in the crowded quarters of the town, and a loan of Rs. 2,300 was advanced by Government to enable the poorer inhabitants to roof their houses with tiles. The municipality maintains only 9 miles of road. There is considerable vehicular traffic in the town owing to its proximity to Mattancherry in the Cochin State. The management of the Vypeen ferry has now been transferred to the Cochin Port Conservancy Board together with the Victoria Jubilee jetty which was reconstructed by the municipality. The strength of the council is 20, all of whom are elected. Its chairman and vice-chairman are elected. Compulsory elementary education was introduced in this municipality in 1924 and the council maintains thirteen elementary schools—seven for boys (of which two are for Mappillas) and six for girls. Several tube wells have been sunk by the council in various

CHAP. XIV. MUNICIPALITIES.

parts of the town and the water from them is purer than that from wells ordinarily used by the people. The population of the town rose to 20,637 in 1921 and to 22,818 in 1931.

Tellicherry municipality.

The working of the Tellicherry municipality, which like the others was constituted in 1866, does not call for any special remarks. Its administration, without being in any way brilliant, has usually been efficient. The chairman however is nominated by Government, the privilege of election having been withdrawn in 1898 'owing to the unsatisfactory state of municipal affairs.' The rate-payers are allowed to elect half of the 18 members of the council. Besides attending in the usual way to the lighting and sanitation, the council has enriched the town by a Jubilee market completed in 1889 at a cost of over Rs. 11,000 and by the Chalil branch dispensary; and has of late years managed the Brennen College with such success that, instead of costing the council more than Rs. 5,000 per annum for its upkeep, as it did in the year they took over charge, it now yields an annual profit of more than Rs. 1,000. For its water-supply the town is still dependent on wells public and private, but the water is reported to be excellent and the best on the coast. The health of the town is usually good; but cholera, small-pox and recently plague are prevalent in the crowded and insanitary Mappilla and Mukkuvan quarter of Chalil. The whole council are now elected and elect their own chairman. Chalil continues to be the black spot in this otherwise fairly healthy town.

Cannanore municipality.

Unlike the other municipalities, Cannanore is not a centre of thriving and progressive trade. Apart from the bay which affords some shelter to small native craft, the town which is not situated upon a river or backwater offers few natural advantages to trade. Its strong fort however and the healthy open plain around it make it an ideal site for a cantonment; and Cannanore was for many years the head-quarters of the Malabar and South Canara brigade. A regiment of Native infantry and a company of British troops are all that remain, and the reduction of the garrison was a severe blow to the town. Much of the trade hitherto attracted to Cannanore by its populous cantonment was diverted to its natural outlet at Tellicherry, and the income of the municipality suffered in consequence. The population of the town dwindled from 31,170 in 1871 to 27,811 in 1901, whereas that of Tellicherry increased from 20,504 to 27,883 in the same period. The extension of the railway to the town has given a welcome impetus to trade, and the income of the municipality which for many years was almost stationary has shown a satisfactory increase in the last few years. Poverty however aggravated by inefficient administration has prevented the council from embarking upon any ambitious schemes of town improvement; and beyond maintaining medical and educational

MUNICIPALITIES.

institutions and attending to conservancy and sanitation, the municipality has done little for the town. Its roads however which are upwards of 23 miles in length are well maintained, and are the best municipal roads in Malabar. The population rose from 27,705 in 1921 to 34,236 in 1931; and the mileage of roads maintained from 23 miles in 1901 to 30 miles in 1931, the difference being due to the transfer to the council of roads previously maintained by the military department.

The old wooden bridge connecting the Payyambalam with the beach has been replaced by a strong bridge with iron girders. The culverts on the busy roads have now been rebuilt with ferro-concrete slabs. The council maintains a high school and a town middle school in addition to several elementary schools. The hospital has been taken over by the Government, but the council has opened a Maternity and a Child Welfare Centre and also a free Ayurvedic dispensary. Protected water-supply has been provided for a small portion of the town. The Edward Memorial Town Hall opened in October 1930 was built largely with municipal funds.

Owing to want of funds the council has been unable to extend the water-supply to other parts of the town, to complete the drainage for the whole town or to introduce free and compulsory elementary education.

CHAPTER XV.

GAZETTEER.

CALICUT TALUK—Beypore—Calicut—Chevayur—Kanniparamba—Kannamangalam—Puthupadi—Tamarasseri. CHIRAKKAL TALUK—Anjarakkandi—Cannanore—Chirakkal—Elimalai—Ettikulam—Irukkur—Madayi—Payyanur—Srikandapuram—Taliparamba—Valarpattanam. COCHIN TALUK—British Cochin. ERNAD TALUK—Ariyakod—Chaliyam—Edakkara—Ferok—Kadalundi—Kondotti—Kottakkal—Malappuram—Mambram—Manjeri—Nilambur—Tirurangadi—Wandur—Pookottur—Pandikkad—Thuvvur—Kalikavu—Karuvarakundu. KOTTAYAM TALUK—Darmadam—Iritti—Kadirur—Kannavaram—Kottayam—Kuttaparamba—Manattana—Pazhassi—Tellicherry. KURUMBRANAD TALUK—Badagara—Chombala—Kottakkal—Kuttipuram—Kuttiyadi—Mahe—Nadapuram—Nadavanur—Pantalayini Kollam—Payyoli—Quilandi. PALGHAT TALUK—Alattur—Kollangod—Palghat—Para—Pudunagaram—Vadakkancheri. PONNANI TALUK—Chavakkad—Chettuvayi—Edappal—Enamakkal—Guruvayur—Kodakkal—Mathilingam—Panniyur—Ponnani—Pudiyangadi—Punattur—Tanur—Tirunavayi—Tirur—Tiiprayar—Tritala. WALAVANAD TALUK—Angadippuram—Attapadi Valley—Cherukkod—Cherpalcheri—Karimpuzha—Kavalappara—Kolattur—Mannarakkad—Mankada Pallipuram—Ottapalam—Pattambi—Perintalmanna—Shoranur—Vaniamkulam. WYNAAD TALUK—Chandanatode—Kalpatta—Korot—Lakkidi—Manantoddy—Meppadi—Panamaram—Pukkot—Sultan's Battery—Talapoya—Tirunelli—Vayittiri.

CALICUT TALUK.

CHAP. XV. CALICUT.

CALICUT, conveniently situated, as befits the head-quarter taluk, in the very centre of the district, is the smallest taluk in Malabar proper, and with 918 inhabitants to the square mile is, after Ponnani, the most thickly populated. Physically it bears a striking resemblance to the three northern taluks; but among the hills that guard it on the east are some of the loftiest peaks in Malabar, Camel's Hump, Vellari Mala and Elambileri. The two chief rivers, the Beypore and Elattur rivers in the south and north respectively, are linked by the Conolly canal; but north of the capital the importance of the canal, like that of the coast road, has been diminished by the extension of the South Indian Railway. The interior is not so well served with communications as the seaboard, but as far as the head of the Tamarasseri pass the great Calicut-Mysore road passes through the taluk. The old roads from Calicut to Ariyakkod, and from Manasseri to Ariyakkod are now impassable; but the latter could be reopened without difficulty. The unsurveyed lands along the foot and on the slopes of the ghats, which measure 92 square miles or nearly one-fourth of the area of the taluk, are covered with valuable private forests, and teem with big game.

The soils are typical of the district and the crops characteristic of South Malabar. Pepper plantations are rare, the industry never having recovered from the devastations of Tipu, who, of the vines in the south of the district, left not one in fifty standing. *Modan* takes the place of *punam* as the principal dry crop, and rubber is being experimented with at the bottom of the Tamarasseri ghat. Rubber is now cultivated on an extensive scale in Kodavur, Puthupadi, Nileswaram, Tiruvambadi and Kumaranallur amsams. Thirty per cent of the population in the taluk are Mappillas. Nevertheless Calicut is comparatively well educated, the percentage of its literates (13 per cent) being exceeded only in Cochin and Kottayam. For revenue purposes the taluk, which with the town is a sub-divisional charge, is divided into 71 amsams. The Tahsildar is relieved of magisterial work by the stationary sub-magistrate stationed at Calicut and by the sub-magistrate at Kunnamangalam.

The modern taluk comprises the ancient nads of Polanad, Beypore, Pulavayi and part of Tamarasseri. The last on the Kurumbranad frontier was subject to the Kottayam Rajas. The Beypore Raja, an offshoot of the Kshatriya family of Parappanad, ruled along the coast line from Beypore to the Kallayi river, and the Pulavayi Nayars held sway in the jungles in the east of the taluk. Both these nads were nominally subject to the suzerainty of the Zamorin, who at a very remote period dispossessed the Porlattiri Raja of Polanad.

At the beginning of the eighteenth century the Zamorin's house saved itself from extinction by adopting three lady members of the Nileswaram family, with which branch alone of the Kolattiri dynasty the Zamorin's family observes death pollution. Some time previously to the adoption, it is alleged a scion of the Kolattiri family, which was then bitterly hostile to the Zamorin, married in the guise of a Nambudiri a princess of the Zamorin's family. The intruder escaped with his wife just in time to avoid the Zamorin's wrath, and, eventually becoming Kolattiri, he settled Nileswaram on his natural heirs. The Zamorin's family, which now numbers over 300 male and female members and is in little danger of extinction, is divided into three main branches, the Eastern, Western and New palaces. Each palace or *Kovilagam* has its own property which is managed by the Valiya Tamburatti or senior lady of the branch. The senior lady and nominal head of the whole family has her own *stanam*, known as the Ambadi Kovilagam, to which a separate estate is attached. The five senior males have also their *stanams* and *stanam* estates, and are known in order of dignity as the Zamorin, the Eralpad, the Munalpad, the Edataralpad and the Nadutaralpad. The New and Western branches have their chief palaces at Calicut, the Eastern branch at Kottakkal in Ernad. The palaces of the Zamorin

CHAP. XV.
CALICUT.

and Ambadi Kovilagam both stand upon the banks of the Talli tank, but are no longer in use. The outhouses of the Zamorin's palace are now used by the Kerala Vidya Sala or Zamorin's college, and the palace of the Ambadi Kovilagam is now inhabited by some Brahmans. The Eralpad has a residence at Karimpuzha in Walavanad. The various branches and *stanams* of the family own immense landed properties all over Malabar, and also enjoy a *malikhana* of Rs. 1,32,163–4–0

Beypore : about six miles from the Calicut railway station at the mouth of the river of the same name ; the fifth port in Malabar : sea customs office ; travellers' bungalow. The port can never be provided with a harbour for European vessels at any reasonable cost ; but even in the driest weather the scour on the bar maintains a depth of six feet of water, and the estuary of the river makes a useful harbour for native craft. But fate seems to be against the place. In 1797 saw mills, in 1805 a canvas factory, in 1833 iron works and later still shipbuilding works were started, but all from one cause or another failed. Lack of fuel was the ruin of the iron foundry which worked till 1861. The town became prosperous when the terminus of the Madras Railway was at Chaliyam island on the opposite bank of the river, but the extension of the railway to Calicut put an end to its shortlived importance. Exports from the port, however, are still considerable, coffee from the Cheruvannur curing works accounting for about half of their average annual value. Tanned skins and hides, tobacco and coconuts are other important exports ; salt, rice, and rails are the chief imports. The tile manufactories which have sprung up of late years near Beypore have already been alluded to. In Beypore amsam are the four palaces of the Beypore branch of the Parappanad family.

Calicut : the capital of Malabar, the sixth town and one of the principal ports of the Madras Presidency. Population 99,273 in 1931. Besides being a municipality, a cantonment and the headquarters of all branches of administration, it is the seat of the District Judge of South Malabar, the registrar of Calicut, and the executive engineer of the west coast division. There are two district munsifs, and two subordinate judges. The town is also the headquarters of the income-tax officer, assistant registrar of co-operative societies, and assistant director of fisheries. The district headquarters hospital and Sir Ramaswami Mudaliyar's lying-in-hospital for women and children are now Government institutions. The municipality maintains dispensaries at Kallayi, Vellayikkod and Kuthuchira besides an Ayurvedic dispensary. The Basel Mission also maintains a hospital. There is a Government veterinary hospital. Among the technical institutions are the Government School of Commerce,* the fishery school and Kerala Soap

* Since abolished.

factory which trains students in soap-making, and the navigation school for fishermen. There is a municipal public library. Educational institutions are numerous, the Government School of Commerce, the Zamorin's College and two high schools being the most important ; and visitors to the town are catered for by a travellers' bungalow and hotel, not to mention two clubs for European and native gentlemen respectively. Calicut is also the headquarters of the Malabar Volunteer Rifles raised in 1885. The regiment is recruited mainly from the populous Eurasian community, and has detachments at Cannanore, Tellicherry and Cochin. One of the Basel Mission high schools has developed into a second-grade college known as the Malabar Christian College. The Malabar-Volunteer Rifles has been absorbed in the Nilgiri-Malabar battalion of the auxiliary force.

The situation of Calicut is low, flat and unhealthy, and its position on the little Kallayi river is a standing puzzle ; but both Tipu and the Madras Railway Company have tried in vain to induce the inhabitants to move six miles further south to the site marked out by nature for a great town at the mouth of the Beypore river. From the sea the lighthouse and the pier are the only indications of the important town that lies hidden in the palm groves along the coast. The town is spread over an area of thirteen square miles, with an average breadth of about two miles, and stretches along the shore for some six miles from the southern boundary of the Panniyankara desam to the West Hill barracks. The Mananchira tank and maidan are the centre of the city. Round them cluster the offices of the Collector and the District Superintendent of Police, the Madras Bank, the Municipal Hospital, the Basel Mission High School, the District Press and many other buildings of importance. Close at hand are the District Court and the railway station, and on the south-east lie the fashionable Nayar and Brahman quarters of Chalapuram and Talli. The warehouses and offices of the mercantile community fringe the shore from the Malabar club to the Kallayi river, and the bungalows of the European residents partly lie facing the sea between the pier and the club, and are partly situated on the low hills on the north and north-eastern boundaries of the town. The bungalow in which Mr. Conolly was murdered in 1855 is now part of the European barracks on West Hill. A flagstaff on East Hill opposite the barracks marks the bungalow of the Collector, which is guarded nightly by a file of the reserve police.

There is no harbour, and steamers have to lie in the open roadstead two miles off the land. Close in shore the anchorage is rendered dangerous by 'Coote's reef,' so called from the Honourable Company's sloop of war *Coote* which was wrecked on the rocks, and popularly supposed to be the site of a sunken

CHAP. XV. CALICUT.

Portuguese town. North-west of the pier is another group of rocks discovered by Captain Hogg of the *Juliana* who lost his ship upon them. Native craft find some shelter in the anchorage under the lee of Coote's reef, and in gales of wind take refuge behind the small mud bank off Varakkal in the extreme north of the town. Shipping facilities have been increased by a small iron screw pile pier, and the lighthouse built in 1847 has lately been replaced by a more modern erection. Government have decided that nothing further can be done for the port at any cost proportionate to its trade. Neverthelesst he trade of Calicut is considerable, and averages annually in value about two crores of rupees. The chief imports and exports, industries and manufactures have already been alluded to in Chapter VI.

According to the Keralolpatti, Calicut (*Kozhikod* or Cock fort) was the share of Cheraman Perumal's territory which fell to the Zamorin on the former's departure for Mecca, and was so called because it was so small that the crow of a cock could be heard all over it. More probable is another story in the same book that the Zamorin invaded Polanad from his own country of Ernad, and by dint of hard fighting for forty-eight years drove out the Porlattiri Raja, and forced him to seek refuge with the Kolattiri. To secure his conquest he built a fort at Velapuram, and the city which grew up round the fort gradually became a place of great trade. This seems to have been due to good Government on the part of the early Zamorins and to the reputation for honesty which they obtained. Hither came the Chinese in great floating hulks with 'huge wooden anchors which hold in all weathers,' and in Marco Polo's time they had the lion's share of the trade. They brought copper in ballast, cloths of silk and gold, gold, silver, cloves and spikenard, and bartered them for 'pepper, cinnamon, ginger, turbit, nuts of India and delicate and beautiful buckrams.' Sixty years later when Ibn Batuta (1342–1347) visited Calicut the Moors were in high favour; and by the beginning of the fifteenth century, they had supplanted the Chinese in the monopoly of trade. The latter did not yield without a struggle. 'The king of Calicut having treated them badly they quitted that city; and returning shortly after, inflicted no small slaughter on the people of Calicut and after that returned no more.' Abdur-razak was the next traveller of note to visit the town. In a passage already quoted (see p. 381) he corroborates the tradition that it was owing to the security of trade that merchants were induced to settle in Calicut, and he notices also that wrecks were not seized here as was the piratical custom elsewhere on the coast.[1]

[1] See *India in the XVth century*, p. 14; and conf. *Pyrard de Laval's Voyage* I, pp. 401–9.

The old pier was dismantled and two new piers have been built. The old lighthouse has been replaced by a new one built near the northern pier.

The arrival of the Portuguese in 1498 and their interference with Moorish trade dealt a great blow to Calicut. Under the influence of the Portuguese and Dutch, Cochin gradually became the trade-centre on the coast, and owing to its less favourable situation Calicut has never recovered its former predominance. The Portuguese erected a fort in 1513. Built by Thomas Fernandez, the engineer of Fort St. Angelo at Cannanore, it was situated on the north bank of the Kallayi river at its entrance to the sea, and was square in shape with flanking bastions at the corners facing the sea. Twelve years later it was abandoned after a long siege successfully withstood; and for many years the Portuguese were content with their coign of vantage at Chaliyam on the Beypore river. No trace of the fort remains; but in 1846 Captain Newbold found 'a ruined doorway, the trace of a fosse and counter-scarp, some mounds marking the southern gateway and the site of a few bastions.' Subsequently the English, French and Danes set up factories in the town. In 1615 a small factory was established by ten men whom Captain Keeling had left at Cranganore, but the Zamorin proved unsympathetic and the venture failed. In 1667, however, two Englishmen were permitted to settle down, and thenceforward trade was carried on steadily. The factory, situated somewhere near the Roman Catholic Church, was purely a trading post, and the resident abstained from interference in politics. The French were established in the town, when Hamilton came in 1703; but they were not prospering and were 'not in a condition to carry on trade.' The French *loge* to the north of the Native club on the sea front was the site of their factory. It was restored to them in 1819. The travellers' bungalow close by stands on the plot of ground granted by the Zamorin to the Danish nation in 1752 on condition of 'payment of customs on all goods imported and exported, supply of munitions of war and aid in case of attack on the Zamorin's territories.' The factor fled in 1788, and till 1817 the factory buildings were used as a hospital. The notorious Captain Kydd's first act of piracy was to make a prize of a small Dutch vessel in the roads at Calicut, and his execution in 1701 did not deter others from following his example. The English ship *Formosa* which left Calicut one night homeward bound was never heard of again. The inhabitants heard heavy firing out to sea next forenoon, and two Dutch cruisers were suspected of having rifled and sunk her.

Relics of the past in the shape of ancient buildings are singularly few. The site of the Velapuram fort has been lost and the very name forgotten; but an ancient palace of the Zamorins

CHAP. XV. CALICUT.

stood in the block of gardens south-east of the Collector's office, now cut in two by the Beypore road, which is still known as Kottaparamba. Here to this day the Zamorins are crowned, and massive slabs of granite are scattered here and there in the gardens. The Mudalakulam tank, now the resort of dhobis, was the kitchen tank, and the Mananchira or Manavikramanchira tank the bathing tank of the palace. A new palace for the Zamorin has been built at Meenchantha during the administration of his estate by the Court of Wards.

Ancient temples are numerous in the town, but none of them call for special remark. One of the holiest is the Varakkal temple, a Bhagavathi *kavu*, on a rocky eminence close to the railway line just beyond the West Hill station, famous for an idol piously supposed to have been the gift of Parasu Raman. New moon day in the month Thulam (October-November) is the great day of the year at Varakkal, and thousands of people collect annually to perform ancestral rites in the temple and to bathe in the sea close at hand. On this day every husband must visit his wife with presents of sweetmeat, plantains and the like. 'Failure to visit on the Varakkal new moon' so runs the proverb 'entails forfeiture of relationship.'

Mosques are even more numerous, there being over forty in the town. The most important are the Jamat mosque on the banks of the Kuttichira tank, the Sheikhinde Palli and the Pazhaya Palli. The second of these was built over the tomb of Sheikh Mammu Koya, an Arab of Himisi in Egypt with a great reputation for sanctity. His first resting place was invaded by the sea; but his bones were recovered and an annual *maulad* or birth feast is held over them. An inscribed slab is let into the wall of the Macchinda mosque in Nagaram desam.

The Anglican and Basel Mission churches, dating from 1863 and 1855 respectively, are of no particular interest. The old cemetry, now closed, near the port office is crowded with old fashioned tombs, the earliest of which goes back to the sixteenth century.

The Roman Catholic church of the 'Mother of God' is perhaps the most interesting building in Calicut.

"On the 4th of March 1724, a Portuguese man-of-war called *Madre de Deos*, Commander Pedro Guedes de Magalhaens, anchored off the Calicut Roads, and he concluded a treaty of peace, on behalf of Pedro Mascarenhas, Conde de Somdomil, the Viceroy and Captain-General of the State of India, with the king Samory in the presence of Monsr. Andre Molandin, Chief of Moye (Mahe), for the Royal Company of France, who became surety for the execution of the treaty as follows :—The erection of 'a church of stone and mortar with a parochial house, vestry, porch and a belfry having a bell weighing 150 lb.'; the grant of 'a separate land for building a strong upstair factory of stone and mortar with lodges below; the immediate demolition of the houses of Moors (Mappillas) authors of the revolution which had just terminated;' the protection of all

Christians against the *Zacaio* (fanaticism) of the Moors; 'that on the arrival of vessels of the most Serene Crown of Portugal the said king is obliged to send four boats of fresh water, four of firewood, with provisions which may be had in the country, and for which the Captains have not to pay anything' and lastly, 'that the whole of the articles will be confirmed by *an Olla in copper*, which Monsr. Molandin will send to the Governors off the State at Goa.'

"By the end of that year, Monsr. Molandin informs the authorities at Goa that 'after a great deal of trouble with these Malaveres,' the Zamorin has deposited 10,000 Calicut fanams and 700 fanams as the price of a bell to be cast at Goa, that the building of the Church has been commenced, and 'that the Zamorin has, in the presence of the Vicar, Bernado da Sa, given a Moor merchant. Bamacheri Isumali' as surety to pay all further expenses for the completion of the work. He quaintly states that 'the heretics here are rabid on account of these procurations for the good of Christianity,' and adds that the *copper plate* is left unexecuted till the fulfilment of all the promises made by the Zamorin, who has paid up all, 'the arrears of rent due to the Factor, the Scrivener, the Vicar, the Topas and the Nair Jaganda (double boat).' By 1725, most probably, the church dedicated to *Madre de Deos* was completed, and the Zamorin granted an horta (garden) in perpetuity for the support of the church. This property appears to have formerly belonged to Talichanor, one of the four hereditary ministers of the King, and its extent is now traditionally known here as forming the greater portion of the old Portuguese town bounded on the north by the French and Danish factories, the latter situated at the Old Jail or Town Market; on the east by the Chetty houses: south, the Moplah mosque of Pattæratu: and west, the sea. But the aspect of the town has so much changed during the last half a century that the exact spots can be hardly identified: the glebe lands are now one of the densest business centres of the town.

"Like in all European factories, the Vicar and the Factor had the right to govern and administer justice over all their dependents. In 1735 it appears 'the Vicar of the Calicut Church imprisoned a Christian, when some Christians backed by some Nairs entered the *Church District, without a pass*, and rescued the prisoner; upon which the Revd. Vicar with the Revd. Padre Factor closed the Church and Factory, and retired to Tanur, until the king Samory gave satisfaction for the outrage.' On the arrival of a Frigate *Nessa Senhora da Estrella*, Captain Antonio de Britto Freyra, the Regedores (ministers) offered the same, when a Covenant was made before Francisco Xavier, First Lieutenant of the Frigate, in the presence of Monsr. Martinville, 'Second factor of Mahim and First of Calicut for the Royal French Company, the Revd. Agostinbo Machado, Administrator of the Factory, and the Revd. Cypriamo de Amorin, Vicar of the Church of this city of Calicut.'

"By this treaty concluded with the Viceroy, Dom Pedro de Noronho, Conde de Villa Verde, the Prime Minister, Nilenda Nambi, with the other Ministers and the King's Treasurer, Changarambi, were to proceed to the beach, receive the said Revd. Padres and accompany them to the Church; to seize the three Nairs, who were concerned in the case, and 'after well punishing them, according

CHAP. XV. CALICUT.

to their custom, make them confess who were the others, Christians as well as Nairs, who had released the prisoner': to complete the factory, rebuild and enlarge the parochial house, and make a straight broad road from the factory to the beach so as to clear the view to the sea; to pay the year's rent due, and to deliver the *Olla of copper*, which the king had obliged himself to grant in confirmation of the treaty settled with the State in 1724."[1]

On the invasion of Malabar in 1766 by Haidar Ali, the Portuguese Vicar and Factor obtained from the Nabob a grant confirming the rents, revenues and benefits of the church and the ancient privileges of the community and an order for the payment of 2,420 fanams yearly to the Padre 'as this is an ancient custom'. Tippu was less complaisant, and in 1788 the Vicar with most of his flock and the church plate took refuge in Tellicherry. On their return in 1792 they found that the Honourable Company 'had caused 500 coconut trees belonging to the church to be cut down' as they rendered 'the English factory close and unhealthy and impeded also the sight of the flag-staff.' The Vicar demanded 'a just indemnification and permission to collect the rent on houses built on church ground agreeably to immemorial custom and privileges as per the Zamorin's grant engraved on copper plate still preserved at Goas.' Both claims were compounded for a monthly allowance of Rs. 50 still paid to the Padre 'for his own maintenance, expenses for servants and repairs of the church.' About the same time the community claimed the 'ancient privileges granted to Christians of being tried by Christians' and protested against the jurisdiction of 'a Deroga and other native officers, Mussalmans and Gentoos who are deemed infidels and who are ignorant of Christian law.' The claim was overruled as incompatible with British rule; but the Vicar was allowed to attend Court, and expound the law of the Christians. Two schools attached to the church were opened soon afterwards.

The building is picturesque, but from an architectural point of view is lacking in merit. The great bell is dated 1750; the smaller and older bell cracked and was re-cast in 1843. The images of the Virgin Mary and the Crucifixion, and a painting of the Madonna and child were brought out by the Portuguese for their Chapel at Tanur, and thence were removed to Calicut. They are reputed to be the work of the best artists of the age, and are still in good preservation. A crown of gold was presented by Mr. D'Souza in fulfilment of a vow made when he was surrounded by a herd of wild elephants between Coimbatore and Palghat. The church was tiled about 1797 and has since been several times restored and enlarged. An orphanage and asylum were added in 1862, a

[1] Logan's *Malabar* II, p. ccexliii.

convent was also established by the Carmelite Mission, and the old parochial schools were converted at the same time into schools for boys and girls. A Bull of Pius IX placed the church in 1878 under the jurisdiction of the Jesuits.

Motor buses connect the town with Nilambur, Malappuram, Vayittiri, Cheruvannur and Tellicherry and motor lorries ply for hire between Calicut and Meppadi. On the outbreak of war the industrial establishment of the Basel German Mission institutions were declared enemy property and taken over by Government. They were subsequently transferred to the Commonwealth Trust, Ltd., a British managed concern. The Malabar Spinning and Weaving Company at Kallayi is an Indian concern with a sound financial position. The Standard Furniture Company also at Kallayi is maintained by an Indian graduate and has been doing successful business.

Chevayur : Three miles north-east of Calicut. Sub-Registrar's office ; Basel Mission leper asylum. The new rifle range of the Calicut detachment is here ; and a rock-cut cave exists in which pottery and parts of a sword were found.

Kanniparamba : Ten miles east of Calicut, on the old road to Ariyakkod and Ootacamund ; celebrated for its *tirtam* or spring of holy water. On certain holy days and festivals such as Sivaratri there is a miraculous flow of water into a small pit on a rocky hill, and high-caste pilgrims assemble by the thousand to cleanse themselves of sin by drinking the water. At other times of the year the pit is dry. In the adjoining desams of Kalpalli and Palangad are an umbrella stone and rock-cut cave respectively.

Puthupadi : At the foot of the ghat, contains a police station, two travellers' bungalows, and a small private hotel much frequented by travellers up and down the ghat. An experimental plantation of Castilloa rubber, the first in Malabar, was started at Ingapuzha near Puthupadi in 1882, but was abandoned soon afterwards. A new plantation of Para rubber has recently been opened.

The police station has been reduced to an outpost. The hotel has been closed.

Kannamangalam : Population 6,896 in 1931, lies about 10 miles to the east of Calicut on the road to Vayittiri. It is the headquarters of a deputy tahsildar and sub-magistrate and has a police station, a sub-jail and a post and telegraph office.

Tamarasseri : Six miles from the foot of the pass of the same name into the Wynaad ; once an important road centre and the meeting place of no less than three of Tipu's gun

CHAP. XV. CALICUT.

roads. Travellers' bungalow chattram; dispensary; police station; post office. Near the hospital is an ancient palace, now disused, belonging to the Kottayam Raja's family.

Inscriptions are fairly common in the taluk. They occur in Karipuram temple of Payimpalasseri amsam and desam; in a temple of Manapuram desam of Parambatta Kavu amsam; in a temple of Pokkur desam of Nadukkil amsam; and in a temple in Talakolattur amsam. Padinnattumuri amsam contains a number of interesting rock-cut caves.

CHIRAKKAL TALUK.

CHAP. XV. CHIRAKKAL

CHIRAKKAL, the most northerly taluk of Malabar on the frontiers of Coorg and South Canara, is included in the northern or Tellicherry division of the district. The terraced character of the laterite formation is conspicuous, and except for the solitary eminence of Mount Deli on the seashore, and for the fact that the hills at the back of the taluk are lower than in the taluks further south, the general features of Chirakkal differ in no way from those of the rest of North Malabar. Except on the borders of Kottayam, the ghat slopes have been practically denuded of valuable timber, and are covered with scrub jungle which extends far down into the plains. The rivers and waterways of the taluk have been dealt with in Chapter I above. The South Indian Railway runs along the coast to South Kanara with stations at Edakkad, Cannanore, Azhikkal or Balipatam, Taliparamba road (a signal station), Kannapuram, Madayi (Pazhayangadi), Kunnimangalam (Elimala) and Payyanur. Except in the south and along the coast, the taluk is badly off for roads, its 93 miles being only a small fraction of the total mileage of the district. The north-east of the taluk is roadless, sparsely inhabited and little known.

Statistics on many points are given in the separate Appendix. Mappillas swarm along the coast, but are rare inland and compose only 24 per cent of the population. Noticeable in the backward parts of the interior are two hill tribes, the Vettuvans and Mavilons. Their civilisation is of the most elementary nature, and an apron of leaves is the sole garment of the Vettuvan women. As elsewhere the soils belong almost entirely to the red ferruginous series. Unoccupied dry lands measure upwards of 440 square miles or nearly two-thirds of the total area. A great proportion of these lands is uncultivable hill, rock and jungle. The large extent in the centre of the taluk devoted to the growing of thatching grass is a peculiarity of Chirakkal. *Punam* is the principal dry cultivation. The pepper grown in the north and north-east, which commercially is known as Taliparamba pepper, is the finest produced in Malabar. Paddy and cocoanuts are the staple wet and garden crops. Cardamoms grow on the hills in some of the eastern amsams, and at Anjarakkandi is a large cinnamon plantation. *Kaipad* wet cultivation is common along the coast, and *nendra* plantains are raised, though

CHAP. XV. CHIRAKKAL.

not to the same extent as in Kottayam. Industries are few. The weaving industries of Taliparamba and Cannanore, and the bellmetal work of Kunnimangalam have already been referred to in Chapter VI. There are no Government forests in the taluk. The usual big game is found on the ghat slopes, and a herd of spotted deer still survives on Mount Deli. Crocodiles are so numerous and grow to such a size in the Mount Deli river as to be a positive danger, and occasionally the whole country side turns out to wage war upon them.

For purposes of administration Chirakkal, which formerly was divided into the two taluks of Kavvayi and Chirakkal, is organised into 76 amsams and 272 desams. The tahsildar is assisted by a deputy tahsildar at Taliparamba.

Anjarakkandi: one of the most interesting amsams in Chirakkal taluk. In 1797 the Honourable Company decided to open at this place a plantation of coffee, cinnamon, pepper, nutmeg, cassia, sugarcane and sandalwood plants, 'such products as from time immemorial formed the valuable articles of exchange between Malabar and the distant nations.' Mr. Murdoch Brown the originator of the scheme, a merchant of Mahe, who had joined the Company's service on the fall of the settlement in 1793, was appointed overseer and manager; and by an agreement signed on December 31, 1797 [1] he agreed that, if the Honourable Court of Directors disapproved, he would take over the plantation on his own account and repay the Company all the money, principal and interest, expended thereon. In 1799 the terms of the agreement were enforced, and the plantation which the Company had found too expensive was handed over to Mr. Brown. A survey was made and the transfer finally effected by Major Macleod in 1802. The estate was leased to Mr. Brown for 99 years and he was granted the following rights :—(*a*) the possession of lands which he had already cleared or purchased on behalf of the Company amounting to 459 acres; (*b*) the right to clear and occupy all waste land within the five taras or desams of the amsam; (*c*) the right to purchase from the owners the lands occupied by private persons amounting to 918 acres. Mr. Brown on his part was responsible for the whole revenue on the five taras amounting to Rs. 5,857, and was to pay back by instalments the expenses already incurred by the Company amounting to 1½ lakhs. In the next year 1803 the plantation was devastated by the Pychy rebels, and Mr. Brown claimed the remission of the amount he had agreed to pay. The matter was left unsettled for 13 years, and finally in 1817 a fresh agreement was drawn up confirming that of 1802, the particulars of which had been lost. One or two unimportant alterations were made. Since then the descendants of Mr. Brown

[1] Logan's *Treaties*, ii. CLIX.

remained in undisturbed possession of the estate, paying in one kist the whole revenue of the amsam. The lease was held to have expired in 1901, and has now been cancelled, and the amsam has been surveyed and settled. The lands which were held by private janmis at the time of the lease to Mr. Brown, and in which the lessee had merely the right of collecting the Government revenue, have been registered as the private *janmam* of the several owners. The lands of which the *janmam* right had been purchased by the East India Company before the date of the lease and handed over to the lessee, as well as the lands purchased by the lessee during the currency of the lease, have been registered as the private *janmam* of the lessee's heirs. The remaining lands, which were waste at the time of the lease, have been registered as Government *janmam*, and occupancy pattas have been issued for them to the lessee's heirs; but by a special concession such of them as have not yet been brought under permanent occupation are treated as unoccupied dry, and charged *janma-bhogam* annually but assessment only when actually cultivated.[1] The estate has hardly maintained its character as a plantation of special products; it is rather an ordinary Malabar janmam estate, albeit a very well managed one. Coffee was first grown here in Malabar and from Anjarakkandi seems to have been introduced into the Wynaad at Manantoddy some time before 1825. A large plot of cinnamon is a feature of the amsam, and Anjarakkandi white pepper is famous in the London market. The Brown family has a large rambling old house on the banks of the Anjarakkandi river. There is a sub-registrar's office in the amsam.

Cannanore : the headquarters of the taluk is the municipality and cantonment of Cannanore (population 27,811), the fourth town, the fourth port and the most important military station in Malabar. Apart from the taluk and military offices, the principal public buildings are a District Munsif's Court, sub-registrar's office, municipal hospital and high school, police station, sea customs' office, and travellers' bungalow. There is also a comfortable hotel. The working of the municipality has been discussed in the preceding chapter. Three miles north of the town on the Baliapatam road is one of the six central jails in the presidency. Population rose to 34,236 in 1931. There are also in the town a board high school, a secondary and training school for women, and three hotels.

Cannanore, though the reduction of its garrison has diminished its importance, is one of the pleasantest places on the Malabar coast. Its climate is cooler than that of Calicut and the sea breezes blow unimpeded over the healthy open maidan, which serves both as a parade ground and a playground

[1] G.O. No. 281, dated 26th March 1906, and No. 510, dated 7th June 1906.

CHAP. XV. CHIRAKKAL.

for the troops, and where excellent golf links have been laid out. The town is large and straggling, and is composed of two detached portions, known locally as the Old town and the Cantonment. Between the two, on a promontory jutting out into the sea, is the old Fort St. Angelo, now enclosing within its walls a modern lighthouse. South of the promontory is a curving bay, fringed with groves of cocoanut palms and the low irregular houses of old Cannanore, among which the white-washed palace of the Ali Raja and a picturesque old mosque are conspicuous. Here Mappillas swarm; and the crooked lanes between their shops and warehouses are often too narrow for any but foot passengers. North and north-east of the fort the barracks, the European churches and cemeteries, the commissariat offices and the little village of Barnacheri are grouped round the extensive maidan, and further north still are the bungalows of the military officers. East of the railway is another open plain and a long line of mouldering barracks, relics of the time when Cannanore was the headquarters of the Malabar and South Canara brigade.

Fort St. Angelo is massively built of laterite, and is triangular in shape with a ditch on the land-ward side and strong flanking bastions. A fort of this name was built here in 1505[1] by Almeida the first Portuguese Viceroy of India, but the present building is of later date. The Dutch, who acquired it from the Portuguese in 1663, sold it to the Ali Raja in 1772, from whom it was taken by storm in 1790. The fort is now occupied by a guard relieved daily from the detachment of British troops stationed at Cannanore. On the little tongue of land, now overgrown with casuarina trees, which projects into the sea on the west, the shoal of crabs must have come forth, which saved the garrison from starvation during the siege of 1507 (see p. 47). On the east at the entrance of the covered way is a well. In 1507 this well was a bowshot from the walls; and during the siege 'every time the Portuguese wished to draw water therefrom they had to cut their way through the besiegers,' till Fernandez, an Engineer, hit upon the expedient of mining a passage as far as the well and drawing off the supply underground. The fort still mounts a few obsolete guns, and until comparatively recent times its dungeons were used as a jail. The Fort St. Angelo is now practically deserted except for the lighthouse. Half of the buildings have tumbled down and the rest have a desolate appearance. The little tongue of land which projects into the sea on the west of the fort still has some old casuarina trees.

---

[1] Or 1507; the exact date is uncertain. The Portuguese had a factory at Cannanore in 1502. The place was then one of the chief-ports for Vijayanagar. (See Varthema's *Travels*, p. 123; Barbosa, p. 150; Linschoten I, p. 67.)

In the old town, as stated above, is the palace of the Ali Raja of Cannanore. The Keralolpatti traces the history of the family back to the inevitable Cheraman Perumal (see p. 38 above); but tradition is tolerably unanimous that the first chieftain was a Nayar, by name Arayan Kulangara Nayar, one of the ministers of the Kolattiri, who embraced Islam and adopted the name Muhammad Ali about the end of the eleventh or beginning of the twelfth century A.D. Owing to his ability he was retained in the service of the Kolattiri; and his successors, known as the Mammali Kidavus, were the hereditary ministers of the Kolattiri. Tradition says that they were admitted to all the Kolattiri's most important councils and that they stood with sword point resting on a box, implying that whatever was determined upon they would find the money therefor. Hamilton speaks of Cannanore being under the sway of 'Adda Raja, a Mahomedan Malabar prince, who upon occasion can bring near 20,000 men into the field.' Ali Mussa, the fifth of the line, is said to have conquered some of the Maldive Islands for the Kolattiri, and to have been rewarded for his services with an annual grant of 18,000 fanams from the revenues of the islands, and with the port of Cannanore and the desams of Kanattur and Kanotchala on the mainland. The Laccadives were probably colonized from Kolattanad at an earlier period. They are said to have been conferred with the title of Ali Raja, 'lord of the deep,'[1] upon the head of the Cannanore family by the Kolattiri in 1550 in return for a fixed tribute. From this time the Ali Rajas prospered. Their trading fleet covered the sea; and by the end of the seventeenth century they were a thorn in the side of their nominal suzerain. Their attitude towards the Honourable Company was usually unfriendly. They intrigued against them with the Dutch and French in turn, and their consistent support of Haidar was one of the most dangerous features of the Mysorean invasion. Finally in 1790 Cannanore, 'that nest of enemies' was stormed by General Abercromby. In spite of her persistent treachery, the Bibi, the lady who was then head of the family, was generously treated, and no distinction was drawn between her and the other ruling princes of Malabar. Her dominions were leased to her in 1793; and three years later by an agreement drawn up on October 28th, 1796[2] she consented to pay 'Rs. 15,000 per annum being the Jumma on the houses and purrams, etc., situated at and near Cannanore, on my trade to the Laccadive Islands, and on my Jenm property on the said islands.' The agreement merely farmed the collection of the land revenue; but, unlike the other Rajas, the Bibi was punctual in her payments, and the lease was never revoked. In course of time its nature

[1] The word Ali in this title is, according to Gundert, properly the Malayalam *azhi*, sea; and not the ordinary Muhammadan name.
[2] Logan's *Treaties, ii,* CXXVI.

CHAP. XV. CHIRAKKAL.

was forgotten, and in the minds of her descendants it assumed the dignity of a treaty. Their pretensions seem to have been admitted, and in 1824 the Bibi was 'regularly supplied with a guard of honour from the military station at Cannanore' and was 'very strict in exacting this homage to her rank.'[1] The Karar lands measuring about 3,092 acres were surveyed and classified in 1907. These were subsequently resettled as ryotwari lands. A lamp is kept constantly burning in one of the rooms of the Arakkal[2] palace, as it is called, the belief being that only so long as it remains alight will the prosperity of the family continue. In olden times the Raja's cat was a burden to the fishermen, one fish from each boat being her portion. Subsequently a toll of two pies on each successful boat was substituted for the fish.

Chirakkal: an amsam about four miles north of Cannanore and quite close to the jail. The palace of the Chirakkal Raja is here, a block of hideous buildings round a large tank. The family is one of the most ancient and honourable in Malabar, and under the title of the Kolattiris appears frequently in the preceding pages. The legendary origin of the family is that one Kshatriya and two Sudra women, strangers from a foreign land, were stranded at Mount Deli. Cheraman Perumal took them all to wife. For the Kshatriya woman he built a palace at Elimala[3] or Mount Deli, and he conferred upon her offspring the title of Elibhupan, ruler of Eli, with the heirdom of the kingdom. Karipad in Kurumattur amsam is the original family seat. Thence they moved to the Eli *kovilagam* or palace near Mount Deli, and the site of one of their residences in this neighbourhood is still marked by a small but ancient temple with an inscription in *vatezhuttu* characters near the big Raman talli temple on the banks of the river, near Kavvayi. Here they were established as the kings of Eli, 'afraid of nobody,' as early as the 13th century when Marco Polo touched at Mount Deli,[4] and their kingdom seems to have included the Malayalam country in the South Canara district and to have stretched as far as the Kotta river on the south. During their residence at the Eli *kovilagam* the family after the fashion of Malabar *tarwads* split up into two main branches, the Udayamangalam and Palli branches. The eldest male of the family was the Kolattiri, who had his own *stanam* property and lived apart from the rest of the family in residences at Madayi, Valarpattanam and other places. The dissensions which rent the family and led to the ultimate dismemberment of Kolattanad have been described in Chapter II above. The Udayamangalam branch is now extinct, and the present Raja belongs

[1] *Thirty years in India* by Major H. Bevan, II. 173.

[2] *Arakkal* means literally 'at the palace.'

[3] According to Gundert the name should be spelt Ezhi. I have kept the more usual spelling, as the derivation is by no means certain.

[4] Yule's *Marco Polo*, Vol. II, Book III, Ch. XXIV.

to one of the numerous offshoots of the Palli branch. He is still a great landed proprietor, and enjoys a *malikhana* of more than Rs. 12,000. The total *malikhana* of the family is Rs. 22,127–1–5. The Chirakkal or Kolattiri family is closely allied with that of the Maharajahs of Travancore. The two families have always observed pollution, when deaths have occurred in either house ; and the Travancore dynasty would have come to an end long ago but for the adoption of heirs from the Chirakkal family.

Mount D'Ely, locally known as Eli-Mala, is the northernmost boundary of Malabar. Mr. Padmanabha Menon in his *History of Kerala* suggests that the name may be a variation of Azhi-mala meaning "the mount near the sea." It is a conspicuous isolated cluster of hills forming a promontory 16 miles north of Cannanore. Gasper Correa says that Vasco-da-Gama's pilots had foretold that the first land to be sighted would be a great mountain on the coast of India in the kingdom of Cannanore which the people of the country called Delielly. Its height is 855 feet. The Arab history of the Muhammadan settlement in Malabar mentions a State called Hili Marawi. The name of Marawi is preserved in Madavi or Madayi (situated 13½ miles north-west of Cannanore upon the river which enters the bay about 7 or 8 miles south-east of Mt. D'Ely) and which is called De Barros the Rio Marabia.

Ettikulam : a small village lying a mile south of Mount Deli ; distinguished only for a small fort built probably by the Portuguese and subsequently held successively by the French and the English. It was once a notorious pirate stronghold.

Irukkur : six miles south-east of Srikandapuram ; an important Mappilla village on the road from Cannanore which joins at Iritti the high road up the Perambadi ghat. Travellers' bungalow ; sub-registrar's office ; police outpost. The Valarpattanam river is navigable for small boats as far as Irukkur, and much timber is floated down from this point to Baliapatam.

Madayi : or Pazhayangadi. Railway station ; travellers' bungalow ; sub-registrar's office. Close to the travellers' bungalow on the west are the lines of an ancient fort, and further north in the midst of a desolate, rocky plain are traces of many walls and buildings and an old tank, still known as the Jews' tank. The fort was probably the Canarese redoubt captured by the British in 1736 ; but may be on or near the site of the old Eli fort of the Kolattiri family, built, according to the Keralolpatti, by Eli Perumal, the eighth of the line. East of the bungalow is the principal temple of the Chirakkal family ; and near thereto is a natural cave extending for some distance under a ledge of laterite rock. The mouth of the cave is very narrow, and it should be entered with care and a bright light.

The writer's explorations were brought to a premature conclusion by a slumbering python. The 'Jews tank' points to an early colony of Jews, probably in the palmy days of the kingdom of Eli. Some manuscripts of Durate Barbosa refer to this colony :—' After this at the foot of the mountain to the south is a town called Mazare, very ancient and well off, in which live Moors and Gentiles and Jews ; these Jews are of the language of the country ; it is a long time that they have dwelt in this place'.[1] There is also an allusion to them in the ancient Malayalam poem, the Payyanur Pattola.

But the most interesting building in Madayi is the beautiful old mosque in the bazaar below the bungalow, which was founded by Malik Ibn Dinar himself. If there be any truth in the tradition of Cheraman Perumal's pilgrimage to Mecca and Malik Ibn Dinar's mission to Malabar, the Arabic inscription within the mosque, which commemorates its erection in A.D. 1124, is of extreme chronological importance. A block of white marble in the mosque is said to have been brought over from Arabia by the founder.

Within the village of Madayi is the hamlet of Payangadi or Pazyangadi (old town or market) with an old tank near which stands the ruins of an ancient fort or palace of the Eli or Kolattiri Rajas. Mr. Sewell in his Archaeological Survey of South India, Vol. I, page 42, conjectures that the tank was probably constructed by the Colony of Jews or Yavanas, and an old Malayalam poem mentions a Buddhist vihara as having existed there.

Payyanur : the northernmost amsam of the Malabar coast line ; celebrated as the seat of the seventeen Nambudiri illams of the Payyanur gramam. These Nambudiris are unique among Brahmans in that they follow the *marumakkattayam* law of inheritance. The gramam was one of the sixty-four founded by Parasu Raman. It has a railway station, police station and sub-registrar's office ; and at Kavvayi, 4 miles off on the coast, there is a travellers' bungalow. The village is now the headquarters of a deputy tahsildar and contains a district board high school.

Srikandapuram : in Chuzhali amsam, ten miles due east of Taliparamba ; once an important point on the trade route from Malabar to Coorg, and still a populous Mappilla village. Mr. Logan identified this place with the 'Zaraftan' of the Tahafut-l-Mujahidin, the site of one of Malik Ibn Dinar's mosques ; and the tradition that the Chuzhali Nambiyar,

---

[1] *The Coasts of East Africa and Malabar*, p. 149. Conf. Yule's *Marco Polo*, Vol. I, Book II, Ch. XXIV, foot-note. Mazare is written in Rowlandson's *Tahafut-l-Mujahidin* 'Hubaee Murawee.' Both are corruptions of the Arabic Hili Marawi, which itself is the equivalent of Madayili, the ancient name of Madayi.

some time warden of the marches and still the most powerful janmi in this part of the taluk, is descended from Cheraman Perumal by his alliance with one of the two Sudra women stranded at Mount Deli lends some colour to the theory.

Taliparamba : fourteen miles north-east of Cannanore ; the headquarters of a Deputy Tahsildar, and District Munsif : sub-registrar's office : police station : travellers' bungalow : dispensary : Basel Mission outstation : post office. There are many sepulchral caves at this place, and two famous temples, the Taliparamba and Trichammaram temples. The *stala puranas* of the former or Lakshmipuram temple are long and elaborate. A king of Oudh built the first temple here over a *lingam* presented to him by Parvati. The temple was restored by Parasu Raman ; and a well within the precincts, which now is kept under lock and key, was filled by him with diamonds and other precious stones. The fine *gopurams* of the temple were partially blown up by the Mysoreans and now make an impressive gateway. An inscription on a granite slab in a bathing shed on the banks of the tank below the temple records the fact that the shed was built in A.D. 1524 (M.E. 700), and another inscription, dated 1778 exists at the foot of a neighbouring banyan tree. On a hill near the temple are the ruins of a small mud fort, one of the Canarese outposts captured by the British in 1736. The festival held at the Trichammaram festival in the month of March attracts thousands of pilgrims. An experimental pepper garden has been established near Taliparamba. There are an agricultural demonstration farm and an agricultural middle school in this village, about two miles from the Deputy Tahsildar's office.

Valarpattanam : : or Baliapatam or Azhikkal, five miles from Cannanore on the coast road, a thriving Mappilla town, a minor port of some importance, and a station on the South Indian Railway. It is situated on the south bank of the river of the same name close to its mouth. Police station ; sub-registrar's office. The town is rich in Malayalam and Mappilla traditions. Vallabha Perumal, the eleventh of the Perumals, here found a lingam, and built a shrine over it and a fort to protect it on the banks of the Neytara river, as the river was then called. Valarpattanam was his chosen seat and the residence appointed by him for the kings of Kerala. In Cheraman Perumal's time it was, with Trikkariyur and Tirunavayi, one of the three holy places of Malabar. Subsequently it became one of the principal places of residence of the Kolattiri ; and the remains of an ancient fort magnificently placed in a commanding position above the Mappilla village still exist on a lofty cliff overhanging the river. Within the fort are the ruins of a temple, possibly the shrine built by Vallabha Perumal ; and in the adjoining waste ground the bodies of deceased Rajahs are still burnt. On the south is one of the

CHAP. XV. CHIRAKKAL.

most famous of the many temples of the Kolattiri dynasty, the Kalarivattukkal or fencing school temple, dedicated to the family goddess Bagavathi. In ancient times Nayars accused of theft or caste offences uuderwent the boiling oil ordeal in Valarpattanam fort.

There are twelve mosques in the town. The oldest and most picturesque is held by some to be one of the original mosques of Malik Ibn Dinar, but Ibn Batuta's story is that it was founded by an early Kolattiri convert to Islam.

"We next came to Dadkanan, which is a large city abounding with gardens, and situated upon a mouth of the sea. In this are found the betel-leaf and nut, the cocoanut and colocassia. Without the city is a large pond for retaining water; about which are gardens. The king is an infidel. His grandfather, who had become Muhammadan, built its mosque and made the pond. The cause of the grandfather's receiving Islamism was a tree, over which he had built the mosque. This tree is a great wonder; its leaves are green, and like those of the fig, except only that they are soft. The tree is called Darakhti Shahadet (the tree of testimony), darakht meaning tree. I was told in these parts that this tree does not generally drop its leaves; but at the season of autumn in every year, one of them changes its colour, first to yellow, then to red; and that upon this is written with the pen of power, 'There is no God but God; Muhammad is the Prophet of God,' and that this leaf alone falls. Very many Muhammadans, who were worthy of belief, told me this; and said that they had witnessed its fall, and had read the writing; and further, that every year, at the time of the fall, credible persons among the Muhammadans, as well as others of the infidels, sat beneath the tree waiting for the fall of the leaf; and when this took place, that the one-half was taken by the Muhammadans, as a blessing, and for the purpose of curing their diseases; and the other by the king of the infidel city, and laid up in his treasury as a blessing; and that this is constantly received among them. Now the grandfather of the present king could read the Arabic; he witnessed therefore the fall of the leaf, read the inscription, and undertsanding its import, became a Muhammadan accordingly. At the time of his death he appointed his son, who was a violent infidel, to succeed him. This man adhered to his own religion, cut down the tree, tore up its roots and effaced every vestige of it. After two years the tree grew, and regained its original state, and in this it now is. This king died suddenly; and none of his infidel descendants, since his time, has done anything to the tree".[1]

Few other places of interest remain to be noticed. Oaths taken in the Pattuvad temple in Pattuvam amsam are still of peculiar sanctity. The party that takes the oath pays 21 fanams to the temple and the other party 22 fanams. A burning lamp is placed in a small shrine attached to the main building, and the oath is administered by the priest in the words

---

[1] Lee's *Travels of Ibn Batuta*, p. 167.

of the order of the civil court read out by the commissioner. The priest certifies to the performance of the oath. Two ancient inscriptions, as yet unread, exist in the Ramantalli temple in the amsam of the same name on the western slope of Mount Deli, another on a broken slab in the Velam temple in Kandakkayi amsam, and yet another in Maniyur temple in the amsam of the same name. A dose of sacred water administered by the priest of the Peralasseri-temple in Makreri amsam is believed to be of peculiar efficiency as an antidote to snake poison.

COCHIN TALUK.

CHAP. XV. COCHIN.

COCHIN is distinct from the rest of Malabar, and consists of the town of British Cochin, and seventeen other tiny patches of British territory, *pattams*, all embedded in the Native States of Travancore and Cochin. It is the smallest taluk of the presidency, containing an area of about two square miles and a population of 21,042 ; and is remarkable for the literacy of its inhabitants, and the numbers of its Christian population. The occupations of the people are mainly industrial, and agriculture is of only secondary importance. But the soils are for the most part rich alluvial deposits such as the coconut leaves, and the gardens of the taluk are of an excellence unsurpassed in Malabar. The few wet lands in and near Cochin town are valuable properties, but more because prices rule high in the town than because the soil is eminently suited for paddy cultivation. Statistics on these and many other points of interest are given in the separate Appendix.

British Cochin—the headquarters of the taluk, and the seat of the officer who unites in his own person the offices of the Deputy Collector and Subordinate Judge. Local affairs are entrusted to a municipal council constituted in 1866. The chief officials are the port officer, an inspector of customs with an assistant, the engineer-in-chief attached to the Harbour Works with an executive engineer and an assistant engineer to help him. There are a post and telegraph office, a municipal hospital, a travellers' bungalow and a police station. A lighthouse exhibits from the south-western bastion of the old fort a group occulting light of 1,250 candle power, visible twelve miles out to sea. The population of Cochin is 19,274. There are at present 14 European mercantile firms, an European Chamber of Commerce and a Conservancy Board in Cochin. The principal banks are the Imperial Bank and the National Bank. The population of the town rose to 20,637 in 1921 and to 22,818 in 1931.

The town is built on a narrow strip of land lying between the backwater and the sea on the south of the mouth of the Cochin river. The southern extremity of the island of Vypeen on the north bank of the river also belongs to the British Government and is included in the municipality.

The Cochin river is now the main outlet to the sea of the immense system of backwaters that run parallel with the coast from Cranganore to Trivandrum : and to it the present town owes not only its importance, but its very existence. The tradition is that in 1341 A.D. the backwater burst through the narrow sand banks which separated them from the sea at Cochin, and made a new outlet; the island Vypeen is said to have been thrown up at the same time, and from that date a new era, known as the Pudu Veppu or era of the new bank, began. The formation of the new island could hardly have been synchronous with the formation of the new outlet; but the features of the coast are constantly altering, the counteraction of river flood and sea current tends continually to form new sand banks and lagoons, and an exceptional monsoon is always liable to result in the closing of existing outlets and the opening of new ones. At the beginning of the Christian era and for some centuries afterwards, Cranganore, now a small village celebrated only for its Cock-festival, was the seat of the Perumals and a trade centre, whose fame had stretched as far as Rome, while Cochin apparently did not exist; and the inference is that either the coast line was what is now the eastern bank of the backwater, or the main outlet to the backwater was at Cranganore. In either case the formation of the island of Vypeen and the scouring of a deep channel at Cochin would be easily explicable; and the Pudu Veppu era, which seems to have been first used by the Christians of the Narakkal church, may commemorate either the establishment of the first church on the island, or the date when the island first became cultivable, which according to the Keralolpatti was about the time traditionally assigned to the era. The name of Vypeen seems to be strictly applicable to the southern extremity of the island, and the scouring of a deep channel at Cochin would naturally have resulted in accretion immediately to the north of the outlet. There is in any case no reason to doubt that the history of Cochin as a seaport began about the 14th century; and that it gradually superseded Cranganore as an emporium of trade; and in course of time the Jews and other settlers in Cranganore seem to have emigrated to its more flourishing rival.

Cochin is the earliest European settlement in India. On December 24th, 1500, a Portuguese fleet under the command of Pedro Alvarez Cabral anchored in what must have seemed to the sailors the finest natural harbour their eyes had ever seen. It was the second Portuguese expedition to India sent by the king of Portugal to follow up the discoveries made by Vasco Da Gama two years before. They had already touched at Calicut; but, after an unsuccessful attempt to open a factory, had come to open rupture with the Zamorin, and had sailed further south in quest of a cargo. Their reception at Cochin was very different. The Raja, the hereditary enemy of the Zamorin, received them with open arms, and afforded them such facilities for trade that within twenty days their ships were full. Cabral then sailed off, leaving a few Portuguese in charge of the small factory he had established. In 1502 the great Vasco Da Gama himself landed at Cochin, and concluded a treaty of commerce with the Raja. On his departure the Zamorin invaded Cochin with 50,000 Nayars, and the Raja had to take refuge with the few Portuguese factors in a small fort in Vypeen. The timely arrival of Francisco d'Albuquerque with a fleet of six vessels on September 2nd, 1503, raised the siege, and the Portuguese then proceeded to build a small fort at the mouth of the river on its south bank for the protection of their trade. This fort dignified by the name of Manuel, the king of Portugal, was the first European fort in India.

Protected by its fort, the Portuguese settlement at Cochin rapidly increased in prosperity, and until Goa was built, was looked upon as the official residence of the Viceroy of all the Indies ; and several of the religious orders of Rome established themselves in the town. The first Viceroy, Francisco de Almeida, arrived in 1505. In 1524 Vasco Da Gama paid his second visit to Cochin, but this time he came only to die. He expired on the 24th December 1524, and was buried probably in the chancel of the present Government church. A few years later however his body was removed to Portugal, and was interred in the family vault at Vidigueira. Quite lately it was removed to a tomb at Belem, the port whence he sailed in quest of the Indies. St. Francis Xavier passed through Cochin on his way to his mission fields near Cape Comorin ; and in 1557 at the request of Sebastian, king of Portugal, one of the churches of Cochin, Santa Cruz, was raised to the dignity of a Cathedral by a bull of Pope Pius IV. In 1577 the first book printed in India was issued at Cochin by the Society of Jesus. In 1585 the town was visited by the English traveller Ralph Fitch, who with a band of adventurers came to India by way of Aleppo, Baghdad and the Persian Gulf. In 1634 with the permission of the Portuguese a small factory was opened at Cochin by the English East India Company.

Cochin at this time was a city of great trade, and second in importance only to Goa in Portuguese India. But the star of the Portuguese was now on the wane and was soon to set for ever in the East. In 1661 the Dutch under Van Goens appeared before the town, and occupied Vypeen, where they established a small fort, called Fort Orange. Their first attacks were repulsed, and on the approach of the monsoon they retired leaving 700 men in Fort Orange. They returned to the attack in October of the same year ; and after a heroic resistance the Portuguese capitulated in January 1663. The English at once received notice to quit, and retired to Ponnani.

The Dutch remained in possession for 132 years and greatly improved the town. One of their first acts was to expel from the place all Portuguese or Spanish priests ; after which, in an unfortunate access of puritanical zeal, they destroyed most of the convents and all the churches, except the church of the Franciscan Friars, which they converted into their own chapel, and the cathedral of Santa Cruz which they retained as a storehouse. The Roman Catholic community, in consequence of these measures, deserted the town in a body, and declined to enter into any mercantile transactions with the Dutch. A compromise was finally effected; and permission was given to the Roman Catholics to erect a church in Vypeen, and to remove to it any of the internal fittings from the church of the Franciscans they might desire. The church now existing in Vypeen was accordingly built, and dedicated to Our Lady of Hope. The altar and old screen of the church are said to have once belonged to the church of S. Francis. In the latter years of the seventeenth century the famous 'Hortus Malabaricus' was compiled at Cochin, by a Carmelite Monk, named Mathaeus, under the auspices of the Governor, Van Rheede.

In 1697 the Dutch, in pursuance of their policy of cutting down expenses, contracted the old Portuguese fort to one-third of its former size, but they strengthened the new works by seven strong bastions named respectively after the names of the seven united Provinces of Holland. In rebuilding the fort they took great care to leave the old Portuguese streets, now called by Dutch names, standing. The most important streets at that time were de Linde (Lime tree) Straat; Heere (Gentleman's) Straat; de Peterceelie Straat (Parsely street): de Bree Straat (Broad street); de Smee Straat (Smith's street); de Osse Straat (Ox street); de Burgen Straat (Burgers street); and de Kalven Straat (Calf street). Cochin in Dutch times is thus described by Dr. Day[1]:—

"The Dutch Cochin fort, according to Stavorinus, was nearly semi-circular, and about a mile and a half in circumference: on the land side were six large bastions, and a cavalier to the eastward: an irregular work on the water side, a substantial loopholed wall terminating at its eastern extremity in a ravelin, before the cavalier: a wet ditch ran round these works, whilst before it was a covered way, and glacis.

"The north, or river side, was defended by batteries, whilst a stone wharf, or more properly speaking a plain wall, was erected on the river face, which served two purposes, to protect its banks from the threatening effects of the freshes, and also for a landing place. Either its construction was very faulty, or the materials were inferior, as in 1821, much of it had fallen in, and extensive repairs were deemed necessary: this may however have been in some degree due to the current of the river setting in against it.

"The sea, or west face, was protected by a ravelin, the east by morasses and a strong wall, and the west by walls and a wet ditch. There were three small gates, one to the west the By-gate,

[1] *Land of the Perumals*, p. 125. For description of the town in Portuguese times see *Voyage of Pyrard deLaval*, I, 435; and *Voyage of Linschoten*, I, 67.

CHAP. XV.
COCHIN.

another to the east called the New-gate, and one on the north, the River-gate. Along each side of the wider streets, and ramparts, were Portia trees (*Thespesia populnea*), left by Portguese, and under their grateful shade, the inhabitants of an evening lounged or promenaded. A small but elegant, public garden was kept up inside the fort, and a larger one near the Governor's house: in the vicinity of which the richer classes possessed Bungalows. There were also others on the neighbouring islands.

"The pieces of artillery in the fort consisted of 95 of iron, six of brass, and two mortars. Five hundred and thirty Europeans [1] and thirty-seven natives were considered a sufficient garrison. This reduction in power caused the Dutch to fall considerably in the estimation of the natives, and they became but little feared by the surrounding people.

"The principal buildings within the fort were the Commandant's house on the north-west bastion, and the only one built on the Dutch model. The Governor's house, was half a mile to the south, divided from the fort by a long sandy plain. There was a hotel at which the Dutch paid a rupee a day for board and lodgings, and persons of other nations two rupees: this was yearly farmed out by the Government.

"The Governor of Cochin, was subordinate to the Supreme Council of Batavia, and if not a member of the Batavian administration, his title was that of Commandant. The Town Council consisted of the Second who was a senior merchant, the Fiscal, the chief of the Military, the Warehouse-keeper, the Dispenser or Purveyor, and all the Junior Merchants (not trades-people, but Government Civilians), who might be in the settlement, either in or out of office. The Council had a Secretary, generally a junior merchant, who also held the post of Malayalam translator. The Chief of the Military had the title of Major, the Commandant of the Artillery that of Captain-Lieutenant."

In 1795 Cochin passed into the hands of the English. The Governor, Mr. Vanspall, made a show of resistance; but a siege train was brought up and a single shell 'planted with excellent skill in the centre of Government house' induced a more chastened frame of mind, and he surrendered on terms on October 20th, 1795.[2] The early history of British rule is not calculated to reflect credit upon the Honourable East India Company. In 1806 fearing that Cochin was to be restored to the Dutch, they blew up the cathedral of Santa Cruz, the fort, and some of the quays and best houses in the place. The massive buttresses which are so conspicuous a feature of the town are said to have been put up at this time, to shore up the houses whose walls had been shaken by the force of the explosion. In the same year Dr. Buchanan visited the town,

---

[1] The European troops maintained in Cochin were rarely above one-quarter or a third Dutch: the remainder were composed of English and French deserters, renegade Germans, and similar broken down adventurers, who came for the purpose of mending, or making their fortunes.

[2] Logan's *Treaties*, ii. XCVI.

and obtained from the Jews and Syrian Christians some valuable manuscripts, notably a Syriac copy of the Bible and a copy of the Pentateuch on goat skins. All the manuscripts collected by Buchanan are now in the University Library at Cambridge. The concluding days of 1808 and the beginning of 1809 were a time of excitement for the town. It was the time of the Nayar rising in Travancore and Native Cochin, The town was fiercely attacked on three sides, but successfully defended by Major Hewitt.

Since then Cochin has enjoyed a period of peace, chequered from the point of view of the inhabitants only by the long drawn out investigations of the Escheat Department into the value of their holdings, and by occasional fires. The fire of 1889 deserves a brief notice. On Friday 4th January 1889 a *pattamar* moored near the Kalvetti bridge caught fire, and breaking loose from her moorings floated down stream on a strong ebb-tide, and colliding with Messrs. Volkart Brothers' jetty set fire to a long thatched shed. Within a few minutes the warehouses of this firm and the adjoining buildings of three other European firms were ablaze; and the strong sea breeze that was blowing carried the flames to the native bazaars in the vicinity. The loss caused by the fire amounted to more than thirteen lakhs. One good result of the fire is that thatched houses are now strictly forbidden in the crowded quarters of the town.

The last half century in particular has been a period of great and progressive activity. The trade of the town increased in value from 34 lakhs in 1858–59 to more than 300 lakhs in 1903–04, to 976 lakhs in 1926, to 1,071 lakhs in 1927, and to 1,040 lakhs in 1930, and Cochin is now the most important port on the West Coast of India, south of Bombay and is the second port in the Madras Presidency. Great as it already is, this trade would be multiplied manyfold could only Cochin be provided with a deep water harbour. For native craft, as it is, the magnificent sheet of smooth water inside the mouth of the river is one of the finest natural harbours in the world; but with only eleven feet of water over the bar at low tide, the big steamers that call here have to lie in the open roadstead 2½ miles from the shore. Various schemes for deepening the bar have been proposed in the last thirty years, only to be rejected on the score of expense. As lately as 1902 a scheme to keep open a channel from the anchorage to the entrance of the backwater by the employment of a powerful suction dredger was referred by the Secretary of State to a firm of harbour experts for report. The report was unfavourable; the scheme was condemned; the cost of constructing a sheltered harbour was pronounced prohibitive; and the question has once more been shelved.[1] The existing waterway can be maintained only by preventing the formation of other outlets in the long reach

[1] G.O. No. 308, Marine, dated 13th July 1903.

CHAP. XV. COCHIN.

of sandspits from Cranganore to Alléppy. Much alarm was thus caused in 1875 when the backwaters broke through into the sea at the Cruz Milagre gap two miles north of the town, and the filling up of the deep channel that was at once formed was a matter of difficulty and expense. Protective works are still maintained here. The well-known Narakkal mud bank (see p. 8) now lies off Mallipuram Flag-staff two miles north of Cochin in east latitude 76° 10′ north longitude 10° 30′. The bank has lately extended seaward, and its value as an anchorage has been much impaired.

The Port of Cochin has been greatly improved during the past few years. The scheme for a deep-water harbour, approved by Government in May 1925, was completed as to the dredging on 13th March 1929, the first cut through the bar 400 feet wide by 32½ feet deep having been completed on 30th March 1928. The outer channel is now about three miles long by 450 feet wide and has an average depth of about 35 feet at low-water. From August to October the bar silts up to about 30 feet at low-water giving with the rise of tide a working depth of 32 feet daily. The channel is redredged every year to 35 feet at low-water in December and January. Vessels up to 29 or even 30 feet can safely use the channel during this time, and the yearly redredging is done without hindrance to traffic. The first ship to navigate the outer channel was the "Padma" from Bombay (Captain Bullen) in June 1928 and the first large home-going steamer the "Croxteth Hall" in August 1928. From that time until March 1930, the harbour was increasingly used by ships and it has been in constant and regular use since March 1930 by all ships. These include vessels of the British India Steam Navigation Company, the Clan Line, the City and Hall Lines, the Asiatic and Scindia Lines, a number of coasting steamship companies, oil vessels and cargo steamers of all nationalities. Vessels up to 29 feet draught and 510 feet length can moor inside and a berth will shortly be available for taking any ship up to 700 feet long by 30 feet draught.

At present vessels lie and swing at flat-topped moorings. The operations of connecting the ship to the moorings and disconnecting are accomplished in a few minutes. The entrance channel is well buoyed and there is a service of European pilots under the Port Officer. Supplies of bunker coal, diesel oil and fuel oil are available, also fresh water from a tank barge. These facilities are being increased. Two private engineering firms can carry out repairs to vessels calling at the port while the harbour department possesses a dry dock capable of taking any of the dredging craft in use in South India.

The railway connection to the port is being converted into broad gauge and it is expected the work will be completed in 1933.

Proposals are now being formulated for the next stage of the works which include the construction of deep-water jetties with broad and metre gauge railway connections, constructing of godowns and transit sheds, the installation of rapid handling cranes and other transport facilities. These improvements will be made on the new reclamation of which 175 acres have been formed up to date by dredgings from the harbour. This reclamation, with the adjacent island of Venduruthy, takes the form of a huge double-sided jetty two miles long and half a mile wide (on the average). It is intended to connect this to the mainland by a railway bridge across the backwater. Reclamation work is still in progress and it is hoped that when completed it will provide sufficient area to allow at least 20, and possibly 30, large vessels to load or unload at the same time besides those in stream. These improvements, it is expected, will be carried out under the controlling authority of the Madras Government and the Cochin Travancore Darbars who, subject to certain conditions, are joint partners in the financing and further development of the harbour. Up to the present the scheme has been financed by the Cochin Port Conservancy Board at a cost of roughly Rs. 75 lakhs, repayment of interest and principal being met by landing and shipping dues. This sum of Rs. 75 lakhs includes the cost of reclamation which has been borne by the Cochin State. The Port Conservancy Board pays the State 5 per cent interest on the cost of the first 100 acres reclaimed and will pay a similar rate on the cost of reclaiming the remaining area from the date of the entrustment of the land by the Cochin Darbar to the Harbour authorities.

With improved railway connections and terminal facilities, Cochin is likely to become one of the really important ports in India. It has unique advantages as a distributing port inland both by water and rail, and its magnificent backwaters, which are 120 square miles in extent, provide room for a deep-water expansion which is hardly equalled in the whole of the east.

Cochin is a picturesque little town in a beautiful setting. On a sunshiny morning the view from the mainland, looking towards the town, is superb. To the north and south, as far as the eye can see, glittering backwaters stretch away in long lines between rows of palm-clad islands. On the right close at hand the Union Jack floating lazily from a lofty flag-staff, and a fine house and garden, mark the island of Bolgotty and the British Residency. Further away across a wide open sheet of water, on which a fleet of *pattamars* rides at anchor, and boats move slowly in every direction, the narrow mouth of the Cochin river reveals a glimpse of the open sea and the steamers in the offing ; and a collection of low red roofs and whitewashed walls on the curving left bank of the stream represents Cochin. The town itself is full of surprises and contracts. Along the quays, where stand the warehouses of the European firms, the long

CHAP. XV. COCHIN.

drawn wall of steam presses and the crowds of coolies laden with bales of coir and barrels of oil bespeak the busy commercial seaport town. But five minutes later the scene changes, and one might almost fancy oneself transported to some old-world continental city, the quaint old Portuguese houses, the grey pile of S. Francis' church, the cool green *maidan* and the general air of peace and quiet all serving to keep up the illusion.

But the bigotry of the Dutch and the vandalism of the Honourable Company have spared few buildings of historical interest in Cochin. The church of S. Francis, of massive but plain construction, is one of the few exceptions, and in it Cochin can boast, if not of the first church built in the country, at any rate of the oldest existing European church in India. Its exact age is uncertain, but it was built early in the sixteenth century. It is haunted of course, and the disconsolated figure of an old woman is seen sometimes in the building, but more commonly seated by the side of an old well in the adjacent *maidan*. The church plate is very valuable and interesting, and was handed over by the Dutch when the town was captured in 1795. The floor was till recently paved with the inscribed and carved tombstones of former Dutch and Portuguese worthies, but in 1887 for safety's sake they were taken up and fixed against the walls. The church was restored in 1779 by the Dutch. Two massive pillars and a few inscribed stones are all that remain of the cathedral of Santa Cruz, which stood on the open ground near the Port office ; but in the last two years a new and hideous cathedral of the same name has been erected by the Roman Catholics in another part of the town. The old Commandant's house still stands on the north-west bastion of the fort near the river bank, and a few hundred yards south of the English Club are the gates of what was once the Governor's residence. The lighthouse stands on the south-west bastion of the fort, and near the Bishop's palace traces of the walls and moat are still visible. The Deputy Collector's office is an interesting building with a history going back to Portuguese times, when it was the residence of the priests attached to the cathedral. In the rising of 1808 the Nayars burst into the buildings and tried to murder Colonel Macaulay, the Resident. When Cochin was a military station, it was the officers' mess and subsequently the upper rooms were the Fiscal's office and the lower were used as a jail. The old cemetery, now closed, bears the date 1724 on its gateway, and is crowded with old-fashioned tombs of many curious forms and shapes.

Cochin merges insensibly into the native town of Muttancheri, belonging to Cochin State, whence steamers ply with Alleppy and with Ernakulam, the terminus of the Shoranur-Cochin Railway. In Muttancheri is an ancient palace where the Cochin Rajas are crowned ; and next door to the palace is the synagogue of the white Jews, the floor paved with beautiful blue and white porcelain tiles, the gift of a former Raja of Cochin. The white and black Jews of Cochin are famous throughout India and are a standing puzzle to the historian. Their own legends affirm that about A.D. 68 after the destruction of the Temple, a large number of Jews and Jewesses migrated from Jerusalem to Malabar and settled for the most part in Cranganore, and that about 300 years later they received from Cheraman Perumal the copper plate charter, to which reference has already been made.[1] But which came first, and whether the black Jews are merely the offspring of alliances between the white Jews and native women are questions which are still hotly discussed. In spite of the fact that the copper plates are in the possession of the white Jews, it seems probable that they are comparatively late arrivals in Cochin, and that the black Jews are the descendants of the original settlers at Cranganore,[2] who were very probably refugees from Muhammadan persecution in Arabia or Persia in the 6th or 7th century. They were attacked at Cranganore by their Muhammadan rivals at the beginning of the 16th century; and finally left it for Cochin in 1565, when the Zamorin defeated the Cochin Raja and destroyed Cranganore.

The outlying *pattams* of Cochin are detached bits of British territory scattered about in Travancore and Cochin, Tumboli pattam being close to Alleppy nearly thirty miles south of the town and Palliport hospital paramba lying fifteen miles north of Cochin. They probably owe their name of *pattams* or rents to the fact that in Dutch times they were leased out to private renters for periods of twenty years. Ramantirutti island is still leased, and at present is held temporarily by Messrs. Aspinwall & Co., who have established a saw mill and timber depot on the island. At Palliport is the Government leper asylum, probably the oldest institution of the kind in India, dating as it does from the days of the Dutch. In 1789 when the Dutch sold to Travancore, Cranganore, Ayacotta and their other possessions in the vicinity, a special exception was made in favour of 'the lepers' house' at Palliport.[3] Messrs. Aspinwall & Co., have closed down their saw-mill and timber depot as they were found to be unprofitable concerns, but they still hold about 29 acres on a lease, terminable at 6 months' notice, while 14 acres are held on perpetual lease. The Leper Hospital at Palliport has been abolished and the site leased to the Bishop of Verapoli for a girls' school.

[1] See p. 33.
[2] See Day's *Land of the Perumals*, Chapter VIII; and the Malabar Quarterly Review, Vol. I.
[3] Logan's *Treaties*, i. CLXVI.

ERNAD TALUK.

CHAP. XV. ERNAD.

ERNAD is at once the largest and most typical taluk in Malabar, and combines in itself the characteristic features of the taluks both of the coast and of the interior. In the north of the taluk opposite Ariyakkod the western ghats take a right angle turn to the east ; and, after running a few miles in this direction, recede northward and enclose in the shape of a horseshoe the Nilambur valley, famous for the finest teak forests in India. In the lofty forest-clad ranges of Camel's Hump and the Kundahs, which overhang this valley, are some of the highest peaks in Southern India. Vavul mala and Vellari mala in the former range both exceed 7,000 feet, and the outstanding peaks of the Kundahs on the Nilgiri boundary, Nilgiri peak Mukurti, Gulikal and Anginda are all upwards of 8,000 feet high. In the plains unconnected with the main range are the outlying hills of Urot mala (1,573 feet) and Pandalur hill, which is about 2,000 feet above sea level. The latter is still well wooded ; but Urot mala or Signal Hill, as it is sometimes called, has long been cleared of anything that can be called forest, and is covered with thickets of lantana and other scrub. On its summit stands a small Hindu temple which was seized by the Ponmundam fanatics in 1885 ; and from this hill communication was opened by heliograph with Calicut, when the telegraph broke down during the disarming operations of the same year. The navigable rivers are the Beypore or Chaliyar puzha and the Kadalundi puzha (see p. 5), and both are important waterways. The latter is mainly used for traffic in cocoanuts and ginger, and down the Beypore river are floated vast quantities of timber and bamboos from the Government and private forests in the Nilambur valley and elsewhere on the ghat slopes. Apart from these rivers, the taluk has excellent communications. The South Indian Railway passes through it parallel with and close to the sea, and the roads, more than 260 miles in length, are on the whole the best in the district. The most important perhaps is that which taps the planting district of the Nilgiri-Wynaad, and brings down the Karkkur ghat to Ferok and Calicut heavy consignments of tea and coffee by way of Nilambur, Manjeri and Kondotti. Important extensions of the road system have been made in the last decade. The 'fanatical zone' has been opened up by three new roads and a great impetus has been given thereby to the timber trade and to cultivation in the remote and jungly amsam of Chembrasseri ;

and three old lines of communication, dating from the time of Tipu, but long abandoned, between Ferok and Tirurangadi, Tirurangadi and Kottakkal, and Ariyakkod and Kondotti have been restored in the last year or two. The Nilambur valley and the slopes of the surrounding hills are covered with dense forest through which big game of every description roam at will. The valley is pierced by an excellent road with bungalows at convenient stages, and there are few places in the presidency where big game shooting of the same quality is so easily accessible. The forests of Amarambalam and Nilambur are described in Chapter V. The new Shoranur-Nilambur railway runs through the "outbreak zone" of this taluk with stations at Thuvur, Vaniyambalam and Nilambur.

Statistics on many points are given in the separate Appendix. The area of the taluk is 979 square miles, but of this nearly a third is hill, forest and jungle, uncultivated, unsurveyed and almost uninhabited. The taluk is comparatively sparsely populated, but is unique in that the Mappillas outnumber the Hindus. For this reason the taluk is educationally backward, nearly 94 per cent of the population being illiterate.

The soils almost without exception belong to the red ferruginous series. Except along the coast, and in the amsams of Nilambur, Mambad and Wandur, the paddy lands are uniformly good, and in the amsams between Kottakkal, Malappuram and Urot mala are unsurpassed in Malabar. Near Tirurangadi the Kadalundi river overflows its banks in the monsoon, and *medha punja* or hot weather wet crops irrigated from wells are the rule. The sandy soils near the coast are particularly favourable for the growth of the cocoanut, and for about half their length the banks of the Beypore and Kadalundi rivers are fringed with luxuriant gardens of cocoa and areca palms. Ginger is grown in most amsams, but flourishes best on the uplands of Vengara, Kannamangalam and the adjoining amsams. Nannambra betel is famous, and in the Calicut market fetches two or three times as much as any other variety. Lemon grass grows wild in the eastern amsams, and the manufacture of its oil has been carried on for the last few years at Pandikkad to the great profit of the local Mappillas ; but the demand for the grass has outrun the supply, and the industry is now at a standstill. Rubber plantations have recently been opened in the Nilambur valley, and on the slopes of the hills near Kalikavu. Iron is smelted by a rude process and in small quantities in Chembrasseri and Tuvvur, and gold washing has been carried on in the Beypore river above Nilambur from time immemorial. The chief trades are those in timber, coir, ginger and dried fish. Kadalundi and Paravvanangadi are both sub-ports, but their trade is insignificant.

Ernad formerly comprised the *nads* of south Parappanad, Ramnad, Cheranad and Ernad, the first named belonging to

CHAP. XV. ERNAD.

the Parappanad Raja, a feudatory of the Zamorin. Nediyiruppu in ancient Ernad is by one account the birth-place of the Zamorin's family; and to this day the second Raja is known as the Eralpad Raja, and the family is sometimes called the Eradi or Nediyiruppu dynasty. The *nad* has belonged to the Zamorin for a very long time, and he is probably the Udayavar of Ernad mentioned in the Jews' and Syrians' deeds, the date of which is certainly not later than the 8th century A.D. The Parappanad family claim to be Kshatriyas by caste, and have often supplied consorts to the rulers of Travancore. They were roughly handled by Tipu, and many of them were forcibly converted to Islam; and since that time they have lived for the most part in Travancore. But they still have a residence near Parappanangadi, and enjoy a *malikhana* of Rs. 4,114-4-8.

For many years after the British occupation Ernad was divided into the taluks of Cheranad and Ernad, but in 1860 they were amalgamated and a Deputy Tahsildar was placed in charge of Cheranad. In 1886 Ernad was combined with Calicut as a Revenue Division, and with part of Walavanad was placed under the Special Assistant Magistrate of Malappuram. The taluk now consists of 94 amsams and 221 desams.

The annals of Ernad have since 1836 been disfigured by frequent Mappilla outrages. Malappuram, Manjeri, Pandikkad, Pandalur and Wandur are the centres of the fanatical zone; but the criminals have in many cases been drawn from the ranks of the rude and uncivilised Mappilla cultivators in the jungles of Chembrasseri. The police stations are scattered at short intervals throughout this tract and during Ramzan the Malabar Special Police carries out extensive patrols.

The most interesting and important places in Ernad are briefly described below:—

Ariyakkod : Eleven miles north-west of Manjeri; formerly one of the centres of the lines of communication by road, and an important point on the shortest and most direct routes connecting the Nilgiri-Wynaad and Ootacamund with Calicut *via* the Karkkur and (now abandoned) Sispara ghats. Roads led hence to Calicut, Tamarasseri, Mambad, Edavanna, Kondotti and Manjeri. All these roads except the last have been long abandoned, but the Kondotti road has recently been restored. The village is beautifully situated on the south bank of the Beypore river beneath the shadow of Chekkunnu mala, and contains a travellers' bungalow, a police station and some very picturesque streets. About two miles from Ariyakkod adjoining the Manjeri road is a remarkable group of hat stones standing on a flat-topped hill called Kottataram kunnu.

Across the river in Trikkalayur desam of Kizhuparamba amsam is a celebrated temple dedicated to Siva and occupying a commanding position on a low hill. It was this temple that was seized by Kolkadan Kutti Assan and a gang of eleven fanatics in December 1884, after their outrage at Malappuram (see pp. 81-82); and a determined resistance was here offered to the British troops. The fanatics were killed by volleys one by one as they fired through the loop holes, and the temple was captured only after the barricaded doors had been blown up by dynamite. The devasvam owns immense properties managed by Krangad Ashtamurthi Nambudiripad of Walavanad taluk, and some of the finest of the Nilambur leased forests are its property. Opposite the temple is the Chenot mosque in which the fanatics prayed before taking up their position. In the same amsam is the Arimbra Kuda mala, a small leased forest in the boundary between the Ernad and Calicut taluks. Ariyakkod and the surrounding country were the scenes of many murders and forcible conversions during the rebellion which broke out in the neighbourhood on the 15th October 1921. The police outposts and lines were burnt and Attupurath Nambudiri and many Hindus murdered. In that outbreak a Hindu woman of Ugrapuram desam showed remarkable courage. On the night of 20th September she saw a gang of Mappilla rebels armed with war knives and sticks advancing towards her house. She sent away the other inmates, her sister and children to the jungle and stayed behind to guard her property. She shut herself in and when the rebels broke open the door she attacked them with a chopper and cut down four of them before she was overpowered, mal-treated and left for dead and her money stolen. She escaped after four days to Chikkod where a relief party had arrived and was sent down by boat to Calicut where she eventually recovered.

Chaliyam : in Kadalundi amsam, an island formed by the Beypore and Kadalundi rivers. It was once the terminus of the Madras Railway, and contained a hotel, a Protestant church and other public buildings ; but its short-lived importance ended when the railway was extended in 1888 to Calicut. On a rocky islet lying south of the entrance to the Beypore river, and connected with the mainland by a groyne, the masonry foundations of a formidable fortress have been excavated. Undoubtedly they are the remains of the fort 'of great solidity and strength' erected by the Portuguese in 1531.[1] To build it they are said to have demolished the tombs of the Moslems and their Jamath mosque for the sake of the stones of which they were built. The fort was long a thorn in the side of the Zamorin, and was the ruin of the trade of the Moors and of Calicut. In 1571 the fort was fiercely

[1] See Linschoten's *Voyages*, I, p. 73.

besieged by the Zamorin assisted by the Moors, and after being driven to feed on dogs and animals 'of a similar vile impure nature' the garrison surrendered, 'safe egress being afforded them.' The fortress was promptly destroyed and the site made 'a barren waste.'

Edakkara: Eight miles from Nilambur and twenty-four from Manjeri. A favourite shooting camp, containing a small rest-house and a fine bungalow belonging to the Tirumulpad. Spotted deer and peafowl are plentiful all the year round in the neighbouring forests; and, as soon as the rains break, bison and sambur come down from the ghat slopes to feed on the new grass. In the hot weather Eddakkara and the Nilambur valley are extremely feverish. The fine bungalow belonging to the Nilambur-Tirumulpad was burnt down on 8th December 1921 by Mappilla rebels.

Ferok: Six miles south of Calicut Railway station; Post office; sub-registrar's office; rest-house. Half a mile south-west of the village are the ruins of Ferokabad commanding two beautiful reaches of the Beypore river which flows immediately north of the fortress. It was built by Tipu Sultan in 1788, as his intended capital in Malabar; but after Martab Khan's defeat at Tirurangadi in 1790, his troops were driven out of the town before the design was fully carried out. He compelled a large portion of the inhabitants of Calicut to settle here, but on the departure of his troops they returned to their former abodes. Two miles above the Mammali Ferry on the Ernad bank of the river lies Chattamparamba, a laterite hill containing numerous tombs of a long forgotten generation; some of them excavated from the laterite rock, others in the shape of huge earthen pots buried in the ground. Agate beads and pottery in abundance have been found in these tombs. The Tile industry at Ferok has been referred to in Chapter VI. The tile works stand on either side of the river and a small rest-house is on the Calicut side of it.

Kadalundi: In Kadalundi amsam. Probably the Tyndis of Ptolemy, 'a village of great note by the sea.' It is now a sub-port and a small fishing village. In the neighbourhood is the Nirumkayicha Kotta temple with a tradition going back to Rama's conquest of Ceylon. The monkeys which swarm within the precincts are said to be the descendants of a portion of Rama's army, left here by him on his return from his expedition. They are fed daily, and are tame.

Kondotti: An important Mappilla village, fourteen miles west of Malappuram consisting of two long bazaars, one on the Calicut road, the other at right angles thereto on the old road leading to Tirurangadi. In this latter are the buildings which are the pride of Kondotti, the *Jaram*, the *Takkiya* and the residence of the local Tangal. This Tangal, the high priest of the Kondotti as opposed to the Ponnani sect of the Mappillas, is the descendant of a Persian, Muhammad Shaha by name, who introduced new forms of Islamic worship into Malabar towards the end of the 18th century. His followers, who are fairly numerous in Kondotti and the surrounding amsams, are called Shiahs (a term which they repudiate) by members of the Ponnani sect, and are accused of the unorthodox practice of prostrating themselves before their Tangal. The *Jaram*; a granite building, was erected by the first Tangal as his last resting place and his remains repose therein. The *Takkiya* is the private chapel of the Tangals, and like the *Jaram* was built by Muhammad Shaha about 1784 A.D. The Tangals have been granted an assignment of revenue to the value of Rs. 2,734 per annum as a personal inam, so long as they remain true and loyal, and have special permission to keep seven pieces of cannon. The public buildings of Kondotti are a sub-registrar's office, a police station, a post office, and a travellers' bungalow finely situated in a hill a mile west of the bazaar. Two hundred Mappilla rebels headed by Variankunnath Kunhamad Haji, a leader in the rebellion of 1921, raided Kondotti on the 28th October, burnt the records of the sub-registrar's office and police station and marched in a body to the Tangal's house where they shot one man. A few shops were looted. The raid was merely spectacular and though the local Mappillas took no part in the rebellion they are believed to have helped the rebels, with supplies and with safe places of refuge for them with a prompt *alibi* when arrested and tried.

Kottakal : Seven miles from Malappuram on the Tirur road ; the old Venkatta kotta ; travellers' bungalow and post office. There is here the fortified palace of the Kizhakke Kovilagam or Eastern Branch of the Zamorin's family. Two miles from Kottakkal in Klari desam is a military encamping ground. Ponmala, half way between Kottakkal and Malappuram, contains a rock-cut cave, and an important Hindu temple with a tank attached in which a single mugger lives in solitary state. The travellers' bungalow belongs to the Kizhakke Kovilagam. There is a well-known Ayurvedic School and hospital here.

Malappuram : Seven miles south of Manjeri. A cantonment and the headquarters of a revenue divisional officer and of a district superintendent of police. The latter has two assistants, one of whom is the Commandant of the Malabar Special Police and the other a deputy superintendent ; sub-registrar's office ; post and telegraph office ; police station ; Roman Catholic and Protestant churches and cemetery ; and police hospital. Tippu had a fort here, but beyond the fact that the

CHAP. XV. ERNAD.

maidan at the foot of the cantonment hill is known as the Kottapadi or Fort Gate maidan, all traces of its site have now disappeared.

Native troops were first sent to Malappuram in consequence of the risings of 1841 and 1843; but, as they proved useless in the outbreaks of 1849 and 1851; a company of European troops' has been stationed here since 1852. At Malappuram, also, are the barracks of the Special Police force, first constituted temporarily in 1885, and made permanent in 1897. The Malappuram Special Police was abolished after the rebellion of 1921 and in their place a company of Malabar Special Police is stationed, their barracks being opposite the sub-collector's office.

Half a mile from the barracks in the Mappilla bazaar, known as old Malappuram, are the Jamat mosque and the residence of the Pukkoya Tangal. The Tangal, like his kinsman the Jaratingal Tangal of Ponnani, is a direct descendant of the Prophet and is held in extraordinary veneration by the Mappilla population. Adjoining the mosque is the mausoleum of the Malappuram Sahids, who about a century ago died to the number of forty-seven in the defence of the mosque against the retainers of Para Nambi, the most powerful Hindu janmi of the locality. A Mappilla war song, the *Sahidu Mala Pattu*, commemorates their exploits.[1] One of the many legends current about the fight is that among the martyrs was an *Asari* or carpenter, a true believer, but not a formal convert. The survivors tried to take up his body for burial, but were unable to lift it until they had admitted him into the fold by performing the right of circumcision. A *Nercha* or festival, which is held every year in the mausoleum in honour of the slain, is attended by thousands of Mappillas; and the offerings made to the Tangal, mostly in copper, amount to many thousands of rupees. In the hills at the back of Old Malappuram are many curious caves running deep into the bowels of the mountain. At the outbreak of 1921, Mr. T. Austin, the sub-collector was cut off in Malappuram with a very small party until the relief party arrived from Calicut on the 26th of August 1921 after the Pookottur fight. The bodies of the assistant superintendent of police Mr. Lancaster and privates Thornay and Kennedy killed in the Pookottur battle lie buried in the cemetery here.

Mambram: Directly opposite to Tirurangadi on the north bank of the river. It is celebrated as the residence of the Mambram Tangals, and contains their *mukham* or mausoleum. The first of these Tangals, Sayid Hussain Ibn Alabi Jiffri Tangal, who is said to have come from Arabia, settled at Mambram in the early part of the 18th century and lived in

[1] See Indian Antiquary, Vol. XXX, p. 505.

the house called Taramal. He died in Hejira 1169, but five years later his place was filled by his nephew and son-in-law, Sayid Alabi Ibn Muhammad, whom the Mappillas served with the utmost devotion. His marriage with Fatima, the first Tangal's daughter, proving unfruitful, he married other wives, including a woman from the Pudiyamalyakkal house in Calicut and one from Quilandi. From the former union is descended the present Tangal, and the Quilandi woman bore him among other children the notorious Sayid Fazl who was compelled to leave India by Mr. Conolly in 1852. The *Mukham*, which contains eleven tombs including those of the first Tangal, and of Sayid Alabi, and their nearest relatives, is a favourite place of pilgrimage. Nearly 70 years ago when Mappilla outbreaks first began in Malabar, it was at Mambram that Mappilla fanaticism was focussed and the Hal Ilakkam or religious frenzy had its origin. Sayid Fazl, the Tangal, frequently preached from the text that it was no sin, but a merit, to kill a landlord who evicted his tenants; and intending *Sahids* or martyrs, before embarking on their desperate enterprise, usually prayed at the shrine and invoked his blessing. To this day the most binding oath a Mappilla can take is one on some portion of the Mambran Tangal's body. In the rebellion of 1921 it was the false report of the destruction of this shrine that led to large crowds of the Mappillas proceeding there on the 21st of August 1921.

Manjeri: the headquarters of the taluk and the seat of the Tahsildar; District Munsif; Sub-Magistrate; hospital; travellers bungalow; overseer's shed; chattram; sub-registrar's office; police station; post and telegraph office and high school. It is the centre of the road system of Ernad, and roads radiate hence in all directions to Ariyakkod, to Feroke Nilambur and the Karkkur ghat *via* Edavanna, Angadippuram and Malappuram. There are three rock-cut caves in the amsam and a hat stone close to the Kondotti road at Pattukulam.

About a quarter of a mile south-east of the taluk office is the Srimutra Kunnu or Kunnath Ambalam dedicated to Durga and situated on a low hill, and just below it is the residence of the Manjeri Karanamulpad. A *vattezhuttu* inscription on its eastern wall records the fact that the temple was built and dedicated by Manavikrava Manavikravan in M.E. 827 (1652 A.D.), and another relates that an adjacent well was sunk and purified by the 'Victorious Vikrava Tirumulpad' in M.E. 833. The temple has a melancholy interest as the scene of three Mappilla outbreaks. In 1784 it and the Karanamulpad's palace were attacked by a large body of Mappillas, and after a three days siege were burnt to the ground. The temple was not fully restored till 1849, in April of which year a new idol was installed. In August of the same year a gang of about thirty Mappilla fanatics occupied and desecrated the temple, and put

CHAP. XV. ERNAD.

to flight two companies of sepoys, killing four privates and Ensign Wyse who lies buried on the taluk office hill. The exploits of the 1849 gang were still the talk of the country in 1896, when the last serious outbreak occurred, and it was doubtless in emulation of the prowess of their fathers that the fanatics selected this temple as the theatre for their death struggle. The outbreaks have been described in Chapter II. The taluk treasury was looted by the rebels on the 22nd August 1921 and more than six lakhs of rupees carried away by them. The treasury strong-box was opened by a notorius criminal of Tirurangadi who happened to be then in the Manjeri sub-jail, and who was specially released by the rebels for this purpose. That day and the next was given up to looting in the village and the Khilafat King Variankunnath Kunhamad Haji who came here on 24th stayed on till 26th, opened the Nambudiri Bank and returned all pledged jewels to their owners.

Nilambur : sixteen miles due north of Manjeri on the Karkkur ghat road ; the seat of the District Forest Officer of South Malabar. Hospital ; police station ; travellers' bungalow ; post and telegraph office. Close to the bungalow is the residence of the Nilambur Taccharakavil Tirumulpad, one of the largest land-holders in the taluk, and the owner of a great part of the valley. There is excellent fishing for carp in the river at Nilambur, and in the upper reaches of its various tributaries ; and in the pool below the Trimulpad's house where they are considered sacred and are fed daily, they attain an immense size. In the Cherupuzha, about 1½ miles from its junction with the Karimpuzha, as the Beypore river is here called, there is an inscription in unknown characters on a block of gneiss, known as the *ezhuttukallu*. The inscription is below the ordinary low-water level, and is visible only in the dry weather. The washing for gold carried on in the river has already been alluded to, and here and there in the amsam are abandoned gold mines. On the banks of the river near the travellers' bungalow stands the grave of Samuel Robert Clogstoun, Lieutenant in the 23rd Regiment M.N.I., who was drowned on August 13th, 1843. The remains of old temples and tanks are scattered here and there in the Nilambur forests, and the tradition is that the amsam was once inhabited by a large colony of Nambudiris who were driven to Karikad desam of Trikkalangod amsam by the unwelcome attentions to their women of an Asuran or demon, named Bagan. In memory of the time when they lived in terror of the demon, the *antarjanams* of the *gramam* to this day refrain from wearing the jingling bangles worn by other Nambudiri women throughout Malabar.

During the rebellion of 1921 a Mappilla sub-inspector and two constables of the Nilgiris were murdered here by the rebels on the 2nd of September. On 1st October of the same year Lieutenant Harvey of the 2nd Dorsets and a private were killed and Col. Herbert wounded. Nilambur is now the terminus of the Shoranur-Nilambur Railway and one company of the Malabar Special Police is stationed here. About 200 Mappilla rebels in the company of the Mappilla sub-inspector of police of Nilambur, marched on the Kovilagam on the 20th of July 1921. Its Hindu watchmen fired on them and in retaliation the rebels killed seventeen of them including two women, broke into the Kovilagam and did considerable damage and after a few days of looting and dacoity in the neighbourhood returned to Pookottur when they gave battle to the English troops marching for the relief of Malappuram. The District Forest Officer Mr. Chandy fed the rebel mob the next day, but during the next two days the forest buildings at Nilambur and Nedungayam were looted and burnt and the District Forest Officer and his family were captured and while the captors were considering whether they should be murdered or forcibly converted to Islam, Mr. Chandy managed to escape with his family to Calicut on the 3rd of August.

Tirurangadi : fourteen miles from Malappuram and four from Parappanangadi on the road connecting the two places. It is a long narrow Mappilla bazaar on the southern bank of the Kadalundi river. It is the 'Tiruvana angadi' of Buchanan, and was at one time the capital of the Cheranad taluk, and is now the seat of a Deputy Tahsildar ; sub-registrar's office ; post office ; police station ; travellers' bungalow. The District Munsif's Court is four miles away at Parappanangadi, where there are also a police station and a post office. Opposite the taluk office are the remains of an old fort, built by the Mysoreans round a palace belonging to the Zamorin. At Tirurangadi took place the only two pitched battles fought in Malabar between the Mysoreans and the British. Here Colonel Humberstone defeated and slew Makhdum Ali, one of Haidar's Generals in 1780, and on the same battlefield near the fort General Hartley gained a decisive victory over Tipu's troops in 1790. Near Tirurangadi on the side of the old Mambram-Kondotti road is a group of hat stones, and there is another group in Koduvayur amsam within the enclosure of an ancient fort near the ferry over the Kadalundi river on the new Ramanatkara road. Of this fort nothing is known. Judging by the moat, which still exists, it must have been of an immense side. Probably it belonged to the Zamorin in the days when Cheranad acknowledged his supremacy.

The rebellion of 1921 broke out here on 20th and 21st of August. Mobs of several thousand Mappilla rebels came in all directions from Tanur, Vengara and other surrounding parts and attacked the police and troops who had arrived there with the District Magistrate Mr. E. F. Thomas, the

CHAP. XV. ERNAD.

District Superintendent of Police Mr. R. H. Hitchcock and Captain McEnroy of the Leinster Regiment for the arrest of certain important Khilafat leaders. Mr. W. J. D. Rowley (a new Assistant Superintendent of Police), Lieutenant W. R. M. Johnstone, one of the Leinster Regiment and Inspector Reedman of the Malappuram Special Police were killed. The bodies of the first two were subsequently recovered and are buried in the deputy tahsildar's office compound near the sub-registrar's office. The above offices, the police station and all the other public buildings were looted, and burnt on the 21st August. The district munsif's court and the railway station at Parappanangadi were also destroyed. Some privates of the Leinster Regiment who were killed in another action near the mosque were buried behind the Tirurangadi shandy.

Wandur : twelve miles north-east of Manjori. Once a halting station on the Sispara ghat road, it contains a large old travellers' bungalow ; a sub-registrar's office ; a police station ; a post office and a Hindu temple with a breach in its wall said to have been caused by Tipu's guns. The old ghat road has lately been restored as far as Kalikavu (rest-house ; police station) in Chembrasseri amsam, and Wandur has thus been linked up with the Mappilla roads from Nilambur *via* Karuvarakundu to Pandikkad and Melattur. In Vellayur desam of Vellayur amsam, where there is a police station, is the Ayilassori rock, bearing an inscription in *vattezhuttu* characters, and locally believed to have been a place of execution in ancient times. On the Sispara ghat, in the wilds of the Silent valley, is the tomb of Mary Elliot. Some rubber plantations are now being opened out near Kalikavu, and on the slopes of the hill enclosing the old ghat road.

The village is now in Kalikavu amsam. There is no police station in Vellayur amsam. The private residence of the present Nilambur Tirumulpad is within 2 miles of Wandur. The public offices here were also looted during the rebellion of 1921. The notorious Variankunnath Kunhamad Haji's gang did great havoc in these parts. The Vaniyambalam railway station on the Shoranur-Nilambur railway is about 2 miles from here.

Pookottur : lies between 25th and 27th milestones on the Calicut-Malappuram Road. On the 20th of August 1921 it was the scene of a battle between the Mappilla rebels and a movable column which was proceeding from Calicut to relieve Malappuram. The engagement was the biggest which occurred during the rebellion. Before the column emerged from the cover afforded by the trees and undergrowth of the gardens on either side of the road at this point the enemy opened fire from all sides and made an assault on the rear which was beaten off. A typical fanatical assault was made along the road on the head of the column, the fanatics dying to a man as usual. A party was sent to reconnoitre the houses on the edge of the paddy flats from which the enemy had advanced, but had to fall back. Stokes mortar guns were tried without effect on these houses. Another party sent to clear these houses was forced back by a mad rush of more rebels who reached the head of the column before obtaining the death they sought. Mr. C. B. Lancaster (Assistant Superintendent of Police, Malappuram) was mortally wounded by a sniper, and Captain McEnroy in the thick of the fighting had a narrow escape, a fanatic in the act of cutting him down being bayonetted by a soldier. The snipers were eventually cleared out and the fanatics made a final charge in which they all perished. About 400 rebels were killed, before the column was able to move on to Malappuram.

Pandikkad : Eight miles east of Manjeri police station ; travellers' bungalow. It was the scene of the outbreak of 1884. During the 1921 rebellion about 2,000 rebels headed by Variankunnath Kunhamad Haji attacked a force of Gurkhas encamped in Pandikkad in the early hours of the morning of the 14th November. One European Officer, Captain Averell was killed but the rebels were repulsed with great loss after a hand to hand fight. The same day the postmaster was caught and killed and the sub-magistrate on special duty narrowly escaped with his life.

Thuvvur : Thirteen miles east of Manjeri. The Shoranur-Nilambur railway line passes through the amsam and has a station here. Thuvvur was the scene of one of the most gruesome of atrocities committed during the 1921 rebellion. Thirty-five persons including two Mappillas who had assisted the troops, were murdered in cold blood and their bodies thrown into a well. A retired head constable's head was sawn in two before being thrown into this well. The band responsible for these outrages was that commanded by Variankunnath Kunhamad Haji.

Kalikavu : Nineteen miles north-east of Manjeri. There is a police station, an amsam-cutcherry and a travellers' bungalow. The amsam contains extensive rubber plantations. During the 1921 rebellion Mr. Stanley Eaton, a planter, was murdered by rebels in August. His body was not recovered. A bone which was found and believed to be that of Mr. Eaton was buried near the bridge and a memorial erected by the Mappillas of Kalikavu.

Karuvarakundu : Twenty miles north-east of Manjeri. Most of the inhabitants are Mappillas. It is situated in the fanatical zone. In 1914 a few fanatics made an attempt on the life of the District Magistrate Mr. (now Sir) Charles Innes. Karuvarakundu is linked with roads from Kalikavu to Thuvur, Melattur and Pandikkad. There is a European rubber plantation at Kerala, two miles to the north-east of Karuvarakundu toll-gate.

KOTTAYAM TALUK.

CHAP. XV. KOTTAYAM.

KOTTAYAM, the central taluk of North Malabar and included in the Tellicherry division, is one of the smaller taluks. From Morampara Hill at the head of the Periya Pass, whence on a clear day a magnificent bird's eye view of the low country as far as the coast is obtained, the taluk presents the aspect of a tumultuous sea of forest clad hills. At the foot of the ghats, which here are some four or five thousand feet high, are the Kanoth and Kottiyur reserves: and, save for occasional *punam* clearings, the forest is unbroken. Further west timber trees grow fewer, forest dies down into scrub jungle, and beyond Kuttaparamba the hills are insignificant and covered with lantana and brushwood. Kanaka Mala, a lofty spur of the ghats, projects into the plains within ten miles of Tellicherry; and, unconnected with the main range, the well-wooded Purazhi ridge is conspicuous in the interior of the taluk. Its slopes are still haunted, it is said, by the demons who in the dark ages prevented his subjects from approaching Harischandra Perumal in his lonely fort on the summit. The site of the fort and the foundations of old buildings are still pointed out. The north-east of the taluk is drained by one of the branches of the Valarpattanam river, its centre by the Anjarakkandi river, and the Mahe river forms part of its southern boundary. The South Indian Railway runs along the coast; and the taluk is covered by a network of roads, many of them dating from the time when the Pychy rebels held the jungles beneath the ghat slopes. Among them is the great highway from Tellicherry up the Perambadi ghat into Coorg; and branching off from this road just beyond Kuttuparamba another important road ascends the Periya Ghat into Wynaad, and leads ultimately to Mysore. South of Tellicherry is a small irregularly shaped tract of French territory.

Statistics on many points will be found in the separate Appendix. The whole of the north-east of the taluk, comprising one-third of its total area, is unsurveyed hill and jungle. The soils and chief crops are typical of North Malabar and need no special mention. As in Chirakkal, *punam* is the most important dry crop, and pepper, which thrives at the back of the taluk, is its characteristic product. '*Nendra*' plantains and tapioca are extensively grown. Mappillas make up one quarter of the population, and chief among the jungle tribes of the ghat slopes are the Kuricchiyans, who are peculiarly numerous in the

Kanoth reserve. With the exception of Cochin, Kottayam is the most literate taluk in Malabar, nearly 22 per cent of its inhabitants being able to read and write. CHAP. XV KOTTAYAM.

The taluk is divided into 49 amsams and 227 desams.

Darmadam (Darmapattanam) : 'the place of charity,' an island formed by the junction of the Tellicherry and Anjarakkandi rivers just north of Tellicherry town, is sacred in the eyes of the Malayalis as the place where Cheraman Perumal took his last farewell of Malabar and sailed for Mecca. The adjoining district of Randattara for this reason was often known as Poyanad 'the place of departure.' Here, according to the Tahafut-ul-Mujahidin, Malik Ibn Dinar founded one of his nine mosques, but not a trace of the building remains. Ibn Batuta's account is different.

"We next come to the city of Fattan, the greater part of the inhabitants of which are Brahmans, who are held in great estimation among the Hindus. In this place there was not one Muhammadan. Without it was a mosque to which the Muhammadan strangers resort. It is said to have been built by certain merchants and afterwards to have been destroyed by one of the Brahmans, who had removed the roof of it to his own house. On the following night, however, this house was entirely burnt, and in it the Brahman, his followers and all his children. They then restored the mosque, and in future abstained from injuring it : whence it became the resort of the Muhammadan strangers."[1]

The vital importance of Darmadam to the trade of Tellicherry has already been referred to more than once in the preceding pages. The island was ceded to the Company in 1734, and save for a few months in 1788–89 the factors never lost their hold on it. One of their small redoubts still exists, and there is also a rock-cut cave.

Iritti : At the foot of the Perambadi Ghat. Police outpost; post office ; travellers' bungalow ; overseers' shed. A fine iron girder bridge, built by the Local Fund Department in 1887, spans at this place one of the two branches of the Valarpattanam river. The river here is very swift and in the monsoon rises in flood almost to the level of the bridge. There is good fishing and shooting in the neighbourhood.

Kadirur : four miles from Tellicherry on the Coorg road; now a small Mappilla bazaar, once a place of importance. In 1801 Dr. Buchanan stayed at 'Cadrur' with Mr. Wilson, Collector of Cotiote and Iruvalinad, in a house which formerly had been the palace of the Pychy Rajas and 'was by the Nairs reckoned a superb building.'[2] Subsequently it was the headquarters of the taluk and the seat of a District Munsiff. There

---

[1] Lee's *Travels of Ibn Batuta*, p. 169. [2] Buchanan's *Journey*, II, 540.

CHAP. XV. KOTTAYAM.

are two sepulchral caves in the adjoining amsam of Ponniam. There is a high school here now run by the District Board, a sub-registrar's office, and a post office.

Kannavam or **Kanot:** Eight miles east of Kuttaparamba on the Periya Ghat road; travellers' bungalow; police outpost and a rural dispensary; Forest Ranger's Office; post office. During the rebellion it was a military outpost, as the ruins of a small redoubt still testify. The Kannavam and Peruvayil Nambiyars, the two most powerful janmis of the locality and two of the principal adherents of the Pychy Raja were captured at Kuttiyadi in 1801, and were marched forthwith to be hanged on 'the hill of Canute (Kanot) which is near their late residence, and the scene of their rebellious oppositions to the Company's authority.' The hill is well known as Fletcher's tote. Their estates were confiscated, and now form the valuable Kanot escheat forest in Kannavam and Manattana amsams. In the forest about a mile from Kannavam are a celebrated temple and three rock-cut caves said to be paved with bricks. The stone bridge over an arm of the Anjarakandi river at Kannavam was built in 1823 by the 2nd battalion of the Madras Pioneers.

Kottayam: a mile from Kuttaparamba on the Cannanore road, contains the Eastern and Southern palaces of the Kottayam Rajas on the banks of a large tank, and a fine but modern temple.

The Kottayam or Puranad (foreign) family is of Kshatriya origin and closely allied to the Rajas of Kurumbranad. They are not one of the ancient dynasties of Malabar, as their name does not appear in the list of chieftains among whom Cheraman Perumal divided up his kingdom; but by the end of the seventeenth century they shared Kottayam taluk with the Iruvalinad Nambiyars, and were in possession of North Wynaad and the small *nad* of Tamarasseri in the Kurumbranad and Calicut taluks. The 'Cotiote,' as the Raja was called, was one of the first with whom the Company entered into formal relations; and during the 18th century he was one of their most consistent supporters, rendering in particular signal services in the wars with Haidar and T.pu. After the cession of Malabar misunderstandings arose, and the Pychy Raja of the Western palace rose in a rebellion (see Chapter II), which terminated only with the death of the Raja in a skirmish at the end of 1805. The property of the rebel and of two other Rajas of the family was declared forfeit, and the Kottayam family has never recovered its former prosperity. Their *malikhana* is Rs. 5,900.

Kuttaparamba: eight miles from Tellicherry on the same road; the headquarters of a Deputy Tahsildar; District Munsiff, and sub-registrar; hospital; police station; post office; travellers' bungalow.

This place was of some importance during the two Pychy rebellions, as a military outpost and cantonment. The travellers' bungalow stands on the site of the old mud fort occupied by the British troops.

Manattana : three miles east of the Peravur rest-house on the branch road from Nedumpoyil Chattram at the foot of the Periya Ghat to Iritti. It was a place of great strategic importance during the Pychy rebellion, and was held by British troops whose redoubt still exists on the top of a low hill. It is situated on the abandoned road to the foot of the Smugglers' pass which one hundred years ago was one of the principal passes into the Wynaad. The road traverses wild jungle and the magnificent Kottiyur reserved forest. Six miles from Manattana in the midst of the wildest part of the jungle is the most famous temple in North Malabar, the Kottiyur or Tricharamanna temple, the scene of a great series of sacrificial rites celebrated by Daksha. Sati Divi, his daughter and the wife of his enemy Siva, despite the protests and warnings of her husband, felt constrained to attend the rites. She travelled by Manattana, and every foot of the road from Manattana to Kottiyur is holy ground. Each stage of her journey is named after one of the conflicting emotions which filled her mind as she made her pilgrim's progress through the forest. Manattana itself means ' the place of perplexity ' and its temple is ' the shrine of despair.' The forest beyond is ' the abode of terror ', and among the many well-known land marks on the road are ' the rock of recreation,' ' the pool of tears,' ' the place of the swoon,' and ' the stream where the serpent was slain.' Sati Divi was ill received by her father, and in despair burnt herself alive ; whereupon Siva in his wrath slew Daksha. Many hundred years afterwards, when the site of the ceremonies had long been forgotten a Kuricchiyan hunting in the forest chanced to whet his arrows on a stone. Blood instantly gushed forth from the stone ; and the Kuricchiyan, whose family still bears the honorific name of Ottupilam, carried news of the portent to the nearest Nambudiri, a member of the Padinnatta Illam. The Nambudiri recognized in the stone a *lingam*, and the discovery of many copper and bronze vessels in the adjacent jungle established the sanctity of the spot as the scene of Daksha's rites. These vessels, which are still used at the time of the festival, have never been cleaned, but are as bright as on the day when Daksha used them.

The Nambudiri priests live in a little way-side temple at Kottiyur, but the true shrine is a quarter of a mile away in the forest across one of the feeder streams of the Valarpattanam river. The usual temple buildings are absent. The *lingam*, still discoloured where the blood flowed forth, stands on a rude platform of piled up stones ; and round about are the long thatched sheds where the pilgrims lodge. For eleven months in the year the scene is inconceivably desolate and dreary ; but during the month Edavam (May-June) upwards of 50,000 Nayars and Tiyans from all parts of Malabar throng the shrine for the twenty-eight days of the annual festival. During the rest of the year the temple is given up to the revels of Siva and Parvati, and the impious Hindu who dares to intrude is consumed instantly to ashes.

The two great ceremonies are the *Neyyattam* and the *Elanirattam*, the pouring of ghee and the pouring of the milk of the green coconut. The former is performed by the Nayars, who attend the festival first, and the latter by Tiyans. In May all roads lead to Kottiyur, and towards the middle of the month the ' ghee pourers,' as the Nayar pilgrims are called, who have spent the previous four weeks in fasting and purificatory rites, assemble in small shrines subordinate to the Kottiyur temple. Thence, clad in white and bearing each upon his head a pot of ghee, they set forth in large bodies headed by a leader. At Manattana the pilgrims from all parts of Malabar meet, and thence to Kottiyur the procession is unbroken. However long their journey, the pilgrims must eat only once, and the more filthy their language, the more orthodox is their conduct. As many as 5,000 pots of ghee are poured over the *lingam* every year.

After the *Neyyattam* ceremony the Nayars depart and it is the turn of the Tiyans. Their preparations are similar to those of the Nayars, and their language *en route* is even more startling. Eruvatti near Kadirur is the place where most of them assemble for their pilgrimage, and their green coconuts are presented gratis by the country people as an offering to the temple. The *Elanirattam* ceremony begins at midnight, and the pilgrims heap up their coconuts in front of the shrine continuously till the evening of the same day. Each Tiyan then marches thrice round the heap and falls prostrate before the *lingam* ; and a certain Nayar sub-caste removes the husks preparatory to the spilling of the milk. The festival finally closes with a mysterious ceremony, in which ghee and mantrams play a great part, performed for two days consecutively by the presiding Nambudiri, and Kottiyur is then deserted for another year.

Pazhassi (Pychy): Five miles from Kuttaparamba on the Coorg road ; the seat of the western branch of the family. Their ' palace ' is now a small tumble-down house inhabited by a lady and her child, sole surviving members of the once powerful Pychy Raja, who shook to its foundations the British supremacy in Malabar. The ruins of four forts on the surrounding hills are relics of the time when Pazhassi was the centre of the rebellion. Mattanur, a neighbouring desam, has a melancholy interest as the scene of the tragedy of 1852 when a Brahman family eighteen in number was cruely murderd by Mappilla fanatics. This awful tragedy occurred on 10th January 1852 when a band of fifteen Mappillas attacked a Nambudiri's illam in this village, butchered all the unhappy inmates including an infant. The fanatics were followed by a large body of Mappilla rabble who then plundered the premises and set fire to it. An adjacent house, also a Brahman's was next attacked where the inmates put up a fight killing two and wounding two more of the attackers and eventually escaped after one or two of them were killed and the house was set on fire. The Hindus of the neighbourhood were so greatly alarmed that the more wealthy among them, like the Pychy and Chavasseri Rajas took their families to the nearest jungle leaving their palaces to the mercy of the Mappillas. Pychy Raja's palace 3 miles from Muttanur was broken into and the family temple defiled, though on the intervention of a Mappilla retainer of the Raja the fanatics abandoned their preparations for setting fire to the palace.

The gang next defiled a Hindu temple on their way to Irukur where they spent the night and next day proceeded to Kallyad to attack the house of a rich and influential landholder by name Anandan. The latter had foreseen the invasion and mustered a guard of 300 retainers for the defence of his house and though Anandan himself escaped during the siege with his family into the jungle and was followed by most of the defenders, eleven of the fanatics who battered the outerdoor and entered the house were killed and two were mortally wounded by the guards inside his house. The outbreak, the only one in North Malabar, was thus quelled even before the authorities could rush to the spot and deal with the rebels. Mr. Strange was soon after appointed Special Commissioner to enquire into the Mappilla outbreaks and suggest remedies; and the first act of Government soon after this event was their approval of Mr. H. V. Connolly's action in acquiescing and helping in the departure of the Tirurangady Thangal, Saiyyid Fazl, and his family and dependents to Arabia on 19th March 1852.

Tellicherry: (population 27,883): the seat of the District Judge, the Divisional officer and District Registrar of North Malabar, and the head-quarters of the taluk, is the chief town of the northern half of the district. In point of size it ranks third after Calicut and Palghat; and its trade is exceeded only by Cochin and the capital A Superintendent of Police, Port officer, District Munsiff and Civil Surgeon are stationed here among other officials. Apart from the public offices the principal institutions are the municipal hospital, the Chalil dispensary, the Brennen College and the travellers' bungalow. The municipality is dealt with in Chapter XIV above, and in Chapter VI allusion has been made to the important coffee and pepper trade of the town. The Madras Bank and three great European firms have branches in Tellicherry, and many of the richest Mappilla merchants on the coast live here. Prominent among them is the Chovakkaran family, descendants of the 'Chocara Mousa,' who in 1784 obtained a monopoly of the

CHAP. XV. KOTTAYAM.

coir of the Laccadive Islands, and in 1792 offered to contract with the Hon. Company for the supply of 6,000 candies of pepper.'[1] There is a comfortable English club, but no hotel. The population in 1931 was 30,349. The town is now connected with Coorg and Mysore by motor buses. There are also bus services from Tellicherry to Manantoddy and Cannanore. There is no superintendent of police at Tellicherry now. There are a port officer and a port conservator, a subordinate judge, two district munsifs and a deputy director of argiculture. There are two high schools, one for boys and the other for girls, the latter being run by the Sacred Heart Convent. There are also two training schools, one for mistresses of the higher elementary grade and the other for masters of the secondary grade.

Tellicherry is a healthy and picturesque town, situated upon a group of low wooded hills running down to the sea, and protected by a natural breakwater of basalt rocks. Its importance is largely fortuitous. The rocks make the roadstead dangerous, and H.M.S. *Superb*, mounting 74 guns, was wrecked upon them in 1781. The small river, only 14 miles long, which bounds the town on the north and east, though in the stormy years of the 18th century it was a useful line of defence and was further strengthened by outworks at various points of advantage, is navigable only for three or four miles, and is of little value for trade. Darmadam or Darmapattanam Island, at the mouth of the Anjarakkandi river, three miles north of the town, would have been a more eligible site ; but at the end of the seventeenth century it was a bone of contention among the Malayali chieftains, and the East India Company preferred to shun complications by settling at Tellicherry. Here in 1683[2] they founded their first regular settlement on the Malabar coast, and opened a factory on a site in the Kurangod Nayar's territory granted by his suzerain, the ruling Prince of Kolattanad. The Company was careful to conciliate the natives by paying scrupulously for all the land and houses they required ; but the Kurangod Nayar refused to be pacified, and in 1704, abetted by one of the recalcitrant princes of Kolattanad, he forced his way into the Company's warehouse. The factors complained to the Prince Regent, and sought permission to prevent similar outrages in the future by fortifying the settlement. The Prince Regent laid the first stone, and the fort was completed by 1708 on a small hill by the sea called Tiruvallappan Kunnu. From this time forward the history of Tellicherry, as recorded in the ponderous tomes of the factory diary in the Collector's office, is the history of the English in Malabar, and need not be recapitulated. Till 1735–36 the factors were continually manœuvring for the possession of Darmadam island ; and the French occupation of Mahe

[1] Joint Commissioners' Report, 137–141.

[2] The exact date is uncertain, at any rate it was some years before 1699.

in 1725 compelled them in self-defence to fortify and garrison Pallikunnu, Morakunnu, Andolla Mala, Mailankunnu and the other outlying hills of Tellicherry. This long line of outposts entailed a numerous garrison, and even in 1737, when peace had been concluded with the Canarese and the military establishment had been reduced, the forces numbered "2 Captains, 4 Ensigns, 19 Sergeants, 16 Corporals, 13 Rounders, 14 Drummers, 91 Europeans, 42 Mustees, 221 Topasses, total 422". Ninety men were required for the fort, 8 for the limit gate, 13 for the banksaul, 9 for the great bastion and 5 for the hospital. The rest were distributed among the various outposts. In times of stress native irregulars were raised. The sepoys were 'cloathed' in 'scarlet coats faced with green perpets' and a belt 'covered with green perpets': the Calli-Quiloners or Mappillas in 'blue coats faced and bound with red'. The pay of the factors was very small. In 1739 the Chief received only £70 a year, the two senior merchants £40 a year each, one junior merchant £30 a year, and one writer £5 a year with an allowance of Rs. 144 (equivalent at that time to £18) for reading divine service. From 1776 to 1784 the factory was reduced to a residency: and on 27th July 1794, in the words of Mr. Logan 'the old Tellicherry factory, which had exercised such abundant influence for good in the annals of the Malayalis for over a century, and which had existed as an oasis of peace and security and good government during all those troublous times ceased to exist as such'. Its abolition had been decreed by Sir John Shore, Governor-General of India. Eliza Draper, Sterne's correspondent, lived for some time in Tellicherry, Daniel Draper, her husband, being chief factor from 1768 to 1770. Tellicherry was for a time the seat of the Northern Superintendent of Malabar, and of the Provincial Court of Circuit.

The small redoubts on most of the outlying hills have long since disappeared, as has the stone wall which surrounded the town, built according to Hamilton, an interloper and no friend of the factors, 'to keep out the enemies of the chief's making'. The fort is in fair preservation. It is built of laterite in the form of a square; and with its massive and lofty loop-holed walls and strong flanking bastions, the cavalier bastion in the south-east corner and the great bastion to the north beyond the Divisional Officer's bungalow, must have been a formidable stronghold in days gone by. A lighthouse now crowns its walls on the seaward side. Round the fort clusters the business part of the town full of old fashioned warehouses and houses built by Portuguese refugees during the Mysorean invasion. On the seashore is the old factory 'banksaul' now used as a salt godown: and the taluk and many of the other public offices are grouped round a small green maidan beneath the great bastion of the fort. Further south is the Mappilla fishing village of Chalil, the plague spot of Tellicherry, and on the north and east the bungalows of

CHAP. XV. KOTTAYAM.

the European residents crown the low hills. Pallikunnu bungalow was built in 1814 by Mr. T. H. Baber, for many years Sub-Collector of Tellicherry, and subsequently a judge of the western court of circuit. He was the suppressor of the Pychy rebellion, and one of the most distinguished of the early officials of Malabar. His name is still a household-word in the town, and lives in Baber's tank. The house is haunted and has a bad reputation, many European merchants, who have owned or inhabited it in the past, having left it bankrupt. Morakunnu bungalow was built by Mr. James Stevens, also a judge of the western court of circuit. The Anglican church beneath the walls of the fort was built in 1869 with funds left by master attendant, Mr. Edward Brennen (who also endowed the Brennen high school) and the foundation stone was laid by Lord Napier of Ettrick. Other churches are those of the Roman Catholics and the Basel Mission, whose first station in Malabar was established in 1839 on Nittur hill by the famous Malayalam scholar, Dr. Gundert. The principal mosque in the town, the Odathil Palli, so called because it was built in a Government garden, was built by Chovakkaran Mussa. The Tiruvangad temple, dedicated to Sri Rama and one of the few temples in Malabar with a golden spire, is the most important temple. It is generally known as the Brass Pagoda from the copper sheeting of its roof. It was one of the outposts of the fort in the eighteenth century. Its ruined walls were restored by Mr. Baber. Attached to the temple is the largest tank in Tellicherry. The tank in front of the Sri Rama temple at Tiruvangad has been repaired. Pallikunnu and the Baber's bungalow in it are now in the possession of Messrs. Volkart Brothers and have lost their evil reputation.

Pre-historic sepulchral remains are also to be found in Kannampalli desam, Kolavalur desam, Peringalam and Tiruvangad amsams and on Purazhi Mala in Mushakkunnu.

KURU BRANAD TALUK.

CHAP. XV KURUMBRANAD.

Kurumbranad is the southern taluk of North Malabar and formed with Chirakkal and Kottayam the old Tellicherry Revenue Division. It is now included in the Calicut Revenue Division. In appearance it is very similar to these two taluks; but the sandy strip of cocoanut land along the coast is broader, and for a few miles inland the country is less hilly and broken. At the back of the taluk along its eastern border is a belt of wild mountainous country from six to eight miles broad, which is unsurveyed and unexplored, and is inhabited only by a few jungle tribes. The prevailing soil is red ferruginous, only 2 per cent of the classified area falling within the arenaceous series. The taluk slopes from the ghats to the sea, and is drained by the Mahe, Kotta and Agalapuzha rivers. Canals connect the Kotta river with Badagara on the north and the Agalapuzha on the south, and the water communication between Badagara, the headquarters of the taluk, and Calicut is uninterrupted. All these rivers are highways of trade; and, as the S. Indian Railway runs through the taluk and there are more than 100 miles of roads, the taluk is well served with communications. The taluk now has about 1.0 miles of road.

Statistics on many points of interest are given in the separate Appendix. The area of the taluk is 505 square miles, but of this only 420 square miles have been surveyed and classified. The settled portion of the taluk is however very closely cultivated. Cocoanut gardens climb the slopes of nearly all the low laterite hills, and the proportion of unoccupied dry land to the classified area is smaller than in any other taluk except Ponnani. The wet lands as usual in North Malabar are inferior to those of the interior taluks of the district; but the gardens are excellent, and one-fourth of all the garden land in Malabar lies in Kurumbranad. *Punam* is the only dry cultivation of importance. There are no reserved forests, but large quantities of valuable timber from private forests near Kuttiyadi are floated down the Kota river to Kottakkal and Kallayi. Nearly 74 per cent of the population are Hindus, the proportion of Mappillas (26 per cent) being rather less than the district average. Nearly 12 per cent of the population can read and write. Seventy-three per cent of the population were Hindus in 1931, and the proportion of Mappillas 27 per cent was rather less than the district average.

CHAP. XV.
KURUMBRANAD.

The taluk was in the days before the British occupation divided into the *nads* of Kadattanad, Payyanad, Payyormala and Kurumbranad, and included part of Tamarasseri.

Kadattanad, the most celebrated of these, lay between the Mahe and Kotta rivers, and was at one time part of the Kolattiri's dominions. The Tekkelamkur or Southern Regent of this family had his headquarters at Puthuppattanam (now Puthuppanam) on the north bank of the Kotta river where traces of his palace are reported still to be visible. The Kadattanad Raja, who traces his descent from a union between a Kolattiri princess and a scion of the royal house of Porlattiri (see p. 404), was by the end of the 17th century only nominally subject to the Kolattiri; and in 1750 A.D., with the latter's consent he formally assumed the title of Raja. Hamilton visited him in 1703, and describes him as the 'Ballanore[1] Burgarie, a formidable prince'. He and his predecessors had been 'Lords of the Sea time out of mind, and all trading vessels between Cape Comorin and Damaan were obliged to carry his passes'. He maintained a fleet of light galleys, and the famous Kottakkal pirates preyed on all vessels that 'traded without their Lord's pass'. The family is now divided into two branches, the Ayanchori and Edavalat Kovilagams, and enjoys a *malikhana* of Rs. 26,441.

In the division of Malabar made by Cheraman Perumal, Payyanad fell to the share of the Raja of Kollam; but he was too weak long to resist the aggressions of the Zamorin, who in historical times was lord paramount of the nad. Payyanad comprised the island now formed by the sea, the Kotta, Elattur and Agalapuzha rivers, and one or two amsams east of the last named.

With the exception of a few amsams in the extreme south which formed part of Tamarassori, the rest of the taluk was divided between the Payyormala Nayars and the Kurumbranad Raja, all of whom acknowledged the suzerainty of the Zamorin. Of the three ruling Nair families (Paleri, Avinnat and Kudali) only two now survive, the Paleri family being extinct. The Avinnat Nayar lives in Mennannyam amsam and desam, and enjoys a *malikhana* of Rs. 4,058–4–2, but his estates are heavily encumbered. The Kudali Nayar, whose tarwad house is in Kalliod amsam, is also in straitened circumstances. His *malikhana* is Rs. 1,766–12–10. The Kurumbranad Raja, who claims to be a Kshatriya by caste, and is nearly allied to the Kottayam family, received his nad from Cheraman Perumal, but in time became feudatory to the Zamorin. He is still one of the greatest landholders in North Malabar, and owns large estates in the Wynaad, which taluk he is said to have invaded

[1] Ballanore=Valunnavar or Ruler; Burgarie=Badagara. See Hamilton's *New Account* I. 301. Also Pyrard de Laval's *Voyage* I. 344, and Buchanan's *Journey*, II–514.

CHAP. XV.
KURUMBRANAD.

at an early period with the Kottayam Raja. The Kurumbranad family which has a *malikhana* of Rs. 5,824, is divided into four branches the Ramankalattu, Muttirakkal, Mallisseri and Kolapreth Kovilagams. The Raja's palace is in Valasseri desam.

Kurumbranad is composed of the old taluks of Kadattanad and Kurumbranad. In 1866 six amsams were transferred to Calicut, and in 1904 the remaining 57 amsams were split up into 104 at the reorganization of village establishments, which followed the settlement.

A short account of some places of interest in the taluk is appended.

Badagara or **Vadakara** (north-bank) so called from its situation just north of the Kotta river; the headquarters of the taluk, the sixth town in Malabar, a port and a thriving centre of trade. Population 11,319. District Munsiff's Court; sub-registrar's office; hospital; police station; travellers' bungalow; chattram and overseer's shed; combined post and telegraph office; sea-customs and port office; railway station. Its population in 1921 was 9,804 and in 1931, 11,259.

The public offices are pleasantly situated on a hill about half a mile from the sea. On the beach there are several substantial warehouses; but the Mappilla town around them is, as usual, dirty and insanitary. The Mappillas, in whose hands the trade of the town is concentrated, number 5,223 or nearly half the total population. The export trade of the town has increased in value from 18¼ lakhs in 1899–1900 to more than 29 lakhs in the year ending June 30th, 1904; but imports have declined in the same period from nearly 14 lakhs to 7·33 lakhs. Cocoanuts and copra are the chief exports; salt and grain the only imports of importance. The town is connected by a canal with the estuary of the Kotta river, but possesses no harbour.

The most interesting feature of the town is the ruined fort near the travellers' bungalow. Tradition has it that it was acquired from the Kolattiri by the Kadattanad family in 1564 A.D., but probably it was built after 1703; for when Hamilton visited the 'Ballanore Burgarie' in that year, his palace was 'meanly built of reeds and covered with cocoanut leaves, but very neat and clean.' The Mysoreans established a monopoly of all goods exported from Malabar, and converted the fort into their chief storehouse. Here, too, they made their last stand in Malabar, and after the fall of Fort St. Angelo at Cannanore in 1790 they were driven out of Badagara and Kuttippuram with the loss of 200 men and 12 guns. The British Government subsequently restored the fort to the Kadattanad Raja, and for a time it was used for the Brahman feeding house, now attached to the Peruvantala temple.

CHAP. XV. KURUMBRANAD.

Badagara was the scene of many of the exploits of Taccholi Othenan, the Robin Hood of North Malabar, and many ballads[1] still sung by coolies at their work commemorate his exploits. Near the Peruvantala temple about half a mile from the town is a masonry well 20 feet 6 inches in diameter, and close thereto a massive block of laterite. One of the legends about Taccholi Othenan is that with this block of laterite under one arm and a jack tree under the other he cleared the well at a bound. The Taccholi *tarwad* house is in Nadakuttayi amsam and desam but the family is now represented by a single female.

Three miles south-east of Badagara and connected with it by a cart track is the Lokanar Kavu, a celebrated temple belonging to the Kadattanad family, which is frequently mentioned in the Taccholi ballads. In the vicinity of the temple are three rock cut caves.

Chombala : Five miles north of Badagara on the Tellicherry road ; since 1848 a Basel Mission station, now containing 404 Christians or more than half of the total Christian population of the taluk. There is a large orphanage—the only one of its kind in Malabar—for 106 Malayali girls, a weaving establishment subordinate to the Cannanore factory which gives work to 62 operatives, a large church built in 1897, and a lower secondary school with accommodation for 160 pupils. Out-stations of the Chombala mission are situated at Mahe, Badagara, Muvarattu, Porambra and Karakad.

Kottakkal : Three miles south of Badagara on the south bank of the Kotta river ; at one time the stronghold of the Kottakkal Kunhali Marakkars, famous pirates whose deeds are the theme of many ballads. Traces of their fort, to which the river owes its name, are still visible. The family originally hailed from Pantalayini Kollam ; but on its destruction by Henry Menezes in 1525, they moved first to Tikkodi and finally to Kottakkal. They obtained their name from the Zamorin ; and, when the Portuguese first settled in Calicut, they surprised a Portuguese vessel, and slaughtered its crew on the rock which lies off Kottakkal about 8 miles to sea. This rock is called in the vernacular Velliyan kallu or the white rock, but since this exploit of the pirates has gone by the name of Sacrifice Rock. Kottakkal was besieged and taken by the Portuguese with the aid of the Zamorin in 1600 and the most famous of the Kunhali Marakkars was then captured and executed at Goa.[2] Subsequently the Marakkars seem to have transferred their allegiance to the Kadattanad Raja ; and, when Hamilton visited Badagara, they seized every vessel which traded without his pass. As late as 1742 the Kottakkal pirates were very busy, and the 'Tiger' Gallivat was especially detailed to look after them.

[1] One of these is translated in Logan's *Malabar*, Vol. I, p. 96.

[2] See *Voyage of Pyrard de Laval*, I, p. 354 and II, 509.

The Marakkars are now in distressed circumstances. The tombs of the founder and of several other members of the family are still pointed out in a mausoleum attached to the Jamat mosque. Kottakkal is now an important timber depot.

Kuttippuram : Two miles further along the Kuttiyadi road, has a small rest-house, but is remarkable only for the Kadattanad Valiya Raja's palace. At the back of the palace, which is quite a modern building, are the ruins of magnificent fort. The walls are in places nearly 50 feet thick and 30 feet high, and the fort which was surrounded by a deep moat, must have been in ancient times well-nigh impregnable. Nevertheless it was captured by Tipu in 1789 after a seige of several days; and its garrison, consisting of 2,000 Nayars and their families, were offered their choice between 'a voluntary profession of the Muhammadan faith and a forcible conversion with deportation from their native lands.'[1] They chose the former, and the next day the males were circumcised, and all were made to eat beef. Kuttippuram fort was one of the last places in Malabar to hold out for Tipu. The Ayancheri and Edavalat *kovilagams*, and the palace of the Elaya Raja of the Kadattanad family are in Puramori amsam, where the Elaya Raja maintains a high school. In the Parambil desam of Ponmeri amsam by the side of the foot-path between Kuttippuram and Badagara are nearly a dozen rock-cut caves hitherto unexplored. A granite slab in the Ponmeri Siva temple bears an inscription in unknown characters.

Kuttiyadi : Seventeen miles from Badagara, and rather more than twenty from Tellicherry; sub-registrar's office; police station; post office and travellers' bungalow. Although within Kadattanad, the country round Kuttiyadi always acknowledged the supremacy of the Kottayam Raja, whose fortified palace stood on the hill now occupied by the public buildings. The fort which mounted four guns fell into the hands of the Mysoreans, but was recaptured in 1790 by the Raja. During the Pychy rebellion Kuttiyadi, which commanded one of the chief passes to the Wynaad in those times, was of great strategic importance, and the fort was for some years held by British troops. In Valayyanur desam is a *tura* or artificial lake fabled to have been excavated by the Pandavas. Four miles from Kuttiyadi at Kavilampara a wooden bridge spanning a mountain torrent, which in the monsoon rushes foaming and seething over a bed of solid gneiss, marks the beginning of the ghat, and at this point the road degenerates into a mere foot-path. The ghat is impassable for carts, but is extensively used for cooly traffic and pack animals.

Mahe : The little French settlement of Mahe lies at the extreme north of the taluk on the southern bank of the Mahe

---

[1] Wilks' *History of Mysore*, II, 126.

CHAP. XV. KURUMBRA-NAD.

river. It comprises ten small desams spread over an area of about two and a half square miles; and there are also attached to the settlement four desams or *aldees* on the northern bank of the river, Chalakkara, Pallur, Chembra and Pandakkal, known collectively as Nalutara; and three detached hills or outposts, called Fort St. George, and Great and Little Kallayi. These *aldees* were handed over to the French Government in 1853 after a prolonged discussion.

The French settlement at Mahe dates from 1725, when the native town of Mayyazhi was captured by M. Mahe de Labourdonnais and rechristened after its captor.[1] In the latter half of the eighteenth century it was thrice taken by the British and restored. In 1793 it capitulated for the fourth time, and was not finally restored to France till the peace of 1817.

The town occupies a most picturesque position on a hill at the mouth of the river. It contains a Roman Catholic Church, to which a large number of visitors are attracted at the festival of Corpus Christi.

The settlement is under the charge of Chef de Service, or Administrateur, subordinate to the Governor of Pondicherry. The French Government maintains four schools and a hospital. The trade of the town is not of great importance, but appears to be increasing.

Nadapuram: Ten miles north-east of Badagara, at the junction of the roads from Tellicherry and Badagara to Kuttiyadi; a Mappilla village of some importance, but little interest. A District Munsiff and sub-registrar are stationed here. There are a police station, a post office, and a travellers' bungalow.

Nadavannur: Fourteen miles from Kuttiyadi on the road which joins that from Quilandi to Tamarasseri; once of importance as the head-quarters of the old Kurumbranad taluk. Travellers' bungalow; police station; sub-registrar's office; post office.

Pantalayini or Pantalayini Kollam: Just north of Quilandi; one of the most historic places in Malabar. It is the Patale of Pliny, the Pandarani of the Portuguese writers, the Flandrina of Friar Odoric, the Fundreeah of the Tahafut-ul-Mujahidin, and the Fandaraina of Ibn Batuta. The Kollam Raja of Payanad here made his capital, and the Zamorin, his conqueror, still has a palace in the desam. According to the Tahafut-lul-Mujahidin, Malik Ibn Dinar founded one of the original of mosques at Fundreeah, and appointed one of his ten sons as *Kazi*. A natural hollow in a rock on the seashore close to the mosque has been chiselled into the likeness of a foot, and this mark is said to be the print of Adam's foot as he landed in India, his next stride taking him to Adam's peak in Ceylon.

[1] See p. 54.

Ibn Batuta describes Kollam as 'a beautiful and large place, abounding with gardens and markets.'[1] Off the town is one of the curious mud banks, peculiar to the West Coast, and Vasco de Gama probably moved to its shelter from Kappat where he first touched in 1498. At that time, it was the great emporium of trade between Mecca and the Malabar, and a stronghold of the Moors. The Portuguese made many attacks upon the town, and it was strongly defended by bastions on the Mayyat Kunnu. Soares defeated a Moorish fleet here in 1504; and in 1525 Menezes stormed the town, burnt the shipping, and captured 250 guns. In 1550, Pantalayini was once more raided and burnt by the Portuguese, and tow-thirds of its inhabitants were put to the sword.

Malik Ibn Dinar's mosque was built in imitation of one at Mecca. It is a venerable building, its dome, which Arab vessels passing up and down the coast never failed in former times to salute, being covered with sheets of copper. In the Jamat mosque, there are three granite slabs with inscriptions. The Mayyat Kunnu is the grave-yard of Kollam (*Mayyat*, corpse) and many of the tombs are very ancient, and some are inscribed. One of the tombs bears an inscription to the effect that 'Ali Ibn Udthorman was obliged to leave this world for ever in the year 166 of Hejira, so called after Muhammad the prophet left Mecca for Medina.' A festival is held every year on the hill in the month Ramullan.

There are several Hindu temples in the vicinity of Pantalayini. In three of these, the Maralur, Pantalayini and Talayil temples, are inscriptions as yet undeciphered.

Payyoli : In Torayur desam of Iringatt amsam : a rising Mappilla town with a sub-registrar's office, post office, police station and a travellers' bungalow. There is a lock here on the canal which joins the Kotta and Agalapuzha rivers. In Kizhur desam of Meladi amsam, about two miles from Payyoli, is the Kizhur Siva temp'e. During the annual festival, celebrated in the month of Vrischigam (November-December), the most important cattle fair in the district is held near the temple. Cattle are brought here for sale from all parts of the district and even from Coimbatore. The village is now in Thurayur amsam and desam. There is now a munsif's court in it.

Quilandi : The headquarters of the Deputy Tahsildar; District Munsiff's court; sub-registrar's office; sea-customs office; combined post and telegraph office; police station; travellers' bungalow; chattram; dispensary. The village, which is close to the Kollam mud bank (see p. 8), was once a flourishing port and the favourite starting and landing place of pilgrims on their way to and from Mecca. The passenger traffic ceased when steamers began to ply, and the trade of

[1] Lee's *Travels of Ibn Batuta*, p. 171.

CHAP. XV. KURUMBRANAD.

Quilandi is now unimportant. There is a fine old mosque founded in 1779 by Sayid Abdulla Bin Sayid Abdulla Haji. The mosque was for a time supported by a voluntary cess, which the Hindu and Muhammadan merchants in Tinnevelly and Malabar agreed to pay on every head of bullock load of merchandise passing through their villages. Regulation XII of 1803 put a stop to the practice ; and in 1828 Government granted an annual allowance of Rs. 1,800 for the upkeep of the mosque and caravansari attached to it. In 1848 at Mr. Conolly's suggestion, certain escheated lands in Manjeri, Pandalur, Karakunnu and Trikkalangod amsams of Ernad, the assessment and janmabhogam on which together amounted to Rs. 1,800 were made over to the tangal in lieu of the money grant, and they have since been confirmed as his inam lands.

In addition to those already mentioned, there are inscriptions on a stone belonging to a ruined temple in Kavil desam, Kavuntara amsam, which is now preserved in the *Uralan's* house ; on the eastern wall of a ruined temple in Kinalur amsam and desam ; on a granite slab in the Siva temple in Tiruvankara desam of Karayad amsam (recently damaged by fire) ; and on a slab in front of the Siva temple in Vellikulangara desam, Uralankal amsam. All these except the last have still to be read. The last records that the *kalasam* (purification) ceremony of the temple was performed in 905 M.E. (1730 A.D.) with great pomp by the best of the Brahmans, and that the temple was built under the auspices of the generous Udayavarma, the sea of courage and the gem of the royal line descended from Khatolkacha (the son of Bhima, one of the Pandavas).

Hat stones (*topi kallu*) and rock-cut caves are fairly numerous in the taluk. The former occur in Velur amsam and desam and in Pampirikunnu desam, Cheruvannur amsam, the latter in Muyippod, Kokkallur, and Velur amsams and desams, in Muchikunnu desam of Mudadi amsam and in Nambrattu and Naduvattur desams of Kizhariyur amsam, as well as in the places mentioned above.

PALGHAT TALUK.

CHAP. XV. PALGHAT.

PALGHAT, the most easterly taluk of Malabar, which forms with Ponnani the Palghat division, is connected with the rest of the district only by Walavanad on its north-western frontier, the other boundaries being Coimbatore on the east, and Cochin State on the east, west and south. Its physical features are determined by the famous Gap, of which the far-reaching effects, both physical and political, upon Malabar have been noted in Chapter I. Like the other plain taluks, Palghat slopes gently down from the east ; but its laterite hills are lower than is usual in Malabar, and the valleys between them not so deep. The highest point in the Vada Malas, north of the Gap, is Kari Mala or Periya Kunjara Mala (6,556 feet) ; but more conspicuous is Kalladikod hill at the extreme end of the range, perhaps the stormiest peak in all Malabar. 'If Kalladikodan grows black,' runs the proverb 'will not the Karuga river be in flood.' Government owns two forests already referred to in Chapter V, the Chenat Nayar and Dhoni reserves, on the slopes and at the foot of these hills. The Tenmalas, south of the Gap, a spur of the Anamalas, are likewise covered with forest, owned mostly by the Kollangod Nambidi and cleared away in places to make room for coffee plantations. The only river of importance is the Bharatha puzha or Ponnani river, which is formed near Parali by the junction of the Kalpati and Kannadi streams, rising respectively in the northen and southern ranges. Further east, it is joined by the Kollangod river. The Ponnani river is too shallow and rocky for traffic ; but the taluk is well supplied with roads radiating from Palghat town, though the majority are in very bad order. The South Indian Railway runs through the northern half of the taluk, and a small branch line leads from Olavakkod junction to the headquarter town. Other stations are Valayar, Kanjikod, Parali and Mankara. Palghat is now connected by rail with Pollachi and Dindigul, the section to Pollachi having been opened in April 1932.

Fourth only in point of size, Palghat pays a larger land revenue than any other taluk of the district except Ponnani. Ninety per cent. of the revenue is paid on wet lands, which yield in excellence only to those of Walavanad and make up no less than 39 per cent. of the surveyed area of the taluk. The rainfall being comparatively small, tanks and ponds in the midst of the paddy fields are used to store up water for the

CHAP. XV. PALGHAT.

second crop. In Polpalli and Panayur amsams, a considerable extent is irrigated by channels from an anicut across the Kannadi river in Cochin territory, and near Palghat is another small irrigation work. Gardens are very few and poor, and the palmyra, the characteristic tree, presents a striking contrast to the groves of graceful coconut palms near the coast. Besides the ordinary modan, samai, and gingelly crops, cholam, ragi, kambu, dholl, castor oil, and other East Coast dry crops are raised in the eastern portions of the taluk ; and near Valayar especially the dry lands, like those of Coimbatore, are under cultivation continued from year to year. The soils are of the usual red ferruginous variety. Timber is the principal industry. Jaggery is made in large quantites from palmyra juice, 2,500 tons having been exported last year to Nellikuppam, and grass mats of excellent quality are made near Palghat.

As in its crops, so in its inhabitants, Palghat forms a sort of transition stage between the eastern and western sides of the presidency. The Nambudiri and Mappilla almost disappear, and their places are taken by Pattar Brahmans and Ravuttans. Pattar *gramams* are scattered all over the taluk, there being as many as twenty in Palghat town alone. They were described by Dr. Buchanan as the neatest and cleanest villages he had seen in India. The Ravuttans are Mussalmans from Tinnevelly, and are quiet law-abiding traders.

The legendary history of the Palghat Gap ascribes its origin to the inevitable Parasu Raman, who, after reclaiming Kerala from the sea, found it imposible to procure inhabitants for the land, as the mountains to the east were impassable. Accordingly, with his own hands, he cut the chasm in the ghats, which now is known as the Palghat Gap. Of the early history of Palghat, little is known ; it is doubtful whether it formed part of the ancient Chera kingdom. Probably, it was a debatable land between the great dynasties east and west of the ghats, and through the gap must have come the many invaders, whose vaunted conquests of Kerala are recorded in many inscriptions. Local traditions assert that the small district of Chittur in the centre of the gap was the price paid by the Palghat Rajas to the Raja of Cochin for his asistance in defending the eastern frontier of the gap against invasion.

The Palghat Rajas, who, at the beginning of the 16th century, were supreme throughout the whole of the modern taluk, and were probably independent even of Cheraman Perumal, if such a person ever existed, as no tradition exists that they received their dominions from that legendary potentate, are believed to have come from Athavanad amsam of Ponnani taluk and to have granted their lands there in exchange for their subsequent dominions to the well-known Nambudiri, Azhuvancheri Tamburakkal. The date of this exchange is uncertain, as also is the date when the family lost caste owing to the connection (explained in various ways) of an early Raja with a Malasar woman. The Rajas played little part in the history of Malabar till the middle of the 18th century, when the continued aggressions of the Zamorin drove them, in an evil hour for their country, to seek the aid of Haidar Ali, then Foujdar of Dindigul, in 1766. The dissensions of the family caused much trouble to the authorities in the early days of the British rule ; and Itti Kombi Acchan who became Raja in 1793 began his career by imprisoning a rival claimant to the throne and ended it by murdering one of his enemies and putting out the eyes of another. A reward of Rs. 5,000 was offered for his arrest, and he died in imprisonment in the Tellicherry fort. The Acchanmar, as the Rajas are called, whose *malikhana* is Rs. 18,099–3–3, are now in straitened circumstances.

The modern taluk comprises the three ancient *nads* of Vadamalapuram, Tenmalapuram and Naduvattam. Till 1890, it formed with Walavanad a Head Assistant Collector's division but in that year the latter taluk was transferred to the Malappuram division, and the Ponnani taluk was added to the Palghat division. The arrangement has its drawbacks as the two parts of the Divisional Officer's charge are separated from one another by the Cochin State. After the recent settlement the 56 amsams of the taluk were increased to 113 containing 138 desams. A Deputy Tahsildar stationed at Alattur assists the Tahsildar.

Statistics on several points of interest are given in the separate Appendix. The following are the most important places in the taluk :—

Alattur : thirteen miles south-west of Palghat on the road to the Cochin frontier ; the headquarters of the Deputy Tahsildar ; District munsiff ; sub-registrar ; police station ; post office ; travellers' bungalow. A dispensary built by private subscriptions is being maintained by the taluk board. There are two schools in the locality, one an incomplete secondary school managed by the District Board and the other a high school managed by one of the members of the Palghat Raja's family. A sub-treasury has been opened and is attached to the deputy tahsildar's office. There is also a Roman Catholic church, and in the neighbourhood are two tile works. In the south of the amsam is the Alattur hill (1,202 feet) or Velimala, one of the great trigonometrical stations of the district. About half way up is a small cave which judging from the remnants of mud partition walls and a small mill, appears at one time to have been inhabited. A little higher up are the remains of a temple and a natural spring. In the adjoining Vadakkettara amsam is the oldest Christian church in the taluk known as the church of the

Malarkot and erected towards the middle of the 18th century by Syrian Christian settlers from Trichur in the Cochin State. The congregation is Syro-Roman and is under the jurisdiction of the Roman Catholic Bishop of Coimbatore.

Kollangod: twelve miles due south of Palghat at the foot of the Tenmalas. It possesses a high school built and maintained by the present representative of the Venganad family, a dispensary also built by him but handed over to the taluk board, a post office, a police station and travellers' bungalow, all situated in the long straggling street which forms one of the principal villages of the taluk. There is a considerable trade in paddy and timber with Coimbatore and Pollachi, and other important industries are coarse weaving, the manufacture of grass mats and bell-metal work. In the Tenmala hills, three and six miles distant respectively from the village, are two natural springs or rather pools receiving the hill drainage. The first of these, the Sitakundu, is said to have been created for bathing purposes by Sita during her wanderings with Rama, the hero of the Ramayana. The other and more distant pool, the Govinda Tirtam, on the Govinda Mala, one of the highest peaks of the range, is said to owe its origin to Devendra.

Kollangod is the seat of the Venganad Nambidi whose family claims descent from an ancient Kshatriya Raja named Vira Ravi. The name Ravi Varma is accordingly still affixed to the names of all the male members of the family. Their former dominions comprised eight amsams in and near Kollangod, and were eventually absorbed by the Zamorin when he conquered Naduvattam. The family still owns 150 square miles of forest on the hills south of Kollangod, where many elephants were captured every year but are now captured only occasionally. The present head of the family (Vasudeva Raja) was granted the personal title of Raja in 1901 and knighted in 1925.

There are several temples in Kollengod, but none of them has any architectural pretentions. The most important is the Kachamkurissi temple dedicated to Vishnu and said to have been built by a great saint named Kasyapa Prajapathi. In this temple all the Nambudris of Malabar, Cochin and Travancore have to receive from the senior member of the Venganad family, as a preliminary to the performance of a *yagam* or sacrifice, the *soma* or moon plant, a skin of a black buck and a piece of wood known as '*karinkalli*' (*Mimosa catechu*). The Valiya Nambidi holds this right as the representative of Gandharva, and in virtue thereof is prohibited from walking bare-footed. He also has the right of entering the *Srikovil* of any temple, and of eating with Brahmans, though he does not wear the *punul*. These privileges are supposed to have been conferred by Parasu Rama with the title of Nambidi, which is borne by the two senior members of the family. Another large temple is the Kottambalam, dedicated to Subramania, which take its name from an old mud fort in the neighbourhood, the ruins of which may still be seen. In the neighbouring amsam of Payalur near the Pirali Bhagavathi temple is a stone platform said to have been used for the assembly of the ancient Sastrikars, the 36,000 armed Brahmans mentioned in the Keralolpatti, who ruled the country after the death of Kulasekhara Perumal. On this platform they held their court and investigated complaints. There is a similar one near the Parakad Bhagavathi temple in Kavasseri amsam.

Palghat: the second town of the district, the fourteenth of the presidency and a municipality; situated on an arm of the Ponnani river, some six or seven miles from the foot of the Vadamalas and linked to the South Indian Railway line by a short branch. Population 44,177. The proportion of Muhammadans is less than that in any other town of Malabar. The town is the headquarters of the Divisional Officer, Subordinate Judge, Tahsildar, Assistant Superintendent of Police and the Local Fund Assistant Engineer; and among the principal public buildings are the municipal hospital and dispensary, travellers' bungalow, District Munsiff's court, police station and post and telegraph offices. For a long time a regiment of native infantry was stationed in the town and the sepoy lines may still be seen in Sultanpetta. The regiment was withdrawn in 1860. Population rose to 45,487 in 1921 and to 49,064 in 1931. The town is also the headquarters of an Assistant Superintendent of police, the district registrar and the district forest officer. Among the public buildings may be mentioned the Government Victoria College, Palghat, and the Moyan Girls' High School.

The municipal affairs of Palghat have already been described at length in Chapter XIV. The municipality covers a very large area in proportion to its population; but the business part of the town lies mainly about three miles to the south of the Olavakkod railway station, and is in shape something like a figure of eight, the loops of which are formed by the 'big bazaar' or Chatturangapetta and Sultanpetta. At or near the neck stand the principal public buildings of the town—the railway station, the Roman Catholic Church, the Victoria College, the Divisional office, the Civil Courts, the hospital, the Municipal office and the English Church. The last four are grouped round a fine open maidan sloping gently up to a low hill which is crowned by a picturesque massive fort. Inside the fort, which is in excellent preservation, are now the offices of the Tahsildar, the district registrar, the district forest officer and the inspector of excise, the sub-jail and a store room which was evidently the old magazine. A new divisional

CHAP. XV. PALGHAT.

office was constructed in 1917 on a site adjoining the sub-collector's bungalow. The Victoria College, which was under the management of the municipality, was taken over by Government and raised to a first grade college in 1918. The District Board has also opened a girls' high school near the sub-collector's bungalow and a retired Civil Assistant Surgeon of Palghat (the late Diwan Bahadur Dr. Krishnan) opened a nursing home close to the municipal hospital which is a very popular institution.

The Basel Mission tile works, which employ 250 hands, and the grass mat industry of Palghat have already been referred to in Chapter VI. The town is still the centre of the tobacco trade of the district, but since the Shoranur-Ernakulam railway was completed its trade in this commodity has diminished.

Historically the interest of the town centres in the fort, which dates back, though not in its present form, to 1766 when Haidar built it to secure his communications between Coimbatore and the West Coast. Subsequently it was entirely re-built on approved European principles; and in 1784 'Palghatcherry' was described by Colonel Fullarton (perhaps because he captured it) as 'a place of the first strength in India'.[1] Square in shape with walls of immense thickness, and strong bastions at the four corners and in the centre, the fort must have seemed almost impregnable in those days. The deep moat, now choked with salt and lotus lilies, was crossed by a single draw-bridge, which was reached by a covered way through the glacis. The path from the draw-bridge to the first gate was screened by a curtain. Nevertheless Colonel Fullarton, thanks to the 'fortunate circumstances attending his attack', stormed the fort on November 15th, 1784, after a siege lasting only eleven days. 'The Honourable Captain (now Sir Thomas) Maitland being on duty in the trenches had taken advantage of a heavy fall of rain to drive the enemy from the covered way which was not palisaded, and pursuing the fugitives through the first and second gateways struck such a panic into the garrison as to cause its immediate surrender.'[2] For reasons, however, already recorded in Chapter II, the English soon evacuated, and their place was taken by the Zamorin's troops. Tipu's soldiers did not trouble to lay regular siege to the fort, but contented themselves with exposing daily the heads of many Brahmans in the sight of the defenders. 'Rather than witness such enormities', it is said, 'the Zamorin chose to abandon Palghatcherry.' In 1790 the fort, which then mounted 60 guns, was finally recaptured by the British.

---

1 *A View of the English Interests in India.* Madras, 1867, pp. 26–30.

2 Wilks' *History of Mysore*, II, 80.

Temples are numerous in Palghat, one being attached to each of the twenty Pattar *gramams* in the town. The largest and most important as well as the most richly endowed is the Kalpati temple dedicated to Siva, a low quadrangular building on the banks of the river of that name. The car festival held in November is the biggest in the taluk and collects about 15,000 people. An inscription on a stone to the east of the temple records that it was built in the Malayalam year 600 (1425 A.D.) by Itti Kombi Raja of Palghat who endowed it with land sowing over 4,000 paras of paddy.

Of the temples not belonging to the Pattars, the most interesting is a group of three to the north-east of the Olavakkod railway station situated near the family house of the Palghat Rajas, now a wretched hovel uninhabited by any member of the family. Of these two are dedicated to Siva, the other to Emur Bhagavathi, the family deity of the Palghat Rajas (Jala durga). The last, which was formerly in the middle of a tank, is said to have been built by a former Raja in consequence of a revelation made to a pious Nambudiri who was grieving over the ruins of a temple which had previously existed there. The hand of the goddess appeared in the middle of the tank at the spot which became the site of the present temple.

The *tarwad* of the Palghat Rajas has split into two very numerous branches; one of which still lives at Palghat and the other and more opulent near Vadakkancheri. The ceremony of enthronement of the Raja (usually owing to the numbers of the family a very old man by the time he attains the *stanam*) takes place on the site of an old temple in the compound of the old Sub-Judge's bungalow near the Divisional Officer's bungalow. On the fifteenth day after the cremation of the deceased Raja, his bones are collected and a sham fight takes place over them, a relic of the days when the Zamorin objected to the burial of a former Raja in the Naduvattam and a battle took place in earnest. The new Raja is then seated on a plank; rice is poured over his head by a Nambudiri priest who hands him a sword and calls upon him to protect the liberties of his subjects and their cows. The five senior members of the family are known as Rajas, the rest as Acchans. Formerly each of the five former used to spend the rest of the day meditating on a blanket in a pandal specially erected for the purpose.

Of the remaining temples in Palghat the only one which deserves mention is a small Jain temple near the Basel Mission tile works which ministers to the spiritual needs of some 15 Jains in Palghat and an equal number in Mundur six miles distant. It is a small rectangular building of stone with a stone roof recently restored by one of the Jains of Mundur. It contains stone images of the Achi-tirtankara and a flesh coloured image of Chandra Prabha (Vishnu). In the compound is a stone image of Ayyappan, also a circular stone well substantially built, one of several according to the Jains built by their community in this locality. The few remaining Jains say that their temple is about 200 years old. There was formerly another near at hand of which, however, only a stone or two is now visible. There were then two large settlements of Jains, one at Muttupattanam which dealt in pearls, and one at Machalapattanam (in which the present temple stands) which dealt in jewels. They were dispersed at Haidar's invasion, and the endowment of the temple was lost. There appears to be little difference between the creed of those who are left and that of their neighbours the Pattar Brahmans. The large Roman Catholic church was built by Dr. Barden, Bishop of Coimbatore in 1862. The first Catholics in Palghat accompanied the Engineers who built the fort. The congregations at Palghat and its out-stations now number about 3,500.

The Basel Mission at Palghat was an out-station of Cannanore from 1853 till 1859 when it became the head-quarters of a missionary. It has a high school and a primary school in Palghat and primary schools at the out-stations of Mankara, Panayur and Vadakkancheri Excluding the three out-stations the total number of the congregation is 478. A high school for boys has been opened by the District Board at Elappulli near Palghat.

Para : about eight miles east of Palghat. Police station and travellers' bungalow on a hill commanding a magnificent view of the Palghat gap and the plains of Coimbatore beyond. In the neighbouring Tenari amsam is a sacred spring formerly known as the Ramaswami Tirtam, but now called the Tenari Tirtam. It is said to have been created by Rama during his peregrinations towards Ceylon at the instance of his brother Lakshmana who, tired of carrying bows and arrows for both, thought of throwing them away but repented. He confessed his sin to his brother, and was ordered a bath in Ganges water by the Rishis. Rama shot an arrow into the ground, and water from the Ganges bubbled up. The water is said to remain at the same level all the year round, and the lower castes are not allowed to bathe therein. Three or four years ago a wall was built round it and a resting place for travellers constructed by a neighbouring landholder. To the east is a small tank now partially filled up, known as the Brahma *Kundam*, where Brahma made a pit in order to offer sacrifice. A bath in it was formerly considered essential before immersion in the Ganges water, but this is no longer considered necessary.

Pudunagaram : about six miles due south of Palghat. It is the most thickly populated village in the taluk excluding

Palghat, and contains the largest Muhammadan element, about one-third of the population being Ravuttans; police station; rest house; sub-registrar's office. There is a large Pattar temple dedicated to Siva; and also a mosque. The trade of the place consists of tobacco, salt, vegetables and timber (principally teak wood).

Vadakkancheri: in the extreme south-west of the taluk close to the Cochin frontier about nineteen miles from Palghat. Police station; travellers' bungalow; Roman Catholic church and Basel Mission chapel. It is surrounded by hills on the south and west, and in appearance approximates more to the amsams further west as it has fewer palmyras and more garden cultivation and cocoanut plantations than the ordinary amsam in the Palghat taluk. It has a considerable Muhammadan element and the mosque is well built with a very ornate pulpit. Coarse clothes are woven in this and the neighbouring amsams and there is some trade in timber. A temple in the vicinity known as Tiruvara has one of the common Brahma *Kundams* or tanks in which Brahma performed sacrifice, a handful of earth from the bed of which is considered essential to the performance of a *yagam* by the Nambudiri Brahmans.

PONNANI TALUK.

CHAP. XV. PONNANI.

PONNANI is the southernmost taluk of Malabar proper, and though separated from Palghat by Cochin State and the Nelliampatti hills, forms with that taluk one of the three main divisions of the district. The shape of the taluk is most extraordinary. Upwards of sixty miles in length and containing within its limits nearly two-fifths of the whole seaboard of Malabar, at its widest part it does not extend inland for more than eighteen miles, and in the south tails off into a narrow strip of sand thirty miles long, but rarely more than five broad. The Bharatha puzha or Ponnani river is the only river of the taluk; but an unbroken line of creeks, backwaters and canals connects the railway system at Tirur with Ponnani, Chavakkad and Chettuvayi and ultimately with British Cochin and Travancore. The South Indian Railway runs through the north of the taluk, and links up the two halves of the Palghat division.

Statistics on many points are given in the separate Appendix. Ponnani is one of the smaller taluks, but it contains no large expanse of unsurveyed hill and jungle; and, except Cochin, is at once the most closely cultivated and the most thickly populated tract in Malabar. In density of population, indeed, it yields in the mofussil only to the Coconada taluk of Godavari. As many as 40 per cent of the inhabitants are Mappillas, and hence the taluk is educationally backward. There are more Nambudiri *illams* than in any other part of Malabar, and most of the Syrian Christians of Malabar are to be found in this taluk. The prevailing soils are sandy, but red loam is found in the interior. Unoccupied dry lands are comparatively scarce, but Palghat and Kurumbranad are the only taluks with more wet lands and gardens respectively. A feature of the wet cultivation is the *punjakol* lagoon cultivation, described in Chapter IV, which is carried on in the Enamakkal and V yyattil lakes and in the many *kayal* lands of the taluk. The sandy soils of the coast are not eminently suited to paddy but in the amsams north of the railway and east of the Malappuram-Tirur road, Ponnani boasts of some of the finest wet lands in Malabar; and here too ginger, modan and other dry crops are raised. Along the seaboard and on the banks of the backwaters the cocoanut is the characteristic tree and thrives with wonderful luxuriance. Its produce in one form or another accounts for the greater part of the export trade of the taluk, and on the coast the bulk of the inhabitants devote themselves to its cultivation, to toddy drawing and to preparing coir yarn and copra. Another common tree on the coast is the cashewnut, introduced by Cabral in 1500 A.D. and still known as the foreign mango. There are no reserved forests in the taluk and big game is scarce; but muggers haunt the backwaters, and an occasional panther lurks in the remote and hilly amsams east of the Challisseri-Shoranur road. The Mappilla rebellion of 1921 extended to the northern part of the taluk. Since the suppression of the rebellion, elementary education has been made compulsory among the Mappillas of this region. Five high schools have also been opened in this taluk, three by the District Board and two by private agency.

Ponnani at one time comprised the three ancient nads of Vettatnad, Kuttanad and Chavakkad and a portion of Cheranad. The last lay along the Ernad and Walavanad frontier and belonged of course to the Zamorin. The Vettatnad Raja, a Kshatriya by caste, who was installed by Cheraman Perumal, ruled in the north-east of the taluk; and in course of time was forced, like his neighbours, to bow the neck to the Zamorin. The sole surviving member of the family died in 1793, and his estates lapsed as the first escheat to the British Government. Kuttanad comprised practically the whole interior of the taluk south of the Ponnani river and the coast line from Ponnani to Veliyangod backwater. Chavakkad extended along the seaboard from Veliyangod to the farthest limit of the taluk. In early times the former belonged to the Cochin Raja, but was wrested from him at an early date by the Zamorin. Chavakkad is said to have been bestowed originally upon the Kakkad Nambudiri, an ancestor of the Punnattur Nambidi family, in gratitude for his patriotic action in slaying at the expense of loss of caste Chola, the second of the Perumals. His descendants at first were the independent princes of Chavakkad; but, too weak long to resist the aggressions of their powerful neighbours the Cochin Raja and the Zamorin, bit by bit they were deprived of their territories. Finally in 1791 the Nambidi was reduced by the Zamorin to the humiliating position of his revenue collector. An allowance of Rs. 20,000 per annum, being estimated at 'about one-fifth of the revenue' of the district, is now paid to him from the Zamorin's *malikhana*.

Prior to the reorganisation of the taluks in 1861, Ponnani consisted of the three taluks of Vettatnad, Kuttanad and Chavakkad. In that year they were amalgamated and the new taluk thus formed was styled the Southern Division and placed under the charge of a general duty Deputy Collector with headquarters at Ponnani. In 1890 it was included in the Palghat Division. A Tahsildar assisted by the Deputy Tahsildar at Tirur and Chavakkad has immediate charge of the taluk. It is divided into 121 amsams and 460 desams.

An account of some of the places of interest in the taluk is appended.

Chavakkad (Chowghat): sixteen miles due south of Ponnani. The seat of the Deputy Tahsildar of Chavakkad; hospital; police station; sub-registrar's office; combined post and telegraph office; District Munsiff's court. The travellers' bungalow and Government distillery, where Messrs. Parry & Co. manufacture all the toddy arrack drunk in Malabar, are on the opposite and western side of the canal in Manatala desam. Attached to the mosque in Manatala is a *jaram* or mausoleum, where rest the remains of Haidros Kutti, some time Haidar Ali's commissioner in these parts, who disgusted with the master's oppression took up arms against him, and died fighting his troops. Another *jaram* near the Chavakkad mosque marks the scene of his death, and both are revered by the local Mappilla population. Half a mile from Kuttingal, as Chavakkad is more correctly called, on the Enamakkal road is a Romo Syrian Christian church, famous as one of the seven churches alleged to have been founded by S. Thomas on the West Coast, and the only one in Malabar. The congregation from the priest downwards implicitly believe in the tradition, and assert that the apostle preached in the church. The legend, as related in a folk song still sung by Syrian Christian women at their work, is briefly as follows. On his way from Arabia to Mylapore in the guise of an architect, S. Thomas landed at Chettuvayi and travelled through Palayur. He passed the temple of the Talliyil Devasvam and entered into conversation with some Nambudiri Brahmans who were bathing in the temple tank. The Brahmans told him of their gods, and boasted how by their powerful *mantrams* they could make them do their will. S. Thomas replied by challenging them to call upon their gods, if they were true gods, to make the water they were throwing over their bodies remain suspended in the air. The Brahmans laughed at the idea; but when at the apostle's bidding the water of the tank rose and stood up in the form of a column, they were instantly converted and baptized then and there. The rest of the Brahmans thus put to shame deserted Palayur in a body. The ruins of the temple are pointed out with great pride not fifty yards from the church, and close by is the tank, now choked with weeds. It is certain that the Brahmans were humiliated in some way in Palayur desam, for to this day they look upon it with horror as an accursed place. Nothing must pass the lips of a Nambudiri in the desam, and as a well known local proverb has it, 'his next bathing place is Viminad,' an adjoining hamlet. Close to the church is a garden known as Jews Hill, some time the site of a Jewish Synagogue. When the Jews left Palayur they are said to have bestowed a neighbouring piece of ground upon a Tiyan on condition that he would place every night a lighted lamp on the site of the Synagogue. The custom was kept up till within the last ten years; but the ignorant and ungrateful descendant of the original Tiyan affirms that he used to light the lamp to drive away a devil. A granite slab bearing a long inscription, in worn out *vattezhuttu* which was found on Jews Hill, is now preserved in the Deputy Tahsildar's office. About half a mile east of the church in Chavakkad desam are the foundations of a fort. When it was captured from the Mysoreans by Col. Hartley in 1790 it mounted 15 guns. The village contains a District Board high school and a taluk board office. •A sub-treasury has been opened in the deputy tahsildar's office.

Chettuvayi (Chetwai) : five miles due south of Kuttingal, the Chettuvayi river and connected backwaters find an outlet to the sea, and the island of Chettuvayi or Manapuram (sandy land), to give it its more ancient and appropriate name, begins. Chettuvayi has a travellers' bungalow, and is a sub-port with a trade valued at Rs. 18,000 annually; but its glory has departed. The Dutch were the first to settle here; but in 1691 A.D. in a fit of economy they retired leaving the English under the ægis of the Zamorin to make 'a good milch cow of it,' as Hamilton quaintly says, by trade in 'ophium.' In 1714 they returned only to be ousted by the Zamorin, and it was not till 1717 that they formally resumed possession. Their fort (traces of which are still visible) was named Fort William, and the death on February 2nd, 1729 of its first commandant, Heer Wilhelm Blasser, Captain Lieutenant, is commemorated by a tombstone now preserved in the Chavakkad Deputy Tahsildar's office. In 1740 the French made an abortive attempt to settle here, and for the next fifty years, till Colonel Hartley finally cleared Manapuram of the Mysoreans in 1790, the port and island were the scene of constant warfare at first between the Dutch and the Zamorin, subsequently between the Dutch and Haidar Ali and Tipu. There is excellent snipe shooting in the vicinity, and muggers abound.

Edappal : A Mappilla village five miles east of Ponnani on the Tritala road. Sub-Registrar's office and post office. Half way between Edappal and the rest house at Vattamkulam, and a quarter of a mile south of the road, is the Sukapuram temple in the desam of the same name, founded by Parasu Rama, and the chief temple of the Sukapuram *gramam*. This *gramam* is one of the sixty-four original *gramams*, and is perhaps identical with the Chovvur *gramam* mentioned in the later Syrian's deed. Every twelve years a ceremony is held in the temple at which the Akkittiripad, Somayajipads and Adittiripads, who in the interval have performed the necessary *yagams* (*adhanam*, *somayagam* and *agnichayanayagam* respectively) are registered as such in the temple books, and are admitted into the select company of their fellows.

Enamakkal : in Venkidanga amsam and desam, connected with Chavakkad by road and Chettuvayi by river ; the site of the dam of the same name which protects the cultivation in the bed of the Trichur lake (see p. 210) from the salt water of the Chettuvayi river An embankment of hewn stone about 200 feet long is said to have been constructed by the united efforts of the Zamorin and Raja of Cochin some time in the 18th century. In 1802 Assistant Collector Mr. Drummond, under an erroneous expectation of benefiting the neighbouring lands, caused the dam to be partially destroyed ; and owing to the influx of salt water a large area of land was thereby thrown out of cultivation. Various attempts were made especially in 1822 and 1842 to construct the dam on the original plan. A project for a new dam lower down the river at Chettuvayi was proposed, and between 1855 and 1858 the work was taken in hand. The idea was abandoned, however, after Rs. 35,000 had been wasted, and since then the original dam has been patched up at the joint expense of the British and Cochin Governments. There is an old Syrian Christian Church in this place and the neighbouring desam of Mullasseri has a sub-registrar's office.

Guruvayur : in the amsam and desam of this name two miles north-east of Kuttingal and connected therewith by road, is one of the most holy temples in all Malabar, consecrated to Krishna and founded, so the story goes and its name implies, by Guru the preceptor of the Devas and Vayi the god of the wind. The temple is square in shape, and is enclosed on the east and south by a lofty laterite wall, on the west by tiled buildings where pilgrims are lodged and fed. and on the north by the Brahman bathing sheds of the tank. The shrine, the *nalambalam* round it, and the *chuttambalam* in the outer courtyard, where the *puranas* are recited and explained, are all roofed with copper, and a conspicuous feature is a lofty bell-metal *dwajastambam* or flag-staff tipped with gold. A wide street, closed to all but the higher castes leads up through rows of Brahman shops to the eastern and main gateway of the temple which is surmounted by a two-storied *gopuram.* The porch and its pillars are elaborately carved with heads of elephants and bulls and other sculptures in bold relief, and its walls are covered with gaudy frescoes depicting the adventures of Arjuna, the Pandava. A Sanskrit inscription on one of the slabs of the *mantapam* recites that the temple within is heaven and that the gateway, the ladder thereto, was built by 'the lord of the seas and the hills' and had been trodden by the feet of many kings. The writing is in comparatively modern Malayalam characters, and by the lord of the seas and hills the Zamorin probably is meant. The *dipastamba* in front of the gateway has two inscriptions recording the fact that it was erected by a native of Travancore in M.E. 1011

(A.D. 1836), and the fragments of another inscription in an unknown tongue may be seen on a broken slab of granite now used as a door-step in the house of Mallisseri Nambudiri. Adjoining the temple on the north is the *arat kulam*, where the idol is bathed with much pomp in the month Kumbham. A writing on the granite door post of the western entrance which is also crowned with a *gopuram* relates that the gateway was erected by Panikka Vittil Ittiraricha Menon, kariyastan in M.E. 922 (1747 A.D.). Pilgrims, especially those subject to rheumatism, resort to the temple in large numbers, and make offerings of rude and flimsy representations in silver and gold of arms, legs, ears and other afflicted parts. Grouped round the temple are the houses of the two *uralars*. or trustees, the Zamorin and the Mallisseri Nambudiri, as well as those of the Eralpad Raja, the Punnattur Nambidi and many of the higher castes. The great Ekadasi festival is held annually about the second week of December and is very largely attended by pilgrims from all parts of Malabar. The place has been constituted a union owing to its increasing importance. Choultries have been constructed on the eastern side of the temple for accommodation of pilgrims.

Kodakkal: nearly three miles from Pudiyangadi on the Tritala road, derives its name from an umbrella stone (*kudakallu*) and its importance from a Basel Mission station. The umbrella stone, which is close to the road side, was explored by Mr. J. Babington in 1819[1] but without tangible result. The covering stone has now fallen from its pedestal. Fragments of a similar stone are shown in the vicinity. The Basel Mission station was founded in 1862, and the Christian population of Triprangod amsam, in which it is situated, now numbers close upon 1,000. Large tile works and a small weaving establishment give work to the congregation: their spiritual needs are provided for in a roomy church; their bodily ailments are attended to in a small dispensary; and their children are educated in a primary school. Close by is an orphanage with accommodation for 100 boys. The Mission has outstations at Ponnani, Tritala, Chalisseri, Chavakkad and Mullasseri. Near the orphanage are the Triprangod Siva temple and a large bathing tank with ruined laterite steps. A strong wall of laterite encloses the building, and in the north-western corner thereof the site of an old palace of the Vettatnad Raja is pointed out. The raised stone foundation of the shrine dedicated to Krishna bears a long inscription still unread. A sub-registrar's office has been opened here.

Mathilagam: in the extreme south of the taluk. Police station, travellers' bungalow and sub-registrar's office. The place derives its name from the old Trikkada *mathilagam* or

---

[1] Reprint Bombay Literary Society Transactions, 1877, p. 342.

temple founded by Parasu Rama for the use of the Trikkannapuram *gramam*, one of the original sixty-four. The temple is said to have been destroyed by the Dutch. Here too according to the Keralolpatti, the Brahmans built a royal palace for the king named Keralan, whom they introduced from Choyamandalam. The police station has been converted into an outpost.

Panniyur : six miles west of Tritala on the Pudiyangadi road. There is here an ancient temple, founded by Parasu Rama for the Panniyur *gramam* or 'pig village.' The Panniyur and Chovvur gramams, which are the only two mentioned in the Syrian's deed, must have been at one time important Brahman settlements in Malabar. But at a remote period the former transferred its allegiance to Vishnu, and one of its members (so tradition has it) having dishonoured Vishnu's idol, the *gramam* is now held in contempt by orthodox Nambudiris. The temple clearly dates from the time of its glory and must have been of immense size ; but now the outer wall has fallen down, the *chuttambalam* or temple court is in ruins and marks of neglect and decay are everywhere visible. The presiding deity is Varahamurti, the third incarnation of Vishnu, but there are many other shrines, including one dedicated to Siva. There is an inscription in an unknown language on a granite slab in front of one of the shrines.

Ponnani : twelve miles south-west of Tirur on the south bank of the Ponnani river at its entrance to the sea. The head-quarters of the taluk, one of the few towns of Malabar, and a minor port. Population 10,562. District Munsif's court ; sub-registrar's office ; police station ; port and sea customs office ; combined post and telegraph office ; travellers' bungalow ; civil hospital and attached thereto an "Edward Coronation" dispensary opened in 1903. The town lies low, and is a squalid collection of small huts and narrow bazaars, where grocers, grain and cloth merchants and native druggists drive a thriving trade. More than 95 per cent of the inhabitants are Mappillas, and, notoriously a dirty race, in Ponnani they live up to their reputation with startling success. Mosques meet one at every turn (there are more than forty in the town), and adjoining each is the inevitable overcrowded grave yard, and often a tank where the faithful bathe in oily water a bright olive green in colour. The drinking water is bad ; there is no sanitation ; and Ponnani is the permanent home of all diseases engendered by filth and impure water, and is periodically scourged by small-pox and cholera. It has recently been constituted a Union. A landlord of the place (Mr. Hariharamangalath Achutha Variar) has opened a high school here. A new rest-house has been constructed in Trikavu, close to the high school.

CHAP. XV. PONNANI.

Historically it is a town of some importance. In Portuguese times a Moorish stronghold, it was raided by Almeida in 1507 A.D., and burnt by Menezes in 1525 A.D. The Portuguese began to build a fortress here in 1585.[1] One of the earliest English factories was founded here some time in the middle of the 17th century. Haidar Ali fortified it soon after his invasion of Malabar, and in 1782 Tipu and M. Lally made a fierce attack on Col. McLeod's entrenchments at Ponnani, but were repulsed after a hard struggle leaving 200 dead upon the field. No trace of Haidar Ali's fort now remains.

As a port Ponnani is handicapped by its dangerous harbour. The bar shifts yearly, and is impeded by shoals and sandbanks. When at the first burst of the monsoon the river comes down in flood, the water is backed up by these sandbanks, and parts of the town are flooded till the rush of water has cleared away the shoals. Deep and dangerous currents are thus formed, and until lately Ponnani was in perpetual danger of erosion. Partly with the proceeds of a special volunatry cess paid by the merchants, a portion of the river bed near the taluk office has been recently reclaimed and protected by a strong sea wall at a cost of Rs. 12,000. On this reclamation the new sea customs office and salt godowns stand ; and for the use of the wharf and the maintenance of the groyne the Landing and Shipping Fees Act (Madras Act III of 1885) was introduced into Ponnani with effect from April 1st, 1905. The wharf was unaffected during the heavy rains of 1924.

Statistics of the trade of the port, which is considerable, and of the principal imports and exports are given in the separate Appendix. Nerarly 500 native vessels enter the port every year, but steamers call only occasionally. More than two lakhs of maunds of salt are landed annually at Ponnani. Under the conservator of Ponnani are the sub-ports of Kuttay, Veliyangod and Chettuvayi. Their trade is unimportant.

Ponnani is celebrated as the residence of the Makhdum Tangal, the spiritual head of all the Muhammadans of Malabar, except the Kondotti schismatics. The Jaratingal Tangal, whose picturesque *jaram* with its copper sheeted cupola is conspicuous on the road from the taluk office to the travellers' bungalow, and the Malappuram Pukkoya Tangal are descendants of the Prophet ; but in all matters of doctrine the authority of the Makhdum Tangal is supreme. He is descended in the female line from an Arab, named Zein-ud-din, who more than 600 years ago is said to have founded the famous Muhammadan college at Ponnani. The students or *mullas*, who come from all parts of Malabar and even from South Canara, are boarded out among the townspeople, and study the Koran in the Jamat mosque. Their course of study

[1] It was apparently never finished. See Linschoten's *Voyage*, II, 169.

is somewhat unsystematic, but those selected by the Tangal to read 'by the big lamp' in the mosque are thenceforth known as *Musaliyars*, and are fit and proper persons to give instruction in the Koran and the commentaries (*Kitab*). Near the Jamat mosque is the *jaram* or mausoleum of the Tangals, an object of profound veneration among the Mappillas.

In Ponnani there is also a well-known temple, called Trikkavu and near it a large tank. According to one account a Chetti and a Moslem overtaken by a violent storm at sea, vowed in their hour of peril that if their lives were spared they would found a temple and a mosque. They landed safely at Ponnani and fulfilled their vows by building, the one this temple and the other the Jamat mosque. Another story ascribes the temple to Parasu Rama. Parasu Rama is said to have made over the temple to the Sukapuram *gramam*, but the Brahmans, too poor to repair the damage done by the Mysoreans, handed it over in their turn to the Zamorin.

Pudiyangadi : or Vettatpudiyangadi three miles from Tirur on the Ponnani road. The head-quarters of a Deputy Tahsildar and Sub-Magistrate ; Police station ;sub-registrar's office. All these buildings and the Deputy Tahsildar's office stand on the site of the Vettat Rajas's palace, of which the bathing tank alone remains. A granite slab on one of the steps of the north door of the Jamat mosque bears an inscription, but the letters are now so worn as to be quite illegible. About a mile from Pudiyangadi on either side of the Ponnani road and about half a mile distant therefrom are famous temples dedicated respectively to Garudan (Vishnu's bird) and Hanuman. The former in Vellamasseri desam of Triprangod amsam is probably the only one of its kind in Malabar ; and, the kite being regarded as the especial enemy of snakes, is largely resorted to by the pious Hindu for protection from leprosy and other loathsome visitations of serpentine displeasure. Dedications to Hanuman are also rare in Malabar, and for that reason the temple in Triprangod desam and amsam is regarded with peculiar veneration. Locally Hanuman is regarded as the God of dyspeptics, and sweetmeats are the offerings in which he takes the greatest delight. The village lost its importance soon after the public offices were transferred to Tirur. A higher elementary school for girls has been opened here and is located in the buildings formerly used by the Deputy Tahsildar and Sub-Magistrate. The district board have also opened a high school here.

Punnatur : in Guruvayur amsam nearly a mile to the north of the 16th milestone on the Tritala road is the historic Punnattur *kotta*, the residence of the Punnattur Nambidi. The estate, which comprises more than 6,000 acres of land scattered over eighty desams of the taluk and also includes land in

Cochin State, has been for some years under the management of the Court of Wards, and the minor is now being educated at the Zamorin's College at Calicut. A debt of nearly two lakhs has in the last thirteen years been reduced to about Rs. 30,000, and a valuable property will be handed over to the Nambidi in 1911. About the *kotta* itself there is nothing remarkable. Erected between 1754 and 1758 A.D., it is a low tiled building enclosing an open courtyard, and with its spacious garden and adjoining temples and tanks is a typical residence of a Malayali nobleman. The *kalari* or fencing school near the main building is an interesting relic of the past, and more modern tastes are consulted by a *nadagasala* or hall for dramatic entertainments. The door which opens into the latter from the *nadu-mittam* or inner courtyard is adorned with the most intricate and skilful carvings. The estate record room contains a wealth of old documents written for the most part on cadjans in *kolezhuttu* characters. Among the most interesting are ancient treatises on carpentry and the cure of snake-bite, and various old *kanam* and other deeds dating from as far back as 1736 A.D. The last are now being arranged and translated into modern Malayalam. Kottapadi, as the eight desams round the *kotta* are called, is noted for the pigs bred and reared by the Syrian Christians. A Sub-registrar's office has been opened at Kottapady close to this village.

Tanur: in Rayirimangalam amsam and desam. An important fishing village, a sub-port and head-quarters of the fish-curing industry. Traveller's bungalow; sea customs office; police out-post; sub-registrar's office; post office; chattram and railway station. The fishermen who form the bulk of the population are, for the most part, New Islamites or Mukkuvan converts to Muhammadanism. There is one fine mosque in the village with a dome roofed with copper and several smaller ones. Tanur was one of the early settlements of the Portuguese, and after the peace of 1513 with the Zamorin a chapel was founded here. St. Francis Xavier visited the place in 1546 and converted the local prince. The Keraladesapuram and Trikkayikkad temples in the vicinity are both well-known. To the former is attached a Brahman feeding establishment which has many inam lands. The latter is a temple founded by Parasu Rama, and the adjoining *madam* is ascribed locally to Sri Sanakaracharya.

Tirunavayi: between Kodakkal and Edakkulam: celebrated for what is perhaps the most historic temple in all Malabar. It is a picturesque building in a clump of trees on the north bank of the Ponnani river, but presents no striking architectural features. The *srikovil* dedicated to Vishnu has been lately roofed with copper by the Kizhakke Kovilagam,

CHAP. XV. PONNANI.

and the venerable wall that surround it rises at the two gateways into massive gopurams roughly handled by the Mysoreans and never since repaired. The river which washes the temple steps is holy, and into its sacred waters are cast the ashes of many a departed Hindu. Of the origin of the temple nothing is known. Tirunavayi is frequently mentioned in the Keralolpatti, and is inseparably bound up with the traditionary history of Malabar. Keralan Perumal, by one account the eponymous hero of Kerala, was anointed in the royal hall at Vakkayur after one of the Mahamakham festivals. It was one of the three holy places [1] of the legendary Cheraman Perumal, and from its 'sandy island' he set out on his pilgrimage to Mecca. The management of the temple and of the Mahamakham festival, described below, thereupon devolved upon the Vellattiri or Walavanad Raja, till the Zamorin with the aid of the Moors established his supremacy in Malabar and usurped the privilege. The former Raja, however, had until quite lately a voice in the management of the temple, and was represented by one of the four Brahman Karalars; but now all rights over the temple are vested in the Zamorin, whose palace, where Brahmans are fed, is quite close to Tirunavayi.

Directly opposite the temple on the other side of the river are a temple dedicated to Brahma, who is rarely thus honoured in Malabar, and the Ottanmar *madam*, a college for Nambudiri Brahman boys. There are only two other such colleges on the West Coast, one at Trichur in the Cochin State and one of less note at Pulayi in Kurumbranad taluk. The *madam* was founded and endowed by the Zamorin, and is supervised by his family priest, the Tirunavayi Vadhyan Nambudiri. About one hundred Nambudiri youths from all parts of Malabar, as well as from Cochin and Travancore, are here taught to repeat, but not necessarily to understand, the Vedas. They come at the age of 12, and stay occasionally till they are 25 years old.

But Tirunavayi has another claim to fame. It is here that the Mahamakham festival, alleged to have been founded by Cheraman Perumal, and performed for the last time in 1743, was celebrated every twelfth year. The Rakshapurushan or protector of the festival was the acknowledged suzerain of Malabar and till the dignity had been assumed, the throne, so to speak, was vacant. Two months before the festival began, the Zamorin summoned all the Lokars or chieftains to be present; and those who acknowledged his supremacy sent flags in token of fealty. But the Walavanad Raja, whose right to hold the festival had been usurped by the Zamorin, sent *chavers*—men who had elected to die in a desparate endeavour to cut their way to the Zamorin through his guards.

---

[1] Trikkariyur, Tirunavayi and Valarpattanam Fort.

The origin of the festival is obscure. The facts that it took place every twelfth year and that during its continuance Malabar was in theory without a head, may connect it with the tradition that the early Perumals reigned only twelve years, and then abdicated. Mr. Logan considered it the occasion of a *kuttam* or general assembly of all Malabar when the people assembled in conclave re-adjusted their feudal ties. Hamilton describes the Mahamakham of 1695 and Mr. Jonathan Duncan some time Governor of Bombay has left an account of it in the first volume of the transactions of the Bombay Literary Society. But Mr. Logan's description of the festival of 1683 founded on records preserved in the archives of the Zamorin's palace cannot be improved upon.

'The western gateway (of the temple) faces a perfectly straight piece of road a little over half a mile in length stretching from the temple gateway westwards to the elevated ridge hemming in the paddy-fields on the west. This road is but little raised above the level of the paddy flat. Directly facing this straight piece of road as the elevated ridge is reached there are three or perhaps four terraces, the outlines of which may still be traced in the face of the precipitous bank.

'A little to one side of the upper terrace, are the ruins of a strongly built powder magazine, and on the flat ground above and on both sides of the avenue shading the public road at this place is ample space for the erection of temporary houses.

'In a neighbouring enclosure under cultivation is a disused well of fine proportions and of most solid construction.

'From the upper terrace alluded to, a commanding view is obtained facing eastwards of the level rice-plain at the foot, of the broad placid river on the right backed by low hills, of higher flat topped laterite plateaus on the left, their lower slopes bosomed in trees, and, in the far distance, of the great chain of western ghats with the Nilgiris in the extreme left front hardly distinguishable in their proverbial colour from the sky above them. It was on this spot, on a smooth plateau [1] of hard laterite rock, raised some 30 to 40 feet above the plain, that the Zamorin used several times in the course of the festival to take his stand with the sword of Cheraman Perumal, the last Emperor, in his hand.

'The sword is and has been for centuries slowly rusting away in its scabbard, but it is not alone on it that the Zamorin depends for his safety, for the plain below him is covered with the 30,000 Nayars of Ernad, the 10,000 of Polanad and numberless petty dependent chieftains, each counting his fighting men by the hundred or the thousand or by thousands. Away on the right across the river are the camps of the second prince of the Zamorin's family and of the dependent Punnattur Raja; the third, fourth, fifth and sixth princes' camps too are close at hand in the left front behind the temple, and behind the terrace itself is the Zamorin's camp.

---

[1] This spot was called Vakkayur and is now occupied by the tile works of the Basel Mission station at Kodakkal.

'The whole scene is being made gay with flags as an elephant is being formally caparisoned with a chain of solid gold with "one hundred and fourteen small links and one clasp making in all one hundred and fifteen"—as the record specifically testifies—and with golden bosses or other ornaments too numerous to be detailed. But this part of the ceremonies is not to be permitted to pass unchallenged, for it signifies in a formal manner the Zamorin's intention to assume the role of Rakshapurashan or protector of the festivities and of the people there assembled. On the instant, therefore, there is a stir among the crowd assembled near the western gate of the temple directly facing at half a mile distance the Zamorin's standing place on the upper terrace.

'From this spot, running due east in a perfectly straight line to the western gate of the temple, is the straight piece of road already described, but the road itself is clear and the armed crowd on the plain, it is seen, are hemmed in by barrel palisading running the full length of the road on both sides. Two spears'length apart the palisades are placed and the armed crowd on either hand, consisting on this occasion of the thirty thousand Ernad Nayars, it is seen, are all carrying spears. The spearmen may not enter that narrow lane, and by the mere weight of their bodies present an impossible obstacle to the free passage of the foemen now bent on cutting down the Zamorin in his pride of place.

'Amid much din and firing of guns the *Morituri*, the *Chaver* Nayars, the elect of four Nayar houses in Walavanad, step forth from the crowd and receive the last blessings and farewells of their friends and relatives. They have just partaken of the last meal they are to eat on earth at the house of the temple representative of their chieftain; they are decked with garlands and smeared with ashes. On this particular occasion it is one of the houses of Putumanna Panikkar who heads the fray. He is joined by seventeen of his friends—Nayar or Mappilla or other arms-bearing caste-men—for all who so wish may fall in with sword and target in support of the men who have elected to die.

'Armed with swords and targets alone they rush at the spearmen thronging the palisades; they wind and turn their bodies, as if they had no bones, casting them forward and backward, high and low, even to the astonishment of the beholders, as worthy Master Johnson describes them in a passage already quoted. But notwithstanding the suppleness of their limbs, notwithstanding their delight and skill and dexterity in weapons, the result is inevitable, and is prosaically recorded in the chronicle thus: "The number of *Chavers* who came and died in the early morning the next day after the elephant began to be adorned with gold trappings—being Putumanna Kantur Menon and followers—was 18."

'At various times during the ten last days of the festival the same thing is repeated. Whenever the Zamorin takes his stand on the terrace, assumes the sword and shakes it, men rush forth from the crowd on the west temple gate only to be impaled on the spears of the guardsmen who relieve each other from day to day.

'On the eleventh day, before the assembly broke up and after the final assault of the chavers had been delivered, the *Ernad*

Elankur Nambiyatiri Tirumulpad (the Zamorin next in succession) and the Tirumanisseri Nambudiri were conveyed in palanquins to the eastern end of the narrow palisaded lane and thence they advanced on foot, prostrating themselves four times towards the Zamorin, once at the eastern end of the lane, twice in the middle, and once at the foot of the terraces. And after due permission was obtained they took their places on the Zamorin's right hand.

'After this, so the chronicle runs, it was the duty of the men who have formed the body-guard to march up with music and pomp to make obeisance. On this occasion, however, a large portion of the body-guard seems to have been displeased, for they dispersed without fulfilling this duty and this story corroborates in a marked way the facts already set forth regarding the independence and important political influence possessed by the Nayars as a body.

'The Ernad Menon and the Calicut Talachanna Nayar with their followers were the only chiefs who made obeisance in due form to the Zamorin on this occasion, and possibly by the time of the next festival (1695 A.D.) of which Hamilton wrote, the dissatisfaction might have increased among his followers and the Zamorin's life even may have been endangered, as Hamilton alleges, probably through lack of men to guard him. Tradition asserts that the *Chavers* who managed on one occasion to get through the guards and up to the Zamorin's seat belonging to the family of the Chandrathil Panikkar.

'The chronicle does not mention the fact, but a current tradition states that the corpses of the slain were customarily kicked by elephants as far as the brink of the fine well, of which mention has been made, and into which they were tumbled promiscuously. The well itself is nearly filled up with debris of sorts, and a search made at the spot would probably elicit conclusive evidence of the truth of his tradition.'

Tirur : five miles south of Tanur ; situated on the railway and the centre of a network of communications. Roads from Ponnani, Malappuram and Tanur meet here, and here the railway comes into contact with the wonderful backwater system of South Malabar. Combined post and telegraph office ; travellers' bungalow ; District Munsiff's court. Near the village in the same amsam is the well-known Trikkandiyur temple dedicated to Siva, ascribed to Parasu Rama and, since the extinction of the Vettat family, managed by the Zamorin. Near the temple are two bathing tanks and a smaller temple dedicated to Vettakorumagan, where Brahmans are fed. This doubtless explains the large colony of Pattar Brahmans in the vicinity, Trikkandiyur is justly celebrated as the birth place of Tunjattu Ramanujan or as he is better known, Tunjattu Ezhuttacchan, 'the father of Malayalam literature,' an oil monger by caste but the reputed son of a Nambudiri father. The site of the house where he was born is known as 'Tunjan kadu' and is still pointed out locally. 'It is even now regarded as a sort of hallowed ground possessing an extraordinary power of inspiration, inasmuch as the children of the

CHAP. XV. PONNANI.

neighbourhood when they are initiated into the mysteries of letters are made to trace the letters of the alphabet in sand taken from the garden'.[1] The date of his birth is not known, but is supposed to have been some 300 years ago in the 8th century of the Kollam era. This village has been made the headquarters of a deputy tahsildar since 1910.

Triprayar : in Nattiga amsam nine miles south of Chettuvayi sub-registrar's office and a famous temple dedicated to Sri Rama and belonging to the Cochin State. An inscription on a granite slab in the *srikovil* has not yet been deciphered and there is another in old Malayalam at the eastern entrance. In Valappad, a Syrian Christian village in the neighbouring Pallipram amsam, there is a police station. There are a District Board high school, a combined post and telegraph office, a local fund dispensary and a rest-house.

Tritala : a small Mappilla bazaar on the same road seventeen miles east of Ponnani and five from Pattambi railway station. Travellers' bungalow : chattram : sub-registrar's office : post office. Four miles south of Tritala a few hundred yards east of the Chalisseri road are the ruined walls of a large fort encircled with a deep moat hewn out of laterite. Local traditions assign the fort to the Mysoreans. They probably did occupy the fort, but if it gave its name to the old *nad* of Kuttanad, it obviously dates from far more ancient times. Inside are carved stones, immense slabs of granite and the foundations of three or four buildings, relics of some ancient temple. At one time the fort was probably the palace of some forgotten Hindu Raja, and, judging by the number of wells in the vicinity, the centre of a large town. Three miles north-east of the ruins and by the side of the Shoranur road is a small domed building known as the Kattil *madam*, built of granite slabs in the form of a Hindu shrine. Its origin is unknown. One account ascribes its construction to *Bhuthas* or spirits ; another more prosaically states that it was intended as the second story of a temple in Nedirimangalam amsam in Walavanad taluk. On the road to Pudiyangadi is pointed out the tomb of the Parayan saint Pakkanar under a very handsome nuxvomica tree. Pakkanar was one of the twelve sons of the mythical Vararuchi, who, in fulfilment of a prophecy, married a pariah girl and by her became the father of twelve children. Eleven of these were abandoned on the roadside and adopted by different castes and all grew up persons of remarkable ability and talents. One son was the founder of the Vemancheri (Nambudiri) *illam* ; and a little further along this same road stands the famous temple at which he performed the

[1] Malabar Quarterly Review. Dec. 1902, p. 285.

horse *yagam* ninety-nine times, and only abstained from the hundredth at the earnest request of Indra, with whom he would have been entitled to change places if he had completed the cycle. On the opposite side of the river is a large rock with a rectangular white mark upon it, distinguishable at considerable distance. Here according to tradition, the Mezhattur Adisseri (as the performer of *yagams* was called) left his cloth to dry one day after bathing. The rock is known to this day as Velliyam Kallu. The stone for all the idols in Malabar temples comes from this (Mezhattur) amsam.

At Tritala is the tomb of Henrietta, wife of Captain James Falconer, H.M.'s 74th Highlanders, who died there on February 24th, 1855.

WALAVANAD TALUK.

CHAP. XV. WALAVANAD

WALAVANAD, which is included in the Malappuram division, resembles physically the other taluks of the district except that it has no seaboard and that in the east the palmyra supplants the cocoanut as the characteristic tree. Its innumerable hills, especially in the western half of the taluk, are perhaps higher than in other taluks and off many of them the laterite covering has worn away, and black masses of bare gneissic rock protrude between patches of stunted tree growth. Further east the country becomes more open and undulates more gently. The Western Ghats, here with an average elevation of not more than 4,000 feet, divide Walavanad on the north from the Silent valley; but at Arakurissi amsam the boundary of the taluk turns sharply northward as far as Anginda Peak, and, making a wide detour round the borders of the Nilgiri and Coimbatore districts as far south as Elival at the north-east extremity of Palghat, includes the mountain valley of Attapadi. In this valley are the highest peaks of Walavanad, Anginda (7,828 feet), Villakotta Hill (6,526 feet) and Periya Kunjara Hill (6,556 feet), and many others between 3,000 and 6,000 feet high, of which the most conspicuous are Chemmantatta mala and the sharp peak of holy Maliswaram standing up in the middle of the valley. Prominent in the plains are the detached hills of Pandalur on the Ernad frontier, Pranakod (1,792 feet) close to Angadippuram, and Anangà mala (1,298 feet) far away to the south near Ottapalam. The slopes of the ghat ranges are still clad with dense forest; but they belong mostly to private janmis, and are rapidly going the way of other forests similarly owned. The Government forests at Tiruvazhamkunnu and in the Attapadi valley have already been referred to in Chapter V. The rivers of the taluk are the Ponnani river, its southern boundary, the upper reaches of the Kadalundi river, and the Tudakal or Tutha river, the most important tributary of the first named, which rising in the Silent valley, drains the greater part of the taluk. The head waters of the Bhavani and its numerous feeder streams drain the Attapadi valley. Timber is floated down the first three rivers, and small boats ascend them for considerable distances except in the hot weather; but their importance as waterways is not great, even the timber traffic following the roads rather than the rivers. There are upwards of 230 miles of made road in the taluk, mostly in fair order, though the steepness of the hills renders them difficult to maintain in good condition,

The South Indian Railway runs along the bank of the Ponnani river. The new Shoranur-Nilambur Railway passes through this taluk with stations at Wallapuzha, Cherukara, Angadipuram and Melattur. Motor buses run throughout the taluk which is well served by communications. The Pulamanthole river has been bridged by the District Board.

In point of size Walavanad yields only to Ernad, but of its 882 square miles less than 600 have been surveyed and settled. The Attapadi valley covers about 200 square miles of the rest, and the balance is accounted for by the hills and jungles east of the Mannarakkad-Palghat road. The soils belong without exception to the red ferruginous series. Cocoa and areca trees are rare, except along the banks of the Tutha and Kadalundi rivers, but the palmyra is common in the south-east. The wet lands are excellent, and a feature of the taluk is the wet cultivation on terraces high up on the hill sides. Modan and gingelly are grown extensively on the unoccupied dry lands, which make up more than half the surveyed area, but neither ginger nor pepper is cultivated to any great extent. Timber is by far the chief industry. Iron smelting, once general in the taluk, is now extinct. Lemon-grass oil was formerly manufactured near Perintalmanna, but now, however, it is not manufactured and the cultivation of the grass has recently been taken up in earnest. In the neighbourhood of Ottapalam a new industry has recently arisen in the extraction of fibre from the stem of the palmyra leaf. Coffee estates were opened some years ago on the slopes of Pandalur hill, but they have long been abandoned. There is now rubber cultivation in the taluk in Kodur, Kuruvambalam, Pottasseri, Thenkara and Attapadi amsams. Chilli cultivation on dry lands is a special feature of this taluk.

Statistics on many points are given in the separate Appendix. About 30 per cent. of the population are Mappillas, a proportion exceeded only in Ernad and Ponnani; and for this reason the taluk lags behind all the others, Ernad and Wynaad excepted, in the matter of education. Part of the Mappilla zone lies in Walavanad.

The whole taluk must at one time have been under the sway of the Vellatiri, also called the Vallabha or Walavanad Raja, the successor of Cheraman Perumal in the management of the Tirunavayi Mahamakham festival. But gradually he was stripped of the greater part of his territory by his powerful neighbour, the Zamorin, who wrested from him in turn the nad of Nedunganad and part of Walavanad. At the time of the Mysorean invasion all that was left to him were Vellatiri comprising roughly the northern half of the taluk, which is divided by the Tutha river from Nedunganad, and the Attapadi valley. The seat of the Walavanad family is in Mankada amsam, and its *malikhana* amounts to Rs. 16,415–1–7.

For some time after the British occupation the Southern Superintendent of Malabar was stationed at Cherpalcheri, and a Collector was posted at Angadippuram. The two taluks of Nedunganad and Walavanad were subsequently formed; and in 1860, they were combined into the modern taluk, the Tahsildar of which is assisted by a Deputy Tahsildar at Ottapalam. For many years Walavanad was included in the Palghat division, but in 1890 it was transferred to the charge of the Special Assistant Collector of Malappuram. The taluk is divided into 317 desams and 118 amsams. There are at present 123 elementary schools run by the taluk board. It also maintains a hospital, three dispensaries and three rural dispensaries.

The following are some of the most important and interesting places :—

Angadippuram : a mile and a half from the taluk office. Celebrated for the Tirumanthan Kunnu temple. Various legends are current about the origin of the temple. According to one tradition a Cheruman woman, while cutting sticks in the forest which once covered the low hill on which the temple stands, sharpened her knife on a stone and drew blood therefrom. News of the portent was carried to the Nambudiris of the neighbourhood and one of their number Kathilamittat Nambudiri erected a pandal over the stone. These Nambudiris are still the hereditary priests of the temple, and their names commemorate the parts they played in its foundation. A copper-roofed shrine, built according to an inscription on one of the beams in 1732 A.D., has now taken the place of the pandal. Another legend is more ambitious, and relates that the temple was built over the very *lingam* that Parvati worshipped daily, presented by Siva to an aged Brahman in reward for his piety. The thicket round the temple is considered to be a part of the old forest and is holy ground, where no twig may be cut.

In the outrage of 1849 the temple was seized by the Mappilla fanatics, who were dislodged after a fierce resistance by detachments of H.M.'s 94th Regiment and the 39th N.I. Two privates, James Hart and William Blake, who were killed in the encounter, were buried near the travellers' bungalow at Perintalmanna. The tomb over their graves was erected by the Walavanad Raja 'as a small return for the service rendered him by their comrades of the Grenadiers.'

At the junction of the Kolattur and Malappuram roads near the temple are the remains of a fort said to have been built by Tipu. The site is cultivated every few years with modan and gingelly, and the mound which now marks the outline of the walls will soon have been levelled with the ground. Opposite the fort on the other side of the Kolattur road is a fine lingam, the sole surviving relic of the Talli temple of the Walavanad dynasty. A Nambudiri *gramam* once existed here; but its members mocked a weary Brahman pilgrim by telling him that he would get food and lodging for the night, if he climbed an adjacent hill and called out Kali. The Brahman climbed the hill and was fed by a beauteous damsel and awoke next morning at Trivandrum, his destination. But the gramam was destroyed that night.

The Puthanangadi mosque, one mile from Angadippuram on the Kolattur road, consists of two buildings side by side. The Walavanad Raja, it is said, alarmed at the continued aggressions of the Zamorin and seeing that he owed his power to the support of the Mappillas, determined to settle Mappillas in Vellatiri; and imported ten families from Tirurangadi. The first act of the Mappillas was to build a mosque, which the Karuvayur Mussad, the Raja's hereditary minister, vowed to pull down. One of the Mappillas, Murikkunnan Pokker, whose laterite tomb is conspicuous in the graveyard, vowed in his turn that, if the Mussad pulled down the mosque, he would cut off the Mussad's head and build two mosques instead of one. Both vows were accomplished.

Attapadi Valley: an extensive mountain valley above the crest of the ghat ranges, seamed with the countless feeder streams of the Bhavani river, and winding in and out of innumerable hills, the higher peaks clothed with splendid forest, the lower slopes stretches of open grass land and bamboo jungle. The Bhavani flows south from the Kundahs through a densely wooded gorge; a few miles above the village of Attapadi it turns north-east, and flows through the more open part of the valley, till it is joined by its tributary the Siruvani on the boundary of the Coimbatore district. At the head of the Siruvani, which rises in the southern corner of the valley, there is a fall down which the water drops sheer from a height of some two thousand feet into a deep pool below. The pool, which is called Muttukulam, is regarded with much superstitious awe, and there are many legends associated with the noises which are said to issue from it. The inhabitants consist of Tamil and Canarese Goundans, and of Badagas, Irulas, Kurumbas and other hill tribes. Villages in the strict sense of the term are unknown. Such dwellings as there are mostly, if not entirely, of a temporary nature shifting yearly with their patches of cultivation. These collections of huts are known as *urs*, and are 105 in number. Paddy is grown in the swamps and valley bottoms; ragi, samai, dholl, modan, plantains, chillies, saffron and ginger on the dry lands. There is no regular land assessment, but the *adhigari* collects about Rs. 1,100 yearly from the *muppans* or headmen of the various villages on account of Government. There is neither police station nor post office; but a full complement of village officers has recently been appointed, and beat constables periodically enter the valley and get the signature of the *adhigari* in their beat books. Timber is the most important product. Twenty-one hills and part of another belong to Government, and the rest are in dispute between three powerful janmis, the Mannarakkad Muppil Nayar, Palat Krishna Menon and the Eralpad Raja. The dispute led to frequent disturbances culminating in actual bloodshed in 1901, and has recently been provisionally settled by the Divisional Officer under section 145 of the Criminal Procedure Code; 44 hills and parts of five others have been awarded to the Mannarakkad Nayar, 16 hills and parts of six others to the Eralpad Raja, 10 hills to Palat Krishna Menon and two to another janmi. The upper slopes of the valley are full of big game, including elephants and ibex; but they are difficult of access, and the valley is very feverish. It was seldom visited by Europeans till recent years. There is one coffee estate in the valley; and a company has now been formed to open up a plantation of rubber. The Government are acquiring a large part of the private forests in order to reserve them and protect the head-waters of the Bhavani; and they are taking special measures to prevent the wanton destruction of fish that goes on in them.

Cherukod: on Ramagiri hill in this desam, seven miles south-west of Cherpalcheri on the Pattambi road, are the remains, consisting of walls, wells and bastions, of what must have been one of the strongest Mysorean forts in Malabar. In 1780 after the defeat of Makhdum Ali at Tirurangadi the Mysoreans fell back on this fort; and, after dislodging them, Col. Humberstone made it his base during his advance on Palghat.

Cherpalcheri: nine miles from Perintalmanna on the high road to Palghat. It was at one time the seat of the Southern Superintendent of Malabar, and subsequently of the Tahsildar of Nedunganad, and finally of the Deputy Tahsildar of Walavanad. The last named officer has now been removed to Ottapalam and Cherpalcheri has in consequence lost much of its former importance. Sub-registrar's office: police station: post office: travellers' bungalow: choultry. The troops which at one time were stationed here to over-awe the jungle Mappillas in the north of the taluk were probably cantoned on what is still known as the Cherpalcheri Fort Hill. Sepulchral urns have been discovered in the nighbouring desam of Nallayi. On the western border of Aliparamba desam just north of the Tutha river between Cherpalcheri and Perintalmanna are traces of the walls of a fort, enclosing a deep well and a Bhagavathi temple. The fort is said to have belonged to the Kuthiravattat Nayar, once one of the Zamorin's most powerful feudatories and still a great landholder. Some old sepulchral urns have been found there. There are high schools for boys and girls in this place; also a rural dispensary.

Karimpuzha : eight miles from Mannarakkad on the cart-track which links the two main roads from Perintalmanna to Mannarakkad and Palghat respectively. The seat of the Eralpad or Second Raja of the Zamorin's family. Attached to the palace is a well-known temple dedicated to Sri Raman. The cloth woven by Tamil Chettis in this desam has some local celebrity. Some *nannangadis* have been found near Karimpuzha. The police outpost at Perumangode about a mile away has since been reopened.

Kavalappara : equidistant from Shoranur and Vaniamkulam near the Pattambi road. It is the residence of the Kavalappara Nayar. The present holder of the estates Kochunni Nayar assumed charge in 1925 on the death of his elder brother during whose minority the estates were managed by the Court of Wards and nursed back into solvency. The family is said to have acquired its estates from Cheraman Perumal on his departure for Mecca. When the Nayar arrived, so the story goes, Cheraman Perumal had distributed all his territory except a block of twelve square miles in Nedunganad, which no one wanted because it was reported to be all rock. The Nayar accepted the tract, and finding it not to be all rock, gave it the name 'Kavalappara'. 'false rock.' The estates, which are extensive, lie partly in Palghat taluk, partly in Walavanad taluk in the amsams round about the house, and partly in Cochin State. In the Walavanad portion Mappillas are not allowed to settle, but there are no less than forty Nambudiri *illams* within a radius of two miles of the house. An experimental farm has been established at Kavalappara, in which attention is being directed both to the improvement of the present methods of cultivating the staple crops, and to the possibility of introducing new crops, such as groundnut, into the district. The *malikhana* of the Valiya Nayar is Rs. 4,567–10–3.

Kolattur : six miles from Perintalmanna ; the scene of the memorable outrages of 1851 and 1873. In the former the Kolattur Variar was dragged out of his fine house near the police station and hacked to pieces, and a detachment of the 94th regiment was driven back in disorder. After the latter the amsams implicated were fined Rs. 42,000, and the money was utilized in opening up the country and in building the police station which has accommodation for travellers. Peafowl, pig and an occasional panther are to be shot in the vicinity, and in the neighbouring amsam of Panga are three rock-cut caves and a *vatezhuttu* inscription of M.E. 934 (1759 A.D.) carved upon a rock. Palur Kotta in Puzhakattiri am am is an old fort of which nothing is known. The estate of the Kolattur Variyar is now managed by an officer taken from the Government service. A new travellers' bungalow has been constructed here.

Mannarakkad (Mannarghat): nineteen miles due east of Perintalmanna; an important village four miles from the foot of the Attapadi ghat with which it is connected by a very bad cart track. This place is the headquarters of the timber trade in Walavanad, the timber from the Attapadi valley and neighbouring hills being exported hence, chiefly by road to Olavakkod. The Mannarakkad Muppil Nayar, the most powerful janmi of these parts and the owner of the greater part of the surrounding forests, was a feudatory of the Walavanad Raja before the Mysorean invasion, bound to supply 2,000 Nayars at need, and the guardian of the Attapadi ghat. Numbers of Chettis live at Mannarakkad and have made large fortunes by buying grain from the cultivators of the Attapadi valley at about one-third of its market price. Sub-registrar's office; police station; post office; travellers' bungalow. At Nattukkal, half way between Mannarakkad and Perintalmanna, where there is a police station and a rest-house, several *nannangadi kudams* or sepulchral urns have been dug up. They have also been found at Topanad on the road to Palghat, at the foot of the Kalladikod hill, and in Thenkara amsam on the way to Attapadi. In Pallikurup desam of Tacchampara amsam, three miles south-east of Mannarakkad, is the temple where the fanatics of 1894 were shot down. This place was one of the chief centres of the Mappilla rebellion of 1921. A union panchayat and a dispensary have been opened here and elementary education has been declared compulsory.

Mankada Pallipuram: In this amsam about a mile from the Anakayam ferry on the Manjeri road is the only hat-stone known to exist in the taluk.

Ottapalam: four miles east of Vaniamkulam on the old trunk road. The headquarters of the Deputy Tahsildar; District Munsif's court; sub-registrar's office; police station; post office; high school; travellers' bungalow; railway station. The Trikkangod temple in the desam of that name near Ottapalam is one of the most famous temples in the taluk, and is almost unique in that the Srikovil or holy of holies is sacred both to Siva and Vishnu. An inscription in an unknown tongue is engraved on a granite slab in the building. The temple is much resorted to by women afflicted with fits or possessed of devils. A subordinate judge's court has been opened here.

Pattambi: fourteen miles from Perintalmanna and the railway station for that place. Travellers' bungalow; police station; post office; two choultries. In the adjoining desam of Perumutiyur is a Sanskrit printing press owned by Punasseri Nambi, one of the richest janmis of the locality. There was a munsif's court in the station and a Sanskrit College, but the former was abolished in 1932.

Perintalmanna : or, as it is more commonly but incorrectly called, Angadippuram ; the taluk headquarters ; District Munsif's court ; sub-registrar's office ; police station ; post and telegraph office ; travellers' bungalow. The village is inhabited chiefly by Mappillas ; but contains a considerable number of Parayans and other East Coast castes, probably dating from the time when troops were quartered here. The District Munsif's court is on the site of the cantonment. From Perintalmanna roads radiate to Kolattur, Manjeri and Malappuram, to Pandikkad and Melattur, Mannarakkad, Cherpalcheri and Pattambi. There is a high school here. The Government treasury was looted in this place early in the outbreak of the Mappilla rebellion of 1921.

Shoranur : nine miles east of Pattambi. Important for its railway station, which is the junction for the Cochin State Railway. Police station and post office. Across the Ponnani river, which here is spanned by a fine bridge, are a palace of the Cochin Raja and a travellers' bungalow.

Vaniamkulam : twelve miles east of Pattambi on the old trunk road from the borders of Coimbatore to Ponnani. Celebrated for the biggest weekly market and cattle fair in Malabar. The market, which belongs to the Kavalappara estate, is leased annually for upwards of Rs. 4,000. Travellers' bungalow ; post office ; Basel Mission out-station and hospital. Sepulchral urns have been dug up on the travellers' bungalow hill, and in the adjacent Panayur desam is a rock-cut cave. Ananga Mala (298 feet) three miles to the northward, is famed for the medicinal herbs and simples which grow on its slopes, and for a ruined temple and tank constructed near a cave where a hermit once lived. The origin of the name is variously explained ; but the legend current locally is that it means the 'immovable hill' and was so called because Hanuman when with his army of monkeys he tried to bridge the straits between Rameswaram and the mainland, strove in vain to uproot it. There is now a travellers' bungalow here.

WYNAAD TALUK.

CHAP. XV. WYNAAD.

THE Wynaad taluk is a continuation of the great Mysore plateau, and lies above the crest of the Westetn Ghats. The country is rugged and picturesque, especially in the south and west where range after range of hills, some with peaks soaring upwards of 7,000 feet into the air, give it a wild and mountainnous appearance. In the centre of the taluk the hills are lower and their slopes are covered with grass, lantana and low bamboo jungle; but in the east the country is flatter and more open. In the north the hills become higher again and their sides are clad with ever-green shola forest. The average height of the plateau is about 3,000 feet above sea level, but many of the mountain peaks attain a much greater height. Vellari Mala (7,364 feet) takes pride of place (the Camel's Hump is just outside the taluk), but Elambileri (6,806) and Balasore or Banasura (6,762) where a legendary giant is said to have built a fort, run it close. The Kabbani river with its many tributaries, itself a tributary of the Cauvery, drains practically the whole country side. The Chaliyar river rising in the south-east corner of the taluk, after leaping down from the crest of the ghat in a magnificent cataract near the Choladi pass, joins the Ponpuzha and the Karimpuzha rivers in the heart of the Nilambur teak plantations. The plateau must at no very remote period have been covered with dense forest, but in the centre of the taluk few trees of value now remain.[1] There is excellent big game shooting in the taluk. Sambhur are plentiful in the hills above Lakkidi, Pukkot and Vayittiri; in the hot weather bison roam on the higher slopes of the ghats, and wild elephants are very numerous in Begur and Chedleth reserves. Roads are numerous in the taluk, the most important being the road from Calicut to Mysore *via* the Tamarasseri ghat, Vayittiri and Sultan's Battery. From this road an important highway branches off at Chundale just beyond Vayittiri to Gudalur and Ootacamund. In the north of the taluk the main road passes through Manantoddy from the Periya ghat to Gundalpet in Mysore. The Tamarasseri and Periya ghats are the only two passes into the Wynaad which are fit for cart traffic. The Kuttiyadi ghat is much used by coolies and pack bullocks; but the other passes, the Ellacheram and Tariyot passes descending on Kuttiyadi, the Smugglers' pass from Dindimal to Manattana, and the Choladi pass into the Nilambur valley are mere foot-paths.

[1] *Vide* Chapter V for a description of the forests of the Wynaad.

Statistics on many points of interest will be found in the separate appendix. The taluk is the most sparsely populated of any in the district, and the population since 1871 has steadily declined. One result of this is that owing to the paucity of their numbers the cultivators have never been so oppressed by their janmis as in the low country. Mappillas are not numerous, but the majority of the few Jains in Malabar live in the Wynaad. The taluk is the home of many of the supposed aborigines of Malabar, such as the Kurumbans and Paniyans, who were, perhaps, driven up from below into its mountain fastnesses by the advance of more civilized tribes. Clearer traces are found here than in the rest of Malabar of an early and rude form of civilization. Animistic beliefs and devil worship are common, and the temples are often mere platforms of stones piled up under the shadow of some lofty tree where bloody sacrifices and weird rites are performed. Every year in the cold weather thousands of coolies, some from the coast, but the majority from Salem and Coimbatore, flock into the taluk for work on the plantations during the picking season.

The soils of the taluk have been described in Chapter I. Paddy is the chief wet crop and ragi the only dry crop of importance. Cardamoms of excellent quality grow in great profusion on the ghat slopes between the Periya and Kuttiyadi passes, but cocoanuts and arecanuts are conspicuous by their absence. Iron ore is common in the taluk but is not worked, and reference has already been made in Chapter I to the extinct gold mining industry. The pioneers of the planting industry in Wynaad made their appearance during the second quarter of last century, prior to which the taluk was practically unknown territory and covered with heavy jungle. The first crop planted was coffee and in some 50 years this industry had reached its height in Wynaad, when leaf disease began to make its appearance and by the end of the century the acreage left unharmed was almost negligible. Various efforts were made to substitute other crops including cinchona and pepper but the former was soon killed by overproduction and consequent low prices while pepper suffered considerably from diseases. The real remedy was found in tea which had been tried on a small scale some time previously. Tea has now entirely replaced coffee and with improved methods of cultivation and the use of scientific research there seems little fear of serious loss from disease. Tea, however, has had its vicissitudes in the form of low prices due to overproduction and at the present time (1932) the industry is passing through a period of deep depression which has now lasted over two years, the end not yet being in sight. Given a return of normal prices, however, the tea industry will continue to be the main source of prosperity in Wynaad.

CHAP. XV. WYNAAD.

Much has been done by the planters to improve the health conditions in Wynaad by anti-malarial measures and the district is now recognized to be much healthier than it was 20 or 30 years ago. Over 12,000 acres of tea are in cultivation in the district giving steady employment to some 15,000 labourers (probably nearer 20,000 under normal conditions) who are well cared for being housed in substantially built quarters and provided with skilled medical attention.

The early history of the Wynaad is involved in obscurity. Tradition points to a time when a line of Vedar kings held sway, and the story goes on to record that an ill-judged capture of a Kshatriya pilgrim to the famous Tirunelli shrine led to the invasion and subjugation of the country by the Kshatriya princes of Kottayam and Kurumbranad. The taluk was parcelled out among their followers, the Padri rock half way between Sultan's Battery and Minangadi being the reputed boundary mark between the respective spheres of influence of the two princes. An interesting legend current locally relates how some Nayars of Travancore who helped to conquer the country declined to settle in the taluk, and returned home only to find themselves refused re-admission to caste and household. They returned to the Wynaad and finding all the eligible tracts already occupied retreated to the jungles on the ghat slopes in the west of the taluk. The Kuricchiyans are said to be their descendants and several points of similarity between the social and religious customs of the two castes are quoted to bear out the story.[1] The influence of the Kottayam family was supreme when the Wynaad finally passed into British hands after the fall of Seringapatam in 1798, and the fierce rebellions of the Pychy Raja of the western branch of the family, which disturbed the peace of the taluk till the end of 1805, have already been described in Chapter II. In 1812, there was a small rebellion of the Kuricchiyans and Kurumbans. The three amsams of Munanad, Cherankod and Nambalakod were transferred to the Nilgiri district in 1877, and the remaining thirteen amsams were split up after the settlement into twenty-three. Till 1859, the taluk was in charge of the Sub-Collector of Tellicherry. In that year a Deputy Collector was stationed at Manantoddy. He is assisted by a Tahsildar at Manantoddy and a Deputy Tahsildar at Vayittiri.

A short account of places of interest or importance in the taluk is appended :—

Chandanatod : nineteen miles from Manantoddy at the top of Periya ghat ; travellers' bungalow and chattram. Chandanatod was once a planting centre, and a small planters' club was established just behind the bungalow. From Periya

[1] Malabar Quarterly Review. 11,274-291, & 359-373.

Peak, 3,663 feet, quite close to the bungalow, a glorious view of the plains and the sea coast can be obtained. A road passing through the Periya reserves near the forest bungalow at Makki connects Korot and Chandanatod. From about three miles on the road to Manantoddy from this village there have sprung up several tea estates on either side of the local fund road. The last estate is about three miles from Manantoddy.

Kalpatta : six miles from Vayittiri on the Mysore road. Rest house ; chattram ; post office.

Korot : fifteen miles from Manantoddy at the head of the Kuttiyadi pass and near the foot of Balasore hill, contains several well-built Mappilla houses, two mosques, a travellers' bungalow and a police outpost.

Lakkidi : thirty-six miles from Calicut at the head of the Tamarasseri ghat ; excellent D.P.W. rest-house and a chattram for native travellers. There is no bazaar, and supplies have to be procured from Vayittiri. The place derives its name from a fort or wooden stockade built here in 1800 by Colonel Stevenson during the military operations against the Pychy Raja. The fort was situated on an eminence adjoining the road opposite the travellers' bungalow.

Manantoddy : fifty miles from Tellicherry and ten from the Mysore frontier ; the headquarters of the taluk ; 2,558 feet above the sea. The District Forest Officer of North Malabar, the Deputy Collector and Tahsildar of the Wynaad, a Sheristadar-Magistrate, and a sub-registrar are stationed here. Police station ; hospital ; combined post and telegraph office ; travellers' bungalow ; D.P.W. shed ; chattram ; Roman Catholic church and cemetery, and a small Protestant church. A well-kept European cemetery is pleasantly situated on the Tellicherry road about a mile from the travellers' bungalow. The Pychy Raja was buried at Manantoddy in 1805, but the site of the grave has been forgotten. There are a few old laterite graves, probably those of officers stationed at Manantoddy in the early part of the last century, hidden in the lantana on the eastern slope of the travellers' bungalow hill.

This place ceased to be the head-quarters of a Deputy Collector from 1924, and the taluk has been placed under the Revenue Divisional Officer of Tellicherry. The old laterite graves on the eastern slope of the travellers' bungalow hill have all disappeared now and the site is partly occupied by a reading room and partly by a secondary school.

For the first half of the nineteenth century Manantoddy was a military station, and it was on this hill that the troops were cantoned. The travellers' bungalow was the officers' mess, and the barracks are utilized for the school. In the Kuricchiyan rebellion of 1812 the station was besieged by the insurgents.

The first regular coffee estate opened in the Wynaad is said to have been established at Manantoddy sometime between 1830 and 1840. The place subsequently became a planting centre, and a club was started in which some of the old residents, remember as many as seventy sitting down to dinner. But leaf disease ruined the industry; the estates in the vicinity can now be numbered on the fingers of one hand; and the club no longer exists.

About two miles from Manantoddy on the banks of the river is the Vallurkavu, the famous Fish Pagoda, dedicated to Durga and supposed to have been one of the four shrines erected to protect the Tirunelli temple. The Carnatic carp and other fish in the pool of the river adjoining the temple are sacred, and to feed them is a method of acquiring merit. This fact points to a Dravidian origin of the temple. Possibly it was at one time a temple of the Valluvars, a servile caste of labourers and fishermen. Thousands of pilgrims come for the temple festival which is held in March.

Six miles due east of Manantoddy is the small village of Kattikulam with a rest-house and a post office. At Bavali on the frontier is a chattram. A road, which branches off in a northerly direction at Kattikulam, after passing for nine miles almost continuously through reserved forests, enters Coorg just beyond Tolpatti, where a small weekly market is held. At Begur, three miles from Kattikulam, are the ranger's quarters and the kraals, where the many wild elephants captured in pits in the Government forests are confined. About a mile from Begur a forest bungalow is beautifully situated on Alattur hill.

Five miles from Kattikulam, a cart-track turns off from the Coorg road in a north-westerly direction and leads through the wildest forest, broken only by occasional paddy flats, to a forest bungalow on the top of Brahmagiri hill.

Meppadi : ten miles east of Vayittiri on the Cherambadi road is another planting centre and contains a club, rest-house, police station, post office and Protestant and Roman Catholic churches. It is now the headquarters of the Planters' Association.

Panamaram : eleven miles from Manantoddy on the Vayittiri road. It was formerly a strong military post and traces of the cantonment can still be seen on the hill beyond the police station. This was the Panamarattu Kotta or the

'Palmyra tree fort.' A detachment of 70 men of the first battalion of the 4th Bombay Infantry under Captain Dickenson was massacred here on October 11th, 1802, by a band of Kuricchiyans under Edachenna Kunjan, one of the proscribed adherents of the Pychy Raja, and 112 muskets, 6 boxes of ammunition and Rs. 6,000 were captured by the rebels. The place was re-occupied in 1804, and it was a force of 200 men from Panamaram that under the command of Mr. Baber and Lieutenant-Colonel Hill shot the Raja in 1805 and put an end to the rebellion. There is a post office, and three miles beyond Panamaram at Kumblakad are a police outpost and a higher elementary school.

Pukkot : half way between Lakkidi and Vayittiri on a loop road. Sambhur are plentiful on the hills north of Pukkot and Lakkidi. There is a lake here, the only one in the Wynaad.

Sultan's Battery : twenty-one miles from Vayittiri and thirteen from the Mysore frontier ; locally known as Ganapathivattam, 'the circle or range of the God Ganapathi,' but called Sultan's Battery from the fact that Tipu Sultan had a fort here on the site, it is said, of the present police station. Travellers' bungalow ; chattram ; police station ; post office. The Ganapathi temple, which belongs to the Kottayam Raja, was destroyed by Tipu, and the idol and a few monolithic stones are all that are left. An inscribed stone, formerly part of the *Dipastamba* or lamp stand, is kept in the *pujari's* house. In the Mariyamman temple, which is also in a ruinous condition, there is a stone with an inscription in old Tamil on both sides. The most interesting, however, of the temples at Sultan's Battery is the Vasti temple, an old Jain temple. Hidden in a lantana thicket a few yards south of the 60th milestone on the Mysore road, its very existence has been forgotten for many years. The upper part has fallen down, and the rest is fast falling into ruin, several trees having forced their way between the great granite slabs of which it is built. There are no Jains now in Sultan's Battery, but there are small colonies of them at Manantoddy, Kalpatta and other places. Sultan's Battery was a military post in the time of the Pychy rebellion, and the troops are said to have been quartered on the Kotta Kunnu or 'Fort hill' near the travellers' bungalow. On another hill called Nalapad Chala Kunnu is another inscribed stone. Four miles south-west of Sultan's Battery on the western slopes of Edakal Mala near the crest is an interesting natural cave or fissure in the rock. The walls of the cave are covered with rude, fanciful drawings, and bear five short inscriptions. Four of them are in archaic characters and one of them is the

CHAP. XV.
WYNAAD.

'writing of the propagator of the family of the householder Sri Vishnu Varman,' or as suggested by Dr. Hultzch "the writing of the glorious Vishnu-Varma, the propagator of the Kutumbiya family" who is the earliest king known by epigraphic research in Malabar.[1] On the peak is the shrine of Mudiampilli, the Goddess of the Wynaad Chetti caste and at the foot of the hill are other small temples. West of the hill are numerous stone circles suspected to contain human remains.

Talapoya : about five miles from Manantoddy, has now risen to importance. It is the headquarters of a group of estates and there is a Planters' Sunday Club and a post office here.

Tirunelli : at the eighth milestone on this road picturesquely placed on a small eminence right under the shadow of Brahmagiri is the famous Tirunelli temple, dedicated by Brahma to Vishnu, and the resort of many a pious Hindu under promise of remission of sins and eternal bliss. The temple, up to which a fine flight of granite steps leads, is a small, square, granite building with many pillared mantapams and a holy of holies roofed with copper and surmounted with a golden spire. At the back of the temple a stream of clear water comes tumbling down from the hill-side in a succession of pools and cataracts, and many of these pools are holy. Their names are Papanasini, the extinguisher of sins, Panchatirtam, Irnamochinitirtam, Gunnikatirtam, Satavinnu, Sahasravinnu and Varaham. The water of the last is brought for temple use in a stone aqueduct half a mile long. The water of Papanasini falls on a rock called Pinnapara where offerings to the spirits of the departed are made. This rock is a bone of an Asuran or demon, named Palana-bhedi, slain by Vishnu, whose body was at his own prayer converted into a rock extending from Tirunelli to Gaya, Tirunelli representing his foot, Godavari his middle, Gaya the head. Just by Gunnikatirtam is a small cave temple dedicated to Siva. The mouth of the temple is closed by a small wooden door with beautifully carved door posts and lintel. This cave temple almost points to a Buddhist or Jain origin for the temple. The two *uralars*, both of the Mussad caste, the Embrandiri priest and a few Nayars and temple servants live round the temple. Preserved in the temple are two old copper plate grants, dating probably from the reign of Bhaskara Ravi Varma who bestowed their privileges upon the Jews of Cochin.[2] The four guardian shrines of Tirunelli are the Vallurkavu in the east, Trichaleri and Tricharakunnu temples on the south

---

[1] The cave has been fully described in Indian Antiquary, XXX, 409.

[2] See p. 33.

and west and a temple dedicated to Subrahmanyan in the Brahmagiri range on the north. On the sides of Brahmagiri are several interesting caves.

Vayitiri : thirty-nine miles from Calicut, a centre of the planting industry, and the headquarters of the Deputy Tahsildar of the Wynaad. Police station; sub-registrar's office; hospital; combined post and telegraph office; small rest-house; chattram; Protestant and Roman Catholic churches. Half way between Vayittiri and Pukkot is a District Munsif's court.

CHAPTER XVI.

THE LACCADIVE ISLANDS AND MINICOY.

The Laccadive Islands—Minicoy—Physical aspects—Flora—Fauna—The people of the Laccadives—People of Minicoy—Industries and Manufactures—Religion—Houses—Boats—Health and Sanitation—Climate and rainfall—History—Fiscal Administration—" Pandaram Lands "—General and Judicial Administration.

CHAP. XVI. THE LACCADIVE ISLANDS AND MINICOY.

The Laccadive Islands.

THE Laccadive Islands are a group of coral formation lying off the Malabar Coast between 8° and 12° N. Latitude and 71·40° and 74° E. Longitude. The four northern islands and two open reefs are attached to the Collectorate of South Canara. The four Southern islands belong to the head of the house of Cannanore; but were sequestered for mismanagement and arrears of peshcash, and have been administered for the last thirty years by the Collector of Malabar. Mr. R. H. Ellis, I.C.S., published in 1924 "A Short Account of the Laccadive Islands and Minicoy" (Government Press, Madras), which contains in its 123 pages all the information that a District Gazetteer usually gives.

Androth, the largest, lies about 125 miles west-south-west of Calicut. It is approximately 1⅔ square miles in extent and has a population of 2,300. Kalpeni, to which are attached the islets of Cheriyam, Tilakam, and Pitti, lies due south of Androth and 150 miles south-west of Calicut. It has 1,500 inhabitants and is about 1 square mile in area.

Kavaratti, which is to the north-west of Kalpeni about 200 miles from Calicut, has an area of 1⅓ square miles and possesses about 2,000 inhabitants. Pitti sandbank about 15 miles to the north-west, and the Suheli reef about 35 miles to the south-west, containing two uninhabited islets named Valiyakara and Cheriyakara, are under the jurisdiction of the Amin of Kavaratti.

Agatti, the westernmost island of the group, at a distance of 220 miles from Calicut, has an area of 1⅛ square miles and a population of 1,200. An uninhabited islet called Kalpitti in the same lagoon, and Bingaram, Tinnakara and Parali enclosed in another reef seven miles to the north are attached to Agatti.

Minicoy.

Minicoy does not belong geographically or ethnologically to the Laccadive group; but is the northernmost of the distinct archipelago known as the Maldive, which is also of coral formation. It lies 250 miles south-west of Calicut and is nearly 2 square miles in extent. The population in 1905 was 2,650. Viringilli or small-pox island, which is uninhabited except in times of epidemic disease, lies in the western corner of the same lagoon.

Physical aspects.

The islands are very similar in physical aspect. They are crescent-shaped banks lying along the eastern arc of oval coral reefs. With the exception of Androth, which lies east and west, they all lie north and south, and have a steep shore on the eastern side, and a more or less extensive lagoon on the west; beyond this there is a gradually sloping bank of dead reef coral which varies from 100 feet to three-quarters of a mile in width, and ends abruptly in a precipice, at which soundings drop suddenly from 20 to 200 fathoms. Androth has no lagoon, but the northern shore provides a limited anchorage, as the reef extends for about a hundred yards beyond the beach. The lagoons protect the other islands on their most exposed side from the fury of the south-west monsoon which would otherwise inundate them, as there is no point of land more than ten or fifteen feet above the level of the sea. It seems probable that the atolls have been formed on the summit of a mountain range, first rising to the surface in the form of shallow oval basins. The activity of the coral polyp has gradually developed the islands on the protected side, and the process can be seen still going on, the lagoons getting shallower every year, particularly in Kalpeni. The brilliant appearance of the lagoons has been thus described :

"In their concentric rings of different colours they remind one of the eyes of a peacock's tail. Nothing else can adequately convey an idea of the brightness of the tints that are blended to form one of these ocean gems. First, there is the central portion of the lagoon, an exquisite chrysophrase green ; then a broad zone of this colour, dotted and speckled with olive green ; then the reef itself, a deep olive brown interspersed with patches of dark green and everywhere frosted with the snowy curls of the breakers ; then a narrower or wider belt of bright apple green ; and beyond the deep purple of the open sea ".[1]

After describing in detail the various theories about the geological formation of these coral islands, Mr. Ellis says :—

"The only definite conclusion that has heen arrived at, then, is that the islands are not as one might think, atolls in process of formation, but the remains of originally more or less perfect atolls, exposed to marine and aerial denudation either by upheaval or by an alteration in sea-level. Actual upheaval is perhaps more probable than an alteration in the sea-level and perhaps occurred about the same time that the Malabar Coast below the Ghats was raised above the sea." (page 9.)

[1] A. Hume in *Stray Feathers*, Vol. IV, p. 428.

CHAP. XVI.
THE LACCADIVE ISLANDS AND MINICOY.

The soil is poor consisting chiefly of disintegrated coral with an admixture of vegetable humus. At a depth of 4 or 5 feet there is a compact but porous crust of limestone conglomerate about a foot thick; and below that a bed of fine sand through which there is a constant filtration of fresh water. The remarkable luxuriance of vegetation in Bingaram and Tinnakara and the islets within the Suheli lagoon is due to the excessive porousness of the coral substratum. In the interior of Androth and Kalpeni are extensive excavations below the limestone crust which are ascribed by latter day degenerates to a race of giants, and in which paddy, varagu, cholam and vegetables, such as yams and sweet potatoes, are grown. The paddy is grown in deep excavations known as *avuls*; ragi and other crops are cultivated on a higher level six or seven feet below that of the adjoining gardens or parambas. These low fields or *tottams* as they are called, probably represent an immense amount of forced labour by the early colonists, who found it difficult to support life without the cereal foods they had been accustomed to on the mainland. It is interesting to note that they are found only in the so-called *tarwad* islands, or islands which contain colonists who claim descent from the Nayars and the higher mainland castes. At the south-east corner of Minicoy there are some fifty small underground chambers, constructed at an unknown period, probably as havens of refuge, when the island was subject to frequent piratical raids. Fresh water is obtainable in all the inhabited islands a few feet below the surface; but, notably at Kavaratti, is not very wholesome. The water in the uninhabited islands is alleged to be brackish.

Flora.

The flora of the islands is somewhat disappointing. The cocoanut is everywhere the dominant feature, but bread-fruit (*Artocarpus incisa*) abounds on most of the islands, and the tamarind, banyan, lime and areca are not uncommon. The *puvarasu* (*Thespesia populnea*), the *punna* (*Calophyllum inophyllum*), and the so-called, 'wild almond' (*Terminalia catappa*) give a supply of small but useful timber. Of the common fruits of the mainland papayas and plantains do fairly well, but there are but few mango or pomegranate trees, and these yield but poorly. The *Morinda citrifolia*, the root of which was once valuable for dyeing purposes, and a species of tree-cotton are abundant in Kalpeni and Androth, and *chonam*, a small fragrant shrub from which a tea-like decoction is made, the bushy *cherutalam* (*Pemphis acidula*), the wild heliotrope (*Tournefolia argentea*) and *Kanni* (*Scœvola Kœnigii*) fringe every beach. The horse-radish tree (*Moringa pterygosperma*), and castor oil plant are also widely distributed, and clumps of *patti* (*Macaranga Roxburghii*) provide material for serviceable rafts. *Kayam*, a tree with a small yellow green leaf, provides a particular hard wood of which the *mokku*, or thole pin to which the oar is attached, is invariably made. This tree though common in the Canara islands is found only in Kavaratti. Ferns in profusion beautify the interior of Androth, and mosses and lichens are found in Minicoy. Among flowers, the prettiest is a white balsam found in the *tottam* at Androth. *Ipomea biloba* and goatsweed are universal, and the red flowered *Ixora* is not uncommon.. In the *tottam* in Androth ragi, varagu, cholam and a coarse kind of paddy are grown, the two first named in quantities sufficient for export in a good season after satisfying the demands of local consumption. Small plots are also grown with varagu in Kalpeni and with cholam in Minicoy. Other common food crops are sweet potatoes and a species of yam called by the islanders *chembu*. In the jungles of Minicoy and Bingaram *ittala* (*Dioscorea oppositifolia*), a tuber yielding a sort of tapioca. abounds.

The screw pine (*Pandanus odoratissimus*) flourishes exceedingly everywhere, and when controlled makes an effective wind-screen for young coconut plantations; but if not rigorously cut back it chokes the trees, as in the south *Pandaram* [1] at Minicoy. No use is made by the islanders of the fruit. Some ceara rubber plants have recently been planted on Minicoy, and are growing satisfactorily.

Fauna.

The only animals besides the goats and cows from time to time imported, are the small brown rat and the domestic cat. The former is a universal pest and does incalculable damage to the cocoanuts in the crowns of which it lives. At different times wood-owls, rat-snakes, and mongooses have been introduced to exterminate them but without success, and rat poison has been but little more effectual. Organised *kuttams* [2] by the islanders twice a week during the monsoon have recently been ordered and the levy of fines by the Amin for non-attendance permitted, and it is hoped that the nuisance may somewhat abate. Two thousand rats are said to have been killed in 1905 in Androth alone.

The land birds are few in number and of the commonest Indian species In Androth, Kalpeni and Minicoy there are numberless crows, but they are not found in Kavaratti or Agatti, thanks it is said to the good offices of a saint (perhaps one of the 'grandes encantadores' of whom Duarte Barboza speaks), who promised also freedom for all times from labour-pains to the women of the former island. From September to April migratory birds, chiefly waders, visit the group, but except in Kalpeni in no great numbers. Pitti sand bank

---

[1] *Pandaram* means "Government," and is used to denote the waste lands not occupied by the original settlers and subsequently claimed by the Raja as crown property—*vide* p.529 *infra*.

[2] *Kuttam* means assembly, and is used of the gatherings of the islanders summoned for some common purpose, such as a rat-hunt or a "Courachy"—*vide* p. 530 *infra*.

CHAP. XVI. THE LACCADIVE ISLANDS AND MINICOY.

becomes, in the interval between the south-west and north-west monsoon, a great breeding place for terns, the eggs of which are plundered by boats from Kavaratti and Amini. The common heron, the turnstone, curlew, whimbrel, sand-piper, yellow wagtail and several varieties of plover have been noticed by naturalists on one or more of the islands.

Harrier hawks and kestrels are occasional visitors, and are caught in limed traps at Androth, where their depredation among the chickens are resented.

Fish are of course abundant, those in the shoal water being often very brilliant in colouring. The bonito (*Thynnus palamys*) provides the Minicoy fisherman with a lucrative industry, worth in a good season as much as 25,000 rupees. Each fish is usually cut up into four pieces, parboiled in salt water and then smoked or sun dried for export to Ceylon, the Nicobars and the Andamans. The scraps are boiled down into a soup known as *min chakkara* (fish sugar), and exported in basins to Penang for sale. Sword-fishes and sharks are frequently harpooned by the islanders, the latter for the sake of their fins, which are an article of trade, but unlike the former they seldom penetrate into the lagoons. A porpoise hunt is somewhat rare, but a "school" is driven now and again into the shallows and there despatched. The flesh is cut up into narrow strips dried in the sun and kept for upwards of a year before being eaten. It is esteemed by the islanders a great delicacy. It is a pity that no attempt is made to cure the hides. Among shell fish the cowry is common, especially at Kalpeni, and hermit crabs infest every beach and act as scavengers. An edible octopus known as *appolu* is caught at night with the aid of flares on the reefs, and a valuable species of sea-slug, the *beche de mer* or trepang of commerce, is procurable. Ambergris is also found in small quantities. Skates, which run to a considerable size, are generally pursued in boats and are killed with the harpoon giving excellent sport.

This island of Pitti is the breeding ground of thousands of sea-birds, and Major Alcock, I.M.S., in his "A Naturalist in Indian Seas" is worth quoting :—

"From the ship it looked like barren sandbank and nothing more, but as our landing party drew near, the boat suddenly became enveloped in a dense crowd of shrieking sea-birds. On landing we found every foot of the ground above high-water mark literally carpeted with young terns of two species, many living and nearly full fledged, many dead and rotting, and many reduced to clean picked skeletons with only the quill feathers still sticking to the wing-bones. There were no traces of nests or of any materials out of which nests could have been made, so that the parent birds must have laid and hatched their eggs on the bare sand. We soon discovered that one great cause of the wholesale destruction of young birds was the voracity of swarms of large hermit crabs, (Coenobita), for again and again we found recently killed birds, in all the beauty of their first speckled plumage, being torn to pieces by a writhing pack of these ghastly crustaceans."

CHAP. XVI. THE LACCADIVE ISLANDS AND MINICOY.

Two varieties of turtle are met with, the green turtle or *murigam* which is killed for its fat, from which a valuable oil is extracted, and the hawksbill or *ama*, which yields the tortoise shell of commerce. The usual method of capture is with the harpoon. The green turtle is common everywhere except in Androth, but the hawksbill is scarce.

Reptiles are unknown save for an occasional gecko or calotes lizard, nor is there any authenticated instance of a poisonous snake being killed on any of the islands.

Insects generally and mosquitoes in particular are rare in Androth, Kalpeni and Kavaratti; in Agatti mosquitoes are kept in check by the fact that their breeding places, the fresh water pits where the coir is soaked, are full of a small fish fry which prey upon, the larvae. In Minicoy however the mosquitoes are an intolerable nuisance. They are scarcely larger than sand flies, and so numberless and pertinacious that the islanders invariably sleep under longcloth curtains to escape them. The mesh of the ordinary mosquito net is not small enough to keep them out, and inspecting officers would be well advised to use 'book muslin,' if they intend to sleep ashore.

The people of the Laccadives.

The inhabitants of Androth, Kalpeni, Kavaratti and Agatti are Mappillas almost indistinguishable except in the matter of physical development from those on the mainland. The admixture of Arab blood seems to be confined to a few of the principal families in the two *tarwad* islands, Kalpeni and Androth. The islanders though Muhammadans perpetuate the old caste distinctions which they observed before their conversion to Islam. The highest caste is called Koya, in its origin merely a religious title. The Koyas represent the aristocracy of the original colonists, and in them vests the proprietorship of most of the cocoanut trees and the *odams* (ships) which constitute the chief outward and visible signs of wealth on the islands. They supply each Amin with a majority of his council of hereditary elders *Karnavans*. The lowest and largest class is that of the Melacheris (lit. high-climbers), also called *Tandels* in Kavaratti, the villeins in the quasi-feudal system of the islands who do the tree-tapping, cocoanut plucking, and menial labour. They hold trees on *kudiyan* service, which involves the shipping of produce on their overlord's boat or *odam*, the thatching of his house and boat-shed, and an obligation to sail on the *odam* to the mainland whenever called upon. Intermediately come the Malumis (pilots), also called Urakars, who represent the skilled navigating class, to which many of the *Karnavans* in Kavaratti belong. Intermarriage between them

CHAP. XVI. THE LACCADIVE ISLANDS AND MINICOY.

and the less prosperous Koyas is now permitted. The Melacheries, the reputed low-class in the islands, are demanding greater freedom of occupation, which the higher classes resent. The relation between them became so strained in Agathi, that the former refused to do any work for the Koyas and a situation arose in the island bordering on anarchy. There were dissensions among the Koyas themselves. The dispute was fortunately compromised in 1920.

Monogamy is the almost universal rule; but divorces can be so easily obtained, that the marriage tie can scarcely be regarded as more binding than *sambandham*[1] among the Hindus on the coast. The women go about freely with their heads uncovered. They continue to live after marriage in their family or *tarwad* houses, where they are visited by their husbands; and the system of inheritance in vogue is *marumakkattayam*[1] or inheritance through the mother, as regards family property, and *makkattayam*, or inheritance through the father, as regards self-acquisitions. These are distinguished on the islands under the terms *Velliyaricha* (Friday) and *Tingalaricha* (Monday) property. With the great facilities for divorce on both sides, very few men have more than one wife, and few men or women who have not been married or divorced several times. The men wear oblong silver amulets containing a text from the Koran, tied as a charm in the waist-string or on the upper arm.

The family house is invariably called *pura* in contradistinction to *vidu*, the wife's house. Intermarriage between the inhabitants of different islands is not uncommon.

Like all uneducated people, the islanders are very superstitious and believe in ghosts and hobgoblins, about the visible manifestations of which many stories are current; and there is an old *mamul* or rule on all the islands forbidding any one to go out after nightfall. Phantom steamers and sailing ships are sometimes seen in the lagoons or rowed out to on the open seas; and in the prayers by the graves of his ancestors, which each sailor makes before setting out on a voyage, we find something akin to the Roman worship of the Manes. The Moidin mosque at Kalpeni and the big West Pandaram at Androth are believed to be haunted. There are *Jarams* (shrines) in Cheriyam and Cheriyakara to which pilgrimages are made and where vows are taken; and it is usual to chant the *fateha*[2] on sighting the Jamath mosque in Androth, beneath the shadow of which is the tomb of Mumba Mulyaka, the Arab apostle[3] to the Laccadives.

---

[1] *Vide* p. 96, *supra*.

[2] The *fateha* is the recital of the first chapter of the Koran, part of the regular form of prayer which a Muhammadan should repeat five times a day (p. 189).

[3] See p. 521.

There are flourishing schools at Androth, Kavaratti and Kalpeni where boys are taught up to the old Primary Examination standard, but elsewhere secular education is neglected. Mosque schools, where the Koran and the rudiments of religion are taught, are common on all the islands.

CHAP. XVI. THE LACCADIVE ISLANDS AND MINICOY.

The language spoken is a dialect of Malayalam more corrupt in the Western islands than in Androth and Kalpeni. It is usually written in Arabic. In the matter of pronunciation the letter ഫ as (p) is a striking shibboleth. One hears "fenkutti," and "fanam" meaning "girl" and "money," where a mainlander would say "penkutti" and "panam."

The islanders, it has been shrewdly said, do not by nature desire anything beyond enough food to support existence comfortably. In exchange for their coir and copra they bring back supplies of rice and tobacco from the mainland, and gratify their passion for personal adornment with bandana handkerchiefs, and amber bead necklaces; while the *Karnavans* buy themselves long silk coats in all colours of the rainbow to distinguish themselves in cutcherry from the rank and file.

The people of Minicoy.

The inhabitants of Minicoy belong to an entirely different race, perhaps descended from the original population of Ceylon, and speak "Mahl," apparently an Aryan language akin to Elu, the earliest form of Sinhalese. The islanders are all Muhammadans and as in the northern islands, of the Sufi sect.

Four caste divisions are recognized; the Malikhans, an exclusive but not particularly influential aristocracy; the Malumis; the Takrus who supply many of the ships sailing in Eastern waters with their Kilasis; and the Raveris (Mahl. *Ra*=toddy, *veri*=drawer), who take the place of the Melacheris in the Northern islands but are not subject to the same disabilities. In the title of Dom, which is borne by the heads of the Malikhans and by the principal nobles in the Maldives, is perhaps to be found the sole surviving trace of the connexion of the Portuguese with the Archipelago.

The men are expert sailors and boat builders, and are to be found on most of the ships in the trade with the East which employ coloured seamen. They are absent from the island sometimes for years together; though if navigating their own boats they generally arrange to return about a month before the south-west monsoon breaks, and remain at home until September. At all other times the number of women largely exceeds that of the men on the island, and it is scarcely surprising that they enjoy more freedom and exercise more authority than probably in any other country east of Suez, except Burma. They are more intelligent than the men and not less energetic. They are sufficiently literate to be able to teach

CHAP. XVI. THE LACCADIVE ISLANDS AND MINICOY.

their children to read and write. They shave their husbands and their babies' heads, are the family laundresses, and yet find time not only to cook the daily food but also to sit in their club-houses twisting coir and gossiping the greater part of the day. In disposition they are merry, and a courtship in Minicoy corresponds more to western nations, than would be expected in a community professing Islam. The bride's consent must in all cases be obtained before the *Kazi* will celebrate a marriage, and runaway matches are not uncommon. Monogamy is the rule, and the wife remains in her mother's house after marriage unless her husband builds her one of her own; the children take their mother's family name.

The dress and coiffure of the Minicoy women are exceedingly picturesque. The Manikas (Malikhan women wear over a coloured silk petticoat long chemises of red silk fastened at the neck and reaching down to their ankles. On their arms are gold bracelets innumerable, and their chignons are curiously like those of Burmese women a resemblance accentuated by the roundness of their faces and the openness of their smiles. The women of the lower castes also dress in red, but are forbidden to wear gold or silver ornaments. The men wear navy blue pantaloons fitting close over the instep, and above them a white cloth fastened round the waist hangs square to the knees. The upper part of the body is bare and the head closely shaved. The Malikhans alone wear the fez or the silk conical cap of the Maldives.

Inheritance is governed by Muhammadan law: but the family house vests in the women, and goes to the youngest daughter if her elder sister's husbands have built separate houses for them.

Both sexes are equally fond of *pan supari* or betel and the bridegroom's wedding gift to his bride takes the form of a silver filigree box from Galle to hold her chewing materials. For internal adminsitration and social purposes the inhabited part of the island is divided up into *attiris* and *varangis*, clubs to which the men and women respectively of the Takru and Raveri castes resort. The men's clubs are on the beach (Mahl. *attiri*) and consist of thatched sheds containing one or more long swinging planks, whereon they sit and gossip and defy the mosquitoes. The *varangis*, which are designed as work rooms for the women, consist of long halls with decorative facades in canvas at the end which is open to the breeze, and with a raised platform backed by looking glasses at the other. The floors are worked with a design in cowries, and coloured glass balls hang from the roof. Here the women sit and twist coir and talk scandal during the mornings and afternoons, but the call of the kitchen empties the *varangis* before sunset. On feast days such as the Perunal following the month of fasting, Eramullan (Ramazan), the sexes mingle freely in public, and the young men and boys of one *attiri* may be seen playing a sort of prisoner's base in the lanes with the grown-up girls of a *varangi*. They are said to be very fond of music, the *tara*, a sort of tambourine, which is peculiar to this and the Maldive islands, being found in every house. On festivals, the drum (Mahl. *beru*) is played by troops of men dressed in holiday attire with sprigs of greenery in their turbans.

Industries and manufactures.

The chief industry of the islanders is coir twisting, in which the women folk of all classes find employment. The cocoanut husks are generally socked in pits in the lagoon, save in Minicoy and to some extent in Agatti also, where the ripple on the water is so strong that fresh water pits have to be resorted to. In Androth, though there is no lagoon, the coral shoal on the northern side is found to be sufficiently protected for the purpose. The lime held in solution, perhaps even more than the sea water, gives the fibre a peculiar fineness and whiteness, and the best class of " Divi " coir commands a price which is not obtainable for any twisted on the coast except that from Anjengo.

There is a good deal of sweet toddy tapping, the juice being boiled down in open pans and exported in the form of jaggery or sweetmeats known as *halva* and *pindika*. Slices of bread-fruit are dipped in the boiling juice and thus preserved are taken on the boats sailing to the mainland, for consumption by the sailors.

There is a large export of cocoanuts and copra also ; but, for many years past, there has been no attempt to extract cocoanut oil except by rough and ready methods for domestic needs, though it would not be difficult to import bullocks to work country mills. Oil for caulking boats is extracted from the fat of the green turtle. The islanders are skilled at making and mending nets, and, particularly in Minicoy, are good shipwrights and carpenters, though when there is elaborate carving to be done, Hindus are generally brought from the coast for the purpose. Kavaratti must at one time have possessed some clever masons, and the mosques on that island are architecturally superior to those on the other islands.

The boys of Agatti and Kavaratti are proficient in the art of making conical silk caps for which they find a ready sale in the Maldives and Ceylon : but the industry is chiefly practised in Calicut, where the materials are more easily procurable, and the market more accessible.

It is not unusual to find Hindu goldsmiths from Malabar making and mending jewels (in Kalpeni the Koya women wear them in great profusion), and the isolation for a number of months from their co-religionists frequently predisposes the workmen to conversion.

CHAP. XVI. THE LACCADIVE ISLANDS AND MINICOY.

There are no bazaars in the northern islands, but it is recognized that voluntary contributions of rice and other necessaries should be made to any house where there is a marriage, or a religious ceremony such as a *maulad*, being performed. In Minicoy, two or three enterprising Mappillas have started trading with rice from the mainland, and are ready to take either cash or coir in exchange. Money passes more freely on the islands than one would have supposed.

Religion.

In the northern islands, and in Androth particularly, the inhabitants pride themselves upon their religious knowledge, and it is not unusual for the Koyas to travel as far a field as Colombo as *murids* or disciples and to earn very considerable sums of money thereby. Many of them have been to Mecca, and some have taken their womenfolk with them. The number of mosques in each island is out of all proportion to the number of inhabitants. In Androth, there are 30, in Kalpeni 19, in Kavaratti 32, and in Agatti 29. In Minicoy, there are only 20. To almost every one of these mosques a grave-yard is attached, with the exception of those built since the sequestration in Pandaram lands, wherein sepulture is forbidden. Nearly every grave has its carved headstone on which the name of the deceased, and the day and month of his death are recorded; but limestone is friable, and the islanders, though they regard a grave-yard with sentimental attachment, are so careless of the monuments of the penultimate generation, that it is not unusual to see among the graves many detruncated headstones and a litter of broken coral.

In Minicoy, the shape of the headstone distinguishes the sex of the person buried below. Some of them are beautifully carved, and all are stained a pale green with a decoction of verdigris made by the action on copper of toddy which has been allowed to ferment.

Houses.

The houses are built of coral stone blocks quarried on the reefs or on the islands, and rudely thatched. In Kalpeni where this is not possible owing to the brittleness of the underlying strata, the walls are made of rubble piled up between slender posts made of the midrib of the cocoanut palm and plastered over, which gives the appearance of rough-cast. Some coral stone is also burnt in pits, and when mixed with sand makes excellent mortar. The roofs are high pitched and the eaves low, making the interiors intolerably dark, except in Agatti where large wooden barred windows admit the light. The Jamat mosque at Androth and Kavaratti and one or two other mosques are roofed with tiles of the Mangalore pattern, but few dwelling houses are tiled. In Kavaratti and Minicoy, the houses are surrounded with high cadjan enclosures, which give more privacy than is sought for elsewhere. In Minicoy, all the rooms open on to the outer verandah and there is much fine timber in the houses of the well-to-do Malikhans.

Boats.

The islanders are expert fishermen and sailors, especially those of Minicoy. In Androth, several of the *Karnavans* possess charts and are skilled navigators, but it is not unusual for a boat returning from the coast to the other northern islands to lose its bearings. Hence they prefer to be becalmed to making a hazardous series of tacks when the wind is contrary. Their *odams* are carvel-built and contain wooden water tanks holding from six weeks to two months' supply. They run well before a wind, and look very picturesque with their black hulls of corded timber set off with a white line just below the bulwarks and their high poops decorated with symbols and sentences in Arabic. The smaller boats used for fishing are strongly built, and carry a sturdy crew of rowers from Agatti to Kavaratti or Kavaratti to Amini between sunset and the following midday. Kavaratti boasts two *odams* registered of 60 tons burden and over, and Androth has several of 30, and one of 40. In the other islands, they are smaller.

In Minicoy, the big boats called *odis* are much larger, some of them upwards of a hundred tons, and in build, if not in rig, more closely resemble the sailing ships of the West. Prior to the first assumption of the islands, the Bibi had a considerable fleet, engaged chiefly in the carrying trade between Minicoy and Bengal. Minicoy nuts commanded a special price in Calcutta, and the cargo for the return journey was chiefly composed of rice bought at Balasore at rates very much lower than those prevailing in Malabar. In 1850, the Bibi possessed five barques and seven *odis* (in addition to the several *bandodis* exclusively engaged in trade with the Maldives and the West Coast); but at the time of Mr. E. C. G. Thomas' visit in 1858, the numbers had been reduced to one barque and three *odis*, and many years have now passed since the last survivor of her fleet, the *Hydros*, was broken up. Stress of competition with vessels of superior build and rig has, during the last half century, diminished the profits and chilled the enterprise of the Minicoy boat-owners. Their vessels no longer go so far afield as Mauritius, the Persian Gulf, Moulmein and Singapore, and their trade is at present practically confined to the Maldives, Galle, the Nicobars, Balasore and Calcutta. Their mas-boats, in which they go out after the bonito (Mahl. *Kalu bili mas, i.e.*, the black-fish), are admirably designed for swift cruising in the neighbourhood of the island. They carry two sails, a large mat-sail almost square but broadening at the base like a church banner, and a small linen try-sail behind. There are also places for rowers. At the stern over the rudder is constructed a platform to hold the anglers, who when the boat gets into a shoal of bonito hook the greedy fish, which are attracted by a shower of live bait and the splashing of oars, and throw them into a well in the middle of the boat. The hooks are for greater expedition unbarbed,

CHAP. XVI. THE LACCADIVE ISLANDS AND MINICOY.

and it is wonderful to see with what precision and speed the fishermen make the most of the short time they are in the shoal. The racing boats for the lagoon are very narrow, finely built and gaudily painted. They carry about sixteen oarsmen and two steersmen in the stern sitting abreast to give the time with the strokes of their short paddles. The islanders are splendid swimmers. In Minicoy, it is not unusual to see diminutive boys astride torpedo-shaped planks, as in the South Seas, going out to the boats anchored far out in the lagoon. In 1885 a fine lighthouse was erected at the south-eastern end of Minicoy and this has greatly reduced the number of wrecks on these islands; but the S.S. *Thrunscoe* went ashore here in 1898. The light-house is 160 feet in height and its flash can be seen at a distance of 19 sea miles.

Health and sanitation.

The standard of personal cleanliness is distinctly higher on the islands than among the Mappillas of the Malabar coast, and in Minicoy and Agatti more particularly some attention is paid to conservancy. The commonest complaints are itch, rheumatism and sore-eyes, the last named due to the glare of the white sand and the irritation set up by the particles of disintegrated coral blown about on the beaches. Cholera and dysentery are epidemic in the islands from time to time and smallpox in a virulent form is a frequent visitor. In Minicoy alone 330 perished of this scourge in the last few months of 1904. Vaccination is freely resorted to, except in Kalpeni and Kavaratti, as its effec are beginning to be appreciated even among the lowest classes. In Minicoy patients discovered to be suffering from smallpox are immediately segregated in the little islet of Viringilli, at the south-western end of the lagoon, and separate burial grounds are maintained for those who die of this disease and also for cholera corpses, lunatics and lepers. In Minicoy there is a settlement at the northern end containing some thirteen lepers cut off from communication with the rest of the island, but supported by monthly doles of rice and vegetab'e and eking out a miserable existence by gardening and fishing in the lagoon. The disease generally takes the tubercular form. The same precautionary measures are not observed elsewhere, but there is only one leper in Androth and two on Kalpeni. The beach is generally resorted to for purpos of nature, and very little attempt is made to clear away refuse from the yards of the houses. The women bathe in the tanks attached to the houses; the men in the sea. Nearly every house has a well attached to it. In Androth and Kalpeni they are little more than water holes, but in Kavaratti and Agatti they hav parapet walls. In the latter and and Minicoy the are some fine bathing tanks adjacent to the mosque. One or two draw-well have been built but they are not yet popular. The islands are over-run with quacks, whose business lies chiefly in the dispensing of febrifuges and aphrodisiacs. Venereal diseases, though not unknown, are uncommon.

Climate and rainfall.

From the meteorological observations taken at Minicoy, it would appear that the maximum shade temperature has a comparatively small range of variation between 88 in May to 70 in November. The rainfall is between 40 and 50 inches annually, which is about one-third of that of Calicut. The wealth of shade provided by the cocoanut and bread-fruit trees, and the sea breezes moderate the solar heat, and the islands are much healthier than the Maldives, where malaria appears to be endemic.

History.

The early history of the islands is even more obscure than that of the mainland. Perhaps the earliest reference to them may be found in the passage from the Periplus already quoted[1] which alludes to the tortoise shell "from the islands off the coast of Limurike." But it is improbable that the Laccadives were inhabited so early as the first century A.D. Local traditions go back of course to Cheraman Perumal, and ascribe the first settlement to the shipwreck on one of the atolls of an expedition which set out from Cranganore in quest of that legendary pilgrim to Mecca. But all that is certain is that the islands were colonized from the mainland, probably from Kolattanad. For a considerable time the islanders remained Hindus, as the existence to this day of strongly marked caste distinctions proves; but, as the group lies directly in the path of Arab trade between the Red Sea and Malabar, the ultimate conversion of the inhabitants to Islam was inevitable.

Ibn Batuta fixes the conversion of the neighbouring Maldive Islands at about four generations before his visit (1343 A.D.) and the claim of the present *Kazi* of Androth to be twenty-sixth in descent from Mumba Mulyaka, the Arab preacher to whom is ascribed the introduction of the true religion into the Laccadives, makes it probable that the change took place in the latter between 1100 and 1200 A.D.

Al Biruni writing about 1030 A.D. speaks of the Dyvah Kanbar or Coir islands and the Dyvah Kuzah or the Cowrie islands, meaning perhaps to distinguish by these terms the Laccadives from the Maldives. Ibn Batuta did not visit the Laccadives, and our materials for the history of the islands prior to the arrival of the Portuguese off the Malabar coast are of the most fragmentary nature.[2]

---

[1] *Vide* p. 28.

[2] They are collected and abstracted in Appendix A (Vol. II, Pt. 11, p. 423) of the Hakluyt edition of the *Voyage of Pyrard de Laval*, who visited the Laccadives in 1607.

CHAP. XVI. THE LACCADIVE ISLANDS AND MINICOY.

Towards the end of the fifteenth century the Kolattiri seems to have established a nominal suzerainty over the group and for the next three hundred years Mappilla merchants at Cannanore had the monopoly of the rich coir trade of the islands. The Portuguese made a settlement on Amini, building a fort and a factory, and engaged in filibustering raids upon the other islands of the group in the first half of the sixteenth century; but the colony was exterminated by poison through the intrigues of the Kolattiri in 1545, and, though bloody reprisals were made, no further attempt was made to establish a footing on the islands.

Shortly afterwards, making a virtue of necessity, the Kolattiri Raja abandoned his nominal suzerainty, and made a grant of the islands in jagir to his hereditary admiral the Ali Raja of Cannanore. subject only to the annual payment of 6,000 fanams as tribute. It is uncertain whether Minicoy was or was not included in the gift. It may have been one of the thirty Maldive islands of which Pyrard de Laval speaks[1] as being tributary to the Raja at the time of his ship-wreck and imprisonment on the group in 1602–1607. In 1627 the Maldive islanders appealed to the Dutch for protection against the aggressions of the Raja, and in 1671 the Governor of Ceylon ordered an accurate survey of both archipelagos, in which the Laccadives are curiously referred to as 'Baxos de Padua.' Fifty years later, however, in 1727, just after the Dutch had formally resolved to withdraw from all interference in native politics, the Ali Raja was again threatening the reconquest of the Maldives, and it may have been at this time that Minicoy was finally alienated. If so the price of the island's submission was probably the promise of protection against the piratical raids of the Kottakkal Kunhali Marakkars.[2]

The Ali Raja continued, nominally at least, tributary to the Chirakkal family till the middle of the eighteenth century, when Haidar's invasion of Malabar enabled him finally to throw off the yoke. In 1786 Amini and the three other northern islands of Kiltan, Kadamat and Chetlat revolted as a protest against the harshness with which the coir monopoly was worked, and tendered allegiance to Tippu, notwithstanding his friendship and alliance with the Bibi, who was at that time the ruling princess of the Cannanore house; and but for strenuous efforts she would have lost Kavaratti also. Tippu would not restore the four islands to her, but he compensated her with a jagir worth Rs. 7,380 from the territories of the Chirakkal Raja and a grant of Rs. 12,000.

[1] *Voyage of Pyrard de Laval* (Hakluyt series), Vol. I, p. 323.

[2] See p. 462.

CHAP. XVI. THE LACCADIVE ISLANDS AND MINICOY.

In 1792 Malabar was ceded to the British, and in spite of her persistent unfriendly and treacherous conduct the Bibi was allowed provisionally to remain in possession of the islands which still acknowledged her supremacy. She was required to pay annually a contribution of only Rs. 10,000, this being the sum which she falsely represented to be a moiety of her profits from the islands. In 1795 Lieutenant Bentley was sent to make a thorough inspection of the islands, and his report, which is most interesting, showed that the Bibi had under-estimated her annual income by nearly a lakh, and that the islanders were anxiously looking to the Company for relief from the intolerable exactions and petty tyranny of her agents. But unfortunately war was again threatening with Tippu, and in a second provisional agreement drawn up on October 28th, 1796, the Bibi once more got off with very easy terms. She contracted to pay "Rs. 15,000 per annum being the jumma on the houses and purrams, etc., situated at and near Cannanore, on my trade to the Laccadive islands, and on my jelm property on the said islands." But she did not relinquish her claims to the four islands which had revolted in 1784, and which after the fall of Seringapatam had been attached to the South Canara district. Finally, after prolonged negotiations she was compensated in 1822, by a reduction of Rs. 5,250 in the sum due from her by the agreement, or Karar, of 1796.

The terrible storm that broke over the islands on April 15th 1847(sic), has already been described.[1] Mr. (afterwards Sir William) Robinson was deputed to visit the Laccadives and report upon the damage which they had sustained; and he was directed by Mr. Conolly to enquire at the same time into the general allegations of oppression which had been brought in the previous year by the Agatti islanders against the Bibi. Among other things he recommended a temporary reduction of the lease amount, and the annual contribution was accordingly reduced to Rs. 3,333⅓ for a period of ten years, on condition that the Bibi undertook to give effect to such reforms in the administration of the islands as the Government might demand. Nevertheless the Bibi's administration showed no improvement, and her payments being in arrears, the islands were sequestered for a period of five years in 1861. They were sequestered again in 1875 for the same reasons, and have never since been restored. They are now inspected annually by a Covenanted Civilian from Malabar, who visits them in a vessel of the Royal Indian Marine. Save for another hurricane in 1867 and riots in Minicoy and Androth in 1889, the history of the last forty years has been entirely uneventful. The sequestration of the islands remained in force till 1908 when the Bibi surrendered her phantom sovereignty with a

[1] See p. 286.

CHAP. XVI. THE LACCADIVE ISLANDS AND MINICOY.

view mainly to clear off arrears of peshkash and to have several useful reforms in the administration and fiscal system introduced. Arrears of peshkash in 1908 rose to 2·17 lakhs and though the Government was willing to order the rendition of the estate if payment was made, there was no possibility of payment. Negotiations were opened with the Azhi Raja in 1900, and again in 1905 which were accepted; but the Raja dying in 1907, the whole question had to be reopened with his successor Imbichi Bibi who finally accepted the terms and the agreement was signed in 1908 and ratified by the Government of India in February 1909; and the islands became part of His Majesty's Indian Dominions as from 1st July 1905.

There were troubles in Minicoy in 1912 over the removal of an unpopular Amin, due really to the management of the *Pandaram* property; and peace was restored by the Collector renting the property to the islanders in common for a long period with the option of renewal.

The German cruiser "Emden" operated off the Laccadives for a short time in September and October 1914, and sank several vessels on the trade routes which ran north and south of Minicoy.

Fiscal administration.

So long as the islands remained independent under Mudalals (chief inhabitants) assisted by the elders of the leading families, there was apparently no form of taxation; nor was there any settled revenue or land-tax in the early period of their subjection to the Ali Raja, when the administration continued in the hands of the principal islanders. The earliest imposition took the form of a *chungam* (toll, *i.e.*, export duty) varying from 6 to 10 per cent on coir, and a like tariff on the rice imported from the mainland. Further, the Ali Raja as Lord of the Deep, set up an exclusive claim to all the valuable sea products—ambergris, tortoise shell, holothuria and cowries—to be obtained from the islands, and rewarded those who found them with bare cooly hire. It was not until 1765, however, that the right of purchase by the *Pandaram* (as the Government of the Ali Raja was commonly called) of all the coir produced was first enunciated, the price being fixed at the time when coir was selling at Rs. 60 to Rs. 70 per candy, at Rs. 30, subject to a 10 per cent export duty and a 10 per cent import duty on the rice in which payment was made. Enormous profits might have been expected from this step; but so harshly was the ordinance worked that the Aminidivis were provoked to rebel, and the disaffection in the remaining islands was with difficulty suppressed. Even granting that considerable smuggling went on, the coir monopoly must, upon the basis of an annual output of 1,000 candies brought to account, have yielded upwards of Rs. 40,000 annually for a series of years, and it remains to the present day the chief source of revenue. When collection of Sea Customs dues on merchandize imported at the port of Cannanore, was assumed by the Company in 1793, coir from the Laccadives was expressly exempted ; but the islanders derived no benefit from the concession and paid tithe as before to the Bibi.

In 1827 the price of coir fell suddenly from Rs. 65 to Rs. 20, and in the quinquennium 1830–34 averaged only Rs. 17¾, touching low water mark in 1834 at Rs. 14–5–0 per candy. In 1835–39 the price rose again to Rs. 27–4–0, but fell in the following five years to Rs. 24–15–2 at about which price it remained stationary during 1845, 1846 and 1847. The Bibi reduced the buying price to Rs. 22 as soon as the market became weak, and favoured by a contemporaneous fall in the price of rice, in which payment was partly made, she reduced the actual remuneration paid to the island to Rs. 10½ per candy. Many accounts were also settled by promissory notes which were never redeemed. In 1832 as prices continued low a new system was introduced. The price of coir was fixed at 5¾ *mudas* (bundles) of rice per candy subject to 21 per cent *mamul* deductions, *i.e.*, 4½ *mudas* net. At the current market rate of Rs. 1–8–0 per *muda* the islanders received only Rs. 6–12–0 per candy, which was actually less than the cost of production. The Bibi probably made Rs. 13,000 annually by the change of system. A considerable retail trade in rice was also conducted on the islands by the Bibi's agents, and as all payments for coir were made in rice the price obtained by the islanders averaged between Rs. 7½ and Rs. 9 prior to 1826, and only Rs. 5 subsequently.

The inevitable result of this oppression was a general deterioration in the quality of the coir twisted, and a stubborn refusal to import more than could be avoided into Cannanore. As early as 1820 classification had been begun in the Aminidivis, to check a tendency to careless twisting ; but the commutation price was adhered to even after the fall in 1826. In 1848 the coir produced at Androth was of such indifferent quality, that in Mr. Robinson's opinion it would have been rejected at Mangalore as below the third-class standard. Numerous malpractices were alleged by the islanders to reduce the payments made still further, such as deduction for dryage, weighment by maund, each maund having to turn the scale, or by candies of 680 instead of 640 lb., extortion of mamuls by the Bibi's agents, and deductions on account of mythical old debts. From 1854–61 the islands were under sequestration, but though the abuses were probably less prevalent, there is no evidence of any change of system during this period. In 1865, however, the commutation price of coir was raised under pressure to Rs. 20, and again in 1868–69 to Rs. 22½, and in 1869–70 the Ali Raja agreed to pay Rs. 25 per candy. To this epoch belongs the petition of the Agatti islanders protesting against a deduction of 2½ per cent for the maintenance charges of the Ali Raja's domestic chaplain, and 2½ per cent for the palace cat! The islands were sequestered again in 1875; and three years later the commutation rates already in force in South Canara were adopted and these prevail to the present day, but the privilege of importing duty-free salt, has been withdrawn and the islanders still regard this as a grievance. The rates are nominally Rs. 21–14–0 for first-class coir, Rs. 17–8–0 for second-class coir, and Rs. 13–2–0 for third-class coir, three-fourths being commuted into rice at Rs. 2 per muda and the balance in cash; but as the price of rice has never been so low as the commutation rate and for some years past has been nearly double that, the islanders have actually received about Rs. 30, Rs. 24 and Rs. 20 per candy, the figures for 1904–05 being approximately Rs. 36, Rs. 30 and Rs. 23. The annual output of coir which Lieutenant Bentley estimated at 1,300 candies in 1795, and Mr. Robinson at 1,350 candies in 1848, has not been consistently maintained. In fasli 1310 (1900–01) 1,357 candies were imported, but in fasli 1312, 998 and in fasli 1313, 931 only. The reason given by the islanders was discouragement due to the inferior rice in which payment was made, the harshness of the classification, and the unnecessarily high deduction of 5 per cent for dryage. The first was a genuine grievance, and measures have been taken to remove it, and at the same time an attempt has been made so to alter the rules that the twisters may directly benefit from improved manufacture instead of the shippers. The coir monopoly continued to be a source of great trouble as much to Government as to the islanders. In view of the steady decrease in revenue Mr. Knapp in 1907 suggested a tree-tax, but Government decided that no change was called for. During the European War and the poor harvest of 1918 and 1919 when the price of rice was abnormally high, the monopoly resulted in large deficit, and in the following year when prices became normal, the question was examined by the inspecting officer and Government finally fixed 3½ thulams of coir as the equivalent for one muda of rice, and also ordered the island officers if required to buy coir on the islands direct from the people at four thulams per muda. This arrangement still continues.

There is no coir monopoly in the island of Minicoy, where the *Pandaram* trees occupy the greater portion of the island. Revenue is derived by taxing the trees on the Valiya pattam and Attiri pattam at a uniform rate of four annas, and by leasing the right of tapping some of the trees in the South *Pandaram*.

The only other form of taxation is a poll-tax (*allora*), payable in coir, of 20 lb. per male and 5 lb. per female, from which, however, all Malikhan and unmarried adults and toddy drawers are exempt as well as one married female in each house. The old taxes on the *odis* and fishing boats are no longer collected. The poll-tax "allora" is now paid in cash at the rate of 12 annas for a married couple, six annas on an unmarried man and four annas on an unmarried woman.

A cocoanut monopoly was introduced in the other islands in 1826 to supplement the falling revenue from coir; but it did not bring in as much as was expected, as the islanders turned to the manufacture of jaggery, or, as in Agatti where the trees are notoriously poor in their yield of juice, the nuts were dried for copra and milled on the spot. The monopoly openly defied in 1848 was abolished in the following year.

The cowry monopoly is a very ancient one and extends even to Minicoy. When cowries were in universal demand as a medium of monetary exchange one seer of cowries was worth to the islanders two seers of rice, and their profits rose or fell with the price of that commodity. With rice at Rs. 2 per *muda* the islanders obtained about Rs. 25 per candy for their shells, equivalent to about half their real market value. In 1826 the commutation rate was reduced to one seer of rice per seer of cowries, but this provoked so much discontent that the Bibi was compelled to raise it to 1½ seers. This rate obtained until 1848, at which period Mr. Robinson calculated the annual imports at 10 to 12 candies, and the profits to the Bibi at between Rs. 500 and Rs. 700 annually. After the sequestration a cash price of As. 4 per seer was fixed, but as this entailed a heavy loss owing to the fall in the market value, it was reduced at Mr. Winterbotham's instance to As. 2 a seer, at which rate the cowries are scarcely worth collecting. It is true that in fasli 1293 (1883–84) 11 candies were brought for sale, but in fasli 1314 the receipts were less than 3 candies. The cowry monopoly was abolished in 1901, as the market price and the demand for the cowries had steadily declined and there was no point in keeping up the monopoly.

The hawksbill turtle, though not so common on the shoals as the green turtle, is nevertheless frequently met with especially in the uninhabited reefs of Suheli and Bingaram and the lagoon of Kalpeni. In 1848 Mr. Robinson estimated the annual receipts of shell at about 100 lb., of which at least 50 per cent was smuggled. As only Rs. 1½ were paid for each shell irrespective of its weight the profits to the Bibi even upon this inconsiderable amount were from Rs. 300 to Rs. 350 per annum. The monopoly continued to yield a considerable sum up to the date of the second assumption of the islands in fasli 1285. In the previous decade an average of over 34 lb. was received annually. In fasli 1283 as much as 104 lb. was received from Kavaratti alone. In 1869–70 the price paid

CHAP. XVI. THE LACCADIVE ISLANDS AND MINICOY.

by the Ali Raja was Rs. 3 per lb., but it had been reduced by 1878 to Rs. 2 per lb., one-fifth of the current market rate for superior shell. Since fasli 1301 not a single tortoise shell has been received at Calicut, with the exception of a few flakes weighing ¼ lb. in fasli 1314, and 1¼ lb. recovered and brought back from Kalpeni by the inspecting officer in December 1905.

The sea-cucumber or holothuria, locally called *atta*, which is fairly common throughout the group, does not appear to have been monopolised until the accidental visit in 1836 of a French vessel having Malay seamen on board revealed its commercial value. Subsequently some coast merchants rented the fishing from the Ali Raja, employing a Malay to do the curing, and for a few years the industry was brisk, as the trepang manufactured was of good quality and fetched as much as Rs. 80 per candy. The trade in the article now is infinitesimal ; as is that in ambergris which is also a monopoly of the Government.

The morinda citron, which is abundant on Androth and Kalpeni, yields a valuable dye and was formerly monopolised at one-fourth of its value. Kavaratti boasts a large number of fine lime trees, yielding fruit of remarkable size. These were formerly gathered by the agents of the Bibi and sent to Cannanore either fresh or pickled. Unfortunately the limes ripen in August and September when communication with the coast is interrupted and the reserves of salt being generally low, a good deal of the fruit is spoiled. This and the morinda citron monopoly were abolished in 1880, and two other monopolies which have fallen into desuetude are those on salt and tobacco, from which at one time the ruler made a considerable profit.

The Ali Raja had further sources of revenue, which if less constant were none the less considerable. The islanders used in the days of sailing ships to be in great demand as pilots, and a tax known as *Malumi maryadi* was levied by the *Pandaram* on their earnings as such, varying from Rs. 3-8-0 to Rs. 7 according to the length of the voyage. Forced loans corresponding to the mediaeval ' benevolences ' were occasionally demanded, and a considerable if fluctuating revenue must have been derived from the nuzzers or presents made by Kazis on their appointment, and from the charges incident to the grant of an audience or the conferring of local titles and other distinctions. In Minicoy permission to build an *odi* to engage in the Bengal trade was only granted upon payment of two hundred rupees, and in Androth a sannad granting the title of ' Patlor ' or ' Muthancheror ' usually cost the recipient double that sum. From Rs. 4 to Rs. 11 was demanded as the price of an interview with the Ali Raja and sumptuary fines were levied for permission to wear ornaments.

Pandaram lands.

The property of the ruling house on each island consists of (*a*) waste land on the shore or at the extremities of the islands, which was not brought under cultivation by the earliest settlers, (*b*) escheats either by the death of the last holder without heirs or by forcible assumption as a punishment for disobedience. The islets of Bingaram and Tinnakara were confiscated in 1764, and Suhelipar in the following year, and there were large escheats in Kavaratti when the rebellion of 1784 failed. In Minicoy, Kavaratti and Kalpeni, where the *Pandaram* lands are most extensive, rubble walls were erected to keep out trespassers; but these have long ago fallen into ruins, except in Minicoy. The islanders until comparatively recent times did not recognize ownership in the soil, but only in the standing trees, and the consequent confusion through the commingling of property, was very great. With the object of getting the waste lands planted up, cowles have been granted on favourable terms, having currency for twelve years, and renewable at the end of that time, subject to a re-pymash; only the bearing trees are taxed and payment is made in coir. The rates are equivalent to As. 5 for trees owned by the *Pandaram* and As. 2–6 for trees planted by the cowledars. This system has been distinctly successful. The Great West *Pandaram* at Androth is full of fine bearing cocoanut trees and the East *Pandaram* in the same island is well-planted up, but the poverty of the soil affects the yield considerably. Entry into the *Pandaram* lands was in old days prohibited except when the annual plucking of cocoanuts or limes took place. The trees round the cutcherry were also reserved and this plot is still spoken of on each island as the Cutcherry Pak (lit. 'forbidden').

The cowle scheme succeeded in Androth and Kalpeni, but on other islands where the cowledars also owned large numbers of private trees, it was a failure as they neglected the *Pandaram* trees. In 1908 and 1909 the lands were inspected and the number of trees to be planted fixed; and the cowledars were warned that failure to plant would be met with a fine of Re. 1 for every 50 *thies* not planted. This too had not the desired effect. So in 1920 it was ordered that where a cowledar had not planted half the number of trees the whole would be cancelled and the land given to the poorer islanders; and this order was enforced at the next inspection by 28 plots being granted to new cowledars. The scheme is now working better.

General and judicial administration.

About the ancient administration of the islands very little is known. The *Karnavans* of the principal families apparently formed themselves into a council of elders with one of their number designated *Mudalal* as chief, and this patriarchal government have survived practically untouched to the present day. The *Mudalal* was from time to time superseded by an alien

CHAP. XVI. THE LACCADIVE ISLANDS AND MINICOY.

kari Takar or agent of the Bibi, but she not infrequently preferred to employ one of the islanders in this capacity. The *kari Takar* was assisted by an accountant and one or two peons, and freely availed himself of the advice of the *Karnavans*, when the interests of his mistress were not in conflict. All offences were summarily tried, whether of a criminal or fiscal nature. No rules of procedure were prescribed and no record of trials maintained. Grave crime has always been rare, and thefts practically unknown. Ordeals were frequently resorted to for the discovery of offenders, and there are traditions of executions for witchcraft and of punishment by mutilation inflicted a hundred years ago. Wholesale confiscation of property known as 'Courachy' or gang robbery was the common punishment for more heinous offences. The house of the offender was surrounded by a mob who plundered it, removing even the jewels from the women's ears, and all the property thus taken was confiscated to the *Pandaram*. In some cases a whole family was exterminated. The Valiya Illat Courachy in Agatti, to which Mr. Robinson refers, was apparently a campaign organized from Cannanore against a family that had settled and become very influential in the island. The last survivor of the house—an unfortunate woman—concealed herself for some days in a cave on the islet of Kalpitti still known as *Kunhi Bi Para*, but was eventually caught and put to death. In Minicoy adultery used to be severely punished, the guilty pair being dragged through the village by a rope and given 101 lashes by the Diwani, or sexton, as we should call him, of the Jamat Mosque.

Oaths were, and still are respected, especially those upon the Koran. Oaths in the name of the Ali Raja were once also considered peculiarly binding.

The islanders possess in a high degree an aptitude for self-government and the present administration is satisfactorily conducted by an Amin assisted by a council of elders (*Karnavans*) on each island. The Amin tries petty civil and criminal cases and refers important ones to the mainland for orders. His accounts and registers are compiled by a gumastah, and he has one or two Nadpals (peons) for collection and court purposes. The Penal Code and Procedure Code have not been extended to the group, but a list of offences sixteen in number has been drawn up, which the Amin is competent to try, the maximum fine he can impose being Rs. 15, or a sentence of imprisonment not exceeding 15 days. A room in the Amin's cutcherry is used as a prison, but the tasks imposed on those under detention are purely nominal. Two or more of the *Karnavans* have to sit as assessors. Appeals are common and the inspecting officer has a great number to dispose of. A second appeal lies from him, or from the headquarter Deputy Collector, who is the ordinary appellate authority, to the Collector. A further appeal to Government through the Board of Revenue is also permitted. In the management of island affairs other than official, the Amin is only *primus inter pares*. Every able-bodied Melacheri, no matter what he is doing, must obey the summons of the conch, and assist in the beaching or launching of the *odams* or at any rat hunt, which the *karnavans* convene. Where there is a catch of porpoise a small sub-committee of *Karnavans* superintends the division of the spoil among the islanders and their decisions are never questioned. Similarly in religious and social questions, the islanders show remarkable docility and obedience to authority. It may be said that this patriarchal system works well on the whole, especially in Androth where the *Karnavans* are men of authority and ability, and in Agatti where the Amin is a man of commanding personality.

INDEX

A

B

C

D

E

F

G

H

L

Q

R

S

T

U

V

DISTRICT GAZETTEERS OF INDIA {IN 245 BINDINGS}

GYAN

ASSAM DISTRICT GAZETTEERS

11 VOLUMES

ISBN: 9788121285933 (PB Set)
Price: 6500/

BENGAL DISTRICT GAZETTEERS

52 VOLUMES

ISBN: 9789362089151 (PB Set)
Price: 35000/

GAZETTEER OF THE BOMBAY PRESIDENCY

27 VOLUMES (IN 35 BINDINGS)

ISBN: 9788121285605 (PB Set)
Price: 90000/

CENTRAL PROVINCES DISTRICT GAZETTEERS

30 VOLUMES (IN 33 BINDINGS)

ISBN: 9789362085399 (PB Set)
Price: 23000/

MADRAS DISTRICT GAZETTEERS

23 VOLUMES (IN 25 BINDINGS)

ISBN: 9789362085627 (PB Set)
Price: 32000/

PUNJAB DISTRICT GAZETTEERS

36 VOLUMES (IN 37 BINDINGS)

ISBN: 9789362084033 (PB Set)
Price: 46000/

RAJPUTANA DISTRICT GAZETTEERS

3 VOLUMES

ISBN: 9789362084781 (PB Set)
Price: 6000/

District Gazetteers of India
{In 245 Bindings}
(Rs. 530000/- Hardcover)
(Rs. 370000/- Softcover)
Crown Size

UNITED PROVINCES OF AGRA AND OUDH DISTRICT GAZETTEERS

49 VOLUMES

ISBN: 9789362082183 (PB Set)
Price: 86404/